AFRICAN HISTORICAL DICTIONARIES
Edited by Jon Woronoff

1. *Cameroon,* by Victor T. LeVine and Roger P. Nye. 1974
2. *The Congo (Brazzaville),* by Virginia Thompson and Richard Adloff, 1974.
3. *Swaziland,* by John J. Grotpeter. 1975
4. *The Gambia,* by Harry A. Gailey. 1975
5. *Botswana,* by Richard P. Stevens. 1975
6 *Somalia,* by Margaret F. Castagno. 1975
7. *Dahomey,* by Samuel Decalo. 1975
8. *Burundi,* by Warren Weinstein. 1976
9. *Togo,* by Samuel Decalo. 1976
10. *Lesotho,* by Gordon Haliburton. 1977
11. *Mali,* by Pascal James Imperato. 1977
12. *Sierra Leone,* by Cyril Patrick Foray. 1977
13. *Chad,* by Samuel Decalo. 1977
14. *Upper Volta,* by Daniel Miles McFarland. 1978
15. *Tanzania,* by Laura S. Kurtz. 1978
16. *Guinea,* by Thomas O'Toole. 1978
17. *Sudan,* by John Voll. 1978
18. *Rhodesia/Zimbabwe,* by R. Kent Rasmussen. 1979
19. *Zambia,* by John J. Grotpeter. 1979
20. *Niger,* by Samuel Decalo. 1979
21. *Equatorial Guinea,* by Max Liniger-Goumaz. 1979
22. *Guinea-Bissau,* by Richard Lobban. 1979
23. *Senegal,* by Lucie G. Colvin. 1981
24. *Morocco,* by William Spencer. 1980
25. *Malaŵi,* by Cynthia A. Crosby. 1980
26. *Angola,* by Phyllis Martin. 1980
27. *The Central African Republic,* by Pierre Kalck. 1980
28. *Algeria,* by Alf Andrew Heggoy. 1981
29. *Kenya,* by Bethwell A. Ogot. 1981
30. *Gabon,* by David E. Gardinier. 1981
31. *Mauritania,* by Alfred G. Gerteiny. 1981
32. *Ethiopia,* by Chris Prouty and Eugene Rosenfeld. 1981
33. *Libya,* by Lorna Hahn. 1981
34. *Mauritius,* by Lindsay Rivière. 1982
35. *Western Sahara,* by Tony Hodges. 1982
36. *Egypt,* by Joan Wucher King. 1984
37. *South Africa,* by Christopher Saunders. 1983

Historical Dictionary of EGYPT

BY JOAN WUCHER KING

African Historical Dictionaries, No. 36

THE SCARECROW PRESS, INC.
Metuchen, N.J., & London 1984

Library of Congress Cataloging in Publication Data

Wucher King, Joan.
Historical dictionary of Egypt.

(African historical dictionaries ; no. 36)
Bibliography: p.
1. Egypt--History--Dictionaries. I. Title. II. Series.
DT45.W83 1984 962'.003'21 83-20247
ISBN 0-8108-1670-9

Manufactured in the United States of America

To the Egyptian people,
who have by their culture
and their sense of life
carried their own unwritten history
in the kindness and generosity
of their welcome

†

CONTENTS

EDITOR'S FOREWORD

Egypt has always been a major center of civilization, and never more than today. For now it is an important member of the African community of nations, a prominent part of the Arab world, and a pillar of broader Islamic and Third World groupings. Indeed, due to its large population, its strategic location, and its dynamic leaders, it is hard to imagine a contemporary history that would not stress its role.

In this historical dictionary, which concentrates on Egypt since the Muslim conquest, the problem has been where to start when describing the busy stream of events that have occurred along the Nile. The best solution was, in a sense, to start with the present and work back. It is the present, and the recent past, that will concern most readers of this volume, and thus the persons, places, and events have been treated in greater depth and appear in greater density for the more recent periods, with the previous history covered as to important rulers, personalities, and events.

Little mention is made of the pre-Islamic period since so much has been written about it. There are, however, entries for certain subjects in the pre-Islamic period whose activities or scope had some relevance to later times. Moreover, oddly as it may seem, there is sometimes less clarity about what has been happening in Egypt during the recent regimes of Gamal Abdal Nasser and Anwar Sadat than at the time of Ramses or Nefertiti. It is not that the facts are unknown, but rather that too many of the presentations are biased and try to read political or ideological interpretations into them. In this book the facts are left largely to speak for themselves.

Joan Wucher King has been living in the Middle East over the past several years. After studying at UCLA and in London, she proceeded to the American University in Cairo, where she did research and taught. Since then she has resided in Saudi Arabia, while making periodic trips to Egypt and Europe. This enabled her to obtain the essential material from various sources.

It is hardly necessary to stress how assiduously Wucher King sought this material or how meticulously she selected and organized it so that others can find in one volume what it took her years to gather. This aspect of the Egypt dictionary will be immediately noticeable to readers. Equally important is her ability to present in lively and readable form what could otherwise be a musty collection of data. She makes the volume not only useful but surprisingly enjoyable.

Jon Woronoff
Series Editor

PREFACE

Because this dictionary is the work of one writer, it perforce reflects an individual viewpoint. The difficult process of selecting the entries was based on what information I felt would be most useful or interesting both to the general reader and to students of Egyptian history in the Islamic period. Though relatively few works have been published on Egypt's Islamic era for the nonspecialist or general reader, the history of Egypt from the Muslim conquest to the present day has a richness of event and personality as compelling as the pharaonic period with which the country is more usually associated.

The Introduction presents an overall background into which the individuals and events featured in the entries can be placed. The Chronology has been structured to include some of the major events that occurred outside Egypt's borders but that influenced the development of events within the country. This larger regional setting adds, I feel, a note of clarification to the changes of regime and ruler in Egypt as well as reflecting the strong links that existed between Egypt and her neighbors at various points in her history.

In gathering material for the dictionary entries, I took care to consult as many sources as possible. It would be satisfying to say that these sources concur with each other, but they often do not. The Islamic historians of the past saw personalities and events in the same way as do many observers of Egypt today--that is, through a filter of their own interests, connections, and world view. More stress has therefore been given to recent analyses of Islamic history in Egypt, though the reader is cautioned that what is considered definitive in terms of final assessments varies even within present-day Islamic historiography.

Individuals who have featured in Egypt's recent history have often been the subject of conflicting verdicts by historians. I have tried as much as possible to describe these persons and their roles in light of both views expressed during their lifetime or period of activity and more recent (and sometimes more distanced) evaluations. The events of the recent past, and particularly from the Nasser regime onward, are still being redefined as new information becomes available. Our understanding of the Suez Crisis in 1956 is significantly different from how that crisis was viewed a decade ago. The difficulty of separating political from historic assessment increases for very recent events, such as the peace initiative begun by President Sadat in 1977.

Shortly after the text of this book was completed the assassination of President Sadat took place. Certain entries relevant to the late President have been updated, but the general conclusions made about Egypt during Sadat's presidency, and contained in the Introduction, are still relevant and have been left intact.

This book is a first attempt to present in dictionary form the complex history of a complex society: Egypt. I hope that it will make this history accessible to students, researchers, and all who have read about, and been interested in, Egypt in the Islamic and modern eras.

A NOTE ON TRANSLITERATION

The system followed in this book for transliterating Arabic names in the pre-Muḥammad ᶜAlī period is based on that used in the second edition of the Encyclopaedia of Islam (London and Leiden, 1960-), with the modifications introduced in C. E. Bosworth's The Islamic Dynasties (Edinburgh, 1967): q for ḳ and j for dj. The elision in sound that occurs in Arabic between the definite article Al and certain initial consonants, such as "s," is indicated by the alteration of "l" to the relevant consonant (aẓ-Ẓāfir instead of al-Ẓāfir). In some cases the article has been omitted in the text after the initial reference, to avoid confusion with the English words an, at, and as.

The Arabic consonant "j" is pronounced as a hard "g" in Egypt. Where "g" has been commonly used in English sources in the transliteration of words beginning with "j," these entries have been listed under "g." Organizations more commonly known by their Arabic names have been so listed.

For names in the post-Muḥammad ᶜAlī period, the modern spelling most commonly occurring in the English texts is used, such as Gamal Abdal Nasser for Jamāl ᶜAbd an-Nāṣir. The latter spelling is technically accurate but unfamiliar to the general and non-Arabic-speaking reader. Modern names that have been presented with various and inconsistent English spellings are more directly transliterated from the Arabic--e.g., Muhiaddin for Mohiadine, Mohieddine, and so on. Cities and countries are given in their standard English form where possible.

DATES

Dates from the conquest of Egypt by ᶜAmr b. al-ᶜĀṣ to the French

Invasion of 1798 are given in their AD and AH forms. AH (Anno Hijrae) refers to the Muslim calendar, which dates from the migration of the Prophet Muḥammad from Mecca to Medina in AH 1(AD 622). This calendar is based on the lunar year, which is approximately eleven days shorter than the solar year.

The dates for some historical events on occasion reflect a compromise between conflicting dates given in major sources. These conflicts occur even for some more recent events. In such cases the most commonly given date, or the date that most closely coincides with related events, has been chosen.

ACKNOWLEDGMENTS

The research, preparation, and writing of this book were done solely by the author, but several people who contributed advice and assistance must be mentioned.

Our friends, colleagues, and students in Egypt are owed a collective and individual thank you. In particular, Alan Mackie kindly made available to me his own work on Egypt's modern politics and economy. Dr. Abbas Hamdani of the University of Minnesota (at Minneapolis) provided guidance and help with the entries covering Egypt's Faṭimid period. The late Dr. Klaus-Friedrich Koch supported and encouraged my initial research on Egypt's Islamic movements, and I am equally grateful to Dr. Soraya al-Torki for her enthusiasm and backing. The friendship of Dr. Karl Stowasser and Dr. John Hunwick yielded many hours of fruitful discussion. Miss Wafaa Abdul Hamid of the American University in Cairo was of great assistance to me during a brief research visit to Cairo in December 1980. In London, Mr. Abdel Majid Farid of the Arab Research Centre, Mr. Nabil Osman, Press Attaché at the Egyptian Embassy, and the librarians of the Islamic Studies section at the School of Oriental and African Studies must all be thanked. Beyond this it would be unfair to single out particular individuals, because all of the people I met in Egypt, and my own experiences there, helped shape my view of the country and its history.

I would like to thank HRH Prince Turki b. Muhammad b. Saud al-Kabir, who made available books from his libraries in Riyadh and London, and other friends in Saudi Arabia who generously gave me the time and opportunity to complete the final draft of this book in London in the summer of 1981.

Gina Rowland, lately of the Department of Arabic of Edinburgh University, provided invaluable help with the proofing of the final text. The hospitality and support of Linda Milne in London made my frequent research trips there both possible and worthwhile. Other acknowledgments are mentioned in the bibliography.

Finally, to my husband, Dr. Geoffrey King, my eternal gratitude for his patient endurance of my lengthy absences in London and my total preoccupation for most of 1981 and '82 with the completion of this dictionary.

It should be noted that none of the individuals named bears any responsibility for the information or opinions contained in this book.

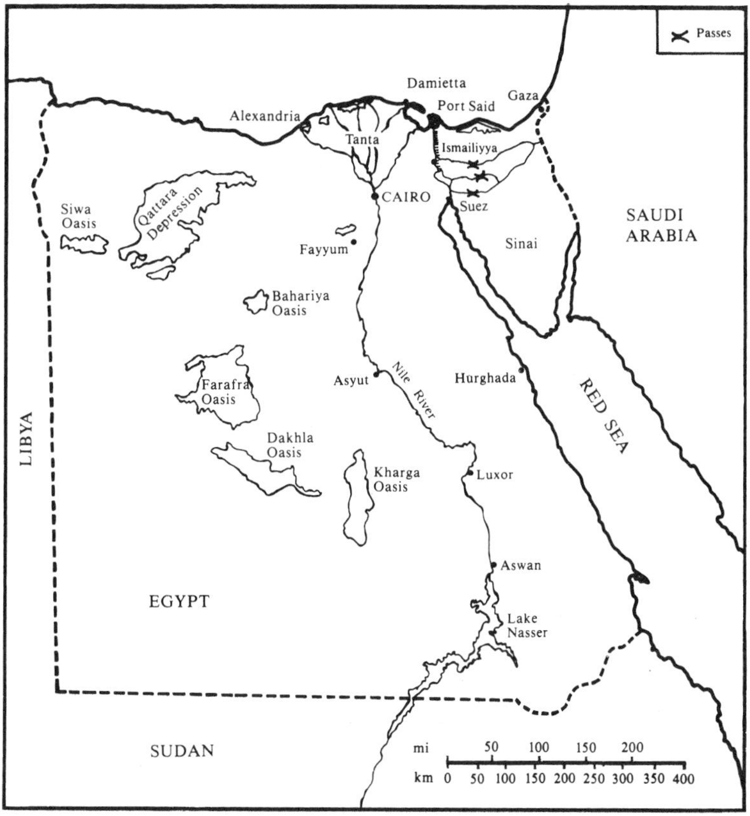
Passes
Damietta
Gaza
Port Said
Alexandria
Tanta
Ismailiyya
CAIRO
Suez
Siwa
Oasis
Qattara
Depression
SAUDI
ARABIA
Sinai
Fayyum
Bahariya
Oasis
Farafra
Oasis
Asyut
Nile River
Hurghada
RED SEA
LIBYA
Dakhla
Oasis
Kharga
Oasis
Luxor
Aswan
EGYPT
Lake
Nasser
SUDAN
mi 50 100 150 200
km 0 50 100 150 200 250 300 350 400

INTRODUCTION

Egypt has one of the oldest civilizations in the world and has left a rich record of its history in the architecture, literature, and art that have survived to modern times. The four thousand years preceding the birth of Christ were, for Egypt, a time of both achievement and obscurity. The extraordinary legacy of the pharaohs has sometimes obscured the fact that Egypt's history did not always move in an uninterrupted line of development. Lengthy periods of invasion and internal dissension occurred as intervals between those dynasties that built and conquered.

The major unifying factor in Egypt's economic and political life throughout its history has been the Nile. In its transit of Egypt the Nile converts what would otherwise have been a desert into a rich agricultural area, one that has supported not only the Egyptians but in later times the populations of Rome and Constantinople, as well as Mecca, Medina, and other cities of the Middle East.

The Greek historian Herodotus' observation that Egypt was the gift of the Nile is apparent to this day, as the visitor to the country can see from the sharp divide of green created by the Nile from the Eastern and Western Deserts that flank the river. Strong, centralized state control, attempted by Egyptian governments throughout the country's history, was a product in part of the need to control Egypt's agricultural system, based exclusively on irrigation water from the Nile. With no regular adequate rainfall, Egypt's agriculture depended on the careful maintenance of irrigation channels to water the land during the period of the year when the river was rising, and on collective techniques to wash areas of land with the silt carried by the Nile. When these irrigation channels were not maintained, or when the Nile failed to rise, the consequence was famine. The impetus for a centrally directed bureaucracy that could oversee and direct this irrigation process was thus present from Egypt's earliest days, and was to continue throughout its history.

Egypt's pharaonic period came to an end with the conquest of Egypt by Alexander the Great in 332 BC, but the concept of absolute political and religious leadership established by the pharaohs was continued by their successors, the Ptolemies. The elaborate Egyptian religion and its associated myths and rituals survived the Ptolemies and their Roman successors, and gained adherents in Rome and other non-Egyptian cities. Egyptian culture, history, and mythology were as interesting to the Ptolemies and Romans as they are to modern observers.

For many people today Egypt is still most strongly associated with its pharaonic past, but in the Christian and Muslim eras Egypt made an equally significant contribution to the regional culture of which it has been part. Christianity took root in Egypt in the early decades of the Christian era, and until the fourth century AD Egypt's capital, Alexandria, was the most important see in Christendom after Rome. The Patriarchs of Alexandria had a prominent role in the development of the Church and of Christian doctrine. The arrival of the Muslims in Egypt brought the country a new religion, Islam, and a new language, Arabic. Egypt went on to become a center of Muslim scholarship and power.

Despite Egypt's regional and cultural importance the Egyptian people themselves had little access to power in their own country. From the Ptolemies down to the time of Gamal Abdal Nasser non-Egyptians ruled Egypt. In the Muslim period the governors, Caliphs, and Sultans who held power in Cairo were foreigners or of foreign origin, as were many of the viziers and powerful court officials.

In time and through marriage many of the Muslim dynasties did establish roots in Egypt. In terms of their interests, however, the majority of Egypt's rulers were concerned with events beyond Egypt's borders.

Throughout the Muslim period the rulers of Egypt displayed a tolerance and acceptance of Egypt's religious minorities that compares favorably with the persecutions suffered by religious minorities in Christian Europe. Christians and Jews were found not only among the scholars and physicians of the Muslim courts but in positions of real power as well. Occasional periods of intolerance were matched by periods in which the favorable treatment of Egypt's minorities was generous to the point of attracting the protests of Egypt's Muslim majority.

The mass of Egyptians below the ruling circles--Muslim, Coptic Christian, and Jewish--benefited from the largess of Egypt's good rulers and suffered the exactions of the rest. Their labor, whether as farmers, artisans, merchants, or traders, was the basis of the nation's wealth. Few historical works have given attention to this mass of Egyptians who were the physical and economic backbone of the ruling dynasties. The passive endurance of the Egyptians in the face of sometimes chaotic, unfair, or ruthless government was not limitless, however. In the nineteenth and twentieth centuries the Egyptian people, through revolt and protest, increasingly gave voice to their demands and to the injustices that marked their national and personal lives.

Egypt's historical evolution underwent two major changes in recent times: the imposition of British control in 1882 and the Free Officers' coup of 1952. Though the British did not reduce Egypt formally to the status of a colony, their involvement in government and administration had an enormous impact on Egypt's political development in the twentieth century. The Free Officers' coup signaled a thorough transformation of Egypt's political life. The power of Egypt's Turco-Circassian ruling elite was broken as this elite was replaced within the nation's power structure by native Egyptians. Egypt became a republic in 1953, and a complete reordering of social, economic, and political life was initiated.

Despite the several changes of religion, language, and government that Egypt has undergone since the pharaonic period, a certain cultural continuity has been maintained at the popular level and in the lifestyle of Egypt's village communities, where many aspects of the life of the peasant farmers have altered only slowly through time. Egypt's pharaonic heritage, which distinguishes it from the other countries of the region, was enlarged and enriched through the Greco-Roman, Byzantine, and Muslim periods. Like all other peoples the Egyptians prize their history, and even the most modern of politicians has found it useful to make references to the country's past greatness and glories. Egypt's history as a Muslim state has linked it with its neighbors, particularly Syria and the Sudan, and Islamic and Arab relationships continue to be important for Egypt's modern regional political role.

Geographical Setting

Egypt's position in the northeastern corner of the African continent has enabled it to act as a bridge between the Islamic and African worlds. The Mediterranean and Red Seas, on Egypt's northern and eastern coasts, gave the country an important role in the trade between Europe and Asia. The land's geographical and maritime advantages were particularly profitable for her rulers prior to the European discovery of a direct route to Asia.

The Sinai peninsula, used by several invaders entering Egypt from the Levant, was divided from the mainland of Egypt by the construction of the Suez Canal. The opening of the Canal in 1869 enhanced Egypt's strategic advantage for Europe, as the new route to India it afforded was shorter and avoided the navigational hazards of the Cape of Good Hope.

Egypt's landmass is nearly 97 percent desert. The Nile River, flowing between the escarpments of the Eastern and Western Deserts, creates a thin band of cultivatable land from the southern region ("Upper Egypt") to Cairo. Beyond Cairo the Nile branches out to create the fan-shaped Delta region, the heartland of the country's agriculture. Egypt's Western Desert, which has oil and mineral deposits, contains five oases and the Qattara depression.

To the west, Egypt shares a border with Libya; this was fixed in 1925 by an agreement between Egypt and Italy, which was then in control of Libya. The eastern region of Libya, known as Cyrenaica in Roman times and Barqa in the Muslim period, maintained links with the Mediterranean cities of Egypt and the Western Desert oases. Egypt's southern border with Sudan was fixed by the 1899 Anglo-Egyptian Condominium.

The border between Egypt and Israel in Sinai is based on the 1906 agreement between Egypt and Turkey delimiting the former's territory in Sinai. The current (1981) border between Egypt and Israel was scheduled to be adjusted under the terms of the Peace Treaty between the two countries; Israel was to return territory seized during the 1967 Arab-Israeli War. The Sinai and its offshore areas, particularly the Gulf of Suez, contain most of Egypt's oil deposits; the peninsula's mineral resources are scheduled to come under full exploitation once Egypt regains full control of the region in 1982.

Historical Background:

Roman and Byzantine Periods (30 BC to c. AD 639)

With the defeat and death of the last Ptolemaic ruler of Egypt, Cleopatra VII, in 30 BC Egypt came under the control of Rome. For several decades previously, Roman influence in Egypt had grown as the power of the Ptolemies weakened through internecine struggle and external challenge. The potential that Egypt possessed as an independent power base for an ambitious governor was demonstrated by Mark Anthony, who came to Egypt in 36 BC and soon used his position in the country and with Cleopatra to mount a challenge against the Roman Emperor Augustus.

After his conquest of Egypt, Augustus placed the country's administration under the control of a military man of the Equestrian rank. Roman senators were forbidden to visit Egypt without permission of the Emperor. At the same time Egypt's new rulers took steps to ensure the regular supply of grain from Egypt to Rome, where its free distribution to the citizens was an important bulwark of the Emperor's power.

Egypt's Roman conquerors, like the country's Greek conquerors three centuries previously, benefited from the Egyptians' ascription of divine character to the country's rulers. Egyptian religious cults, particularly that of Isis, gained a following among the Romans. The city of Alexandria, whose foundation dated from the time of the conquest of Egypt by Alexander the Great, maintained its leading role in the Mediterranean world for several centuries, though it was steadily eclipsed by Constantinople after that city's foundation in the fourth century AD.

Throughout the Roman and Byzantine periods Alexandria dominated Egypt's political, cultural, and religious life. The city's contentious population was involved in revolts against Roman control from the first century AD onward. Communal tensions between the city's Jewish and Hellenic elements became more complex with the foundation of Christianity in Egypt, reputedly by the Apostle Mark in c. AD 54. As Christianity established itself in Egypt, conflicts arose between and among Alexandria's Christian, Jewish, and pagan communities over the desire of Egypt's Christians to suppress the country's Hellenistic and pre-Christian past. The Christians in Egypt were themselves targets of several official persecutions prior to the establishment of religious toleration in the Roman Empire under the Edict of Milan in 312.

Popular sentiment toward Christianity in Alexandria and in Egypt was encouraged by the activism and leadership of the Patriarch of Alexandria. Alexandria was displaced by Constantinople as the second-most-important Christian see (after Rome) by a Church Council vote in 381. Despite this the city retained its importance as a center of Christian theology and learning. The Patriarch of Alexandria was supported by a large establishment of clerics and monks; as Egypt increasingly became a Christian country, the Patriarch's power correspondingly increased. The popularity of monasticism in Egypt also played a role in shaping the development of Christianity as a social force in the country. The Egyptian monks were especially active campaigners against Hellenism, secularism, and the relaxed mores of Alexandrian life. The organized monastic communities assumed administrative and economic, in addition to their religious, functions.

The Christian community in Egypt was split by doctrinal disputes of early Christianity over the nature of Christ. Without going into the complexities of the Monophysite, Arian, and Nestorian controversies, it is sufficient to say that the Egyptians tended to favor the doctrine that was out of favor in Rome and, later, Constantinople. The lead in this religious opposition was increasingly provided by the Patriarch of Alexandria. In 451, during the reign of the Patriarch Dioscorus, the Christian Church in Egypt broke away from the Orthodox Church. Thereafter the Patriarch of Alexandria, appointed by the Byzantine Emperor, was out of harmony with the majority of Christians in Egypt. The Coptic Church, as the Egyptian Christian Church is known in the West, elected its own Patriarch.

Throughout the Roman and Byzantine periods the administration of Egypt was subject to the control of Rome or Constantinople. Reforms carried out by Diocletian in the third century AD separated Egypt's military and civilian administration in an effort to halt the series of military challenges to the Roman Emperor's control of the province. Justinian in the sixth century instituted reforms to correct some of the abuses that had developed in the taxation and administrative systems of Egypt.

Outside the settled regions tribes in Upper Egypt rebelled on occasion and in AD 270 gave their support to the Palmyrene invasion of Egypt. Attempts to suppress these tribes were only partially successful, and many of them continued to be active and difficult until the time of the Muslim Conquest. Rebellions against Roman power originating in Alexandria, though more frequent than these tribal revolts, were usually more quickly suppressed.

The importance of religious questions in Egypt in the period before the rise of Islam mirrored the concern with religion found in both Rome and Constantinople. The continued involvement of the Byzantine Emperors with religious issues kept theological controversies in Egypt and elsewhere active. Religion, combined with the resentment of Egyptians over taxes and the control of their country by foreigners, created a climate of hostility in Egypt toward the Byzantines. This hostility eased the path of Egypt's Persian conquerors in 616, whose short-lived invasion met with little opposition in Egypt. The reconquest in 629 of Egypt and the provinces by the Byzantine Emperor Heraclius preceded by a mere ten years the arrival of the Arab Muslim armies in Sinai.

Muslim Conquest to Tūlūnid Period (c. 639-868AD/ 18-254AH)

The disorders that afflicted Egyptian society in the last centuries of Roman-Byzantine rule partially explain the ease with which the Persians conquered the country and also explain why the Muslims were able, in under two years, to overturn a government that had held power in Egypt for the preceding six centuries. The Muslims were helped not only by their own drive for conquest but also by the enormous disaffection felt by many Egyptians for their Byzantine rulers.

The early Islamic period in Egypt, under the Umayyad and early ᶜAbbāsid governors, saw the consolidation of a Muslim rule that leaned heavily on established Roman and Byzantine administrative practices. The fate of the wealthy country added to the Arab realm by the military campaign of ᶜAmr b. al-ᶜĀṣ was linked with political developments outside Egypt's borders. Egypt's new capital, al-Fusṭāṭ, founded by ᶜAmr, became the country's administrative headquarters.

Egypt was used by the Muslims as a source of grain, mirroring its role under the Romans. The greatest part of Egypt's revenues were sent by Egypt's Umayyad governors to Damascus and, after the rise of the ᶜAbbāsids, to Baghdad. During this early period Egypt's value as a source of food, skilled labor, and manufacturing and trading wealth was recognized, though the country itself was relatively isolated from the power struggles for leadership of the Islamic community surrounding the rise of the Umayyads in AD661/41AH and the ᶜAbbāsids in 749/132. The progress of Islam within Egypt was slow, but it steadily won adherents as the country's Muslim rulers maintained and consolidated their control and expanded their presence in rural areas.

The Islamicization of Egypt was partly helped by the settlement of Arab tribes in the country, particularly the large-scale settlement supported by the Umayyad Caliph Hishām in 727/109. In turn the Egyptians contributed their own character and culture to the nascent Islamic state. The gap between ruler and ruled remained, however, and, fueled by continuing Byzantine attacks on Arab positions along the Mediterranean coast, a series of revolts took place against tax measures, especially by the Copts. These revolts, which occurred under both the Umayyads and the ^{c}Abbāsids, were not limited to the Copts but were joined by members of Egypt's growing Muslim community unhappy with the exactions of the government.

The visit to Egypt by the ^{c}Abbāsid Caliph al-Ma'mūn in 832/217 was followed by a vigorous military suppression of dissent in Egypt, and the introduction of much-needed reforms in the tax structure. The continued vulnerability of Egypt to attacks by the Byzantines, as well as the ^{c}Abbāsids' own problems in their home base, Iraq, undoubtedly influenced their decision to bring more order in, and control over, Egypt. With the rise of the Ṭūlūnids, the first autonomous dynasty in the country, Egypt's role as a wealthy but politically marginal province of the Islamic realm came to an end.

Ṭūlūnid Period
(868-905/254-92)

In 868/247 a court official of the ^{c}Abbāsid Caliph Mu^{c}tazz was given land revenues in Egypt as iqṭā^{c}, or grant, and the official's stepson, Aḥmad Ibn Ṭūlūn, was appointed to govern the country on his relative's behalf. The rule of Ibn Ṭūlūn, of Central Asian origin, though technically under the sovereignty of the ^{c}Abbāsid Caliphate, was in fact nearly autonomous in policy and practice. Within a short time after his appointment Ibn Ṭūlūn gained ascendancy over the ^{c}Abbāsid's minister of finances in Egypt, al-Mudabbir. Ibn Ṭūlūn extended his control to Syria. In Egypt he greatly enriched the capital with public works whose construction was financed by the revenue he withheld from Baghdad. The dynastic struggles of the central ^{c}Abbāsid court, and the challenge presented to the ^{c}Abbāsids by the Zanj rebellion in southern Iraq, prevented Baghdad from successfully countering Ibn Ṭūlūn's increasing independence.

Khumārawayh, the son and successor of Ibn Ṭūlūn, gained recognition from Baghdad of his family's control of Egypt and land grants in Syria and northern Mesopotamia in 892/279. This grant marked the acme of Ṭūlūnid power. Seven years later the Ṭūlūnid territories were decreased and their tribute increased by the ^{c}Abbāsid Caliph. The fairly rapid rise and fall of the Ṭūlūnids was repeated in Egypt by their successors, the Ikhshīdids, and by other dynasties in the Islamic world. After the founder of the dynasty had enlarged his domains by conquest, he was succeeded by sons and grandsons who had neither the personal nor military capacity to continue the pattern of leadership established during the phase of initial expansion. In the case of the Ṭūlūnid dynasty the emergence of a strong military and religious challenge in Syria from the Shīᶜa Qaramatians, plus the rebelliousness of the Ṭūlūnid troops, made uneasy the tenure in office of Ibn Ṭūlūn's descendants.

In 905/292 the Ṭūlūnids were displaced from power in Egypt by an ᶜAbbāsid army, and a thirty-year period of direct ᶜAbbāsid control of Egypt followed. During this period a family of administrators of Persian origin, the Madhārā'ī, were extremely powerful in Egypt.

The Ikhshīdids
(935-69/323-58)

Muḥammad b. Ṭughj was appointed governor of Egypt in 935/323 during the reign of the ᶜAbbāsid Caliph ar-Rāḍī, who subsequently granted him the Central Asian princely title of "the Ikhshīd." The Ikhshīd's career had many parallels with that of Aḥmad b. Ṭūlūn, though his installation as military strongman had the support of Baghdad, where concern was felt about the rising power of the Shīᶜa Fāṭimid dynasty in North Africa. The Fāṭimids had twice raided Egypt in the thirty years of direct ᶜAbbāsid control prior to the appointment of the Ikhshīd and launched a third raid against Egypt in the year of the Ikhshīd's arrival in the country.

Five years after coming to power the Ikhshīd had gained control of Palestine and southern Syria, as well as Mecca and Medina, though his successors were challenged in Syria by the rise of another autonomous dynasty, the Ḥamdānids. The Ikhshīdids who succeeded Muḥammad b. Ṭughj faced not only internal disturbances against the regime but also a major earthquake and plague. The Nubians launched two attacks in Upper Egypt and had to be subdued by military campaigns, while in the west the activities and intentions of the Fāṭimids were a constant threat.

Muḥammad b. Ṭughj was succeeded by two sons, Ūnūjūr and ᶜAlī, but real power was in the hands of Kāfūr, a former slave of the Ikhshīd. Kāfūr took power in his own name in 966/355. The end of the Ikhshidīd dynasty came at a time of increasing activity by the Qaramatians and Byzantines in Syria, and of weakness and division in the Ikhshidīd court in Egypt. The rapid decline of the dynasty following Kāfūr's death in 968/357 provided an opportunity for the Fāṭimids to realize their longstanding goal of establishing themselves in Egypt.

The Fāṭimids
(969-1171/358-567)

The Fāṭimids were the only Shīᶜa dynasty to hold power in Egypt. Because of their Shīᶜa beliefs the Fāṭimids contested both the religious and the political positions of the Sunnī ᶜAbbāsid Caliphs in Baghdad. The Fāṭimids used a combination of military power and religious propaganda in their conquest of Egypt and continued to rely on both their army and an extensive network of missionaries to expand their influence in the Levant and Arabia. Important and lucrative trade links were maintained by the Fāṭimids, whose wealth was reflected in the royal city they founded, al-Qāhira, Cairo. Cairo, built to the north of the former capital, al-Fusṭāṭ, replaced the latter as administrative center. The Fāṭimid period saw the development of the finest art forms and an extensive literature. For the Egyptians, however, the reign of the Fāṭimids was largely an unhappy time. The country's administration and taxation system hastened the deterioration of Egypt's agriculture, with disastrous consequences when a series of natural catastrophes brought famine and plague to the country. Suffering additionally from the disunity and in-fighting of the various regiments of the Fāṭimid army, Egypt was reduced to a state of anarchy barely a century after the establishment of the Fāṭimids there.

Of all the Fāṭimid Caliphs al-Ḥākim (996-1021/386-411) has gained notoriety for a series of decrees that, accepted at face value, suggest eccentricity and even a lack of sanity. However extraordinary his decisions and character, al-Ḥākim managed to hold on to power for some twenty-five years, surviving a severe famine and internal disturbances in Egypt. A peace treaty with the Byzantines was concluded, and though the Fāṭimids lost ground in Libya to their former Zīrid allies, they temporarily gained ascendancy in areas of northern Syria.

In 1021/411 al-Ḥākim disappeared, presumably murdered. Egypt passed into the control of the new Caliph's regent, Sitt al-Mulk, sister of al-Ḥākim; following her death a succession of viziers served the Caliph and largely controlled the court. Viziers continued to dominate the government during the reign of the Caliph al-Mustanṣir, whose lengthy rule (1036-94/427-87) witnessed the decline in Fāṭimid power both internally and externally. Egypt was impoverished and depopulated by a seven-year famine, and the power of the Fāṭimid Caliphate was threatened by the open mutiny of its troops in Syria and Egypt. The Zīrids in North Africa broke completely with the Fāṭimids, who lost control of the territories that had been the basis of their expansion into Egypt. In 1057-59/448-51 the Fāṭimid Caliphate was proclaimed first in Mosul, then in the ᶜAbbāsid capital, Baghdad. This unwitting and largely unplanned extension of their power by a self-proclaimed ally faltered when the Fāṭimids were unable materially to support their new position in Baghdad against a Saljūq Turkish reconquest of the city. Yemen remained a nominal vassal of the Fāṭimids under the Ṣulayḥid dynasty (1038-1138/429-532), which ruled in Sana from 1063/455 until its overthrow.

The struggle for power by the Berber, Turkish, and Sūdān regiments of the Fāṭimid army reached its climax in 1072-73/464-65, when Egypt was in the grip of famine and the Treasury was plundered by the army. To restore order to the country the court of al-Mustanṣir invited its Armenian general, Badr al-Jamālī, to return to Egypt from his campaigns in Syria. Badr arrived in Cairo in 1074/466, restoring order by a vigorous suppression of army dissidents. He enjoyed less success in his campaigns to retake Syria from the Saljūq Turks, who from 1068/461 had been making steady gains in the area, both directly and through their allies.

Badr united under his control the leading civilian and military posts of the Fāṭimid state. After his death, which preceded by a short time that of the Caliph al-Mustanṣir, the history of Fāṭimid Egypt was as much marked by the power struggles of viziers as it was by the achievements of any particular Caliph. The weakness of the Fāṭimid Caliphs created opportunities for ambitious court members to exercise de facto control of the government. These opportunities were, in consequence, fought over and seized with a vigor that seriously disrupted the government of the Fāṭimid state. In the later Fāṭimid period religious support for the Caliphate was split by movements in support of rival claimants to the office: the Nizārīs over the succession of al-Mustaᶜlī in 1094/487 and the Ṭayyibiyya over the succession of al-Ḥāfiẓ in 1131/525.

The struggles and dissensions at the Egyptian court were made more serious by the arrival in the Near East of the Crusaders, who reached Syria in 1096/490, determined to regain Jerusalem and the Holy Land for Christianity. The Fāṭimids finally took Jerusalem in 1098/491 but lost it to the Crusaders, along with Jaffa, in the following year. Palestine and the coastal cities of the Levant were in Crusader hands by 1118/512, when the Crusader King Baldwin launched an unsuccessful attack on Egypt itself.

The last Fāṭimid possession in Palestine, Ascalon, fell to the Crusaders in 1153/548, by which time the weaknesses of the Fāṭimid state in Egypt were manifest not only to the Crusaders but to the vigorous Zangid ruler of Damascus, Nūr ad-Dīn. In 1163/558 the Fāṭimid vizier Shāwar, ousted from office in one of the endless power struggles at court, appealed to Nūr ad-Dīn for support. Nūr ad-Dīn sent his general Shīrkūh to Egypt; Shāwar was reinstated in office only to use the Crusaders then to force Shīrkūh out of Egypt. Two campaigns later, in 1168/564, Shīrkūh entered Egypt permanently. The Crusaders on campaign there were compelled to withdraw, and Shāwar was deposed and killed. Nūr ad-Dīn's general took power in Egypt as the nominal vizier of the last Fāṭimid Caliph, al-ᶜĀḍid.

The Ayyūbids
(1171-1250/567-648)

Shīrkūh's nephew Ṣalāḥ ad-Dīn was closely associated with his uncle during Shīrkūh's campaigns in Egypt and succeeded Shīrkūh as vizier upon the latter's death in 1169/564. Ṣalāḥ ad-Dīn, founder of the Ayyūbid dynasty, is among the most remarkable of Muslim historical figures. The military campaigns of Ṣalāḥ ad-Dīn and his generals gave him enormous territorial gains and began the expulsion of the

Crusaders from the Middle East. His exemplary character as a soldier and as a ruler impressed not only his Muslim contemporaries but also his Crusader opponents.

Egypt was returned to Sunnī, or orthodox, Islam shortly before the death of the last Shī^{c}a Fāṭimid Caliph, al-^{c}Āḍid, in 1171/567. Thereafter Egypt was under the nominal sovereignty of the Zangid ruler Nūr ad-Dīn, on whose behalf Ṣalāḥ ad-Dīn continued to rule Egypt. Following Nūr ad-Dīn's death in 1174/569 Ṣalāḥ ad-Dīn began his advance on Syria, where he eventually displaced Nūr ad-Dīn's son and heir, Ismā^{c}īl. Ṣalāḥ ad-Dīn's major attack on the Crusaders began in 1187/583 with an important victory at Hattīn, followed by a sweep of Acre, Tiberias, and several other cities in Syria and Palestine. Though the Crusaders retook Acre in 1191/587, this initial Ayyūbid thrust greatly reduced their power.

Ṣalāḥ ad-Dīn's brother, al-^{c}Ādil, reunited Egypt and Syria under his rule in 1200/596, following a seven-year period of tension between the sons of Ṣalāḥ ad-Dīn, who had inherited control of Egypt, Damascus, and Aleppo upon their father's death. During al-^{c}Ādil's reign the Crusaders began a new attack on Egypt, which was subsequently defeated by al-^{c}Ādil's son, al-Kāmil, in 1221/618. Al-Kāmil enjoyed cordial relations with the Crusader King Frederick II of Sicily. When Frederick arrived in the Levant at the head of a new Crusade, the two monarchs negotiated a treaty that ceded control of Jerusalem to Frederick. The deep unpopularity of the treaty with the Muslims and many of the Christians of the area did not prevent al-Kāmil from using the respite it granted him to move against his brother and other relatives in Syria. The last major Ayyūbid ruler, aṣ-Ṣāliḥ, was preparing to meet a new Crusade launched by King Louis IX of France when he died in 1249/647. His son, Tūrān Shāh, held power briefly while the Crusader armies were defeated, until his assassination by his father's Mamluks in 1250/648. Tūrān Shāh's assassination brought the Ayyūbid period in Egypt to an end. Power passed to the widow of aṣ-Ṣāliḥ, Shajar ad-Durr, who consolidated her position by contracting a marriage with the Mamluk commander Aybak.

It was during the Ayyūbid period that Mamluks, troops of slave origin, came to play a large role in the army. The Ayyūbid army, which had a strong Kurdish contingent, was altered by the Sultan aṣ-Ṣāliḥ. He maintained a Mamluk regiment on the island of Roda (Rawḍa) at Cairo. Mamluks had been found in the armies of earlier rulers in Egypt, but it was this Sultan who established their preeminence in the army of the Ayyūbids. The Mamluks' rise to power can be explained by the same factor that led to the instability and in-fighting of the Ayyūbids in Egypt and Syria: a keen competition for power, which rendered everyone suspect. The Mamluks, owing no allegiance save to their master, were seen as a reliable source of support in the leadership struggles between the Ayyūbids. The Mamluks ultimately proved stronger and more cohesive than the Ayyūbid regime they were meant to be defending.

The Mamluks (1250-1517/648-922)

For the first two years of their joint reign Shajar ad-Durr and Aybak ruled with a nominal Ayyūbid Sultan, al-Ashraf II, before deposing him and exercising power directly. The judgment of historians on Shajar ad-Durr's actual role during her seven years in power varies. As the only woman to rule Egypt in her own name during the Muslim period Shajar ad-Durr's actual power has been questioned by historians. Relations between the Sultana and her consort deteriorated, and in 1257/655 she had Aybak murdered, an act that cost her her own life shortly thereafter.

Mamluk rule in Egypt has traditionally been divided between the Baḥrī period, from 1250/648 to 1382/784, and the Burjī (or Circassian) period, which began in 1382/784 and ended with the Ottoman conquest of Egypt. The Baḥrī period takes its name from the regimental headquarters of these Mamluks, the island of Roda on the Nile (river = baḥr in Arabic); the Burjīs take their name from their headquarters in the Citadel towers (in Arabic, burj) of Cairo. The Baḥrī Mamluk Sultans adhered to a hereditary principle from the reign of the Sultan Qalā'ūn onward. The Burjīs were a largely unstable, occasionally violent, and rapacious regime, whose time in office brought Egypt to the edge of fiscal and administrative ruin, easing the eventual takeover of the Ottomans. Both the Baḥrī and Burjī periods were characterized by the extreme insecurity in office of the Sultan; reigns of a few months were more common than reigns of several years.

The character of Mamluk rule in Egypt was influenced by the internal disruptions in the Islamic world caused by the successive invasions of the Mongols and of Tīmūr. Sweeping down from their homeland in Asia on a Muslim world divided between petty princedoms, the Mongols left behind them the shattered remains of the Islamic East, areas of which even today have never recovered their population or vitality. Baghdad, the center of the ᶜAbbāsid Caliphate of Islam, was destroyed and the Caliph murdered by the Mongols in 1258/656.

The Mamluks defeated the Mongols in battle at ᶜAyn Jālūt in Syria in 1260/658. This victory saved Egypt from the devastation suffered by the Islamic countries to her east, but it was too late to save Aleppo and Damascus from destruction. The Baḥrī Mamluk Sultan Baybars established the ᶜAbbāsid Caliphate in Cairo shortly after ᶜAyn Jālūt, investing a distant relative of the last Caliph in Baghdad. The Egyptian Caliphate survived until the Ottoman conquest and was used by the Mamluk Sultans to confer legitimacy on their control of Egypt and Syria.

The Baḥrī Mamluk Sultan Baybars (r. 1260-77/658-76) did much through his military conquests to reunite the Syrian territories lost to the Mongols, Crusaders, or minor dynasts of the region. In the scope of his military exploits Baybars resembles his Ayyūbid predecessor Ṣalāḥ ad-Dīn. The next major Baḥrī Sultan, Qalā'ūn, continued the military advances of Baybars, both in Nubia and the Levant, and his son Khalīl completed the expulsion of the Crusaders from the Levantine coast after defeating them in a major engagement at Acre in 1291/690. The Mongols were far from quiescent during this time, reappearing in Mamluk territory twice in the thirteenth century. In 1271/669 the Mongols were turned back from Syria by Baybars, and in 1299/698, preparatory to another offensive on Mamluk lands, the Mongols briefly seized Homs and Damascus. This last offensive was halted by the Baḥrī Sultan Baybars II in 1303/702.

The disruption caused by the Mongols in Syria was matched by the misery, destruction, and dislocations caused by the plague. An especially severe outbreak of Black Death hit Egypt in 1348/749. The plague affected Cairo and the provinces in the same way that it afflicted the cities of medieval Europe, decimating not only the civilian population but also the ranks of the Mamluks and the army. The growing instability that characterized the closing years of the Baḥrī period may be traced to the unsettling effects of this plague and the subsequent cycle of famine and disease.

The Burjī Mamluks had an ethnic background different from their Baḥrī predecessors, with much less emphasis on the maintenance of any form of hereditary principle. The refusal of the Burjīs to effect an alliance with the Ottoman Turks in the north against yet another invader from Central Asia, Tīmūr, had disastrous consequences for both regimes. Tīmūr entered Mamluk territory in 1400/803 and embarked on a program of destruction, pillage, and killing on a terrible scale. His death in 1405/808 brought to an end the threat he posed to the Mamluks in Egypt, but he had inflicted a major defeat on the Ottomans in 1402/805. In consequence the dislocation of the Ottomans prevented them from posing a direct challenge to the Mamluks until several decades later.

The fiscal exactions of the Burjī Sultans, particularly Barsbāy (1422-37/825-41) and Qā'it Bay (1468-96/872-901), brought the Egyptians enormous hardships. The establishment of monopolies by the Burjī Sultans on some basic commodities caused shortages and price rises. Attempts by the Sultans to gain control of trade, artificially adjust the currency, and meet the continuing financial demands of their courts and Mamluks emptied the state treasuries nearly as fast as increased revenues were collected or exacted. As the Burjīs fought among themselves for control of the Sultanate and plundered the remaining healthy sections of the Egyptian economy, the Ottomans were gradually rebuilding their position in the north.

In 1453/857 the Ottomans took Constantinople, bringing the beleaguered Byzantine Empire to an end. Just over a decade later the Ottomans came into conflict with the Mamluks over their expansion into territory claimed by the Mamluks as under their sphere of influence. The intervention of the Mamluk Sultan Qā'it Bay in the leadership contest between the Ottoman Sultan Bāyazīd and his brother

Jem in 1481/886 won the Mamluks no friends in the Ottoman court. Concurrently, the expanding commercial interests of the Portuguese in commodities and territories hithertofore exploited by the Mamluks was to bring these two powers into conflict early in the sixteenth/tenth century.

A short period of hostilities between the Mamluks and Ottomans ended without resolution in 1491/896. The Ottomans then concentrated on meeting the challenge posed to their rule in Anatolia. The expansionist Selīm II came to power in Istanbul in 1512/918; two years later he led the Ottomans to victory over the Persians in the battle of Chaldiran. Having settled this challenge from Persia, Selīm turned his attention to the Mamluks. After a steady advance across Mamluk territory Selīm and the Ottoman armies met the Mamluks in battle at Marj Dābiq in 1516/922. The Mamluks, under the command of the Sultan Qānṣūḥ al-Ghawrī, were defeated; within a year the Ottomans were in control of Egypt.

Ottoman Egypt (1517-1798/922-1213)

The Ottoman Sultan ruled Egypt through his Viceroy, who was supported by an Ottoman garrison, but during the three centuries of their rule the Ottomans never entirely freed their administration in Egypt, or the Egyptians, from the Mamluks. This was to prove their undoing.

The defection of some leading Mamluks to the Ottomans prior to the battle of Marj Dābiq helped ensure the survival of the Mamluks as a political force in Egypt. The first Ottoman governor was one of these Mamluk defectors, and Mamluks were members of the beylicate, from which certain high Ottoman offices were filled. The potential for disruptiveness represented by the maintenance of Mamluk households in Egypt was compounded by the rebelliousness of regiments within the Ottoman garrison itself. The garrison and the beylicate, meant to balance the power of the Ottoman governor in Egypt, slowly gained ascendancy over him.

As the power of the Ottoman governor declined, the importance of the offices held by the beylicate increased, leading to competition within the beylicate for dominance and for control of the important positions available to the beys. This competition was exacerbated by the formation of two great factions within the beylicate in the seventeenth/eleventh century, the Qāsimiyya and the Faqāriyya, who formed alliances with different regiments of the Ottoman garrison. A period of complex alliances and conflicts within the Ottoman garrison preceded the Great Rebellion of 1711/1123, after which the Qāsimiyya enjoyed supremacy in the beylicate. Following the usual pattern of these factional struggles, the Qāsimiyya became divided and were vanquished by the Faqāriyya, who were in turn displaced by their former allies, the Qāzdughliyya.

Although the feuding of the beys and the garrison occasionally produced populist leaders, such as Küçük Mehmed, in general the motivation of the individuals involved was personal advancement within the established power structures. The Ottoman governing structures in Egypt ultimately proved incapable of containing the beys, however much power it afforded them. In the 1760s/1180s a Qāzdughliyya bey, ᶜAlī, assumed independent power in Egypt, deposed the Ottoman governor, and embarked on military campaigns in Upper Egypt and Syria. His Mamluk commander in Syria, Abu'dh-Dhahab, was encouraged by the Ottomans to overturn ᶜAlī, whereupon he assumed the governorship in 1772/1186. Following Abu'dh-Dhahab's death a Mamluk duumvir took power in 1775/1189. They suffered the usual reverses but held office until expelled by an Ottoman expeditionary force in 1786/1200. The duumvir regained power after the withdrawal of the Ottoman army and the death of the Ottoman appointee, and ruled Egypt until the French Invasion.

In retrospect, the Ottomans appear to have miscalculated in allowing the Mamluks to retain much of their original power at the time of the conquest by Selīm. Subsequent attempts by Egypt's Ottoman governors to suppress the Mamluks never enjoyed more than temporary success. As the Ottomans were forced throughout this time to counter strong military challenges from Persia, Russia, and some European states, they were unable, in the seventeenth and eighteenth centuries, to impose the kind of military solution in Egypt needed to break the Mamluks' power.

Dynasty of Muhammad Ali (1805-1952)

The arrival of a French expeditionary force in Egypt under the command of Napoleon Bonaparte in 1798 began a period of transformation in Egypt and in Egypt's role within the Middle East and in relation to Europe. Although the French were forced to retreat from Egypt in 1801 following their defeat by a combination of British, Ottoman, and Mamluk attacks, their brief period of control thoroughly upset Egypt's political balance. After a period of anarchy Muhammad Ali, commander of an Albanian regiment of the Ottoman army in Egypt, was invited in 1805 by a delegation of Cairenes to establish himself in power and restore order. Muhammad Ali moved against the Mamluks, exterminating most of them in a massacre in the Citadel of Cairo in 1811. Over the next three decades his European-trained army, under the command of his son Ibrahim Pasha, extended Egyptian control to Arabia, parts of the Sudan and Syria, and into Ottoman territory in Anatolia. In 1839 his armies inflicted a crushing defeat on the Ottomans at the Battle of Nizib, and with the surrender of the Ottoman fleet to the Egyptians shortly thereafter Muhammad Ali seemed set to replace the Ottomans as the dominant power in the Islamic world. At this point the European powers intervened, alarmed at the rise of a strong and vital state in the region. An expansionist Egypt was far more threatening to European interests than an enfeebled Ottoman Empire, and pressure was brought to bear by the European states. Muhammad Ali was left, in 1841, with control of the Sudan and with hereditary rights in Egypt, but his other territorial conquests were removed to Ottoman control.

Aside from Muhammad Ali's remarkable military progress, he began a program of modernization of all areas of Egyptian life. Educational contacts with Europe, the expansion of technical education in Egypt, European training for Egypt's army, reforms in the civil service and local administration, development of Egypt's agriculture, and the foundation of some (generally unsuccessful) public industries were all introduced during his reign. There were few aspects of education, the economy, or the military that were not subject to reform. His promotion of agriculture, particularly cash-crop cultivation, led to the development in 1820 of the first long-staple cotton plant, which became the basis of Egypt's growth as a cotton-exporter later in the nineteenth century.

Muhammad Ali was succeeded in 1848 by his grandson Abbas I, whose reign was largely devoted to reversing many of his grandfather's modernization and Westernization policies. His successors, Sa^{c}id (1854-63) and Ismail (1863-79), recommenced and continued the expansive policies of Muhammad Ali. The Suez Canal, opened in 1869, was but one of a number of concessions granted by these rulers to European companies to create the modern infrastructure of Egypt. In the process, however, both rulers, but especially Ismail, built up enormous debts to the European banks, as program after program consistently exceeded Egypt's ability to pay. Ismail's autonomy in Egypt was increased through his payment of hefty subventions to the Ottoman Porte, which itself was in deep financial trouble. Awarded the princely title "Khedive" in 1867, he embarked on a successful but costly expansion into Africa. Ill-advised by his court officials, and overambitious in his schemes for Egypt's modernization, Ismail led Egypt firmly toward bankruptcy. In 1875 Ismail was forced to sell his, Egypt's, shares in the Suez Canal to the British government. Egypt's finances were placed under international control, and this control was expanded in 1878 to include management of Ismail's personal finances and European representation in the Egyptian cabinet.

The formation of a cabinet with European ministers proved the undoing of Ismail, providing the deeply discontented native Egyptian officer corps with a rallying point of opposition. The first nationalist groupings were founded in 1879, with membership drawn from the native officers and from prominent Egyptians unhappy with the growing control of their government by foreigners. The nationalist movement reached its culmination in the Arabi Rebellion of 1882. The threat to continued European control of Egypt's finances created by the formation of a nationalist-dominated ministry in 1882 led to British military intervention that summer. The nationalist officer Colonel Arabi led Egypt's unsuccessful defense. Following his surrender in September 1882 the nationalist movement was crushed, Arabi and his supporters exiled, and the British established in de facto if indirect control of the Egyptian government.

The Sudan was lost to Mahdist forces in 1885, though Egypt (and Britain on Egypt's behalf) maintained its claims there. A joint British-Egyptian offensive reestablished control of the Sudan in 1896-98. Under the terms of the 1899 Condominium between Egypt and Britain, the Sudan was administered and controlled largely by the British, with the Egyptian Khedive retaining nominal sovereignty. The status of the Sudan was to become a major point of contention between Egypt and Britain after World War I and remained unresolved until after the 1952 Revolution.

The legal basis for Britain's position in Egypt was not clearly defined. Egypt was treated like a Protectorate of the British crown, a status it was formally accorded at the outbreak of the First World War. French claims in Egypt, originating with the establishment of international financial control in 1875-76, were not settled until the Entente Cordiale of 1904, when France surrendered its claims in Egypt in exchange for British recognition of its position in North Africa. The Khedive Abbas II issued a rescript the next year acknowledging Britain's preeminence in Egypt, but this did not constitute a guideline for British behavior in the country. The fiction of Ottoman sovereignty in Egypt was maintained by the appointment of an Ottoman representative in Egypt in 1885, a post that lasted until the First World War.

Though not a colony, Egypt had, from 1883 until 1922, little control over the management of its government and little freedom to make decisions out of line with British interests. Sir Evelyn Baring (later Lord Cromer), who served in Egypt from 1883 to 1907, gave strong direction to every area of Egyptian public life. He managed to outface the young Khedive, Abbas II (1892-1914), in the early years of the latter's reign when Abbas was filled with a natural resentment at his powerlessness. Abbas' early attempts to give official and public encouragement to the nationalists were quickly and thoroughly halted by Cromer, who soon gained ascendancy over the Khedive.

The establishment of a British Protectorate in Egypt in 1914 made formal a situation of British control that had existed in fact for the past thirty years and brought to an end the Ottoman Sultan's nominal sovereignty over Egypt. Restrictions were introduced on the political rights of Egyptians at a time when the exercise of those rights was just reaching full expression. Egypt patiently endured the exactions and requisitions of the war, but as the conflict drew to a close Egyptian nationalists began to agitate for a restoration of their national rights and a termination of the Protectorate.

The leading nationalist party of the pre-Revolutionary period, the Wafd, had its origins in the formation of a delegation (in Arabic, wafd) by the politician Sa^{c}d Zaghlul in 1918. This delegation sought to present Egypt's case for terminating the Protectorate to the British government and to the Versailles Peace Conference. The British government's refusal to receive not only Zaghlul's nationalist delegation but also (at first) a delegation headed by the then Prime Minister, Rushdi Pasha, started a cycle of public reaction that ended with the British government's decision to exile Zaghlul. Public outrage found expression in the Rebellion of 1919, in which Egyptians of every social and economic background participated.

The 1919 Rebellion, though vigorously suppressed, indicated a widespread disaffection for British rule in Egypt. The British government dispatched the Milner Mission to Egypt at the end of 1919 to study conditions there and make recommendations for future British policy. The Mission was boycotted by supporters of the Wafd and Zaghlul (virtually all non-Palace elements). Zaghlul himself, in Paris after his release from exile in April 1919, finally consented to meet with the Mission in London, in the summer of 1920.

The Milner Mission report recommended termination of the Protectorate combined with certain guarantees of the British position in Egypt. The British government, unhappy with the results of the Mission, requested the Egyptian ruler, Fuad, to send an official delegation to London to discuss the future relationship between the two countries. In March 1921 the moderate nationalist Adli Pasha accepted the Palace's invitation to form a government and lead the delegation to London. Fuad's appointment of Adli was a masterpiece of Egyptian Palace politics, for whether Fuad intended it or not, the appointment caused an irrevocable split in the nationalist movement that crippled it for the next three decades. Adli was bitterly denounced by Zaghlul for collaborating with the British; Zaghlul returned to Egypt in April 1921 to a tumultuous popular welcome. The Wafd Party and its backers organized demonstrations against the Adli government that were fueled by Zaghlul's rhetoric. In response Adli's supporters, and those politicians unhappy with Zaghlul's radicalism and tactics, formed their own political grouping to back the Adli ministry.

Zaghlul was deported again at the end of 1921, following the breakdown in negotiations between Adli and the British. In the end it was the pressure applied on the British government by their High Commissioner in Egypt, Allenby, that finally led to the issuing of the 1922 Declaration. The Declaration terminated Egypt's Protectorate status and granted the country a qualified independence. Preparations were then made for the drafting of a Constitution and for Egypt's first free elections. The Constitution was promulgated in April 1923, and later that year Zaghlul returned to Egypt from his exile.

The Wafd Party had the support of many Egyptians from the days of the 1919 Rebellion and was untarnished by any association with the British. The powerful platform and personality of Zaghlul, twice a victim of British persecution, had no equal in the other Egyptian parties. In Egypt's first, and probably most straightforward, elections, in January 1924, the Wafd won a crushing victory at the polls. To the dismay of the Palace and the British, Zaghlul formed a government. Egypt's first postindependence ministry held office less than eleven months before the assassination of the British Sirdar, Sir Lee Stack, led to the fall of the Zaghlul government.

For the British and the Palace, the Wafd represented popular forces neither of them favored. The Palace sought a maintenance of its position at the head of Egypt's political life, while the British were committed to a maintenance of their strong influence over events in Egypt. This combination of anti-Wafd forces was sufficiently strong to ensure that the party formed only two short-lived governments in the period prior to 1936, despite the party's success at the polls in every free election held during this time. Only when the British wanted a strong and popular negotiating team, as in 1929, did they favor the Wafd and pressure the Palace to allow it to form a government.

The Egyptian governments that held power from 1925 to 1929 did so under sufferance of the Palace, which tired of even such limited democracy in 1930 and asked Sidqi Pasha to form a government. The Sidqi ministry abrogated the 1923 Constitution and promulgated a new Constitution that expanded the Palace's power and reshaped the Parliament along more conservative lines. This period of restriction eased only after 1934, when the illness of King Fuad permitted a deal to be struck among the political groups in Egypt for a gradual return to normal political life. This was supported eventually by the British, who were anxious, in the light of international events, to conclude a new treaty with Egypt and were therefore favorable to the return to power of the Wafd, with their enormous popular support. The British and the Wafd government formed after the May 1936 elections successfully negotiated a new Anglo-Egyptian Treaty in August 1936, four months after the death of King Fuad. The treaty terminated the last vestiges of British political control in Egypt, though it left unsettled the future of the Sudan and was less than satisfactory on the question of the continued British military presence in Egypt.

The Wafd government's dealings with the British aroused the criticism of some more radical nationalists in Egypt. Street clashes in Cairo and elsewhere involving these younger nationalists demonstrated the existence of a gap between the Wafd and segments of nationalist opinion on the popular level. This gap was to widen and deepen in the 1940s, but even in the mid-1930s the political debate in Egypt was being joined by religious groupings, such as the Ikhwan al-Muslimun, and nationalist radicals, such as Misr al-Fatat, with slight allegiance to the established political order.

Egypt's new king, Faruq, was young and popular, but he soon displayed the autocratic tendencies of his father. The Wafd was dismissed at the end of 1937, and a series of pro-Palace or Palace-backed parties formed governments for the next five years. The Wafd itself, rent by internal struggles and the establishment of a breakaway Wafdist grouping, was kept out of these governments. As in the past, the Wafd gathered popular support while in opposition, and in consequence a climate of political instability prevailed. This instability in Egypt became critical for Britain as the Second World War intensified. The British sought the formation of a Wafd government, feeling that the Wafd, which still enjoyed more popular support than any of the other Egyptian parties, would be more effective in leading Egypt's participation in the British war effort. The British Ambassador, Sir Miles Lampson, finally forced the issue in February 1942 by offering Faruq the choice (backed by tanks) between abdication and a Wafd government. Faruq was compromised by his capitulation and the British by the humiliation they dealt him.

Egypt remained nonbelligerent until the very end of the Second World War but provided support of men and material for the British and Allied war effort. The economic boom that accompanied the employment of many Egyptians by the British and in service and manufacturing industries did not survive the war. The Wafd was dismissed in October 1944 and was kept from power for the next six years by the Palace and by a series of governments out of touch with popular demands. The postwar period was dominated politically by popular movements of the left and by the Ikhwan al-Muslimun. These groups led and participated in the wave of civil disturbances in Egypt from 1945 until 1949, when they were the target of a vigorous government suppression.

The poor performance of the Egyptian army against the Israelis in Palestine in 1948 damaged the Egyptian government's credibility not only with ordinary Egyptians but more importantly with a cadre of reform-minded and nationalist young officers who constituted themselves shortly thereafter as the Free Officers. Their political development owed more to the radical nationalists and to the religious revivalists of the Ikhwan than to any of the mainstream Egyptian parties.

Egypt's last elections before the Revolution were held in January 1950 and returned the Wafd to power. The issues of the Sudan and the presence of British troops in the Canal Zone, which had led to the breakdown in postwar negotiations between the British and Egyptian governments, once again became a sticking point in discussions about a new treaty. After several months of fruitless attempts at negotiations the Wafd government decided to abrogate the 1936 Anglo-Egyptian Treaty in October 1951. Shortly afterward the Egyptian government launched a popular paramilitary campaign against British troops in the Canal Zone. A British counterattack on the Ismailiyya police station on 25 January 1952 resulted in heavy casualties among the Egyptian defenders. The next day crowds of Egyptians took to the streets of Cairo, burning buildings and businesses with foreign associations. "Black Saturday," as the 26th of January came to be known, gave a brief glimpse of the rage and tensions that existed in Egypt below the increasingly artificial surface of national political life.

In the wake of the burning of Cairo, Egypt's political parties failed to restore the political situation--or themselves. A reformist ministry headed by Hilali Pasha fell under Palace pressure, and the country's balance of power between the Palace and the parties showed signs of further degeneration at the time of the Free Officers' coup of 23 July.

The Revolution and Its Aftermath

The 1952 Revolution was at its foundation a coup d'état; many of the revolutionary aspects of the regime did not manifest themselves until Gamal Abdal Nasser gained ascendancy over General Naguib, titular leader of the Free Officers, in 1954. Even before the emergence of Nasser, however, new political and policy directions were taken by the Revolutionary Command Council. The early years of the Revolution saw a final resolution of Egyptian and British claims on the issues of the Sudan (which eventually gained its independence from both Egypt and Britain), British troop withdrawals, the introduction of agrarian reform, and the abolition of the monarchy (which had passed from King Faruq to his infant son when the former abdicated shortly after the coup).

Political parties were abolished in January 1953. The only independent force permitted to remain active was the Islamic religious grouping Ikhwan al-Muslimun, in exchange for the organization's acknowledgment of tacit cooperation. Political coordination between the Free Officers and the Ikhwan, with its large popular base, broke down over the Ikhwan's determination to gain a controlling voice in the new government's executive decisions and legislation.

The struggle between the Revolutionary Command Council (established in 1953 from the Free Officers' Executive) and the Ikhwan on the one hand, and between Nasser and his supporters in the RCC against Naguib on the other, became open in 1954. The Ikhwan was banned in January, following a series of antiregime demonstrations. Naguib's resignation from all his offices was announced by the RCC the next month, only to be countermanded later that month and in March by the reinstatement of Naguib as President and Prime Minister, which was followed in April by the removal of Naguib from the premiership. The Ikhwan was allowed to resume its activities. In October an assassination attempt against Nasser by an Ikhwan member gave Nasser the opportunity to move against his political opponents. The Ikhwan was proscribed, and General Naguib was stripped of the presidency and placed under house arrest. A series of arrests and trials of Ikhwan members temporarily silenced the religious opposition.

Nasser ruled Egypt from November 1954 until his death in September 1970, overseeing major changes in Egypt's foreign and domestic policies. Internationally and regionally Nasser's activist role--denouncing the Baghdad Pact, nationalizing the Suez Canal, intervening in the Yemen Civil War, and supporting liberation movements in Africa and the Arab world--was shaped by his determination to gain the leadership of the region and to mute the impact of the superpowers' conflict on the regimes of the area. But his espousal of a variety of Third World political doctrines, positive neutralism, nonalignment, and Arab socialism, put Egypt in opposition to the West and to many Arab governments. Periodic bouts of Arab unity, such as the formation of the United Arab Republic of Egypt and Syria in 1958, were followed by periods in which Egypt's relations with its neighbors were openly hostile. Nasser's uneasy links with the Soviet Union guaranteed American opposition to his government, despite Nasser's efforts in the late 1950s and early 1960s to balance Egypt between the superpowers.

Domestically Nasser emerged as a leader with the same autocratic and absolutist tendencies as his pre-Revolutionary predecessors, but with a determination to remove the corruption, injustice and inequity that afflicted so many aspects of life in Egypt before 1952. During the early 1960s, Nasser's government moved Egypt toward an increasingly socialist economic policy, especially in 1961-63, and an increasingly restrictive political climate. The formation of a succession of government parties, combined with a continuing suppression of the regime's political opponents of all ideological persuasions, did little to encourage political debate in Egypt. The Ikhwan enjoyed a brief revival in the mid-1960s after many of its members imprisoned in 1954 reached the end of their prison sentences and were released. Combining with other opponents of the Nasser regime, the Ikhwan began to agitate against the government until it was the subject in 1965-66 of another official crackdown mirroring that of 1954.

Nasser's leadership of Egypt during the 1956 Suez War, in which Egypt faced an invasion by Israel, France, and Britain, had played a major role in his elevation as a Third World leader threatened by Western imperialism. In many important ways Nasser maintained this role even when the international situation became more complex and when his voice in international councils was increasingly challenged by other Arab countries resentful of his dominance. His inability or unwillingness to cede a larger role to the new revolutionary governments of the region was matched in Egypt by his lack of patience with critics of his policies. Nasser and those members of his inner circle who lasted the course of his presidency set Egyptian policy with slight reference to popular or dissident opinion.

Despite his autocracy Nasser and his government did work to improve the economic lot of ordinary Egyptians. However ill-advised some of the regime's economic policies, these policies were directed toward ameliorating some of the gross unfairness in the distribution of Egypt's national income and toward building an economy that offered greater opportunities for more Egyptians. Additionally Nasser's relations with the Egyptian people, and indeed with other Arabs in neighboring countries, were helped by his masterly and powerful oratory and by his leadership of the most populous and militarily important Arab state.

The disastrous defeat of the Egyptian and Arab armies in the 1967 Arab-Israeli War led Nasser to offer his resignation. It was rejected by the Egyptian people, and from June 1967 until 1970 the Egyptian government undertook a political retrenching and re-examination of its policies. Domestically the defeat was used to purge the army and remove the powerful Commander-in-Chief, Amer. Political reforms were promised and some slight changes instituted, but the regime was extremely cautious in its efforts to broaden its popular political base. A War of Attrition against Israel, begun in 1969, revealed Egypt's continued inability to respond effectively to Israel's superior air power. Russia was pressed to improve its arms supplies, and the Arab oil-producing states to pay for them. At the time of Nasser's death his government had accepted a peace plan put forth by U.S. Secretary of State Rogers. The situation with Israel was far from resolved, however, and the absence of an heir of Nasser's stature seemed to presage the start of a period of internal instability.

Anwar Sadat, relatively unknown at the time he succeeded President Nasser in September 1970, was originally meant to serve as an interim leader until Nasser's inner circle resolved their own political ambitions with regard to the presidency. Sadat confounded expectations and quickly established his own dominance. In May 1971 he ordered the arrest of many of the powerful figures of the late 1960s, ending their potential opposition to his regime. At the same time Sadat promised a liberalization, or "Corrective Revolution," domestically and announced that 1971 would be a year of decision with regard to Israel. The failure of the government to take any steps to resolve the Arab-Israeli dispute led to student unrest in 1972. In July of that year Sadat began reversing Egypt's policy of technical and military cooperation with the Soviet Union by ordering Soviet technicians to leave the country.

The 1973 Arab-Israeli War, though less than a clearcut victory for the Arabs militarily, changed the political balance of the region. The support given to the front-line states by the Arab oil embargo could not balance the immediate advantage enjoyed by Israel in the rapid resupply of weapons by America in the course of the fighting, but in the medium and long term, the embargo focused the West's attention on the other political actors of the region. The 1973 war began a long-overdue adjustment of Western attitudes toward the Arab-Israeli conflict, which was ultimately to work to Egypt's benefit in its efforts to replace the Soviet alliance with an American one.

Sadat's domestic reputation was greatly improved after the 1973 war, and he was able to use his new popularity to introduce a series of economic changes known as the Open Door (Infitah) Policy in 1974. The return to elements of capitalism in Egypt's economy was paired with political and social reforms that loosened many of the restrictions and terminated many of the politically based prison sentences imposed in the last decade of the Nasser period.

Despite the introduction of Infitah, and the contributions made by the OAPEC states to rebuilding the Egyptian economy after the 1973 war, economic conditions in Egypt continued poor in 1974-77. Egypt's population growth meant that the country faced an increasingly massive deficit in foreign exchange to pay for necessary imports of basic foodstuffs. Egypt's defense expenditures and its large and poorly productive public sector and bureaucratic establishment compounded the economic problems. Popular protests among industrial workers in 1975, and against the regime's plans to remove subsidies in 1977 (in response to IMF pressure), forced the readjustment of some of the government's economic plans without halting Sadat's commitment to his Open Door strategy.

Coincident with the regime's economic difficulties, both Egypt and the other confrontation states and Israel were the objects of efforts by the United States, with the occasional support of the Soviet Union, to resolve the situation between the Arab states and Israel. Egypt's acceptance of disengagement agreements with Israel negotiated by the United States was not popular with her Arab allies. The increasing Egyptian tilt toward the United States, much in evidence during 1974-75, became manifest with the final break in treaty relations between Egypt and the Soviet Union in March 1976. Efforts by the United States and the Soviet Union to resolve the Arab-Israeli dispute in 1977 met strong Israeli resistance and objections, particularly after the election of a Likud government in May of that year.

The decision of President Sadat to go to Jerusalem in November 1977 and make a direct approach to the Israelis for peace was the most controversial action by an Egyptian leader in recent times. By his actions Sadat split Egypt from the rest of the Arab world and closely linked Egypt's, and his own, destiny in the immediate future with the progress of his peace initiative. The international and regional repercussions of Sadat's initiative and the subsequent Camp David Accords have yet (1982) to be fully settled, but Camp David forced a realignment of the Arab states and a strong U.S. identification with the peace negotiations.

President Sadat's foreign policy, like that of Nasser before him, tended to dominate his regime, but the domestic problems faced by Egypt continued severe and largely unresolved. Inflation caused by the structural weaknesses of the Egyptian economy and the influx of foreign capital under the Open Door Policy have caused an upward pressure on prices at a time when the wages of the vast majority of Egyptians have remained at their low, preinflationary levels. Remittances from Egyptian workers in the other Arab states and oil revenues have given the government some room to maneuver in the short term, while the need to rationalize and restructure elements of the Egyptian economy remains.

The liberalization of Egyptian political life in 1976-77 was followed in 1978 by a renewal of restrictions on political activity. Religious opposition to the regime had been building since 1973, though it was the Egyptian government itself that encouraged Islamic revivalist groups to resume their activities as a counter to the strength of the left wing on Egypt's university campuses in the early 1970s.

The present Egyptian government faces economic and political difficulties domestically, and internationally it is tied in a new and inherently risky relationship with an Israeli state actively committed to a policy of expansionism and regional dominance. Egypt's official isolation from its Arab neighbors, and its inability so far to influence or moderate the attitudes of its Israeli partner in the peace process with regard to the Palestinian issue, has already exacerbated the serious conflicts between Israel and the other Arab states. The former no longer has to fear, and the latter no longer can count on, the Egyptian army, which by virtue of its strategic position and size provided the only regional counterweight to the demonstrated superiority in tactics and equipment of the Israeli armed forces.

The domestic repercussions of these international factors were not as serious as the economic problems and political issues with which the Sadat government had to cope. Egypt's potential as a regional economic power, with the population base and infrastructure for a new industrial expansion, remains largely untapped. Realizing this potential could have enabled the government to counter the internal criticism that its domestic and international policies have engendered. However, the high profile awarded by the Sadat government to the Camp David peace process made progress in the peace negotiations with Israel, and on Palestinian autonomy, essential.

On 6 October 1981 President Anwar Sadat was assassinated while reviewing a parade celebrating Egypt's victory in the 1973 war with Israel. The event shocked many foreign friends and observers of Egypt. It followed a period of government repression of Sadat's critics in political and religious circles, and a much lengthier time during which opposition to the government and its policies had been both manifest and mounting.

Egypt's new President, Husni Mubarak, must face the same range of domestic and international problems that marked the last years of the Sadat presidency. The early indications given of his policy seem to acknowledge the especially pressing nature of Egypt's domestic and economic troubles. At the same time President Mubarak is committed to carrying on with the Camp David process at a time when that process is questioned by Arab and international opinion, and by Israeli action in the region. Given the radical transformation in Egypt's international and domestic stance during Sadat's presidency, many of the directions he charted for Egypt's future are now filled with uncertainty. The choices made by President Mubarak, however these may be buoyed by the goodwill of Egypt's friends, allies, and sympathizers, will be both complex and difficult.

CHRONOLOGY

[NB: Events listed take place in Egypt unless otherwise stated.]

30 BC	Start of Roman Period
AD 38-41	Communal disturbances in Alexandria
c. 54	Foundation of Christianity in Egypt by the Apostle Mark
55	Revolts in Alexandria
66	Religious disturbances in Alexandria
69	Egyptian Prefect Tiberius Julius Alexander supports Vespasian's attempt to become Roman Emperor
115-17	Revolt of Jews in Egypt
130	Inter-Christian disturbances
153	Plague; tax revolt
172	Plague; Bucolic Rebellion; tax revolt
175	Revolt of Avidius Cassius
c. 180	Cathecal School of Alexandria founded by Pantaenus
193	Revolt of Pescennius Niger
200	Roman Emperor Severus grants municipalities some self-government; persecution of Christians in Alexandria
212	Egyptians given Roman citizenship by Emperor Caracalla
215	Clement, Patriarch of Alexandria, dies
250	Anti-Christian campaign by Emperor Decius
252-54	Revolt of Emelianus; death of Patriarch Origen (253)
257-60	Anti-Christian campaign
270	Egypt temporarily added to the Kingdom of Palmyra
271-73	Revolt of Firmus

284	Reforms of Diocletian; new taxation system; Latin replaces Greek as administrative language; beginning of Coptic calendar
297	Revolt of Domitius Domitianus; military command reorganized
302-11	Diocletian's persecution of the Christians in Egypt
312	Emperor Constantine issues Edict of Milan, granting toleration to all religions
c. 320	Establishment of monastic system by Pachomius
325	First Church Council, at Nicaea, condemns Arianism
330	Dedication of Constantinople; power shifts from West to East in the Roman Empire
373	Death of Athanasius, Patriarch of Alexandria
381	Alexandria replaced by Constantinople as second Christian center
391	Serapeum, pagan cult center, destroyed by Christians
415	Murder of the Greek philosopher Hypatia by Christian monks; Byzantines introduce new administrative reforms
431	Council of Ephesus meets to consider Christian doctrinal disputes
444	Death of Cyril, Patriarch of Alexandria
449	Second, "Robber," Council of Ephesus; Egyptian Patriarch Dioscorus forces settlement of theological disputes between Egypt and other Christian centers
451	Council of Chalcedon; Dioscorus, Patriarch of Alexandria, deposed; Egyptian Coptic Church breaks away
453	Campaign against southern tribes in Egypt
482	Henaticon (Act of Union) promulgated by Emperor Zeno
541	Start of thirty-year plague and famine
550	Patriarchate established as executive administrative office by Byantium
565	Revolt of Blemmyes tribe

610	Emperor Heraclius takes power with Egyptian support
616	Persians advance on Egypt
619	Persians take Alexandria
629	Heraclius restores Byzantine control of Egypt
c. AD639/18AH	^{c}Amr b. al-^{c}Āṣ enters Egypt
640/19	Pelusium, Bilbays, Fayyum taken by ^{c}Amr; Siege of Heliopolis, Babylon; first settlement at al-Fusṭāṭ; Patriarch Cyrus of Alexandria negotiates with ^{c}Amr
641/20	Alexandria surrenders; ^{c}Abdallāh b. Sa^{c}d campaigns in Upper Egypt; canal cleared from Nile valley to port of Qulzum (near modern Suez); Cyrus concludes treaty with ^{c}Amr
642/21	Alexandria formally turned over to Muslims
642-43/22	^{c}Amr leads expedition against western Libya; al-Fusṭāṭ becomes Egypt's capital
644/23	^{c}Abdallāh b. Sa^{c}d appointed governor of Upper Egypt
645/24	^{c}Abdallāh b. Sa^{c}d appointed governor of all Egypt; Byzantine navy led by Manuel attacks Alexandria in support of rebellion; ^{c}Amr temporarily reinstated as governor of Egypt
646/25	Alexandria retaken by Muslims
647-48/27	^{c}Abdallāh campaigns in North Africa after being restored to power as governor of Egypt
651-52/31-32	^{c}Abdallāh campaigns in Nubia, Dongola
652/31	Nubians conclude treaty with Muslims; new Byzantine attack on Alexandria
655/35	Byzantine navy defeated by Muslims at Dhat aṣ Ṣawārī
656 or 658/36 or 38	Death of ^{c}Abdallāh
658/38	^{c}Amr returns to Egypt as governor for the ^{c}Umayyad Caliph Mu^{c}awiya, deposing the Caliph ^{c}Alī's appointee
661/41	Beginning of Umayyad period in Egypt
663-64/43	Death of ^{c}Amr

683-84/64-65	Difficulties in Umayyad succession; Egypt temporarily under sovereignty of ^{c}Abdallāh b. az-Zubayr
685/65	^{c}Abd al-^{c}Azīz b. Marwān appointed governor of Egypt; administrative reforms introduced
690/70	Serious flooding of Nile forces temporary relocation of Egyptian capital from al-Fusṭāṭ to Ḥulwān (Helwan)
698/79	Ifrīqiyya (central North Africa) made independent province
704-05/85	^{c}Abdallāh b. ^{c}Abd al-Malik b. Marwān appointed governor
706/87	Arabic made official language of administration in Egypt
709/90	Qurra b. Sharīk appointed governor (to 714/96)
715/96	Nilometer constructed on Rawda
718/99	Muslims fail in their attempt to take Byzantine capital of Constantinople as Muslim-Byzantine hostilities continue
725/107	Tax revolt in Egypt
727/109	Beginning of settlement of Qays tribe in Egypt
733/116	Coptic disturbances end after several years of trouble
736/118	Byzantine attack on Egypt's Mediterranean coast
739/121	Byzantine attack on Damietta
747/130	Umayyad navy defeated by Byzantines
750/132	Umayyad Caliph Marwān II killed at Fayyum in Egypt; civil troubles in Egypt, al-Fusṭāṭ burned; beginning of ^{c}Abbāsid period; great disturbances in Syria, Palestine
761/145	Canal linking Nile valley and Red Sea closed on orders of ^{c}Abbāsid Caliph al-Manṣūr
778/161	Increasingly fierce fighting between ^{c}Abbāsids and Byzantines
780/163-64	Unrest in Egypt over army requisitions
781/165	^{c}Abbāsids force three-year truce on Byzantines
786/170	Beginning of reign of ^{c}Abbāsid Caliph Hārūn ar-Rashīd; twenty-four governors in Egypt during his twenty-three years in power
794-95/178-79	Unrest among army in Egypt

813-33/198-218	Coptic uprising and general Muslim and Christian revolts over taxes (peaking in 831/216)
827/211	Campaign of pacification in Egypt by ^{c}Abbasid general Ibn Ṭāḥir
831/216	^{c}Abbāsid Caliph al-Ma'mūn visits Egypt accompanied by his general Afshīn to quell revolts there; reforms in tax system introduced
853/238	Major Byzantine attack on Damietta; seizure of Cyprus by Byzantines as they renew their Mediterranean offensive against ^{c}Abbāsids
856/242	Administrative reforms bring more centralization in Egypt
858/244	Revolt of Beja tribe in Upper Egypt suppressed by General Muḥammad b. al-Qummi
859/245	Byzantines again threaten Damietta
861/247	Al-Mudabbir sent from Baghdad to reform Egypt's financial administration
863/249	Byzantines inflict two defeats on Arabs in Mesopotamia
868/254	Aḥmad b. Ṭūlūn appointed governor; persecution of Shī^{c}a in Egypt
870/256-57	Rebellion in Palestine; abortive attempt by Ibn Ṭūlūn to invade Syria
870/256	Al Qaṭā'i^{c}, residential-administrative complex, constructed by Ibn Ṭūlūn
870-83/256-70	Zanj rebellion in southern Iraq threatens ^{c}Abbāsid Caliphate
872/258	Egypt and Syria's financial administration given to Ibn Ṭūlūn
878/265	Ibn Ṭūlūn conquers Syria after unsuccessful attempt to depose him is made by ^{c}Abbāsid court
882/269	Ibn Ṭūlūn tries to persuade ^{c}Abbāsid Caliph to relocate in Egypt
884/270	Khumārawayh succeeds his father as Ṭūlūnid ruler in Egypt and Syria; drives ^{c}Abbāsid troops from Syria
887/273	Uprising of Ṭūlūnid troops suppressed

892/279	^{c}Abbāsid Caliph al-Mu^{c}taḍid grants Khumārawayh extension of his Iqṭā^{c}
896/282	Jaysh becomes third Ṭūlūnid ruler
897/283	Hārūn displaces Jaysh as Ṭūlūnid ruler with Muḥammad b. Abba as his regent
899/286	^{c}Abbāsid Caliph decreases Ṭūlūnid territories, increases their tribute
901-03/288-89 and 905/292	Revolts in Syria against Ṭūlūnids; Qaramatian Shī^{c}a rebels active
905/292	Hārūn murdered; Shaybān succeeds as Ṭūlūnid ruler; Egypt and Syria restored to direct ^{c}Abbāsid control; period of Madhārā'ī family's control as financial administrators (until 935/323); brief seizure of government by Muḥammad b. Khalānjī
913-14/301-02	Fāṭimids briefly seize Alexandria
919-21/307-09	Raids by Fāṭimids
935/323	Muḥammad b. Tughj "the Ikhshīd" appointed governor of Egypt; beginning of Ikhshīdid period; Fāṭimid raid into Egypt
939/328	The Ikhshīd takes Palestine and parts of southern Syria after a battle with Ibn Ra'iq; Ḥamdānids active in north Syria
940/329	Aleppo in Syria joined to Egypt after campaign by Kāfūr on behalf of the Ikhshīd
942/330	Syria rejoined to Egypt following death of Ibn Ra'iq; Mecca, Medina incorporated with Egypt
944/333	Ḥamdānids arise as power in northern Syria; ^{c}Abbāsid Caliph tries to flee to Ikhshīdids; Ḥamdānid chief Sayf al-Dawla takes Homs and Aleppo from Ikhshidids; Byzantines advance on Muslim lands in Upper Mesopotamia
946/334	Ūnūjūr succeeds his father, Muḥammad b. Ṭughj, as ruler of Egypt; de facto power exercised by his tutor Kāfūr; rebellion in Egypt; after one-year truce, fighting recommences with Ḥamdānids

947/335	Treaty between Ikhshidids and Ḥamdānids defines their respective territories in Syria
949/337	Nubians attack oases demanding trade concessions; disturbances in Egypt
954/343	Fire at al-Fusṭāṭ; civil disturbances against regime (with involvement of Ūnūjūr)
955/344	Major earthquake followed by plague; troubles in Nubia, with Aswan briefly seized by Nubian troops; civil disturbances
961/349	ᶜAlī succeeds his brother Ūnūjūr as Ikhshīdid ruler, with Kāfūr still in complete control of government; several outbreaks of famine during ᶜAlī's five-year nominal rule
963-68/352-57	Series of civil disturbances in Egypt
965/354	Cilicia, Cyprus taken by Byzantines
966/355	Kāfūr succeeds to power in his own name as Ikhshīdid ruler of Egypt; Byzantines campaign in Euphrates region between Aleppo (Syria) and Mosul (Iraq)
968/357	Death of Kāfūr; Aḥmad Abu'l-Fawāris briefly on throne; Al-Ḥasan b. ᶜUbayd Allāh briefly on throne; Qaramatians take Damascus from the Ikhshīdids
969/358	Fāṭimid armies under Jawhar aṣ-Ṣiqillī take Egypt; al-Qāhira (Cairo) founded; Byzantines seize parts of northern Syria, annex Antioch; Aleppo becomes Byzantine vassal
970/359	Foundation of al-Azhar Mosque; Mecca, Medina give allegiance to Fāṭimids
971/360	Qaramatians, advancing on Egypt from Syria, defeated in battle
973/362	Fāṭimid Caliph al-Muᶜizz transfers Fāṭimid Caliphate to Egypt; Qaramatians repelled after they attack Cairo
974/364	Fāṭimids briefly reoccupy Damascus (first taken in 971/361 for a short period) before losing it to Turkish military chief Alptakīn
975/365	Advance of Byzantine Emperor Tzimisces toward Jerusalem halted at Tripoli by Fāṭimid armies; death of al-Muᶜizz; al-ᶜAzīz new Fāṭimid Caliph

976-78/366-68	Campaigns by Fāṭimids in Syria; Damascus taken, Alp-takīn defeated, some limited territorial gains
979/369	Communal disturbances in Egypt; vizier Ya^{c}qūb b. Killis in difficulties
983/373	Fāṭimids campaign in Syria, defeat Qassām who earlier seized Damascus
984/373	Famine in Egypt; vizier Ya^{c}qūb b. Killis again eclipsed
987/377	Yemen gives its allegiance to Fāṭimids; treaty concluded with Byzantines over trading rights and recognition in Constantinople; Zīrids, Fāṭimid allies, annex Tripolitania in North Africa
991/380	Death of Ya^{c}qūb b. Killis, long-serving Fāṭimid vizier; three viziers follow in rapid succession; Badjkur, Fāṭimid supporter in Syria, attacks Aleppo
992/381	Al-Ḥusayn b. al-Ḥasan appointed vizier
992-93/382	Al-^{c}Azīz campaigns in Syria; his general, Mangūtakīn, lays siege to Aleppo
994-05/384	Further campaigns by al-^{c}Azīz in Syria; second siege by Mangūtakīn
995/385	Anti-Christian disturbances under vizierate of ^{c}Īsā b. Nasṭūrus, a Christian appointee; Byzantines reassert their control of Aleppo (Syria)
996/386	Al-Ḥākim succeeds to Fāṭimid Caliphate; Ibn ^{c}Ammar vizier; ^{c}Īsā b. Nasṭūrus murdered
997/387	Fāṭimids defeat Byzantines in naval battle; Barjawān displaces Ibn ^{c}Ammar as vizier
998/388	Byzantines start peace negotiations with Fāṭimids
999/389	Disturbances in Syria, where Byzantine Emperor Basil is on campaign; Fāṭimid campaign in Cyrenaica and Tripoli
1000/390	Barjawān murdered
1001/391	Ten-year peace treaty signed between Byzantines and Fāṭimids
1005/396	Rebellion in Cyrenaica; disturbances in Alexandria
1007-08/398	Famine

1009/400	Church of the Holy Sepulcher, Jerusalem, destroyed on orders of al-Ḥākim
1012/403	Zīrids autonomous in Cyrenaica; revolt against Fāṭimids in Palestine
1015/406	Byzantines break commercial relations with Fāṭimids
1017/408	Fāṭimid governor appointed in Aleppo; Darāzī proclaims divinity of al-Ḥākim
1020/410	Rebellion in Egypt, al-Fusṭāṭ burned on orders of al-Ḥākim
1021/411	Fāṭimid Caliph al-Ḥākim disappears; Caliphate passes to his son, aẓ-Ẓāhir, with al-Ḥākim's sister, Sitt al-Mulk, as regent
1023-24/413-14	Challenge of ᶜAbd ar-Raḥmān, Fāṭimid governor of Damascus, defeated; start of severe two-year famine; Aleppo breaks away under Ṣāliḥ b. Mirdās; Fāṭimids make diplomatic approaches to Byzantines
1027/418	Aḥmad al-Jajarā'iᶜ effective ruler as vizier; disturbances in Egypt
1036/427	Al-Mustanṣir becomes Caliph; attempt to reopen canal linking Nile valley and Red Sea
1037/429	Difficulties in Syria; ten-year treaty with Byzantines recognizing their right to appoint Patriarch of Jerusalem
1038/429	Fatimid General Anushtakīn takes Damascus, Aleppo; Sulayhīd dynasty supporting Faṭimids in Yemen
1041/433	Aleppo falls to Mirdāsids once more; Zīrids break with Fāṭimids
1043/434	Internal disturbances in Egypt; imposter as-Sikkīn appears, claiming to be lost Fāṭimid Caliph al-Ḥākim
1045/436	Tustarī becomes vizier until his death two years later
1047/439	Peace treaty with Byzantines renewed
1048-49/440-01	Campaign by Fāṭimids against Mirdāsids in Syria
1050/441	Al-Yāzūrī becomes vizier
1054/445	Famine; Byzantine Emperor Constantine Monomachus approached for food supplies

1055/446	Famine continues; unsuccessful negotiations with Monomachus' successor, Zoë, for food
1056/447	Jerusalem briefly closed to Western pilgrims
1057-58/448-49	Al-Basāsīrī proclaims Fāṭimid Caliphate in Mosul; Aleppo temporarily back in Fāṭimid hands
1058/450	Al-Yāzūrī displaced as vizier by Ibn al-Maghrabī
1059/450	Fāṭimid Caliphate proclaimed in Baghdad by al-Basāsīrī
1060/451	Al-Basāsīrī flees Baghdad as Saljūq Turks take city
1060/452	Aleppo reverts to Mirdāsid control
1062/454	Internal dissensions within Fāṭimid army between Turkish and Sūdān regiments
1063-64/455-56	Fāṭimids campaign in Syria
1065/457	Start of especially severe seven-year famine in Egypt
1066-68/458-60	Fāṭimids campaign in Syria
1067/459	Dissension in Fāṭimid army worsens
1068/461	Turcoman tribes under command of Atsiz active in Palestine
1069/462	Fāṭimid regiments fighting each other in Damascus; Aleppo submits to Saljūq Turks (and is eventually placed under Saljūq control)
1071/463	Atsiz takes Jerusalem with his Turcoman troops; Battle of Manzikert, Byzantines defeated by Saljūq Sultan, Turkic tribes enter Anatolia; Normans in Silicy take Palermo from Arabs
1072/464	Complete civil chaos in Cairo and Egypt; ᶜAbbāsid supporter temporarily in power
1074/466	Fāṭimid General Badr al-Jamālī comes to Cairo to restore order; vigorous suppression of dissident army units
1076/468	Atsiz takes Damascus
1077/469	Atsiz and his Turcoman troops menace Cairo; turned back by Badr al-Jāmalī
1078/471	Campaign by Badr al-Jāmalī in Syria
1079/472	ᶜUqaylids take Aleppo as Saljūq vassals; Damascus has Saljūq governor

1080/473	Fāṭimid Caliph no longer mentioned in prayers at Mecca
1085-86/478-79	Further campaigns in Syria by Badr al-Jamālī on behalf of Fāṭimids; Saljūq governor in Aleppo
1089-90/482	Badr al-Jamālī on campaign in Syria
1091/484	Muslims lose Sicily to Normans
1094/487	Badr al-Jamālī dies, succeeded by his son al-Afḍal; al-Mustaᶜlī becomes Fāṭimid Caliph, causing schism by supporters of his brother, Nizār; Saljūq power in Syria declining
1096/490	Crusaders reach Syria
1097/490	Fāṭimids retake Tyre after local rebellion
1098/491	Crusaders, Fāṭimids negotiate at Antioch; al-Afḍal takes Jerusalem from Saljūqs' allies
1099/492	Fāṭimids lose Jaffa, Jerusalem to Crusaders; al-Afḍal defeated at Ascalon
1101/495	Al-Āmir comes to power as Fāṭimid Caliph; Palestine falls to Crusaders
1103/497	Acre falls to Crusaders
1108-09/502-03	Tripoli taken from Fāṭimids by Crusaders
1110/504	Beirut, Sidon fall to Crusaders
1118/512	First Crusader attack on Egypt, led by Baldwin I, Frankish King of Jerusalem, withdraws
1121/515	Death of al-Afḍal; al-Batā'ihī becomes vizier
1124/518	Crusaders take Tyre; Fāṭimid fleet defeated by Venetians
1125/519	Abū Najāḥ b. Qannā' becomes powerful in Egyptian court
1128/522	Zangids, former Saljūq military commanders, take Aleppo
1130/524-25	Al-Āmir dies; his cousin (later the Fāṭimid Caliph al-Ḥāfiz) appointed Regent for al-Āmir's unborn child; al-Ḥāfiz imprisoned by vizier Kutayfāt
1131-32/525-26	With help of chamberlain Yānīs, al-Ḥāfiz escapes, Kutayfāt killed; al-Ḥāfiz declares himself successor to al-Āmir; schism as supporters of al-Āmir's direct line reject Caliphate of al-Ḥāfiz; Yānis killed

1135/530	Attempt to reopen Red Sea canal; Bahrām becomes vizier after execution of his predecessor, al-Ḥasan, son of al-Ḥāfiz
1137/532	Rebellion of vizier Riḍwān
1143/537	Treaty between Fāṭimids and Normans
1144/539	Ibn Maṣāl acting vizier
1147/522	Former vizier, Riḍwān, dies while in rebellion against al-Ḥāfiz
1148/543	Nizārī disturbances in Egypt
1149/544	Aẓ-Ẓāfir succeeds to Fāṭimid Caliphate; Ibn Maṣal briefly serves as vizier, overturned by Sallār
1150/545	Fāṭimid vizier Sallār makes unsuccessful approach to Nūr ad-Dīn, Zangid ruler of northern Syria, for help against the Crusaders; Fāṭimid fleet attacks Crusader coastal towns
1153/548	Ascalon, last Fāṭimid possession outside Egypt, falls to Crusaders; Normans attack Egypt; Sallār murdered; ᶜAbbās new vizier
1154/549	Fāṭimid Caliph aẓ-Ẓāfir murdered by ᶜAbbās and his son; Fā'iz succeeds to Caliphate; Nūr ad-Dīn takes Damascus; Ṣāliḥ Ṭalā'iᶜ summoned to Cairo by Fāṭimid court to depose ᶜAbbās
1158/553	Ṣāliḥ Ṭalā'iᶜ campaigns in Palestine, takes Gaza and Hebron from Crusaders; Byzantines ask Fāṭimid help against Normans in Sicily
1160/555	Al-ᶜĀḍid becomes Fāṭimid Caliph; Baldwin III, Crusader king, threatens to invade Egypt and is bought off with tribute, subsequently unpaid
1161-63/556-58	Ṣāliḥ Ṭalā'iᶜ killed, his son Ruzzīk becomes vizier; Amalric raids Egypt twice, receives tribute
1163/558	Shāwar displaces Ruzzīk as vizier and is in turn displaced by Dirgham; Shāwar seeks help from Nūr ad-Dīn of Damascus to regain power
1164/559	Shīrkūh, general of Nūr ad-Dīn, invades Egypt on behalf of Shāwar, who then turns against him; Shīrkūh meets

	Crusaders in battle at Bilbays before both parties withdraw from Egypt
1167/563	Second campaign of Shīrkūh in Egypt; Crusaders, defending vizierate of Shāwar, defeated by Shīrkūh in battle at Ashmunayn; Alexandria seized by Shīrkūh, who installs his nephew Ṣalāḥ ad-Dīn as governor; Amalric and Shīrkūh negotiate mutual withdrawal from Egypt following former's successful siege of Alexandria; Egypt made tributary to Crusaders
1168/564	Bilbays sacked by Crusaders on campaign in Egypt following suspicions about Shāwar's loyalty; al-Fusṭāṭ burned by Shāwar to prevent it falling into Crusader hands; Fāṭimid court asks Nūr ad-Dīn for help against Crusaders; Shīrkūh returns to Egypt and Crusaders withdraw
1169/564	Shīrkūh becomes vizier to al-ᶜĀḍid, Shāwar executed shortly afterward; death of Shīrkūh, Ṣalāḥ ad-Dīn becomes vizier; Byzantine attack on Egyptian coast repulsed
1170/566	Earthquake in Syria; Ṣalāḥ ad-Dīn campaigns in southern Palestine
1171/567	Egypt restored to Sunnī (Orthodox) Islam shortly before death of last Fāṭimid Caliph, al-ᶜĀḍid; beginning of Ayyūbid period
1171-73/567-69	Inconclusive campaign against Crusaders in Syria; Ṣalāḥ ad-Dīn withdraws from siege of Montreal castle
1172-73/568	Ayyūbid campaign under Tūrān Shāh, brother of Ṣalāḥ ad-Dīn, against supporters of Fāṭimids in exile in Upper Egypt; Ṣalāḥ ad-Dīn's control extended to southern Arabia by Tūrān Shāh; growing friction between Nūr ad-Dīn and Ṣalāḥ ad-Dīn over latter's withdrawal from siege of Kerak
1174/569	Death of Ṣalāḥ ad-Dīn's nominal sovereign, the Zangid ruler Nūr ad-Dīn, and of powerful Crusader King Amalric; power struggle in Syria; Ṣalāḥ ad-Dīn takes power in Damascus; Norman fleet attacks Egypt but is defeated; Kanūz tribe invades Upper Egypt, met by al-ᶜĀdil,

	brother of Ṣalāḥ ad-Dīn; unsuccessful siege of Aleppo by Ṣalāḥ ad-Dīn
1175/570	Siege at Homs in Syria, followed by more territorial gains for Ayyūbids in Syria; Zangid forces defeated at Hama; truce between Ayyūbids and Zangids; Ṣalāḥ ad-Dīn declares himself Sultan of Egypt and Syria and is recognized by the ᶜAbbāsid Caliph in Baghdad
1176/571	Zangid forces break truce and attack Ṣalāḥ ad-Dīn's army near Aleppo; after defeat of Zangids at Aleppo, treaty between Nūr ad-Dīn's son, Ismāᶜīl, and Ayyūbids, recognizing Ṣalāḥ ad-Dīn's conquests and allowing Ismāᶜīl to remain in control of Aleppo; truce between Assassins and Ayyūbids; Crusaders defeat Ayyūbid forces under Tūrān Shāh in Baqaᶜā Valley (Lebanon); Byzantines suffer massive defeat at hands of Saljūqs in Battle of Myriocephalum, leading to further weakening of Christian power in East
1177/572	Alliance between Byzantines and Crusaders breaks down; Ṣalāḥ ad-Dīn campaigns in Palestine, lays siege to Ascalon; major defeat of Ayyūbids by Crusaders at Mongiscard; Ṣalāḥ ad-Dīn and his army retreat to Egypt
1179/574	Armies of Baldwin IV defeated at Banyās and Marj ᶜAyūn in Syria by armies of Ṣalāḥ ad-Dīn
1180/575-76	Drought and famine in Syria force truce on all parties
1181/577	Raynald de Chatillon, Crusader knight, breaks truce and attacks Muslim pilgrimage caravan; Ismāᶜīl, Nūr ad-Dīn's son, dies in Aleppo
1182-83/578	Start of new Ayyūbid campaign in Syria and Palestine; Raynald launches his fleet against Ayyūbid possessions on Red Sea coast and the Ḥijāz, sinking shipload of pilgrims bound for Mecca
1183/579	Ṣalāḥ ad-Dīn finally takes Aleppo; unsuccessful siege of Kerak; Citadel in Cairo under fortification; Ayyūbid campaigns in North Africa
1184/580	Second Ayyūbid siege of Kerak; raids in Palestine
1185/581	Treaty between Ṣalāḥ ad-Dīn and Crusaders; Ṣalāḥ ad-

	Dīn's armies take Diyarbakr and Mayyafariqin, though Mosul holds out; Raynald's fleet attacked
1186/582	ᶜIzz ad-Dīn, Amīr of Mosul, becomes vassal of Ṣalāḥ ad-Dīn; Raynald breaks truce with Ayyūbids, plundering pilgrimage caravan; Citadel, new Ayyūbid administrative-residential complex in Cairo, completed
1187/583	Great sweep by Ṣalāḥ ad-Dīn and Ayyūbid armies against Crusaders; Tiberias taken, victory at Battle of Ḥaṭṭīn, followed by surrender of Acre, Galilee, Samaria, Nablus; Jaffa taken by storm; Sidon, Beirut, Ascalon, Gaza fall; Jerusalem taken after brief siege
1188/584	Latakiya, Jabalah, Sihyawn fall as Ayyūbids raid coastal cities held by Crusaders; Kerak falls after one-year siege; Shawbak taken; Ṣalāḥ ad-Dīn on campaign in northern Syria
1189/585	Siege of Crusader fort, Beaufort; Crusader King Guy marches on Acre; new Crusade being mounted in Europe
1190/586	Fighting around Acre between Crusaders and Ayyūbids
1191/587	Crusaders, with strong reinforcements from Europe, retake Acre; Ayyūbids defeated in battle at Arsuf; Ascalon sacked by Ṣalāḥ ad-Dīn to prevent its use as Crusader base; friendly negotiations between Richard Coeur de Lion and al-ᶜĀdil (Safadin), brother of Ṣalāḥ ad-Dīn
1192/588	Crusaders menace Jerusalem but withdraw to Ascalon, which they refortify; treaty negotiated between al-ᶜĀdil and Crusaders over Jerusalem and territorial claims; Crusaders capture Ayyūbid fort at Daron in Palestine; fierce fighting at Jaffa; treaty eventually concluded between Ayyūbids and Crusaders for five-year truce
1193/589	Death of Ṣalāḥ ad-Dīn; territories divided among his sons and relations; al-ᶜAzīz inherits his father's Egyptian territories; al-Afḍal assumes power in Damascus; az-Zahīr in power in Aleppo; al-ᶜĀdil on campaign
1194/590	Al-ᶜAzīz invades Syria but retreats after gaining territory in Palestine

1196/592	Al-ᶜĀdil deposes his nephew al-Afḍal in Damascus and rules on behalf of al-ᶜAzīz
1197/593	Al-ᶜĀdil campaigns in Syria against Crusaders
1198/595	Death of al-ᶜAzīz; al-Manṣūr succeeds his father in Egypt
1199/596	Deposed al-Afḍal gains support in Egypt, allies with his brother, Ẓāhir, Amīr of Aleppo; al-Afḍal and az-Ẓāhir besiege their uncle al-ᶜĀdil in Damascus before falling out with each other
1200/596	Al-ᶜĀdil pursues al-Afḍal to Egypt and defeats him at battle in Bilbays; al-ᶜĀdil takes power in Egypt and Syria; Ẓāhir defeated in attempt to take Damascus
1203-04/599-601	Crusaders invade, then sack, Constantinople; enduring bitterness between eastern and western Christian communities results
1207-08/604	Citadel in Cairo refurbished by al-ᶜĀdil; ᶜAbbāsid Caliph recognizes al-ᶜĀdil's control of Egypt and greater Syria
1217/614	Crusader activity in Palestine; al-ᶜĀdil dispatches his army
1218/615	Crusaders attack Damietta on Egypt's Mediterranean coast, capturing its fort; death of al-ᶜĀdil; al-Kāmil, his son, succeeds him in Egypt; another son, al-Muᶜaẓẓam, comes to power in Syria
1219/616	Crusaders under command of Pelagius occupy Damietta; plot against al-Kāmil is uncovered; Ayyūbid fortresses in Palestine and city of Jerusalem are stripped of their fortifications in anticipation of trade-off with Crusaders; al-Kāmil's offer of peace terms is rejected
1221/618	Ayyūbid armies defeat Crusaders at Battle of Mansura in Nile Delta; eight-year peace treaty
1226/623	Al-Kāmil negotiates with Emperor Frederick of Sicily while planning to depose his brother al-Muᶜaẓẓam
1227/624	Al-Muᶜaẓẓam dies, his son Da'ud taking power in Damascus
1229/626	Following several months of negotiations, treaty is con-

cluded between al-Kāmil and Frederick of Sicily, granting the Emperor Jerusalem and several cities in Palestine; Ayyūbid Empire reunited as al-Ashraf Muẓaffar ad-Dīn, brother of al-Kāmil and Amīr of Diyarbakr, takes Damascus from Da'ud, ruling it in al-Kāmil's name

1231-35/629-33 Aṣ-Ṣāliḥ, son of al-Kāmil, campaigns in Syria, Iraq; Turkic tribes active in eastern Ayyūbid territory

1238/635 Al-Kāmil in Damascus after annexing city and suppressing plot of his brother, Isma^{c}il, who had taken power in Damascus following the death of al-Ashraf; death of al-Kāmil; his son al-^{c}Ādil II comes to power in Egypt, his other son, Ṣāliḥ, takes Damascus from yet another rebellious relative, Jaqaq, who had seized the city following al-Kāmil's death

1239/636 Ismā^{c}īl regains Damascus; aṣ-Ṣāliḥ turns his armies toward Egypt

1240/637 Aṣ-Ṣāliḥ takes power in Egypt from his brother al-^{c}Ādil II; Crusaders under Tibald, defeated at Gaza in 1239/636, withdraw from Palestine

1244/642 Khwārazmian Turks, Ayyūbid allies, take Jerusalem; Battle of Gaza between Crusaders and the Ayyūbids and Khwārazmians; victorious Ayyūbid army under the command of Baybars then campaigns in southern Syria; continuing difficulties between aṣ-Ṣāliḥ and ^{c}Imād ad-Dīn of Damascus throughout this year

1245/643 Aṣ-Ṣāliḥ's army with Khwārazmian support lays siege to Damascus; Ismā^{c}īl capitulates, is given principality of Baalbek

1246/644 Khwārazmians turn against aṣ-Ṣāliḥ and back Ismā^{c}īl in his attempt to retake Damascus; Khwārazmians vanquished en route to Homs, Ismā^{c}īl forceably retired to Baalbek

1247/645 Ayyūbids take Tiberias, Ascalon from Crusaders

1248/646 Tūrān Shāh, son of aṣ-Ṣāliḥ, on campaign in Iraq

1249/647 Crusaders under Louis IX land at Damietta

1250/647 Crusaders advance to meet the Ayyūbids in battle at

Mansura; death of aṣ-Ṣāliḥ concealed by his widow, Shajar ad-Durr, who sends for his heir, Tūrān Shāh; after desultory negotiations Crusaders defeated at Mansura, with Louis IX and many Crusader knights captured and ransomed; Ayyūbid ruler of Aleppo seizes Damascus

648 — Tūrān Shāh murdered by his father's Mamluks; Shajar ad-Durr, the Sultana, marries the Mamluk Aybak; al-Ashraf Muẓaffar, a young Ayyūbid prince, holds nominal power for two years; beginning of Baḥrī Mamluk period

1251/648 — Aybak turns back Ayyūbid challenge

1253/651 — Aybak gains recognition of his position in Egypt from the ^{c}Abbāsid Caliph

1254/652 — Disturbances in Egypt, coup attempt against Aybak

1255/653 — Aybak and Crusaders conclude truce

1256/654 — Mongols suppress Nizārī followers in Persia in their advance toward Iraq and Syria

1257/655 — Aybak murdered by Shajar ad-Durr's supporters; Shajar ad-Durr assassinated in turn; Aybak's son ^{c}Alī becomes Sultan; Mūsā, Ayyūbid ruler of Kerak, defeated in attack on Egypt

1258/656 — Mongol hordes under Hūlāgū sack and destroy Baghdad; ^{c}Abbāsid Caliphate in Baghdad ended and Caliph killed

1259/657 — Mongols enter Syria; Qutuz becomes Sultan after deposing ^{c}Alī

1260/658 — Aleppo, Damascus sacked by Mongols; Nablus and Gaza occupied; Qutuz leads strong Mamluk army toward Mongol positions, takes Gaza and inflicts major defeat on Mongols at Battle of ^{c}Ayn Jālūt; Damascus, Aleppo subsequently retaken by Mamluks; Mongols massacre defenders of Aleppo in revenge for death of their commander, Kitbughā Noyon, shortly before their withdrawal from Syria; Qutuz assassinated by his commander, Baybars, who becomes Sultan; Syria annexed

1261/659	ᶜAbbāsid Caliphate reestablished in Cairo; Baybars defeats challenge by the Mamluk Amīr Sinjār al-Ḥalabī
1262/660	Kerak regained from Ayyūbid ruler, Mūsā (al-Mugīth ᶜUmar)
1263/660	Baybars campaigns in Palestine
1264/662	Homs annexed by Baybars; commercial and other contacts pursued with several European states
1265/664	Caesarea, Haifa taken by Baybars
1266/664	Conquests in Galilee by Baybars; Safad, Toron fall to Mamluks; Commander Qalā'ūn takes Cilicia
1268/666	Jaffa, Beaufort, Crac, and Antioch fall to Baybars; Baybars offers one-year truce, which is accepted
1269/667	Baybars defeats Crusaders outside Acre
1271/669	Campaigns by Baybars in Syria; Crusaders offer ten-year truce; Mongols active in Syria, eventually turned back by Baybars; Mamluk fleet sent to Cyprus but defeated at Limassol
1272/670	Peace treaty concluded with Acre, granting Crusaders rights for ten years in coastal area between Acre and Sidon; supresses Assassins
1275/673-74	Campaigns by Mamluks in Nubia, Armenia
1276/675	Beginning of campaign by Baybars in Asia Minor; after two successful battles against Mongols, Baybars withdraws
1277/676	Baraka (Berke) Khan, Baybars' son, becomes Mamluk Sultan
1279-80/678	Baraka Khan displaced by Salāmish; Salāmish turned out of office by Qalā'ūn; Qalā'ūn defeats challenge by Sunqur al-Ashqar and Syrian Mamluks; Mongol army attacks Aleppo, retreats from Syria as Qalā'ūn assembles his own forces
1281/679-80	Qalā'ūn gains allegiance of Sunqur; truce between Mamluks and Knights Templar; Mongols defeated in battle at Homs

1283/682	Mamluk truce with Acre renewed, maintaining most of Crusaders' coastal possessions
1285/684	Crusader fort of Marqab, allied to Mongols, taken by Mamluk troops after siege; Crusader ruler of Tyre concludes truce with Mamluks
1287/686	Latakiya falls to Mamluks
1288/867	Qalā'ūn seeks to attract eastern trade
1289/688	Campaign by Mamluk armies in Nubia; truce with Crusaders broken and Tripoli taken; truce protecting Crusader position in Acre renewed
1290/689	Italian Crusaders arrive at Acre; Muslim population of city harassed and murdered; Qalā'ūn prepares to march on Acre but dies at start of campaign; Khalīl, son of Qalā'ūn, becomes Sultan; Khalīl suppresses plot in Cairo against him
1291/690	Khalīl rejects Crusader offer of negotiations over Acre; Khalīl expels Crusaders from Acre after major battle; Crusader coastal towns of Tyre, Sidon, Beirut all fall; further campaign against Haifa and Crusader forts
1293/692	Crusader raid on Alexandria; Khalīl orders expansion of Egyptian fleet in preparation for attack on Crusader naval bases in Cyprus; Khalīl assassinated
1294/693	An-Nāṣir Muḥammad, Khalīl's brother, becomes Mamluk Sultan
1295/694	Kitbughā deposes an-Nāṣir Muḥammad; plague strikes Egypt
1297/696	Lājīn overturns Kitbughā
1299/698	Mamluk faction deposes Lājīn and reinstalls an-Nāṣir Muḥammad as Sultan; Mongols approach Syria, take Homs, Damascus
1300/699	Mamluks regain their Syrian territories as Mongols withdraw; Mamluks campaign against Mongol allies in Syria, attack Armenia
1302/701	New Mongol offensive against Syria in preparation

1303/702	Mamluk commander Baybars II defeats Mongols at Battle of Marj aṣ-Ṣuffār; major earthquake hits Egypt
1304/703	Mamluk expedition to Nubia
1308/707	Mongols reappear in Syria, advance toward Jerusalem, but withdraw
1309/708	Baybars II deposes an-Nāṣir Muḥammad, takes power as Sultan; Baybars strongly challenged when an-Nāṣir Muḥammad uses his exile to gather army of supporters; Baybars flees Cairo
1310/709	An-Nāṣir Muḥammad regains his throne
1311/711	New Egyptian campaign in Nubia
1320/720	Coptic revolts in Egypt
1323/723	Dongola captured by Mamluk armies; truce between Armenia and Egypt
1330/731	Byzantines forced to recognize Ottoman Turkish victories at Bursa and in northwestern Anatolia following their defeat in attempt to retake this area
1340/740	Abū Bakr becomes Mamluk Sultan following death of his father, an-Nāṣir Muḥammad
1341/742	Kūjūk becomes Sultan after his brother Abū Bakr deposed by vizier Qūsūn
1342/743	Aḥmad becomes Sultan after his brother Kūjūk deposed following fall from power of Qūsūn; Ismā^{c}īl becomes Sultan after his brother Aḥmad is deposed by Mamluk court
1344/749	Ismā^{c}īl campaigns against Aḥmad and his supporters at Kerak
1345/746	Sha^{c}bān becomes Sultan after his brother Ismā^{c}īl's death
1346/747	Ḥājjī I becomes Sultan after his brother Sha^{c}bān is assassinated
1347/748	Ḥasan becomes Sultan after his brother Ḥājjī I is deposed
1348/749	Black Death and subsequent famine decimate population, Mamluks

1351/752	Ṣāliḥ becomes Sultan after his brother Ḥasan is deposed; Mamluk faction backing him soon quarrels within itself
1354/755	Ḥasan restored to power after his brother Ṣāliḥ is deposed
1357/758	Ottoman Turks cross into Europe for first time
1360/761	Ottomans expand their territorial control in the Balkans
1361/762	Muḥammad becomes Sultan after his uncle Ḥasan is assassinated
1363/764	Sha^cbān II becomes Sultan after his cousin Muḥammad is deposed
1365/766	Crusaders attack Alexandria, which they brutally sack then abandon as Mamluk army advances on city; Ottoman Turks advancing northward in Balkans; Egyptian troops in Nubia
1366/768	Revolt against the Amīr Yilbughā, powerful figure in Egyptian court
1370/772	Peace treaty signed between Mamluks and Crusaders in Cyprus
1371/773	Ottoman Turks on campaign in southern Serbia
1375/777	Armenia falls to Mamluks
1376/778	cAlī becomes Sultan after his father, Shacbān II, is assassinated
1380/782	Tīmūr, leading invasion of Central Asian tribes, takes control of Persia
1382/783	Ḥājjī II becomes Sultan after death of his brother cAlī
1382/784	Barqūq becomes Sultan, first Sultan of Burjī (or Circassian) Mamluks, after deposing Ḥājjī II
1385/788	Ottoman Turks take Sophia (Bulgaria); Tīmūr in Caucasia
1387/789	Tīmūr and his army on Syrian border; discontent in Syria and among Mamluk Amīrs
1389/791	Ḥājjī II returned to office as Mamluk Sultan after his predecessor Barqūq is deposed by Yilbughā, Syrian Mamluk Amīr

1390/792	Barqūq regains power as Mamluk Sultan, driving his opponents from Cairo
1393/795	Contacts between Mamluks and Ottomans as Tīmūr advances
1394/796	Ottoman Turks campaign in Greece
1396/799	Ottoman Turks defeat King of Hungary in battle at Nicopolis, on Danube
1399/801	Faraj becomes Mamluk Sultan following death of his father, Barqūq; disturbances in Syria as new offensive by Tīmūr reaches Mamluk borders; Ottomans take Malatya on northern border of Greater Syria, Mamluks, Ottomans divided in the face of Tīmūr's advance
1400/803	Tīmūr enters Mamluk territory; takes Malatya, Baghdad, then Aleppo
1401/804	Damascus falls to Tīmūr with great destruction and loss of life; Faraj negotiates with Tīmūr
1402/805	Ottoman Turks defeated by Tīmūr and his army in battle near Ankara
1403/806	Plague and famine strike Egypt
1404/807	Tīmūr withdraws to Central Asia
1405/808	Faraj temporarily displaced as Sultan by his brother ᶜAbd al-ᶜAzīz, backed by Mamluk faction; Faraj regains power shortly thereafter; Tīmūr's death removes threat of new invasions from Central Asia
1411/814	Rebellion of Amīrs Shaykh and Nawrūz against Faraj; serious and continuing famine in Egypt and Syria
1412/815	The ᶜAbbāsid Caliph in Egypt, al-Mustaᶜīn, becomes Sultan for six-month period following death of Faraj; Shaykh (al-Mu'ayyad Shaykh) eventually takes power; order restored in Egypt and provinces, though famine continues throughout Mu'ayyad Shaykh's reign
1413/816	Ottoman Turkish Sultan Muḥammad I (Mehmed I) begins reunification of Ottoman territories
1414/817	Antipiracy treaty between Egypt and Cyprus

1419/822	Campaigns of Ibrāhīm, son of Mu'ayyad Shaykh, against Tīmūrid forces near eastern borders of Mamluk territories
1421/824	Following death of Mu'ayyad Shaykh, great instability in Cairo; Shaykh's son Aḥmad rules briefly before being deposed by Ṭaṭār; following death of Ṭaṭār, Muḥammad becomes Sultan
1422/825	Barsbāy emerges as new Mamluk Sultan after power struggle; in north Ottoman Turks lay siege to Constantinople
1423/826	Barsbāy imposes monopoly on trade in sugar as economic conditions in Egypt continue to decline
1425/828	Mamluks seize customs post at Jeddah to gain greater revenue from eastern trade; Mamluk position in the Hijaz strengthened; Barsbāy bans circulation of foreign coins in Egypt
1426-27/829-30	Reconquest and sack of Cyprus by Mamluks
1429/832	Barsbāy establishes pepper monopoly
1430/833	Ottomans take Macedonia and Thessalonica as their territorial expansion continues; famine, plague strike Egypt
1432/835	Mamluk armies campaign in Syria, Mesopotamia
1433/836	Treaty between Mamluks and Turcoman tribes brings to close period of hostilities between them
1435-36/839	Ottoman Turks take Albania
1437/841	Yūsuf, son of Barsbāy, becomes Sultan upon his father's death
1438/842	Yūsuf's three-month reign brought to end by his tutor, Jaqmaq, who becomes Sultan; rebellion in Egypt suppressed; Byzantines seek alliance or union with Rome as defense against Ottoman encirclement
1443/847	Following Ottoman Turkish territorial gains in Macedonia and Transylvania, and fighting on Hungarian border, Crusade is launched against Ottomans
1444/848	Further rebellions and disturbances in Egypt and Syria

	suppressed by Sultan Jaqmaq; unsuccessful Mamluk naval attack on Rhodes; in north Ottoman Turks inflict total defeat on European Crusaders and their local allies at Varna
1448/852	Ottoman Turks extend their territories in Balkans
1453/857	ᶜUthmān, son of Jaqmaq, becomes Sultan upon his father's death; Ināl becomes Sultan after ᶜUthmān is deposed; Ottoman Turks take Constantinople; end of Byzantine Empire
1454/858	Disturbances in Mamluk's Anatolian territories
1455/859	Ināl suppresses rebellion in Egypt against his rule
1459/863	Serbia annexed by Ottomans
1469/864	End of Ināl's unsuccessful involvement in attempts to influence succession in Cyprus; Ottoman Turks take Morea
1461/865	Ināl ensures succession of his son Aḥmad; Aḥmad overthrown by Khūshqadam
1466-70/870-75	Ottomans and Mamluks come into conflict over Dulgadir Province of central Anatolia, where Ottomans sought control and Mamluks gave their support to local rulers; Ottomans eventually establish their sovereignty in region
1467/872	Bilbay becomes Sultan upon death of his predecessor Khūshqadam
1467-68/872	Timurbughā becomes Sultan after Bilbay is deposed; Timurbughā hands over power to his ally Qā'it Bay; beginning of four year war with Albistān in Asia Minor
1475/880	Ottoman Turks take southern Crimea
1479/884	Ottoman Turks end sixteen-year war with Venice
1480/885	Ottoman Turks take Otranto in southern Italy
1481/886	Qā'it Bay shelters Jem, claimant to Ottoman Sultanate, incurring wrath of Jem's brother, new Ottoman Sultan Bāyazīd II
1482/887	Jem, with support of Qā'it Bay, campaigns in Anatolia
1490/895	Economic conditions in Egypt deteriorating gravely; Qā'it Bay imposes capital levy to replenish Treasury

1491/896	Close of six-year period of hostilities between Mamluks and Ottomans; Mamluks maintain control of Kayseri and Cilicia under agreement with Bāyazīd
1492/897	Bad outbreak of plague strikes Egypt
1495/900	Factional struggles among Mamluks bring disorder to Egypt and Syria
1496/901	Nāṣir Muḥammad II becomes Sultan following death of his father, Qā'it Bay
1496/901-03	Ottoman-Polish war for control of Moldavia
1498/903	Qānṣūḥ al-Ashraf becomes Sultan after his nephew Nāṣir Muḥammad II murdered; Portuguese explorer Vasco da Gama discovers route to India, beginning of direct European intervention in spice trade formerly monopolized by Mamluks
1499/904	Mamluk troops in revolt, general internal disturbances in Egypt
1500/905	Jānbalāt becomes Sultan after Qānṣūḥ al-Ashraf deposed; Ottomans advance into Crimea; Portuguese establish presence in Calcutta
1501/906	Tūmān Bay I becomes Sultan after Jānbalāt deposed; Qānṣūḥ al-Ghawrī becomes Sultan after Tūmān Bay driven from office
1502-03/907-08	Ottoman Turks conclude treaties with Venice, Hungary
1505/911	Portuguese take Socotra in Gulf of Aden; Mamluk shipping increasingly subject to Portuguese harassment
1508/914	Al-Ghawrī dispatches Mamluk fleet to India
1509/915	Portuguese inflict major naval defeat on Mamluks; naval encounters between Mamluks and Portuguese recommence after years
1512/918	Selīm the Grim becomes new Ottoman Sultan
1514/920	Ottoman Turks defeat Persian Ṣafavid Shah at Chaldirān, ending twelve-year challenge to their power
1515/921	Ottomans take Diyarbakr
1516/922	Ottomans under Selīm march on Syria; Mamluks defeated

	at Battle of Marj Dābiq; Sultan Qānṣūḥ al-Ghawrī dies during battle; Mamluk forces retreat to Egypt, where Tūmān Bay II becomes Sultan
1517/922-23	Cairo falls to Ottomans under Selīm; Tūmān Bay leads unsuccessful defense of Egypt; beginning of Ottoman period in Egypt; Khā'ir Bay, former Mamluk governor in Syria, appointed governor in Egypt; Egypt separated administratively from Syria; Egypt's standing commercial treaties with Europe renewed
1520/926	Sawakin, Red Sea port, taken by Ottomans
1522/928-29	Death of Khā'ir Bay; disturbances in Egypt; Ottomans take Rhodes
1524/930	Revolt of Aḥmad Pasha, Ottoman governor of Egypt
1525/931	Ottoman vizier Ibrāhīm Pasha in Egypt to restore order; Ottoman legal code introduced
1526/932	First Ottoman cadastral survey carried out in Egypt
1528/934	Capitulatory agreements between Egypt and Europe renewed but Egypt placed henceforth under Ottoman capitulatory arrangements with Europe
1530/936	Egyptian fleet assembled by Ottoman governor Sulaymān Pasha
1534/941	Ottomans take Tunis, establishing Mediterranean base there
1538/945	Sulaymān Pasha, serving second term as Ottoman governor of Egypt, takes port of Aden
1541/948	Portuguese attack Red Sea port of Sawakin, but their assault on Suez repulsed
1550/957	Ottoman cadastral survey in Egypt revised
1551/958	Ottomans take Tripoli (Libya)
1566/974	Ottomans unsuccessful after lengthy campaign against Malta
1567/975	Governorship of Sinān Pasha in Egypt
1569/977	Sinān Pasha on campaign in Yemen on behalf of Ottoman Sultan

1570/978	Beginning of three-year Ottoman campaign in Cyprus
1574/982	Governorship of Maṣeh Pasha in Egypt
1576/984	Upper Egypt placed under direct Ottoman administration
1586/994	Military revolt by Sipahi corps of Ottoman garrison in Egypt; Ottoman governor imprisoned in Cairo; in east Ottoman Turks gradually expand into Persian territory
1589/997	New disturbances among Ottoman troops in Egypt
1598/1007	Further revolt of Sipahi corps in Egypt
1601/1010	More disturbances in Ottoman garrison in Egypt
1603-18/1012-27	Ottoman-Persian War
1605/1013-14	Ottoman governor in Egypt, Ibrāhīm Pasha, assassinated by Sipahis
1607/1016	Ottoman troops in revolt in Egypt; new Ottoman governor, Mehmed Pasha, begins vigorous suppression
1609/1017-18	Rebellious Ottoman troops, including Sipahis, active in Delta; Mehmed Pasha finally brings them to order
1610/1019	New Ottoman legal code promulgated in Egypt
1618-22/1027-31	With fighting against Persia continuing, period of disturbance at Ottoman court; Sultan ᶜUthman II murdered in 1622/1031
1619/1027-28	Devastating plague, famine strike Egypt
1623/1032	Ottoman troops in Egypt successfully reject replacement of Ottoman governor, Musṭāfa Pasha; ᶜAlī Pasha, new appointee from Istanbul, sent back
1630/1039	Rise of Faqāriyya faction of beylicate in Egypt
1631/1040	Ottoman governor of Egypt Mūsā Pasha forced to retire by Egyptian beys; Faqāriyya chief Riḍwān holds office of Amīr al-Ḥājj
1635-38/1041-45	In series of battles Ottomans regain Iraqi territory lost to Persians fifteen years previously
1639/1049	Ottomans and Persians sign peace treaty fixing their common border

1640/1050	Unsuccessful attempt by Ottoman governor to suppress Riḍwān
1643/1053	Outbreak of plague in Egypt, followed by famine
1647/1057	Second faction of beylicate in Egypt, Qāsimiyya are eclipsed by Faqāriyya when Qāsimiyya leader Qānṣūḥ is imprisoned and put to death
1656/1067	Faqāriyya faction leader Riḍwān dies; position of faction begins to decline; Ottomans begin twenty-two year siege of Crete
1659/1070	Ottoman governor and Qasīmiyya campaign against Faqāriyya in Upper Egypt
1660/1071	Faqāriyya proscribed by Ottoman governor Musṭāfa Pasha; ascendancy of Aḥmad Bey, "The Bosniak," leader of Qāsimiyya faction of Egyptian beylicate
1662/1073	Aḥmad Bey, Qāsimiyya leader, assassinated on orders of Ottoman governor of Egypt
1683/1094	Start of twenty-six years of Ottoman campaigns in central Europe
1692/1103	Re-emergence of Faqāriyya faction under Ibrāhīm Bey as dominant power in Egyptian beylicate, in alliance with leader of Ottoman Janissary corps in Egypt, Küçük Mehmed
1694/1105	Plague and famine strike Egypt; Küçük Mehmed assassinated; Muṣṭafā al-Qāzduglī implicated
1695/1106	Faqāriyya power wanes following death of their leader, Ibrāhīm Bey
1698/1109-10	Janissaries creating difficulties in Cairo
1699/1110	Ottoman Sultan concludes Treaty of Carlowitz with European powers, loses most of his territorial claims against Hungary
1706/1118	Janissary corps in Egypt involved in fresh disturbances; Janissary leadership contested by Afranj Aḥmad, ally of Faqāriyya faction of Egyptian beylicate
1711/1123	Great Insurrection; Faqāriyya and Qāsimiyya beys, with

their allies in Ottoman corps, fight for supremacy; after seventy days of battles and talks between parties Qāsimiyya emerge triumphant; Ismā^{c}īl Bey and Abū Shanab, head of Qāsimiyya faction, establish their dominance in beylicate

1714/1126 Ismā^{c}īl Bey arranges assassination of Faqāriyya leader, Qayṭās Bey

1718/1130 Death of Abū Shanab leaves Ismā^{c}īl Bey in sole command of Qāsimiyya faction; tension develops as supporters of Abū Shanab find themselves eclipsed within beylicate; in Europe Ottomans recover their position in Morea, lost under Treaty of Carlowitz, by defeating province's Venetian rulers

1724/1137 Ismā^{c}īl Bey assassinated; six years of power struggles within Egyptian beylicate commence; short-lived alliance struck between Abū Shanab faction of Qāsimiyya under Sharkas Bey and Faqāriyya under Dhu'l-Faqār

1730/1143 Last struggle between Qāsimiyya and Faqāriyya; Sharkas Bey dies following battle, and Dhu'l-Faqār is assassinated; Faqāriyya faction emerge as dominant power in beylicate, under leadership of ^{c}Uthmān Bey; Qāzdughliyya faction under Ibrāhīm Kāhya begin to act as rivals to their former Faqāriyya allies

1739/1152 Ibrāhīm Kāhya, Qāzdughliyya leader, breaks with ^{c}Uthmān; following assassination attempt, ^{c}Uthmān leaves Egypt; in Europe, Ottomans recover Serbian territories after defeating Austrians in battle

1746/1159 After Persians renew their offensive against Ottomans, Ottoman Sultan is forced to recognize border established in 1639/1049 between Ottoman territory and Persia

1748/1161 Qāzdughliyya Mamluk household under Ibrāhīm Kāhya, in alliance with smaller household under Riḍwān Kahya, dominates beylicate, which they proceed to fill with their nominees

1754/1168 Ibrāhīm Kāhya dies; six years of instability in Egyptian beylicate follow

1757/1171	^{c}Alī Bey the Elder becomes Shaykh al-Balad, supreme within Egyptian beylicate
1760/1173	^{c}Abd ar-Raḥmān Kāhya, head of Qāzdughliyya Mamluk faction, deposes ^{c}Alī Bey the Elder and names ^{c}Alī Bey "Bulut Kapan" (Cloud Catcher) as Shaykh al-Balad [NB: latter-named Shaykh al-Balad henceforth referred to as Alī Bey]
1763/1176	^{c}Alī Bey gains ascendancy within Egyptian beylicate
1766/1180	^{c}Alī Bey temporarily ousted and exiled by Mamluks Kashkash and Khalīl Bey
1767/1181	^{c}Alī Bey, in alliance with last Qāsimiyya bey, Ṣāliḥ, and with help of Hawwāra chief Humām, defeats Khalīl and Kashkash in battle; ^{c}Alī Bey restored to power in Cairo
1768/1182	^{c}Alī Bey secures expulsion of Ottoman governor of Egypt, and gains recognition for his de facto control of Egypt, from Ottoman Porte; campaign mounted in Gaza against Khalīl and Kashkash; Ṣāliḥ Bey assassinated
1768-74/1182-88	Ottoman-Russian War; Ottoman navy destroyed early in war, and Russia's gradual advance on Ottoman territory recognized by Treaty of Küçük Kaynardji (1774/1188)
1769/1183	Hawwāra tribal rebellion in Upper Egypt crushed by ^{c}Alī Bey's troops
1770-71/1184-85	Abu'dh-Dhahab, Commander of ^{c}Alī Bey's forces, on campaign in Syria; Abu'dh-Dhahab encouraged to turn against ^{c}Alī Bey by Ottoman court
1772/1186	^{c}Alī Bey driven out of Egypt by Abu'dh-Dhahab; Abu'dh-Dhahab becomes Shaykh al-Balad and ruler of Egypt on behalf of Ottoman Porte (formally in 1773/1187)
1773/1187	^{c}Alī Bey dies while attempting to regain power in Egypt
1775/1189	Campaign by Abu'dh-Dhahab in Palestine; death of Abu'dh-Dhahab; power struggle in Egypt within beylicate; Ottoman Sultan and Russians sign peace treaty, granting Russians territorial and navigation rights; Mamluk duumvir of Murād Bey and Ibrāhīm Bey establish their supremacy in Egyptian beylicate

1777/1191	Ismā^{c}īl Bey and other Mamluks of ^{c}Alī Bey (the ^{c}Alawiyya) temporarily displace duumvir from power in Cairo
1778/1192	Ibrāhīm Bey and Murād Bey regain power after Ismā^{c}īl fails to control beylicate and situation in Cairo
1781/1195	Ibrāhīm Bey and Murād Bey, after campaign against ^{c}Alawiyya in Upper Egypt, are forced to cede large areas of region to ^{c}Alawiyya
1783/1197	Russia annexes Crimean territory of Ottoman Empire
1784/1197	Ibrāhīm Bey temporarily ousted from power in Egypt by Murād Bey but regains his position and is reconciled with Murād Bey following year
1786/1200	Plague strikes Egypt; Ottoman Sultan sends Ḥasan Pasha to Egypt to restore Ottoman control; Ismā^{c}īl Bey recalled to Cairo from Upper Egypt and installed in power by Ḥasan Pasha following withdrawal of Murād Bey and Ibrāhīm Bey from Egyptian capital
1787/1201	Disturbances in Cairo
1790-91/1205-06	Uprisings and disturbances as new outbreak of plague hits Egypt; Ismā^{c}īl dies of plague; Murād Bey and Ibrāhīm Bey regain power
1792/1206	Further Russian territorial gains at expense of Ottoman Empire
1798/1213	Napoleon Bonaparte and French army land in Egypt (July 1798); advance on Cairo after defeating Mamluks at Battle of the Pyramids; Cairo taken by French; Murād and Ibrāhīm Bey flee Cairo; British Admiral Nelson sinks French fleet at Abu Qir (August); Ottomans declare war; Napoleon establishes consultative body of notables in Cairo; rebellion against French in Cairo (October)
1799/1214	Napoleon's invasion of Syria turned back at Acre (May); French campaign against Mamluks in Upper Egypt; Ottomans attack Abu Qir (July); Napoleon leaves Egypt (August), turning command over to General Klêber
1800	Klêber and Sir Sidney Smith (for British) negotiate the Convention of Al-Arish, providing for French withdrawal

from Egypt (January); British Admiral Keith refuses to accept Convention, presses campaign against French on behalf of Ottomans (March); Kléber assassinated in June, Baron de Menou assumes command of French forces

1801 British and Ottoman offensive against French; British, Ottomans land (March); French forces in Cairo, under command of Belliard, surrender (June), forcing capitulation of Menou in Alexandria (August); French withdrawal negotiated; French forces leave Egypt in October; Murād Bey, one of Mamluk duumvir ruling Egypt before French invasion, tries to regain power

1802 Khusrau Pasha, Ottoman appointee as governor of Egypt, challenged by Muḥammad Bey al-Alfī on behalf of Mamluks; fighting between Mamluk and Ottoman forces in Egypt; massacre of Mamluks by Ottomans after battle at Abū Qir, British rescue Mamluk survivors of battle

1803 Muḥammad Bey al-Alfī travels to England to seek British help for Mamluks against Ottomans; Khusrau Pasha, Ottoman governor, unable to bring Mamluks under control, deserted by his commander, Ṭāhir Pasha (May); before his death Ṭāhir Pasha requests Ottoman Porte to send new governor to Egypt; Ṭāhir's successor as commander of Albanian regiment, gives his support to Mamluk challenger ^{c}Uthman al-Bardīsi; al-Bardīsi installed in power; Khusrau defeated in battle with Muḥammad ^{c}Alī (July); new governor, ^{c}Ali Pasha Jazairilī, sent from Istanbul, assassinated after arrival in Egypt

---

Author's note: Diacritical markings stop with Muhammad Ali dynasty in the dictionary, and, for the sake of consistency with that, I have begun dropping them in the chronology at this point.

1804 After Muhammad Ali turns against al-Bardisi, another new Ottoman governor, Khurshid Pasha, attempts to establish his power in Cairo; Muhammad Ali campaigns in Upper Egypt and achieves mastery of military situation

1805	Chaos and disturbances continue in Cairo; Muhammad Ali approached by delegation of Cairenes and asked to restore order to city; Muhammad Ali returns to Cairo, besieges Khurshid Pasha in Citadel; Ottoman envoy arrives in Egypt to resolve situation there; Khurshid surrenders, leaves Egypt that summer; Muhammad Ali appointed governor of Egypt on behalf of Ottoman Sultan
1806	Muhammad Ali campaigns in Delta against his opponents
1807	British invade Egypt briefly on behalf of deposed Mamluks, turned back by Muhammad Ali; Ottomans, seeking to rid Egypt of Muhammad Ali, ask him to campaign in Arabia
1808	First Egyptian educational mission to Europe; start of two year campaign by Muhammad Ali in Upper Egypt
1809	In Europe publication of Description de l'Égypte begins, containing observations of scholarly team that accompanied the 1798 French invasion of Egypt
1811	Muhammad Ali massacres nearly 470 Mamluks after trapping them in Citadel in Cairo; Ibrahim Pasha, son of Muhammad Ali, campaigns in Upper Egypt against remaining Mamluks and tribes of region; Tusun, another son of Muhammad Ali, embarks on campaign against the Al Saud, Wahhabi rulers of Arabia, on behalf of Ottoman Sultan
1813-14	Muhammad Ali captures Qunfudah, Turabah in Arabia, personally leads Egyptian pilgrimage caravan to Mecca; cadastral survey and reform of taxation in Egypt
1815	Following series of military reverses in Arabia, Tusun and the Al Saud ruler Abdallah I conclude truce in July
1816	Muhammad Ali replaces Tusun with Ibrahim in Arabia; hostilities against the Al Saud recommence at end of 1816; first school of engineering opened in Egypt
1818	Ibrahim Pasha defeats the Al Saud at their capital, Diriyah in Najd (central Arabia)
1819	Ibrahim Pasha made governor of Jeddah by Ottoman Sul-

	tan; in Egypt work begins on Mahmudiyya Canal linking Alexandria with Western Nile Delta
1820	In Egypt, Louis Alex Jumel develops prototype of long-staple Egyptian cotton plant
1820-21	Muhammad Ali's son Ismail leads conquest of Nubia; Ibrahim Pasha recalled from Jeddah to lead Nubian campaign, which eventually takes Sennar and Kordofan in Sudan
1821	Muhammad Ali establishes government printing press; Ottoman Porte grants Muhammad Ali governorship of Crete; Greece in rebellion over Ottoman control
1822	Campaign by Egyptian forces in Crete and Cyprus, with Egyptian navy under command of Ismail Jabal Tariq; Egyptians recruited to regular army corps
1824	Ibrahim's campaign extended to Morea; withdrawal of Egyptian troops from Najd (central Arabia) following Wahhabi attack on their positions
1825	A. B. Clot (Clot Bey) arrives in Egypt to establish country's first secular medical school; Ibrahim takes port of Navarino for the Ottomans
1827	Egyptian and Ottoman navy defeated in battle at Navarino
1828	Egyptian official gazette begins publication; Egyptian forces withdraw from Greece
1829	Muhammad Ali establishes consultative council, Majlis al-Mashawarra
1830	Greece gains independence from Ottoman control
1831	Syria invaded by Muhammad Ali's armies under command of Ibrahim Pasha
1832	Jaffa, Jerusalem, Acre, Damascus, and Tripoli fall to Ibrahim; Ottoman army defeated at Homs; Ibrahim in alliance with Amir Bashir of Lebanon; Ibrahim Pasha defeats Ottoman vizier and his army at Konya, advances into Anatolia
1833	Egyptian army reaches Kutahiya in Anatolia; European powers intervene and Convention of Kutahiya is promul-

gated by Ottoman Sultan (May); Egypt granted control of Syria

1834 Discontent in Palestine with Ibrahim Pasha's rule; in Egypt work begins on Delta barrage but is later abandoned

1835 Serious plague hits Egypt; Muhammad Ali establishes Department of Public Works; Municipal Improvements Council formed in Alexandria; regular steamship service commences between Marseilles and Alexandria; in Arabia, Muhammad Ali's armies defeated in their second attempt in two years to invade Asir (southwest Arabia)

1836 Opening of regular steamship links between Suez and Bombay; in Arabia, Egyptian expeditionary force arrives to subdue Najd (central Arabia) following revival of Saudi Wahhabi state at Riyadh

1837 In Arabia, Egyptians capture Riyadh; Al Saud counterattack leads to stalemate; Egyptian army campaigns in Asir, Yemen; Druze revolt in Syria against conscription

1838 In Arabia, Khurshid Pasha, Muhammad Ali's Minister of War, captures Saudi Imam, Faysal, suppressing Saudi challenge to renewed Egyptian control of Najd; Khurshid Pasha attempts to gain influence in Amirates of Arabian Gulf; in Syria there is general discontent with Egyptian rule

1839 In northern Syria, Ottoman army is defeated at Nizib by Ibrahim Pasha (June); following death of Ottoman Sultan shortly thereafter, Ottoman fleet surrenders to Muhammad Ali; in Arabia, Egyptian governor of Eastern Province is assassinated and Egyptian troops are moved back into area; British take Aden, for use as coaling station for their ships and as counter to Muhammad Ali's power in peninsula

1840 Alarmed by eclipse of Ottoman Empire by Muhammad Ali, European powers intervene at the Convention of London to protect position of Ottoman Sultan; in Syria, Ibrahim Pasha is beset by rebellion against his rule and by European warships off Syrian coast; Ibrahim and Egyptian

	forces evacuate Syria (November-December); Egyptian troops withdrawn from Arabia and Yemen
1841	Treaty of London between Ottoman Sultan and European powers closes Dardenelles (under Ottoman control) to warships during peacetime (June); by series of firmāns, or decrees, Ottoman Sultan formally adds Sudan to Egypt and makes Muhammad Ali's position in Egypt hereditary, while removing Crete and Syria from his control
1845	Commercial courts established in Egypt
1846	Muhammad Ali leases Red Sea ports of Sawakin and Massawa from Ottoman Sultan
1848	Muhammad Ali gravely ill; Ibrahim Pasha becomes Viceroy of Egypt in September but dies two months later; Abbas Pasha, grandson of Muhammad Ali and son of Tusun, succeeds Ibrahim as Viceroy
1849	Death of Muhammad Ali; promulgation of Code of Abbas based on general legal code drawn up in 1854
1851	Negotiations between Egypt and Ottoman Porte over promulgation of new Ottoman legal code, Tanẓimāt, in Egypt; railway concession granted to Egypt
1854	Crimean War between Ottomans, French, and British against Russians, Egyptian troops, fleet, sent to fight for Ottomans; Abbas murdered, succeeded by his uncle Saᶜid, son of Muhammad Ali; new legal code introduced; first Suez Canal concession granted but delayed through British opposition
1855	Alexandria-Cairo rail link established; Egyptian land law reformed with regard to inheritance of property; communal taxes abolished
1856	Saᶜid visits Sudan; administration of Sudan reformed and decentralized; further work on Egyptian railroad network; Ferdinand de Lesseps granted new concession for Suez Canal; Treaty of Paris ends Crimean War
1857	Saᶜid grants concession for Nile steamship service and for telegraph system; first ministries established under Privy Council; Egyptians admitted to officer corps of

Egyptian army; Egyptian Museum founded; judicial reforms remove Europeans from Egyptian jurisdiction; Arabic given preference as administrative language

1858 Rail link opened between Cairo, Alexandria, and Suez; further reform of land law with regard to usufruct rights; taxation in rural areas made individual rather than collective responsibility; new Ottoman legal code

1859 Institut de l'Egypte reopened; work begins on Suez Canal

1861 Start of American Civil War brings enormous expansion in world demand for Egyptian cotton

1860-62 Sa^{c}id secures Egypt's first international loans

1863 Death of Sa^{c}id Pasha; Ismail Pasha, son of Ibrahim Pasha, becomes Viceroy; Ottoman Sultan makes state visit to Egypt

1864 Egyptian government buys up country's private postal concession

1865 Ottoman Sultan issues firmān returning ports of Sawakin and Massawa to Egyptian control after seventeen years of Ottoman control

1866 Assembly of Delegates established; Ismail's heirs are granted right of succession to governorship of Egypt by Ottoman Sultan; final ratification of Suez Canal concession

1867 Egyptian postal service operational; Nubar Pasha, Egyptian Minister, proposes reform of consular courts; Ismail granted title "Khedive" by Ottoman Sultan; Ismail visits Europe

1869 Suez Canal opened; municipal government in Alexandria; National Library founded; Samuel Baker appointed Governor-General of Equatorial Sudan; Massawa becomes base for inland expansion of Egyptian control in Sudan; second tour of Europe by Ismail

1870 Egyptian forces occupy Zaila on the Red Sea coast; Ismail lays claim to Somali coast down to Ras Assir; Khedival Mail Line takes over from privately operated Nile Steamship Company; Assembly of Delegates meets

1871	Al-Afghani comes to Egypt for first time; Muqabala Law introduced as revenue-raising measure
1872	Public lectures by Al-Afghani in Cairo; Ottoman Sultan abolishes 1869 restrictions on Ismail's borrowing power
1873	Ismail granted virtual autonomy within Egypt by decree of Ottoman Sultan; Samuel Baker annexes large areas of Equatorial Lakes region for Egypt; legal reforms
1874	Nubar Pasha forms ministry; Dafur annexed by Egypt after campaign by Zubayr Pasha and his private army backed by Khedive
1875	British resist Egyptian occupation of Zanzibar's mainland territories in East Africa; Cave Mission sent to Egypt to investigate country's finances; Ismail's shares in Suez Canal sold to British government; Egyptian troops occupy Harar in Ethiopia but are defeated by Ethiopian troops at Gundet; Khedival Geographical Society established; new legal code promulgated in Egypt
1876	Mixed Courts established by Nubar Pasha, Egyptian Minister; Caisse de la Dette Publique formed to provide European management of Egypt finances; dual control of Egyptian revenue and expenditure by Britain and France; elections for Assembly of Delegates; Al-Ahram newspaper founded; Egyptian withdrawal from parts of Equatorial Province in face of military reverses
1877	Anglo-Egyptian antislavery convention; start of two-year drought; Gordon appointed Governor-General of the Sudan
1878	Assembly of Delegates in session from March to June; International Commission meets to examine Egypt's debt repayments; Civil List established for Ismail; on demand of Egypt's creditors Ismail issues Rescript for formation of European Cabinet under Nubar Pasha; Congress of Berlin redraws Ottoman territorial boundaries
1879	First nationalist grouping, Hizb al-Watani, founded; Egyptian army officers protest pay, promotion, conditions, and European cabinet; Malet becomes British Agent and Consul-General in Egypt; Egyptian Assembly meets (January-July); Al-Afghani deported from Egypt for par-

ticipation in nationalist activities; Nubar Pasha deposed as Prime Minister with Tawfiq, Ismail's son, acting briefly in this post (March-April); following Ismail's confrontation with Europeans, Sharif Pasha forms government (April-June); Ismail deposed as Khedive (June); Tawfiq succeeds his father as Khedive; after his constitutional draft rejected Sharif Pasha resigns and Riyad Pasha forms government (September); Anglo-French Dual Control reestablished; Nationalist Manifesto issued (November)

1880 Wilfred Blunt comes to Egypt, beginning his association with nationalist movement; Law of Liquidation formalizes Egypt's debt repayment obligations; conscription extended to all Ottoman subjects in Egypt

1881 Increasing discontent among Egyptian army officers over proposed changes in conscription and promotion leads to dismissal of Rifki Pasha, War Minister (February); Nationalist Petition circulated; drought badly affects countryside; near-coup of nationalist army officers led by Colonel Arabi leads to fall of Riyad's ministry (September), whereupon Sharif forms a government; in response to nationalist demands, elections for a new Assembly of Delegates held (November); changes introduced in landownership laws; in Sudan, Mahdist movement gains momentum

1882 Egyptian Assembly meets (January-March); joint note from Britain and France delivered to Egyptian government (January); Sharif government falls (January); Organic Law establishes elected, salaried legislature (February); Constitution drafted by Sharif Pasha adopted by Assembly (February); Sami al-Barudi forms government with Arabi as Minister of War (February); electoral law passed expanding voter representation (March); dispute between Arabi and Khedive Tawfiq over exile of anti-Arabi officers (May); second Anglo-French joint note delivered, Barudi cabinet resigns (May); Raghib Pasha forms government (June-September); British fleet off Alexandria; European powers' conference in Istanbul

(July); British bombardment of Alexandria (July); Arabi leads defense of Egypt as British land troops in country (September); Egyptian nationalist forces defeated in battle at Tall al-Kabir and Ismailiyya as British forces under Sir Garnet Wolseley advance on Cairo, forcing Arabi to surrender (September); Sharif forms government (September to January 1884); Egyptian army disbanded (September); several Egyptian nationalists, including Abduh and Nadim, deported; after trial Arabi deported to Ceylon; Egyptian army reorganized under command of Sir Evelyn Wood (December)

1883 Constitution of 1882 abrogated; Dual Control abolished (January); Dufferin Report (March) outlines administrative and legislative reforms; Legislative Council and Legislative Assembly established under Organic Law (May); Sir Evelyn Baring becomes British Agent and Consul-General (September); British representation of Suez Canal Company board increased (November)

1884 Al-Urwat al-Wuthqa, Arabic political newspaper edited by Al-Afghani and Abduh, begins publication in Paris; Nubar Pasha forms government after resignation of Sharif Pasha (Jan.); Northbrook Com. formed to examine Egypt's financial situation after failure of London conference held to discuss Egypt's debt (August); British make arrangements to evacuate Egyptian troops from Sudan; establishment of Native Tribunals

1885 Khartoum falls to the Mahdist army, with massacre of General Gordon and his troops (January); London Convention (March) restructures Egyptian debt after Cromer reports massive budget deficit; following withdrawal of Egyptian troops from the Sudan, Nubia placed under military administration; negotiations between Britain and Turkey over Egypt; Ghazi Mukhtar Pasha becomes Ottoman representative in Egypt (November)

1886 The corvée (forced labor) system abolished save for emergency irrigation work

1887 Drummond Wolfe Convention concluded between Ottoman Porte and British government (May); Ottoman Sultan placed under pressure from other European states not to ratify Convention; Egyptian finances begin to recover; Nubar Pasha attempts restructuring of police

1888 Nubar Pasha dismissed; Riyad Pasha forms government; Emin Pasha withdraws from Equatorial Province

1889 Muhammad Abduh returns from exile and his North African and Lebanese travels; Mahdist invasion of Upper Egypt defeated at Toskhi; newspapers Al-Muqattam and Al-Mu'ayyad founded

1890 Alexandria municipal government established; opening of Delta barrage

1891 Riyad Pasha's government falls; Mustafa Fahmi forms new government

1892 Abbas II becomes Khedive following death of his father, Tawfiq (January); Sir Evelyn Baring elevated to the peerage, becomes Lord Cromer; Cromer and Abbas in dispute over Khedive's wish to have Tigane Pasha as his Prime Minister (November)

1893 Abbas dismisses Fahmi Pasha, asks Husayn Fakhri to form government; Fakhri dismissed shortly thereafter following intense pressure from Cromer and British (January); Riyad Pasha forms government; Mustafa Kamil leads group of young nationalists in attack of offices of Al-Muqattam (pro-British paper); semiclandestine nationalist grouping around young Khedive and sympathizers begins meeting; Egyptian budget in surplus for first time since Sa^{c}id's reign

1894 Heated exchange between Abbas and British Sirdar Kitchener results in official apology being forced from Khedive (January); Riyad dismissed, Nubar forms government (April); Mustafa Kamil becomes associated with nationalist grouping around Khedive

1895 After pressure from Cromer, Mustafa Fahmi Pasha brought back to form government (November); new Anti-Slavery Convention (November)

1896-97 Reconquest of Sudan begins; Dafur taken; Ethiopian vic-

	tories, near southern Sudanese border, and French ambitions threaten Egyptian claims in area; <u>Al-Manar</u>, important Islamic journal, founded
1898	Khedival Agricultural Society founded; in Sudan, Mahdist forces decisively defeated in battle at Karari (September); Fashoda Incident, as French and Ethiopian troops enter Sudan; French eventually withdraw their forces from region claimed by Britain for Egypt
1899	Anglo-Egyptian Condominium (January) establishes joint control of Sudan; French relinquish their claims to Sudan and agree on its southern border (March); Arabi returns from exile; Muhammad Abduh becomes Mufti of Egypt and begins reform of al-Azhar
1900	Publication of Qasim Amin's book on role of women in Islam provokes great public controversy in religious circles; <u>Al-Liwa</u>, nationalist paper, begins publication
1901	Arabi pardoned by Khedive Abbas
1902	First Nile barrage at Assyut completed; Aswan Dam opened (December); Agricultural Credit Bank founded
1904	<u>Entente Cordiale</u> signed (April); France relinquishes claims in Egypt
1905	Khedive Abbas issues decree recognizing special position of British in Egypt (January); Egypt granted measure of financial independence and some control of its revenues; Caisse de la Dette Publique reorganized; death of Muhammad Abduh
1906	Tabah Incident, as Ottomans lay claim to southern Sinai (February); Dinshaway Incident and trial of Egyptian villagers involved provokes widespread anti-British feeling in Egypt (June-July); Ottoman-Egyptian agreement on Suez border concluded (October); subscription campaign for Egyptian university started
1907	Egyptian Legislative Assembly dissolved (March); Cromer resigns (March); Umma Party proposed (June); Eldon Gorst becomes British Agent and Consul-General (July); after national congress Nationalist Party organized (No-

vember); Constitutional Reform Party founded (December); start of agricultural-cooperatives movement under Umar Lutfi Bey

1908 Death of Mustafa Kamil (February); Farid emerges as head of Nationalist Party; Egyptian university formally founded by Prince Fuad; Young Turk revolt (July) forces Ottoman Sultan Abdal Hamid to restore parliamentary life in Turkey and enormously influences nationalist movements throughout Middle East; Young Egypt Congress (November); Mustafa Fahmi resigns; Butrus Ghali Pasha, a Copt, invited to form government (November)

1909 Legislative Assembly reconvenes (February); Press Censorship Law reintroduced (March); second Young Egypt Congress (September)

1910 Extension of Suez Canal Company concession rejected by Legislative Assembly (February); assassination of Prime Minister Butrus Ghali Pasha (February); Sa^{c}id Pasha forms government (March); U.S. President Theodore Roosevelt visits Cairo (March); Coptic Congress formed; Farid, head of Nationalist Party, arrested for sedition

1911 Eldon Gorst resigns (June); Kitchener, new British Agent and Consul-General, arrives in Cairo (September); death of Arabi Pasha (September); Ottoman-Italian war in Libya begins (September); Egyptian army occupies Sollum on Mediterranean coast (December); Coptic Congress disbanded

1912 Gulf of Sollum formally annexed to Egypt (April); Farid, head of Nationalist Party, goes into exile (August); raising of Aswan Dam (December); Egyptian funded debt liquidated; Five Feddan Law promulgated

1913 Organic Law creates single-chamber legislature (July)

1914 Legislative Assembly meets (January-June); Sa^{c}d Zaghlul elected to vice-presidency of Assembly; Rushdi Pasha forms new government (May); assassination attempt on Abbas (July); Khedive travels to Istanbul; Milne Cheetham becomes Acting British Agent (August); British Protectorate over Egypt declared (December); Abbas deposed as Khedive, replaced by his uncle, Husayn Kamil, who takes title of Sultan; Sir John Grenfell Maxwell becomes military commander in Egypt; Sir Henry McMahon appointed High Commissioner (December)

1915 Ottoman attack on Suez Canal defeated (February); two assassination attempts on Husayn Kamil (April and July); McMahon gives undertaking on British intentions in Middle East and on Arab independence (October); Ottoman attacks on Sinai; Sanussi attack Egypt from Libya (November)

1916 British advance in Sinai (April); Sykes-Picot secret agreement on creation of British and French spheres of influence in Middle East (May); British occupy Sinai (August); Sir Reginald Wingate appointed British High Commissioner in Egypt (November)

1917 Death of Husayn Kamil; Fuad, Husayn Kamil's brother and a son of Ismail Pasha, becomes Sultan (October); Balfour Declaration on Palestine (November); Allenby defeats Ottoman army at Gaza (November)

1918 Armistice of Mudros ends Turkey's involvement in the War (October); British constitutional commission proposes changes in Egyptian legislature (November); World War I ends (11 November); Egyptian nationalists under Zaghlul form delegation (wafd) to present case for Egypt's independence to London (October-November); British government refuses to receive delegation; Tawkilat campaign

1919 Wingate goes to Britain (January); British government continues refusal to meet with Zaghlul's delegation (February); Rushdi Pasha resigns as Prime Minister (March); British deport Zaghlul, Hamid al-Basil, Sidqi, and Muhammad Mahmud (March); open rebellion against British rule (March-April); Allenby brought in as Special High Commissioner; Rushdi attempts to form new government (April); Wafdist Central Committee formed (April); Zaghlul released from exile, allowed to proceed to Paris (April); U.S. recognizes British protectorate in Egypt (April); Sa^{c}id Pasha forms government (May to

November); assassination attempt on Sa^{c}id (September); Wahba Pasha forms government (December); arrival in Egypt of Milner Mission, charged by British government with investigating causes of March rebellion (December); assassination attempt on Wahba (December); boycott of Milner Mission organized by Wafd Party (December)

1920 Milner Mission in Egypt (to March); Nasim Pasha forms government (May to March 1921); assassination attempt on Nasim (June); Milner and Wafd meet in London (June-July and October-November); trial of Vengeance Society members for various acts of terrorism in Egypt (October); Milner Report completed (December); Banque Misr founded; Socialist Party organized

1921 Milner Report published; British seek formation of Egyptian government delegation to discuss termination of Protectorate (February); Adli forms government prior to organizing official Egyptian delegation (March-November); Zaghlul returns to Egypt (April), splits with Adli over negotiations with British; Lawyer's Syndicate gives Adli its support, then after fresh elections reverses its decision; Adli and delegation go to London (June); Society of Independent Egypt formed to back Adli (August); Anglo-Egyptian negotiations stall on issues of Sudan and military; British Labour MPs tour Egypt at invitation of Wafd (September-October); Adli resigns, Tharwat Pasha tries to form government (December); nearly continuous street violence in Egypt through this year leads to numerous arrests; Zaghlul deported for second time (December); split in Wafd hierarchy over party's opposition to Adli; General Agricultural Syndicate founded

1922 After pressure from Allenby, British issue Declaration granting Egypt limited independence (February); Tharwat succeeds in forming ministry (March); Sultan Fuad's title changes to King; Constitutional Commission established under Rushdi Pasha (April); government crackdown on Wafd leadership (July); Constitution completed (October); Liberal Constitutionalist Party founded (October); anti-British demonstrations (December to February 1923); Nasim Pasha forms government (December)

1923 Adli refuses to form government following resignation of Nasim (February); Ibrahim Pasha forms government (March); New Constitution promulgated with electoral law (April); Wafdist student group formed (June); martial law terminated after nine years (July); Zaghlul released from exile

1924 First elections under 1923 Constitution, Zaghlul and Wafd Party in landslide victory, Zaghlul forms government (January); first session of Parliament (March-December); disturbances in Egypt and Sudan over British presence in Sudan (June-August); Zaghlul goes to London, Anglo-Egyptian discussions on Sudan and Suez Canal (September-October); assassination in Cairo of Sir Lee Stack, Governor-General of Sudan (November); British government presents ultimatum to Zaghlul government (November); British seizure of Alexandria customs post, fall of Zaghlul government (November), Ziwar Pasha forms government; Ittihad Party founded (December)

1925 New seating of Parliament with renewed Wafd majority elects Zaghlul as its president (March) and is dissolved by King; Allenby resigns (May); trial of Lee Stack Assassins (May); Lloyd becomes High Commissioner (October); Cairo University opens; Fuad seeks Caliphate; promulgation of restrictive electoral law (December)

1926 Major trial of antigovernment terrorists; 1925 Electoral Law revoked (February); elections return Wafd majority to Parliament (May); terrorism trial ends with chief Wafdist defendants acquitted (May); Adli forms government after Zaghlul pressured to decline (June); Zaghlul becomes president of Lower House (June); Mahmil incident at Mecca

1927 Adli resigns, Tharwat forms government (April); Army Crisis (May-June); Tharwat-Chamberlain negotiations (July-August); death of Zaghlul (August); leadership of Wafd Party passes to Nahhas Pasha; Tharwat-Chamberlain Draft Treaty (November)

1928 Tharwat resigns after cabinet refuses to consider his treaty (March); Nahhas forms government (March-June);

Assemblies Bill postponed after intense pressure from British High Commissioner (April); following allegations of financial misdealing Nahhas dismissed and Mahmud Pasha forms government (June); Parliament dissolved, Constitution suspended (July); dissolved Parliament meets unofficially, passes no-confidence motion against Mahmud government (November); Ikhwan al-Muslimun founded

1929 Nahhas and colleagues acquitted of charges of financial misdealing (February); Nile Waters Agreement concluded after three months of negotiations (May); jurisdiction of Mixed courts revised (May); Lloyd resigns (July), Lorraine named new Consul-General (August); Mahmud-Henderson talks (July-August) result in draft treaty; Adli forms government to supervise elections (October); Constitution restored (November); elections return huge Wafd majority, Nahhas forms government (December); Personal Status Laws reformed

1930 Wafd replaces local government administrators (January); new negotiations with London (April-May); Nahhas government dismissed by King, Sidqi Pasha forms government (June); Parliament adjourned, political activities curbed, Wafd calls congress of Egypt's elected representatives to protest these actions (June); Parliament suspended amid widespread civil disturbances (July); electoral law altered (September); new Constitution (October); Sha^{c}b Party formed by Sidqi (November)

1931 Wafd-Liberal Constitutionalist coalition formed (March); elections under new Constitution boycotted by coalition and many Egyptians (May-June); discussions among opposition parties on formation of national cabinet as alternative to Sidqi government (December)

1932 Badari Case provokes criticism of local administration; Butler Report on labor in Egypt published; Credit Agricole established to help small farmers; first major split in Wafd Party leadership, breakaway Wafd group formed (November); Parliament meets (December)

1933 Sidqi forms new cabinet (January); Lampson appointed High Commissioner (August); Yahya Pasha forms government (September); labor legislation introduced; further measures for easing credit problems in rural areas as impact of world depression hits Egypt's farmers; Misr al-Fatat political party formed

1934 Sir Miles Lampson arrives in Egypt (January); new raising of Aswan Dam; Nasim forms government (November); 1930 Constitution abrogated, Parliament suspended (November)

1935 Wafd-Nasim negotiations over restoration of political activity (June); anti-British demonstrations (November); National Front of Egyptian opposition parties succeeds in securing reinstatement of 1923 Constitution (December); Blue Shirts, Wafdist paramilitary organization, formed; Workmen's Compensation legislation introduced

1936 Street violence between paramilitary political groups (January onward); Ali Mahir forms caretaker government (January-May); Fuad dies, succeeded as King by his son Faruq (April; Faruq's coronation July 1937); Regency Council formed for Faruq's minority; elections return Wafd majority, Nahhas forms government (May); Anglo-Egyptian Treaty concluded after six months of negotiation (August); first general admission to the Military Academy (September) attracts many of the future Free Officers; new Parliament meets (November), ratifies Anglo-Egyptian Treaty; restrictions on paramilitary groups (December); Lampson's title changes from High Commissioner to Ambassador (December)

1937 Pilgrim caravan goes to Mecca for first time since 1926, following restoration of Saudi-Egyptian relations; dam completed for Sudan water storage on Nile (March); Montreux Convention (April-May) acts on Egypt's legal and international status; Egypt joins League of Nations (May); reform of Suez Canal Company agreements (June); alterations in Egypt's capitulations drafted at Montreux approved by Egyptian Paraliament (July); leadership struggle in Wafd, Nahhas forms new cabinet (July-August); capitulations abolished (October); Ali Mahir appointed Faruq's chief political adviser (October); assassination attempt on Nahhas (November); Nuqrashi Pasha splits from Wafd leadership; Faruq dismisses Wafd, Mahmud forms government (December)

1938 Ahmad Mahir splits from Wafd leadership (January); Nuqrashi and Ahmad Mahir found Sa^{c}dist Party (January); Parliament dissolved (February); Shirt organizations proscribed (March); elections for Parliament held on basis of redrawn constituencies, suppression of Wafd on local level (March-April); Mahmud forms new cabinet (April); Parliament opens with non-Wafd majority (May); Mahmud reshuffles his cabinet (June); Congress for the Defence of Palestine formed by Egyptian parliamentarians (October)

1939 London Palestine Conference (February); Ali Mahir forms government (August); outbreak of World War II, Egypt breaks relations with Germany (September); Palace suggestion for deploying a territorial army rejected by Britain (September); martial law imposed under "State of Siege" (October)

1940 Regulation of trade union activity (March); Ali Mahir resigns after failing to form government of national unity (June); Italy bombs Egyptian territory, Egypt breaks relations (June); Caisse de la Dette Publique wound up (July); Sabri Pasha forms government (July-November); Sa^{c}dist Party members resign from Sabri cabinet over government's failure to declare war (September); Sirri Pasha forms "nonbelligerent" government after death of Sabri (November)

1941 General Masri captured after unsuccessful attempt to defect to German army in Libya (May); Sirri forms new cabinet (June-July)

1942 Sirri resigns after Faruq objects to declaration of war on Vichy France (February); Palace Incident, British force King to ask Wafd leader Nahhas to form government (February); Parliament dissolved as Nahhas calls new elections (March); Masri released (March); Nahhas orders crackdown on anti-Wafd politicians and Axis sympathizers (March-April); Ubaid, longstanding member of Wafd Executive, resigns (May); Egypt nearly falls to Axis powers (July); Battle of Al-Alamayn, anti-British disturbances in Egypt (Summer); Alexandria university opens; Wafd government introduces social-insurance legislation

1943 Ubaid publishes The Black Book, detailing allegations of Wafd leadership's corruption; French intervention in Lebanon provokes sharp anti-European reaction in Egypt

1944 Anti-Wafd agitation grows; Alexandria Protocol on formation of Arab League signed (October); King dismisses Nahhas, Ahmad Mahir forms government (October)

1945 Elections boycotted by Wafd (January); Parliament vote to declare war on Axis, Ahmad Mahir assassinated shortly thereafter by Axis sympathizer (February); Nuqrashi forms government (February); Arab League established (March); attempts made by Egypt to renegotiate 1936 Anglo-Egyptian treaty (December); censorship lifted

1946 Osman Pasha, pro-British Finance Minister, assassinated (January); to protest Britain's continued military presence in Egypt, National Committee of Workers and Students formed (February); political, civil violence sweep Egypt with many deaths; Sidqi forms government (February); British announcement of preparedness to withdraw British troops from Egypt to Canal Zone (May); government crackdown on political opponents (July); Sidqi and British Foreign Minister Bevin negotiate (May-July); draft treaty concluded (October); ratification founders over conflicting interpretations of clauses on Sudan; student disturbances (November); Nuqrashi reinstated as Prime Minister (December)

1947 Egypt gains Arab League support for its position on Sudan (January); pullback of British troops from Egypt (January-March) to Canal Zone; Egypt brings Sudan dispute before UN (August); Industrial Bank founded, Companies' Law passed; civil disturbances and bombing continue in Cairo, Alexandria, and towns and rural areas; union of Political Party and Group Youth (September)

1948 Two assassination attempts on Wafd leader Nahhas (April); Nuqrashi imposes martial law and becomes Egypt's military governor as British withdraw mandate for Palestine and Nuqrashi announces Egyptian invasion of Palestine (May); after initial Egyptian successes at Gaza and Beersheba, four-week truce arranged under UN auspices (end of May); mixed and consular courts closed (June and October); British announce plans for Sudanese autonomy (June); Egyptian army in Palestine suffers military reverses (October-November); police crackdown on Ikhwan terrorists begins (November) after seizure of Jeep belonging to Ikhwan Secret/Special Section; Cairo Police Chief assassinated (December); Ikhwan banned, following which Nuqrashi assassinated (December); Al-Hadi Pasha becomes Prime Minister (December), continues Nuqrashi's antiterrorism campaign

1949 Israeli activity in Sinai (January); armistice concluded between Israel and Egypt under UN auspices (February) providing for military evacuation of Faluja and other towns, establishment of demarcation line; Hasan al-Banna, head of Ikhwan al-Muslimun, assassinated (February); Al-Hadi dismissed, Sirri forms government (July); new agreement with Suez Canal Company

1950 Elections return Wafd, though not by absolute majority; Nahhas forms government (January); trial of suspected Ikhwan terrorists (March); Western powers issue Tripartate Declaration (May); Point Four Agreement between Egypt and United States (May); new labor legislation (June-July); Nasser elected head of secret Free Officers' Executive (December)

1951 Arms scandal trial (January) over lack of Army supplies during Palestine War; restrictions on union activity (February); land distribution to peasants (May); Sterling Reserves Agreement (July); Allied Middle Eastern Command established (October); after many months of unsuccessful negotiation Nahhas announces Egypt's unilateral abrogation of 1936 Anglo-Egyptian treaty (October); anti-British demonstrations, attacks on British property

(October-November); student demonstrations in Cairo and elsewhere (November-December); Liberation Squads active (November); General Naguib, Free Officer candidate, elected president of Officers' Club (December)

1952 British troops attack Ismailiyya police headquarters, leading to burning of Cairo next day (26 January); Ali Mahir forms government following dismissal of Wafd (January-March); arrest of suspected participants and instigators of Cairo fires (February); Hilali forms government (March-June); Parliament formally suspended (March); Britain releases some sterling reserves to shore up Hilali government (April); Sirri forms government (June-July) when Hilali falls from favor with Palace; Hilali brought back to form government (21 July); Free Officers seize power under titular leadership of General Naguib (23 July); Ali Mahir asked to form government; Faruq abdicates in favor of his infant son Ahmad Fuad II (July); Regency Council established with Free Officer representation (August); Six Principles of the Revolution announced, along with plans for agrarian reform and lifting of censorship (August); vigorous suppression of labor disorders (August); resignation of Ali Mahir over agrarian-reform proposals, Naguib becomes Prime Minister (September); purge of army command (September); Party Reorganization Law forces Nahhas to resign from Wafd leadership (October); Free Officer Mehanna removed from Regency Council (October); censorship reimposed (October); 1923 Constitution suspended (December); Naguib meets with Sudanese political leaders to discuss Sudan's future (Autumn-Winter 1952-53)

1953 Political parties disbanded (January); Naguib announces provisional constitution, start of three-year transitional period leading to restoration of democracy (January-February); short-lived constitutional commission established (January); creation of government political group, Liberation Rally, announced (January; established in March); Revolutionary Command Council assumes executive and administrative power (January); arrest of anti-regime plotters in military (January); Naguib assumes supreme power (February); Anglo-Egyptian Sudan Agreement (February); Constitutional Charter promulgated (February); trial of military conspirators against regime (March); monarchy abolished and Egypt declared republic (June); Naguib becomes President, Amer appointed Commander-in-Chief, Nasser and several of his RCC supporters join Naguib's cabinet (June); all royal properties nationalized (July); trials of political opponents of regime begin (September); Israeli attack on Gaza camp (August)

1954 Negotiations with British begin on withdrawal of British troops from Egypt (January); Ikhwan al-Muslimun proscribed after street clashes in Cairo and elsewhere (January); RCC announces removal of Naguib from presidency and premiership (February); Nasser becomes Premier, Naguib regains presidency (February); Naguib regains premiership, announces forthcoming elections, creation of Constituent Assembly, press freedom (March); Nasser regains premiership, RCC takes ministerial portfolios, announces cancellation of promised elections (April); Mutual concessions on Canal Zone by Egypt, Britain (May-June); Ikhwan allowed to resume nonpolitical activities; Anglo-Egyptian Evacuation Agreement concluded (July; signed in October); Arab League meeting on proposed Baghdad Pact (October); Lavon Incident (October); assassination attempt on Nasser (October); Naguib stripped of presidency, placed under house arrest (November); Ikhwan al-Muslimun suppressed (November-December); Nasser actively campaigns against Baghdad Pact and extraregional military agreements

1955 Arab League meeting on Baghdad Pact (January) fails to avert February signing; trial of Israeli saboteurs (January); Gaza Incident (February); border dispute with Israel (March); Bandung Conference brings Nasser into association with nonaligned movement (April); third-party negotiations with Israel over disputed border (June); France announces new arms supplies for Israel (July); New Sterling Reserves Agreement (August); Egypt announces intention to purchase arms from Czechoslovakia after series of Israeli border attacks (September); Egypt concludes military pacts with Saudi Arabia, Syria (October); fighting in Gaza (November); U.S. approaches Israel, Egypt for negotiations (December)

1956 Financing for Egypt's High Dam project approved by International Bank for Reconstruction and Development (February); RCC officially disbanded, martial law and censorship abolished (June); referendum to approve new Constitution and Nasser's election as President (June); Liberation Rally to be replaced with National Union; Brioni meeting between Nasser and Tito (July); United States and Britain withdraw their offer to support financing of the High Dam project (July), Nasser nationalizes Suez Canal, intending to use revenues therefrom to pay for High Dam (July); Egypt refuses to participate in international negotiations in London on Canal (August-September); Jordan asks Egypt for military aid following Israeli border attacks (October); Egypt, Jordan, and Syria sign defensive pact (October); Security Council debate on Egypt's Suez Canal nationalization (October); Suez War: Israel invades Egypt (29 October), followed by Anglo-French invasion (5 November); UN cease-fire; UN Emergency Force troops arrive (November), as Western troops complete withdrawal (December); Israel only partially withdraws from Egyptian territory; Nasser government abolishes religious courts in Egypt

1957 Economic Agency created (January); nationalization of foreign property (January); Arab Solidarity Pact signed by Egypt, Syria, Jordan and Saudi Arabia (January); Suez Canal clearance (April-September) under supervision of Egyptian Suez Canal Authority; National Union organized, with Nasser as its president (May); National Planning Committee takes over all economic planning; elections for National Assembly (July); government crackdown on Wafdists, communists (July-August); Haykal becomes editor of Al-Ahram; Egypt and Syria announce economic-cooperation measures (September); Egyptian troops sent to Syria at Syrian government's request;

Afro-Asian People's Solidarity Conference (December to January, 1958)

1958 Industrialization plan (January); following negotiations between Nasser and Syrian political leaders, United Arab Republic formed by the two countries (February) with Nasser as President; border dispute with Sudan (February); Yemen joins UAR under title United Arab States (March); provisional UAR Constitution announced (March); Iraqi Revolution (July); Jordan and Egypt break relations (July); USSR agrees to High Dam financing (October); Tunisia breaks relations (October); UAR cabinet formed (October); French relations with Egypt partially restored (November); revolution in Sudan brings to power government more favorable to Egypt (November)

1959 Egyptian-Iraqi relations sour (March); Arab Oil Conference (April); Egyptian-government suppression of left-wing critics; relations with Jordan restored (August); UAR cabinet reshuffle (August); King Saud visits Egypt (September); Amer made governor of Northern Region (Syria) of UAR (October); Nile Waters Agreement between Egypt and Sudan (November); Egypt compensates French and British Suez Canal Company claims; final settlement of Sterling Reserves with Britain

1960 Bank nationalizations (February); Arab Economic Council (March); boycott of Egyptian ship, the Cleopatra, by U.S. unions (April-May); press nationalization (May); UAR National Assembly meets (July); Jordan breaks relations with Egypt again (August); UAR cabinet changes (September); relations with Britain partially restored (December; fully restored in following year)

1961 Casablanca Conference (January) increased African involvement with UAR, nonaligned movement; relations restored with Tunisia; further nationalizations and introduction of Socialist Laws (June-July); Arab Security Forces Agreement (June); at Belgrade Conference (August) Egypt expresses her commitment to nonalignment; Syria breaks from UAR (September); Nasser forms new cabinet (October); United Arab States (with Yemen) dissolved (December); numerous meetings, throughout year, of various African political groupings with which Egypt is involved

1962 Elections for Congress of Popular Forces (February); Charter of National Action presented (May); Presidential Council formed; Arab Economic Unity Agreement (June); Arab Socialist Union (ASU) founded (July); Arab League meeting in Shtoura (Lebanon) condemns Egyptian interference in Syria (August); Ali Sabri becomes chief minister of Presidential Council (September); Egypt sends troops to Yemen to assist revolutionary regime there (October); Saudi-Egyptian relations severed after Egypt bombs Saudi border area (November)

1963 Pro-Egyptian governments take power in Iraq, Syria (February-March); federation talks between Egypt, Syria, and Iraq (March-April); relations with France restored (April) ten months after Algerian revolution, which Egypt had supported, ended; further nationalizations (April-November); elections held for Arab Socialist Union (May); Tripartate Federation talks break down between Egypt and Syria (July); break in relations with Morocco after Egypt intervenes in border dispute between Morocco and new revolutionary regime in Algeria (September); Egypt rejoins Arab League after one-year boycott

1964 Arab Summits (January and September) meet to consider Israeli plans to divert water from River Jordan for its own territory; new Constitution introduced, elections held for National Assembly (March); Ali Sabri forms new government (March); federation discussions (April); relations with Jordan restored after three-year break (March); Joint Egyptian-Iraqi Presidential Council formed (May); PLO formed as Palestine's representative grouping (May); Council for Arab Economic Unity opened in Cairo (June); Coordinating Council established with Yemen (July); federation with Iraq discussed (September-November); Nonaligned Conference meets in Cairo (October); Nasser supplies Egyptian arms to Congolese rebels (November); Yemen cease-fire (November) after Saudi-Egyptian accord two months previously; Yemen fighting resumes (December)

1965 Arab Common Market established (January); Nasser returned to presidency in referendum (March); Bandung Conference (April) meets to consider progress of non-aligned movement over ten years that followed first Conference; U.S. resumes food shipments, halted for six months (June); Nasser and King Faysal of Saudi Arabia meet in Jedda to discuss Yemen War (August), as relations between two countries temporarily improve; Zaqaria Muhiaddin becomes Prime Minister (October); wave of internal disturbances, building over several months, comes to climax with widespread arrests of Ikhwan members, dissidents, and some trade-union activists (September-October); allegations by government of Ikhwan plot to overthrow regime; Casablanca Summit boycotted by Tunisia (September); Harad Conference (November); Saudi and Egypt once more try to negotiate settlement to Yemen War; Harad Conference adjourns without firm settlement (December); trials of Ikhwan members begin (December)

1966 U.S. aid program for Egypt announced (January); trials of Ikhwan members continued (January-March and August); following Kamchiche incident Committee for the Liquidation of Feudalism established (May); Nasser's decision to boycott Algiers Summit (July) marks downturn in inter-Arab relations; Egyptian and Saudi Arabian representatives meet in Kuwait to discuss Yemen (August); Sulayman becomes Egyptian Prime Minister (September); Egypt experiencing difficulties in negotiating food aid from U.S., IMF loan; Syria's new pro-Egyptian government concludes Defense Pact with Egypt (November); Israeli attack on Jordanian village (November) causes split in Arab ranks over Egypt and Syria's failure to come to Jordan's defense; trial of accused communists opens in Cairo (December)

1967 Raids into Syria, Jordan by Israel (February-March); Israel shoots down Syrian planes in response to what it describes as increasing Syrian backing for Palestinian commandos (April); mobilization of Israeli troops alleged, Egypt requests withdrawal of UN forces, moves troops into Sinai, closes Straits of Tiran (May); Jordan signs defense pact with Egypt (late May); U.S./UN diplomatic approaches to Egypt, Israel; Nasser announces visit of Zaqaria Muhiaddin to Washington to negotiate (June); two days before his departure, Israel launches devastating air attack on Egypt, Syria, Iraq, and Jordan, destroying or immobilizing most of their air forces (5 June); four days later Israel and Egypt conclude cease-fire agreement; entire Sinai peninsula in Israeli hands, Suez Canal blocked with wrecked ships; Nasser offers his resignation, which is rejected by popular acclaim; Nasser becomes Prime Minister, forms new government (19 June), and assumes leadership of ASU; OAPEC states place boycott on oil sales to U.S., Great Britain, and Netherlands for their unqualified support of Israel; Egypt breaks relations with U.S. and several European states; General Amer and other members of High Command dismissed (June); Khartoum Conference (August-September); arrest of alleged military plotters, suicide of General Amer (September); Soviet Union replaces Egyptian weaponry; fighting in Canal Zone (September-October); Accomplishment Plan; Egypt sinks Israeli ship, the Eilat, Israel destroys Egyptian oil refineries (October); Egypt withdraws from Yemen (November-December)

1968 Trials of military plotters (January and August); anti-government disturbances (January and November); Ali Sabri reinstated as Secretary-General of ASU (January); Manifesto of 30 March, government reorganization; Soviet-Egyptian agreement (March); UN mediator Gunnar Jarring arrives in Cairo (March); referendum on government's proposed reforms (May); Nasser asks for more Russian arms (July); Israel shells Suez (September); educational-reform law withdrawn after popular protest (November); universities closed (December)

1969 Elections for National Assembly (January); War of Attrition (March to Summer 1970); Nasser sends military aid to Nigeria; ASU shake-up; Sabri dismissed (September); Rabat Summit (December) over future Arab response to

Israel ends in split between Nasser and many of other Arab states and failure of Egypt to obtain renewed commitments of material and financial aid; further changes in executive, judiciary; first Rogers peace initiatives as War of Attrition goes in Israel's favor

1970 Israeli air strikes in Egypt (February and April); confrontation states meet in Cairo to discuss strategy (February); Islamic Foreign Ministers Conference (March); Nasser gets SAM antiaircraft missiles from Soviet Union (March); union between Sudan, Egypt, and Libya discussed (April-May); intensive Israeli raids on Suez Canal (May-June); Aswan Dam opened (July); second Rogers Plan and ninety-day cease-fire accepted by Egypt (July), Israel (August); Israel withdraws from negotiations after cease-fire violations by Egypt are charged (September); Emergency Arab Summit meets in Cairo in September after civil war in Jordan between PLO and Jordanian army (September), Nasser mediates; death of Nasser (28 September); Sadat becomes Provisional President, Mahmud Fawzi appointed Prime Minister (October); Ali Sabri, Husayn Shafi named Vice-Presidents; Sadat confirmed as President by referendum; federation discussions between Egypt, Libya, Syria (November)

1971 Gunnar Jarring's mediation efforts, Sadat cease-fire (February); confederation plans with Libya and Syria announced (April); arrest of Ali Sabri and other opponents of Sadat (May); "Corrective Revolution" announced, with new program of national action, purge of Arab Socialist Union (May); Organization of the Islamic Congress founded (May); Soviet-Egyptian Friendship Treaty (May); new Constitution approved by referendum (September); renewal of tensions in Canal Zone (September); elections for People's Assembly (renamed National Assembly) (November); 1971 was "Year of Decision" with regard to Israel

1972 Antigovernment demonstrations at Cairo University over inaction during "Year of Decision" (January); Aziz Sidqi becomes Prime Minister (January); Russian technicians

	ordered by Sadat to leave Egypt (July); unified leadership of Egypt and Libya announced (August)
1973	Arms deal concluded with Russia (February); Sadat assumes offices of Prime Minister and Military Governor-General (March); invasion of 30,000 Libyans supporting federation of Libya with Egypt (July); war with Israel; Egypt and Syria launch invasion (6 October) of territories taken by Israel in 1967 War; Israeli counterattack (14 October) leads to encirclement of Egyptian army in Sinai; in face of rapid resupply of weapons to Israel by United States, Sadat unilaterally accepts cease-fire (22 October), though Syria continues fighting; Six Point Agreement accepted by Egypt, Israel (November), becoming basis for first Disengagement Agreement (concluded two months later); Kissinger visits Cairo, Sadat decides to restore relations with United States (November); Geneva Conference meets briefly (December)
1974	Egyptian-Israeli Disengagement (Separation of Forces) Agreement (January); amnesty of many political prisoners (January); legislative foundation for Open Door Policy, Law No. 43, promulgated (April); U.S. President Nixon visits Egypt (June); Higazi becomes Prime Minister (September); Rabat Summit (October) discusses role of PLO; October Paper, Sadat's first comprehensive policy statement, promises political and economic liberalization; press censorship lifted, new guidelines for ASU set (October); after Higazi tours Arab Gulf states, Gulf Organization for the Development of Egypt established (November)
1975	Labor and civil disturbances spurred by domestic economic problems (January, March); Salim forms government (April); Suez Canal reopens (June); People's Assembly votes for abolition of many nationalization measures introduced under Nasser (July); Second Egyptian-Israeli Disengagement Agreement (September); Sadat visits United States (October); U.S. announces major aid program for Egypt
1976	Soviet-Egyptian treaty relationship terminated (March);

ASU allowed to form political platforms within its overall structure (March); Soviet naval facilities terminated (April); Sadat returned as President in referendum (September); first elections on limited multiparty basis (October-November); Salim forms new government (October); negotiations with IMF for loan proceed with difficulty; Cairo, Riyadh Summits lead to cease-fire in Lebanon (October); Syria and Egypt announce plans to unify their executives and decision-making (December)

1977 January riots over removal of subsidies leads to reinstatement of subsidies and rethinking of economic strategy; Salim forms new government (May); Israeli elections return extreme right-wing Likud leader, Begin, as Prime Minister (May); Egyptian Parliament passes law permitting formation of political parties (June); border fighting between Egypt and Libya; assassination of former Waqfs Minister by Islamic radical group (August); Sadat declares ten-year moritorium on Soviet debt repayment (August); U.S.-Soviet declaration on Middle East (October); cabinet reshuffle (October); Sadat goes to Jerusalem (November); resignation of Foreign Ministers Fahmy, Riad; International Peace Conference in Cairo called by Sadat (December); Begin-Sadat Summit (December)

1978 Bilateral talks between Egypt and Israel; cabinet reshuffle (May); restrictions on activities of political parties passed by referendum (May); following slowing of negotiations Leeds Castle Meeting (July) attempts to break negotiating deadlock; Sadat forms National Democratic Party (July); Camp David Accords reached with active U.S. participation (September); Khalil becomes Prime Minister (October); Baghdad Summit of Arab states votes sanctions against Egypt if bilateral peace treaty is concluded (November); target date for peace treaty set by Camp David Accords passes (December); Sadat awarded Nobel Peace Prize jointly with Begin

1979 Egyptian-Israeli Peace Treaty signed in Washington (March), approved in Egypt by referendum (April); Second Baghdad Summit imposes sanctions on Egypt (March);

	commencement of negotiations on Palestinian autonomy (May); elections for Peoples' Assembly (June); town of Al-Arish and western third of Sinai returned to Egypt (July); Sadat-Begin talks at Haifa (September); despite autonomy talks Israel continues to establish settlements on occupied Palestinian territory
1980	Israeli Ambassador presents his credentials amid protest by some groups in Egypt (February); General Shazli, in exile, organizes opposition group (March); Constitutional amendment voted by People's Assembly making Sadat President for his lifetime (April); Palestinian autonomy talks suspended by Sadat as Israeli settlements on Palestinian land continue to be established (April); Sadat becomes Prime Minister, forms new government (May); proscription of communal activities; Suez Canal expansion opened; Iran-Iraq war (September); joint Egyptian-American military maneuvers (November)
1981	Assassination of President Sadat (October); Husni Mubarak assumes presidency with Fuad Muhiaddin as his prime minister

THE DICTIONARY

-A-

ABBAS I PASHA (r. 1848-54). Ruler of Egypt as Viceroy for the Ottoman Porte, the power Abbas exercised was virtually that of an independent ruler, in line with the autonomy established by his grandfather Muhammad Ali. However, Abbas discontinued most of the Westernizing and modernizing policies of Muhammad Ali, and dismissed many of the Europeans hired by his grandfather to restructure elements of Egypt's military and educational institutions. He did, however, grant the British a concession to build a railway linking Alexandria, Cairo, and Suez.

During Abbas' reign, protracted negotiations took place between Egypt and the Ottoman Porte over the introduction of a new Ottoman legal code, the Tanẓimat. An Egyptian delegation went to Istanbul in 1851, and though a compromise was eventually reached, the formal introduction of the Ottoman Code did not occur until after the death of Abbas. Despite these difficulties in his relationship with the Porte, which stemmed mainly from his desire to preserve his autonomy, Abbas sent an Egyptian regiment to fight on the Ottoman side during the Crimean War.

Egypt's economy made a substantial recovery from the indebtedness caused by Muḥammad Ali's military campaigns and development programs, as Abbas' government withdrew from active involvement in the public sector. Abbas was advised, though not particularly guided, by a Council that included Nubar Pasha and Joseph Hekeyan Bay, to whom he delegated a great deal of responsibility. His personal life is generally described as unsavory; he was murdered, in obscure circumstances, in 1854.

ABBAS HILMI II (r. 1892-1914). Khedive of Egypt, Abbas came to power at the age of seventeen. Despite his youth Abbas made a determined, if short-lived, attempt to lessen British influence in Egypt. In January 1893 he dismissed the pro-British Prime Minister, Mustafa Fahmi, and appointed Husayn Fakhri Pasha, who was regarded by the British as a francophile nationalist. This followed Abbas' earlier attempt to appoint Tigane Pasha, and rid himself of Fahmi, in the autumn of 1892, an act sharply vetoed by the British Agent Cromer. Cromer also opposed Fakhri; after some controversy between the Palace and the Residence, Riyad Pasha was brought in to form a government. In January 1884 a bitter exchange between Abbas and the Sirdar (Commander-in-Chief) of the Anglo-Egyptian army, Lord Kitchener, ended with Abbas having to make what was, for him, a humiliating public gesture of apology. This incident, which led to Riyad's replacement by Nubar that spring, created an atmosphere of permanent hostility between Abbas and Cromer.

Cromer secured the reinstatement of Fahmi at the end of 1895, after Nubar Pasha had lost the support of the Palace. Thereafter the residency managed to keep nationalist sympathizers firmly out of positions of power. Abbas in turn gave both his covert and active support to the nationalist groupings that resumed activity in the first decade of his reign. He was for a time in close communication with Mustafa Kamil, the brilliant young lawyer who dominated the nationalist movement. Various nationalist journals received Palace backing and funding, and Abbas himself headed a semisecret nationalist grouping, the Society for the Revival of the Nation. The Khedive and the nationalists of more radical stripe did eventually come into conflict over the form the future government of Egypt would take and also, it is said, over the growing popularity of individuals like Mustafa Kamil. By 1900 a split had developed between the Palace and the radical nationalists, coincident with Abbas' growing resignation to the realities of his own position in Egypt.

During Abbas' reign the British reconquered the Sudan, in

1898, defeating the Mahdist government that had ruled this former Egyptian province for thirteen years. The Anglo-Egyptian Condominium, signed in 1899, recognized the Khedive's titular authority in the Sudan, but the administrative structure, and actual power, remained in British hands. French claims in Egypt, dating to the days of Dual Control, were finally waived in favor of the British under the terms of the 1904 Entente Cordiale. Abbas formally recognized Britain's special position in Egypt in a 1905 Khedival decree. By the time Cromer's consulship was drawing to its close Abbas and Egypt had been brought under ever stronger British control.

The severe penalties imposed on the villagers of Dinshaway in 1906 for a shooting incident involving British officers caused a tremendous outpouring of nationalist feeling in Egypt. Abbas made new approaches to the nationalists through the Palace physician, Dr. Mahmud Sadiq Ramadan. Cromer was replaced by Sir Eldon Gorst in 1907, a year that saw the creation of three major and several minor political groupings. Gorst, more sympathetic to the national aspirations of Egyptians than his predecessor, was still not an active supporter of nationalist politicians. He worked closely and well with Abbas, and urged on the Khedive a program of moderate reforms. Gorst was able to coopt much of the appeal of nationalist programs to middle- and upper-class supporters. The death of Mustafa Kamil in 1908, the subsequent leadership struggles in the Nationalist Party, and the assassination of the first Coptic Prime Minister of Egypt, Butrus Ghali Pasha, in 1910 by a Nationalist supporter, left the nationalist movement unable to counter this shift in policy by Abbas.

It was unfortunate that Gorst's successor in 1911 was Lord Kitchener, with whom Abbas had such bitter (and unforgotten) words two decades previously. Kitchener introduced several restrictions on the powers of the Khedive, in the granting of honors and in the control of religious endowments, and removed from Abbas the automatic right to preside at cabinet meetings.

Under the Organic Law of 1913 Kitchener established a new and more effective legislature.

Following an assassination attempt in July 1914 Abbas went to Istanbul for medical treatment. He was there in December when the British established a Protectorate over Egypt and announced his deposition on 14 December 1914. Thereafter Abbas tried to remain in Istanbul, but political factors combined against him. He eventually settled in Switzerland and in 1918 affiliated with the growing Axis activity. Abbas did not surrender his claims to the throne until 1931, though he was not reconciled to this decision and apparently nurtured hopes of a restoration. He died in Switzerland in 1944.

^{c}ABBĀS b. ABU'L-FUTUH (d.1154/549). Fāṭimid vizier, ^{c}Abbās and his son Naṣr (d.1155/550) were important figures in the court of the Fāṭimid Caliph aẓ-Ẓāfir (r.1149-54/544-549), whom they eventually murdered. ^{c}Abbās was the stepson of Sallār, the Fāṭimid general and vizier, who had seized the latter office in 1150/544. ^{c}Abbās, who resided in court with his son (a great favorite of the Caliph), was appointed by Sallār to be commandant of the Fāṭimid forces at Ascalon in 1153/548. Shortly after he took up this appointment, Naṣr murdered Sallār and ^{c}Abbās took the vizierate. Father and son were consumed by jealousy over their respective roles at court, and to resolve this tension between them they decided to murder the Caliph aẓ-Ẓāfir, which they did in 1154/549, placing Ẓāfir's young son Fā'iz on the throne. Both men had to flee shortly afterward to Syria, in advance of the arrival in Cairo of as-Salih Tala'i^{c}, who had been summoned by the court after Ẓāfir's assassination. ^{c}Abbās was killed by the Crusaders, who trapped and seized Naṣr, returning him to face the judgment of the Fāṭimid court.

^{c}ABBĀSID EGYPT (750-969/133-297). The shift in the center of power in the Islamic world from the Umayyad dynasty in Damascus to the ^{c}Abbāsid dynasty in Iraq was marked in Egypt by the campaign of the general Ṣāliḥ b. ^{c}Alī, who conquered the country on behalf of the ^{c}Abbāsids. During the ^{c}Abbāsid period there was a continuing, rapid changeover of governors; eighty appointees held power, some for several terms. Administrative instability and internal discontent, which flourished in Egypt and elsewhere in the ᶜAbbāsid world during this time, paved the way for the eventual emergence of autonomous dynasties in Egypt, the Ṭūlūnids and the Ikhshīdids.

A major cause of discontent during ᶜAbbāsid times was the revenue demands from Baghdad; heavy exactions for the army led to unrest in 780/163-64 and in 794-95/178-79. Communal taxes also aroused opposition, and from 813/198 to approximately 833/218 there were several Christian revolts of a general nature against taxes, as well as revolts by Christians and Muslims together. It required a visit by the ᶜAbbāsid Caliph al-Ma'mūn and his general Afshīn in 832/217 to calm the situation.

The ᶜAbbāsids pursued a policy of settling Arab tribes in Egypt, such as the Qays, which doubtless helped to tie the country more closely to the center (and also relieved population pressure in the central Islamic lands) but which created problems as these tribes attempted to establish their own power bases within Egypt. They were involved in the unrest of 780/163-64, when two military campaigns were sent against them, and in 827/212 the ᶜAbbāsid general Ibn Ṭāhir led his armies against the tribes. Nubia was generally quiet in the ᶜAbbāsid period, but a revolt there, also with tribal involvement, was suppressed in 858/244 by the ᶜAbbāsid general Muḥammad b. al-Qummī. Possibly seeking to profit from Egypt's internal disorders, the Byzantines launched major but unsuccessful attacks on Damietta, on the Mediterranean coast, in 853/238 and 859/244.

The ᶜAbbāsid governors and financial administrators were largely at the mercy of court politics in Baghdad. Their brief tenure in office precluded any effective program and policies beyond this. The decline in government led to the appointment, in 861/247, of Aḥmad b. al-Mudabbir to reform the administration and tax system in Egypt. The reforms of al-Mudabbir were interrupted by the arrival in Egypt, in 868/254, of Aḥmad b.

Ṭūlūn; after an initial struggle with al-Mudabbir, Ibn Ṭūlūn gained ascendancy in Egypt and eventually autonomy vis-à-vis Baghdad. The Zanj revolt in southern Iraq prevented the ^{c}Abbāsids from responding more strongly to Ibn Ṭūlūn. Direct ^{c}Abbāsid control of Egypt was reestablished in 905/292, and for thirty years, until the rise of the next autonomous dynasty, the Ikhshīdids, substantial power was exercised by a family of administrators, the Madhārā^{c}ī. In 935/323 Muḥammad b. Ṭughj, more commonly known as the Ikhshīd, was sent by Baghdad to head a stronger government in Egypt, deemed necessary in view of the increasing strength of the Fāṭimids to the west. The Ikhshīdid dynasty once more brought to an end direct ^{c}Abbāsid control of Egypt, and with the conquest of the Ikhshīdid state in 969/358 by the general Jawhar aṣ-Ṣiqillī, Egypt became part of the Fāṭimid Empire.

During the ^{c}Abbāsid period al-Fusṭāṭ, the capital of Islamic Egypt, was extended by the construction of al-^{c}Askar at the beginning of ^{c}Abbāsid rule, and by al-Qaṭā'i^{c}, built by Aḥmad b. Ṭūlūn. Egypt underwent a slow but increasing conversion to Islam, though Christians continued to hold high and important government offices.

<u>^{c}Abbāsid Governors of Egypt</u>

(List adapted from Eduard von Zimbaur's <u>Manuel de généaologie et de chronologie pour l'histoire de l'Islam</u>, Hanover, 1927)

750/133	Ṣāliḥ b. ^{c}Alī al-^{c}Abbas
751/133	Abū ^{c}Awn ^{c}Abd al-Malik b. Yazīd al-Khurāsānī
753/136	Ṣāliḥ b. ^{c}Alī (second term)
755/137	Abū ^{c}Awn (second term)
758/141	Mūsā b. Ka^{c}b at-Tamīmī
759/141	Muḥammad b. al-Ash^{c}ath al-Khuzā'ī
759/142	Nawfal b. Muḥammad al-Furāt
760/143	Humayd b. Qaḥtaba at-Tāy
762/144	Abū Khālid Yazīd b. Hātim al-Muhallabī
764/147	^{c}Abd ar-Raḥmān b. Yazīd (as deputy for Abū Khālid)

769/152	Muḥammad b. Saʿīd (through his deputy ʿAbdallāh b. ʿAbd ar-Raḥmān)
772/155	Muḥammad b. ʿAbd ar-Raḥmān
772/155	ʿAbd aṣ-Ṣamad b. ʿAlī al-ʿAbbās
772/155	Mūsā b. ʿUlayy al-Lakhmī
776/159	Matar
776/159	Abū Ḍamra Muḥammad b. Sulaymān
778/161	ʿĪsā b. Luqmān al-Jumahī
778-79/162	Abū Ḍamra Muḥammad (second term)
778-79/162	Salāma b. Rijā
779/162	Wāḍiḥ
779/162	Manṣūr b. Yazīd ar-Ru'aynī
779/162	Abū Ṣāliḥ Yaḥyā b. Saʿīd al-Harashī
780/164	Sālim b. Sawāda at-Tamīmī
781/165	Ibrāhīm b. Ṣāliḥ al-ʿAbbās
784/167	Mūsā b. Muṣʿab al-Khathamī
785/168	ʿAssāma b. ʿAmr al-Ma'āfirī
785/169	Al-Faḍl b. Ṣāliḥ al-ʿAbbās
786/169	ʿAlī b. Sulaymān al-ʿAbbās
787/171	Mūsā b. ʿĪsa
789/172	Maslama b. Yaḥyā al-Bajallī
789/173	Muḥammad b. Zuhayr al-ʿAzdī
790/174	Dā'ūd b. Yazīd al-Muhallabī
791/175	Mūsā b. ʿĪsa (second term)
792/176	Ibrāhīm b. Ṣāliḥ (second term)
792/176	Jaʿfar b. Yaḥyā b. Barmak (through his deputy ʿUmar b. Mihrān)
793/176	ʿAbdallāh b. Musayyib ad-Dabbī
793/177	Isḥāq b. Sulaymān al-ʿAbbās
794/178	Harthama b. A'yān
794/178	ʿAbd al-Malik b. Ṣāliḥ (through his deputy ʿAbdallāh b. Musayyib, serving a second term)
795/179	ʿUbaydallāh b. al-Mahdī
795/179	Mūsā b. ʿĪsa (third term, through his son and deputy Yaḥyā)

796/180	cUbaydallāh b. al-Mahdī (second term)
797/181	Ismācīl b. Ṣāliḥ al-cAbbās
798/182	Ismācīl b. cĪsa
798/182	Al-Layth al-Faḍl
803/187	Aḥmad b. Ismācīl al-cAbbās
805/189	cUbaydallāh b. Muḥammad
806/190	Al-Ḥusayn b. Jamīl
808/192	Mālik b. Dalham al-Kalbī
809/193	Al-Ḥasan b. at-Takhtāḥ
810/194	Ḥātim b. Harthama b. A'yān
811/195	Jābir b. al-Ashcath at-Tāy
811-12/196	Rabīca b. Qays
812/192	cAbbād b. Muḥammad al-Balkhī
813/198	Al-Muṭṭālib b. cAbdallāh al-Khuzā'ī
814/198	Al-cAbbās b. Mūsā
814/199	Al-Muṭṭālib b. cAbdallāh
816/200	As-Sarī b. al-Ḥakam az-Zuttī
820/205	Abū Naṣr Muḥammad b. as-Sarī
822/206	cUbaydallāh b. as-Sarī
826/211	cAbdallāh b. Ṭāhir b. al-Husayn or cAbbās b. Hāshim (disagreement in sources Ṭāhir was active in suppressing local rebellions at this time)
829/213	cĪsā b. Yazīd al-Jalūdī
(period of revolt)	
829/214	cUmayr b. al-Walīd at-Tamīmī al-Baghīsī
829/214	cĪsā b. Yazīd (second term)
830/215	cAbdawayh b. Jabala
831/216	cĪsā b. al-Manṣūr ar-Rāfī'ī
832/217	cAbd al-Malik Naṣr b. cAbdallah aṣ-Ṣafidī (Kaydur)
834/219	Al-Mazaffar b. Naṣr b. cAbdallāh Kaydur
834/219	Mūsā b. Abū'l-cAbbās Thābit al-Ḥanafī
839/224	Mālik b. Kaydur aṣ-Ṣafadī
841/226	cAlī b. Yaḥyā al-Armanī
843/229	cĪsā b. al-Manṣūr (second term)
848/223	Harthama b. an-Naḍr al-Jabalī
849/234	Ḥātim b. Harthama b. an-Naḍr

849/234	^{c}Alī b. Yaḥyā (second term)
850/235	Isḥāq b. Yaḥyā al-Khuṭṭalānī
851/236	Khūṭ ^{c}Abd al-Wāḥid b. Yaḥyā al-Manṣūr
852/238	^{c}Anbasa b. Isḥāq aḍ-Ḍabbī
856/242	Yazīd b. ^{c}Abdallāh at-Turkī
867/253	Muzāḥim b. Khāqān at-Turkī
868/254	Aḥmad b. Muzāḥim at-Turkī
868/254	Yarkūj/Arghūz b. Ulugh Ṭarkhān at-Turkī
868-905/254-292	The Ṭūlūnids
905/292	Abū Mūsā ^{c}Īsā b. Muḥammad an-Nawsharī
	Rebellion of Muḥammad b. Khalanjī
910/297	Abū'l-^{c}Abbās b. Bustām (died shortly after appointment)
910/297	Abū Mansur Takin (Tekin) b. ^{c}Abdallah al-Khazarī
915/303	Abū'l-Ḥasan Duqā al-^{c}Awar ar-Rūmī
919/307	Takīn b. ^{c}Abdallāh (second term)
921/309	Abū Qābūs Maḥmūd b. Ḥamak (three days only)
921/309	Takīn b. ^{c}Abdullāh (third term)
921/309	Abū'l-Ḥasan Hilāl b. Badr
923/311	Abū'l-^{c}Abbās Aḥmad b. Kayghalygh
924/311	Takīn b. ^{c}Abdallāh (fourth term)
933/321	Muḥammad b. Takīn
933/321	Abū'l-^{c}Abbās Aḥmad b. Kayghalygh (second term

The Ikhshīdids (935-69/323-58)

^{c}ABDALLĀH b. ^{c}ABD AL-MALIK b. MARWĀN (r. 704-09/84-90). Umayyad governor of Egypt, ^{c}Abdallāh brought to his post his reputation as an experienced and successful military commander. He sought during his term of office to abolish or modify many of the practices of his uncle and predecessor, ^{c}Abd al-^{c}Azīz b. Marwān (d. 704/85) and introduced Arabic as the official court language, though it spread rather more slowly outside the confines of the court. A famine struck Egypt during his reign. ^{c}Abdallāh was recalled to Damascus following allegations of corruption and power-seeking.

ᶜABDALLĀH b. SAᶜD b. ABĪ SARḤ (r. 644-56/23-35). First Muslim governor of Upper Egypt, ᶜAbdallāh had been associated with the Prophet Muḥammad from the earliest days of his ministry. ᶜAbdallāh was appointed by the Caliph ᶜUmar (d. 644/23). He was elevated to the governorship of all Egypt by ᶜUmar's successor, his foster brother ᶜUthmān, in 645/24 over ᶜAmr b. al-ᶜĀṣ, Arab conqueror of Egypt, who had ruled the country since his initial conquests five years previously. ᶜAbdallāh was temporarily eclipsed in 645/25, when ᶜAmr was reinstated to lead the defense of Egypt against an attack by the Byzantine Emperor Constans, but he managed to regain his position thereafter and repulsed a second Byzantine attack on Alexandria in 652/31. He went on to inflict a major defeat on the Byzantine navy in the Battle of Dhāt as-Sawārī in 655/35, in combination with the forces of the future Umayyad Caliph Muᶜāwiya (who later reinstated ᶜAmr in the governorship of Egypt).

ᶜAbdallāh helped consolidate Egypt's southern borders through a treaty concluded with the Kingdom of Nubia in 652/31, following a year's campaigning. He had previously campaigned in Barqa (east Libya) in 645-46/25 and 647-48/27. Revenues from Egypt greatly increased during his tenure in office, though his tax measures were, inevitably, exceedingly unpopular with the Egyptians, especially as they were largely diverted to military expenditures outside Egypt. In 656/35 ᶜAbdallāh was prevented from returning to Egypt by internal disturbances there, following a period when he had been out of the country supporting the Caliph ᶜUthmān, who was facing serious challenges to his reign.

ᶜABD AL-ᶜAZĪZ b. MARWĀN (d. 704/85). Umayyad governor of Egypt from 685/65 until his death, ᶜAbd al-ᶜAzīz was initially appointed by his father, the Caliph Marwān I, an appointment confirmed by his brother, ᶜAbd al-Malik, when the latter came to power as Caliph in 685/65. ᶜAbd al-ᶜAzīz is described in the sources as extremely competent in his rule, though he suffered the jealousies of his brother, ᶜAbd al-Malik, who wished to secure the succession to the Caliphate for his own sons rather than his brother. There appear to have been a number of plots against ᶜAbd al-ᶜAzīz on this account, which proved rather pointless, for in the end he predeceased his brother, who was then able to pass power on to his sons. The deliberate exclusion of ᶜAbd al-ᶜAzīz from power outside Egypt freed him to devote his attention to the country's administration, and he introduced a number of important changes. Forced to relocate to Helwan (Ḥulwān) during flooding and plague in al-Fusṭāṭ, ᶜAbd al-ᶜAzīz developed that town. He later commissioned the construction of a Nilometer to measure the Nile's flow.

ᶜAbd al-ᶜAzīz disbanded the Muslim garrison at al-Fusṭāṭ, as well as other garrisons established throughout the country among which the troops were rotated. The soldiers were settled in rural areas and along the coast, given stipends, and encouraged to integrate with the local population. They were on occasion given supervisory functions with regard to local officials, who also enjoyed ᶜAbd al-ᶜAzīz' favor.

ᶜABD AL-ᶜAZĪZ (AL MANṢŪR ᶜIZZ AD-DĪN ᶜABD AL-ᶜAZĪZ) (r. 1405/808). Burjī Mamluk Sultan, son of the Sultan Barqūq, ᶜAbd al-ᶜAzīz briefly held power during the reign of his older brother Faraj. He was placed on the throne by a faction of Burjī Mamluks headed by Yashbāk and Baybars who felt that Faraj was backing the Turkish Mamluks against them. ᶜAbd al-ᶜAzīz was displaced after two or three months of fighting among the various Mamluk factions, when Faraj managed to regain power. ᶜAbd al-ᶜAzīz and his brothers were imprisoned in Alexandria by Faraj, to prevent their being used as figurehead sultans by the still discontented Mamluk factions; they later died in prison.

ABDUH, SHAYKH MUHAMMAD (1849-1905). One of the most important Muslim religious figures of the nineteenth century, Shaykh Muhammad Abduh had a profound influence on the development of Islamic thought in this century.

Abduh came from a religious family and received his education in the traditional Quran schools in Tanta, Egypt. He studied at al-Azhar from 1866, pursuing in his personal life an active religious search involving both a study of the theology and original sources of Islam and affiliation with the Sufi tariqas, which are such an important part of popular Islam in Egypt. Abduh became associated with Jamal ad-Din al-Afghani, who first came to Egypt in 1871 preaching a combination of pan-Islamicism, Islamic revivalism, and political redirection of Islamic societies. As an editor of the official gazette Abduh also was in contact with the prominent journalists of his day, such as Abdullah Nadim and James Sanua. When Al-Afghani founded a nationalist-oriented masonic lodge in Egypt in the late 1870s, Abduh joined that, as well as the Hizb al-Watani, or Nationalist Party, organized in 1879. He participated in the drafting of the nationalists' manifesto. Though Abduh turned away from some of the more violent aspects of the nationalist movement in this period, his commitment to it was strong enough for him to be deported from Egypt in the wake of the 1882 Arabi Rebellion. He joined Al-Afghani in exile in Paris, and in 1884 the two men joined forces to produce Al-Urwat al-Wuthqa ("The Indissoluable Bond"), a short-lived but extremely influential anticolonialist, pan-Islamic journal.

Abduh returned to Egypt in 1889, after four years of travel in North Africa and the Levant; he devoted himself after his return to the reform of Islamic law in Egypt and to the modernization and renewal of al-Azhar, the Islamic university where he had himself been educated. His initial attempts to bring its curriculum more in line with modern needs were resisted, although, outside al-Azhar, he gained respect among, and acceptability to, the British (and to Lord Cromer). Abduh was appointed a judge in the native tribunals, and eventually named Mufti (chief religious judge and legal authority) in 1899. He eventually succeeded in forming an administrative council at al-Azhar, which directed the reforms he had sought. Abduh was nominated for, and participated actively in, the Legislative Council from 1899 until his death, but his relationship with Egypt's more radical nationalists was uneasy in his later years. He also did not enjoy the support of the more conservative clergy of al-Azhar, who felt threatened by the reforms he sought. Conversely, he attracted many moderate and dedicated nationalists to his teachings on Islamic reform, resulting in the formation of the Imam Party, forerunner of the Umma Party.

Though Abduh was not fully successful in achieving the ambitious goals he set for himself, initially politically but later religiously, there is no doubt of his influence on the development of religious thought in Egypt in the twentieth century. He sought, in his teachings and writings, to come to terms with the problems arising from the contact between Islam and the West and emphasized the need for a revitalization and strengthening of Islam. His belief that there must be a return to the original purity of Islam in the interpretation of its teachings and practices was combined with a selective attitude toward what the West could offer a Muslim society. Abduh's insistence that there could be no true conflict between Islam and what was valid within Western science gave inspiration to many of Egypt's modern religious thinkers.

ABŪ BAKR (AL-MANṢŪR ṢAYF AD-DĪN ABŪ BAKR) (r.1340/741). Baḥrī Mamluk Sultan, son and first successor of an-Nāṣir Muḥammad in the line of eight sons who ruled ephemerally in the eleven years following their father's death. Abū Bakr's reign of a few months was terminated by his brother Kūjūk. Nominated as his father's successor shortly before the latter's death, as the best among an indifferent lot, Abū Bakr lived up to expectations by a quick display of cruelty directed toward old members of his father's court. Kūjūk's accession was aided by the powerful Mamluk Qūsūn, who was particularly alienated by Abū Bakr. Qūsūn arranged for Abū Bakr and some of his brothers to be exiled to Qūṣ in Upper Egypt, where he was later executed on Qūsūn's orders.

ABU'DH-DHAHAB (MUHAMMAD BEY) (d.1775/1189). Shaykh al-Balad in Egypt from 1773/1187 until his death, Abu'dh-Dhahab was the Mamluk of ᶜAli Bey (Shaykh al-Balad and de facto ruler of Egypt from 1768/1181 until his overthrow by Abu'dh-Dhahab). Abu'dh-Dhahab was originally a Mamluk of ᶜAlī Bey and was raised to the beylicate shortly after ᶜAlī became Shaykh al-Balad, in 1764/1178.

Abu'dh-Dhahab commanded the army that suppressed a major rebellion of the Hawwāra tribe in 1769/1183. He then went on to campaign in Syria in 1770-71/1184-85, before coming to an understanding with the Ottoman Porte whereby he would remove ᶜAlī Bey from power in Egypt in exchange for his own appointment as Shaykh al-Balad. In 1172/1186 he turned his armies against Egypt and defeated ᶜAlī Bey in battle at the Delta village of Salāḥiyya, after which he received the promised position. The intense internal competition prevailing among the Mamluk factions at this time was not greatly affected by the changeover. A powerful duumvir of two leading Mamluks, Murād Bey and Ibrāhīm Bey, managed to seize power and restore some order when Abu'dh-Dhahab died while on campaign in Palestine against a rebel chief formerly allied to ᶜAlī Bey.

ABŪ NAḌḌĀRA see JAMES SANUA

ACCOMPLISHMENT PLAN (1967-70). The failure to meet many of the ambitious goals of Egypt's 1965-70 Five-Year Plan, and the dislocations caused to the economy by military expenditure prior to the 1967 Arab-Israeli War, led to the establishment of the Accomplishment Plan, which stressed the completion of projects already underway but froze all new development schemes. The Accomplishment Plan aimed at a 5-percent growth rate in GNP per annum (compared with 7.2 percent in the original 1960-70 Plan), with a total investment of £Eg 1,085 million (compared with the £Eg 1,513 million invested in the 1960-65 period). The 1967 Arab-Israeli War, which occurred shortly after the Accomplishment Plan was announced, forced a complete re-thinking on the government's part, and the plan was eventually replaced by a series of annual development appropriations, which effectively brought long-term economic planning to a halt.

AL-ᶜĀḌID (r. 1160-71/555-67). Last Fāṭimid Caliph to rule Egypt, al-^{c}Āḍid was a boy of nine when he was placed on the throne by the vizier aṣ-Ṣāliḥ Talā'i^{c}, who sought to further consolidate his position by marrying al-^{c}Āḍid to his daughter. Aṣ-Ṣāliḥ Talā'i^{c}, despite these precautions, was murdered within a year of the Caliph's accession, at the instigation of al-^{c}Āḍid's aunt, a powerful figure in the court. The vizierate then passed to Aṣ-Ṣāliḥ Talā'i^{c}'s son, ar-Rizzīk, who was himself displaced in 1163/558 by Shāwar, then shortly afterward by Dirgham.

In terms of the power al-^{c}Āḍid exercised, the activities of the viziers who ostensibly served him suggest that he held little control of the government, and slight autonomy. The involvement of Egypt with the Crusaders and with the strong Zangid ruler of Damascus, Nūr ad-Dīn, was established in the course of the power struggle between the viziers Dirgham and Shāwar. When the latter was displaced in 1163/558, he sought the support of Nūr ad-Dīn; the following year Nūr ad-Dīn sent an army to Egypt under the command of Shīrkūh, which defeated and killed Dirgham and installed Shāwar in power. Shāwar then used the Crusaders to rid himself of Shīrkūh.

In 1167/563, following a Crusader siege of Shīrkūh's forces under the command of Ṣalāḥ ad-Dīn in Alexandria, which had been captured during Shīrkūh's second campaign against his ungrateful erstwhile ally, the Crusaders and Shīrkūh negotiated their withdrawal to Syria, though not before the Crusader commander Amalric had made Egypt a tributary. The Crusader chiefs were allowed a meeting with the young Caliph, providing the chronicles with a vivid description of his exotic and luxurious court. Egypt's tributary relationship with Amalric was unpopular, and it was not long before Shāwar showed signs of restiveness over his new allies. The Crusaders sent an army to Egypt in 1168/564; Bilbays, in the eastern Delta, was destroyed. Shāwar set fire to al-Fusṭāṭ and announced his intention to do the same to Cairo rather than let the city fall into Crusader hands. At this point al-^{c}Āḍid and the court appealed to Nūr ad-Dīn to save them. The arrival of Shīrkūh, at the head of Nūr ad-Dīn's armies, on the Egyptian border was followed by a Crusader withdrawal. Shīrkūh took power as vizier to al-ᶜĀḍid early in 1169/564 and had Shāwar murdered shortly thereafter, with the agreement of al-ᶜĀḍid; when Shīrkūh died two months later, his nephew Ṣalāḥ ad-Dīn succeeded him as vizier, though both men remained nominally in the service of Nūr ad-Dīn.

In the closing two years of al-ᶜĀḍid's reign the Caliph was a virtual recluse; his vizier, Ṣalāḥ ad-Dīn, repulsed a Crusader attack on Damietta in 1169/564 and went on to campaign in southern Palestine against the Crusaders in the following year. He restored order within Egypt, suppressing the rebellious remnants of the Fāṭimid army. In 1171/567, as al-ᶜĀḍid lay dying, Ṣalāḥ ad-Dīn formally restored Egypt to the Sunnī Islamic doctrine, bringing to an end two centuries of Shīᶜa rule in Egypt.

AL-ᶜĀDIL I (AL-MALIK AL-ᶜĀDIL I SAYF AD-DĪN) (r.1200-18/596-615). Ayyūbid ruler of Egypt and Syria, brother of Ṣalāḥ ad-Dīn, al-ᶜĀdil was known to the Crusaders as Safadin. He accompanied Ṣalāḥ ad-Dīn to Egypt on their uncle Shīrkūh's third expedition against the Crusaders in 1169/564. Following Ṣalāḥ ad-Dīn's assumption of power as vizier in Egypt after Shīrkūh's death al-ᶜĀdil acted as his deputy as governor of the country during Ṣalāḥ ad-Dīn's absence. In 1183-86/579-82 al-ᶜĀdil held the governorship of Aleppo, Syria, returning to Egypt to rule the country as regent for Ṣalāḥ ad-Dīn's son al-ᶜAzīz until 1192/588.

During this time al-ᶜĀdil superintended the construction and fortification of the Citadel in Cairo (finished in 1207-08/604), as well as participating in several of the military campaigns of his brother against the Crusaders. In 1192/588 he successfully negotiated a treaty with the Crusaders, granting them trading privileges in Alexandria, control over land seized in the previous years' fighting, and making Jerusalem an open city. He was in that year appointed governor of Diyār Bakr and Balqā', which he remained in control of, in addition to Kerak, at the time of his brother's death.

Ṣalāḥ ad-Dīn's death in 1193/589 resulted in his conquered territories being split between his sons and other family members, but the principal inheritors were al-^{c}Azīz in Egypt and al-Afḍal in Damascus. Al-^{c}Ādil, ruling in Kerak, spent a great deal of time mediating between these two antagonists. He eventually gave his support to the more capable of the two, al-^{c}Azīz, taking power in Damascus as the latter's deputy when he defeated his nephew al-Afḍal in 1196/592; four years later he took power in Egypt from al-^{c}Azīz's nominal successor, al-Manṣūr, who was under challenge from his deposed uncle, al-Afḍal. Al-^{c}Ādil's joint rule of Egypt and Syria was recognized by the ^{c}Abbāsid Caliph in 1207/603.

Al-^{c}Ādil's rule was marked by a genuine concern for public welfare and a benevolent attitude toward his subjects. More importantly, he saved the Ayyūbid state founded by his brother Ṣalāḥ ad-Dīn from being rent asunder by internecine struggle between his heirs, and it was this strengthened Ayyūbid state that was able to meet successfully a Crusader invasion launched in the last year of al-^{c}Ādil's reign, which was defeated by his son and successor, al-Kāmil.

AL-^{c}ĀDIL II (AL-MALIK AL-^{c}ĀDIL II SAYF AD-DĪN) (r. 1238-40/635-37). Ayyūbid ruler of Egypt, al-^{c}Ādil II was the son and successor to al-Kāmil. After a period of strong leadership under his grandfather and father al-^{c}Ādil's reign marked the beginning of the internal, internecine struggles that were to weaken and eventually bring to an end Ayyūbid power in Egypt. At the time of his accession, Ayyūbid control in Syria was in tumult. Al-^{c}Ādil left the resolution of this to his brother aṣ-Ṣāliḥ, and devoted himself to pleasure-seeking to a degree which alienated his commanders. He maintained his position against his more capable brother aṣ-Ṣāliḥ through an alliance with his cousin Prince Dā'ūd of Kerak; when Dā'ūd shifted his allegiance to aṣ-Ṣāliḥ, al-^{c}Ādil was unable to match their power base or popularity in court circles. Aṣ-Ṣāliḥ deposed his brother and placed him under house arrest; al-^{c}Ādil was eventually executed in

1247/645, for, it is reported, refusing to change residences as ordered.

AL-^{c}ĀDIL b. AS-SALLĀR see AS-SALLĀR

ADLI PASHA YEGEN (d. 1933). Egyptian nationalist politician who served three times as Prime Minister in the 1920s, forming governments in 1921 (March-November), 1926-27 (June-April) and briefly from October 1929 until the elections of December 1929.

Adli was the appointed Vice-President of the Legislative Assembly formed in 1914, Zaghlul holding the second, elected, vice-presidency. Disputes over precedence soon developed. Adli's political life thereafter was dominated by his relation with Zaghlul, as the forces opposed to Zaghlul personally, and to the more ardent nationalists, grouped around Adli. Adli was serving as Minister of Education in 1918 (in the Rushdi government) when he was apparently invited to join Zaghlul in the original Egyptian nationalist delegation (Wafd) seeking to present the case for the termination of the Protectorate to Britain and eventual representation at the Versailles Peace Conference. His participation was not approved by some of the delegates, and his name was dropped. Increasingly identified with pro-Palace moderate nationalist elements, Adli's decision to accept the Palace's invitation to form a government in 1921 and lead official negotiations with the British led to open antagonism with Zaghlul, who had returned to Egypt in triumph that April after a period in exile.

The Egyptian nationalist movement, especially at its elite level, split between supporters of the two men, with dissidents from Zaghlul's Wafd Party forming the Society of Independent Egypt to back Adli and his ministry. Despite this support Adli strove as far as possible to avoid further provocation of the popular Zaghlul. His reluctance to make concessions that would be attacked by Zaghlul and the Wafd is held partly responsible for the breakdown in negotiations on Egyptian independence between Adli and Curzon in the summer of 1921. Zaghlul refused

Adli's invitation to participate in these talks. Adli subsequently resigned in the face of increasing nationalist pressure on his government. Zaghlul was deported for a second time shortly after Adli's government fell.

Adli went on to found the Liberal Constitutionalist Party in 1922, meant to be a support group for the government of Tharwat Pasha. He refused an invitation to form a government in February 1923, though he was subsequently appointed a senator in the Egyptian Parliament. Adli formed his second government after the elections of May 1926, which returned a huge Wafdist majority to the Parliament. The British were unwilling to countenance Zaghlul forming a government after allegations of Wafd involvement in the Lee Stack Affair, but Adli, despite British support, still had to manage a Wafd-dominated Parliament with Zaghlul as its president. The impossibility of this situation led to his resignation, in April 1927, to make way for, once more, Tharwat Pasha.

Adli's third and brief term as Prime Minister in the closing months of 1929 came at a time when lengthy but unsuccessful negotiations were being held between Egypt and Britain over a new treaty. Adli's government acted as a caretaker between the resignation of his predecessor, Muhammad Mahmud Pasha, and the elections that December. Prior to his death he was active in the political opposition to the Sidqi regime and led attempts to form a coalition cabinet to replace it.

ADLY PASHA see ADLI PASHA

AL-AFḌAL b. BADR AL-JAMĀLĪ (1066-1121/458-515). Son and successor to the vizier Badr al-Jamālī, al-Afḍal was associated with his father from 1089/482 in the latter's efforts to restore the power and unity of the Fāṭimid state in Egypt following a long period of decline. He succeeded his father as vizier and Commander-in-Chief of the army (Āmir al-Juyūsh) upon Badr's death in 1094/487.

To secure his control of the country al-Afḍal engineered the succession of the malleable al-Mustaᶜlī to the Fāṭimid Caliphate in 1094/487, causing a major split in the Shī^{c}a community. The supporters of the claims of al-Musta^{c}lī's older brother, Nizār, rose in battle against the new Caliph. Al-Afḍal was forced to campaign against them in Egypt, after which most of them regrouped in the Levant. For many decades they remained a continuing danger to the Fāṭimids. Al-Musta^{c}lī was confined to the Palace as al-Afḍal took charge of the government.

During the reign of al-Musta^{c}lī the Crusaders reached Syria, in 1096/489-90. At the time the Levant and parts of Syria were occupied by the Arṭukid allies of the Saljūq Turks, who had seized Fāṭimid-claimed territory. Al-Afḍal entered into negotiations with the Crusaders in 1098/491, possibly with the idea of forming a military alliance against the Turks, and in that year took Jerusalem from the Saljūqs. However, in 1099/492 the Crusaders turned against the Fāṭimids and swept them out of Jerusalem, massacring the city's Muslim and Christian citizens. They went on to defeat al-Afḍal in battle at Ascalon.

On the death of al-Musta^{c}lī in 1101/495, the year Palestine fell to the Crusaders, al-Afḍal selected al-Āmir to succeed him; as al-Āmir was only five at the time, he was expected to pose little threat to al-Afḍal's ambitions. The Crusader advance continued with the fall of Acre in 1103/497, the seizure of Tripoli in 1108/502, and an attack on Egypt itself in 1118/512 led by Baldwin I, King of Jerusalem. Though this attack was repelled, al-Afḍal's unimpressive military record in defense of Fāṭimid territory, and al-Āmir's growing impatience with the restrictions placed on him by his overly watchful vizier, led to al-Afḍal's assassination probably on orders of al-Āmir, though it was blamed on Nizārī assassins and occasionally also linked to the ambitions of the Amīr al-Baṭā'ihī, who desired to replace him. Al-Afḍal's efforts to improve aspects of Egypt's fiscal administration show a certain dedication to continuing the reforms of his father, but his time in power is more characterized by Egypt's absolute military decline vis-à-vis the Crusaders.

AL-AFGHANI, JAMAL AD-DIN (1838-1897). Among the earliest

advocates of pan-Islamic politics and Islamic revitalization, Al-Afghani was a major influence on the development of nationalism in nineteenth-century Egypt. He first came to Cairo in 1870 after a checkered political career in Kabul and travels in India. He then served at the Ottoman Porte before returning to Cairo, a return speeded by the controversies aroused by his public lectures in Istanbul.

Granted a stipend by the Khedive, Al-Afghani soon attracted a following of young scholars from the al-Azhar, including Muhammad Abduh, and enjoyed the support of many nationalist political and military leaders. A Masonic lodge founded by Al-Afghani in 1876 had a membership of 300, including every prominent individual with a nationalist connection: Abduh, Sharif, Burtrus Ghali, Zaghlul, and the heir-presumptive to the Khedivate, Tawfiq. Afghani used all the platforms available to him to argue passionately for Islamic political unity in the face of the European colonial threat.

Afghani's involvement in the circulation of the Nationalist Manifesto in 1879 led to his deportation from Egypt. He then traveled to India and London before making his way to Paris. In 1884 Abduh joined him in Paris and the two cooperated in the publication of a pan-Islamic, anticolonialist journal, Al-Urwat al-Wuthqa ("The Indissoluable Bond"), which drew contributions from several nationalist authors and the editors.

After Abduh departed for North Africa in 1885, Al-Afghani went to Persia; his association with the court there ended in 1887, when he was deported. He eventually received an invitation from the Ottoman Sultan to settle in Istanbul in 1892. Conditions there were less than ideal, though Al-Afghani was refused permission to leave.

Al-Afghani's intellectual heirs in Egypt are numerous, but most direct influence can be seen in the Nationalist Party under Mustafa Kamil. Al-Afghani's belief in the political strength of a revitalized Islam was later to be echoed in Egypt by many in the nationalist movement, particularly in aspects of Misr al-Fatat's ideology and the Young Men's Muslim Association.

ARFANJ AḤMAD (d. 1711/1123). A leader of the Janissary corps in Egypt, Afranj Aḥmad was a crucial figure in the Great Insurrection of 1711/1123, which saw the fall of the Faqāriyya faction of the beylicate, with whom Afranj was allied. Afranj Ahmad first seized leadership of the Janissaries in 1703-04/1116 but was deposed following a Janissary insurrection in 1706/1118. In 1709/1121 he managed to assert control over the Janissary leadership as the corps stood in increasing opposition to the rest of the Ottoman garrison. This opposition was a longstanding phenomenon, but the grave weakening of the position of the Ottoman governor in Egypt, and the heightened rivalry between the factions in the beylicate, exacerbated tensions with the garrison.

Early in 1711/1123 Afranj survived an attempt by pro-Qāsimiyya Janissaries to depose him and break the corps' traditional links with the Faqāriyya. Thereafter he suppressed the opposition against him in the corps and led the Janissaries in the fighting against the other Ottoman corps and the Qāsimiyya faction during the Great Insurrection. This period of general chaos was not brought to an end for over two months, during which the Faqāriyya and the Janissaries were bested. Afranj Aḥmad was killed after the fighting when he was caught while attempting an escape from Cairo.

AFRO-ASIAN PEOPLES' SOLIDARITY CONFERENCE. First held in Cairo 26 December 1957-1 January 1958, the Conference was an outgrowth of the earlier Bandung Conference. The AAPSC program was structured around opposition to colonial and imperialist influences and control in the Third World. It supported a number of national liberation movements there. Egypt's involvement with the AAPSC was part of Nasser's post-Bandung strategy to gain a major voice in the leadership of the Third World. Following the first meeting of the Conference, in which forty-six countries participated, a permanent Secretariat was established in Cairo under the leadership of Yusuf Sibai'i. The Secretariat coordinated the activities of member states of the Conference with regard to anticolonialist activities, acting as a brake on the more extreme elements within the anticolonialist movement. Anwar Sadat served as chairman of the first AAPSC Conference and was active in the organization.

Egypt's dominance within the AAPSC was affected by the gradual withdrawal of European colonial powers from the region and the emergence of new regimes with independent national policies and interests. This broadened the movement's ideological base, although the AAPSC has tended to concentrate on programs of social and economic cooperation of benefit to all members. There are currently seventy-five countries in the AAPSC, which is headquartered in Cairo under the Secretary-General, Abdur Rahman Sharqawi.

AGHA. Ottoman title given to military commanders in Ottoman Egypt (1517-1798/922-1213) and used as well by some Ottoman administrative officers.

AGRARIAN REFORM LAW. First major legislation introduced after the Revolution of 1952, the law was the cornerstone of the Free Officers' initial program of social and political reform. Law No. 178 (9 September 1952) limited individual landholdings to 200 feddans (1 feddan equals 4.201 square meters or slightly over 1 acre) plus 100 additional feddans for family members. Land confiscated by the government was to be redistributed by the High Committee for Agrarian Reform headed by Sayyid Marei. Cooperative societies, already established, were to be incorporated into the scheme for administration of reform measures and agricultural planning. Initial problems with titles and land registration were handled through the HCAR, which acted as a semiautonomous body until its formation into a Ministry in 1956. In all, over 2,100 large landowners, holding more than one million feddans, were affected by the law, which aimed at redistributing some 730,000 feddans over a five-year period.

The law's main articles provided for indemnification for expropriated land in negotiable government bonds, carrying an annual interest rate of 3 percent for thirty years, with compensation at a rate of seven times the land tax, thus hitting the large landowners, who for years had kept land taxes artificially low. The expropriated land would be distributed to landless peasants, with a five-feddan-per-family limit. This redistributed land would be paid for over thirty years, at 3-percent interest with a 15-percent charge for costs and conveyancing. Agricultural workers were to have their wages set by a special committee and would be permitted to form unions. Ceilings on rents, whether in cash or in kind, were also established.

The Agrarian Reform Law was modified in 1958 and 1959, extending the period for purchase-payment from thirty to forty years and reducing the interest rates of loans from 3 percent to 1.5 percent, with a 5-percent reduction in conveyancing charges, measures to ease some of the difficulties experienced by peasant families in profiting from the law's provisions.

In 1961, in the wake of the Socialist Laws, far-reaching changes were introduced. The ceiling on private ownership dropped from 200 to 100 feddans, with the 100 feddans to include waste and fallow land as well as land under cultivation. Provisions limited rental rights to smallholders, and the exchange value for appropriated land was expressed in non-negotiable fifteen-year Treasury Bonds carrying 4-percent interest. Late in 1961, the remaining conveyancing charges were dropped. The ceiling on private land holding was reduced once more to fifty feddans in 1969.

AGRICULTURAL COOPERATIVES. The use of agricultural cooperatives to assist the government in its efforts to control Egypt's vital agricultural sector has been a central feature of Egyptian government agricultural policy since the 1952 Revolution, though cooperatives as such long predated the Revolution.

The first cooperatives in Egypt were established in 1907 by Umar Lutfi, though these early cooperatives were mainly designed to protect the economic interests of Egypt's larger landholders. A General Central Syndicate was established to control credit, supplies, and marketing, and a 1923 law outlined provisions for their organization and procedures. In 1927, the Wafd proposed legislation offering self-regulation to the cooperatives, but less than two years later, the government instituted more centralized controls.

Before the Revolution entry fees for most of the cooperatives were so high that (at least prior to World War II) few small farmers were associated with them. Marketing functions remained the main purpose of the cooperative movement until 1944, when new legislation gave the government more direct supervisory control of cooperatives. The development of the Agricultural Cooperative Bank in 1949 permitted more farmers to join the movement, and by 1952, 750,000 farmers were members of the 1,727 cooperatives then in existence.

After 1952 membership in an existing cooperative was no longer on a voluntary basis for small landholders, and representatives of the Ministry of Agrarian Reform participated in cooperative management at local levels. In addition to their old functions of supply and marketing, the post-1952 cooperatives also introduced new crops and techniques, provided loans, and distributed seeds and fertilizer. Crop yields, particularly of cotton and sugar, dramatically improved under the reformed system. Aside from their agricultural role, the cooperatives were also used by the government as a means of disseminating political information and as a base for building rural support.

With the introduction of the Socialist Laws in 1961, membership in a cooperative was made compulsory for all landholders. Despite the government's intentions the cooperative movement after the Revolution was troubled by bureaucratization within local power structures. In 1969 legislation was enacted to ensure more centralized control and distribute the benefits of the cooperative system more evenly at the local level.

In 1980 there were over 4,800 cooperatives, whose links with the center have enabled the government to keep control over an agricultural sector that is increasingly dominated by smallholdings. Every farmer is obliged to grow crops selected by the government on a certain portion of his land, based on a quota system. In turn the government sells these goods through a state marketing system, and provides cooperative farmers with free water, subsidized pesticides, and fertilizer.

AGRICULTURAL SOCIETY. Founded in 1898 by a group of Egyptian landowners, the Agricultural Society was the first organization formed in Egypt to encourage the development of new agricultural techniques. The society hired an Englishman, Laurence Balls, as a research botanist in 1904, and in the forty-three years that he held the post much of the foundation for Egyptian cotton research was established. In 1914, at the urging of Lord Kitchener, a Department of Agriculture was set up and took over some of the Agricultural Society's functions and personnel. A Cotton Research Board was eventually established in 1920.

AGRICULTURE. Egypt has been, and likely always will be, a predominantly agricultural country. It was Egypt's agricultural wealth as much as its strategic importance that attracted a succession of conquerors to the country, and in the early centuries of Roman rule Egypt was the Empire's major supplier of grain. This role of food supplier remained important despite the shift in power within the empire from Rome to Constantinople. The establishment of the monastic system in rural areas of Egypt, and the incorporation of large rural areas under the supervision of the monasteries, and of large landholders with set tax liabilities, provided for a certain continuity in supply in the agricultural sector during a time when Egypt's capital, Alexandria, was torn by religious and political strife.

The grain harvest was important to Egypt's Arab conquerors; one of the first acts of ^{c}Amr b. al-^{c}Āṣ was to clear an ancient canal from the Nile valley to the port of Qulzum, near present-day Suez, to speed the transport of grain to Mecca and Medina. This canal, begun in 641/20, was later closed by the new ^{c}Abbāsid Caliph al-Mansūr in 761/143 to punish the residents of those cities, but in fact the interests of Egypt's rulers had shifted from agricultural production to the revenue they could earn by taxing that production. A revised system of stiff land taxes was introduced by the administrator al-Mudabbir in 861/247, but harsh policies toward the cultivators merely drove them off the land. The arrival in Egypt of Ibn Ṭūlūn (868/254) helped the situation in the agricultural sector, as revenues were used to repair and improve the infrastructure, land-tenure conditions were eased, and cultivated area increased through new land grants.

During Fāṭimid times (969-1171/358-567) and despite the early reforms of the administrator Ya^cqūb b. Killis, agriculture began a long period of stasis that was not fully reversed until the nineteenth century and the beginning of reforms in the land law. The practice of tax farming, which was already present in modified form and which under previous regimes also had bound tax collectors to maintain irrigation and other vital elements of rural infrastructure, deteriorated as the government placed few nonfiscal responsibilities with the tax farmer. As a result irrigation works were neglected, and, combined with several disastrous failures of the Nile, the Fāṭimid period became increasingly marred by severe famines. In 1054/405 food shortages were so severe that the Byzantine Emperor had to be approached for supplies. A seven-year famine that began in 1065/457 nearly brought about the collapse of the Fāṭimid state.

The rise of the Ayyūbids in power in Egypt (1171-1250/567-648) brought some improvements in both the tax structure and in the maintenance of the irrigation vital to agriculture. However, the Ayyūbid's successors, the Mamluks, pursued a policy of exploitation that rivaled that of the Fāṭimids, and famine once again made its appearance. The recurrence of famine in Mamluk times was also linked to the outbreak in Egypt of the plague; in 1348/749 and again in 1401/803 Egypt lost many of its farmers to especially serious plagues. Outbreaks of the plague recurred for decades, and the rural areas took several centuries to recover their population. In the meantime the incidence of famine increased through sheer lack of manpower to grow food necessary to feed the urban centers. Finally, in later Mamluk times Egypt's agriculture was damaged by the desire of some Burjī Mamluk Sultans to impose a monopoly on every commodity in which there might be a profit, which resulted in shortages and hardships in rural areas. Despite the sporadically favorable attentions of the Ottomans to rural revenue collection, agriculture continued to decline. The impoverished rural areas saw an increase in brigandage as their populations had to suffer the exactions of the Ottoman tax farmers and members of the Ottoman garrison.

The rise to power of Muhammad Ali in 1805 marked the commencement of a new era in Egyptian agriculture, with reforms in landholding, taxation, tax collection, and cultivation of cotton in commercial quantities. The conversion of Egypt's agriculture through the development of cash crops led to a rapid development in the country's infrastructure in both rural and urban areas. This impetus given by Muhammad Ali to cash-crop agriculture was supported by the British when they assumed de facto control of Egypt. The corvée, or forced labor, used to maintain irrigation works was abolished in the 1880s. Higher levels of foreign investment, and official encouragement, led to tremendous agricultural growth. A series of barrages and dams were constructed to make more efficient use of the Nile waters for agriculture, particularly the raising of dams at Aswan in 1902, 1912, and 1934. The British also introduced legislation that attempted to protect the Egyptian smallholder. However, agriculture in the decades prior to the Revolution was increasingly burdened by a surplus rural population whose presence helped depress agricultural wages and also by an exceedingly inequitable distribution of land. The cash crops on which Egypt depended for export earnings from late-nineteenth century onward made her a victim of international economic forces well beyond her control. The slump in demand in each postwar period, plus the Depression of the 1930s, badly affected the Egyptian economy and the earnings of Egyptian farmers.

At the time of the 1952 Revolution the agricultural sector in Egypt was dominated by a tiny minority of large and medium landholders (6 percent) and a vast number of smallholders (94 percent) owning just 35 percent of Egypt's arable land, as well as landless laborers. Though the irrigation works carried out in the nineteenth century helped expand arable land from 4.767 million feddans in 1881 to a total crop area of over 7.7 million feddans, this expansion could not keep up with population growth and with the demand for land, which kept its price high and effectively out of the reach of most peasants. Larger landholders were protected by extremely favorable taxation systems.

Given the situation in the countryside, it is not surprising that the immediate priority of the Free Officers upon coming to power in 1952 was land reform. It was an issue that directly touched most of Egypt's population. At the same time land reform was combined with direct government involvement, through cooperatives and local councils, to ensure more centralized control over the agricultural sector. This allowed the government to alter crop patterns and production, though even the dramatically improved crop yields that resulted did not lessen Egypt's growing dependence on food imports to feed its rapidly growing population.

The unpredictability of water supplies from the Nile hindered, in the government's view, its capacity to make long-range plans for agriculture. Accordingly, the regime gave strong support and high priority to the Aswan High Dam project, which would provide not only stable water supplies but a substantial expansion in arable land available for cultivation. The Dam, completed in 1970, increased land under perennial cultivation by 25 percent. Problems with salinity and water seepage have been severe, however, and many of the Dam's long-term advantages will have to wait until the completion of a massive tile drainage scheme currently (1980) underway to counteract the effects of increased salinity.

Since the Revolution agricultural production has been increasing at the average rate of 2 percent per annum, with consumption increasing 2.8 percent per annum. Agriculture declined in importance relative to industrialization in post-1956 government planning until quite recently. To reverse this trend, at least partially, the government of President Anwar Sadat announced in 1980 that the improvement of agricultural productivity would be accorded high priority, along with the search for ways to increase Egypt's arable land.

Aside from a massive program of population control, which will take several generations to effect, the only medium-term solution for the gap between Egypt's agricultural productivity and its consumption, apart from ever increasing food imports, is through the farming of reclaimed, marginal lands. But given the previous poor record of land reclamation--£E380 million invested for 1 million feddans over twenty years has yielded only 400,000 feddans of arable land, one quarter of which is marginal--it appears that most of this gap will have to be closed through even more intensive cultivation of existing land resources. In the long term the government hopes to add 2 or 3 million feddans to Egypt's crop area by the year 2000 through reclamation and reuse.

AḤMAD (AḤMAD ᶜABŪ'L-FAWĀRIS) (r. 968-69/357-58). Last ruler of the Ikhshīdid dynasty in Egypt, Aḥmad came to the throne as a boy of eleven, following the death of Kāfūr, the former slave who had controlled the country first indirectly and then directly for over twenty years. Aḥmad was a grandson of the founder of the dynasty, Muḥammad b. Ṭughj, and was selected by a group of court officials as a malleable candidate. Shortly after his investiture Aḥmad was temporarily unseated by his cousin al-Ḥasan b. ᶜUbayd Allāh, who had the support of the army. The obvious weakness of Ikhshīdid control in Egypt attracted the attention of the Fāṭimids, who, advancing from Cyrenaica (eastern Libya) achieved their longstanding goal of conquering Egypt in the following year (969/358).

AḤMAD (AL-MALIK AN-NĀṢIR SHIHĀB AD-DĪN AḤMAD) (r. 1342/743). Baḥrī Mamluk Sultan, son and third successor to an-Nāṣir Muḥammad, Aḥmad was in office for approximately six months until his cruelty aroused opposition in the court. After he was deposed, Aḥmad fled to Kerak to mount a campaign to regain his throne. In this he enjoyed the covert support of his successor Ismā^{c}īl's own vizier. Ismā^{c}īl launched an attack on Aḥmad when the vizier's duplicity was uncovered in 1344/744. The two brothers met in battle at Kerak where Aḥmad was defeated with his troops. He died shortly afterwards in prison, strangled by guards on his brother's orders.

AḤMAD IBN ṬŪLŪN see IBN ṬŪLŪN

AḤMAD IBN AL-MUDABBIR see AL-MUDABBIR

AḤMAD (AL-MUẒAFFAR AḤMAD) (r. 1421/815). Burjī Mamluk Sultan, Aḥmad was an infant when appointed as heir by his father, the Sultan Mu'ayyad Shaykh, shortly before the latter's death. Mu'ayyad's son-in-law, Altunbughā, was appointed regent, with Ṭaṭār as deputy regent, Altunbughā being on campaign in Syria at the time of his appointment. Ṭaṭār took advantage of Altunbughā's absence to guide the infant Sultan's hand over a proclamation declaring Ṭaṭār regent in lieu of Altunbughā. A rebellion of the Syrian Amīrs broke out over this act; Altunbughā, after initially giving his support to the rebellion, was convinced by Ṭaṭār to abandon his claim, whereupon he was rewarded by being executed by Ṭaṭār. Aḥmad was deposed shortly thereafter when Ṭaṭār took power in his own name.

AḤMAD (AL-MU'AYYAD SHIHĀB AD-DĪN AḤMAD) (r. 1461/865). Burjī Mamluk Sultan, Aḥmad was the son and successor to the Sultan Ināl. Aḥmad was unable to command the loyalty of his father's Mamluk faction, the Ashrafiyya, who wished to see the governor of Damascus, Jānim, on the throne; they were further antagonized by Aḥmad's commitment to reform, particularly his interest in putting an end to financial misdealings by Mamluk administrators. He resigned when Khūshqadam gained ascendancy and was briefly imprisoned in Alexandria.

AḤMAD BEY ("THE BOSNIAK") (d. 1662/1073). A leader of the Qāsimiyya faction of the beylicate in Ottoman Egypt, Aḥmad and the Ottoman Viceroy, Muṣṭafā Pasha, contrived the defeat and suppression of the Faqāriyya faction, the Qāsimiyya's rivals for supremacy in the beylicate. The Viceroy appointed Aḥmad governor of Upper Egypt in 1658/1069, replacing the Faqāriyya governor, Muḥammad Bey, who rose in revolt. The failure of the divided Faqāriyya leadership to rally to Muḥammad's defense sealed his fate. Aḥmad was subsequently appointed Qā'im Maqām, or acting Viceroy; in this position he gained the support of the ᶜAzaban Ottoman regiments and the governor himself in the conflict over supremacy in the beylicate between the two leading factions. This struggle saw the Qāsimiyya triumph over the Faqāriyya; the Viceroy replaced the Faqāriyya governors of several important provinces with Qāsimiyya appointees. In the face of this combined opposition the Faqāriyya fled, some establishing themselves as local powers in remoter regions of Egypt. Aḥmad led a largely successful campaign against these exiles, and by the late 1660/1071 he had suppressed most of his Faqāriyya enemies. Aḥmad was assassinated two years later at the behest of the new Viceroy, who was troubled by Aḥmad's undisputed supremacy and power in the beylicate. With both factions' leadership gone the beylicate was fairly quiescent for two decades.

AḤMAD PASHA KHĀ'IN (d. 1524/930-31). Ottoman governor of Egypt from 1523/929, Aḥmad Pasha had been an important figure within the Ottoman court prior to his appointment. Defeated in his attempt to become vizier to the Ottoman Sultan, he soon tried to turn his position in Egypt into virtual independence from the Porte, aided by the discontented Egyptian Mamluks. He aroused local opposition, however, through his autocracy and the forceable seizure of some individuals' wealth. The Ottoman Sultan was angered by his display of autonomy; Qara Mūsā was nominated to replace him. Aḥmad met this challenge by attempting to gain support from some of the Ottomans' Christian opponents.

He forcibly took over the Citadel from the Janissary regiment, and also declared himself Sultan. Efforts by the Porte to sow dissension among his supporters may have caused an assassination attempt on Aḥmad, which left him wounded. He fled to the south, but the tribe he sheltered with betrayed him to Ayās Pasha, who had been sent with an army to depose and execute Aḥmad.

Aḥmad's downfall was partially engineered by the Ottoman vizier, Ibrāhīm Pasha. Aḥmad and Ibrāhīm had both sought the vizierate in Istanbul before it was awarded to the latter, causing Aḥmad great bitterness and Ibrāhīm some concern at the existence of a strong rival.

AḤMAD AL-BADAWĪ (c. 1199-1276/596-675). Devoted to this most popular saintly figure of traditional Islam in Egypt, the shrine of Aḥmad al-Badawī in Tanta is the object of a massive annual pilgrimage. Born in Morocco, Aḥmad al-Badawī traveled to Mecca and to Iraq before receiving a vision, in 1230/634, instructing him to go to Tanta. His reputation as a mystic and visionary quickly spread beyond that city. The Aḥmadiyya Ṣūfī movement, based on his teachings, started after his death and gained a wide following. The Aḥmadiyya was occasionally subject to official censure, though the indigenous popular enthusiasm it generated enabled it to survive. Several Mamluk Sultans were supporters of the Aḥmadiyya. Along with other elements of organized Islam in Egypt, the Aḥmadiyya grew in strength with the decline of Ottoman rule and appear to have been associated with some rural and popular protest movements. At a time when the country's political life was extremely confused, these religious groups took over many sociopolitical functions at the local level. Following the establishment of Muhammad Ali's rule (1805-48) the brotherhood largely reverted to its religious and social role. There are numerous stories and folk-tales in Egypt relating Aḥmad al-Badawī's life and miraculous deeds.

AHMAD FUAD see FUAD II

AḤMADIYYA see AḤMAD AL-BADAWĪ

AL-AHRAM ("The Pyramids"). Egyptian daily newspaper, the most widely read Arabic-language paper in the Middle East, Al-Ahram was founded in 1876 by the Taqla brothers, immigrants from the Lebanon. Prior to the Revolution Al-Ahram was one among many Egyptian daily newspapers and pursued a moderate nationalist editorial policy. After 1952, however, and especially with the appointment of Muhammad Husayn Heykal as its editor in 1957, Al-Ahram became the semiofficial voice of Egypt's leadership, largely because of the close relationship between Heykal and Nasser. In 1960, along with all other major newspapers, Al-Ahram was nationalized. Heykal's weekly column in the paper was widely consulted as an indication of future government policy, as he was credited with being the inspiration for much of Nasser's ideological thought. Following policy disagreements with Sadat, Heykal was removed from his post as editor-in-chief and replaced by Ali Amin in 1974.

Al-Ahram maintains an extensive network of foreign correspondents and publishes a weekly financial supplement. The current editor (1980) of Al-Ahram is Ibrahim Nafih; its circulation (despite a 1979 Arab boycott on its distribution outside Egypt) is estimated at 400,000.

ALEXANDRIA. The second-largest city in Egypt, Alexandria was founded in 332 BC by the Greek conqueror of Egypt, Alexander the Great. It was the country's capital until the Muslim conquest, when that role was taken over by the newly founded (in 641/20) city of al-Fuṣṭāṭ.

Alexandria was originally laid out on a Greek-city model by Deinocrates, walled with a double harbor flanking the island of Pharos. Following its establishment Alexandria quickly became a center of Hellenistic culture and learning and by 200 BC was the largest city in the world, though it was later surpassed in size by Rome. Its lighthouse was considered one of the seven wonders of the world. Alexandria's senate, established by Alexander, was abolished at the advent of Roman rule in 30 BC and not restored until AD 195. Difficulties between Alexandria's

Greek and Jewish populations led to troubles and minor uprisings under Caligula (AD 38), Claudius (AD 41), and Nero (AD 55). With the growth of Christianity in Egypt new communal tensions arose between the city's Christians, Jews, and Greek pagans. A major Jewish revolt in AD 115-16 led to wholesale slaughter on all sides. Fifteen years later new riots between Christian factions resulted in the death of the Roman Prefect, and under the locally proclaimed Emperors Aemilianus (AD 252-54) and Domitianus (AD 295-97) there were great internal disturbances preceeding the reestablishment of Roman control.

Alexandria's instability during the Roman period may be partially traced to its move away from the centers of power in the Empire, but this instability was also greatly fed by the city's involvement with the major theological controversies that swept Christianity in the third to seventh centuries AD, and in which it was a leading participant. The Alexandrians tended to ally themselves initially with whatever theological faction was opposed to the religious establishment of the day, and through this, expressed as well their desire for political autonomy. The accession of a new Patriarch appointed by the center on occasion marked a period of general discontent by the factions opposed to him, though by the middle of the fifth century the Patriarch Dioscorus himself led the Alexandrian opposition at the Council of Ephesus. Following the Council of Chalcedon in 451, which rejected the Alexandrian Monophysite position, the Church in Alexandria and Egypt formally broke away. The subsequent murder of the Byzantine candidate for the Patriarchate led to a complete rupture with Constantinople in theological matters. Thereafter troops were occasionally required to install new bishops. In 550 the Patriarch was made head of the secular administration and provided with troops to support his expanded authority.

Alexandria's Hellenistic character, and its reputation in philosophy and secular learning, did not survive the sharp hostility of Egypt's Christians toward what they saw as the country's unacceptable pagan inheritance. The burning in 391 of the pagan cult center, the Serapeum, and the murder of the distinguished woman philosopher Hypatia by an Alexandrian mob occurred in an atmosphere of growing intolerance toward divergent and heterogeneous philosophies. Such an atmosphere made compromise between the Alexandrian Christian and pagan communities impossible.

The approximately ten years of Sassanian Persian control of Egypt and Alexandria, which ended in 629, made slight impression on a city profoundly disaffected toward its Byzantine government and inwardly directed toward its own religious enthusiasms. Byzantine control was reestablished by the Emperor Heraclius, but just over a decade later, in 641/20, the Muslim general ^{c}Amr b. al-^{c}Āṣ was laying siege to the city. He found there a population ready to welcome anyone who could deliver them from Byzantine control; and the Byzantine Patriarch, Cyrus, was prepared to negotiate a reasonable surrender. Under the terms agreed to by ^{c}Amr and Cyrus, the city's Greek population was given a year to evacuate, following which the Muslims would take possession.

Alexandria's troubled reputation may have contributed to ^{c}Amr's decision to establish the country's capital at al-Fusṭāṭ (now part of modern Cairo). Al-Fusṭāṭ also had the advantage of a canal cleared by ^{c}Amr and linking the Nile with the Red Sea, a reflection of the shift from a Mediterranean to an Arabian focus of the country's new rulers. A brief attempt by the Byzantines to retake Alexandria in 645/24, in support of a rebellion of Christians, was defeated by ^{c}Amr. Later Byzantine attacks on the city and on Egypt's Mediterranean coast were repelled, though sometimes after causing considerable damage.

Alexandria was ruled as an independent province from Ṭūlūnid to Fāṭimid times, the autonomy of its governors varying with the rulers' willingness to control them. Alexandria's main importance was in textile manufacture and as a major center of trade, from which Egypt's rulers derived substantial revenues. Despite increasing control from Cairo after the rise of the Ayyūbids in 1171/567, Alexandria maintained its importance in the areas of textiles and trade. European merchants were encouraged and invited to use the city as an outlet for the extensive trade routes on which much of the wealth of the Muslim world depended. Alexandria also remained a place of escape from the hotter, drier climes of Cairo in summer, and a place of imprisonment for unsuccessful holders of, or contenders for, power during Mamluk times. The use of Damietta, east of Alexandria, as a landing point for the Crusader invasions of Egypt spared Alexandria much destruction, but the city was eventually brutally sacked in 1365/766 by a Crusade led by King Peter, with heavy loss of native Christian, Jewish, and Muslim lives in the city.

Alexandria's links with Europe and its location on the Mediterranean helped maintain its importance under the Muhammad Ali dynasty in the nineteenth century. The development of a cash-crop, export-oriented agriculture, and particularly the growth in importance of cotton, helped revitalize a city that had always depended on trade and its European and Levantine connections in its banking, shipping, and business interests. Muhammad Ali (r. 1805-48) encouraged the establishment of European traders; as early as 1834 there was some form of municipal council in the city, though its functions are not known. A similar attempt to establish local government by the Viceroy Sa^{c}id in the 1860s eventually came to a halt under his successor, Ismail, in 1868, though the city's merchant community, foreign and indigenous, assumed the direction, management, and financing of a range of municipal services.

Much of the infrastructure built in the mid-nineteenth century, especially the rail service, opened in 1858, helped to link more closely Egypt's two main cities, Alexandria and Cairo, with the city of Suez, whose development was spurred by the construction of the Suez Canal, opened in 1869. Alexandria's role as the country's summer capital, combined with its economic importance and strategic value, had transformed the city by the end of the nineteenth century. In 1890 Alexandria became the only Egyptian city to be granted the right to form a municipal government.

As Egypt's second city, Alexandria has a character that remains quite distinct from Cairo. Possibly because it was physically distanced from the mainstream nationalist politics of Cairo, and through its more international character, Alexandria tended to receive, in the twentieth century, political and social ideas that diverged sometimes broadly from the ideologies of the major Egyptian nationalist parties. The association of the city with the industrial development of the Delta region, particularly with the textile industry, may explain the appearance in Alexandria of the first socialist and communist parties in Egypt. At the same time, broadly drawn nationalist issues (the Sudan, British troop withdrawals) were as actively supported in Alexandria as in Cairo.

Alexandria also became identified as a center of artistic activity, particularly in the visual arts. Its university and medical faculty, founded in 1942, are known throughout the Arab world. Though Alexandria has not been able to match Cairo's political position, either in pre- or post-Revolutionary Egypt, it has maintained its importance in trade, commerce, the arts, and education.

ALEXANDRIA PROTOCOL. Signed 7 October 1944 by Egypt, Transjordan, Iraq, Syria, and Lebanon, the Alexandria Protocol provided for the establishment of a league of sovereign Arab states. The protocol was drafted after a Preparatory Conference in which these states, plus Saudi Arabia and Yemen, participated. The protocol also pledged league members to support the independence of Palestine and the Lebanon and provided for a subcommittee to be established to draft the first treaty proposals. These proposals, which were to be completed by 3 March 1945, formed the basis for the foundation of the Arab League.

The convening of the Preparatory Conference that drafted the Alexandria Protocol was arranged by Nahhas Pasha, Prime Minister of the highly controversial 1942-44 Wafdist government. It was intended to counter moves by Iraq to form an Arab federation under its leadership, and also to protect Nahhas' own declining political position in Egypt. In the event, Nahhas was dismissed shortly after the protocol was signed, though Egypt went on to play a leading role in the organization and staffing of the Arab League.

ᶜALĪ (ABŪ'L ḤASAN ᶜALĪ) (r. 961-66/349-55). Third Ikhshīdid ruler of Egypt, ᶜAlī succeeded his brother Ūnūjūr after the latter's unseemly and possibly assisted demise. Like his brother he was completely under the control of Kāfūr, the slave appointed by his father to be tutor to both sons. Although twenty-three at the time of his accession, he was given a pension of 400,000 dinars and "retired," leaving the administration of Egypt completely in Kāfūr's hands.

There were several outbreaks of famine during ᶜAlī's reign, and the rebellions and other disturbances that immediately followed the catastrophic earthquake during Ūnūjūr's reign continued. Forbidden by Kāfūr to see anyone, it was reported that ᶜAlī soon developed bitter feelings toward him. Upon ᶜAlī's death Kāfūr secured power in his own name.

ᶜALĪ (AL-MANṢŪR NŪR AD-DĪN ᶜALĪ) (r. 1257-59/655-57). Baḥrī Mamluk Sultan, ᶜAlī was the son and successor of Aybak, whose marriage to the Sultana Shajar ad-Durr marked the transition from Ayyūbid to Mamluk Egypt. The murder of his father by his stepmother, Shajar ad-Durr, led to her murder in turn, and ᶜAlī was placed in power by a group of Mamluks who wished to ensure their continued supremacy in running Egypt. ᶜAlī's deputy, Qutuz, drove those Mamluks opposed to ᶜAlī's candidacy out of Egypt. He then turned against his charge and took power in his own name, after turning back an Ayyūbid attack on Egypt led by Mūsā of Kerak.

ᶜALĪ (AL-MANṢŪR ᶜALĀ' AD-DĪN ᶜALĪ) (r. 1376-82/778-83). Baḥrī Mamluk Sultan, ᶜAlī was a boy of six when placed on the throne after his father, Shaᶜbān II, had been murdered by his own palace guards. At the time of his accession there was complete anarchy and disorder in Cairo, with the Mamluks seizing what they wanted. There was a plan by the court to put the ᶜAbbāsid Caliph al-Mutawakkil I on the throne, but factional fighting among the Mamluks prevented any clear-cut resolution of the internal situation. The return of the Amīr Barqūq from exile in 1378/780 intensified the brutal internecine struggles among the Mamluks. Barqūq, following his appointment as army commander, sought the regency for, and control over, the young ᶜAlī, which he finally gained in 1380/782. ᶜAlī died of plague two years later.

ᶜALĪ BEY (r. c.1763-72/1176-86). Shaykh al-Balad and de facto ruler of Egypt, ᶜAlī Bey was from the Qāzdughliyya faction of the beylicate. He was raised to the beylicate shortly after the death of his master, Ibrāhīm Kahya (d.1754/1167). ᶜAlī was made Shaykh al-Balad by the new head of the Qāzdughliyya, ᶜAbd ar-Raḥmān Kahya, following the disgrace of his predecessor, also named ᶜAlī Bey. As was the fashion for beys seeking ri'āsa or paramount influence, ᶜAlī built up a large household of Mamluks and carefully assembled a following loyal to him by packing the beylicate with his supporters, until in 1763/1176 he received their acknowledgment of his leadership.

ᶜAlī was assisted in his search for power by his chief Mamluk, Muḥammad (known as Abu'dh-Dhahab), whom he raised to the beylicate in 1764/1178. A vigorous suppression of his real and potential opponents followed, and ᶜAbd ar-Raḥmān was sent into exile. ᶜAlī was temporarily eclipsed and twice exiled himself, in 1765/1179 and 1767/1181, but regained his position. In 1768/1182, the same year his position as Shaykh al-Balad was recognized by the Ottoman Porte, he secured the removal of the Ottoman Viceroy, who had been plotting against him. He put down a final challenge to his rule, led by two Qāzdughliyya Mamluks, Kakash and Khalīl Bey, and in 1769/1183 he deposed the new Ottoman Viceroy shortly after the latter's arrival in Egypt.

Thereafter ᶜAlī did not much conceal his ambition to have a virtually independent position in Egypt while remaining (superficially) loyal to the Ottoman state. He minted coins in his own name and gradually directed the reestablishment of Egypt's traditional dominance in the surrounding regions, campaigning in Upper Egypt and the Hijaz.

ᶜAlī's deputy, Abu'dh-Dhahab, subdued the Hawwāra tribes, who were in revolt in Upper Egypt in 1769/1183. ᶜAlī Bey's armies then installed a supporter in Mecca. This was followed in 1770-71/1184-85 by a campaign in Syria. This Syrian expansion aroused the concern of the Ottoman Sultan about ᶜAlī's further ambitions. Abu'dh-Dhahab was encouraged to turn against his master: he led his army back to Cairo and against ᶜAlī Bey, who was forced to flee the capital in 1772/1186. ᶜAlī raised an army of supporters in Acre but was killed during the defeat of his army in their attempts to retake Egypt in 1773/1187.

ALI, GENERAL KAMIL HASAN (1921-). A commander of the Egyptian Armored Brigade in the 1967 Arab-Israeli War, General Ali was one of the few military figures to emerge untarnished from that fighting. After 1967 he moved up rapidly in the military hierarchy, becoming Major General and Chief of Staff in the Armored Corps in 1970. In 1972 Ali was promoted to Director of the Armored Corps and in 1975 joined the government as Assistant Minister of War and Chief of Intelligence. In 1978 General Ali was made Minister of Defense and Military Production and was promoted to Commander-in-Chief of the Armed Forces. He has been an active participant in the negotiations with Israel over the Peace Treaty and Palestinian autonomy. In May 1980 General Ali assumed the offices of Deputy Prime Minister and Minister for Foreign Affairs. Following the assassination of President Sadat, Ali was retained in both posts in the cabinet formed by President Mubarak in October 1981.

ALI YUSUF, SHAYKH (1863-1913). Egyptian religious writer and supporter of the 1890s revival of Egypt's nationalist movement, Shaykh Ali was the editor of the journal Al-Muayyad. He was helped to found this journal in 1889 by Saᶜd Zaghlul and a number of other nationalists, to counter the pro-British Al-Muqattam and to provide a platform for Egyptians concerned with national as well as Islamic issues. Al-Muayyad enjoyed a good circulation in Egypt and elsewhere in the Arab world. Brought to trial on sedition charges in 1896, Shaykh Ali was helped by the lenient prosecutor, Muhammad Farid, a later associate of the nationalist leader Mustafa Kamil.

Shaykh Ali's support for the nationalist movement in the 1890s followed closely the attitude of the Palace. During the period of cooperation between the Khedive and Mustafa Kamil, for instance, Kamil was afforded an open platform in Al-Muayyad; as the Khedive began to weaken in his support for Kamil and constitutionalism, the latter found his access to the pages of Shaykh Ali's journal increasingly restricted.

With the gradual resignation of the Khedive to a continuation of British rule in Egypt, Shaykh Ali began to moderate the journal's political stance and to give greater focus to the topics of Islam and Islamic reformism. Shaykh Ali was one of the founders of the Constitutional Reform Party, a pro-Palace political grouping established in 1907.

^{c}ALĪDS see SHĪ^{c}A

ALLENBY, FIELD MARSHAL LORD (1861-1936). High Commissioner of Egypt from 1919 until 1925, Allenby was appointed Special High Commissioner at the time of the 1919 Rebellion. He advocated Zaghlul's release from exile, realizing that this was the only way to ease the tense atmosphere in Egypt. Following this, Allenby acted firmly to suppress a number of industrial strikes in April 1919 and to restore order to the cities.

Allenby adopted a policy largely conciliatory to the more moderate nationalist elements, though not to Zaghlul; a witness to the disruption caused by Zaghlul after his return to Egypt in April 1921, he gave his approval to a second exile of the Wafd leader in December of that year, imposed by the Palace.

The opposition of Zaghlul and the more radical nationalists had made it impossible for the 1921 government of Adli Pasha to negotiate successfully with the British over the ending of the Protectorate, something sought by all groups in Egypt, from the Palace to the Wafdists. Allenby finally resolved the situation by traveling to London in February 1922 and making clear his decision to resign unless the British government ended the Protectorate and made some firmer commitments to Egypt's eventual independence.

On 28 February 1922 the British issued a declaration terminating the Protectorate and restoring Egypt to a nominal independence, within certain limitations. Allenby presided over the stormy emergence of parliamentary life in Egypt. The drafting of the new Constitution in 1922 provoked considerable controversy. Allenby's support for the advocates of constitutional government did not endear him to Fuad, and his handling of the Wafdists, particularly Zaghlul and his circle of supporters who were kept in exile during this period, lost him the support of those nationalists affiliated with the Wafd. Further, his insistence at the time of the 1922 Declaration that Fuad surrender his claims to the Sudanese throne left Allenby in opposition to both the Palace and a broad spectrum of nationalist opinion.

With the release of Zaghlul from exile in 1923 the political scene in Egypt was dominated by the Wafd Party, of which he was leader. The Wafd swept to victory in Egypt's first elections, in January 1924, and Allenby was faced with a Wafd government with which he had only slight sympathy. The situation between Allenby and the new government was not eased by the lack of progress in negotiations over the Sudan; the nationalist disturbances there involving the army, and popular demonstrations within Egypt over the Sudan issue, were worrying to the British government. In Egypt anti-British sentiment was growing, and reached its denouement with the assassination of the Sirdar and Governor-General of the Sudan, Sir Lee Stack, in November 1924.

As part of the British response to the assassination Allenby presented Zaghlul and the Wafd government with an ultimatum that exacted a heavy fine and required them to make certain territorial concessions with regard to the Sudan and to the division of Nile waters between the two countries. Zaghlul rejected these last two concessions, and Allenby ordered the occupation of the Alexandria customs shed. The Wafd government fell and was replaced by a pro-Palace government under Ziwar Pasha in December 1924.

Following the Lee Stack assassination Allenby worked to keep Zaghlul (whose Wafd Party he blamed for the act) from power, though at the time of the new seating of Parliament in March 1925 Zaghlul was elected its president, leading to the dissolution of the legislature by King Fuad that June. The establishment of an Army Council, though intended by Allenby as a reform measure, was seen by the nationalists as one more British action compromising Egyptian independence, which they felt was already overly limited by the terms of the 1922 Declaration. Allenby announced his resignation in May 1925, his relationship with both the Palace and with the nationalists having been damaged by his desire to strike a middle line between the two. Allenby's support for Egyptian independence in the framework of British imperial interests was without attraction for the Wafd or the Palace. The conflict of these two contributed to the tensions in Egypt during Allenby's service there.

A^cMĀL. Administrative unit of Fāṭimid Egypt, the A^cmāl system was organized in the closing years of the reign of al-Mustanṣir (1036-94/427-87) by his vizier, Badr al-Jamālī, who did much to revitalize the administration of the Fāṭimid state in the period of its decline. The series of famines that marred al-Mustanṣir's reign had made apparent the defects of the old administrative system, particularly its failure to ensure proper maintenance of the irrigation system vital to the country's agriculture. However, land taxes continued to be collected through a tax-farming system similar to that which had brought about the deterioration in rural infrastructure.

The original twenty-six A^cmāl created at the time of Badr al-Jamālī declined in number as the land under each A^{c}māl was expanded. During the reign of Qalā'ūn (1280-90/678-89) there were fifteen A^{c}māl, and in the Ottoman period the country's administration was reorganized under twelve A^{c}māl. The ^{c}amīl (pl. ^{c}ummal) found in Egypt from Umayyad times were usually officials in the provinces with fiscal and administrative responsibilities, though the title altered in time to apply variously to village chiefs, tax collectors, and sometimes governors.

AMER, ABDAL HAKIM (1919-1967). Deputy Supreme Commander of the Egyptian Army at the time of the 1967 Arab-Israeli War, Amer was the second-most-powerful figure in Egypt from the Revolution of 1952 until his death by his own hand in 1967.

Amer was among the original group of Free Officers who led the 1952 Revolution and was reputed to be Nasser's closest confidante and companion in the pre- and post-Revolutionary period. Within the Revolutionary Command Council Amer's position was promoted by Nasser, who secured for Amer the title of Commander-in-Chief from General Naguib in June 1953. The transfer of this military office from Naguib to Amer marked the beginning of Naguib's decline within the RCC hierarchy.

Amer became an ardent promoter of Army interests in the new government, and in 1954 he was made Minister of War. Amer's powerful position within the military helped Nasser survive politically the resignation, reinstatement, and eventual house arrest of General Naguib during 1954, as Nasser emerged as ruler of Egypt.

Though the 1956 Suez War cannot be described as a clear-cut military victory for Egypt, the moral victory gained by Egypt over the former colonial powers and Israel heightened the importance of the military, and with it, General Amer. However, Amer's performance during the war lost him the support of some of his colleagues. Nasser continued to back Amer, despite calls in some quarters for his demotion. With the formation of the United Arab Republic by Egypt and Syria in February 1958 Amer was appointed Chief Coordinator of the Northern Region (Syria), in addition to serving as Field Marshal, Vice-President of Syria, and Minister of Defense. In October 1959 he was made governor of Syria. As the person responsible for implementation of the regime's policies in Syria, he attracted the enmity of those Syrians who opposed the increasingly left-wing tenor of the government's programs. The growing unpopularity of Egyptian domination of the bureaucracy and administration became pronounced in 1961. In September of that year Amer was expelled from Syria following the seizure of Damascus by Syrian army units opposed to continuing the link between their country and Egypt. Amer continued to serve as Minister of War in Egypt until March 1964, when he resigned to become First Vice-President and Deputy Commander-in-Chief. During this time he supervised Egypt's deepening involvement in Yemen, and early in 1963, Amer personally led a major Egyptian offensive against royalist supporters there.

Amer's political career in Egypt was strongly linked to his army role, and in his military capacity he served in some political posts. In September 1957 Amer was appointed to the Executive Committee of the National Union, one of the post-Revolution political groupings established by the regime to gain mass support for the government's programs. But by 1961, when he returned from Syria, there was reputedly a growing rift between Nasser and Amer over the increasing socialism of government policy, and more importantly, over the strength and autonomy of Amer himself. His position with the Army helped Amer avoid the fate of political obscurity that befell many of the original Free Officers who fell out with Nasser after the Revolution; thus he was made First Vice-President in 1964. But within the administration his once-dominant voice was increasingly challenged by more left-wing elements opposed to Amer's power, political caution, and militarism.

In 1966 Nasser named Amer chairman of the politically controversial Committee for the Liquidation of Feudalism, which was charged with investigating the holdovers of pre-Revolutionary social and political practices in the countryside. Amer's restrained criticisms during the hearings antagonized the left wing of the Arab Socialist Union, whose power within the government was growing. But any political troubles that beset Amer in his last years plaed in comparison to the reverses he suffered as a result of Egypt's disastrous defeat in the 1967 Arab-Israeli War. The Egyptian army's lack of preparedness, despite a series of provocative actions by both sides in the months preceding the outbreak of hostilities, left most of Egypt's aircraft destroyed on the ground and the course of the fighting dominated by Israel's control of the air. Amer and those associated with him in the High Command were removed in June 1967. Along with a number of other officers Amer was arrested in August 1967 and charged with involvement in a plot to overthrow Nasser. His suicide was announced the following month.

^{c}ĀMIL see A^{c}MĀL

AMIN, AHMAD (1886-1954). Egyptian scholar and writer on Arabic literature and modern methods of historiography, Amin was appointed the first head of the Cultural Section of the Arab League in 1947 and served in this post until his death. He had previously taught Arab literature at Cairo University for almost twenty years. Amin's three-volume work on the history of Islam and his shorter dictionary of Egyptian folklore are among his better-known works, though he also studied the evolution of political thought in nineteenth century Islam and participated in the editing of several literary journals. Amin was an advocate of the cultural renewal of Islam through harmonization with modern trends, and he wrote extensively on the need for the application of scholarly methods to the study of Islamic history and culture.

AMIN, ALI (1912-1974). Egyptian newspaper editor, Ali Amin was co-owner with his twin brother, Mustafa, of an extensive press empire prior to the 1952 Revolution, after which he continued to play a prominent role in Egyptian journalism until his self-imposed exile in 1965. Both Ali and his brother had been quite close to Nasser in the early years of his government, and both men acted as unofficial ambassadors on Nasser's behalf.

Ali Amin received his education in England and upon his return to Egypt served in various ministries while writing anonymously for several journals. In 1944 he became associated with his brother in the publication of Akhbar al-Yawm (1944-65), Akhair Sa^{c}a (1946-65), and Al-Akhbar (1952-65). At the time of his brother Mustafa's arrest in 1965 Ali fled to England, where he lived in exile until his pardon by President Sadat in 1974. Upon his return he briefly joined the staff of Al-Ahram as Editor-in-Chief and columnist, replacing Muhammad Husayn Haykal. Amin then served as Chairman of the Board of Al-Akhbar.

AMIN, MUSTAFA (1912-). Twin brother of Ali Amin, Mustafa Amin was co-proprietor with him of a wide range of Egyptian journals. Their father decided that the twins should be educated separately, and Mustafa was educated in the United States while his brother was sent to England. When he returned to Egypt in 1927, Mustafa began writing for several journals and newspapers. In 1938 he became editor of Akhair Sa^{c}a (a post he held until 1946, when he and his brother became co-publishers), editor of Al-Ithnain (1941-45), and assistant editor of Al-Ahram (1940-44). (See AMIN, ALI, for a list of the journals he published with his brother.) In 1965 Mustafa Amin was arrested and charged with being an American spy, and was sentenced to life imprisonment after a trial in 1966. He was subsequently pardoned and released from prison in 1974 by President Anwar Sadat, becoming Editor-in-Chief of Akhbar al-Yawm and Al-Akhbar, until 1976, when he became staff writer for the former paper.

AMIN, QASIM (1863 or 1865-1908). A lawyer and writer on Islamic modernism, Amin was greatly influenced by the liberal trend in Muhammad Abduh's thinking. His books on the emancipation of women, The Liberation of the Woman [Ar. Taḥrīr al-Mar'ah] and The New Woman [Ar. Al-Mar'a al-Jadīda] published in 1899 and

1901 respectively, argued that originally Islam had acted to improve the condition of women and that a return to the true precepts of Islam, combined with improvements in education, legal and social rights, would accord woman her proper position in Muslim society. The publication of this work aroused great controversy in Egypt in conservative religious circles, though a section of Egyptian nationalists gave their support to Amin's arguments. Many of the ideas put forth by Amin in this work were to reappear subsequently in the writings of other, more recent, advocates of greater rights for women in Islamic societies, though his most direct influence was on the work of the Egyptian feminist writer, Malak Hifni Nasif.

AMĪR. A title used by leading Mamluk military commanders during the Mamluk period in Egypt (1250-1517/648-922), Amīr means prince, commander, or governor. It was used variously throughout the Islamic period for governors of provinces, military chiefs, members of the Caliphal family, and autonomous rulers of petty principalities and major regions.

AL-ĀMIR (r. 1101-30/495-524). Fāṭimid Caliph of Egypt, al-Āmir was the son and successor of al-Mustaᶜlī and only five at the time of his accession. For the first twenty years of his reign al-Āmir was completely under the control of his vizier, al-Afḍal.

The level of military activity against the Crusaders was intense in the early years of the Caliph's reign. The Fāṭimid possessions in Palestine were lost in 1101/495, with Acre falling in 1103/497. In Syria the Crusaders took Tripoli (in 1108/502) and Tyre (in 1124/518); the Fāṭimid navy was badly defeated by the Venetians in 1124/518. During al-Āmir's reign the Crusaders under Baldwin I made their first foray into Egypt but were compelled to withdraw a year later, in 1118/512.

Tension between al-Āmir and al-Afḍal inevitably grew as the Caliph came to resent the latter's absolute domination of his life and his government. Al-Afḍal was assassinated in 1121/515, an act in which the Caliph was doubtless involved. Al-Afḍal's successor, al-Baṭā'ihī, fared no better: after four years in power he was imprisoned by the Caliph's order in 1125/519 and executed shortly afterwards. A Christian, Abū Najāḥ b. Qannā', then rose to some prominence in the court. He survived for about four years, until 1129/523, when he incurred al-Āmir's disfavor. Al-Āmir ruled without a vizier until the end of his reign. His death plunged the Fāṭimids into another religious controversy as the Caliphal succession was disputed.

Al-Āmir's reign is described as onerous and bloody. He met his death at the hands of assassins of the Nizarī sect, who had become a serious menace to internal security in Egypt during his rule.

AMĪR AL-ḤAJJ. Title given to the Mamluk who led the annual Pilgrimage Caravan to Mecca and Medina during Mamluk times, the Amīr al-Ḥajj became an important political post in Ottoman Egypt. The office was, in the period before the Caliphate moved to Egypt, held directly by the Caliph or his appointed representative, and attracted a good deal of prestige.

When the ᶜAbbāsid Caliphate was moved from Baghdad to Cairo in 1261/659, the appointment of the pilgrimage caravan's leader was made by the Mamluk Sultans, which reflected their growing dominance in the Hijaz region. The Amir al-Hajj was responsible for protecting and policing the pilgrim caravans to Mecca and Medina, over which cities the Mamluk Sultans claimed pre-eminence, and the Amīr was also responsible for the safe delivery of the Kiswa (curtain), which covered the Kaᶜba in Mecca. He was supported by troops and administrative staff during the journey. The pilgrimage itself provided an opportunity for the Amīr to make a great deal of money, especially as the basic outgoings were largely covered by a special subvention from the Sultan.

With the establishment of Ottoman control in Egypt in 1517/922 the Amīr al-Ḥajj became, with the Shaykh al-Balad, one of the premier positions open to members of the beylicate. Appointment as Amīr al-Ḥajj was actively sought by the leaders of contending factions wanting to establish their supremacy within the beylicate. The power of both positions grew with the decline in the power of the Ottoman governor.

The rise to power of Muhammad Ali in 1805 reduced the office of the Amīr al-Ḥajj to a largely ceremonial and honorific nature, especially after the Egyptian withdrawal from Arabia in the late 1830s. The functions of the office altered greatly in the twentieth century, first with the revitalized Hashemite control of the Hijaz, and the dislocations of the first world war, and then, the restoration of Wahhabi control over the region by Ibn Saud in 1925-26. Difficulties between the Saudi and Egyptian governments led to a ten-year pause in the caravans, which, when they were resumed in 1936, operated under Saudi sovereignty. The office was eventually abolished by the Egyptian government in 1954.

AMĪRĪYYA see TAYYIBĪYYA

ᶜAMR b. AL-ᶜĀṢ AS-SAHMĪ (c. 573-664/43 AH). Muslim conqueror of Egypt, ᶜAmr was one of the greatest of the early Muslim generals and instrumental in the establishment of the Umayyad dynasty.

After a victorious campaign in Palestine, ᶜAmr opened his campaign against Egypt, probably in 639/18, though the exact dates are uncertain. He entered the Sinai during the spring of 640/19, and by July he had crossed the Eastern Desert to the Nile valley. He took the Fayyum, an oasis area to the west of the Nile. Reinforcements were eventually sent to him under the command of Ibn az-Zubayr. ᶜAmr then laid siege to Babylon (on a site south of present-day Cairo) in July 640/19, after meeting its defenders in battle at Heliopolis, north of the city. Babylon fell a few months later, and ᶜAmr founded a garrison city nearby, al-Fusṭāṭ, which was eventually to become Egypt's capital. He also began the clearing of an ancient canal, completed four years later, to ease the transport of grain from the Nile valley to the Red Sea and from there to the Hijaz (western Arabia).

After Babylon was secured, ᶜAmr turned his attention to

Alexandria, Egypt's capital for nearly a thousand years. He laid siege to it in 641/20 until the city was surrendered to him by its Patriarch, Cyrus, under a treaty that required the Byzantine government and the city's Greek residents to evacuate within a year.

^{c}Amr's control of Egypt was divided by the Caliph ^{c}Umar (634-44/13-23), who shortly before his death appointed ^{c}Abdallāh ibn Sa^{c}d ibn Abī Sarḥ as governor of Upper Egypt. This appointment was confirmed and extended to all Egypt by ^{c}Umar's successor, ^{c}Uthmān (who was also ^{c}Abdallāh's foster brother). ^{c}Uthmān recalled ^{c}Amr in 645/24. However, the reappearance of the Byzantine navy at Alexandria at the end of 645/25, and the consequent slaughter of the Arab garrison there, led to ^{c}Amr's reinstatement. He defeated the Byzantine forces in battle at Nikiu. Alexandria was eventually retaken early in 646/25.

After his military victory ^{c}Amr was again recalled after refusing to divide his power with ^{c}Abdallāh, as requested by ^{c}Uthmān. Instead ^{c}Amr became one of the major actors in the fight for the succession to supreme power in the new Islamic state between ^{c}Alī, the fourth Caliph, and Mu^{c}āwiya, founder of the Umayyad dynasty. ^{c}Amr's brilliant defense of Mu^{c}āwiya's cause at the Battle of Siffīn was continued in the subsequent arbitration between the two contenders in 659-61/38-40. During this period of negotiations ^{c}Amr took power in Egypt on Mu^{c}āwiya's behalf, deposing ^{c}Alī's nominated governor, Muḥammad b. Abū Bakr, and prevented the country from affiliating itself with ^{c}Alī's cause. He ruled the country until his death.

ANGLO-EGYPTIAN CONDOMINIUM. Established by an agreement signed by Britain and Egypt in January 1899, the Condominium referred to the administrative division between Egypt and Britain with regard to the Sudan. Executive powers were concentrated in the hands of a British Governor-General appointed by the Egyptian Khedive upon nomination by the British government. Egyptian law was to be implemented in the Sudan by discretion of the Governor-General. The Egyptian and British flags were to be jointly displayed. The Condominium was symbolic as far as the actual rule of the country by the British was concerned, for in fact the Sudan was administered as a virtual colony and only the most minor Egyptian interference was tolerated.

The Condominium, together with Egypt's clouded de jure position in the Sudan, was the source of considerable internal political controversy in Egypt in the post-1922 period. The Unilateral Declaration giving Egypt its independence in that year forced King Fuad to compromise his claims to the throne of the Sudan. This was accepted neither by the Egyptian court nor by the majority of nationalists committed to the "Unity of the Nile Valley"--i.e., the reunification of Egypt and Sudan under the Egyptian Crown, based on the Ottoman decree of 1841 that granted Muhammad Ali and his line control of the Sudan.

The negotiations between Britain and Egypt that preceded the Unilateral Declaration therefore continued. Egypt wanted undisputed juridical sovereignty over the territory, whereas the Sudan, under the terms of the Condominium, was excluded from the jurisdiction of the Egyptian courts, either consular or mixed. The control over water allocation for the Sudan was another issue between Britain and Egypt, as was the position of the Egyptian and British armies in the country. The assassination of the Sirdar and Governor-General of the Sudan, Sir Lee Stack, by an Egyptian nationalist in November 1924, brought a temporary halt to these negotiations and resulted in the imposition of certain unilateral measures by Britain with respect to the Sudan. The Sudan's status was not radically altered by the 1936 Anglo-Egyptian treaty, in which Egypt agreed to continue to provide finance and the British continued to control the country. The question of ultimate sovereignty was shelved and the Condominium left largely intact.

After World War II the long-term misunderstandings between Egypt and Britain over the Sudan were typified by the Sidqi-Bevin negotiations in the Autumn of 1946, with Egypt announcing that agreement had been reached for a united Egypt and Sudan under the Egyptian crown, and the British announcing there would be no change in the Sudan's status. In January 1947 Egypt attempted to rally Arab League support and that August Egypt made an unsuccessful appeal to the United Nations to resolve its dispute with England over the Sudan.

In June 1948 the British government announced its intention of giving the Sudan a measure of self-government that largely abrogated the Condominium. Despite protests from Egypt a Legislative Assembly with elected representatives was formed. The return of a Wafd government to power in January 1950 saw renewed efforts on both sides to resolve their differences on the Sudan issue, but the collapse in negotiations led to the decision in October 1951 by the Nahhas government to abrogate the 1936 Anglo-Egyptian Treaty and by implication, the Condominium, and declare Faruq king of Egypt and the Sudan. This act gained no recognition from the British, who in 1952 introduced further measures for eventual Sudanese self-government.

The Egyptian Revolution of July 1952 enabled the British, in the following year, to negotiate a new treaty (the Anglo-Egyptian Sudan Treaty), which provided for the termination of the Condominium through the election of a parliament and the formation of the first Sudanese cabinet.

ANGLO-EGYPTIAN EVACUATION AGREEMENT. Signed in October 1954 and based on a draft agreement initiated that July, the Evacuation Agreement was intended to provide for the phased withdrawal of British troops from the Canal Zone over a period of twenty months, maintenance of British bases in the Zone by civilian contractors, and reactivation of a British military base in the event of circumstances of apparent danger to the Middle East or Turkey. The Royal Air Force would have overflight facilities, and both parties agreed to reratify an 1888 Convention guaranteeing freedom of navigation through the Suez Canal. The agreement aroused opposition in Egypt from some individuals and from the Ikhwan al-Muslimun on the basis that it prolonged, rather than terminated, the British military presence in the country by indirect means. During the talks, Nasser and the British negotiator Anthony Nutting struck up a friendship that doubtless helped ease the progress of the negotiations, and won for Egypt, in Nutting, a powerful and sympathetic backer in the Foreign Office.

ANGLO-EGYPTIAN SUDAN AGREEMENT. Concluded between Egypt and Britain, and signed in February 1953, the Sudan Agreement followed both countries' decision to separate negotiations about the status of the Sudan from those about the future of the British in Suez. Shortly after the 1952 Revolution, Egypt announced its support of Sudanese independence, and talks were held thereafter between General Naguib and Sudanese political leaders. Under the Agreement, the Governor-General of the Sudan was to have his exercise of power limited by the election of a parliament that would function under the guidance of an internationally drawn commission. Two other commissions would assist the cabinet and the Governor-General's office. The negotiations provided that, after a three-year transitional period, the Sudanese Constituent Assembly would choose between total independence or linkage with Egypt in some form. The Sudanese Assembly elected in 1953 decided, immediately prior to the 1956 granting of independence, to become a fully independent state unaffiliated with Egypt in any formal way.

ANGLO-EGYPTIAN TREATY. Negotiated between the Egyptian government of Mustafa Nahhas and the British government, the Anglo-Egyptian Treaty was signed in August 1936. The treaty was an attempt to rectify the anomalous situation created by Britain's unilateral declaration of Egyptian independence in 1922, in which certain areas of Egyptian sovereignty were "reserved" by the British.

The 1936 treaty provided for (1) close cooperation in time of war; (2) gradual modification of the British occupation, in line with increasing Egyptian powers of self-defense, leading to the eventual confinement of British troops to the Canal Zone; and

(3) a twenty-year duration to the treaty provisions. No substantive negotiations took place on the Sudan, where Egypt was granted a minimal and notional increase in prerogative.

Both parties were committed in advance to a further alliance in 1956, but Egypt would then have the right to submit to third-party negotiation the subject of the continued presence of British troops. The British occupation of Egypt was formally ended by the treaty, yet her troops were not to be withdrawn until the strength of the Egyptian forces were improved. The Royal Air Force was granted rights of overflight, and the British reserved the right to reoccupy Egypt, with unrestricted use of Egyptian ports and roads, in the event of a war. In fact the treaty did not physically or fully terminate the British military occupation.

In exchange for these concessions Egypt finally gained more control of its own security forces. The Military Academy was opened to a broader class of students than had previously been the case (among the first graduates under the more open admissions criteria were Gamal Abdal Nasser, Anwar Sadat, and the Free Officers who were to overthrow the civilian government of the country sixteen years later). The treaty also imposed certain costs on Egypt in the maintenance of communications and in the Sudan.

As a consequence of this treaty the British government requested the League of Nations to admit Egypt, which it did in May 1937. Britain also arranged Egypt's participation in the Montreux Convention in April and May of that year, which helped to end, eventually, the capitulations in Egypt. Despite certain immediate gains the Anglo-Egyptian Treaty as a whole was felt by some nationalists to reflect badly on the Wafd government that negotiated it.

After the Second World War, Egypt approached the British to have the treaty altered to reflect nationalist demands regarding British troop levels in Egypt and the status of the Sudan. Negotiations early in 1945, and again in 1946, failed to yield positive results, though the 1946 talks did produce a draft treaty, subsequently rejected by the Egyptian cabinet of Sidqi, who led the Egyptian negotiating team. The 1936 treaty was unilaterally abrogated by the Wafd government of Nahhas in October 1951, following yet another breakdown in negotiations, though this abrogation was not recognized by the British. The 1936 treaty was effectively ended with two treaties, in 1953 and 1954, on the issues of the Sudan and British troop withdrawals.

APHRODITO PAPYRII. Found in 1901 in Kum Ish Guh, fifty kilometers north of Sohag in Upper Egypt, the papyrii recorded the correspondence from the governor of Egypt, Qurra b. Sharīk (r. 709-14/90-96) to his Prefect, Basilius, who headed the Upper Egyptian district of Aphrodito. The papyrii provide valuable information on tax and administration during the Umayyad period in Egypt, showing the administrative organization of the country and the maintenance, in somewhat altered form, of the ancient nome administrative divisions of rural areas.

APPANAGE see IQṬĀ[c]

ARAB BOYCOTT. In the aftermath of President Anwar Sadat's visit to Jerusalem in November 1977 the Arab states discussed the imposition of certain economic and political penalties on Egypt if that country went ahead with plans to normalize relations with Israel. In November 1978 a summit meeting of Arab leaders in Baghdad voted to impose an economic boycott on Egypt, applying such measures as would affect the government and avoid, as far as possible, harming the large number of Egyptian migrant workers in the Arab countries and guaranteeing that their salaries would not be affected. The boycott was conditional on Egypt actually signing a peace treaty, which it did in March 1979. As Egypt moved to establish diplomatic relations with Israel, the other Arab states broke off diplomatic relations, especially in the period immediately preceding the arrival of the Israeli ambassador, whose credentials were accepted in February 1980. Air links between Egypt and other Arab capitals were partially severed. The boycott has been more effective at the official level, and particularly in inter-Arab groupings. Large-scale joint ventures funded by the OAPEC states have for the most part come to a halt, though funding committed prior to the boycott has in most cases been continued as has certain private investment. The boycott has not had an appreciable effect on the position of Egyptian migrant workers, who continue to play a major role in the labor forces of many of the OAPEC states.

ARAB CONQUEST OF EGYPT (639-41/18-20). At the height of the first Muslim expansion northward out of the Hijaz, the Caliph ^{c}Umar b. al-Khaṭṭāb had reputedly instructed his generals to conquer no land that was not within the land area of Syria, Palestine, and Iraq. ^{c}Amr b. al-^{c}Āṣ, who was, with Khālid b. al-Walīd, one of the two great Muslim generals of the period, advanced on Sinai late in 639/18, before informing ^{c}Umar of his plan to continue on to Egypt. ^{c}Umar, it is reported, wrote back instructing ^{c}Amr to turn back if he had not reached Egypt by the time his letter arrived, but if he had, to proceed. ^{c}Amr waited until he was in Egyptian territory before opening the letter. This westerly expansion of Islam from its birthplace in western Arabia, whether intended by the Caliph or not, was to substantially increase Islam's territorial and regional weight.

The route ^{c}Amr took to conquer Egypt was influenced by his own familiarity with the country. Prior to his conversion to Islam, ^{c}Amr had led trade caravans through the region and knew the routes into the country's heartland. The path ^{c}Amr and his army (reportedly merely 3,500 men and of mixed religious and tribal background) followed led them across the Eastern Desert to the Fayyum, an oasis to the west of the Nile valley. At some point he was joined by an additional 7,000 troops under the command of Ibn az-Zubayr, sent by the Caliph to reinforce ^{c}Amr. The next attack was on Babylon, at the south end of the Nile Delta. First meeting a force of its defenders at Heliopolis, ^{c}Amr then proceeded to lay siege to Babylon in July 640/19. After the fall of Babylon the Muslim armies advanced on Alexandria, the renowned Mediterranean port. After a lengthy siege the city was surrendered in 641/20 under a treaty that gave the government and Greek citizens one year to evacuate. These negotiations, led by Cyrus, the Byzantine Patriarch of Alexandria, brought to an end 600 years of Romano-Byzantine rule of Egypt, but it was an end hastened by the Byzantines' own decaying administrative control of the country and the disaffection felt by the country's Coptic Christian population for their Orthodox Christian rulers in Constantinople. At the same time, the conquest of Egypt by the Arab Islamic armies brought them into direct confrontation with the Byzantines. The threat represented by the possession of a Mediterranean base at Alexandria was soon answered by Byzantine attacks on that city, all of which the Arabs successfully defeated. (See entry ᶜAMR b. AL-ᶜĀṢ-AS-SAHMĪ.)

ARAB ECONOMIC COUNCIL (1960). The first moves towards an Arab common market were made by Egypt through the Arab League. Since 1958, the Egyptian Arab League delegation had been pressing member states to establish administrative and fiscal structures to encourage economic unity and cooperation among the Arab states both in trade and economic development. The Arab Economic Council, established in Cairo in 1960, was meant to work toward the easing of Arab corporate investment and trade in the region. The formation of an Arab Development Agency was proposed. The Council was also meant to examine ways of increasing the representation of Arab states within World Bank affiliates such as the International Bank for Reconstruction and Development.

ARAB ECONOMIC UNITY AGREEMENT. The 1962 agreement between Egypt, Morocco, Jordan, Kuwait, and Syria, under Arab League sponsorship, initiated a series of economic policies in common commencing in 1964. Iraq and Yemen joined in the agreement the following year; Sudan, Libya, and the UAE eventually participated, as well.

The signatories agreed to tariff reductions of 10 percent annually over a period of ten years, to a program of regional planning, and to the establishment of pan-Arab enterprises. The Council set up under the agreement, and headquartered in Cairo, was also meant to supervise various regional, bilateral, and multilateral arrangements aimed at the creation of unified customs and tariff structures, import/export policies, and economic legislation. Domestic measures were to include implementation of tax and economic policies, as well as social-security systems. In August 1964 the AEUC adopted a resolution providing for a customs union and removal of trade restrictions between member countries by 1973. A common market between the signatories was established in January 1965. Though progress was made in the negotiations covering the areas defined by the AEUC, implementation of these proposals was hampered by regional political developments.

ARAB FEDERATIONS. Since the breakup of the union between Egypt and Syria in 1961, Egypt has been involved in discussions for three other Arab federations. Egypt, Syria, and Iraq agreed in April 1963 to form a federal union with a common constitution, following pro-Nasser coups in both countries. Further discussions did not lead to the formation of a federation on this basis. In 1964 negotiations were held between Egypt and Iraq about a federation that would include these two countries and Yemen. (See TRIPARTITE TALKS.)

A further federation of Libya, Egypt, and Sudan was discussed, and Syria announced her intention to join in November 1970. A Union of Arab Republics without the Sudan was declared in April 1971, endorsed by the three countries in referendums held in September of that year, but never implemented. This last federation attempt caused a deterioration in relations between Egypt and Libya when the latter tried to force implementation of the federation after Egypt's decision not to participate. (See FEDERATION OF ARAB REPUBLICS.) New (1981) discussions on a federation between Egypt and Sudan have resulted in proposals for currency and tariff coordination prior to the creation of unified political structures.

ARAB-ISRAELI WAR (1948). Prior to the establishment of the state of Israel on Palestinian territory in 1948 the Egyptian government along with other Arab states had expressed their official opposition to the division of Palestine. Though Egypt was opposed to the division of Palestinian territory under UN resolution 181 (1947), the Prime Minister Nuqrashi Pasha was reluctant to involve Egypt's small and ill-equipped army with the Arab League forces that were meant to lead the attack to regain Palestine. However, his government was under strong pressure from domestic political and religious groups opposed to the establishment of a foreign and non-Muslim state on Arab land. The Egyptian army crossed into Palestinian territory on 15 May 1948. Fighting between the Egyptians and the Israeli army continued, despite a short-lived truce, until January 1949, when an armistice was signed through UN mediation.

The lack of weaponry, ammunition, and supplies greatly hindered the Egyptian war effort, and blame for the shortages was placed by many of the younger officers on the government, which, it was felt, had pocketed the funds meant for arms purchases. The performance of the Egyptian high command, with few exceptions, provoked widespread criticism inside the army and among ordinary Egyptians. In 1951 a trial was held of officials charged with negligence over the supply of military equipment, but this failed to satisfy public criticism.

In consequence of the armistice Egypt was left with a small piece of territory in Palestine, the Gaza Strip, leaving most of its border in Sinai exposed to the Israelis in the Negev (in Arabic, Naqab). The vulnerability of this border was demonstrated by the ease with which the Israelis were able to sweep over it, and across Sinai, in 1956 and 1967. The 1948 fighting also created a discontented younger officer corps, among whom the Free Officers featured prominently. They were able in the following years to make use of sentiment in the army against the regime's performance in the 1948 fighting to develop their own position and cohesiveness. After the Revolution several senior officers were brought to trial for their role in Egypt's 1948 defeat.

ARAB-ISRAELI WAR (JUNE WAR, SIX-DAY WAR) (1967). After several months of increasing tension between Israel and the Arab states a series of Israeli air attacks on Syrian planes and the reported mobilization of Israeli troops in April and May caused Syria to call on Egypt to implement its part of the Egyptian-Syrian Defense Pact, concluded between the two states in November 1966. Egypt therefore announced on 15 May 1967 its dispatch of troops to Sinai. The UN forces there could not effect the partial pull-back requested by Egypt, and on 16 May were therefore requested to withdraw completely. On 22 May came Nasser's decision to close the Straits of Tiran to Israel, in response to complaints by her Arab allies that Israel was receiving war supplies at Eilat. At the end of May, Jordan, which had suffered a number of Israeli reprisal attacks, signed a defense treaty with Egypt. At the beginning of June, Syria and Egypt had about 200, 000 available troops, compared with 264, 000 Israeli mobilized troops and reserves. Diplomatic efforts by the United States to resolve the dispute were proceeding, and a certain amount of optimism was generated by Nasser's decision to send Zaqaria Muhiaddin to Washington to negotiate. However, on 5 June 1967 the Israeli government launched a full-scale and devastating air attack on the Syrian, Jordanian, and Egyptian airfields, as well as Habaniyyah in Iraq. The air forces of the first three countries were almost completely destroyed, and in the fighting that followed, Israel controlled the skies. Some estimates put initial Egyptian losses at 300 of its 430 combat aircraft. Israeli armored forces bisected the Gaza Strip, cutting off Egyptian forces there from supplies, with Gaza itself fully occupied on 6 June 1967. On 7 June the Israelis launched an air attack on Egyptian fortifications at Sharm ash Shaykh in Sinai, ending Egypt's two-week blockade of the Straits of Tiran.

Some 200 miles to the northwest the Israeli army reached the Suez Canal, cutting off a sizable part of the Egyptian army in the Sinai from the mainland. Attacks were also launched against Egyptian cities on the mainland along the Canal, causing heavy damage and an outflow of refugees. The Suez Canal itself was blocked with sunken and destroyed vessels. About 20,000 Egyptian soldiers died, many of them while en route back to Egypt after being dispatched by their captors across Sinai without adequate provisions.

A cease-fire was eventually signed between Egypt and Israel on 8 June, but the economic, military, and political consequences for Egypt were devastating and stretched far beyond that. The revenue from the Suez Canal was lost, as was the revenue from the oilfields at Sharm ash-Shaykh. Israeli troops continued to occupy all of Sinai, while Egypt was faced with the vast expense of rebuilding its shattered airforce and army. Politically the defeat brought about the downfall of General Amer, once Nasser's closest political ally within the regime, nearly toppled Nasser himself, and certainly affected his position of leadership in the Arab world. The consequences of the war were equally serious for Jordan, whose West Bank territories were occupied and from which thousands of Palestinian refugees fled or were forced to flee (some for their second exile since 1948), and for Syria, which lost the strategically crucial Golan Heights. A short-lived embargo by the Arab oil-producers against Israel's supporters marked the beginning of a more politicized role for these states, which paralleled the increased regional involvement, post-1967, of the United States.

In spite of the UN-arranged cease-fire, a de facto state of war existed between Egypt and Israel, with sporadic hostilities on both sides. In October 1967 the Egyptians sank the Israeli destroyer Eilat, and in retaliation Israel bombed Egypt's oil refineries at Suez. These had supplied 80 percent of Egypt's domestic oil needs, and the bombing also heavily damaged the harbor. The unresolved tension eventually led to the War of Attrition in 1969, with serious clashes, including air attacks on Egyptian industrial and civilian areas. The two superpowers and several other states presented various plans for resolving the Arab-Israeli conflict, with the Rogers Plan finally gaining acceptance in 1970.

The defeat of the Arabs in the 1967 war had profound repercussions in all the Arab states, but particularly in Egypt. The sense of victory that followed the 1956 Suez War, however questionable in military terms, was replaced by a long period of consternation and doubt. Egypt found its political voice increasingly challenged, as was its leadership role. However, the negotiations among the Arab states that followed the war did permit the resolution of the conflict with Saudi Arabia over Yemen: the closing of five years of hostilities between the two countries helped heal a major rift in the Arab world.

ARAB-ISRAELI WAR (OCTOBER WAR, RAMADAN WAR, YOM KIPPUR WAR) (1973). The third major confrontation between the Arab nations and Israel followed a period of planning among the Arab states, with coordination between Egypt and Syria and Egyptian pressure on the Soviet Union to replace arms and equipment lost in the 1967 war.

Fighting began on 6 October 1973, with a massive Egyptian assault across the Suez Canal and a simultaneous Syrian attack on the Golan Heights. The Sinai campaign by Egypt was met by a major Israeli counterattack, which swept north and south of the position held by the Egyptian Third Army, severing its links with the mainland. The Arab armies' initial successes were quickly diminished by their failure to match the Israeli army's rapid resupply of weapons from its American ally. Additionally a threat of Russian intervention on the Arab side escalated this conflict into one with extraregional implications and brought the active involvement of U.S. Secretary of State Henry Kissinger. The Israeli army had crossed the Suez Canal and reached Kilometer 101 by the time the cease-fire was accepted by Egypt and Israel on 22 October 1973.

The Israeli army launched a minor and partially successful counterattack on Egyptian positions in the Sinai after the cease-fire in an attempt to consolidate their final position. Egypt's acceptance of the cease-fire without prior consultation with the Syrians left their ally to face an Israeli army whose fighting forces could now concetrate on one front. Under the first disengagement agreement, concluded in January 1974, the Egyptians gained a small strip of land in the Sinai bordering the Suez Canal. But the 1973 fighting left many issues between Israel and Egypt unresolved, despite the subsequent disengagement agreements.

It would appear that Egypt had seen the war as an attempt to achieve limited military objectives, whereas its partners, both active and supportive, had more ambitious military and political goals. However qualified the military victories of the 1973 war, it helped to strengthen greatly the domestic position of President Anwar Sadat. In the aftermath of the war Sadat was able to use his new popularity to introduce a series of reforms and retrenchments in Egyptian internal and foreign policy that were a distinct departure from the policies of his predecessor, Gamal Abdal Nasser. The 1973 war also saw the emergence of a more unified Arab strategy in the oil embargo announced by the OAPEC states; though such a boycott had followed the 1967 war, it was limited and largely ineffective economically or politically. The 1973 embargo helped redefine the Arab states' international political role and began a process of global readjustment that has not yet been completed.

ARAB LEAGUE. Established by Egypt, Iraq, Saudi Arabia, Yemen, Transjordan, Syria, and Lebanon in March 1945, the Arab League's membership (which included representation for the Palestinians) was eventually expanded by Libya (1953), Sudan (1956), Tunisia and Morocco (1958), Kuwait (1961), Algeria (1962), and South Yemen (1968). The UAE, Bahrain, Somalia, and Mauritania joined in the 1970s; there are today twenty-one Arab League members, excluding Egypt.

Egypt's involvement in the formation of the Arab League was intended at least partially to counter the Arab-union proposals made in 1943 by the Iraqi Prime Minister Nuri al-Sa^{c}id. The concept of a league of Arab states was first put forth by Egypt (though the idea enjoyed British support) in 1944, as the expanding Zionist claims on Palestine and French intervention in

Lebanon in the previous year helped form certain pan-Arab sentiments and recognition of the need for mutual support. In September 1944 a conference of leaders of the Arab states presided over by the Egyptian Prime Minister Nahhas was held in Alexandria. The Alexandria Protocol, drafted at this Conference and issued in October 1944, laid the foundations for the formation of the Arab League. Collective security arrangements were agreed on in 1950.

From the beginning Egypt had a dominant voice in the league. The headquarters of the Arab League were established as a permanent secretariat in Cairo, and the league's first Secretary-General, Muhammad Abdel Khalik Hassuna, plus many of its officials, were Egyptian. After the 1952 Revolution in Egypt the Arab League became a forum through which Egypt sought to influence other states in the region in line with its new foreign and domestic policy priorities. Egyptian opposition to the Baghdad Pact (1955) was channeled through the league as well as its rejection of other policies pursued by Arab League member states that it viewed as conflicting with Egyptian and pan-Arab goals. These measures did not have any real power to change actions, but they did carry a political impact that was difficult to ignore, especially when combined with Egyptian government propaganda and influence in other member countries, aided by the rhetoric and charisma of President Nasser.

With the emergence of a revolutionary regime in Iraq and the granting of independence to the French North African colonies, the dominance of Egypt in the league was increasingly challenged, and the Arab League became a forum for venting the political differences of an ideologically heterogeneous Arab world. In August 1962 a concerted move to relocate the Arab League outside Egypt, and a meeting of Arab states at Shtoura, Lebanon, in which Egypt was condemned for intervening in Syrian affairs, led to Egypt withdrawing its active membership from 1962 until March 1963, snubbing the next meeting of the Arab League, in February 1963. Similar boycotts of league meetings were undertaken by other Arab states; but despite the political constraints on, and conflicts within, the league, it managed to serve through the 1960s and 70s as a useful forum for the exchange of views among the Arab states and more particularly as a source of regional information on social and technical matters. The large number of Egyptian staff serving the Arab League, plus the location of the league's Secretariat in Cairo combined throughout this time to continue Egypt's influence in the league.

In March 1979 the league's headquarters were shifted to Tunisia as a sign of the Arab states' disapproval of the Egyptian-Israeli agreements at Camp David and the subsequent bilateral peace treaty. The last Egyptian head of the Arab League, Mahmud Riyad, served from 1972-1979.

ARAB NATIONALISM. A political philosophy based on the community of interests among the Arab states in the realm of politics, culture, and foreign relations, Arab nationalism sees some form of unity or Arab nationhood among the Arab states as necessary to achieve and preserve their power. Supporters of Arab nationalism have offered differing views on how much or how little these concepts of unity should or could be substituted for the discrete political identity of individual Arab states. National self-determination of the Arab people and their right to be free from outside interference or aggression are other aspects of the Arab nationalist ideology, particularly as found in Egypt.

Prior to the 1952 Revolution, Egypt was relatively uninvolved with pan-Arabism; its national politics largely tended to reflect Egyptian concerns in a situation where many of its nationalist issues were still unresolved. The one great exception to this was the country's involvement in the Palestine fighting in 1948. Though the Egyptian government may have been partially motivated by Egypt's fear of losing territory to the newly created Israeli state, it also had to respond to great popular demand in Egypt for action to be taken on religious and political grounds. Egypt's participation in the Arab League from 1945 onwards also helped link her loosely to her Arab neighbors, but her outstanding problems with Britain over troop withdrawals and the Sudan tended to focus the attention of Egypt's leaders outside the region. Alone among the mass political groupings, the Ikhwan al-Muslimun maintained active links with branches in neighboring Arab states.

After the 1952 Revolution, Egypt became much more directly involved with pan-Arab issues, such as regional security, defense against Israel, the Baghdad Pact (1955), anticolonialism, economic and labor issues. The Arab nationalist movement in Lebanon and Syria, as well as in the Gulf States, came increasingly under the influence of the philosophies and policies adopted by the Nasser regime.

At the same time Egypt had commitments to other ideologies, such as positive neutralism and the nonaligned movement, that occasionally supplemented but also often transcended purely Arab issues. As Nasser's relations with the other Arab states became more convoluted in the late 1950s-early 1960s, his association with the Arab nationalist movement became less clear-cut, especially with the increasing activism of other Arab states that competed for political and ideological leadership with Egypt in the region. The development of Arab Nationalist ideology by the Ba^{c}ath parties of Syria and Iraq went beyond the more constrained views of Nasser, particularly in political and regional policy.

The use of, and appeal to, Arab nationalism by Nasser owed much to his desire to build an anti-imperialist sentiment within the region (with Egypt taking the leadership of this sentiment) and to maintain a united front against Israel in the post-1956 period. During the war in the Yemen (1962-67) Arab nationalism was also used to attack the government in Saudi Arabia as being out of line with the more progressive Arab regimes, and appeals to Arab nationalism were used by Nasser to gain a following in the Gulf, particularly among the oil-workers there.

The diffuseness of Arab nationalist ideology has led to extremely varied interpretations of its meaning for social and political action. The "Arab" component has always been a powerful image, with its association of a shared Arab identity, cultural, linguistic, and historic. Ultimately, however, "nationalism" has frequently proved a stronger drawing card in terms of domestic political support, not only for Nasser but for other Arab leaders in the region.

ARAB OIL CONFERENCE. Called by the Arab League in April 1959, the conference received a proposal by Egypt to encourage OAPEC, the oil-producing Arab states, to devote 5 percent of their annual oil revenues to a central financial organization. The organization would be charged with investing the money in development projects in various Arab states (particularly, but not exclusively, the United Arab Republic of Egypt and Syria). The need for Arab capital to bring Egypt up to its full potential as an economic power was discussed extensively by Egypt's economists in the late 1950s. In the aftermath of the 1959 Conference, and following the formation of the Arab Economic Council, an Arab Development Agency was established to attract OAPEC investment capital.

The outbreak of fighting in Yemen soured Egypt's relations with OAPEC and the oil-producing states and halted discussions on this idea. Nonetheless, modifications of these proposals reappeared in the 1967 Khartoum Conference, with Egypt suggesting that the oil-producers should fund the military and economic refurbishing of the confrontation states. The amount of aid received by Egypt from OAPEC sources was criticized by Nasser in 1969, when he made an unsuccessful bid to raise the financial commitments of these states. The levels of funding established prior to 1973 increased markedly after the Arab-Israeli War, with the eventual creation of a Gulf Fund for the Development of Egypt.

ARAB SECURITY FORCES. In July 1961 Egypt participated with Tunisia, Sudan, Jordan, and Saudi Arabia in a defense force to protect Kuwait against the territorial claims of its neighbor, Iraq. Egypt's involvement with one rival (Tunisia) and two monarchies against republican Iraq was justified on the basis of the need to replace British troops in Kuwait with Arab soldiers in order to grant Kuwait Arab League membership. In fact, the pact followed two years of hostile relations between Iraq and Egypt, the two leading revolutionary countries of the region.

The alliance effected by Egypt did not survive more than a few weeks. Egypt's participation was deeply unpopular with both Saudi Arabia and Jordan, and her troops were eventually asked to withdraw in advance of the rest of the Security Forces contingent.

ARAB SOCIALISM. Broadly defined, Arab socialism was a political doctrine put forth by the Egyptian government at the time the Charter of National Action was presented in 1962, in which the long-term goal of political development in Egypt was seen as the creation of a government with socialist economic policies and an Arab-nationalist foreign policy. The government accepted the commitment to achieve a level of political and economic cooperation within the region, structured around its cultural and linguistic identity. The emphasis on socialist economic measures arose from the government's increasing reliance on the public sector to lead Egypt's development efforts. This wedding of "Arabism" and socialism found political expression in the Arab Socialist Union, also created at this time, which in addition to acting as a mass political party was also meant to provide ideological direction to the government.

ARAB SOCIALIST PARTY. The Arab Socialist Party was founded in 1977 to support President Anwar Sadat after the latter's decision to allow the return of political parties in Egypt. An earlier incarnation of the Arab Socialist Party, the "center grouping" of the Arab Socialist Union, had won a majority (280 out of 342 seats) in the 1976 election. The party was headed by the then Prime Minister, Mamduh Muhammad Salam, with Fu[c]ad Muhiaddin (in 1981, Prime Minister under President Husni Mubarak) and Muhammad Mahmud as Secretaries-General.

In the parliamentary reshuffle of June-July 1978, following

the restrictions on political activity voted in a referendum that May, the centrist party gained an additional twenty-two seats. It merged in October 1978 with a new grouping, the National Democratic Party, formed by President Sadat.

ARAB SOCIALIST UNION. The only legal political party in Egypt from 1962 until the introduction of a limited multiparty system in 1976 (with the establishment of platforms in the ASU), the Arab Socialist Union was created after the introduction of the Charter of National Action as a mass political grouping. The ASU Executive gained some political importance in the following years, most especially in the two years prior to the 1967 Arab-Israeli War, when, under the leadership of Ali Sabri, the ASU became a base for the more left-wing elements in the regime. Its political role was formalized with the introduction of the provisional Constitution in 1964.

Although the government intended to have the ASU act as a mass political party, in its actual functioning it differed little from its executive-dominated predecessor, the National Union. The party was pyramidic in structure, its 7,000 units subject to thorough control from the top, the Higher Executive Committee. Fifty percent of party posts were allocated to farmers and workers, and groupings were also established in the party on the basis of craft associations. Elections from the ASU units to the National Conference of the party first took place in May 1963; Gamal Abdal Nasser became the ASU's first president. Nasser was also responsible for the appointment of the first Higher Executive Committee, meant to draft ASU policy. Ali Sabri, who served on the HEC from 1962, and as Secretary-General of the ASU from 1965, was the dominant figure in the organization. Nasser, in the mid-1960s, apparently considered resigning his presidency to devote himself to the ASU, a plan he subsequently abandoned.

By the middle of the 1960s the government claimed a membership of 2.5 million for the ASU, drawn from Egypt's five "working forces"--peasants, workers, soldiers, intellectuals, and national capitalists. Membership eventually reached 5 million (divided among the 7, 000 local committees), but only a small proportion of this figure could be considered "active." Despite the membership figures and popularist image the party remained highly elitist in structure, dominated by its 100-member executive.

Ali Sabri was replaced by Nasser for six months following the 1967 war, and again in 1969, with the ASU Secretary-General's post eventually passing to Mustafa Khalil. The arrest of Sabri and some of his colleagues in May 1971 marked the beginning of the ASU's decline in the Egyptian political structure. In August 1974 new guidelines were introduced for the ASU that sharply limited its role and power. The decision by President Sadat to allow the emergence of political platforms within the ASU in 1976 saw the creation of a right, center, and left-wing platform (manabir), on the basis of which the 1976 elections were contested. Shortly after these elections the ASU political role was abolished and independent political groupings were allowed to form. The ASU was reduced to a supervisory role outside political action per se. Most of Egypt's contemporary political parties derive from the 1976 diversification of the ASU. The vestiges of the ASU's political role were abolished by a constitutional amendment in April 1980.

ARAB SOLIDARITY TREATY. Agreement concluded in 1957 among Egypt, Syria, Saudi Arabia, and Jordan for military cooperation over a ten-year period. The treaty was meant as an alternative to the Baghdad Pact and owed much of its impetus to the victory of the Egyptians in the Suez War and Nasser's consequent rise to leadership within the Arab world. Jordan accepted Nasser's offer of aid, along with that of Saudi Arabia, following the formation of a nationalist government in Jordan under Sulayman Nablusi. The treaty eventually foundered with the falling away of Saudi and Jordanian support for the Egyptians and with the dismissal of the Nablusi government in Jordan in April 1957. From July until November of that year relations between Jordan and Egypt were extremely bitter.

ARAB SUMMITS. In January 1964 Arab leaders met in Cairo to consider Israel's intention of diverting waters from the Jordan River, vital to Jordan's agriculture, to irrigate the Negev (in Arabic, Naqab). Eleven heads of state participated, and a communiqué was issued, announcing the formation of an Arab Unified Military Command under General Amer. The conference also brought together King Hussein of Jordan and President Nasser, who restored their relations, broken since 1961, the following March. A special agency was established by the January summit, composed of representatives of the Arab heads of state and Ahmad Shukari, representing the Palestinians.

An Arab summit met in Alexandria in September 1964, also to consider the Jordan-waters issue and to endorse the formation of a Palestine Liberation Organization. Egypt secured from the summit a declaration from the delegates denouncing the British for their activities in South Arabia (Aden and the Protectorates). Things went less smoothly for Egypt at the 1965 Casablanca Summit. Coming at a time of poor relations between Egypt and Tunisia in particular, at the summit Nasser answered criticism from the other Arab leaders for his attempts to dominate the policies and leadership of the Arab region, and for his failure and unwillingness to confront Israel directly.

In the aftermath of the 1967 Arab-Israeli War a summit was held in Khartoum in August 1967 to decide policy toward Israel, which became one of no peace, no war. The Arab states were effectively freezing themselves into a state of non-relationship with Israel following their defeat 3 months previously. But a settlement of the differences between Egypt and Saudi Arabia over the Yemen was initiated, and it was further decided that the Arab oil-producers would provide Egypt with a subvention of £95 million to replace the revenues lost through the closure of the Suez Canal. The OAPEC states decided to resume full oil production and to lift the embargo they had imposed on the British, Americans, and Germans for their active support of the Israelis during the 1967 war. The Rabat Summit in 1969 went less easily for Nasser. The confrontation with Israel and domestic economic problems had greatly handicapped the Egyptian government, and it was only partially successful in obtaining more funding from the OAPEC states. Nasser's final participation in an Arab summit was in Cairo just days before his death on 29 September 1970. Arab leaders met in an attempt to resolve the crisis between King Hussein of Jordan and Yasser Arafat of the Palestine Liberation Organization, following the suppression of the PLO in Jordan earlier in the month. Both Nasser and King Faysal of Saudi Arabia worked hard to resolve the enormous and sensitive political issues involved.

The use of summits as a means of resolving inter-Arab differences and developing common policies continued in the 1970s, despite the pursuit by the Arab countries of diverse political and economic goals that did not always harmonize. Of the post-1970 summits the 1974 Rabat Summit on the PLO and the 1976 Riyadh and Cairo summits on Lebanon were important. The 1978 Baghdad Summit, which imposed a boycott on Egypt for its involvement in peace negotiations with Israel, was significant in its uniting of radical and moderate Arab states against Egypt. The consensus obtained at this summit has not (1981) lasted, although Egypt has continued to be barred from Arab summits.

ARABI, COLONEL AHMAD (prop. ᶜUrābī) (1840-1911). Leader of the 1882 uprising in Egypt against growing European control of the country, Arabi was one of the early heroes of the Egyptian nationalist movement. Arabi came from fairly humble rural origins and was recruited into the army during the reign of Saᶜid (r.1854-63) as part of his program to Egyptianize the armed forces. The program was continued under Saᶜid's successor, Ismail, and succeeded in creating a sizable Egyptian officer corps. Under the Khedive Tawfig, official policy continued to favor those officers of Turco-Circassian background, especially with the appointment of Rifqi Pasha as Minister of War in 1879.

This policy created resentment among the native Egyptian army officers, Arabi among them, and he began to gather support from these officers, both openly and clandestinely, to push for better pay and promotion for Egyptians. There was a minor revolt in the army over these issues in 1879, in which Arabi was involved. He became closely linked at this time with the nascent nationalist movement protesting against the presence of Europeans in Ismail's government. Arabi was also associated with the drafting of the first nationalist manifesto, which attracted wide support among Egyptian officers. In mid-January 1881, Arabi and two other officers presented a petition of grievances to Rifqi Pasha. Rifqi apparently planned to have Arabi murdered when he arranged for Arabi's detention two weeks later. Arabi was rescued by his regiment, Rifqi was dismissed, and the nationalist Sami al-Barudi became Minister of War. Sami al-Barudi became a strong backer of Arabi and the Egyptian officers, which gave Arabi a wider base nationally and in the army. Arabi was involved in the first nationalist party, the Hizb al-Watani, which was active in the first three years of the reign of the Khedive Tawfiq. The activities of Arabi and the nationalists mounted as domestic opposition to the ministry of Riyad Pasha became increasingly vocal. Discontent in the army, leading to a near-coup in September 1881 forced the Khedive to ask the moderate nationalist Sharif Pasha to form a ministry and to reconvene the Assembly of Delegates. The appointment of Arabi as Deputy Minister of War in Sharif's government, and as Minister in Barudi's cabinet in February 1882, marked the high point of Arabi's political career. The following month, long overdue promotions for the Egyptian officers were announced.

Arabi's decision, in the spring of 1882, to deport some fifty officers plotting against the nationalist government led to his decisive confrontation with the Khedive, and ultimately with the British. The Khedive's refusal in May 1882 to countersign the deportation order led to bitterness between Arabi and his supporters and the Khedive. Following the delivery of a Franco-British ultimatum in May and the resignation of the Sami ministry, Arabi took control of the government and prepared to confront a threatened European invasion of Egypt.

In the course of the "revolt" that took his name Arabi was not able truly to command the situation. His inability to present Egypt's case to international opinion, despite the active support of the British orientalist Wilfred Blunt, led him into a one-sided confrontation with British military power from which Egypt was bound to emerge defeated. After the British invasion of Egypt, Arabi was arrested and tried for sedition. His exile in Ceylon (Sri Lanka) ended in 1901, and he returned to Egypt virtually forgotten by a younger generation of nationalists.

ARABI REVOLT/"NATIONAL MOVEMENT OF 1882." The origins of the first Egyptian struggle for nationalist goals in modern times can be traced to several factors: the discontent of the Arabic-speaking Egyptian officers with a military system that favored their Turco-Circassian colleagues and that had already led to an officers' rebellion in 1879; a nascent, partly clandestine but articulate nationalist party; widespread popular discontent with the growth of European financial and political control via the Caisse de la Dette Publique; and the active and growing interference of the European powers in Egyptian politics. The nationalist party, the Hizb al-Watani, founded in 1879, was the platform around which the leaders and supporters opposed to European domination gathered. The militancy of the army sharpened during the 1879-81 period under the government of Riyad Pasha and his Minister of War, Rifqi Pasha, whose policy of open discrimination against native officers created dangerous resentments.

In January 1881 Colonel Ahmad Arabi, Ali Fahmi, and Abdel Hilmi presented the Khedive Tawfiq with a petition protesting a proposed law that would have increased the difficulties faced by Egyptians trying to enter the Military Academy. Rifqi Pasha tried to have Arabi dismissed; Arabi was detained and his execution threatened. Rifqi's own dismissal was forced by Arabi and his supporters in February 1881; his replacement was the nationalist Sami al-Barudi. In September 1881 Arabi placed troops around the Khedive's palace and demanded the appointment of a more nationalist ministry. Sharif Pasha then formed a government, replacing Riyad Pasha. Arabi was appointed Deputy Minister of War after some delay; he held the post of minister under the government of Sharif's successor, Sami al-Barudi. The Assembly of Delegates was called into session late in 1881, under the presidency of Muhammad Sultan Pasha, thus fulfilling another demand of the nationalists.

The early months of 1882 were memorable for the nationalist movement in Egypt. In January the British and French governments, under pressure from the new French Prime Minister, Gambetta, delivered to the Egyptian legislature a Joint Note, in effect an ultimatum threatening intervention if anything was done by the legislature to threaten the Khedive Tawfiq's position. Sharif Pasha, already in difficulties with the Khedive, resigned, and Sami al-Barudi formed a government.

The sense of outrage in Egypt following the delivery of this note hardened nationalist attitudes. The Assembly made evident its desire for greater control of Egypt's finances, a Constitution was promulgated in February, and in March the Assembly passed an electoral law that would have expanded its size and functions. The Egyptian officer corps were awarded long overdue promotions.

In April 1882 a group of fifty officers, including Rifqi Pasha, were arrested and charged with a murder plot against Arabi. Following intense pressure from the British Agent Malet, the Khedive Tawfiq refused to sign the order exiling the officers. A confrontation followed in May between the Khedive and Arabi, in which the former backed down and the latter gained a great moral victory. However, the delivery of the second Anglo-French Joint Note in May forced the dismissal of the Sami government, although the two countries failed to secure the exile of Arabi. Raghib Pasha became Prime Minister in June, but in fact Arabi, as Minister of War, was the real head of government.

The changing circumstances in Egypt were alarming for the

British and French, not only because they threatened to undo the arrangements by which these two countries controlled the Egyptian economy, but also because of the large amount of private European investment in Egypt. The growing popularity of a military figure so clearly opposed to their continued presence in the country represented real danger to their interests. Claiming that there was a threat to civil order, the two governments had sent a fleet to Alexandria in May. An outbreak of violence in the city in June, and the Egyptian government's refusal to stop fortifying Alexandria, led to a British bombardment in July. Arabi's response to this was limited by a lack of weaponry and an overly optimistic military strategy. On 13 July Egypt declared war on Britian, but two days later the Khedive sought British protection, which was gladly offered, while Arabi was proclaimed a rebel by the Ottoman Sultan. The French (much to their later regret) did not wish to associate themselves with direct British military action, leaving the British in sole command of the European initiative. At the end of July, a Grand National Council of nationalist supporters demanded the Khedive's resignation and pledged full backing to Arabi as leader of the Egyptian resistance. Over French protests at violation of the Suez Canal's neutral status, the British made a number of landings of troops in the zone during August.

The British eventually triumphed in a surprise attack in September 1882, moving in from Ismailiyya on the Red Sea and from Tall al-Kabir on the Mediterranean coast. Arabi was compelled to retreat inland from Alexandria; the British routed the nationalist forces and pursued Arabi in his retreat. Arabi surrendered on 14 September 1882 to General Drury Lowe.

Arabi was tried for sedition, a rather incongruous charge considering he was a government official defending his own country against foreign financial and political control, quite apart from his actions in countering a straightforward military invasion. Wilfred Blunt arranged for Arabi to be defended by a British barrister, A. M. Broadly, who negotiated an eighteen-year exile for his client.

After the Arabi Revolt the British assumed de facto control of Egypt. The Egyptian army was disbanded at the end of September, and Sharif Pasha was brought back to head a cooperative ministry; Lord Dufferin became British Consul-General. In 1883, with the abrogation of the Constitution and the institution of an Organic Law drafted in consequence of the Dufferin Report, British control of the country in all but de jure status became complete.

ARABIC LANGUAGE IN EGYPT. When the Arab forces settled in Egypt in the aftermath of the Muslim conquest of the country (639-41/18-20), they were concentrated in al-Fusṭāṭ and several scattered garrison towns. Arabs who held administrative office in the Coptic-speaking countryside were able to govern through Coptic local officials and initially contributed little to the propagation of Arabic influence in the provinces.

The formal introduction of the Arabic language to Egypt occurred during the governorship of ᶜAbdallāh b. ᶜAbd al-Malik b. Marwān (r. 704-09/85-90), though his predecessor, ᶜAbd al-Azīz, had also instituted measures to foster the integration of the Arabs and the Arabic language with the Egyptians. However, both Greek (used by the Arabs' Byzantine predecessors) and Arabic were used commonly into the eighth century AD/second century AH for administrative work.

The chief factor in the spread of Arabic as a language, a process more widespread and deeper than the previous transformation of Egypt into a Greek-speaking country, was the conversion of Egypt to Islam and also the gradual settlement in the Egyptian countryside of Arab tribes. These tribes came to Egypt with the regular army, were deliberately settled there, or casually migrated to Egypt in this early period. These tribes and groups gradually advanced southward along the borders of the cultivated areas of the Nile valley, sometimes settling and sometimes continuing their nomadic existence by bartering with settled indigenous groups. In time the rate of intermarriage between the Arab tribes and the native population grew, easing the Egyptianization of the Arabs and the Arabization of the settled Egyptians. By the tenth century/fourth century an Arabic liturgy was developed by the Coptic Church, indicating how extensively the use of Arabic had spread by then. Turkish was introduced as an administrative language under the Ottomans in the sixteenth/tenth centuries. Arabic was reinstated as the language of government under Sa^{c}id (1854-63) though Turkish continued to be used in certain court and élite circles down to the twentieth century.

ARIANISM. A sectarian movement in Egyptian Christianity, Arianism maintained that Christ was not an eternal, but a created, being and therefore was not divine in nature. The movement originated with Arius (c. 250-336), a presbyter of Alexandria, who argued further that the Holy Spirit, the third member of the Christian Trinity, was also a created being. The theological disputes that arose from this teaching were especially violent, with the Patriarch of Alexandria, Athanaseus, refusing communion to Arius.

The dispute finally forced the intervention of the Byzantine Emperor, Constantine I, who called the Nicean Council in 324 to discuss Arianism. The council rejected Arianism, although the beliefs it represented gained favor in the eastern Christian world and even with the Emperor Constantine himself. It is held by some historians that the view Arianism offered of Jesus as a human prophet rather than as a divine son of God may have in part eased the acceptance of Islam in the region, as Islam gave acknowledgment to Christ's historic role, though not his divinity. Certainly Arianism and the other heterodox movements divided the region's Christians. Their mutual acrimony and their hostility to the views of Rome and/or Constantinople played a role in Islam's advance.

ARMY CRISIS. Tharwat Pasha formed a government in April 1927, following the resignation of Adli Pasha over a dispute with some Wafdist politicians involving questions about the size of the Egyptian army (which the Wafd wanted to expand) and Britain's powers over it (which the Wafd wanted to curtail). Shortly after his government was formed, the British High Commissioner,

Lord Lloyd, approached him on these issues. Though Tharwat attempted to resist what he perceived as British interference, Lloyd countered with an ultimatum. The ultimatum, presented 25 May, included a number of demands such as the supervision of the Egyptian army by a British Inspector-General, the funding by Egypt of the costs of frontier defense and administration, and the establishment of a formalized relationship between the Minister of War and an Anglo-Egyptian Officers' committee.

The Army Crisis lasted until June 1927, when the Tharwat government, with the agreement of the Wafd Party leader Zaghlul, accepted Lord Lloyd's demands. It served to underline, however, how incomplete was the "independence" granted Egypt under the 1922 Declaration.

AL-ASHRAF II MŪSA (AL-ASHRAF II MUẒAFFAR AD-DĪN) (r.1250-52/648-50). Last Sultan of the Ayyūbid dynasty in Egypt, al-Ashraf ruled in name only, real power being exercised by the Sultana Shajar ad-Durr and her consort, Aybak, Commander-in-Chief of the army. Al-Ashraf II was a young cousin of Tūrān Shāh, his immediate predecessor, who had been murdered by a group of disaffected Mamluks. His appointment was doubtless intended to confer the legitimacy of continuity with the Ayyūbids, though al-Ashraf was deposed as soon as Shajar ad-Durr and her consort had secured their position.

AL-^{c}ASKAR ("The Cantonments"). Closed quarter northeast of al-Fusṭāṭ, al-^{c}Askar was built by the first ^{c}Abbāsid governors of Egypt as an official residence and military suburb discrete from the original Muslim settlement of al-Fusṭāṭ. Al-^{c}Askar with a large mosque, residences, and a commercial quarter, maintained its position until the arrival of Aḥmad b. Ṭūlūn in 868/254. Ibn Ṭūlūn built his own residential suburb, al-Qaṭā'i^{c}. Al-Qaṭā'i^{c} did not survive the reconquest of Egypt by the ^{c}Abbāsids in 905/292. The governor's residence was moved by them back to al-^{c}Askar, though the region had by then merged geographically and economically with al-Fusṭāṭ.

ASSASSINS see NIZĀRĪ

ASSEMBLIES BILL. Introduced prior to the formation of the March 1928 Wafd government of Nahhas, the Assemblies Bill sought to ease Egypt's political life by permitting freer political association and meetings. The bill was strongly opposed by the British High Commissioner, Lord Lloyd, who felt such an opening in Egyptian political life would challenge the British position in Egypt. He pressed the King not to sign the bill if it passed. This interference by Britain was strongly attacked by Nahhas, though he eventually agreed to defer consideration of the bill until the next legislative session. The initial support given by Nahhas to this liberalization in political life was one of the factors that led the British government to support the dismissal of his government that June by the King.

ASSEMBLY OF DELEGATES (MAJLIS SHŪRĀ AN-NUWWĀB)/CHAMBER OF DEPUTIES. Established in 1866 by decree of the Khedive Ismail, the Assembly held its first session in the same year. The original decree created a body of seventy-five members, elected for a three-year term by indirect ballot. Articles were also promulgated defining the Assembly's functions and activities. Despite the seeming move toward constitutionalism that the creation of the Assembly represented, in fact the body in no way compromised the Khedive's power. Its functions appear to have been purely consultative, though the Assembly did exert some influence on policies relating to local practices and power relations. Selected by the village shaykhs and community leaders, the members of the Assembly had to be of good character, at least twenty-five years of age, born in Egypt, and neither a soldier nor a bureaucrat.

The Assembly met irregularly, being called into session on the decision of the Khedive. The 1870 session examined the budget, and the 1876 Assembly was called to discuss the repeal of the extension of the Muqabala law. Ismail briefly suspended the Assembly under European pressure before he was deposed in 1879, after granting it the right to give prior approval to all taxation measures. This Assembly, whose growing nationalist tenor had aroused European concern, was subsequently dissolved though some members continued to meet informally. Tawfiq, Ismail's successor, was forced to revive the Assembly in 1881 after intense pressure from the nationalists and a near-coup by the army in September. Elections for the Assembly took place that November, and the first session opened in December 1881.

The delivery of the Joint Note to the Egyptian government in January by the French and British signaled the transformation of the Assembly by the nationalist struggle that was shortly to erupt into open rebellion against foreign control. An organic law was passed that provided for the establishment of an elected, paid legislature, a constitution was promulgated, a more democratic electoral law was adopted, and a number of Egyptian and nationalist army officers were promoted--all before the Assembly closed its 1882 session on 23 March. The Assembly also came into conflict with the Caisse de la Dette Publique, the European commission charged with the supervision of Egypt's revenue and expenditure, over the Assembly's determination to become more involved in budget matters. Along with other nationalists, members of the Assembly met in July and August 1882 to express support for Colonel Arabi.

The Assembly of Delegates was dissolved in the autumn of 1882, following the defeat of Colonel Arabi by a British invasion force.

ASU see ARAB SOCIALIST UNION

ASWAN DAMS (pre-1970). One of the concerns of the British government after taking control in Egypt in 1883 was to improve its irrigation, not only for internal purposes but to extend the land available for cash-crop cultivation and increase Egypt's agricultural revenues. A series of engineers were recruited from Britain and the Indian Civil Service to examine the possibilities of damming the Nile at Aswan and elsewhere along the river, working under the direction of Colin Scott-Moncrieff. Existing barrages were extended, repaired, or completed, and the important Delta barrage was opened in 1890. Work on the first Aswan dam was begun in 1895, and drew on the survey work done by William Willcocks from 1890 to 1894.

Part of the funding for this dam was provided by the British financier Sir Ernst Cassel, whose large landholding at Kom Ombo, north of Aswan, greatly benefited from the dam's construction. The Aswan dam's first stage was completed in 1902. Four other barrages were constructed on the Nile between 1902 and 1928.

The dam was raised in 1912 and 1934, forcing an ever larger relocation of the Nubian communities whose lands were in the flood areas created. Agriculturally the dam permitted a rise in crop yields through gradual conversion to perennial irrigation, though certain drawbacks were experienced in the more rapid exhaustion of the soil, an increase in water-borne disease, and a rise in the water table due to inadequate drainage.

ASWAN HIGH DAM. Located some five miles south of the original, British-constructed, dam at Aswan, the High Dam was the major development project of the Nasser regime. Capital investment in the dam project is estimated to have run between $960 million and $1.5 billion; the financing of the project created far-reaching international and domestic repercussions for the Nasser regime.

The Egyptian government decided on the High Dam project (the idea of which had previously been actively promoted by a Greek agriculturalist, Adrian Daninos) in 1954. Approaches were made to the United States and Britain, as well as to the International Bank for Reconstruction and Development, in which these two countries had a dominant voice. The lack of policy agreement between the U.S. and Egypt on the matter of weapons sales, and the subsequent Egyptian decision to purchase arms from Czechoslovakia, did not appear to affect an initial IBRD decision, in February 1956, to provide financing. However, in July of that year the U.S. and the British government withdrew from participation in the scheme after Egypt rejected their demand for external supervision of its economy. Egypt responded by nationalizing the Suez Canal that same month and declaring that its revenues would be used to finance the High Dam project. In October-November 1956 Egypt fought off an invasion by Israel, Britain, and France in consequence of this decision. Thereafter, implementation of the High Dam scheme became, both politically and economically, an urgent task of Nasser's government.

The Soviet Union finally agreed to initial credits of $320 million in 1958, and participated in all stages of the High Dam's design and construction. The Egyptian government created a special bureaucratic authority to oversee the project. Construction of the dam forced the relocation of the population of Nubia, who were resettled in the regions north of the dam and around Kom Ombo. Problems related to the submersion of Egyptian antiquities in the lake scheduled to form behind the dam were solved with the participation of Unesco, which launched a worldwide appeal for funds to raise and relocate three major buildings, two at Abu Simbal (moved in 1968) and the temple complex at Philae, reopened in a new location in 1980.

The High Dam was officially opened in July 1970, shortly before the death of President Nasser. After its completion the Aswan High Dam fronted one of the world's largest reservoirs, Lake Nasser, covering 2,000 square miles. It increased the cropping pattern on 5.4 million of Egypt's 12 million feddans, brought 973,000 feddans under perennial irrigation, and provided water that could potentially irrigate 1.3 million feddans of new land. Along with the original Aswan Dam downstream, the High Dam provides 60 percent of Egypt's electric needs, with expansion of the dam's hydroelectric capacity planned.

The negative consequences of the dam are similar to those experienced with the original Aswan Dam: a marked increase in salinity and waterlogging, plus a rise in the water table that has threatened the foundation of structures much farther up the Nile. Some of these problems should be solved by the introduction of tile drainage, which is planned by the government for the early 1980s. However, the loss of silt that used to be carried down the Nile in its annual flood has only partially been compensated for by mechanically removing this silt and transporting it upriver.

ATABEG. (Ar., ATABĀK AL-ᶜASAKĪR) An important military office in Mamluk times (1250-1517/647-922), the title derives from the Turkish ātā (father) and beg (lord) and was originally applied to the guardians of the young Saljūq Turkish princes. The title gained currency in Ayyūbid times and was used by Aybak, consort of Shajar ad-Durr (1250-57/647-52); as Atabeg al-ᶜAsakīr he was both Commander-in-Chief (Amir al-Kabir) and Commander of the Guards. This latter, military concept of the post of Atabeg was more popular in Mamluk times. Atabeg was also a title used by regents of young Sultans; in the Burjī Mamluk period the Atabeg on occasion succeeded or dominated the Sultan, whose protector and viceroy he nominally was.

ATHANASIUS (c.296-373). Patriarch of Alexandria, Athanasius was a leader of the orthodox faction in the doctrinal disputes that broke the unity of the early Christian Church in Egypt. His lack of popularity with both the Byzantine court and other bishops led to his exile on several occasions. During his lifetime he managed to suppress the supporters of the Arian movement, though his Melkite, orthodox position was displaced in Egypt by Monophysitism after his death.

Athanasius participated in the Council of Nicea (325) called by the Emperor Constantine I, in which he managed to unite the clergy present in a condemnation of Arianism, though in his later life he worked unsuccessfully to reconcile the more moderate Arian faction with the orthodox position at the Council of Alexandria in 362. Athanasius' writings on theology and moral topics were extremely popular in their day and among later Christian scholars, and he was a staunch advocate of monasticism. Author of a celebrated biography of St. Anthony, Athanasius is one of the four "Doctors" of the Church, a title given in recognition of his theological scholarship.

AWLĀD AN-NĀS see MAMLUK

AYBAK (AL-MUcIZZ cIZZ AD-DĪN AYBAK) (r. 1250-57/648-55). Husband and co-ruler of Egypt with the Sultana Shajar ad-Durr, Aybak was initially appointed her Commander-in-Chief. His marriage to her was a means of legitimatizing the rule of a woman Sultan, whose sole control would have been otherwise unacceptable to some of the Mamluks and to the Caliph in Baghdad. Some of the more powerful Mamluks plotted Aybak's overthrow in 1254/652, but were forced into exile. Aybak then accumulated enough supporters among the other Mamluks to challenge his wife's power openly. His threat to marry a daughter of the ruler of Mosul and establish hegemony within Egypt led to Shajar ad-Durr's decision to terminate his life. Aybak's and Shajar ad-Durr's reign marked the ending of the Ayyūbid period in Egypt and the transition to Mamluk rule.

cAYN JĀLŪT, BATTLE OF. cAyn Jālūt, fought in 1260/658, was the decisive military encounter between the Mamluks of Egypt and the Mongol forces of Hülegü under the command of Kitbughā Noyon. Prior to the battle the Mongols had been advancing across the Muslim world, leaving general destruction and chaos in their wake. Baghdad, the center of the cAbbāsid Caliphate, was destroyed in 1258/656 and the Caliph killed. Aleppo, Damascus, Nablus, and Gaza were taken in 1260/658. The Mongols then turned their attention to the rich province of Egypt.

The Mongol leader Hülegü sent an ambassador to Cairo in the spring of 1260/658, demanding that the Mamluks submit to him. The Sultan Qutuz responded by executing the emissary, making hostilities inevitable. On 3 September 1260/658 the Mongols and Mamluks met in battle at cAyn Jālūt ("The Spring of Goliath") in Palestine. Qutuz relied on superior numbers, strategy, and cunning to lure the Mongol army toward the main Mamluk positions, capturing and executing Kitbughā Noyon. The Mamluks inflicted the first defeat the Mongols had experienced in their sweep across the Islamic and Arab lands, and saved Egypt from the devastation the Mongols had inflicted elsewhere on the territory they conquered.

In the aftermath of the battle Quṭuz was murdered by his commander, Baybars, who went on to reestablish the ᶜAbbāsid Caliphate in Cairo in 1261/659. Egypt became the dominant actor in the shattered Islamic world for nearly two centuries, and within Egypt, the Mamluks were assured of their supremacy. The Mongols, involved in settling internal matters following their defeat, were to reappear in Syria a decade later.

AYYŪBID EGYPT (1171-1250/564-648). The rulers of Ayyūbid Egypt were drawn from the descendants of Ṣalāḥ ad-Dīn and his brother al-ᶜAdil, who were of Kurdish origin. The founder of the Ayyūbids, Ṣalāḥ ad-Dīn, first came to Egypt with his uncle Shīrkūh, who was in the service of Nūr ad-Dīn, Zangid ruler of Damascus. Shīrkūh had been sent by Nūr ad-Dīn to reinstall the Fāṭimid vizier Shāwar to power, which he did in 1164/559. The Fāṭimids in Egypt were in their final decline, and it is possible that the ambitious Nūr ad-Dīn was attempting to cultivate an ally able to further his own plans there. Shāwar's goals did not include submission to Nūr ad-Dīn, and he used the Crusaders to arrange for Shīrkūh's expulsion from the country. A second invasion by Shīrkūh, which saw Ṣalāḥ ad-Dīn briefly installed as governor of Alexandria, took place in 1167/563. The situation in Egypt was confused by struggles for power, the absolute decline of the Fāṭimids, and the growing menace of the Crusaders, who were used once more during Shīrkūh's second campaign to drive him from the country. One year later Shīrkūh mounted a third, successful, campaign in Egypt, this time against Shāwar's erstwhile Crusader allies, who had turned against him. He gained control of Egypt and executed Shāwar, dying himself shortly thereafter in 1169/564; his power as vizier to the Fāṭimid Caliph al-ᶜĀḍid then passed to his nephew Ṣalāḥ ad-Dīn. It was the latter who, shortly before al-ᶜĀḍid's death in 1171/567, restored Egypt to Sunnī Islam after two centuries of Shīᶜa rule of the country.

Until the death of his nominal sovereign, Nūr ad-Dīn of Damascus, in 1174/569, Ṣalāḥ ad-Dīn's freedom of action was somewhat limited. He embarked on an inconclusive campaign against the Crusaders in Syria in 1171-73/567-69; at the same time he had to deal with the supporters of the Fāṭimids, who menaced Upper Egypt and Alexandria. A campaign against Fāṭimid supporters in the south was led by Tūrān Shāh in 1172-73/568. During this time he developed a strong army drawn from the ranks of his countrymen.

Nūr ad-Dīn's death in 1174/569 removed the constraints on Ṣalāḥ ad-Dīn's ambitions. In 1175/570 he defeated the supporters of Nūr ad-Dīn's son and successor at battle in Hama, Syria, and was invested with control of Egypt, Syria, Palestine, Maghreb, Nubia, and the Hijaz by the ᶜAbbāsid Caliph. The Assassin cult in Syria was attacked in 1176/571; thereafter Ṣalāḥ ad-Dīn met and defeated various challenges from the minor Muslim princes of the area.

The Crusaders remained, through this time, a real menace, and Ṣalāḥ ad-Dīn's goal was to drive them from the Holy Land. A bitter two-year attack on Muslim shipping and pilgrim caravans by the Crusader Raynald de Chatillon took place in 1182-83/578-79; Raynald's navy was eventually sunk at Qulzum on the Red Sea in 1185/581. Ṣalāḥ ad-Dīn defeated the Crusaders in a major land battle at Ḥaṭṭīn in 1187/583, driving them from Jerusalem and several other cities and confining them to a small coastal strip. In 1192/588, after the Crusaders had retaken Acre but failed to take Jerusalem, a treaty was concluded between the Ayyūbids and the Crusaders that recognized past Ayyūbid gains, declared Jerusalem open to unarmed Christian pilgrims, and granted the Europeans certain trading rights in Alexandria.

After his death Ṣalāḥ ad-Dīn was succeeded in Egypt by his son al-ᶜAzīz. Al-ᶜAzīz soon fell into dispute with his brother al-Afḍal, who had been placed in control of Damascus in Syria. Ṣalāḥ ad-Dīn's brother al-ᶜĀdil, who had been closely associated with him in the rule of Egypt and who was in power in Kerak, was finally forced to intervene. He united Egypt and Syria under his rule in 1200/596. The sons and relations of al-ᶜĀdil ruled the tripartate Ayyūbid state in Egypt, Syria, and Diyarbakr, with minor branches of the state through the Levant and Yemen.

The Ayyūbid period in Egypt saw several encounters with the Crusaders. In 1218/615 the Crusaders landed at Damietta (Dimyāt) on the Egyptian Mediterranean coast, marching inland until their defeat in battle at Mansura in 1221/618. A new Crusade under Frederick II entered the Levant in 1229/626 but ended with a treaty negotiated by the Ayyūbid Sultan al-Kāmil I, by which the Crusaders gained Jerusalem, Nazareth, and Bethlehem. But this easy relationship, based on the friendship established between al-Kāmil and Frederick, did not survive his departure from the area. In 1240/637, the year the Ayyūbid Sultan aṣ-Ṣāliḥ came to power, a Crusader force under Tibald was defeated at Gaza. Four years later the Crusaders were driven from Jerusalem by a force of Khwarāzmian Turks allied with the Ayyūbids. In the same year, 1244/642, the Ayyūbid armies themselves were on campaign in southern Syria, and in 1245/643 Damascus, under the Amīr Ismāᶜīl, fell. The Khwarāzmians, who had turned ambitious, were defeated in 1246/644, and an Ayyūbid campaign in Syria-Palestine in the next year took Tiberias and Ascalon. Aṣ-Ṣāliḥ's son Tūrān Shāh led a campaign into north Syria and Iraq beginning in 1248/646.

The intensity of Ayyūbid activity in the Levant encouraged the next Crusader invasion, this time of Egypt, in 1249/647. Led by Louis IX, "The Pious," this Crusade followed the same path as the 1218/615 invasion, and like the earlier Crusade was eventually defeated at Mansura. Aṣ-Ṣāliḥ died shortly before this battle, in 1250/647, whereupon his widow summoned Tūrān Shāh from Iraq. Tūrān Shāh participated in the battle but did not long survive it, being murdered afterward by his father's Mamluks, whom he had managed to alienate thoroughly. He was succeeded in 1250/648 by his father's widow, Shajar ad-Durr, whose reign effectively brought to an end the Ayyūbid regime in Egypt.

At their foundation, the Ayyūbid dynasty was imbued with a

vision of a drive against the Crusaders that combined military and diplomatic action. At certain periods, the rulers of this dynasty gave every evidence of preferring the latter to the former, a desire not shared by most of their Crusader opponents. The family's rivalries continued active. From the time of aṣ-Ṣāliḥ, who formed his own regiment of Mamluks, the consequences of this rivalry became manifest. With the constant threat of a power struggle in the family, a personal regiment of troops owing total loyalty had great attraction.

Financially the costs of the military establishment maintained by the Ayyūbids were met by taxation, though these costs must have been high. However the power of the Saljuqs and the Mongols in the east, aside from the Crusader menace, meant that the army had to be maintained at a high level of troop preparedness.

Politically the large number of princes holding power in the Ayyūbid state after the death of Ṣalāḥ ad-Dīn also created certain centrifugal forces that were never completely suppressed.

Domestically, though the Ayyūbids were staunch supporters of orthodox Islam, they were generally tolerant in their policies toward their Christian and Jewish subjects. Not all the financial or administrative measures introduced by Ṣalāḥ ad-Dīn were successful, but in general Egypt enjoyed prosperity and peace during this period, with strict and fair fiscal management and the encouragement of trade. These policies had to support a military establishment that was to prove, under later and less competent rule, increasingly difficult to maintain.

Ayyubid Rulers in Egypt:

[For individual entries, look under names underlined]

1171/567	Al-Malik an-Nāṣir I Ṣalāḥ ad-Dīn
1193/589	Al-Malik al-ᶜAzīz ᶜImād ad-Dīn
1198/595	Al-Malik al-Manṣūr Nāṣir ad-Dīn
1200/596	Al-Malik al-ᶜĀdil I Sayf ad-Dīn
1218/615	Al-Malik al-Kāmil I Nāṣir ad-Dīn

1238/635	Al-Malik al-ᶜĀdil II Sayf ad-Dīn
1240/637	Al-Malik aṣ-Ṣāliḥ Najm ad-Dīn Ayyūb
1249/647	Al-Malik al-Muᶜaẓẓam Tūrān Shāh
1250-52/648-50	Al-Malik al-Ashraf II Muẓaffar ad-Dīn

AL-AZHAR. The oldest university in the Muslim world, al-Azhar was founded in 970/359 by the Fatimid general Jawhar aṣ-Ṣiqillī as a Friday mosque and shortly afterwards, under the Caliph al-ᶜAzīz, became a university and teaching center for the propagation of the Ismāᶜīli Shīᶜa doctrine of the Fāṭimid Caliphate. Because of its association with the Shīᶜa, the Ayyūbids initially proscribed al-Azhar when they reestablished Sunnī orthodoxy in Egypt in 1171/566. However, under the Baḥrī Mamluk dynasty, and beginning during the reign of Baybars I (1260-77/658-676), al-Azhar was transformed into a center for religious studies within the Sunnī Islamic tradition, becoming in time one of the leading universities in the Islamic world. Egypt's Ottoman governors continued the strong patronage the institution enjoyed under the Mamluks, making grants and constructing buildings. The students at the university were supported by a religious endowment and pursued studies in the classic disciplines of grammar, law, Quranic, and Ḥadith studies as well as related subjects.

The Shaykhs of al-Azhar, scholars who had attracted a personal following inside and outside the university, became increasingly important in Egypt during the later Ottoman period (eighteenth century/twelfth century) when they assumed, with other religious functionaries, informal leadership roles in a politically fragmented Egyptian society. The arrival of Napoleon and the French army in 1798 emphasized this role of the ᶜulamā' and Shaykhs of al-Azhar, whose approval was sought by the French. In turn, some of these religious figures from al-Azhar studied and observed the researches of the European scholars accompanying Napoleon and were to play an important role in the dissemination of their ideas. Others, like ᶜUmar Makram, emerged as leaders of popular resistance against both foreign influence and the chaos caused by the power struggles among the Mamluks in the wake of the French withdrawal in 1801. But educationally, the university suffered the effects of the previous century of decline.

Throughout the nineteenth century there was a growth in the political awareness of some faculty and students at al-Azhar, the most notable of whom, Muhammad Abduh, was subsequently to lead a sustained campaign to reform its curriculum and teaching methods. From 1896 to 1908, after long deliberations in which Abduh had been a leader (until his death in 1905), the university undertook a reform of its curriculum and administration. The university was subjected to further regulation in the 1930s and again during the 1950s.

The Shaykh, or head of al-Azhar, is a powerful figure in the Egyptian Muslim community; several scholars, such as Shaykh al-Maraghani, who held this office in the period prior to the 1952 Revolution were important political figures as well. In general, however, the Shaykhs of al-Azhar have tended to be extremely cautious in their dealings with the government.

After the 1952 Revolution al-Azhar, like many other religious institutions that depended on the established system of religious endowments (waqfs) for their funding, was affected by government controls on the disbursals of waqfs. Al-Azhar was also the subject of government educational reform measures promulgated in 1961, establishing four graduate faculties in Islamic Law, Foundations of Religion, Arabic Studies, and General Relations and Administration. Control of the university was divided between the Rector, with administrative responsibilities, and a Shaykh, who had religious duties. Al-Azhar was incorporated into the Egyptian university system, with such secular faculties as medicine allowed, however, to retain their emphasis on traditional Islamic teaching. The Grand Shaykh of al-Azhar is currently (1980) Dr. Muhammad Abdur Rahman Bisar. Al-Azhar has, through the large numbers of foreign students who train there, an enormous and continuing impact on the Muslim world.

AL-ᶜAZĪZ (r. 975-96/365-86). Second Fāṭimid Caliph to reign in Egypt, al-ᶜAzīz's rule saw the expansion of Fāṭimid activity to Syria and the Hijaz. The Qaramatians were active as a military power in the area, and Turkish troops under Alptakīn were in Damascus at the time of al-ᶜAzīz's accession. In 976/366 the Hijaz was annexed and the Fāṭimid general Jawhar aṣ-Ṣiqillī was sent to meet Alptakīn and his Qaramatian allies, who were challenging the Fāṭimids' claims in Syria. Confronted by their overwhelming military superiority, Jawhar was forced to negotiate and retreat. On his way back to Egypt he was met by al-ᶜAzīz and reinforcements. The two thereupon defeated Alptakīn at the Battle of Ramlah in 978/368. In his later campaigns in Syria, al-ᶜAzīz was less successful, being hampered by the confused and contentious political situation in the province and the backing afforded some of the local petty lords by the Byzantines, who had their own interests in northern Syria. He finally succeeded in gaining control of most Syrian territory south of Aleppo.

The administration of Egypt during al-ᶜAzīz's reign was in the skilled hands of Yaᶜqūb b. Killis, who was the first individual to be awarded the title of vizier, in 979/367. The prominent position of this Jewish convert to Islam, and the subsequent promotion to the vizierate of the Christian ᶜĪsā b. Nastūrus give ample indication of the lack of religious prejudice of the Fāṭimid Caliphs. Unfortunately this situation did not obtain with the population in general, and there was an outbreak of anti-Christian rioting during Nastūrus' vizierate (995-96/385-86). Internal order was also not helped by al-ᶜAzīz' decision to settle members of two fierce nomadic tribes, the Banī Hilāl and the Banī Sulaym, in Upper Egypt following his defeat of them in the fighting against the Qaramatians in 978/368. Both tribes were to prove extremely problematic for the stability of the region. Al-ᶜAzīz began the recruiting of Turks into his army, something which was to prove detrimental in future to the army's cohesiveness and stability.

Al-ᶜAzīz was a great patron of the arts and constructed several major monuments in Cairo. He encouraged scholarship of all kinds. The Coptic theologian Severus, as well as representatives from other Christian sects, participated in theological debates before him. The Caliph died while on campaign to secure territory around Aleppo and Antioch.

AL-ᶜAZĪZ (AL-ᶜAZĪZ ᶜIMĀD AD-DĪN) (r. 1193-98/589-95). Son of Ṣalāḥ ad-Dīn and inheritor of the Egyptian part of his empire, al-ᶜAzīz and his brother al-Afḍal in Damascus soon fell out over their relative positions and goals (involving each other's territory). Shortly after taking office al-ᶜAzīz invaded Syria with the intention of unseating his brother; he withdrew after gaining certain territorial concessions in Palestine. Their uncle al-ᶜĀdil and members of their father's court, particularly al-Qāḍī al-Fāḍl, attempted to mediate between the brothers, but the situation was not really resolved until al-ᶜĀdil decided that his nephew in Cairo was more competent and overthrew al-Afḍal in Damascus in 1196/592. He ruled the city as Viceroy for al-ᶜAzīz until the latter's death in 1198/595; eventually al-ᶜĀdil took power in both Cairo and Damascus, in 1200/596. Al-ᶜAzīz' reign, apart from being dominated by his struggle with his brother, saw the extension of the habitable area of Cairo, though the economy remained fragile. He was advised by his father's counsellor al-Qāḍī al-Fāḍl and assisted by his deputy Qarāqūsh.

-B-

BABYLON (BĀBALYŪN). Greco-Roman city to the south of the garrison town of al-Fusṭāṭ established at the time of the Muslim conquest of Egypt, Babylon was of pharaonic foundation. A canal (al-Khalīj al-Misrī in Arabic) ran from this city, linking the Nile with the Red Sea, though it had fallen into disuse at the time of the Conquest. The Emperor Trajan (98-117) had built a fort on the site to which the Muslim general ᶜAmr b. al-ᶜĀs laid siege; remains of this fortress, Qaṣr ash-Shamᶜā, still stand. Between the fortress and the present location of the Nile lies a district of modern Cairo, but at the time of the Arab conquest, the Nile washed the walls of the fort, which was linked by a bridge with the fortified island of Roda (ar-Rawḍa). Babylon appears to have been a town of moderate import, with its own bishopric and links with the Nile valley and the Delta.

Following the Conquest ᶜAmr redug the canal, and the two cities, al-Fusṭāṭ and Babylon, continued for a time their discrete existence until the latter was absorbed by the former.

BADARI CASE. In 1932, a government official in the Badari district of Upper Egypt was murdered by two youths. Though they were found guilty, the case was brought to the Court of Cassation on appeal. While supporting the verdict of guilty, the court case described various mitigating circumstances, including the murdered official's previous arrest and maltreatment of his attackers. The appeal case revealed many of the more unsavory aspects of rural administration and justice in Egypt and was exploited by the major nationalist newspapers. Eventually the case rebounded unfavorably against the government of Sidqi, especially when his Minister of Justice, Ali Mahir, commuted the sentences of the accused. Sidqi formed a new cabinet in 1933, dropping Mahir and some of his supporters from the government.

BADR AL-HAMĀMĪ. Tulunid general who defected to the ᶜAbbasid cause in 905/293. Badr had earlier participated in an ᶜAbbāsid campaign against Qaramatian rebels in Syria. Badr al-Hamāmī joined forces with the ᶜAbbāsid general Muḥammad b. Sulaymān in the invasion and reconquest of Egypt. With the toppling of the Ṭūlūnids, Sulaymān turned against Badr and sought to have him stripped of power, but the difficulties of suppressing internal disturbances in Egypt resulted in Badr's being restored to favor, particularly with his ability to control the rebellious Sūdān corps. Badr al-Hamāmī's defection to the ᶜAbbasids came at a time when there was nearly complete disintegration of Ṭūlūnid power, with a two-year revolt against Ṭūlūnid control in Syria, beginning in 901/288, and great instability in Cairo.

BADR AL-JAMĀLĪ (d. 1094/487). Military and administrative rebuilder of the Fāṭimid state in Egypt, Badr al-Jamālī was originally a Mamluk of the Fāṭimid ruler of Tripoli (Syria) Ibn ᶜAmmār. Badr had served as governor of Damascus and commander in Acre before being called into the service of the Fāṭimid Caliph al-Mustanṣir in 1073/465. An Armenian by birth, Badr commanded a powerful guard of his countrymen and had a reputation as a disciplinarian. This reputation proved necessary when Badr arrived in Cairo in 1074/466, to find a situation of complete civil and military anarchy. A severe seven-year famine and a rebellious and divided army had decimated the population, storehouses, and treasury. With the support of the court Badr suppressed the army and silenced the military cliques running and ruining the country. He was appointed head of the secular government, commander-in-chief, and vizier.

Outside Egypt, despite Badr's succession to power, the Fāṭimids steadily lost ground to the Saljūqs, who gained control of Syria in 1076-79/468-72. The Saljūq general Atsiz threatened Cairo in 1077/469 but was forced to retreat. Subsequently Badr made three unsuccessful attempts to retake Syria.

Within Egypt, Badr restored order in Cairo and Alexandria, and among the tribes in the south of the country. He reformed the revenue-collecting system, which increased by one-third the monies available to the Treasury. Part of this he applied to fortifying Cairo with a new wall and city gates, three of which survive to this day. In the last years of his reign Badr's son al-Afḍal participated in his father's government. Upon Badr's death his titles of Amīr al-Juyūsh (Commander-in-Chief of the Fāṭimid armies) and vizier passed to al-Afḍal.

BAGHDAD PACT. A military alliance linking Turkey and Iraq was announced in January 1955 and immediately drew sharp and sustained Egyptian criticism. Nasser called a meeting of the Arab League to protest against the pact and the link it would establish between Iraq (a member of the neutral Arab League) and NATO (via Turkey, a NATO member). Nasser's attack on the Baghdad Pact was based on the entrée he felt it provided for Western military ambitions in the Arab world. He saw the pact as superfluous in view of the existence of an Arab League collective-security agreement, signed in 1950, and emphasized the dangers to Arab governments that looked for military support in the West rather than among the states of the region. The pact was nonetheless signed a month later (February, 1955). Pakistan, Iran and Great Britain subsequently joined the Baghdad Pact countries. In October 1955 Egypt signed a defense pact with Syria, Saudi Arabia, and the Yemen to demonstrate Arab independence from Western defensive alliances. Egyptian opposition to the pact, combined with that of Saudi Arabia and Syria, deterred Jordan from joining it at the end of 1955.

The strong line taken by Nasser with regard to the Baghdad Pact grew out of his own espousal of the doctrine of nonalignment and of neutralism, both of which rejected a role for the European powers in the region. Nasser's active role in organizing Arab rejection of the pact led to a sharp deterioration in his relations with the United States.

The Suez War in October 1956 greatly damaged the British position in the Middle East, and, by implication, the Baghdad Pact, with which it was linked. Iraq finally withdrew from the pact in March 1959, following a period of intensive anti-British propaganda from Egypt; Iraq's revolution eight months previously had overturned its pro-British monarchy and government.

BAGHDADI, ABDAL LATIF AL- (1917-). Free officer and government minister during the presidency of Gamal Abdal Nasser, Baghdadi was an Air Force officer and a member of the Executive Committee of the Free Officers at the time of the 1952 Revolution. Baghdadi was appointed to the Revolutionary Command Council and presided over the 1953 tribunal examining the activities of pre-revolutionary politicians. He served as Minister of War and the Navy in 1953-54, and was made Minister for Municipal and Rural Affairs in 1954. In 1957 Baghdadi was appointed to the Executive of the National Union, the government political party, and after Egypt and Syria formed the United Arab

Republic in February 1958 Baghdadi became a junior vice-president and Minister of Planning. He was speaker of the Egyptian National Assembly from its foundation in 1957 until the formation of a joint legislature by Egypt and Syria.

In addition to these ministerial posts Baghdadi served on the High Council of National Planning, cultivating links with Egypt's private sector. Baghdadi was appointed Minister of Planning and Finance in 1961-62, a critical time for Egypt's economic strategy as the government became increasingly committed to public-sector development. In 1962 Baghdadi was made a member of the Permanent Committee for National Defense, and during 1962-64 served on the Presidency Council, a nominally executive body within the government. He withdrew from the government following policy disagreements with Nasser.

Along with many others of the original Free Officers, Baghdadi was thus eclipsed within Nasser's political circle. He maintained his personal loyalty to Nasser despite this, and a rapprochement between the two men shortly before Nasser's death resulted in discussions about his possible return to government. Along with other Free Officers, Baghdadi presented a 1972 petition asking the government of Anwar Sadat to reduce Egypt's dependence on the Soviet Union and to restore free political life. He retired in 1974 but in February 1980 joined the general opposition movement to the presentation of credentials by the Israeli ambassador to Egypt.

BAHĀ AD-DĪN ZUHAYR/BAHĀ ZUHAYR (1186-1258/581-656). Pen name of the Arab poet, companion, and vizier of the Ayyūbid Sultan aṣ-Ṣāliḥ, Bahā ad-Dīn was born in Mecca, coming to Egypt as a child. He entered the service of aṣ-Ṣāliḥ, traveling with him on his campaigns in Syria and Iraq in 1232/629. When aṣ-Ṣāliḥ was detained in Palestine on orders from his brother al-ᶜĀdil II in 1239/637, the poet remained with him and was rewarded for his loyalty by being appointed vizier when aṣ-Ṣāliḥ became Sultan in the following year. Bahā ad-Dīn was with the Sultan in the fighting against the Crusaders at Mansura in 1249/

647. In the confusion following aṣ-Ṣāliḥ's death that year Bahā ad-Dīn was forced into exile in Syria. He gained permission to return to Egypt shortly before his death. His main work, the Dīwān, has been studied by both Arab and European literary scholars.

BAHRĀM (r. 1135-37/529-31 and 1139-40/533-35). Vizier to the Fāṭimid Caliph al-Ḥāfiz, Bahrām was an Armenian Christian by birth. He had been commander of an Armenian regiment and was serving as a provincial governor at the time he was summoned to the service of al-Ḥāfiz's vizier and son, al-Ḥasan. Al-Ḥasan's seizure of the vizierate had provoked a rebellion by his brother Ḥaydara. Al-Ḥasan was assassinated shortly thereafter. Bahrām was then offered the vizierate by the Caliph, a post that at the time amounted to nearly absolute power in Egypt. The favor Bahrām showed to his Armenian Christian countrymen eventually led to a rebellion by Riḍwān and by the Muslim troops, and in 1137/531 Bahrām was forced to leave Cairo. He secured the Caliph's protection, and permission to retire to a monastery, after unsuccessfully mounting a brief resistance to Riḍwān in Upper Egypt. Following the fall of Riḍwān, Bahrām was recalled to service as adviser, though without the title vizier, in 1139/533. He died a year later.

BAḤRĪ MAMLUKS. Rulers of Egypt from 1250/648 to 1390/792, the Baḥrī Mamluks derived their name from their original headquarters on the island of Roda (ar-Rawḍa) on the Nile (Baḥr an-Nīl). The original Baḥrī corps of Mamluks, or soldiers of slave origin, were formed by the Ayyūbid Sultan aṣ-Ṣāliḥ and were of Kuman Turkic origin. These slave soldiers, found widely in the Islamic world, were purchased as young children and manumitted at the end of their training, while retaining their loyalty to their original masters. They became the mainstay of many Islamic regimes, and it was perhaps inevitable that in time they should dispense with the figurehead and take power in their own name.

In Egypt the death of the Baḥrī Mamluks' patron aṣ-Ṣāliḥ in 1250/647 brought his son Tūrān Shāh back to Egypt with his own group of Mamluks. The favor that Tūrān Shāh showed the latter led to his assassination by the Baḥrīs, and in 1250/648 power passed for the first and only time in the Islamic period in Egypt to a woman, Shajar ad-Durr, the widow of aṣ-Ṣāliḥ. For two years she and her consort, the Baḥrī Mamluk Aybak, ruled behind the fiction of a nominal Ayyūbid Sultan, al-Ashraf II; thereafter they ruled in their own name.

At the time of aṣ-Ṣāliḥ's death the Mamluks were involved in a battle against the Crusaders at Mansura, which they won. The Crusaders were driven back toward the coast, and some of their leaders, including Louis IX of France, were captured and ransomed. In 1264/661 commercial agreements were concluded with several Christian states, but hostilities between the Mamluks and Crusaders continued. Antioch was razed after successful Mamluk campaigns in Palestine and Syria (also to subdue the Assassins) by Baybars. A peace treaty between the Crusaders and the Sultan Baybars was concluded in 1271/669. A further truce was signed between the Mamluks and the Knights Templar in 1281/680, but this was broken in 1289/688, when Tripoli was seized by the Mamluk Sultan Qalā'ūn. This Sultan's son Khalīl inflicted a major defeat on the Crusaders at Acre in 1291/690, expelling them from Palestine. The Crusaders made their last appearance during the Baḥrī period in 1365/766, when they razed Alexandria. The attack, while enormously destructive, was unsuccessful, though the Crusaders went on to challenge the Mamluk position in Cyprus and Little Armenia.

The most significant military role the Mamluks played was not, however, against the Crusaders, but against the Mongols. The Mongol horde had reached and sacked Baghdad in 1258/656. Damascus and Aleppo were badly damaged in 1260/658. In that year the Mamluk Sultan Qutuz met and inflicted a major defeat on the Mongols at the battle of ᶜAyn Jālūt in Palestine, saving Egypt from destruction. The Sultan Qalā'ūn met the Mongols in battle at Homs, Syria, in 1281/679, and a third wave of Mongol invaders was finally defeated by the commander Baybars (later to become the Sultan Baybars II) at the Battle of Marj aṣ-Ṣuffār, near Damascus, in 1303/702. Until the end of the Bahrī period the Mamluk territories remained secure.

The Mongol invasions of the Islamic world had destroyed the center of the ᶜAbbāsid Caliphate in Baghdad. The ᶜAbbāsid Caliph, to whom all Sunnī monarchs in the Islamic world gave their nominal allegiance, was murdered by the Mongols when they seized Baghdad in 1258/656. The Bahrī Mamluk Sultan Baybars reestablished the Caliphate in Cairo in 1261/659 in the person of a distant relation of the last, murdered, ᶜAbbāsid Caliph. Although this Egyptian "shadow" Caliphate did not have the total spiritual authority of the Baghdad Caliphate, it was used by the Bahrī Mamluks and their Burjī Mamluk successors to validate their control of Egypt.

The quality and leadership of the individual Bahrī Mamluk Sultans show many variations, from the great military leader Baybars I to the series of Mamluks who held power briefly and forgettably as the Bahrī Mamluk period drew to an end. The Bahrī Mamluks did maintain a hereditary principle in the transfer of power. The Sultan Qalā'ūn and his successors ruled Egypt for nearly a century. Qalā'ūn and his descendants, particularly an-Nāṣir Muḥammad, made many contributions to the public welfare, building hospitals, schools, and mosques.

Internally, the costs of the military campaigns conducted by the Mamluks imposed a heavy burden on the treasury, with consequent rises in taxation. A Coptic revolt in 1320/720 may have signaled rising and broader public disaffection with the Bahrī Mamluks, whose end was hastened by a steady, bitter, and violent struggle for power among the Mamluk backers of various increasingly powerless Bahrī heirs of Qalā'ūn. A devastating outbreak of the Black Death, or plague, and consequent famine in 1348/749 weakened internal order as the population and army were decimated. As a new wave of invaders from Central Asia under Tīmūr began their advance on Egypt in the 1380s/780s, the Burjī Mamluks emerged as defenders of Egypt and eventual supplanters of their Bahrī Mamluk patrons.

Baḥrī Mamluk Sultans:

[For individual entries, look under names underlined]

1250/648	Shajar ad-Durr (with) al-Mu^{c}izz ^{c}Izz ad-Dīn Aybak
1257/655	Al-Manṣūr Nūr ad-Dīn ^{c}Alī
1259/657	Al-Muẓaffar Sayf ad-Dīn Quṭuz
1260/658	Aẓ-Ẓāhir Rukn ad-Dīn Baybars I al-Bunduqdārī
1277/676	As-Sa^{c}īd Nāṣir ad-Dīn Baraka Khan
1280/678	Al-^{c}Ādil Badr ad-Dīn Salāmish
1280/678	Al-Manṣūr Sayf ad-Dīn Qalā'ūn al-Alfī
1290/689	Al-Ashraf Ṣalāh ad-Dīn Khalīl
1294/693	An-Nāṣir Nāṣir ad-Dīn Muḥammad (first reign)
1295/694	Al-^{c}Ādil Zayn ad-Dīn Kitbughā
1297/696	Al-Manṣūr Ḥusām ad-Dīn Lājīn
1299/698	An-Nāṣir Muḥammad (second reign)
1309/708	Al-Muẓaffar Rukn ad-Dīn Baybars II al-Jāshankīr
1309/709	An-Nāṣir Muḥammad (third reign)
1340/741	Al-Manṣūr Sayf ad-Dīn Abū Bakr
1341/742	Al-Ashraf ^{c}Alā' ad-Dīn Kūjūk
1342/743	An-Naṣir Shihāb ad-Dīn Aḥmad
1342/743	As-Ṣāliḥ ^{c}Imād ad-Dīn Ismā^{c}īl
1345/746	Al-Kāmil Sayf ad-Dīn Sha^{c}bān I
1346/747	Al-Muẓaffar Sayf ad-Dīn Ḥājjī I
1347/748	An-Nāṣir Nāṣir ad-Dīn al-Ḥasan
1351/752	Aṣ-Ṣāliḥ Ṣalāḥ ad-Dīn Ṣāliḥ
1354/755	Al-Ḥasan (second reign)
1361/762	Al-Manṣūr Ṣalāḥ ad-Dīn Muḥammad
1363/764	Al-Ashraf Nāṣir ad-Dīn Sha^{c}bān II
1376/778	Al-Manṣūr ^{c}Alā' ad-Dīn ^{c}Alī
1382/783	Aṣ-Ṣāliḥ Ṣalāḥ ad-Dīn Ḥājjī II (first reign)
1382/784	Aẓ-Ẓāhir Sayf ad-Dīn Barqūq (Burjī)
1389-90/791-92	Ḥājjī II (second reign)

BAKER, SAMUEL WHITE (1821-1893). A British explorer, Baker

first came to the African continent in 1861. He attracted the support of the new Khedive, Ismail (1863-79), who appointed him to head a Khedival expedition charged with annexing the Equatorial sources of the Nile. Baker brought Egyptian claims to Lake Albert and to within 100 miles of Lake Victoria, paving the way for later, more substantial European exploration in Africa. In 1869 Ismail appointed Baker Governor-General of Equatorial Sudan. Baker's four years in office were marred by nearly continuous warfare arising from poor central control of the region's tribal areas, as well as difficulties with the Egyptian administration. His tenure as Governor-General involved him in several campaigns to bring order to the province and an end to the slave trade. He left the Sudan at the end of his appointment.

AL-BALAWĪ (ABŪ MUḤAMMAD ᶜABDALLĀH b. MUḤAMMAD) (tenth century/fourth century). Historian of the Ṭūlūnid period in Egypt (868-905/254-92). Al-Balawī's writings are among the oldest historical works on Egypt. His history of Ibn Ṭūlūn is considered the major source for this period in Egypt, but the work also contains general material important to the history of the area during the ᶜAbbāsid period, drawing on Ṭūlūnid official documents. For Egyptian historiography the main value of al-Balawī's work lies in the full record he provides of Ibn Ṭūlūn's life.

BANDUNG CONFERENCE. A meeting of Third World leaders of the nonaligned movement in Bandung, Indonesia, in April 1955, the conference brought Nasser into close contact with Chou En-lai of the People's Republic of China and President Sukarno of Indonesia, and strengthened his links with Presidents Nehru of India and Tito of Yugoslavia. The Bandung Conference helped develop the orientation of Nasser's foreign policy within the Arab world as one of neutralism and noninvolvement in the conflict between the major powers and support for national liberation movements within colonial countries. The conference also, in a certain sense, marked Nasser's own emergence as an Arab leader of stature, particularly in view of the generous treatment he received from other established leaders in the Third World. The "Spirit of Bandung" became a part of his appeals to the other Arab and Third World states to resist alignment with the West in particular and to join with Egypt in the nonaligned neutralist movement. The initial cohesion of the South at Bandung did not survive well the changes in political leadership and ideology in the Third World. The 1965 Bandung Conference, held to review the progress made by the South toward the goals set in 1955, reflected the changed personnel and goals of the preceding decade.

BANK MISR/BANQUE MISR. Founded in 1920 by a group of Egyptian industrialists led by Talat Harb, Bank Misr was intended to be a source of capital to develop Egyptian industry. The bank, which initially drew its funding from the country's large landowners and businessmen, was designed to counter both foreign banks and the traditional tendency of money to be invested in land, but it was not wholly successful in this. The bank, formed during the period of prosperity following the First World War, was envisaged by its founders as being a purely Egyptian bank, able to fund an independent economic policy.

Despite the worldwide recession in the 1930s, and consequent shortage of investment capital, Bank Misr widened its activities through alliance with foreign capital, liberating itself in the process from dependence on capital from Egypt's landed interests. With the bank's aid a shipping line, hotel company, printing works, airline, film company, and, most important, textile companies at Mahalla al-Kubra and Kafr al-Dawa were founded. By the 1930s, Bank Misr had also gained an important economic role in Egypt and campaigned actively for legislation favorable to Egyptian industry.

Before its nationalization in 1960 Bank Misr was a dominant institution in the Egyptian economy through its control of a stable of companies that produced over 25 percent of Egypt's cotton textiles, as well as iron and steel companies, petroleum production, and the national airline. Its policy of providing starting-up capital in exchange for effective operational and directoral control gave it a strong position in Egypt's private sector.

The "Misr Group" of companies, after the bank's nationalization, remained organizationally under the control of the bank's directors, who were increasingly appointed from the public sector. The bank has retained its original function of providing capital for development, particularly in domestic trade and some aspects of agricultural credit.

AL-BANNA, HASAN (1906-1949). Founder of the Society of Muslim Brethren, the Ikhwan al-Muslimun (in Arabic, Ikhwān al-Muslimūn), Hasan al-Banna led one of the most influential Islamic revivalist movements of the twentieth century.

Like Muhammad Abduh a century before, Hasan al-Banna received his early education in traditional Quran schools and, also like Abduh, appears to have studied many aspects of popular Islam in Egypt before embarking on his revivalist mission. At the time Al-Banna was completing his teacher training Egypt was being torn apart by the competition for power among its political elite. Al-Banna began his mission by preaching in Cairo cafes and other public gathering places about the need for a revitalized Islam to underwrite Egypt's national life. He was sent to teach in Ismailiyya, on Egypt's Red Sea coast. It was there, in 1928, that the Ikhwan al-Muslimun was started.

From the beginning Al-Banna combined his religious teaching with social-welfare measures, starting up schools, clinics, and small businesses that became local centers for the spread of Ikhwan teaching. By the time he was allowed to return to Cairo in 1932 he had founded a mosque and two schools, and the group had a headquarters building. The rapidity of the movement's spread thereafter can be traced to the forcefulness of Al-Banna's own personality and preaching, his message of religious and personal renewal within a revived Islam, and the obvious vacuum that existed at certain levels of Egyptian society and political life for a personality, message, and organization of this type.

Al-Banna's development as a political leader seems to have occurred initially as an adjunct to his religious role, but, with his identification of Islam as a charter for religious and social action, it was unlikely that the two would be very far apart. Additionally, as his movement grew in strength of numbers he inevitably acquired a national profile. By 1936 he was sufficiently confident to address a long, counseling letter to the new king, Faruq, detailing his ideas on the latter's responsibilities as monarch of an Islamic country and the role and problems of religion in an Islamic state.

From 1936 until the end of World War II the Ikhwan under Al-Banna's leadership enjoyed an enormous expansion in membership, and with the establishment of the Special Section, which concentrated on paramilitary and occasional terrorist activities, it became a force within Egyptian national politics on official and clandestine levels. Simultaneously, Al-Banna ceased to have the thoroughgoing control of the group that he had enjoyed in earlier days, and conflict within the leadership led to the breakaway of several disaffected elements. Al-Banna was himself arrested and detained briefly in 1941 for opposing Egyptian involvement in the British war effort. During this period a number of young army officers, including Anwar Sadat, established personal contacts with Al-Banna that were to lay the foundation for the future Ikhwan-Free Officer cooperation before and after the 1952 Revolution. Al-Banna was also consulted more frequently by the political leadership of the day, causing charges to be raised in some quarters of the Ikhwan who were unhappy with any links, however faint, with Egypt's political establishment.

In the urban violence and terrorism that beset Egypt in the postwar period the Ikhwan's Special Section was a major actor, and at the outbreak of the 1948 Palestine War members of the section were formed into commando groups, possibly with the assistance of the Free Officers, and joined the fighting in Palestine. The antigovernment activities of the Ikhwan did not harm its popularity, though Al-Banna was careful to keep the hierarchy distanced from the violence. The group gained further from the effectiveness of its commando units in the Palestine fighting, which stood in marked contrast to the performance of the army high command.

The Egyptian government was throughout this period concerned with the Ikhwan militants' propensity to violence and with the threat the group represented to the mainstream political parties, whose supporters it increasingly attracted. In December 1948 the Prime Minister, Nuqrashi Pasha, decided to ban the group following the assassination of the Cairo police chief. Nuqrashi was assassinated in retribution by an Ikhwan member late in December 1948. Al-Banna's involvement with the antigovernment, and particularly the terrorist, activities of the Ikhwan is not clear, but many in the Egyptian government held him to blame for instigating such acts. In retaliation for the assassinations by the Ikhwan Al-Banna was himself assassinated, probably by a police agent, in February 1949.

At the time of his murder Al-Banna's organization was estimated as having about a million active or sympathizing members, but the group's original power and cohesion were badly, if temporarily, damaged by Al-Banna's death. It is a testament to how closely the Ikhwan was linked to him that the leadership struggle that followed took nearly two years to resolve and was marked by great bitterness and factionalism. Only the link that Al-Banna and the Free Officers had established remained strong, possibly because the latter were counting on the Ikhwan to provide them with the popular base they needed in Egypt.

Al-Banna's philosophy derived strongly from that trend in the work of Muhammad Abduh and his disciple Rashid Rida that sought a return to the original purity of Islam and found in that pure Islam a model for social and political action unmatched by contemporary political philosophies. Al-Banna combined his theoretical writings with an activist commitment to social reform at a time when basic social services were sorely needed in Egypt among less-well-off urban elements. His message and work marked Al-Banna and the Ikhwan as something rather different from the self-seeking politicians and parties that seemed to dominate, with few exceptions, national political life in the post-1936 period.

BAR LEV LINE. Series of fortified bunkers constructed in northwest Sinai by the Israelis in October 1968 the Bar Lev Line was intended to give them a commanding position in the Sinai to control the routes from the Suez Canal. The overrunning of the previously impregnable Bar Lev Line in the first thrust of the Egyptian offensive in the 1973 war achieved one of the major objectives of Egypt's military strategy in that war. The Bar Lev fortifications were maintained by Israel until the 1975 Egyptian-Israeli Disengagement Agreement, under which Israel withdrew from their forward Sinai positions.

BARABRA. The Barabra are, ethnically, the Nubians settled in the area around Aswan and in northern Sudan; the term covers a number of tribes within this region. The relationship of the Barabra to the Muslim areas to the north dates almost from the time of the Arab Conquest of Egypt (see NUBIA). An interesting subgroup within the Barabra are the descendants of Bosnian mercenaries sent to the area by Selīm I, Ottoman conqueror of Egypt. These soldiers formed themselves into a distinct clan known locally as the Kushaf and appear to have maintained an identity separate from the rest of the Barabra until the time of Muhammad Ali.

BARAKA KHAN (AṢ-ṢA^{c}ĪD NĀṢIR AD-DĪN BARAKA KHAN) (r. 1277-80/676-78). Baḥrī Mamluk Sultan, son and successor to Baybars I and son-in-law of Qalā'ūn, Baraka Khan had to step into a role of his father's creation, a role to which he was inadequate. He was strongly under the influence of Qalā'ūn, who had his own ambitions which did not coincide with Baraka Khan remaining in power. Alienating the Mamluk hierarchy that had served his father so well, Baraka Khan eventually provoked a

Mamluk rebellion against his rule. He was placed under siege in the Citadel until he agreed to abdicate and retire to Kerak. After his abdication Baraka Khan decided to campaign against Armenia; he got no farther than Damascus, where he died in 1281/679.

AL-BARDĪSĪ, ᶜUTHMĀN (d. 1805/1220). With Ibrāhīm Bey and others ᶜUthmān al-Bardīsī led the last attempt by Egypt's Mamluks to regain political control of the country following the withdrawal of the French in 1801. Al-Bardīsī benefited from the decision in 1803 of Muḥammad ᶜAlī, leader of the Albanian regiment, to support him. Muḥammad ᶜAlī deserted his former chief, Khusrau Pasha, the Ottoman governor, and pursued the latter to the coast, where Khusrau and his defenders were defeated. With Khusrau imprisoned in Damietta by Muḥammad ᶜAlī, al-Bardīsī assumed the office of Shaykh al-Balad, de facto Mamluk governor of Egypt. His chief rival, Muḥammad Bay al-Alfī was in England and thus unable to oppose him.

Al-Bardīsī was soon placed under pressure from Muḥammad ᶜAlī, however, and by the competing claims of Muḥammad Bay al-Alfī, who returned to Cairo in 1804. Muḥammad ᶜAlī sought a large amount of back pay for his regiment, and Al-Bardīsī attempted to raise the funds through stringent taxation, gaining him wide unpopularity. Al-Bardīsī's inability to control the Mamluks also aroused public feeling against him in Cairo. In March 1804 al-Bardīsī and his supporters fled to the south of Egypt after being attacked by Muḥammad ᶜAlī and his troops in the Citadel of Cairo. He died in exile the year after Muḥammad ᶜAlī assumed power.

BARING, SIR EVELYN see CROMER, LORD

BARJAWĀN (d. 1000/390). Tutor to the Fāṭimid Caliph al-Ḥākim at the time of his accession in 996/386, Barjawān was initially overshadowed by the vizier Ibn ᶜAmmār. In a one-year power struggle Barjawān managed to displace the vizier, first through effecting an alliance with the Fāṭimid governor of Damascus (a

Turk who was subsequently defeated by Ibn ^{c}Ammār's armies), then with the cooperation of a disenchanted Berber officer, and finally through the dislocation of Ibn ^{c}Ammār's Berber supporters in the street fighting between Turkish and Berber regiments in 996/386. Although the contest between the two men profited from the conflict between the Berber (Ibn ^{c}Ammār) and Turkish (supporting Barjawān) elements in the Fāṭimid army, in fact Barjawān's own ethnic origins are uncertain.

Ibn ^{c}Ammār was forced to flee in 997/387, giving Barjawān a free hand as vizier and control over his young master. His three years in office were devoted to consolidating the Fāṭimid empire in North Africa against the centrifugal forces of the Berbers, who had found that their past support for the Fāṭimid's expansion into Egypt had yielded them no great power within the state. In the east the Fāṭimids and Byzantines began negotiations on a treaty in 998/388 with regard to their respective claims in Syria. This eventually brought to an end a period of hostilities between the two powers over the territory. The next year Barjawān put down a rebellion in Syria that had been spurred by his suppression of Ibn ^{c}Ammār's supporters there.

Barjawān's power finally aroused the jealousy of al-Ḥākim, who had him murdered by Raydān, a court figure anxious to supplant Barjawān.

BARQŪQ (AZ-ẒĀHIR SAYF AD-DĪN BARQŪQ) (r. 1382-89 and 1390-99/784-91 and 792-801). First of the Burjī Mamluk rulers of Egypt, Barqūq overthrew the Baḥrī Mamluk Sultan Ḥājjī II and was himself displaced by Ḥājjī's supporters seven years later, although he returned to power shortly thereafter. Barqūq rose rapidly in the closing years of the Baḥrī Mamluk dynasty of Qalā'ūn, becoming Commander-in-Chief and acquiring enough power to name the final Sultans of this line.

Barqūq's first reign as Sultan coincided with the growing menace posed by the arrival of Tīmūr and his army, who by 1387/789 had reached the Syrian border. In this first wave of his attack Tīmūr did not advance into territory where he directly threatened Barqūq. But the advent of Tīmūr led to many minor rebellions in Syria, and in 1389/791 Barqūq was temporarily eclipsed by Yilbughā, the governor of Aleppo, who had already seized land in Syria. The two met in battle near Cairo in 1389/791, and Barqūq, defeated, was forced to retire to Kerak.

In the interval of Barqūq's exile, Yilbughā put Ḥājjī back on the throne, but was then overturned by another Syrian Mamluk, Mintash, with whom he had been allied; Ḥājjī remained in his figurehead position. Taking advantage of the confused situation in Egypt, Barqūq escaped from exile, organized an army of supporters, and marched on Egypt, where he met Mintash in battle at Gaza. It is reported in some sources that Barqūq's kindly treatment of Ḥājjī II, whom he captured in Mintash's camp, won him many supporters.

During his second reign Barqūq was approached by an emissary from Tīmūr, seeking a friendly alliance. Barqūq put this emissary to death and instead was in contact with the Ottoman Sultan Bāyazīd, which may have acted to stave off temporarily the threat from Tīmūr. Barqūq then went on a tour of the provincial areas under Mamluk control, checking their defenses against a potential attack.

Internally, Barqūq reorganized Egypt's administration through the establishment of a diwān, or consultative council, of Mamluks, and lessened the powers of certain court officials. He appointed the famous Islamic historian Ibn Khaldūn as Chief Qādī (judge) of the Mālikī school in 1384/786, during his first reign, and left behind several buildings in Cairo that are still extant.

BARSBĀY (AL-ASHRAF SAYF AD-DĪN BARSBĀY) (r. 1422-37/825-41). Burjī Mamluk Sultan, originally a Mamluk of Barqūq, Barsbāy was one of the longer-reigning Sultans of the Burjī period.

Barsbāy's reign was marked as much by economic as by military events, for his greed during his tenure of office seemed unbounded. He sought to establish monopolies on such commodities as sugar and pepper and to dominate the major trade links with India. He also tried to gain personal control of Egypt's currency.

Barsbāy conducted a campaign against Cyprus in 1426-27/829-30, making that island a tributary of the Mamluks. Relations with the Turcomans over Iraq resulted in several irresolute military encounters and a treaty in 1433/836, which recognized Egyptian sovereignty in a general way. This sovereignty was, however, challenged by the Tīmūrids, who pressed for permission to provide the Kiswa, or covering, for the Kaᶜba in Mecca, a privilege always claimed by the Mamluks as defenders of the holy cities. This last dispute was not resolved during Barsbāy's reign, despite lengthy and acrimonious negotiations.

Within Egypt, Barsbāy engaged on a program of fortification against the growing menace of European pirates and also as a defense against any attacks by European traders, many of whose privileges he revoked and whose property he impounded. In an attempt to reassert Mamluk control in the Hijaz, and thus gain more revenue, Barsbāy sent a regiment there and opened a port at Jeddah in 1425/828. After unloading, the merchants were meant to proceed to Egypt for the further collection of taxes. In the event the difficulties of implementing this plan led to one substantive collection of taxes in Jeddah, of which the Sultan took half.

Although Barsbāy's ascendancy in Egypt brought to an end a period of instability, his greed, as expressed in his economic policies, brought the country great hardship. The difficulties faced by Christians and Jews were compounded by an edict forbidding them to hold public office (usually designed to be overcome through the payment of a bribe), while within the Mamluk regiments themselves the competition for power continued. In the last years of Barsbāy's reign the plague returned to Egypt and claimed the Sultan as one of its victims.

AL-BARUDI PASHA see SAMI AL-BARUDI, MAHMUD

AL-BASĀSĪRĪ, ABU'L-ḤĀRITH (d.1060/451). Turkish Būyid military leader who gave his allegiance to the Fāṭimid Caliph al-Mustanṣir, al-Basāsīrī was originally connected with the Sunnī ᶜAbbāsid Caliphal court in Baghdad. His relations at court were exceedingly bad with the vizier, and he was eventually forced to leave Baghdad when that vizier effected an alliance with the Saljūq Turks under Toghrul Beg. Whether because of his treatment at court, or through his innate leanings toward Shīʿa Islam, al-Basāsīrī then approached the Fāṭimid court for assistance in taking Iraq in their name. The Caliph al-Mustanṣir and his vizier, al-Yāzūrī, eventually agreed to provide al-Basāsīrī with funds and coordinated their arrangements with him through their local dāʿī, or missionary, al-Mu'ayyad.

Al-Basāsīrī took Mosul (Mawṣil) in 1057/448, gaining support locally and militarily through the intense propaganda efforts of al-Mu'ayyad. Though his control of this city was lost twice afterward to the Saljūq Toghrul Beg, al-Basāsīrī recaptured it and went on to take Baghdad, where the Fāṭimid Shīʿa Caliph was proclaimed in January 1059/450. By this act al-Basāsīrī brought the Fāṭimid state to its greatest territorial extent, but it was a short-lived victory. The Sunnī ʿAbbāsid Caliph al-Qāʿim escaped when Baghdad was captured, and this displeased the Fāṭimid Caliph al-Mustanṣir, who had wanted al-Qāʿim brought to Cairo and kept under house arrest. Therefore al-Basāsīrī's requests for assistance when his control of Baghdad was threatened by the re-emergence of the Saljūqs were not met with favor. Additionally, al-Yāzūrī had been replaced as vizier by Ibn al-Maghrabī, who had formerly been in al-Basāsīrī's employ and who was not disposed to help his former employer. In 1059/451 al-Basāsīrī was forced to flee Baghdad when the Saljūqs marched on the city. He was intercepted by them and a battle was joined, during which he was captured and executed.

BAY see BEY

BAYLICATE see BEYLICATE

BAYBARS I (AẒ-ẒĀHIR RUKN AD-DĪN BAYBARS I AL-BUNDUQDĀRĪ) (r. 1260-77/658-76). Baḥrī Mamluk Sultan and the real founder of the Baḥrī Mamluk dynasty, Baybars began his career in Egypt as a Mamluk of the Ayyūbid Sultan aṣ-Ṣāliḥ. In 1244/642 Baybars led the Ayyūbid armies of aṣ-Ṣāliḥ on campaign in Palestine and Syria against the Crusaders and against the Khwarazmian Turks, formerly allies of the Ayyūbids.

At the time of aṣ-Ṣāliḥ's death in 1250/647 Baybars was leading the Ayyūbid forces at Mansura against the Crusaders under Louis IX, in whose defeat he played a crucial role. He was among the Mamluks who murdered Tūrān Shah, aṣ-Ṣāliḥ's son and successor, in the same year. After this he went into exile during the reign of Aybak, reappearing at the Battle of ᶜAyn Jālūt in 1260/658 as a commander of the Mamluk forces who defeated the Mongols. Once again he participated in an assassination, this time of the Sultan Qutuz, and took power as Sultan.

A year after ᶜAyn Jālūt, in 1261/659, Baybars reestablished the ᶜAbbāsid Caliphate, destroyed when the Mongols had sacked Baghdad, in Cairo. The last Caliph's uncle took the office as the Caliph al-Mustanṣir. He appears to have differed with Baybars over a plan to retake Baghdad. Baybars provided al-Mustanṣir with a small expeditionary force, but the Caliph died on campaign shortly afterward, before he ever left Egyptian territory. He was succeeded by the more cooperative al-Ḥākim I. After ordering the reconstruction of the fortifications protecting Mamluk lines, Baybars went on a brief campaign in Syria. In 1263/662, his armies took Kerak from its Ayyūbid ruler.

Baybars concluded commercial treaties with several Christian states in 1264/661, the year he annexed Homs, but in the next year he began a six-year campaign against the Crusaders in the Levant. Caesarea was taken in 1265/563, Safad in 1266/664, Jaffa and Antioch in 1268/666, and Crac, a major stronghold of the Crusaders, concluded a peace treaty with Baybars three years later. Baybars also concluded a treaty with the King of Little Armenia in 1275/674 that made broad territorial concessions to the Mamluks. In the course of these campaigns Baybars gradually took over the remaining Ayyūbid principalities in Syria, met a brief Mongol challenge in 1271-72/669-70, subdued the Assassins, and laid the foundations for future Mamluk control over Syria. In the south Nubia was subdued in 1275/674 by a Mamluk army.

Baybars introduced extensive administrative reorganization in Egypt, establishing an efficient postal service connecting all parts of his domain, and reorganized the Mamluk military structure along Mongol lines. He was the first ruler of Egypt to appoint four Qāḍīs (judges) to represent each of the four legal schools within Sunnī Islam. Many schools and public buildings were constructed, and Baybars restored the barracks of the Mamluks on the island of Roda (ar-Rawḍa). During his lengthy career he led a total of thirty-eight campaigns in the Levant; his military exploits are comparable with those of Ṣalāḥ ad-Dīn. He died while on campaign in Asia Minor. Baybars' military achievements survived to modern times in the popular Egyptian folktale aẓ-Ẓāhir, or the Sīrat Baybars.

BAYBARS II (AL-MUẒAFFAR RUKN AD-DĪN BAYBARS II AL-JĀSHANKĪR) (r. 1309/708). Baḥrī Mamluk Sultan, Baybars II was a Circassian Mamluk of the Sultan Qalā'ūn. Baybars rose rapidly in the hierarchy under Kitbughā and Lājīn and eventually shared de facto power in Egypt with the vizier Sallār al-Manṣūrī during the second reign of Nāṣir Muḥammad (1299-1309/698-708).

Baybars II entered Damascus in 1303/702 and met the Mongols in battle at Marj aṣ-Ṣuffār. This brought to a halt nearly five years of Mongol pressure on the Mamluk territories in Syria, and the battle, which was joined by both the Sultan and the ᶜAbbāsid Caliph al-Mustakfī I, was one of the decisive military encounters of the period. Back in Egypt, however, a major earthquake in the same year brought the usual destruction and famine. To this earthquake may be related an uprising in the south of the country by the Arab tribes, but in any event Baybars II acted swiftly to suppress it.

Inevitably Baybars began to seek supremacy within his ten-year partnership with the vizier Sallār al-Manṣūrī. The contest became bitter enough for Nāṣir Muḥammad to decide to flee the country. Baybars II was pronounced Sultan, with Sallār serving as vizier and a constant source of intrigue at court. Hearing that Nāṣir Muḥammad, who had retired to Kerak, had organized an army to reinstall himself in power, Baybars fled. Though initially pardoned by Nāṣir Muḥammad, he was strangled on the latter's orders when he was returned to Cairo.

BAYBARS AL-MANṢŪRĪ (d.1325/725). Historian of Mamluk Egypt, Baybars al-Manṣūrī was himself a Mamluk in the service of the Sultan Qalā'ūn, rising to high office during the reign of Qalā'ūn's son, Nāṣir Muḥammad. Baybars saw much active service during Qalā'ūn's reign and was appointed governor of Kerak, where he served five years before being deposed by the Sultan Khalīl in 1291/690. Nāṣir Muḥammad elevated Baybars to high administrative and military positions (1294-95/693-94). Deposed when Nāṣir Muḥammad fell, Baybars regained prominence during that Sultan's second reign (1299-1309/698-708) until unseated in a power struggle at court.

Baybars al-Manṣūrī was instrumental in helping Nāṣir Muḥammad regain his throne for a third and final time in 1309/709; in return he was appointed the Sultan's second-in-command. However, his career underwent a reversal, common enough in Mamluk times, and he was imprisoned for five years in 1312/712.

Baybars wrote a lengthy study of Islam's development, and his discussions of the Mamluks are naturally informed by his own firsthand experiences, much like Ibn Khaldūn at a later date. He also was the author of a shorter history that concentrated on the Mamluks.

BEG see BEY

BERKE KHAN see BARAKA KHAN

BEY/BEG (ar. BAY). A Ottoman ranking with the meaning "lord," "Bey" was therefore roughly equivalent to the Mamluk title "Amīr." The duties of the beys varied widely and depended as much on the power and position of the individual bey as any clearly defined role. In the Ottoman hierarchy, beys ranked below Pashas. As with the latter title, "bey" often came to be used as an honorific. The title was abolished after the 1952 Revolution in Egypt.

BEYLICATE. The Beylicate in Egypt was a group of high military officers who worked technically in association with the Ottoman governor. In the exercise of their duties (which covered different aspects and areas of administration, and changed through the Ottoman period) the Beylicate was supported by their households of Mamluks. By the seventeenth/eleventh century, the Beylicate as a group and individually began actively to challenge the position of the governor. By the eighteenth/twelfth century, the Beylicate became the source of several independent rulers.

The twenty-four members of the Beylicate were largely but not exclusively Circassian in origin, and had the prerogative for the two high offices of the Ottoman hierarchy, Amīr al-Ḥajj (leader of the pilgrim caravan) and Shaykh al-Balad, as well as for the office of Qā'im Maqām (acting Viceroy) and Deftedar (financial controller). Beys were also appointed as governors of Upper Egypt (Ḥākim aṣ-Ṣaᶜīd) and in other Egyptian provinces. Elevation to the beylicate involved payment of a hefty stipend, the Khidmat as-Sanjāqiyya.

In time the beys began to form power structures paralleling that of the Viceroy and his Ottoman establishment. Their military functions, carried out as sirdars, or commanders of units, and guardians of the tribute convoy to Istanbul, permitted them to form alliances with elements within the Ottoman corps. As the beys were drawn from the supporters of whichever faction or group was dominant, the beylicate itself reflected the ascendancy of either the Qāsimiyya, Faqāriyya, or Qāzdughliyya as these factions rose and fell in power. Additionally, the beylicate, being a flexible institution with few defined roles, permitted an ambitious bey to seize opportunities as they arose, both within the government and among his peers.

The importance of individual beys waxed and waned as their factions fought for supremacy (in Arabic, rī'asa), and toward the end of the Ottoman period the only way for the Ottoman Viceroy to maintain any semblance of power was to exploit these factional struggles. Nonetheless, by the middle of the eighteenth century the emergence of ᶜAlī Bey, in 1763/1176-77, marked the final triumph of the beys over the Viceroys. ᶜAlī secured the dismissal of the Ottoman governor during his reign, and his successors dominated the remaining three decades of Ottoman rule until the ascendancy of Muḥammad ᶜAlī.

BILBAY (AZ-ẒĀHIR SAYF AD-DĪN BILBAY) (r. 1467/862). Burjī Mamluk Sultan who headed the Ẓāhirite faction of Mamluks, Bilbay held power for two months in the interregnum between the death of Khūshqadam and the rise of Qā'it Bay, before being displaced by Timurbughā. It is alleged in some sources that Bilbay was insane; after his deposition he was imprisoned in Alexandria.

BILHARZ, THEODORE and BILHARZIA see CLOT BEY

BLACK BOOK see UBAID, WILLIAM MAKRAM

BLACK SATURDAY/THE BURNING OF CAIRO. On 26 January 1952, in reaction to a British attack on the Ismailiyya police headquarters that resulted in fifty Egyptian deaths and many injuries, a mob burned sections of the city of Cairo, concentrating on British property and establishments with foreign associations. It appears that there were organized elements in the crowd, on both the left and right wing, and possibly involvement by some of the country's politicians with the initial outbreak of violence, though no one apparently foresaw the extent of the destruction. The King and the leaders of the Wafd Party, which was in power at the time, blamed each other for the failure to call in troops earlier. By the time the Egyptian army was alerted most of the damage had been done.

Black Saturday nearly occasioned another British military occupation, but this was narrowly averted by the Egyptian army's restoration of order. A total of £3.4 million damage was done to British and foreign property, and probably sixty or seventy people lost their lives, including nine British nationals. The Wafd government of Nahhas fell, and Ali Mahir formed a short-lived government. The political and domestic instability which followed were among the factors leading to the eventual coup d'état on 23 July.

BLUE SHIRTS (AL-QIMṢĀN AZ-ZARQĀ). Paramilitary youth group set up in December 1935 by students supporting the Wafd Party, the Blue Shirts were meant to counter the growing appeal of the Green Shirts, a similar youth organization established by Ahmad Husayn's Misr al-Fatat (Young Egypt) Party. The Blue Shirts were closely allied to Nahhas and Ubaid in the Wafd leadership.

Both the Blue Shirts and Green Shirts were especially active after the 1936 Anglo-Egyptian Treaty, which proved disappointing to many Egyptian nationalists. The shirt organizations were disarmed in December 1936 and some of their paramilitary features, such as armbands, forbidden. The Blue Shirts revived in the autumn of 1937 following the expulsion of Nuqrashi Pasha (who opposed them) from the Wafd Party and the growing tension between King Faruq and the Wafd government of Nahhas. The organization was proscribed once more when Mahmud Pasha formed a government in December 1937, following a series of violent street clashes between, and agitation by, the two groups. The Blue Shirts dissolved themselves thereafter, having lost the support of their own leadership and in view of the government's opposition.

BLUNT, WILFRED SCAWEN (1840-1922). English writer, explorer, and supporter of the Egyptian nationalist cause, Blunt was for many years the effective British opposition to the policies of Britain, and particularly of Lord Cromer, in Egypt. A friend of Ahmad Arabi and Muhammad Abduh, an adviser to the first nationalist party (whose platform and program he helped draft and publicize in England), and a mediator between the nationalists and the British government, Blunt played an important role in the events surrounding the British invasion of Egypt and subsequent de facto colonization of the country.

Widely traveled in the Middle East, Blunt bought a home near Cairo in 1881. He initiated discussions with various nationalist leaders and intervened continually both publicly and privately with the British government on the Egyptian question. In the aftermath of the Arabi Rebellion, he was banned from Egypt for three years. Following the Dinshaway Incident in 1906 Blunt was responsible for arranging a meeting between the new British Prime Minister, Campbell Bannerman, and the nationalist leader Mustafa Kamil, in which the latter secured the promise of increased autonomy for the Egyptian government. Blunt returned several times to Egypt, and his wife died at their home there in 1915.

Among Blunt's writings on Egypt and Islam The Secret History of the British Occupation of Egypt detailed the financial involvements of private British interests in the Egyptian economy, involvements that led these interests to press for a British occupation of Egypt. Blunt was regarded in Britain as overly sympathetic to the Egyptian nationalists, and his efforts on their behalf were largely dismissed by the supporters of Cromer in the British government.

BONAPARTE, NAPOLEON (1769-1821). Napoleon invaded Egypt in July 1798 in a brief but extremely important military occupation that was instrumental in starting Egypt's involvement with Europe and in reshaping the entire political and social structure of the country. The organization and equipment of Napoleon's troops had tremendous influence on Muhammad Ali, who emerged as leader of Egypt in 1805. The Egyptian army was subsequently remodeled on European lines, and possibly Napoleon's vision of himself as European leader became translated by Muhammad Ali into a similar role for himself within the Islamic world.

The scientists and observers who accompanied Napoleon began an encyclopedic study of Egypt, La Déscription de L'Égypte, a project that enjoyed Napoleon's enthusiastic support (he founded an institute to collect data on Egypt). His own attempts to present himself to the Egyptians as a leader in sympathy with Islam were not readily accepted by the majority of Egyptians, who rose in revolt during his stay. His leadership was rejected outright by the Mamluks and the beylicate, who fled Cairo to mount various campaigns against the French. Defeated in his attempt to conquer Syria from Egypt, Napoleon left the country in the summer of 1799, turning over command to General Kléber. The previous year he had established a diwan, or consultative council of notables, but the hopes this act represented, of French presence, were not realized.

BRIONI DECLARATION. In July 1956 President Nasser and President Tito met at Brioni, in Yugoslavia, where they were later joined by Prime Minister Nehru. Following their discussions the leaders issued a communiqué stressing their commitment to Positive Neutralism as a foreign policy. The ideology evolved at the Brioni Meeting helped define the Egyptian dedication to the nonaligned movement following the 1955 Bandung Conference, in which Tito and Prime Minister Nehru had also featured prominently. The Brioni Declaration, in addition to affirming the signatories' commitment to peaceful coexistence, collective security and nuclear disarmament, also addressed the specific problems of the Middle East and the centrality of the Palestinian issue in resolving them.

The significance of the Declaration lay as much in the coordination and cooperation of Tito and Nasser as in the commitments themselves. The relationship between these two leaders was extremely influential in shaping Nasser's thinking on both foreign and domestic issues.

BREAD RIOTS see JANUARY RIOTS

BUREAUCRACY. Virtually since earliest pharaonic times the need to control the agricultural pattern of a country completely dependent on irrigation for its water supplies helped create a bureaucratic system that in its own way is as characteristic of Egypt as the Pyramids. The bureaucratic system built up through the years, decades, centuries, and millennia has proved a remarkably durable one, long surviving the rulers who attempted to change it. The Egyptian bureaucracy always had as its object the extremely centralized control of a riverine society, the collection of revenue, and the supervision of agricultural production. Centralized control of the bureaucracy itself was established by the organization of key networks within the administrative structure. Despite the vagaries of civil wars, rebellions, and changes of regime, nothing substantially interrupted Egypt's bureaucratic lifelines. In times of difficulties the profile of the bureaucratic system may have lowered, but the structure remained to reassert itself when the famine, civil strife, or struggle for power was over and central authority was reestablished. Egypt's Muslim conquerors were thus heirs to a bureaucracy whose development long preceded their arrival in the country, and which they were able to direct to their own ends.

At various points in the Muslim period individual administrators and families of administrators would arise and gain prominence and even exercise near-supreme power; some of these families gained cultural and intellectual renown. But as a rule the majority of Egypt's bureaucrats--Muslim, Christian, and Jewish--were the executors of policies set by the viziers and rulers above them. The strength of the Egyptian bureaucracy enabled it to make the transition into the Muslim period with only slight alterations. The most fundamental changes took place at the level of personnel, as the pace of Islamicization heightened and the Muslims gradually replaced some (though by no means all) Christian and Jewish bureaucrats, and Arabic replaced Greek as Egypt's administrative language.

The relationship between the center and the bureaucracy varied as regimes changed; the degree of control sought by individual rulers, changes in economic policy, and the condition of the country and the economy all influenced the bureaucracy's freedom to act. For example, during the Ottoman period (1517-1798/922-1213) there were structural reforms of the bureaucracy accompanied by the long struggle of the ancien régime of Mamluks to regain power through those bureaucratic posts they held or controlled. The Ottomans themselves affected the bureaucracy in a formalistic way, adding certain refinements to the rigidity of a well-established system, with their own systems of tax collection and revenue assessment, and a political focus outside Egypt.

Muhammad Ali sought to reform the bureaucracy, in line with his reform of many other aspects of Egyptian life, by introducing higher standards of education, more modern administrative techniques, and a government printing press to keep bureaucrats informed about policy and procedure. Under the reign of his grandson Ismail an increasing number of Europeans joined the bureaucracy in administrative and supervisory capacities, especially following the imposition of Dual Control in 1876 by France and Great Britain. This trend naturally increased after the formal intervention of Britain militarily in 1882, an intervention occasioned by Egyptian nationalist resistance to the growing influence of Europeans in Egypt's government and administration. From 1883 until 1936 this foreign presence created an upper level of European bureaucratic control, imposing certain alterations in the decision-making process within the bureaucracy, but, more importantly, depriving several generations of Egyptians of the practical experience of managing their own administration. Under the British, ministerial structures were established mirroring their British counterparts. Agriculture and Waqfs (religious endowments) were placed under autonomous ministries by Kitchener.

Beginning with the Declaration of 1922, whereby Britain unilaterally granted Egypt a limited independence, and especially after the Anglo-Egyptian Treaty of 1936, the bureaucracy began a process of re-Egyptianization. This became a point of conflict between Britain and Egypt, as the former tried to preserve the position and prerogatives of its nationals and the latter pressed for their replacement. The issue was not really resolved until after the Second World War, when natural wastage and retirement permitted the former British administrators to be nearly completely replaced by Egyptians.

Even before the Revolution of 1952 the Egyptian bureaucracy was a major employer of the country's educated youth, but the bureaucracy really came into its own as a political force in the post-Revolutionary period, as it became charged with the responsibility for implementation of the government's economic planning and policies. The bureaucracy enlarged and expanded its role as employer for the thousands of graduates of Egyptian universities when the Nasser regime promised government jobs to these graduates. It afforded many individuals the chance to build a power base outside the executive and military wings of the government, and by the 1960s the bureaucracy was the civilian counterweight to the military, though the latter had many representatives scattered in the higher levels of the former.

Nasser divided the bureaucracy into functional fiefdoms to prevent the accumulation of too much power in any one sector or level. While the division did not always succeed in this task, the organization of the bureaucracy as well as the sometimes intense conflicts between the various ministries did serve as a brake to consistent action. The criteria of bureaucratic survival in the post-Revolutionary period became loyalty, not performance. Those government organizations that did depend on effective action, such as the Suez Canal Authority, were placed outside the bureaucracy proper. Reforms introduced in the early 1960s, with their automatic pay raises and regulated staffing levels, hindered rather than helped efforts at improving bureaucratic efficiency.

The Nasser government's promise of a job to every university graduate helped push the number of bureaucrats to one million by the early 1970s. Some of these bureaucrats have been given official leave to be employed in the labor-importing countries of the Arabian Gulf and Libya, temporarily relieving pressure on the job market at home. But the Sadat government's renewed commitment, made in 1979, to increasing public employment for graduates presaged a further expansion of the bureaucratic sector.

Criticism of the bureaucracy, particularly its performance in the public-sector companies and in the social services, became rife in the wake of President Sadat's liberalizations in 1974. Lengthy newspaper exposés during this period and afterward have drawn popular and official attention to the full dimensions of the problems within Egypt's bureaucracies. The advent of the Open Door Policy, with its commitment to free-market capitalism, has also created certain pressures on the bureaucracy to increase the standards of its performance and efficiency. Despite changes in the economy in recent years the bureaucracy remains the preferred form of employment for many young Egyptians, representing a secure (if low-paid) job with social-welfare benefits not available to many other Egyptians.

BURJĪ/CIRCASSIAN MAMLUKS (1382-1517/784-922). The Baḥrī Mamluk Sultan Qalā'ūn established a regiment of Mamluks headquartered in the fortified towers (in Arabic, burj) of the Citadel overlooking Cairo. These Burjī Mamluks, as they have been termed by some historians, were largely Circassian in origin, and like their Baḥrī predecessors eventually took power from the rulers they were meant to protect.

The Burjī Mamluk period is noteworthy for two major events outside Egypt: the final disappearance of the threat posed by Tīmūr to the survival of Egypt by his death in 1405/808 and the growing power of the Ottomans, who by 1517/922 were to take Egypt from the Burjīs. These two events mark the opening and closing episodes of the period; between these events Egypt was afflicted by lengthy periods of anarchy as numbers of individual Burjī Mamluks tried to gain and hold on to power. Those who did manage to hold on to power for any length of time betrayed a rapaciousness remarkable even by the standards of a country that had had more than its fair share of greedy rulers. In consequence one finds rebellions in Egypt and the provinces in 1399/801 (spurred on by the proximity of Tīmūr and the Mongols), in 1412/815, 1444/848, and in 1490/895. Famine and plague in 1403/806, the 1430s/830s, and 1492/897 decimated and impoverished the population and the Mamluks themselves.

Despite the rather grim situation in Egypt the Burjī period saw a flowering of Islamic historiography, with al-Maqrizi, Ibn Taghrī-Birdī, Baybars al-Manṣūri, and as-Siyūtī. The Sultans Barqūq, Qā'it Bay, and Qānṣuh al-Ghawrī left important monuments. Trade links with India were improved, a new port was opened at Jeddah, and heavy duties on trade helped fill the coffers of the Sultan, which military and court expenditures rapidly emptied. During the reign of Barsbay, the Burjī Mamluks added Cyprus and parts of Little Armenia to their territories. Internally, the latter half of the Burjī period saw the imposition of monopolies on several vital commodities, with negative consequences for their supply and price.

The Burjī Mamluks eventually divided into four major factions structured on the primary households of Mamluks established by past Sultans. These factions, the Ashrafiyya (Barsbāy), Ẓāhiriyya (Barqūq and Jaqmaq), Mu'ayyadiyya (Mu'ayyad Shaykh), and Nāṣiriyya (Faraj), with their nearly continual in-fighting, contributed much to the domestic chaos in Cairo and instability at court during this period. Nor were the Burjis able to appreciate fully or respond to the true dimensions of the threat posed to them by the Ottomans. The Burjī Sultan Qā'it Bay gave his support to Jem, who was contending for the Ottoman throne against his brother Bāyazīd in 1481/886. This proved to be a bad choice, as Bāyazīd emerged victorious and no friend of the Mamluks. The two powers fought inconclusively between 1485/890 and 1490/896.

The Burjīs were also unable to meet the military challenge presented by the Portuguese navy, which was moving in to dominate the sea routes along which the vital spice trade was carried. The Portuguese took Socotra in the Gulf of Aden in 1505/910, defeated the Mamluks, and all but destroyed their navy in a series of battles between 1505/914 and 1509/914. The accession of the Ottoman Sultan Selīm I ("the Grim") in 1512/918 decided the Ottomans on the expansionist course that carried them to Cairo. Al-Ghawrī watched, his treasury rapidly dwindling, as the Ottomans defeated their immediate opponents, the Persians, and then turned against Egypt. Selīm was able to profit from the rivalry between the Mamluk governors in Syria and their Egyptian colleagues, securing the defection of Kha'ir Bay, governor of Aleppo, and a number of Syrian Mamluks.

The Burjī Mamluks and the Ottomans met in battle at Marj Dābiq, north of Aleppo, Syria, in 1516/921. The Mamluks were utterly routed by the Ottomans, who had mastered the use of artillery which the bulk of al-Ghawrī's army, traditionally trained Mamluks, rejected as ungentlemanly. Selīm offered al-Ghawrī's successor, the last Burjī Mamluk Sultan, Tūmān Bay, the chance to surrender, but many of the Mamluks around Tūmān Bay, and eventually the new Sultan himself, refused. Selīm entered Cairo in January 1517/922, and the conquest of Egypt was completed by the spring of that year.

Burjī Mamluk Sultans:

[For individual entries, look under names underlined]

1382/784	Aẓ-Ẓāhir Sayf ad-Dīn Barqūq (first reign)
1389/791	Ḥājjī II (Baḥrī, second reign)
1390/792	Barqūq (second reign)
1399/801	An-Nāṣir Nāṣir ad-Dīn Faraj (first reign)
1405/808	Al-Manṣūr ᶜIzz ad-Dīn ᶜAbd al-ᶜAzīz
1405/808	Faraj (second reign)
1412/815	Al-ᶜĀdil al-Mustaᶜīn (ᶜAbbāsid Caliph)
1412/815	Al-Mu'ayyad Sayf ad-Dīn Shaykh
1421/824	Al-Muẓaffar Aḥmad
1421/824	Aẓ-Ẓāhir Sayf ad-Dīn Ṭaṭār
1421/824	Aṣ-Ṣālih Nāṣir ad-Dīn Muḥammad
1422/825	Al-Ashraf Sayf ad-Dīn Barsbāy
1437/841	Al-ᶜAzīz Jamāl ad-Dīn Yūsuf
1438/842	Aẓ-Ẓāhir Sayf ad-Dīn Jaqmaq
1453/857	Al-Manṣūr Fakhr ad-Dīn ᶜUthmān
1453/857	Al-Ashraf Sayf ad-Dīn Ināl
1461/865	Al-Mu'ayyad Shihāb ad-Dīn Aḥmad

1461/865	Aẓ-Ẓāhir Sayf ad-Dīn Khūshqadam
1467/872	Aẓ-Ẓāhir Sayf ad-Dīn Bilbay
1468/872	Aẓ-Ẓāhir Timurbughā
1468/872	Al-Ashraf Sayf ad-Dīn Qā'it Bay
1496/901	An-Nāṣir Muḥammad
1498/903	Aẓ-Ẓāhir Qānṣūḥ
1500/905	Al-Ashraf Jānbalāt
1501/906	Al-ᶜĀdil Sayf ad-Dīn Tūmān Bay
1501/906	Al-Ashraf Qānṣūḥ al-Ghawrī
1517/922	Al-Ashraf Tūmān Bay

BUTLER COMMISSION REPORT. In 1931 the Sidqi government in Egypt asked the ILO to examine the conditions of workers in Egypt. The findings of the investigator, Harold Butler, were published in 1932. The Butler Report, the first systematic study of Egypt's labor situation, studied seasonal labor in the agricultural sector, rural-urban migration, and child labor. The report also examined unemployment, the problems caused by urban migration, and described working conditions in the different economic sectors. Butler put forth various recommendations for comprehensive protective legislation. In 1933 the first general labor law was passed, followed in 1936 by a noncompulsory workmen's compensation scheme. Compulsory workmen's compensation was not introduced until 1942, under the Wafd government of Nahhas.

BUTRUS GHALI PASHA (1846-1910). Prime Minister of Egypt from 1908 until his assassination in 1910, Butrus Ghali was the most prominent Copt among nationalist politicians of his era. He began his political service under the Khedive Tawfiq, serving as Minister of Justice, Finance, and Foreign Affairs at various times, prior to his appointment as Prime Minister by Abbas in 1908. His conciliatory attitude toward the British aroused the opposition of the Nationalists, particularly Muhammad Farid.

As Foreign Minister in the government of his predecessor, Mustafa Fahmi, Butrus Ghali handled the negotiations over the Anglo-Egyptian Condominium in the Sudan. Butrus Ghali was

Minister of Justice at the time of the Dinshaway Incident in 1906 and was involved in the controversial trial of the accused Egyptian villagers. During his terms as Prime Minister he entered into negotiations for prolongation of the Suez Canal Company lease. His assassination in February 1910 followed his decision to support a proposed extension to the Suez Canal Company's concession for forty years beyond the expiry of the original concession in 1968, in exchange for increased payments to Egypt. His re-activation of press censorship was also unpopular.

Butrus Ghali Pasha was extremely active in the attempts to reform and modernize the Coptic Church in the latter part of the nineteenth century. The death of this prominent Copt caused a split in the nationalist movement between Copts and Muslims (his assassin was a Muslim) that took several years to heal.

BUTRUS GHALI, BUTRUS (1922-). Deputy Foreign Minister in the government of Anwar Sadat, appointed in 1977, Butrus Ghali went on to become Minister of State for Foreign Affairs in 1978, an appointment renewed in the new cabinet formed in May 1980, and in the October 1981 cabinet formed by President Mubarak after the assassination of Anwar Sadat.

Butrus Ghali was originally a university professor of political science at a number of educational institutions in Egypt and overseas. He was one of the first faculty members at the School of Economics and Political Science established at Cairo University in 1961 and is a member of the Center for Arab, African, and Asian Studies under the High Council for Arts, Letters, and Social Sciences. He also served as editor of the bimonthly on international politics published by the newspaper Al-Ahram and has participated in a number of international legal commissions. Butrus Ghali accompanied President Sadat on his journey to Jerusalem in November 1977 and has been one of the major negotiators during the various stages of the Egyptian-Israeli peace talks.

BUTRUS GHALI, MIRIT. Egyptian nationalist politician and reformer, Mirit Butrus Ghali published, in 1938, a political program called Policy of Tomorrow, combining social reform with the encouragement of private enterprise, carried out along set lines of development. He became linked in 1945 with a reformist front organization, the Gama^{c}at al-Nahda al-Qawmiyya (Association of National Renaissance), which proposed a twenty-five-year program of agrarian reforms, nationalization of landholding and inheritance patterns, and other measures connected with land use that prefigured aspects of Egypt's first proposed agrarian-reform law introduced after the 1952 Revolution. In 1950, continuing his involvement with land reform, Butrus Ghali introduced a bill to the Egyptian parliament calling for a 100-feddan limit on individual landholding.

Following the ban on political involvement by pre-Revolutionary politicians in January 1953 Butrus Ghali retired from political life and is now active in the affairs of the Coptic Church and in research on Coptic studies and archaeology.

-C-

CAIRO (AL-QĀHIRA). Capital of Egypt, Cairo was founded in 969/358 by the Fāṭimid general Jawhar aṣ-Ṣiqillī following his conquest of the country. At the time of its foundation al-Fusṭāṭ was the main commercial and residential center, and al-Qāhira was envisaged as a royal city. It was divided into four ḥaras, or quarters, with splendid Caliphal palaces, gardens, parade grounds, and baths, all enclosed in fortifications. Contemporary accounts of the city by travelers from other parts of the Islamic world provide glowing descriptions of its splendor, but in fact al-Qāhira was for many decades commercially eclipsed by al-Fusṭāṭ, being rather the center of the Fāṭimids' ceremonial and court life. New walls and gates were added during the vizierate of Badr al-Jamālī (1074-94/466-90); three of these gates--Bāb an-Nāṣir, Bāb al-Futūḥ, and Bāb az-Ẓuwayla--survive.

At the end of the Fāṭimid period, when Cairo was under threat of the Crusaders, the vizier Shāwar burned al-Fusṭāṭ (in 1168/564) and threatened to do the same to Cairo. Al-Fusṭāṭ never fully recovered from this, and over the next few centuries gradually lost position to Cairo.

With the arrival of the Ayyūbids in power in 1171/567 Cairo's character as a royal city changed. New buildings rose within the original Fāṭimid walls, and the four quarters of the city were fortified with walls and towers. In 1176/572 Ṣalāḥ ad-Dīn began construction of the Citadel to the southeast, which was to become the residence of his successors and one of the main army barracks.

The growth in Cairo's population, despite successive outbreaks of plague, continued through the Mamluk period, and Cairo remained one of the two or three great centers of the Islamic world, with its schools, universities, and courts. The city developed an artistic and intellectual tradition that attracted visitors and scholars from all parts of the Muslim world.

The advent of the Muhammad Ali dynasty in the nineteenth century brought further transformations to Cairo, as the city expanded territorially and became increasingly linked with the other major cities in Egypt and with the outside world. Large areas of Cairo on the East Bank of the Nile had lakes, some used for ceremonial and recreational purposes but others left behind as the Nile flood receded each year, creating an unhealthy atmosphere in the city. The drainage and filling in of these areas near Izbakiyya and Bab al-Luq in modern Cairo in the 1820s added to the land available for building in the city and permitted improvement of sanitation. During the reign of the Khedive Ismail a European-style quarter was built in the area, along with a magnificent Opera House (finished in 1869). Railroad links with Alexandria and Suez were completed in 1855-56. At the time of the British occupation of the country Cairo was veritably a potpourri of all the architectural styles from the different periods in its history, giving the city an architectural heritage that was and is unique in the Islamic world.

As Egypt expanded economically in the late nineteenth and twentieth centuries, there was a substantial rise in rural migration to the cities, but particularly to Cairo. This surge in urban population growth, fueled by the population pressure in rural areas that was forcing people off the land, helped create much of the urban density characteristic of modern Cairo, as the limits of its lateral growth were slowed and intense habitation began. Its population in 1980 was estimated as approaching 14 million (from approximately 4 million in 1967), with variations in density from the relatively open suburbs, especially on the West Bank of the Nile, to the densely crowded older city areas. The average population density in the city varies from 12,000 to 110,000 per square kilometer.

Though Cairo has many serious problems of population, housing, services, and transport, it has never lost its position as one of the premier cities in the Islamic world in terms of volume of cultural riches it has to offer: universities, publishers, film industry, artists, and writers. Cairo's role as the headquarters of many pan-Islamic and Third World groupings has faded somewhat as alternative headquarters have been developed, and especially since the Arab Boycott saw the removal of the Arab League headquarters to Tunis, though its importance as an Arab capital has continued.

CAIRO ARAB SUMMIT (1964) see ARAB SUMMITS

CAISSE DE LA DETTE PUBLIQUE. A fiscal supervisory body, the Caisse was established in 1876 by Egypt's creditors to regulate and restore order to Egypt's economy through the management of its revenues and to ensure repayment of the massive external debt built up by the Khedive Ismail. The British first sent an investigatory team to Egypt in 1875; the Cave Mission made certain recommendations for the creation of a system of international controls. This was followed by a French mission shortly afterward.

In November 1876 an Anglo-French mission on behalf of Egypt's creditors set up the Caisse, with one British and one French economic adviser. The Caisse also had Italian and Austrian representatives, with Germany and Russia gaining representation in 1885. In 1878 Major Baring (later Lord Cromer) was made a member of the Caisse when it extended its control to the Khedive's personal finances and estates.

Ismail accepted the Caisse's demands (through a Commission of Inquiry) for the formation of a "European" ministry in 1878, with European-controlled finance and public-works ministries, under Nubar Pasha. This "European" ministry, or cabinet, was the cause of the nationalist uproar which eventually led Ismail to dismiss it, an action that led to his own deposition by the Ottoman Sultan under European pressure.

The Caisse's initial plan of operation called for a combination of the entire Egyptian debt, floating and funded, into a unified debt of £91 million, at 7-percent interest. This was announced by Ismail at the time of the Caisse's creation. British opposition caused fresh negotiations to take place between their representative, Goschen, and Joubert for the French, and resulted in a reduction of the combined debt to £59 million through the removal of private French debts. The revenues collected by the Caisse would go toward paying this debt off, but the original payments schedule had to be revised in 1879 after it became apparent that the first revenue estimates were overly optimistic--£9.5 million per annum--while the government's revenue was actually one million pounds lower. In all, the Caisse took over half Egypt's annual revenues to pay off the interest and capital on its debt, which was an enormous drain on the Egyptian economy.

The Caisse's original functions were limited to receiving these assigned revenues on behalf of the creditors, but these functions expanded considerably in the early years of the group's existence. The crises of 1879-82 are directly linked to the resentment of Egypt's nationalists, both in the military and in the government, over their country's loss of real fiscal autonomy. A Commission of Liquidation in 1880 ameliorated conditions, but the Caisse ultimately managed to gain control of every aspect of the Egyptian domestic economy and its revenue sources. Its operations were slightly modified following the London Convention of 1885.

The arrangements under which the Caisse operated were changed with the Entente Cordiale of 1904, which reestablished the principle that the Caisse should be limited to receiving land tax revenues, returning certain surplus funds to Egypt's general administration. Its consent would no longer be required to issue new loans, nor would it continue to be empowered to limit administrative expenses. The entire funded debt of Egypt was to be liquidated in 1912, with the Caisse commissioners put on retainers.

Under the terms of the Montreux Convention (1937) the vestiges of the Caisse were to be wound up, which they eventually were in 1940.

CALIPHATE (EGYPTIAN) (1261-1517/659-923). The original role of the Caliphate in Islam--to provide leadership of the Muslim community following the death of the Prophet Muḥammad--had become in the course of Islam's expansion a political role as well. The Caliphate, first under the al-Khulafā' al-Rāshidūn, or rightly guided Caliphs (632-61/11-40), the Umayyads in Damascus (661-750/41-132), and finally and especially under the ᶜAbbāsids in Baghdad (749-1258/132-656) was in titular control of a vast empire. The power, or rather the authority, of the Caliphate derived from the lack of separation within Islam between the religious and political spheres. Additionally, the Caliphate maintained its moral power, even when the Islamic world was no longer politically united under its auspices. The Caliph, by his concordance and approval on their accession, maintained the link between the rulers of Egypt (however autonomous) and the center of Sunnī Islam at Baghdad. The Caliph's position was not without its problems, however. Ibn Ṭūlūn invited the ᶜAbbāsid Caliph al-Muᶜtamid to Egypt in 882/269 to escape the difficulties the latter was experiencing at his court in Baghdad.

The legitimatizing function of the Caliph was limited to those dynasts and rulers who belonged to the Sunnī, orthodox mainstream of Islam. In Egypt the Shīᶜa Fāṭimids (969-1171/358-567) had their own Caliph, who ruled in opposition to the Sunnī Caliph in Baghdad. With Ṣalāḥ ad-Dīn's restoration of Sunnī Islam in 1171/567 Egypt's nominal allegiance was once again rendered to the Caliph in Baghdad.

By the time of the Mongol destruction of the city of Baghdad, and of its ᶜAbbāsid Caliphate, in 1258/656 the Islamic world had already witnessed the shift of the Caliphate from Medina to Damascus to Baghdad, and (despite a brief revival of their power at the end of the twelfth/sixth century) the increasing domination of the Caliphs by the military men who were meant to be their protectors, but who ended by becoming their masters. The move, therefore, of the Caliphate (in the person of a distant relation of the last, murdered, ᶜAbbāsid Caliph) to Cairo in 1261/659 by the Mamluk Sultan Baybars completed in one sense the evolution of this office. Baybars saw, in the establishment of the Caliphate in Egypt, a means of providing the Mamluk Sultans with legitimacy in their control of what was in the post-Mongol period one of the preeminent Muslim countries and the center of their larger territorial holdings.

The first Egyptian ᶜAbbāsid Caliph took the name al-Mustanṣir and began his reign by attempting to assert his independence from Baybars. He insisted on leading a campaign to regain Baghdad; Baybars gave this his most grudging support, and al-Mustanṣir died several months later while on the march.

The subsequent Egyptian Caliphs lent moral authority, and little else, to the Sultans, although one Caliph, al-Mustaᶜīn, ruled briefly in 1412/815 during a six-month period when the various Mamluk contenders for the Sultanate fought it out. Otherwise the Caliphs in Egypt were minor court pensioners with a few ceremonial functions to perform on the accession of a new Sultan; they occasionally accompanied the Mamluks into battle.

In 1517/923 the last Egyptian Caliph was deposed by the Ottoman conqueror of Egypt, Selīm, and sent back to Istanbul. Some sources assert that at the time al-Mutawakkil III, the Caliph, transferred the rights and privileges of the Caliphate of Islam to Selīm. This is disputed by other, more authoritative sources. Nonetheless, the Caliphate was claimed by the Ottoman Sultans, and the abolition of the Caliphate in Turkey in 1924 by the Turkish republican government provoked an outcry throughout the Muslim world. Both King Fuad and his son, Faruq, made efforts to claim the Caliphate, but their candidacy was rejected in the strongest terms by the other Arab and Islamic states.

Egyptian Caliphs:

1261/659	Al-Mustanṣir
1261/660	Al-Ḥākim I
1302/701	Al-Mustakfī I
1340/740	Al-Wāthiq I
1341/741	Al-Ḥākim II
1352/753	Al-Mu^{c}tadid I
1362/763	Al-Mutawakkil I (first time)
1377/779	Al-Mu^{c}taṣim (first time)
1377/779	Al-Mutawakkil I (second time)
1383/785	Al-Wāthiq II
1386/788	Al-Mu^{c}taṣim (second time)
1389/791	Al-Mutawakkil I (third time)
1406/808	Al-Musta^{c}īn
1414/816	Al-Mu^{c}taḍid II
1441/845	Al-Mustakfī II
1451/855	Al-Qā'im
1455/859	Al-Mustanjid
1479/884	Al-Mutawakkil II
1497/903	Al-Mustamsik (first time)
1508/914	Al-Mutawakkil III (first time)
1516/922	Al-Mustamsik (second time)
1517/923	Al-Mutawakkil III (second time)

CAMP DAVID AGREEMENTS. President Anwar Sadat of Egypt and Israeli Premier Menachem Begin met in the United States with U.S. President Jimmy Carter in September 1978 to settle the difficulties that had arisen between Egypt and Israel in the course of their original negotiations over peace. The parties agreed to the following points within the overall text: the basis for settling the dispute between Israel and its neighbors was to be UN Resolution 242 and that negotiations between Israel and its neighbors should be carried out in the framework of a comprehensive, just, and durable peace based on Resolutions 242 and 338.

The negotiating framework was meant to be open to all parties to the Arab-Israeli conflict, and on the subject of the West Bank and Gaza, Egypt, Israel, and Jordan (which was not a party to the Camp David accords or the subsequent peace treaty), together with a representative of the Palestinian people, would negotiate. The Camp David meeting followed a six-month period when direct peace talks between Egypt and Israel had been interrupted by the issues of the Israeli settlements in Sinai and the West Bank, the Israeli invasion of southern Lebanon, the inconclusive Leeds Castle meeting (July 1978), and the real prospect of a breakdown in any further negotiations.

To bring these negotiations on the West Bank and Gaza to fruition Egypt and Israel agreed on transitional arrangements that would occur over a five-year period. In order to provide autonomy for the inhabitants under these arrangements the Israeli military government and its civilian administration would be withdrawn as soon as a self-governing authority had been freely elected by the inhabitants of the two areas. Egypt, Israel, and Jordan would agree on the mode of establishing the elected, self-governing authority in the West Bank and Gaza, with the negotiating teams having possible Palestinian representation and being responsible for reaching an agreement as to the powers and authorities of the self-governing authority in the West Bank and Gaza. A withdrawal of Israeli troops would take place, with those remaining deployed in specific agreed locations. A future agreement would also be concluded making provision for internal and external security and policing.

Once a self-governing authority was established, a five-year transition period would begin. No later than the third year of this period, negotiations would take place to determine the relationship of the West Bank and Gaza to their neighbors, as well as their final status, and to conclude a peace treaty between Jordan and Israel by the end of the transitional period. The negotiators would be divided into separate committees concerned with the financial status and relationship of the West Bank and Gaza, and with the peace treaty.

The Peace Treaty negotiations, based on UN Security Council Resolution 242, would deal with border and security arrangements and would be structured to protect Palestinian interests and rights, particularly the refugee problem.

Egypt and Israel agreed to resolve their disputes peacefully, and to attempt to negotiate and sign a peace treaty within three months, while inviting other parties to join the negotiations. Under the terms of Camp David, Egypt and Israel agreed to establish a claims commission and explore areas of economic cooperation. The U.S. would participate in future negotiations, and any Peace Treaty that emerged would be put before the UN Security Council for approval. Egypt received (a) full sovereignty over the border between itself and mandated Palestine, (b) the promised withdrawal of Israel from the Sinai, (c) the use, for commercial purposes only, of the Sinai airfields seized by Israel in 1967, and (d) stationing of UN troops to oversee border security. Both parties agreed on the construction of a road across the Sinai to Jordan, with free access by all parties, and Israel gained the right of free passage through the Suez Canal and the Straits of Tiran.

The Peace Treaty based on the Camp David Accords was signed in March 1979 and approved by the Egyptians in a referendum in April 1979. The first partial Israeli pullback in Sinai occurred in June 1979. Relations between Egypt and Israel were established in February 1980, with the exchange of ambassadors, but negotiations, "the Camp David process," on all other aspects of the treaties and accords relating to the position of the Palestinians and the West Bank have been continually stalled by conflicting Egyptian and Israeli interpretations of the meaning of the various provisions of the accords especially on the issue of future Israeli settlements on the West Bank, and Israeli understanding of the term "autonomy." Egypt has been unsuccessful in convincing any other front-line Arab states to join these negotiations, which have been widely and persistently condemned by the Arab world for their failure to address the Palestinian issue.

The assassination of President Anwar Sadat on 6 October 1981 has not lessened official Egyptian commitment to the Camp David process. Whether this process can be maintained in the post-

Sadat period, and in the face of domestic opposition from certain quarters in both countries, remains problematic.

CAPITULATIONS. A series of legal concessions made by the Egyptian government to various European powers, the capitulations granted nationals of these countries extraterritoriality in Egypt. Several of the capitulations in Egypt were originally granted by the Ottoman Sultan, Egypt having been part of the Ottoman capitulatory system since the sixteenth century. This was renewed by the Ottoman Sultan in 1841, covering legal and tax status.

Under the capitulations criminal offenses committed by foreigners were not under the jurisdiction of Egyptian courts but were tried under the courts and law of the offender's native country: this resulted in the establishment of courts in the various consulates of the foreign countries represented in Egypt. The capitulatory system had its origin in the principle of the personal rather than territorial nature of law, in the sense that individuals had the right to be tried for offenses by their own nationals. In practice, however, the results of the extraterritoriality granted foreigners under the capitulations were to give Europeans in Egypt virtual freedom from all Egyptian law.

In 1867, following his purchase from the Ottoman Sultan of the right to negotiate with foreign powers, the Khedive Ismail addressed notes to each of the governments with which Egypt had a capitulatory agreement, expressing Egypt's desire for an immediate legal reform to obviate the need for the consular courts. Nubar Pasha proposed a system of mixed courts, in which Egyptian judges sat with their European colleagues. Though mixed courts were instituted in 1875-76, criminal cases continued to be heard in consular courts.

Efforts by the Minister of Justice, Husayn Fakhri Pasha, to reform the legal system in the late 1870s, the introduction of a new Civil Code in 1883, and the general opposition of several Egyptian governments did not affect the overall operation of the capitulatory system, which was finally abolished in Egypt under the terms of the 1937 Montreux Convention.

CAVE MISSION. The growing indebtedness of the Khedive Ismail to his European creditors led a group of British bankers to press their government to investigate the fiscal situation in Egypt. In 1875 Stephen Cave and Sir John Stokes were sent to Egypt at the request of the Khedive; after an examination of the country's revenues (which were at that time not separated from those of Ismail himself) and expenditures, the mission recommended placing Egypt's finances under the control of an international commission composed of the country's creditors. According to the mission's findings, Egypt's expenditures for the previous ten years were £158 million, with revenues of only £95 million; £41 million were committed to interest payments on loans dating from 1862, with increased borrowing nearly every year thereafter. Cave made a number of sharp but reasonable judgments on the pace and quality of Egypt's development.

The Cave Mission, followed by a similar group sent by the French government, led to the establishment of Dual Control of the Egyptian economy in the following year. This began a period of ever-increasing British involvement, spurred initially by financial interests and gradually developing into full political control.

CHAMBER OF DEPUTIES see ASSEMBLY OF DELEGATES

CHAMPOLLION, JEAN FRANÇOIS (1790-1832). With Thomas Young, Jean François Champollion began the deciphering of the famous Rosetta Stone in 1821, eventually breaking the code of the hieroglyphs and making possible the modern study of Egyptology. Champollion was among the scientists and scholars who accompanied the French invasion of Egypt in 1798 and in 1811-14 published _L'Égypte sous les pharaohs_, the first modern study by a European of pharaonic Egypt. Through his association with the French Institute in Cairo, he had great influence on the evolution of the discipline of Egyptology in Egypt and was the founder of Egyptological studies in France. Champollion's career inside and outside Egypt was in many ways demonstrative of the important cultural links forged between Egypt and Europe during Muhammad Ali's time.

CHARTER OF NATIONAL ACTION. The Charter of National Action (1962) was a comprehensive policy statement on Egypt's political future, issued after the breakup of the union with Syria and a rethinking of Egypt's political goals. On 21 May 1962 the charter was presented to the Congress of Popular Forces by President Nasser. The charter consolidated and clarified the country's legal and economic situation after the introduction of the Socialist Laws the previous year; it promised that the government would ensure essential social control over economic development, and detailed the regime's ideological precepts. The charter also provided for the formation of a new political grouping, the Arab Socialist Union, and for the election of a National Assembly whose members would be drawn from the ASU.

The "Guide for Revolutionary Action" outlined in the charter provided that (a) basic economic infrastructure would be publicly owned, (b) the bulk of all types of industry would be either under public ownership or public-sector control, (c) all imports and three-quarters of all exports would be controlled by the government, (d) banks and insurance companies that were still in private hands would be nationalized, and (e) nonexploitative private land ownership would be allowed to continue. The solution to Egypt's long-term socioeconomic problems was to be found in a massive increase in industrialization and a consequent rise in the GNP. The charter also confirmed Egypt's regional links and pledged Egypt to maintain regional security and support liberation movements in the rest of the Third World.

The Charter of National Action was the major ideological statement of the last half of the Nasser regime; it acknowledged that in the past no consistent radical program or ideology had been evolved since the presentation of the Six Points in 1952. The emphasis placed by the charter on socialism and secularism provoked a reaction among the religious, some of whom led antigovernment demonstrations and were joined by many other opponents of the regime, who united behind their leadership. Despite this opposition, implementation of the charter continued; in March 1964 the first elections were held.

The failure of the regime to deliver many of the social benefits promised in the charter, as well as the further clamp-down on free political expression during this period, may have helped spur the series of industrial and popular protests that afflicted Egypt in 1964-66. The Arab Socialist Union continued to be a dominant force in government-directed political life until 1971, when the organization, and the charter principles, began to be reexamined by the Sadat regime.

CHEETHAM, MILNE (1869-1938). Counsellor of the British government in Egypt from 1910 to 1919, Milne Cheetham was Acting High Commissioner and Minister Plenipotentiary in 1914-15 and in the absence of Sir Henry McMahon and Sir Reginald Wingate thereafter. Cheetham was regarded as a reasonable and efficient administrator who oversaw the transition from the Khedive Abbas II to the Sultan Husayn Kamil, and the establishment of the British Protectorate in 1914. Cheetham was successful in resisting British attempts to annex Egypt formally, perceiving that as being out of line with nationalist sentiments in Egypt and with long-term British policy in the area. He did, however, support the exile of Zaghlul in 1919, an action that touched off the worst rebellion against the British since their occupation of the country.

CIRCASSIAN MAMLUKS see BURJĪ MAMLUKS

CITADEL (QAL^{c}Ā). Fortified administrative and residential compound in Cairo whose construction was started by the first Ayyūbid Sultan, Ṣalāḥ ad-Dīn (1171-93/566-89), and completed during the reign of the Sultan al-Kāmil (1218-38/615-35). The Citadel was partially modeled on Syrian castle forms, and its construction was supervised at various points by Qarāqūsh and al-^{c}Ādil. It was the former who sank the well that provided the Citadel's original water supply.

The gradual removal of the administration of Egypt to the Citadel was not completed until Mamluk times, though even thereafter certain administrative functions, such as those pertaining to southern Egypt, remained in al-Fusṭāṭ. From 1207/

604 the Citadel was the official residence of Egypt's rulers, a role it played down to Muhammad Ali's time. Successive dynasties added to the Citadel's walls and towers, most notably the Baḥrī Mamluk Sultan an-Nāṣir Muḥammad, who during his third reign (1309-40/709-41) also built a massive aqueduct to carry Nile water to the Citadel. The Citadel was the residence of the Circassian Mamluks, whose familiar name, "Burjī," derives from its towers (Ar. burj). Muhammad Ali began an enormous Ottoman-style mosque on the Citadel (completed in 1857), whose domes and spires have become a characteristic feature of Cairo's skyline.

CLEOPATRA BOYCOTT. In April 1960 the American Seafarers International Union organized a boycott on the unloading in New York of the Egyptian ship Cleopatra, in protest against the Arab boycott on ships dealing with Israel and alleged harassment of American seamen in Arab ports. The boycott was lifted in May 1960 following intense pressure on the unions by the U.S. government and condemnation of the boycott by U.S. Senator Fulbright. A counter-boycott was organized by the Arab trade unions in several countries. The incident was aggravated by the passage, shortly after the commencement of the boycott, of a foreign-aid bill in the U.S. Senate that contained various penalty clauses against Egypt.

CLOT BEY (ANTOINE BARTHELEMY CLOT) (d. 1860). One of a group of European experts recruited by the Viceroy Muhammad Ali to introduce European methods and technology to Egypt, Clot Bey established the first Egyptian medical school where European medicine was taught on a strictly secular basis. Clot Bey also laid the foundations of the Egyptian health service in Qasr al-Aini hospital and wrote a valuable study on early nineteenth-century Egypt. One of the doctors brought in by Clot Bey, Theodore Bilharz, was the first to identify the water-borne parasite disease endemic in Egypt, schistosomiasis, which became known in Egypt as bilharzia.

Clot Bey's career was temporarily halted during the tenure

of Abbas I (1848-54), who dismissed most of Muhammad Ali's European advisers. Though Clot Bey was recalled in 1856 by Sa^{c}id, Abbas' successor, he was able to serve for only a year before his retirement.

CODE OF ABBAS. Muhammad Ali (r.1805-48) introduced a series of laws in Egypt between 1833 and 1844 that, following his death, were published in codified form and named after his successor, Abbas. The Code of Abbas conflicted on several points with the Ottoman Tanzimat, a reformed and modernized legal code that the Ottoman Porte introduced in 1841 and insisted Egypt adopt. The Egyptians argued that the Code of Abbas, with its stress on agricultural and political crimes, was more adapted to Egyptian circumstances than the Ottoman code, which was rejected also because it gave supreme authority over executions to the Ottoman Sultan rather than the Egyptian Viceroy. Abbas sent delegates to the Porte in 1851 to negotiate a compromise. In 1852 an agreement was completed whereby Abbas was given control over executions in Egypt for seven years in exchange for acceptance of a modified Tanzimat. This new code was introduced under the reign of Sa^{c}id (1854-63).

How much of the Ottoman Tanzimat was actually implemented is uncertain; many of its penalties were altered during Sa^{c}id's reign. The Egyptian legal code subsequently underwent modification in 1875 and 1883. (See TANẒĪMAT.)

COMMISSION OF INQUIRY see NORTHBROOK COMMISSION

COMMISSION OF PUBLIC DEBT see CAISSE DE LA DETTE PUBLIQUE

COMMISSION DES ARTS ET DES SCIENCES see DESCRIPTION DE L'EGYPTE

COMMITTEE FOR THE LIQUIDATION OF FEUDALISM. Set up in 1966 by the Egyptian government under the chairmanship of General Abdal Hakim Amer, the committee was charged with investigating the holdovers of feudal landownership and social patterns in Egyptian rural areas, following the assassination of a representative of the Arab Socialist Union (the government's political party) in the town of Kamchiche.

The assassination and the establishment of the committee followed a long period of unrest in rural areas, partially spurred by Islamic groups, against the Nasser regime and its policies. The assassination was believed by the authorities to demonstrate, and the committee duly confirmed, that the Agrarian Reform Law had not been entirely successful in weakening the hold of the many large Egyptian landowners and some local officials who opposed the reforms that the regime wanted to introduce. The committee's caution in tackling the issue was, however, widely criticized by Egypt's leftists, especially as it failed to examine the more severe structural weaknesses of the agrarian reform on the local level. The committee did confiscate about 25,000 feddans of land that it found had been illegally withheld from agrarian reform.

COMMUNIST PARTY see EGYPTIAN COMMUNIST PARTY

CONDOMINIUM (SUDAN) see ANGLO-EGYPTIAN CONDOMINIUM

CONFEDERATION OF ARAB REPUBLICS see FEDERATION

CONGRESS FOR THE DEFENSE OF PALESTINE. Pan-Arab grouping organized in 1938 by a faction of Egyptian parliamentarians, the congress was meant to lead resistance to the increase of Jewish settlers in Palestine and long-term Zionist plans for the region. In concert with a number of other countries Egyptian members of the congress attended the London Round Table Conference in February-March 1939 to press the Arab case in Palestine, but the congress did not succeed in developing a concerted or effective Egyptian government policy on Palestine.

CONGRESS OF EGYPTIAN TRADE UNIONS. The congress' members, left-wing trade unions, were basically dissatisfied with the conservative and cautious line adopted by previous trade-union syndicates. In addition to introducing demands for reforms in the conditions of Egyptian workers, the congress, formed in 1945, also participated in the popular agitation of the post-war years for land reform and political power-sharing. Along with students from Egypt's schools and universities, the congress at various points in the 1945-47 period was a member of popular-front organizations opposed to the government. The congress operated in association with another leftist grouping, the Preparatory Committee for the Congress of Egyptian Trade Unions.

CONGRESS OF POPULAR FORCES see NATIONAL CONGRESS OF POPULAR FORCES

CONSTITUTION OF 1882. Drafted by the Egyptian Prime Minister Sharif Pasha and presented to the Assembly in January 1882, the Constitution was an attempt to build national political institutions in the face of Europe's threats to Egypt's autonomy. It provided for the establishment of a Chamber of Deputies elected for five-year terms with a salary of £E100 per annum. A president of the chamber would be selected by the Khedive from three names put forward by the chamber. Sessions of the parliament would be open to the public, and in Arabic. Ministers chosen by the Khedive would be responsible to the chamber, who would also have the right to approve the budget, any new taxes, and foreign treaties and commitments.

New legislation could originate from either the cabinet or the chamber. The initial draft of the Constitution was modified by the Assembly President, Sultan Pasha, after certain objections from the Palace and the nationalists, and the Constitution was signed by the Khedive Tawfiq on 7 February 1882. A month later, the Assembly passed an electoral law. The workings of this constitution were never properly tested. The Arabi Revolt and the subsequent invasion of Egypt by the British resulted in a suspension of normal political life. Following their imposition of control on Egypt, the British abrogated the 1882 Constitution.

CONSTITUTION OF 1923. Drafted by a thirty-two-member Constitutional Commission appointed by Egyptian Prime Minister Tharwat Pasha and chaired by Rushdi Pasha, the postindependence Egyptian Constitution was completed in October 1922. The final version was modified by British objections to clauses relating to the Sudan and by the objections of the Palace to what it saw as limitations imposed on its power. After the appropriate compromises were made the Constitution was promulgated on 19 April 1923. The legislature was to have two chambers, a Senate, half of whose members would be replaced every five years and up to 40 percent of whose members could be nominated by the King, and a Chamber of Deputies elected by indirect popular vote. There would be one senator for every 180,000, and one deputy for every 60,000 citizens. The King had the right to select and appoint the Prime Minister and the Senate president, to dismiss the cabinet, and to dissolve parliament (something done with increasing frequency in the 1920s). He could also return draft laws to parliament for recommendation. The cabinet was to be drawn from the two chambers and was collectively responsible to the lower house.

The Egyptian 1923 Constitution was strongly influenced by the Belgian constitution, save that its checks on royal power, though elaborate, were largely ineffective. This may be traced to the composition of the original constitutional commission, in which the King's men had the strongest voice and a powerful defender in the chairman. During the reign of Fuad no session of parliament held under the 1923 Constitution ever sat its full term. The Constitution was suspended in parts from July 1928 until October 1929 and replaced by a new Constitution (see below) from October 1930 until December 1935, when it was restored. In 1938 changes were introduced during the ministry of Mahmud Pasha that substantially increased the Palace's power with regard to the number of senators who could be royal appointees. The 1923 Constitution was suspended in December 1952, five months after the Revolution.

CONSTITUTION OF 1930. Introduced by the government of Sidqi Pasha, the 1930 Constitution replaced the 1923 Constitution, which the Palace felt gave too much power to Egypt's elected representatives. In addition to increasing the executive's role and powers substantially, the Constitution removed from the parliament its right to bring down the cabinet on a vote of confidence. Polling would be done in two stages, a process that the government hoped would control popular sentiment and prevent the Wafd Party in particular from winning any more elections. In the event, the Wafd and the Liberal Constitutionalists refused to participate in elections held under this Constitution. The 1930 Constitution was rescinded in November 1934, a year before the restoration of the 1923 Constitution.

CONSTITUTION OF 1956 (REPUBLICAN CONSTITUTION). Following the declaration of Egypt as a Republic on 18 June 1953, a Constitutional Charter was introduced while a new Constitution was being drafted, largely under the direction of the Revolutionary Command Council. Under this 1956 Constitution Egypt was proclaimed to be an Arab nation, with a presidential (as opposed to ministerial) executive. A single-chamber National Assembly was created, with a government political party, the National Union, under strong presidential control. Members of the Assembly were to be nominated by the National Union and elected by popular vote. The Constitution also provided for a centralized executive; local affairs were to remain in the hands of local executive councils answerable to the center.

Gamal Abdal Nasser was elected the first President of Egypt under a referendum on 23 July 1956, in which the voters approved a further referendum item providing for a new Constitution to be implemented in the future.

Under the 1956 Constitution the National Assembly was to have 350 members, with the President, as head of state, serving a six-year term. After the initial 1956 referendum, which returned Gamal Abdal Nasser as President, future Presidents would be nominated by the National Assembly and confirmed by plebiscite. Women were given the right to vote, and popular rights, such as those of speech, property, and person, were acknowledged within certain limits. The President would appoint a cabinet responsible to him and had control over nominations of parliamentary candidates. Under the 1956 Constitution the President was vested with power to promulgate laws until the National Assembly was elected. Though legislative power was vested in the National Assembly, the entire system was directed toward the President. Through the President's control of the executive of the National Union there was little within the political system that this Constitution did not place under his control, either directly or indirectly.

CONSTITUTION OF 1964 (PROVISIONAL). Following the breakup of the union with Syria, Egypt (retaining the title of the United Arab Republic) introduced a new 164-article Constitution defining the UAR as a democratic socialist state with Islam as the state religion and Arabic as the national language. Though the March 1964 Provisional Constitution roughly followed the lines of the Charter of National Action, it was not a constitution as such but a decree establishing certain administrative procedures, such as an executive cabinet that would govern the country until a new constitution was drawn up by the National Assembly. Nasser's presidency was confirmed by the Assembly that January.

The President, together with the Vice-President(s) of his choice, would make all government policy in consultation with the cabinet and was responsible for public-security regulations. Cabinet members would guide and coordinate ministerial work and draft legislation for the President to consider. The extreme concentration of power in the hands of the executive under this Constitution continued the trend developed in the previous, 1956, Constitution.

CONSTITUTION OF 1971. The 1971 Constitution, introduced under the presidency of Anwar Sadat, provided for a legislative body, the People's Assembly, and a continuation of the strong executive found in previous Constitutions. It was passed by referendum in September 1971.

The People's Assembly, with 360 members (ten of whom could be presidential appointees), would draw its candidates from the ASU, though this one-party system was altered in 1976. The President was to serve no more than two six-year terms, though in 1981 the Constitution was amended to enable Anwar Sadat to hold Egypt's presidency for life.

The 1971 Constitution introduced administrative changes, including the division of Egypt into twenty-five governates, whose governors would be appointed by presidential decree on the advice of the Minister for Local Government. Administrative personnel participating in the governor's council would be elected from each district. And though the 1971 Constitution drew strongly on its 1964 predecessor, it defined more clearly local government organization and representation and established the responsibilities of the elected councils and mudirs (mayors) at the village level in the maintenance of local order and implementation of government policies and programs. The President of Egypt was entitled to increase the number of elected and appointed representatives to the People's Assembly. Alterations to the Constitution are done through referendum based on presidential decree.

CONSTITUTIONAL CHARTER. After the suspension of the 1923 Constitution in December 1952 the government introduced a Provisional Constitutional Charter in February 1953. The charter vested executive and legislative power in the Revolutionary Command Council and the cabinet, both of which were under the overall supervision of the Chairman of the RCC (then General Naguib).

The 1953 Constitutional Charter retained the monarchy in the form of a Regency Council, though this was eventually abolished in June 1953. The charter was a temporary legal device until a new Constitution, reflecting the altered political realities of Egypt, could be drafted. This would occur at the end of a three-year transitional period, following which a democratic system would be established. In the meantime, the charter banned political parties and provided for the creation of a new political grouping, the Liberation Rally.

CONSTITUTIONAL COMMISSION. A Constitutional Commission, established by decree of King Fuad in April 1922, was composed of thirty-two appointed members under the chairmanship of Rushdi Pasha. The membership, drawn from politicians, landowners, religious and public figures, broadly represented the Palace's views and those of the moderates within the nationalist movement. The commission was placed under strong Palace pressure to refrain from including articles that would in any way curtail the King's prerogatives and power; at the same time it had to satisfy mainstream sentiment among the nationalists, who wanted to see the creation of genuinely representative institutions. The Commission was also placed under pressure by the British, who objected to constitutional clauses affecting the Sudan and previous British and Egyptian arrangements over it. The commission was sharply opposed by the Wafd, whose leader, Zaghlul, was in exile during its sessions. Egyptian domestic opposition (led by the Wafd) ensured that the constitution drafting process was surrounded by considerable controversy. The commission presented in October 1922 a Constitution that attempted to satisfy all parties; after some adjustments it was promulgated by King Fuad on 19 April 1923.

CONSTITUTIONAL REFORM PARTY (ḤIZB AL-IṢLĀḤ ᶜALA'L-MABĀDI' AD-DUSTŪRIYYĪN). Founded in December 1907 as a political party to support the Palace, the Constitutional Reform Party was started by Shaykh Ali Yusuf, editor of the newspaper Al-Muayyad. The party stood in opposition both to the moderate Umma Party and to the more radical Nationalist Party of Mustafa Kamil, whose relations with the Palace had been on the decline for several years. Many members of the Khedive Abbas' family joined the party, but Abbas himself waited until the death of Kamil in February 1908 before joining himself. Despite its rather illustrious membership the Constitutional Reform Party was rather an extension of the political concerns of Shaykh Ali Yusuf, and did not really formulate a popular policy or platform, or try to attract a mass following. It advocated increased Egyptian participation in government but its views on constitutional matters were far more conservative than the other major prewar parties, particularly the Nationalists.

CONSULTATIVE COUNCILS. These were provincial legislative units established by the Organic Law of May 1883. Each of the fourteen provinces was to have a small council, meeting under direction of the provincial governor. These council members would be selected by electors representing the different communities in the province. The councils were to be responsible for the supervision and administration of local public-works projects, agricultural marketing, and irrigation. The councils would have a minimum of three and maximum of eight members, depending on the size of the province. In 1890 a council was formed for the municipality of Alexandria, with Cairo getting a council in 1949. The councils were the idea of Lord Dufferin, who participated in the drafting of the Organic Law.

CONVENTION OF KUTAHIYA. Signed in May 1833 between representatives of Muhammad Ali, Viceroy of Egypt, and the Ottoman Porte, the Convention recognized Muhammad Ali's control of Greater Syria, in exchange for his withdrawal from Ottoman territory. Muhammad Ali's conquest of this region was gained through the military successes of his son Ibrahim Pasha from 1831 onward, when the Egyptian invasion of Syria began. By February 1833 Ibrahim had inflicted three defeats on the Ottomans, two in Anatolia itself, and had advanced as far as Kutahiya when ordered to stop by his father. The details of the Convention were shaped by the active intervention of British, French, and Russian diplomats, in response to the Ottoman Sultan's concern that his position in Anatolia itself was under threat from Ibrahim's advance. Following the signing of the Convention, Ibrahim Pasha was appointed governor of Syria on his father's behalf.

CONVENTION OF LONDON. Signed with the Ottoman Porte in July 1840 by Britain, Russia, Prussia, and Austria, the Convention bound the Ottoman Sultan to guarantee the closure of the Dardanelles to foreign warships in peacetime, in exchange for their protection of his position. Additionally, the Convention promised Muhammad Ali hereditary control of Egypt in exchange for his withdrawal from territories claimed by the Sultan and his recognition of the Sultan's suzerainty over him. A final agreement between Muhammad Ali and the Sultan on these points was not concluded until 1841. The intervention of the European powers through the London Convention signaled their determination to curb sharply the powers of Muhammad Ali following his military victory at Nizib and the subsequent surrender of the Ottoman fleet in the previous year.

CONVENTION OF LONDON. Signed in March 1885 following nearly a year of preliminary discussions by the British and Egypt's other European creditors, the Convention of London allowed Egypt to raise a £9 million loan to meet outstanding financial commitments and temporarily scheduled slightly lower funded-debt repayments. In exchange Britian agreed to allow a reexamination of Egypt's international financial position if Egypt's interest payments on its unified debt were not resumed in two years' time. The signing of the convention placed a great burden on Cromer, the British Consul-General, to ensure that the health of the Egyptian economy was sufficiently restored by 1887 to avoid further controls being instituted by the other European powers. Egypt started its first full interest payments in April 1887, meeting the deadline and avoiding the threatened examination of its finances.

COPTIC CONGRESS. Formed in 1910 following the assassination of Butrus Ghali Pasha, Egypt's first Coptic Prime Minister, the Coptic Congress was organized by a Coptic political grouping, the Party of Independent Egyptians. It was an expression of the Coptic community's discontent with the development of nationalist politics in a way that seemed to exclude their particular, communal needs. Meant to function as a pressure group pushing Coptic interests, the Congress met with a low level of official acceptance. It held meetings in Assyut in 1910 and 1911; a number of resolutions were adopted regarding the position of Copts in Egypt and the conflicts between their religious beliefs and the Egyptian legal system, which favored, in their view, Islamic practice. The Congress and the party dissolved shortly thereafter under British pressure.

COPTIC LANGUAGE. The Coptic language is derived from late Egyptian, though its script is based on the Greek alphabet, with the addition of seven demotic (late hieroglyphic) characters. Its origins date to the third century AD, when it was developed to make the Christian Scriptures available to Egyptians. It became the liturgical language of the Coptic Church after the Council of Chalcedon in 451, when the Coptic Church officially broke away from the Orthodox Church. Subsequently Coptic was used for theological writing, liturgy, and religious purposes of a more general nature, permitting the development of a strongly national coloring to Egyptian Christianity. It developed four (in some sources, five) regional dialects and was used to translate many Greek and Gnostic manuscripts. As a spoken language this Egyptian vernacular tongue was found among the Christian community until the twelfth century, after which parts of the liturgy were explained in Arabic, and Coptic texts appeared with Arabic translations. In Upper Egypt spoken Coptic appeared to persist among the Christian communities there until about the seventeenth century.

COPTIC LEGION. Formed by Napoleon Bonaparte after his invasion of Egypt in 1798, the Coptic Legion was recruited by General Donzelot, French governor of Middle Egypt, and headed by Yaqub Tadrus. Tadrus died in 1801 before reaching France, but the Coptic Legion participated in several European battles of the Napoleonic Wars under the leadership of some prominent members of the Egyptian Coptic community.

COPTS. The vast majority of Egypt's Christians belong to the Coptic Church, whose origins represent a fusion of the doctrinal issues that were a source of such controversy within the early Christian Church in Egypt, and indigenous Egyptian sentiment. The development of Coptic Christianity was also influenced by the early and rapid spread in Egypt of monasticism and by the development of Christianity as an adjunct to state policy in the later Roman-Byzantine Empire.

The Evangelist Mark is regarded as the founder of Christianity in Egypt. In its early years the religion engaged in a lengthy struggle against the indigenous pagan religious practices descended from ancient times that were still found in the country, as well as against Hellenism, which was established in Alexandria and other urban centers. To counter the appeal of Greek philosophy the Christian leadership in Egypt established the Cathecal School of Alexandria (the Didascalia), which provided intellectual refutations of Greek philosophers and sophisticated advocacy of Christianity. Monks and preachers spread throughout the countryside to preach the Christian message among ordinary Egyptians and in time were of great effect. Nonetheless, the transformation of Egypt into a Christian country was not an entirely smooth process; there was resistance from the pagan and Hellenized elements of the population and divisions within the Christian Church itself between advocates of the various theological schools evolving at this time. Egypt's sizable Jewish population, particularly in Alexandria, also became a target of the Christians' fervor and antagonism, with unhappy results for civil order in Alexandria and elsewhere. The burning in 391 of the pagan cult center, the Serapeum, and the murder in 415 of the distinguished woman philosopher Hypatia by a Christian mob of monks and laymen signaled a growing and violent Christianity in Alexandria in active confrontation with that city's pagan past. The dominance of a new religion was gained at the expense of the intellectual heterogeneity that had distinguished the city.

The pre-Islamic period was for the Copts marked by two major events: the beginning of the Coptic calendar in AD 284, in commemoration of the persecution suffered by Egypt's Christians, and the establishment of an independent Egyptian Church in 451, following the Council of Chalcedon, which condemned the Monophysite theology accepted by the majority of Christians in Egypt.

Thereafter the relations between Egypt's Copts and Constantinople were strained. The Copts refused to recognize the religious authority of the Patriarchs of Alexandria appointed by the Byzantine state, and when those clerics were given, in 550, administrative jurisdiction in the office of the Patriarchate, popular opposition became widespread against the political as well as religious dominance of Egypt by outsiders. This opposition may in part account for the acceptance of the Muslim conquest by the Copts, who saw the Muslims initially as liberators from the Byzantine yoke. The Coptic Patriarch was forced, along with other Coptic clergy, to leave Alexandria in 550, though he did not transfer his official residence from there until the mid ninth century, when Damirah in the Nile valley became the Patriarch's residence.

Muslim converts among the Copts began to appear slowly; whatever official encouragement was offered by the Muslim governors was later assisted by the imposition of the Muslim system of communal taxes paid on top of general tax assessments. These taxes were a source of bitter resentment among Egypt's Christians, and in 813-33/198-218 there was a Coptic revolt against their fiscal and probably other, noneconomic, conditions. Despite this, from earliest Muslim times Copts were found in quite high and responsible positions within the Muslim administration, and as tax and revenue collectors at the local level.

The Coptic Patriarch was appointed by the Muslim governor of Egypt, on the recommendation of the clergy, in Umayyad and ᶜAbbāsid times, but eventually his selection passed over to the Coptic clergy themselves, with their elected choice confirmed by the ruler. The Copts and the Jews were subject to occasional persecutions, particularly for a period during the reign of the Fāṭimid Caliph al-Ḥākim (996-1021/386-411), but this persecution was atypical. In the rest of the Fāṭimid period the Copts enjoyed especially favored treatment by Egypt's rulers, so much so that there were occasional uprisings by Muslims in protest.

The reestablishment of Sunnī Islamic orthodoxy in Egypt under the Ayyūbids in 1171/567 brought to power a regime that was neither hostile nor particularly sympathetic to Egypt's Copts. From this time onward, and possibly associated with the gradual defeat of the Crusaders and their departure from

Arab lands, the Copts steadily lost ground to the Muslims. A Coptic revolt in 1320/720, during the reign of an-Nāṣir Muḥammad, was quickly suppressed. Various Mamluk Sultans introduced restrictions on the number of Copts in government service, but these restrictions were usually designed to be waived in consideration of a fee. The Christian communities in Egypt became concentrated in but by no means confined to the southern half of the country, with individual monasteries and clergy continuing the intellectual traditions of the Church while the Christian lay population became, in terms of culture, language, and custom, virtually indistinguishable on the surface from their Muslim countrymen.

The arrival of the French in 1798 changed the focus of the Coptic community in Egypt. The dominance of European Christian governments in Egypt and elsewhere in the Islamic world, which increasingly manifested itself henceforth, was bound to have an effect on the indigenous Christian populations of these countries. This rise in self-consciousness among Egypt's Copts led them, in the nineteenth century, in two quite distinct directions. There was a move among lay Copts for a reform of the Church's administrative structure, spurred by the series of changes introduced under the Patriarch Cyril IV (1854-61) and resulting in the establishment of a laymen's representative body, the Maglis (Majlis) al-Milli. This body first met in 1874 and was formally incorporated in 1885. Second, the Copts, by carefully refusing to ally or overly identify with the European powers in Egypt, generally succeeded in assuming an active role in Egypt's political life at the national level.

In 1908 Egypt's first Coptic Prime Minister, Butrus Ghali Pasha, was appointed. His assassination two years later led to a temporary breakdown in relations between Muslim and Coptic nationalists, but by the 1920s Coptic politicians appeared at the highest levels of political life in Egypt and in all political groupings.

Since the nineteenth century the relationship between the Coptic religious hierarchy and the lay community had undergone periods of controversy and change. The monastic tradition, which has figured so importantly in Coptic religious life, has also served to isolate the Coptic clergy from the layman and led to the development of quite differing views about the role of the Church in both religious and secular affairs. The prominence and power of the Coptic laymen involved in Church activities has in the past, and to this day, acted to balance the religious authority of the clergy.

Until quite recently communal tensions between Egypt's Coptic and Muslim populations have lacked the sustained quality found in other societies with substantial religious minorities. The completely indigenous nature of Coptic Christianity had rendered it relatively impervious to attack in the pre-Revolutionary period by, for instance, Islamic fundamentalist groups, such as the Ikhwan al-Muslimun, who admitted the Church's truly Egyptian character. The 1970s, however, saw a rise in the acts of violence between the communities, and against Christian property by newer and more radical Muslim groupings. This violence became especially pronounced in 1979-81, leading to a government suppression in September 1981 of Muslim and Coptic religious leaders, some of whom were accused of inciting communal sentiments.

Estimates of the size of Egypt's Coptic population today vary between a low of 6 percent and a high of 10-15 percent of the population. The Coptic Church has branches in East Africa and Palestine, though the Ethiopian Church, probably its most historically rich linkage, broke away in 1937. The Church's hierarchy is headed by the Coptic Patriarch, with nineteen bishops superintending the work of the Church's priests, deacons and monks.

CORRECTIVE REVOLUTION. A series of presidential decrees issued by President Anwar Sadat starting in May 1971, the Corrective Revolution aimed to disassemble some of the elaborate security apparatus established during the Nasser period and to create a greater amount of personal and political freedom in Egypt. These decrees followed Sadat's successful defeat of an conspiracy against him. Under the decrees, many of the detention centers from the Nasser period were to be closed, and certain unilateral police powers were abrogated. Despite these reforms it is not fully clear to what extent the secret-police network was completely overhauled; internal security concerns have certainly continued to play an important role in government policy, and periods of liberalization have alternated with periods of stricter control. Sadat's call for a constitution and a greater voice for people in discussing the future of the country have been followed since then by the dissolution of the Arab Socialist Union's political functions and the creation in 1977 of a limited multiparty system. This system was soon placed under increasingly tight regulation, particularly after there had been a high level of popular discontent with the regime's economic programs and political dissatisfaction with the peace treaty with Israel. A permanent constitution was introduced in September 1971.

COTTON. The potential of cotton as a cash crop was first recognized by Muhammad Ali (r. 1805-48), who invested in the production of the first two varieties of high-yield cotton plants, the Shmouni and Sikel strains. Long-staple cotton, which was especially prized for the high-quality finished textiles it yielded, was discovered by Louis Alex Jumel, a French engineer, who cultivated it from an ornamental shrub in 1820.

Egypt's role as an international cotton producer was established during the American Civil War, when Egypt was the beneficiary of a British investigation of potential cotton-growing areas to compensate for the drying up of American supplies. Though this initial boom faltered when American cotton once more became available, the cotton-producing industry eventually recovered, to become by the turn of the century Egypt's largest earner of foreign capital in agriculture.

In the 1920s the General Agricultural Syndicate succeeded in getting various protective measures passed by the Egyptian government to defend the financial position of Egyptian cotton-growers against the fluctuations in the world market and to gain more direct control over the trade in cotton. At this time, with the assistance of Bank Misr, textile factories were built or expanded to export more Egyptian cotton in finished form and enable the country to enjoy a higher share in the profitability of the commodity. The enormous textile complexes at Mahalla al-Kubra and Kafr al-Dawaa became an important part of Egypt's manufacturing base.

Despite the legislative measures passed for the protection of the cotton trade Egypt's cotton exports remained tied to international market forces that were well beyond Egypt's control. The First and Second World Wars and the Korean War brought vast profits as demands for the material rose; the subsequent slumps caused widespread financial hardship in Egypt. President Nasser's decision to use Egypt's cotton production to pay off some of its industrial and other loans from the COMECON countries removed much Egyptian cotton from international markets until the mid-1970s, when President Anwar Sadat abrogated the Soviet-Egyptian treaties relating to these exports. Egypt now imports short-staple cotton, which is finished at existing textile plants for its own domestic needs, and exports about one-third of its highly prized long-staple crop to European and American textile companies.

COUNCIL OF MINISTERS (MAGLIS/MAJLIS AN-NUZZAR). Established by the Khedive Ismail in August 1878, the Council of Ministers was granted at its foundation a measure of power and independence thanks largely to the pressure of Egypt's European creditors, who stood behind its formation.

On the insistence of these creditors Europeans joined the Council in the Public Works and Finance ministries; it was hoped that by controlling these ministries Egypt's creditors would be able to keep tighter rein on the country's revenues and expenditures. This "European cabinet" provoked intense nationalist criticism, which rose to such a level that Ismail accepted Prime Minister Nubar Pasha's resignation in February 1879 and dismissed his cabinet that April. After his own deposition two months later, the new Khedive, Tawfiq, made the council answerable directly to him. This Council, under Riyad Pasha, was replaced in September 1881 by a moderate nationalist ministry headed by Sharif Pasha, who was in turn replaced by Sami al-Barudi in January 1882. A constitution introduced the following month attempted to transfer ministerial responsibility to the legislature, but this planned reform was interrupted by the Arabi Rebellion and the subsequent invasion of Egypt by Britain.

Ministerial government continued after the British occupation in 1882, under the watchful eye and occasional intervention of Lord Cromer. Egyptian ministers were assisted, or, more exactly, directed by European advisers, who in fact set much of the administrative policy within the various ministries.

COUNCIL OF THE NATION see NATIONAL ASSEMBLY

CROMER, LORD (SIR EVELYN BARING) (1841-1917). British Agent and Consul-General in Egypt from 1883 until his retirement in 1907, Lord Cromer was one of the most influential figures in preindependence Egypt. He was first appointed to Egypt in 1877 as a member of the Caisse de la Dette Publique and in 1879 became the British representative on the Caisse, superintending Egypt's debt repayments. A few months later he was transferred to India, returning to Egypt in September 1883, a year after the British occupation of the country. He became Lord Cromer in 1892.

In his twenty-four years as British Agent in Egypt, Lord Cromer ruled the country in a de facto, if not de jure, manner, using his position to secure the appointment and dismissal of ministers serving the Egyptian Khedive. His disdain for the Egyptian nationalist movement was combined with a paternalistic concern for the lot of the poorest of the cultivating classes.

The direction Cromer gave to Egyptian policy was shaped by the country's external debt obligations, and in this area he made great progress in restoring the country's international fiscal position. His social programs were less highly regarded, particularly his seeming neglect of both education and industrial development, two areas for which Egypt was to pay dearly in the future. Cromer supervised the restructuring of the post-Occupation government, army and services, and the reorganization of the country's administrative structure. A large part of Egypt's available revenues were directed toward public works, particularly for necessary improvements in irrigation and water storage; many capable British engineers were recruited to the Public Works Ministry.

The achievements of Cromer were, in the eyes of Egypt's nationalists, more than counterbalanced by his failure to come to terms with their demands for a political voice in their own country. Starting with the Egyptian position in the Sudan in the mid-1880s, Cromer and the various governments of the day were often in disagreement. The resignations of Sharif in 1885, Nubar in 1888, Riyad in 1888, Fakhri in 1893 (shortly after his appointment), and Riyad in 1894, were all in some way related to difficulties with, or objections by, Cromer. The installation in 1895 of the cooperative Mustafa Fahmi (who served until after Cromer's retirement) did not entirely ease the situation, as Cromer and the Khedive Abbas were never on good terms.

Cromer, who did not speak Arabic, was assisted by Harry Boyle. For eighteen years Boyle acted as Oriental Secretary to Cromer and through his command of Arabic was able to keep Cromer in touch with a wider segment of Egyptian opinion than he was normally exposed to in his dealings with the Palace and ministers. Despite this assistance, however, Cromer had few links with the nationalists and slight sympathy with their demands. Though he kept the press free, feeling it a necessary safety valve, he tended to react badly to Egyptian or other criticism of his performance.

Cromer's personal manner, and disregard of what many nationalists saw as necessary political and social reforms, made him a less than popular figure with many Egyptians. The Dinshaway Incident in 1906, in which a number of villagers were executed following the death of a British officer on a hunting trip, aroused strong anti-British and anti-Cromer feelings, and likely contributed to his decision to resign in 1907.

Cromer's major achievement was the repair of Egypt's international credit position to the satisfaction of her external creditors, and throughout his long tenure in office Cromer showed great skill in managing Egypt's fiscal situation, if one leaves aside the fairness or the size of the payments Egypt was required to make. His achievements in other areas were mixed; he favored and instituted programs of benefit to poorer Egyptians, yet he refused to support the establishment of a university or the entry of Egyptians into higher levels of the administration. His treatment of the Khedive, Abbas, and of many Egyptian political figures was bound to arouse resentment, as was his dampening of all efforts for even the most minor of political reforms. Cromer had a strong vision of Egypt's national role and future development, but being an imperial vision, it was out of line with the wishes or needs of Egypt's growing nationalist movement.

CRUSADES. The arrival of the Crusaders in the Islamic world in 1096/489 began a period of major changes in the balance of power throughout the region, and especially for Egypt's Fāṭimid dynasty.

The first Crusaders reached Syria when Fāṭimid control in that province was fast diminishing in the face of a determined Saljūq Turkish advance. It has been suggested that the Fāṭimids may have seen in the Crusaders a potential ally against these Turkish princes challenging their control of the Levant (or claimed control, the Fāṭimid position in many parts of the region having never been substantively established). But the Crusader capture of Jerusalem in 1099/492, one year after its seizure by the Fāṭimids, plus the pillage and massacre of the city's Muslim, Christian, and Jewish population by these Crusaders, pointed out the weakness of any alliance; the Crusaders evidenced ambitions quite contradictory to those of the Fāṭimids. The Crusaders were moving toward an invasion of Egypt as early as

1101/495, the year most of Palestine fell; Acre followed in 1103/497. In 1108/502 the Crusaders took the port of Tripoli, and by 1109/503 the Fāṭimids were left with only a few footholds in the region. The Crusader King Baldwin embarked on an invasion of Egypt in 1117/511 but died during a battle at Al-Arish the following year, forcing a Crusader withdrawal.

The Crusader chief Amalric invaded Egypt several times during the reign of the last Fāṭimid Caliph, al-ᶜĀḍid (r. 1159-71/554-67), initially to gain tribute, then in support of the vizier, Shāwar, and finally in a bid to impose more direct control of Egypt, which had been made a tributary of the Crusaders. The arrival of the general Shīrkūh (in the service of Nūr ad-Dīn, Zangid prince of Damascus and a former ally of Shāwar) in 1168/564 was enough to make Amalric withdraw his forces, but not before the city of Bilbays had been sacked and burned by the Crusaders and al-Fusṭāṭ, the oldest section of Cairo, burned by Shāwar himself as a warning to the Crusaders of what he would do to the rest of Cairo if they advanced farther.

It was Shīrkūh's nephew Ṣalāḥ ad-Dīn, founder of the Ayyūbid dynasty in Egypt, who inflicted the first in a series of major reverses on the Crusaders. It was not until the mid-1180s/570s that Ṣalāḥ ad-Dīn, who had been temporarily involved in settling the challenges to his control of Egypt and expansion into Syria, addressed himself to the presence of the Crusaders in the Islamic world. In 1185/581 the naval force of Raynald de Chatillon, who had been pillaging Muslim shipping and pilgrim caravans, was sunk at Qulzum, near modern Suez. In 1187/583 Ṣalāḥ ad-Dīn drove the Crusaders from Tiberias, then inflicted a major defeat on them at the Battle of Ḥaṭṭīn (the Horns of Hattin), west of Tiberias. Acre and Jerusalem also fell to the forces of Ṣalāḥ ad-Dīn, though the Crusaders retook the former in 1191/587 and sought unsuccessfully to regain Jerusalem. The Treaty of Ramlah, concluded in 1192/598, recognized Ayyūbid gains, the status of Jerusalem as an open city, and certain trading rights for the Crusaders.

In 1218/615 a Crusade led by the Papal Legate Pelagius landed in Damietta (on Egypt's Mediterranean coast), which he succeeded in taking in the following year. Pelagius foolishly rejected an offer of compromise made by the Ayyūbid Sultan al-Kāmil when they reached Mansura in the Egyptian Delta. This Crusade was eventually driven back to Damietta in 1221/618, after which an eight-year peace treaty was signed. A minor Crusade against Egypt was launched under Tibald in 1240/637 but was defeated in battle at Gaza.

In 1229/626 a Crusade led by Frederick II arrived in the Levant. The Crusade had been cursed by the Pope, who opposed it, but Frederick managed to secure through skillful negotiations a series of far-ranging concessions including Nazareth, Bethlehem, and Jerusalem, with a corridor linking the latter to the port of Acre. He was helped in this by his friendship with the Ayyūbid Sultan, al-Kāmil. Crusader control of Jerusalem lasted until 1244/642, when a group of Khwarāzmian Turks allied with the Ayyūbids took the city. Ayyūbid troops under the command of the Mamluk Baybars campaigned in the Levant, seizing first Gaza, then Jerusalem from the Khwarāzmians. By 1247/645 the Ayyūbids had retaken Ascalon and greatly reduced the Crusader territories.

The reverses suffered by the Crusaders coincided with the decision to launch a new Crusader invasion, this time of Egypt, under the direction of Louis IX ("The Pious") of France. This Crusade reached Egypt in 1249/647, followed the same route taken by Pelagius--Damietta to Mansura--and like the earlier Crusade was defeated by the Egyptian army there, in 1250/648.

The Baḥrī Mamluks came to power in Egypt shortly after this last defeat of the Crusaders, in which they had been instrumental. It was the Baḥrī Mamluks who, following their defeat of the Mongols, drove the remnants of the Crusaders out of the Levant in a series of battles starting, in 1268/666, with a campaign in Syria against Antioch. An eight-year-old truce with the Crusaders was broken in 1289/688, when Tripoli was taken, and in 1291/690 the Mamluks regained Acre, Beirut, Sidon, and Haifa.

Though a Crusader outpost remained in north Syria until 1302/701, the Crusader threat to Egypt and the Levant had been effectively countered. A Crusader attack in 1365/766 on Alexandria resulted in a great loss of life and destruction of property but did not advance beyond that city.

In the Islamic world the Crusaders' presence frequently brought as much misery to Christians in the region as to Muslims. But the actions and behavior of many of the Crusaders helped create anti-Christian sentiments that damaged communal relations and left a bitter harvest in areas where the Crusaders had been active. The most profound impact of the Crusaders was probably on the internal politics of Europe rather than on the Arab world, for they carried back to their own countries little of the achievements of Islamic culture, the arts, architectural styles, philosophies, and science of the Muslims, who were far in advance of their northern neighbors in intellectual and cultural matters at this time.

CYRIL (d. c.444). Patriarch of Alexandria (c.412-44) and a major theologian of his era, Cyril's writings were used by some of his supporters to secure the eventual triumph of Monophysite Christianity in Egypt. Cyril himself stayed carefully within the lines of orthodoxy accepted by the Byzantine state. He was an ardent Christian polemicist; during his reign the Egyptian monastic community made a sustained attack on Alexandria's Jewish, Hellenic, and pagan population, including the brutal murder of the philosopher Hypatia. Cyril managed through intimidation and, some sources claim, bribery in bringing the Council of Ephesus (431) to his side in the doctrinal controversies that the council had been called to consider, and played a forceful role in the council debates. Cyril wrote numerous tracts on theological and historical topics and was active in the suppression of Nestorian and other heterodox Christian philosophies.

CYRIL IV ("THE REFORMER"). Important nineteenth-century Coptic Patriarch, Cyril was in power from 1854 to 1861. He initiated a series of reforms that made a lasting impact on the structure and function of the Coptic clergy and introduced sweeping changes in religious education. He adopted an active ecumenical policy and attempted to correct what he saw as some of the non-Christian practices of the Coptic community in Egypt by initiating a wave of iconoclasm directed against the images displayed in Coptic churches and homes. Under his Patriarchate the Coptic Church established one of the first nongovernmental Arabic printing presses in Egypt. The forces set in motion by Cyril both among the clergy and Coptic laity took several decades to settle but led ultimately to a new level of lay involvement with the ecclesiastical administration of the Church.

CYRUS (d. 641/20). Patriarch of Alexandria, Cyrus was the head of Egypt's religious and civil administration at the time of the Muslim conquest of Egypt and negotiated that country's surrender to the Muslim general ᶜAmr b. al-ᶜĀṣ.

Cyrus had been working since his appointment in 631/11 to convince Egypt's Christians to compromise with the Orthodox beliefs of the Byzantine center and to reintegrate themselves with the Greek Church. Taking power after the brief interlude of Persian rule ending in 629, Cyrus also sought to increase Egypt's flagging revenues paid to Constantinople.

Despite his efforts Cyrus remained unpopular with Egypt's Copts, something that doubtless eased the Muslims' progress through the country. Cyrus negotiated the surrender of Babylon in 640/19, after the city had been placed under siege by the Muslim armies, an act that so enraged the Byzantine Emperor Heraclius that he had Cyrus recalled. Fortunately for Cyrus, Heraclius died shortly thereafter and Cyrus was able to return to Egypt in September 641/20. He assiduously courted Alexandria's Copts while concluding in November 641/20 a treaty with ᶜAmr, surrendering the city in a year's time to permit the evacuation of its Greek community. The city's inhabitants at first rejected this arrangement but relented in the face of an inevitable Arab occupation. Cyrus died before the treaty was implemented.

-D-

DĀ^{c}Ī. Missionaries for the Shī^{c}a Ismā^{c}īlī faith of Egypt's Fāṭimid dynasty (969-1171/358-567), the Dā^{c}ī also played important roles in the administration of the Fāṭimid state and were a major support of the power of the Caliph. The Fāṭimid Caliph funded the Dā^{c}ī, and the missionaries were trained at al-Azhar in Cairo prior to being sent to propagate the Fāṭimid's sect of Shī^{c}a Islam in the Sunnī and Shī^{c}a areas of the Levant. In their preaching the Dā^{c}ī stressed the legitimacy of the ^{c}Alīd claim to the Caliphate (and thus of the Fāṭimid Caliphs in Cairo) and, by implication, the illegitimacy of Sunnī orthodoxy of the ^{c}Abbāsid Caliphs. They also initiated and taught students in the mystical practices associated with Ismā^{c}īlī beliefs. These missionaries were headed by a Dā^{c}ī al-Du^{c}āt (chief Dā^{c}ī), based in Cairo, whose position was equivalent to, and at times identical with, that of the vizier.

The successes of the Dā^{c}ī in converting large numbers of Muslims in the Yemen, Iraq, Syria, and elsewhere can be traced to the military and political position of the early Fāṭimid state in Egypt, the general discontent in many Islamic countries with the Sunnī ^{c}Abbāsid Caliph in Baghdad, and their personal persuasiveness. Dā^{c}ī traveled on diplomatic and military missions as well, and the chief Dā^{c}ī in Iraq, al-Mu'ayyad, played a major role in the brief seizure of Baghdad by the Fāṭimid supporter al-Basāsīrī in 1059/450. The Dā^{c}ī represented a useful, extended network of missionaries, sympathizers, and intelligence-gatherers throughout the Muslim world. By the time of the passing of the Fāṭimid state in Egypt the Dā^{c}ī were active from the Levant to Yemen and India. The various schismatic movements which arose in Egypt during the Fātimid period divided the Dā^{c}ī and in consequence weakened their support for the Caliph.

AD-DARAZĪ (MUḤAMMAD b. ISMĀ^{c}ĪL AD-DARAZĪ) (d. 1019/410). Dā^{c}ī of the Ismā^{c}īlī faith and a founder of the Druze religion, ad-Darazī arrived in Egypt in c. 1016-17/407-08, in the troubled closing years of the reign of the Fāṭimid Caliph, al-Ḥākim. A Turk by birth he soon gained the Caliph's confidence and with it, a high position in al-Ḥākim's court. Shortly thereafter, ad-Darazī provoked considerable controversy by proclaiming that al-Ḥākim was divine. In his writing, ad-Darazī claimed that the spirit of ᶜAlī (the fourth Caliph of Islam and the last accepted by the Shīᶜa) had passed into al-Ḥākim. The opposition of the Egyptian Dāᶜī to his preachings, and his own competition with another proponent of al-Ḥākim's divinity, Ḥamza b. ᶜAlī, eventually led to violence. Some sources say he was killed in Egypt, but he is also said to have made his way to Syria, where he died in exile. The subsequent mysterious disappearance of al-Ḥākim in 1021/411 fueled rather than stilled the supporters of his claims to divinity.

AL-DAWAA/AL-DAᶜWĀ ("The Call"). One of the more influential mass circulation journals of the modern Islamic revivalist movement in Egypt, Al-Dawaa is published in Cairo but read in many other Arab countries. A journal by this name was published by a group of Muslim Brethren during the pre-1954 period and provided an opposition voice to the moderate leadership of the Supreme Guide of the Ikhwan, Hudaybi. Its editor, then and now Salih Ashmawi, was himself a contender for the leadership of the Ikhwan against Hudaybi. The contemporary (1980) Al-Dawaa is under the direction of Umar Tilmasanni, and is one of the few journals in Egypt that has been openly and consistently critical of the Camp David process. Tilmasanni was arrested in September 1981 during a government crackdown on religious dissidents, and the journal was proscribed.

DAWISH, SHAYKH ABDAL AZIZ (d. 1929). Political figure associated with the nationalist leader Mustafa Kamil, Shaykh Dawish was editor of the Nationalist Party's newspaper, Al-Liwa, following the death of its founder Mustafa Kamil in 1908. Shaykh Dawish's defense of the Ottoman Sultan and support for pan-Islamicism were not popular among many segments of the Egyptian nationalist movement. His attacks on the British produced slight reaction apart from the antagonism of the Residency. But Shaykh Dawish's articles attacking Egypt's Copts drew hostile reaction and press censorship. The assassination in 1910 of Butrus Ghali Pasha, Egypt's first Coptic Prime Minister, increased official sentiment against Shaykh Dawish and Al-Liwa. The journal itself became the object of a successful take-over bid by opponents of Dawish and Muhammad Farid, head of the nationalist party who had appointed, and thoroughly supported, Dawish and his editorial line.

During the war (1914-18) Dawish took refuge in Turkey where he was active with pan-Islamic groups. He returned quietly to Egypt in 1924, after a stay in Germany. Dawish worked for a short time in the Ministry of Education before his death, and participated in the founding of the Young Men's Muslim Association.

DECLARATION OF 1904 see ENTENTE CORDIALE

DECLARATION OF 1922 (UNILATERAL DECLARATION OF EGYPTIAN INDEPENDENCE). On 28 February 1922 the British government announced unilaterally that the British Protectorate over Egypt was terminated and that Egypt was formally independent with the exception of four areas that Britain reserved: foreign relations, communications, the military, and the Sudan.

The issuance of the declaration followed a period of inconclusive negotiations between the British and Egyptian governments. The Egyptian Prime Minister, Adli Pasha, could not secure agreement with Britain over Egypt's position on the issues of the Protectorate and her future role in the Sudan. Adli and the moderate nationalists got the British High Commissioner Allenby to agree to secure the more general issue of Egypt's independence. Allenby threatened to resign, bringing the issue of Egyptian independence to public discussion. The government of Lloyd George did not want to end the Protectorate, which had been in force since the outbreak of the First World War, but his actions produced a quick official response: two weeks later the declaration was issued.

The declaration, while it met the immediate demands of the nationalists for an end to the Protectorate, was highly unsatisfactory in the "reserved points" clause, which so restricted Egypt's national freedoms as to compromise gravely its sovereignty. Before the decade was up the British were under pressure from Egyptian nationalist circles to renegotiate the relationship between the two countries, which finally took place in 1936 with the Anglo-Egyptian Treaty.

DEMOTIC. The native popular language of Egypt in the Ptolemaic through Roman period, Demotic used a simplified hieroglyphic script. The difficulties in mastering the written language limited literacy to a priestly class. With the advent of Christianity in Egypt the inadequacies of Demotic, with its absence of vowels, led to the evolution of Coptic, which combined Demotic and Greek characters and was used to translate the Christian scriptures.

DESCRIPTION DE L'ÉGYPTE. An encyclopedic study of the arts, sciences, history, people, and culture of Egypt, the Description was the combined work of the team of 165 scholars and scientists who accompanied the French expedition to Egypt in 1798, the Commission des sciences et des arts. Napoleon had assembled this team specifically to undertake such a study and also to make policy and administrative recommendations to him. A month after his arrival in Egypt, Napoleon announced the establishment of a French Institute in Cairo. A vast amount of material on every aspect of Egypt was collected by the team during their brief stay. The institute was forced to close temporarily in 1801, but the accumulated drawings, maps, and notes were removed. Published in volumes from 1812 to 1829, the Description remains one of the most valuable general studies on Egypt before the advent of Muhammad Ali.

DINSHAWAY INCIDENT. In June 1906 a group of British officers on a shooting trip in the Delta accidentally shot the wife of a local official at Dinshaway. A flight followed, during which two British officers and several Egyptians were shot or killed. The trial of the Egyptians involved resulted in four of the accused being hanged and four sentenced to life imprisonment, with flogging and imprisonment for the remaining defendants. The severe sentences aroused a storm of protest in Egypt and overseas. The sentences were intended by the British to discourage future incidents and to frighten pro-nationalist agitators and supporters into submission but instead gave many hitherto apolitical Egyptians second thoughts about the nature of British rule in their country and reunited (albeit temporarily) the Khedive Abbas with the nationalist movement. The story of the incident and the attendant injustice of the sentencing became a part of Egyptian nationalist folklore, spreading throughout Egypt on the village level. The Dinshaway Incident and Egyptian reaction to the sentences (handed down by a military court) were used by the nationalist leader Mustafa Kamil to press the British government for a broadening of Egyptian self-government.

DIOSCORUS (r. 444-51). Successor to Cyril, Patriarch of Alexandria, Dioscorus was the first Patriarch of Alexandria to espouse the Monophysite creed, which became the doctrine of the Coptic Church in Egypt. Dioscorus moved far beyond the theological balance of Monophysitism and Orthodoxy effected by Cyril, arguing for the single completely divine nature of Christ. Dioscorus had the support of the Byzantine Emperor Theodosius II, who, at his urging, called the Council of Ephesus in AD 449. At this council Dioscorus secured the acceptance of the Monophysite position by the assembled bishops. Allegations of irregularities led to the holding of a new council at Chalcedon, in 451, which condemned the Monophysite position and deposed Dioscorus. These findings were rejected by Egypt's Christians and led to the establishment of the Coptic Church.

DISENGAGEMENT AGREEMENT see ARAB-ISRAELI WAR (1973); EGYPTIAN-ISRAELI INTERIM AGREEMENT (1975)

DĪWĀN. Probably of Persian origin (though this is disputed), Dīwān is equivalent to a ministry or administrative department. It is also used on occasion to denote a collective of administrators, military chiefs, religious leaders and so on acting in a consultative role to the ruler--such as the Dīwān Bonaparte attempted to establish in Egypt.

DRUMMOND WOLFE CONVENTION. Sir Henry Drummond Wolfe was sent in 1884 to Istanbul by the British government to negotiate with the Ottomans the position of the British in Egypt following their occupation of the country in 1882. The first convention signed between the British and the Porte in 1885 established an agenda and a framework for discussions, and Sir Henry and Ghazi Mukhtar Pasha began eighteen months of negotiations.

The second convention initialed by the negotiators in May 1887 provided for the evacuation of British troops within three years and of British officers in the Egyptian army in five years; this withdrawal could be halted if there was any appearance of danger of instability. The negotiations were not able to resolve the conflicting claims of the parties with regard to the Sudan, and there was only a notional reference to necessary administrative reforms. Mukhtar Pasha failed to get British agreement on an increase in the number of Turkish officers serving with the Egyptian army, though under the terms of the convention the Turkish officers were meant to participate with their British counterparts in a special commission overseeing army administration and reorganization.

France and Russia raised strong objections to the convention, which the Sultan himself was reluctant to sign for fear of legitimatizing the British occupation of Egypt and setting a precedent whereby other European powers could seize Ottoman lands and gain his recognition of their position later. Britain had seen the convention as a means of enabling it to reduce its troop levels while ensuring its supremacy politically, as well as the right of automatic re-entry in time of war.

At the close of the negotiations Britain was left in Egypt without formal Turkish agreement but under no compulsion to withdraw her troops. Ghazi Mukhtar Pasha remained in Egypt as representative of the Ottoman Porte and gave encouragement to those nationalist groups in Egypt who wished to forge stronger links with the Porte as a way of lessening Britain's hegemony in the country.

DRUZE see AD-DARAZĪ

DUAL CONTROL. Dual Control was a system of European management of the Egyptian economy, established by an Anglo-French mission sent to Egypt in November 1876 and headed by George, Lord Goschen and A. Joubert.

The Goschen-Joubert negotiations followed the British refusal to participate in the commission, the Caisse de la Dette Publique, meant to serve as a vehicle for Anglo-French administration of Egypt's economy. Britain objected that the unified Egyptian debt that the Caisse was to ensure was paid off gave more benefit to Egypt's private French creditors than to its official British creditors. The unified debt was finally reduced from £91 to £59 millions, largely of official debts. Thereafter, under the Caisse, Dual Control was exercised with Egyptian revenue under British supervision and expenditure under French management. The British and French controllers worked in conjunction with the Caisse in the management of Egypt's economy and the settlement of its international financial obligations. The role of both the controllers and the Caisse came under increasing criticism as there emerged a strong nationalist movement in 1879. The brief resignation of the controllers in 1879 came in the midst of Egyptian reaction to the country's control by foreign interests, which, combined with domestic political unrest, culminated in the nationalist disturbances of 1882.

The French decision not to participate in the military suppression of the "Arabi Rebellion" in 1882, despite its active role in the drafting of the Joint Notes that helped spur it, left the British alone in physical occupation of the country in the autumn of 1882. In February 1883 Sir Auckland Colvin was nominated by the British as the sole financial adviser. The French maintained their representation on the Caisse and the Suez Canal Company Board, but their influence on Egyptian political events was to become increasingly negligible.

DUFFERIN REPORT. Lord Dufferin was British Ambassador to the Ottoman Porte at the time of the British invasion of Egypt in 1882 and was subsequently sent to Egypt in November 1882 to examine the situation and make recommendations. He published a report in March 1883 outlining the general principles under which Egypt should be administered at the national and local levels and addressing the problem of the involvement of the British with Egypt in the future. His solution, a compromise between those who advocated returning full sovereignty to the Egyptians and those who wished Britain to annex the country, was really a "veiled" protectorate. Certain carefully limited representative institutions would be maintained. A thirty-member legislative council was to be created, with an eighty-two-member legislative assembly, half of whose members would be appointed and whose powers would be limited to "examining" bills and, in the case of the Assembly, approving new taxes. The ministerial system was to be retained, with some Europeans in key positions, and the Khedive would remain head of the country. On the provincial level consultative councils would assist the governors in local administration. The British Resident was to have a strong role in keeping these institutions acting in line with British interests in Egypt. Though the report was intended to examine ways of terminating the British position in Egypt, the substance of its recommendations involved expanding this position. Additionally, the report assigned more than £4 million of Egypt's already overstretched revenues to pay for the British suppression of the Arabi Rebellion and subsequent British military occupation. His other recommendations, on military, administrative, and security reforms, were largely implemented over the next several years. Following the publication of the Dufferin Report, Sir Evelyn Baring, later Lord Cromer, was appointed British Agent and Consul-General in Egypt. The report was the basis of the Organic Law of 1883, drafted under Lord Dufferin's supervision.

-E-

EBEID, MAKRAM and WILLIAM EBEID see UBAID

ECONOMIC ORGANIZATIONS AND AGENCIES. Government bodies which were established to supervise and administer the transfer of the bulk of Egyptian industry from the private to the public sector. The first Economic Agency, created in January 1957, was concerned with the supervision of public and mixed companies and also was charged with management of the foreign investment nationalized in the post-Suez period. Prior to the 1961 nationalizations many of the (Bank) Misr complex of companies and the communications interests of Egyptian industrialist Ahmad Abbud had been placed under the Economic Agency. This expansion caused the capital of the Economic Agency to grow from £17 million in 1957 to £59 million in 1959; and following the nationalizations of December 1960 the Economic Agency controlled £80 million in capital of over 60 companies employing more than 80,000 workers.

The Economic Agency's role changed following the public-agency reorganizations in 1961. The Socialist Laws introduced that year brought many more companies into the public sector, and thirty-eight new sector organizations were created to supervise them. The 367 companies involved were grouped according to industrial categories, under the control of the individual agencies, or General Organizations as they came to be known later. Overall supervision was vested in the High Council for Public Agencies, under the direction of the president of Egypt.

Since the 1974 liberalizations of the economy the role of the Economic Organizations has been relaxed. Since 1975, some General Organizations have been phased out in favor of sectoral councils, and individual companies have been granted more autonomy with regard to decision making vis-à-vis the remaining General Organizations. These were to have their functions redefined in the light of intended changes in the public and private sector balance.

Another group known as the Economic Organization, or Economic Development Organization, was created in 1946 to coordinate development planning and in the 1952-61 period had responsibility for the development and social-services budgets as well as for the raising of capital for development financing.

ECONOMY. The Egyptian economy in the nineteenth and twentieth centuries prior to the 1952 Revolution was characterized by the government's laissez-faire approach to development and economic activity and by the continuing dominance of cash-crop agriculture. The brief experiment with industrialization through state capitalism attempted by Muhammad Ali concentrated on the production of military goods and the processing of cotton. Demand for the former collapsed with the reduction in the size of Egypt's army imposed in 1841. Growth in the latter had to face the opposition of European countries who preferred to import raw materials rather than processed goods. Additionally, the lack of trained skilled manpower could not support this early attempt at industrialization. The rapid buildup of both foreign investment and external debt during the reign of the Khedive Ismail (1863-79) permitted a faster development of Egypt's infrastructure and economy (particularly for the agricultural sector) but at the eventual expense of its independence both physically and financially.

Under the British, agricultural development, including agricultural exports, received the most favored treatment, with necessary improvements in irrigation being carried out and the construction of the Aswan Dam to increase the amount of land available for cultivation. These policies did nothing to encourage Egypt's nascent industrial sector (largely linked to the processing of commodities) but favored those who already had a position in land. The cost-effectiveness of large landholding for production and export, in combination with lenient tax rates and credit facilities for major landholders, left Egypt, by 1952, with 6 percent of the population holding 65 percent of the country's land. Few of the economic advantages of export agriculture touched the majority of Egyptian cultivators.

In view of the limited economic opportunities afforded by agriculture, the British were sharply criticized by Egypt's nationalists for failing to encourage industrial development. To correct this Talat Harb and a group of Egyptian industrialists and landowners formed Bank Misr in 1920 to provide capital for indigenous industry. In the period 1938-51 industrial production rose 138 percent. Its starting base was so small, however, that this growth still gave industry only a 15-percent share of Egypt's GNP in 1951. Neither the development of industry nor that of agriculture in the pre-Revolutionary period met the problems of the inequities in Egypt's distribution of wealth or of the need to provide jobs for a growing number of people in a country whose population was soaring. Real per-capita income in Egypt actually fell from U.S. $109.50 in 1907 to U.S. $63.50 in 1950.

An immediate objective of the leaders of the 1952 Revolution was to correct some of these distortions in the Egyptian economy. That they chose to address the problem through agrarian reform underlines how important that sector was in terms of its size and its share of the overall economy. The attitude of the Free Officers toward the industrial sector prior to 1957-58 did not seem well defined; the private sector was initially left fairly untouched. The nationalization of British, French, and other foreign interests in Egypt after the Suez War led to the creation of the Economic Agency to manage them for the public sector. This initial public management of companies was later broadened as the government began nationalizing companies in the private sector, which by the late 1950s was being blamed for its failure to invest in Egypt's development efforts. Following the nationalizations of 1961 under the provisions of the Socialist Laws, Egypt was left with a largely public-sector economy in the industrial sphere and the continued dominance of the national economy by a moderately reformed agricultural sector, with private-sector enterprises, on a small or artisan scale, dealing in both goods and services.

Between 1956 and 1963 the Egyptian economy registered a modest 3-percent annual increase in the per-capita GNP; but the Yemen War (which began in 1962), the increasingly high share of the budget devoted to defense (rising from 3.5 percent of GNP in 1950-51 to 12.3 percent in 1965), and Egypt's galloping population growth, all acted to drag down the growth rate of the economy. Increasingly, bureaucratic inefficiency and mismanagement began to plague the nationalized and public-sector companies as well as the agricultural sector in the pre-1967 period. Overlarge, overadministered, overstaffed, and under- or badly planned, the industrial sector's performance was in decline by the 1967 Arab-Israeli War; the economy itself was virtually bankrupt.

Economic performance between mid-1967 and the 1973 war was erratic, as Egypt suffered the loss of Suez Canal revenues and those from the Sinai oil fields. The continuing high defense bill, worsened by the need to replace the vast amount of equipment lost in 1967, was only partly met by increased subsidies from the Arab oil producers. The managers of Egypt's industries were unhappy with the degree of political interference in the running of the public sector, and overall planning, essential for the public sector, was replaced by yearly appropriations and assessments that did not permit the sector or its managers to benefit from forward planning.

The publication of President Sadat's October Paper in 1974 marked a major shift in government policy toward the public and private sectors. There was to be an increased emphasis on private-sector investment in the economy, and strong encouragement of foreign investment. Though some of the October Paper's reforms had been discussed as early as 1968, they now had official sanction and the active support of the new Prime Minister, Abdal Aziz Higazi. Law 43, issued in 1974, was the start of the "Open Door" policy through which President Sadat hoped to transform the Egyptian economy.

Such a transformation was not a smooth process. The problems faced by the country's industrial sector, particularly low wages and rising prices, led to a series of violent strikes in January and March 1975. That April Sadat replaced the Higazi government.

Despite the renewed cease-fire in the area, the reopening of the Suez Canal, and the return of the Abu Rudais oil fields to Egypt, the foreign investment sought by the government did not materialize quickly enough. By the end of 1976 only $75 million in foreign investment capital had come to Egypt at a time when the country was increasingly unable to meet its external indebtedness. The Sadat government finally approached the IMF at the end of 1976. The IMF demanded as an initial corrective measure that Egypt remove the subsidies on consumer foodstuffs and durables, which since the Revolution had kept food in the urban areas at a set, low price. The removal of these subsidies touched off the 1977 January Riots; they were quickly replaced and the OAPEC states approached for supplementary financing, which they provided.

Since the 1977 riots the government has adopted a more gradualist line, and the economy on a national level has profited from increase in revenues from the Suez Canal, from Egypt's modest oil exports, and from worker remittances sent by the 2 million or so Egyptians currently working in the other Arab states. The withdrawal of Arab economic investment in the wake of the Camp David Accords has affected only new investments, as most of the OAPEC states have continued to honor the commitments they made before 1977. From the near-bankruptcy of the country at the beginning of 1977, Egypt's foreign-exchange reserves for 1980 are estimated at $7.6 billion. However, import bills, particularly for food (70 percent of which is imported), continue to run slightly in excess of this. The government has not been successful in controlling the money supply or in resolving the politically difficult issue of subsidies, which continue to take an enormous amount of the national budget. However, Western commercial banks have taken an increasingly active role in raising loans for Egypt. Income distribution in Egypt, despite the longstanding limitations on salary levels introduced under Nasser and maintained under Sadat, remains highly unequal, both between urban and rural areas and within the urban areas themselves.

EDUCATION. Before the era of Muhammad Ali (1805-48) education for the majority of students in Egypt was conducted through religious schools, where the emphasis was on the memorization of the Quran, and study of the sayings and traditions associated with the Prophet Muḥammad. Education for girls, limited to those classes of society able to hire private tutors, was uncommon. Military education was under the supervision of, and confined to, the Mamluk households. Higher education in religious studies was available at al-Azhar, founded during the Fāṭimid dynasty, which had become a major institute for the training of religious scholars and personnel from throughout the Islamic world.

Muhammad Ali established a special diwan to advise him on education in 1836. He had earlier introduced secular training to his military recruits and officers, based on the European model, and also sent Egyptian students to Europe to study languages, arts and sciences. Strong official encouragement was given to translation of important books into Arabic. The separation of general from religious education developed in both Egypt and elsewhere in the Islamic world at this time. Faculties were established in medicine and the sciences and were all in operation by the 1840s. The reigns of Sa^{c}id (1854-63) and Ismail (1863-79) saw the arrival in Egypt of many Europeans who brought with them European schools and teachers. These schools, frequently under the direction of Christian religious orders, offered a high-quality secular education to Egyptian pupils: by 1914, at a time when general school enrollments were still quite low, these schools had more than 48,000 pupils, most of whom went on to fill important positions and government posts. Higher institutes for training teachers (1880) and lawyers (1886) were established and later incorporated into the university system. Ali Mubarak and Rifa^{c}a Tahtawi were both active in the development of education in Egypt.

A pair of specialized schools, the Dar al-^{c}Ulūm and the School of Qāḍīs, were opened in 1872 and 1907 respectively, to provide training for Arabic teachers and religious functionaries. Al-Azhar itself became the object of a campaign led by Shaykh Muhammad Abduh to bring its curriculum and teaching methods in line with modern needs. Despite the resistance of the highly conservative faculty the university slowly began to reform at the turn of the century, with the institution of established degree procedures.

The attitude of the British toward education in Egypt during their period of control of the country (1883-1922) has been criticized for neglecting all but elementary education, which they did work to improve and expand. This criticism applies especially to Lord Cromer, who during his term in office (1883-1907) consistently opposed the establishment of a national university. The teaching personnel recruited in England by British administrators in the Ministry of Education were also felt by many Egyptians to be inappropriate as teachers in an Egyptian setting, and conflicts within the Ministry between British and Egyptian administrators (seldom resolved in favor of the latter) over the style and substance of mass education increased in intensity as the years advanced. The Ministry attracted some of the brightest young Egyptians, but many of these had to wait until Egyptianization of the bureaucracy in the 1920s and 1930s permitted them to reach the administrative rank long denied them by the presence of so many European administrators.

A subscription campaign for an Egyptian national university was started in 1906 and enjoyed the active support of the Royal Family. King Fuad University opened in 1925, uniting the national university with the faculties of law, medicine, and engineering established earlier in Cairo. Before the 1952 Revolution further universities were founded in Alexandria (1942) and Ayn Shams (1950). Though the educational system from 1922 to 1952 was improving, it was still far from adequate in its ability to provide mass education. Students of ability had to be sent to school in Cairo, Alexandria, or the larger towns, limiting the higher levels of schooling to the better-off sectors of society or else (as for many of the students in the 1930s and 40s, including some of the Free Officers) made higher and secondary education a time of personal and financial hardship.

After the Revolution there was an expansion in school facilities for all children between six and twelve, with postprimary schools offering vocational training in agriculture, commerce, and domestic studies. Entrance to the four-year preparatory schools is by examination, and successful graduates of the preparatory schools are admitted to a three-year secondary school. At the end of this secondary education students sit the Thanawiyya ^{c}Amma exam, which determines whether they will gain a place at one of the national universities.

There are currently twenty universities in Egypt, including al-Azhar, whose enrollment figures individually are sometimes in the tens of thousands. As a university degree is essential for a job in the government bureaucracy (a government job is guaranteed to every university-leaver), competition for university places is intense (as are demands for the expansion of their number). In consequence classes of 2-3, 000 students, even in medicine, are not uncommon despite criticisms of the quality of the students passed through in such numbers; efforts to curtail enrollment have aroused controversy and even rioting, as happened in March 1968.

Egypt's universities produce thousands of teachers and doctors for the labor-importing OAPEC countries, where they sometimes compose the majority of the teaching force, and there is no doubt that such mass higher education has been of benefit to the country in terms of the remittances sent back by these workers. At the same time the difficulties of enforcing the law on compulsory schooling in Egypt's rural areas have left the country with a slowly declining 60-percent illiteracy rate; functional illiteracy may be higher. In the area of mass education, in fact, adult literacy programs, particularly those provided for recent arrivals from the rural areas in Cairo and other cities, may prove more effective in countering illiteracy than the past emphasis on rural primary education. Estimates of school enrollment in the late 1970s were that 70 percent of primary-school age and 40 percent of secondary-school age children were registered, though actual attendance figures may be considerably lower, as are the numbers of those completing schooling.

EGYPTIAN-AMERICAN RURAL IMPROVEMENT SERVICE (EARIS). Major land-reclamation project, EARIS commenced work in 1953 in Bahaira province and in two other sites, with Egyptian capital of £E5,450,000 and American capital of £E3,469,000. EARIS was hoping to eventually reclaim and develop 37,000 feddans, and the project was part of U.S. government policy of attempting to win the new military regime's support through backing what it saw as gradual, noncommunist social-welfare programs. Administrative complications notwithstanding, the EARIS project ran into problems with a lack of settlers, low crop yields, and political complications after the 1956 Suez War, which led to a gradual winding down of the program.

EGYPTIAN COMMUNIST PARTY. The three major communist groupings in Egypt--the Egyptian Communist Party, the Unified Egyptian Communist Party, and the Worker's Vanguard, formed a Committee of Coordination in the spring of 1957 and by that autumn had altered their name to the Committee of Unity. By January 1958, all three groups had merged to form the Egyptian Communist Party. The Party was active in addressing what it felt were the many unresolved ideological issues in Egypt--the role of the military, the social and economic development of society, and future political evolution in Egypt. Although the Party enjoyed a good audience in certain left-wing and intellectual circles, it can in fairness be said the Communist Party had slight impact on the government.

The post-Revolutionary Communist Party had no obvious links with an earlier Socialist (later Communist) Party, which existed briefly in the 1920s before it was suppressed by the government. Various groups with the label "communist" did appear in the

1930s and 40s but made no lasting impression on the political scene except to attract sharp and immediate official suppression. Communist involvement in the Front Organizations formed after the Second World War was important but its role as a minor party is probably best compared with the role of Ahmad Husayn's "Socialists"; the Ikhwan al Muslimun far outstripped both of them in popular support.

The 1958 incarnation of the Communist Party did not have a very easy relationship with the Nasser regime, despite Nasser's occasionally close ties with the Soviet Union; these seldom extended to toleration of left-wing socialists at home. Along with its Syrian equivalent, it was forced to affiliate with the National Union. With elements of the religious revivalists, the communists were the frequent targets of government crackdowns and arrests, particularly in 1959-64, followed unpredictably by periods of relaxation and toleration. In 1965 the Communist Party officially disbanded to join the Arab Socialist Union. Membership in the Communist Party is currently (1980) forbidden to Egyptians under the new political regulations announced in 1978; clandestine communist groups were accused by the government of involvement in the January 1977 riots.

EGYPTIAN FEDERATION OF INDUSTRIES. Established in 1924 by Talat Harb and a group of foreign and Egyptian industrialists, the federation sought to promote the development of Egypt's industrial sector and to put forward legislation to protect Egypt's nascent manufacturing industries. By the 1940s the EFI had become the spokesman for a strong minority of Egypt's elite who wished to lessen the continued domination of the country's political life and economic policies by the landed aristocracy. Ismail Sidqi, who served as Prime Minister of Egypt in the 1930s, was active in the federation, with which many other Egyptian politicians were associated. The federation consistently opposed the introduction of comprehensive labor legislation in Egypt, though such legislation was gradually introduced in piecemeal fashion by the 1936 and 1942 Wafd governments. The increase in the federation's Egyptian membership prior to 1952 helped shape the slightly more nationalist tenor of the EFI in the 1940s. The federation welcomed the investment incentives introduced in 1953-54, though it was cautious in its dealings with the new regime. The Egyptian Federation of Industries was in 1958 brought under control of the Ministry of Industry, which appointed its own nominees to the federation's board as well as named its chairman. The federation, under the leadership (1981) of Dr. Mahmud Ali Hasan, still acts to represent the interests of industry to the government.

EGYPTIAN TRADE UNION FEDERATION see GENERAL FEDERATION OF TRADE UNIONS

EGYPTIAN-ISRAELI INTERIM AGREEMENT/SECOND DISENGAGEMENT AGREEMENT. After intensive shuttle diplomacy by the U.S. Secretary of State Henry Kissinger, Egypt and Israel agreed in September 1975 to (1) partial pullback of Israeli troops in Sinai from the Mitla and Giddi passes, (2) return of the Abu Rudais oil fields in exchange for a mutual pledge to refrain from the threat or use of force or military blockade, and (3) the unimpeded passage of nonmilitary cargoes destined for Israel through the Suez Canal. The American government was to supervise an electronic early-warning system set up in Sinai, consisting of five listening posts, three manned by the U.S., one by Egypt, and one by Israel. To secure Israel's agreement, the United States made a number of concessions including, most significantly, a pledge not to negotiate directly with the PLO until that organization recognized Israel's right to exist and accepted UN Resolutions 242 and 338. For Egypt, the agreement helped consolidate the foothold it had gained in Sinai under the first disengagement agreement. U.S. involvement in the negotiations met a longstanding aim of Sadat to draw the Americans firmly into closer relations with Egypt, lessening Egypt's former dependence on Soviet initiatives in the area.

EGYPTIAN-ISRAELI PEACE TREATY. Concluded by Egypt and Israel on 26 March 1979 on the basis of the Camp David Accords, the Peace Treaty was signed through the efforts of U.S. President Carter to overcome Israeli objections to its terms. The treaty was not to be merely bilateral but was open to the participation of all parties in the region interested in peace.

The treaty provided that the state of war between Egypt and Israel was to be ended and that Israel would withdraw to the Mandate lines between itself and Egypt. This withdrawal would not, however, affect negotiations over the future of Gaza. Both parties committed themselves to respecting each other's national sovereignty, agreeing to live in peace and refrain from acts or threats of violence, belligerency, or hostility. Relations would be fully normalized in all areas.

The Israeli withdrawal would be accomplished in three phases over a three-year period. The second phase put Israeli troops behind a line stretching from Al Arish to Ras Muhammad; the third withdrawal would be to the international boundary. During this three-year period a UN presence would be maintained and a joint commission would supervise the withdrawal.

The Israelis were granted free passage through the Suez Canal and the Straits of Tiran. Both parties were enjoined from signing treaties that would in any way conflict with the peace treaty; further, obligations under the peace treaty would have preference over all existing commitments. Disputes between the two parties would be resolved by negotiation or arbitration, and a Claims Commission was to be established to ensure settlement of financial claims to each other's mutual agreement.

Negotiations on Palestinian autonomy were to begin in April 1979, with the invited participation of Jordan; failing Jordan's attendance the two signatories would negotiate alone. A target date of one year later was set for completion of the autonomy talks, following which elections in the West Bank and Gaza should be held and a self-governing authority elected. Once elections were held, the five-year transition period mentioned in the Camp David Accords would begin.

The autonomy talks have made slight progress since then, reaching an impasse on two main points: the withdrawal of the Israelis to the pre-1967 borders (evacuating their settlements in Gaza and the West Bank) and the definition of "autonomy." No elections for the self-governing authority have been held and Egypt has suspended the talks on several occasions to reflect official displeasure with Israeli government policies (1981).

EGYPTIAN-SYRIAN DEFENSE PACT. In November 1966 Egypt and Syria signed a five-year mutual defense pact in which the parties were required to come to each other's assistance if either was threatened. During the months following the conclusion of the pact tensions rose markedly between the Arab states and Israel. A massive retaliatory raid into Jordan by Israel in 1966 had been followed by further raids against both Jordan and Syria early in 1967. These raids and some armed border skirmishes were escalated by the shooting down of six Syrian aircraft by Israel in April, in retaliation for Syria's alleged increased backing of Palestinian fighters. Mutual inflammatory rhetoric was exchanged, including several weeks of statements by Israeli leaders advocating the overthrow of the Syrian regime. In May 1967 Syria charged that Israel was mobilizing her troops prior to an attack on the Golan Heights, and requested Egypt to fulfill its part of the Defense Pact. This pattern of action and reaction was to culminate in the closing of the Straits of Tiran by Egypt in retaliation for Israel's actions toward Syria. In turn, Israel attacked Egypt on 6 June on the grounds (among others) that the Straits closures represented an unacceptable military threat. The Defense Pact lapsed in 1971, but Syria and Egypt continued to coordinate defensive and offensive strategy in some areas down to the 1973 war, when they launched a joint offensive.

L'ÉGYPTIENNE/AL-MIṢRIYYA. First women's magazine, L'Égyptienne was printed from 1925 to 1940. Founded by the Egyptian feminists and nationalists Hoda Shaarawi and Ceza Nabarawi, the magazine largely reflected the liberal middle- and upper-class sentiments of its authors and readership, but was nonetheless the first magazine to address directly the problems of the Arab woman's role in a changing society. The magazine gave strong support to women's education, liberalizations in the Personal Status laws regarding women's rights and protection of women workers.

ELECTORAL COMMISSION. Established by the government of Ziwar Pasha in 1925, the commission was under the chairmanship of Sidqi Pasha. It was formed to consider various ways of limiting the franchise (and reducing the Wafd Party's chances of automatic victory in each election). The Electoral Commission proposed wealth, property, and educational qualifications. The number of electors was reduced by half, and the principle of indirect suffrage was recommended to reduce the impact of the Wafd's appeal for the mass of voters. A restrictive electoral law was introduced in December 1925 but rescinded prior to the 1926 elections after general protest. Electoral restrictions were finally introduced and implemented by the 1930 Sidqi government.

ELEPHANTINE. Small island in the Nile at the present-day city of Aswan, Elephantine has been mentioned since pharaonic times. With Kom Ombo upriver, it was regarded as the northern border of Nubia. Papyrii relating to the immediate pre-Ptolemaic period, discovered on Elephantine in 1904-08, provide an important record of Egypt during this period. In Muslim times the governors of Elephantine were leaders of the caravans to the Sudan and charged with the trade in the precious commodities brought in from central Africa.

EMIN PASHA (EDUARD CARL SCHNITZER) (1840-1892). Originally a medical officer in the service of the Ottoman Porte, Emin Pasha, an Austrian, joined the service of C. G. Gordon, Governor-General of the Sudan for the Khedive Ismail, in 1876. In 1878 Emin Pasha was made governor of the Equatorial Provinces, charged with consolidating Egyptian claims in the southern Sudan and gaining control of the ivory trade. He was an effective governor and enthusiastic explorer of the region. By 1881, and the outbreak of the Mahdist Rebellion, Emin Pasha had begun to organize a government in the area, despite nonexistent infrastructure. For the next six years Emin Pasha was under threat from the Mahdists; in 1885 Sudan was evacuated by the Egyptians, who advised him to withdraw. Neither Mahdists nor Egyptians seemed able to persuade Emin to leave Equatorial Province. In 1888 the British and Egyptian governments sent the explorer H. M. Stanley to convince Emin to withdraw; he finally withdrew after mutiny of his own men and renewed hostilities by the Mahdists forced him to retreat from the territory in 1889. He remained in Africa until his death three years later.

ENTENTE CORDIALE (DECLARATION OF 1904). Agreement between Britain and France that brought to an end nearly thirty years of uncertainty about their respective positions in Egypt, the Entente recognized Britain's de facto control of Egypt in exchange for British recognition of French claims in Morocco. Signed in April 1904, it reestablished that the Caisse (charged with supervising the paying off of that debt) would only receive certain Egyptian revenues on behalf of the bondholders and not have the right to interfere with other aspects of administration in the country. The consent of the Caisse would no longer be required for the issue of new loans, and it would have no power to limit the government's administrative expenditure. The entire funded debt of Egypt was to be liquidated by 1912. Many Egyptian nationalists who relied on French sympathy and support (most notably Mustafa Kamil) were dismayed by this agreement. Eldon Gorst, later Lord Cromer's successor, negotiated the Entente on England's behalf and one year later secured from the Khedive Abbas a letter recognizing England's special position in Egypt.

EUROPEAN CABINET see RESCRIPT OF 1878; COUNCIL OF MINISTERS

EVACUATION AGREEMENT see ANGLO-EGYPTIAN EVACUATION AGREEMENT

EZBEK AL-TUTUSH see IZBAK AT-TUTUSH

-F-

FAHMY, ISMAIL (1922-). Egyptian Foreign Minister from 1976 to November 1977, Ismail Fahmy served in the Egyptian diplomatic service until 1969. In 1972 he was given his first ministerial appointment, Tourism, and in 1973 was made acting Foreign Minister. President Sadat made him his Secretary for Information in February 1974, and in 1975-77, Fahmy was vice-president of the Council of Ministers. In November 1976 he was appointed Foreign Minister. He broke with Sadat in November 1977 over the President's planned visit to Jerusalem and he has been out of the government since then.

FAHMI PASHA, MUSTAFA (d. 1914). Prime Minister in the reigns of Tawfiq and Abbas II, Fahmy was a strong supporter of British interests in Egypt. Mustafa Fahmy served as Foreign Minister during the 1882 Arabi Revolt, appointed largely for his acceptability as a negotiator with the foreign powers. Though he did not especially favor the Turco-Circassian elite that Arabi was trying to displace, he was not in sympathy with the nationalist line of Arabi and his supporters.

Fahmy formed his first government in 1891 following the resignation of Riyad Pasha, but he was unpopular with the new Khedive, Abbas Hilmi II, who came to power in 1892 filled with nationalist sentiments. Abbas tried to replace Fahmy with Tigane Pasha or Husayn Fakhri when Fahmy fell ill in 1893; Tigane and Fakhri proved unacceptable to Lord Cromer, who permitted Abbas to appoint Riyad Pasha. Riyad, then Nubar, served in the Prime Ministership over the next two years, both experiencing difficulties in their relations with the Palace and/or Cromer. Cromer then had Fahmy reappointed to the Prime Ministership in November 1895; he held office until 1908 before making way for a government headed by Butrus Ghali Pasha.

Fahmy is viewed as being overly sympathetic to Cromer and as offering little resistance to Cromer's attempts to influence government policy. Fahmy was much resented by Abbas II, who finally succeeded in having him removed from power after Sir

Eldon Gorst took over as High Commissioner in 1907. Shortly before his death in 1914 the British again approached Fahmy about forming a government, but he was unable to do so.

AL FĀ'IZ (r. 1154-60/549-55). Fāṭimid Caliph, infant son and successor of aẓ-Ẓāfir, al-Fā'iz was placed on the throne by aẓ-Ẓāfir's vizier and assassin, ᶜAbbās. ᶜAbbās attempted to govern independently but was soon displaced by the governor of South Egypt, aṣ-Ṣāliḥ Talā'iᶜ, who was summoned to Cairo by the harīm following aẓ-Ẓāfir's murder. Ṣāliḥ Talā'iᶜ brought ᶜAbbās and his son to justice and went on to campaign in Palestine in 1158/553, taking Gaza and Hebron. During his reign al-Fā'iz was kept from all visible involvement in the government. After his death he was succeeded by his cousin al-ᶜĀḍid.

FAKHRI, HUSAYN (1843-1910). Prime Minister for a short time during the reign of Abbas II, Fakhri was asked by Abbas to form a government as a corrective to the overly pro-British Prime Minister, Mustafa Fahmy. Abbas had previously tried to replace Fahmy with Tigane Pasha, a choice rejected by Cromer on the grounds of Tigane's religion but in reality to quash any ideas Abbas might have had about steering a course independent of the Consul-General.

Fakhri had served as Minister of Justice in the reign of Tawfiq (1879-92), working actively for the reform of the Egyptian legal system. Though regarded as a moderate by most Egyptian politicians, Fakhri was in Cromer's eyes a francophile nationalist. Abbas' appointment of him without prior consultation with Cromer was strongly protested. During his one month in office nationalist demonstrators attacked the offices of the pro-British newspaper Al Muqattam, in retaliation for an ultimatum delivered by Cromer to the Khedive demanding Fakhri's dismissal and an apology. Riyad Pasha was finally called in to form a government, and Fakhri became president of the Council of Ministers (1894-1905) and Minister of the Interior (1895-1908).

FAQĀRIYYA. One of the leading houses of the Egyptian beylicate in the seventeenth and eighteenth centuries, the Faqāriyya were composed of Circassian Mamluks allied with the Nisf Sa^c^d, an indigenous grouping of merchants and artisans. The Faqāriyya were dominant in the early internal struggles for power among the beys, between 1630/1039 and 1656/1066. Under the leadership of Riḍwān Bey al-Faqārī the faction managed to maintain its preeminence, but after his death in 1656/1060 the leadership of the Faqāriyya became disunited. This lack of unity permitted the Ottoman Viceroy, in collaboration with the Faqāriyya's rivals, the Qāsimiyya, to proscribe the Faqāriyya in 1660/1070, following their defeat during a rebellion by the leaders of the faction.

Both the Faqāriyya and Qāsimiyya were unusually quiescent after the assassination of the Qāsimiyya leader by the Ottoman governor in 1662/1070-01, but in the 1690s/1100s the Faqāriyya under Ibrāhīm Bey were again active. With the help of the Qāzdughliyya military faction, Ibrāhīm gained supremacy in the beylicate from 1692/1103 until his death three years later, after which the situation within the beylicate became unclear once more.

Sixteen years of instability in Egypt culminated in the Great Insurrection of 1711/1123, which saw the defeat of the Faqāriyya and their Janissary allies, now under the command of Afranj Aḥmad. The Faqāriyya rose once more in 1730/1143 to crush the divided Qāsimiyya, after which they themselves, rent by divisions, were defeated and silenced by the Qāzdughliyya in 1748/1161.

FARAJ (AN-NĀṢIR NĀṢIR AD-DĪN FARAJ) (r. 1399-1405/801-08 and 1405-12/808-15). Burjī Mamluk Sultan, son of Barqūq, Faraj initially reigned under a regency that was terminated when the two guardians appointed to him could not resolve their differences. His first reign was interrupted for three months; his incompetent younger brother, ^c^Abd al-^c^Azīz, took power, after which Faraj was restored and went on to rule for another seven years.

At the beginning of Faraj's first reign the Ottoman Sultan Bāyazīd I broke his alliance with Barqūq and seized Malatya. Faraj and his regents also had to face a rebellion in Syria, which was becoming increasingly destabilized by the presence of Tīmūr and his army, which had entered Syrian territory in 1400/803, sacking Damascus one year later. Faraj, accompanied by the historian Ibn Khaldūn, journeyed to Syria to meet with Tīmūr; however the situation was saved not by Faraj's presence but by Tīmūr's decision to turn northward, away from Egypt. Upon Tīmūr's death in 1405/808 the immediate threat posed by his forces finally receded.

Faraj's second reign was dominated by the renewed rebelliousness of the Amīrs in Syria, Jaqam (killed soon after proclaiming himself Sultan in 1407/809) and Nawrūz. His commander, Shaykh, was sent to replace the latter, but joined him instead. The two rebels resisted three separate attempts to suppress them.

Faraj's reign saw a weakening of the Egyptian administration and economy; a serious famine and plague in 1403/806 brought predictable hardship in both rural and urban areas and a massive death toll among civilians and Mamluks. The challenges to Faraj in Syria limited his ability, it would seem, to handle the situation in Egypt; the country's economy was in tatters by the time of Faraj's death. Unable to defeat Shaykh and Nawrūz, Faraj was forced to retreat to Damascus, where he learned of his deposition in favor of the ᶜAbbāsid Caliph, al-Mustaᶜīn in 1412/815. Faraj was executed in Damascus.

FARID, MUHAMMAD (1868-1919). Egyptian nationalist leader, Muhammad Farid was a lawyer by training. In 1891 he was appointed to the Native Court of Appeals but left to join the bar. As deputy public prosecutor in the 1896 sedition trial of Shaykh Ali Yusuf, Farid's lenient prosecution angered Cromer, and the latter's reaction prompted Farid's decision after the trial to retire from the bar. He naturally enjoyed good relations thereafter with Shaykh Ali, who published a nationalist paper associated with the Palace. Farid was also linked with the nationalist grouping headed by the Khedive and with the young Mustafa Kamil, who was to dominate the Egyptian nationalist movement by the turn of the century. In fact the growing prominence of Kamil, who initially had enjoyed the support of Shaykh Ali, led to a cooling of Shaykh Ali's relations with both Kamil and Farid. Shaykh Ali began restricting Kamil's access to his newspaper, Al-Mu'ayyad, whereupon Farid used his own funds to finance the establishment of Al-Liwa. The paper, which began printing in 1899, was the platform for the Nationalist Party and for Kamil and Farid.

Though relations with Shaykh Ali and the Palace were strained from the time of Al-Liwa's foundation, the Dinshaway Incident in 1906 led Farid to form a delegation to appeal to the Khedive to mend his relationship with Kamil. This move was temporarily successful.

After Kamil's death in 1908, Farid became head of the Nationalist Party over the opposition of Kamil's family. Working in cooperation with the new editor of Al-Liwa, Shaykh Dawish, Farid was to make up in controversy what he lacked in Kamil's charisma. During the early years of his leadership Farid proposed a series of legal and economic reforms to protect Egyptian agriculture. With Umar Lutfi, Farid supported the creation of agricultural cooperatives. However, his attacks on the Copts and his support for Turkey were not well received domestically and were received with indifference by the Turks. The fortunes of the Nationalists declined after the 1910 assassination of the Coptic Prime Minister, Butrus Ghali, by a member or supporter of the Nationalist Party, Ibrahim Wardani.

Farid was sentenced to six months' imprisonment in 1912 for publishing seditious material, and he subsequently left Egypt. A brief journey to Istanbul proved unsatisfactory, and Farid settled in Geneva. Meanwhile the poor relations between Abbas and the new High Commissioner, Kitchener (appointed in 1911), led to attempts to reconcile Abbas and Farid to strengthen the former's hand in his dealings with Kitchener.

Following his deposition in 1914 Abbas joined Farid in Switzerland. The two men gave support to the oncoming Axis cause late in the war, which was not an entirely popular move in Egypt. Farid was not invited to join the new nationalist grouping, the Wafd, when it was forming in 1918-19; he died in exile in Berlin.

FARUQ (d. 1965). Son of Fuad I and King of Egypt from his coronation in July 1937 until the Revolution of 1952, Faruq was barely seventeen at the time of his father's death in April 1936. The young king was initially very popular in Egypt but in a short time assumed the autocratic manner of his father and a lifestyle found increasingly unacceptable by many of his subjects. His lack of leadership in the many crises that Egypt faced prior to the Revolution enabled forces beyond the control of the Palace and the government to gain control of Egypt's national life.

Faruq dismissed the Wafd government of Nahhas Pasha at the end of 1937, following a prolonged period of street violence and internal dissension within the Wafd leadership, but domestic politics were rapidly overtaken by the deteriorating international situation. Italian colonial ambitions in Libya and Ethiopia alarmed the British government, who were deeply unhappy with the number of Italians found among Faruq's inner circle. Very quickly Faruq's relationship with the British Ambassador, Sir Miles Lampson, came to parallel the relationship between his predecessor Abbas II and Lord Cromer, with Lampson's high-handed treatment of Faruq matched by Faruq's resentment of Lampson. This built to a crisis by 1942, and saw Lampson and the British government trying to force Faruq to accept a Wafdist government. Though the British had not especially backed the Wafd up to this point, they felt that the Wafd, which was still the most popular national party, would be more effective in leading Egypt and its involvement in the British war effort. Since war broke out, Faruq had refused to ask Nahhas, the Wafd leader, to form a government; instead, through 1940-41 a series of largely ineffective governments were formed by Palace sympathizers. Lampson eventually decided to take strong action.

Surrounding Abdin Palace with tanks on 4 February, Lampson walked in with a letter of abdication, which he intended to force Faruq to sign unless the King agreed to have Nahhas form a government. Faruq capitulated, and the Wafd came to power. Faruq's humiliation aroused resentment, particularly in the army.

As the war drew to its close Faruq dismissed the Wafd in October 1944. Faruq and his Palace circle began to intervene more actively in national politics. The Wafd Party was kept firmly out of power until 1950. All efforts at political and economic reform met with the Palace's disfavor, with the result that much national political debate was shifted to the streets. The civil disturbances that marred the postwar period in Egypt continued until 1949, when a long period of government repression finally brought a fragile peace. The poor performance of the Egyptian army in the Palestine fighting in 1948 rebounded on the government and on Faruq himself. His decision to divorce his popular wife, Farida, his personal life, and a later honeymoon during Ramadan, the Muslim holy month of fasting, also aroused much adverse popular comment.

Faruq's "reconciliation" with the Wafd and Nahhas in 1950, when they were returned to power in elections held in January, showed all the talent of his father for keeping his opponents off-guard. His withdrawal into a life of indulgence permitted him to make a peace of sorts with the British, though the Wafd were still struggling to gain recognition of Faruq's rights to rule the Sudan. The rapid deterioration in Egypt's internal situation during the first half of 1952, following the burning of Cairo, revealed Faruq's true weakness and incapacity to act. A series of governments were brought in and dismissed, while Faruq's credibility sank to new lows. At the time of the Free Officers' coup of 23 July, Faruq was in Alexandria; he abdicated in favor of his infant son, Ahmad Fuad II, on 26 July, when it became clear that the British would not rescue him. Faruq was allowed to leave Egypt unharmed and with most of his wealth. He settled in Europe, where he died in obscurity in 1965.

FĀṬIMID EGYPT (969-1171/358-567). The only Shīʿa dynasty to hold power in Egypt, the Fāṭimid dynasty was founded by ʿAbdallāh al-Mahdī in 909/297. ʿAbdallāh (known as ʿUbayd Allāh in some sources) claimed descent from the Prophet Muḥammad's daughter Fāṭima (wife of the fourth Caliph, ʿAlī). Initially based in Syria, he established a base in North Africa (al-Mahdiyya), seized Sicily, and made tributaries of a number of Berber tribes in the area. As early as 913-14/301-02 the Fāṭimids were raiding Egypt, and they briefly took Alexandria. A second attack, in 919-21/307-09, was turned back, but Fāṭimid strength in North Africa doubtless influenced the decision of the ʿAbbāsid Caliph in Baghdad to install a military strongman, Muḥammad b. Tughj al-Ikhshīd, as governor of Egypt in 935/323. His descendants, the Ikhshīdids, went into eclipse after the death of their powerful vizier and ruler Kāfūr, in 968/357. By the time the Fāṭimid general Jawhar aṣ-Ṣiqillī marched on Egypt in 969/358 he was easily able to defeat the disunited Ikhshīdid defenders.

Jawhar established a new capital three miles to the north of al-Fusṭāṭ, al-Qāhira ("The Victorious"). By his victory he also established a Shīʿa Caliph in Cairo, who was in direct competition with the Sunnī ʿAbbāsid Caliph in Baghdad for legitimacy, power, and territory. The full territorial ambitions of the Fāṭimids beyond Egypt have been questioned by modern historians of the period, but after their defeat of an initial challenge by the Qaramatians of Eastern Arabia the Fāṭimids had by 978/368 secured areas of Syria and the Hijaz. Their control of Syrian territory was acknowledged by the Byzantine Emperor in a treaty signed in 987/377, though Aleppo broke away in 1023/414 and the province was in general rebellion in 1037/429. During this period the Fāṭimids also experienced difficulties with their territories in North Africa, with a major rebellion in Cyrenaica (eastern Libya) in 1005-06/396. Their position in Libya was eventually supplanted by their former allies, the Zīrids.

The unique nature of the Fāṭimid's religious claims, and the effectiveness of their network of missionaries, probably won them more converts than their qualified military successes. In 1057-59/448-51 the Buyid general Arslān al-Basāsīrī proclaimed the Fāṭimid Caliph al-Mustanṣir in Mosul and Baghdad, though the Fāṭimids did not have the men, money, or real desire to back this unexpected extension of their power. Similarly, they gained the allegiance of the Yemen during the Ṣulayḥī dynasty's ascendancy (1038-1139/429-532).

By 1070/462 Fāṭimid power outside Egypt was diminished by the Normans (who established themselves in Sicily and south Italy after 1071/463); by Turcoman troops under a former Fāṭimid officer, Atsiz (who threatened Egypt in 1077/496 after seizing Damascus and portions of Fāṭimid territories in Syria); by the Saljūqs (advancing from Baghdad, which they took from al-Basāsīrī in 1060/451); and finally the Crusaders, who landed in Syria in 1096/490. It is possible that the Fāṭimids hoped that the Crusaders might be used, wittingly or otherwise, to reduce the threat posed by the Saljūq Turks. Embassies were sent to the Crusaders at Antioch in 1098/491, the year the Fāṭimids took Jerusalem; whatever the Fāṭimids' plans, the Crusaders took Jerusalem from them in the next year. By the reign of al-Ḥāfiz in 1130/524 much of the Fāṭimid territory in the Levant had been lost, though a brief Crusader attack on Egypt had been repulsed in 1118/512. The final Fāṭimid holding in Syria, Ascalon, fell to the Crusaders in 1153/548.

The last decade of Fāṭimid rule saw increasing Crusader activity in Egypt itself. Between 1161/556 and 1163/558 Amalric raided Egypt and received tribute. Dissension in the Egyptian court brought the Zangid ruler of Damascus, Nūr ad-Dīn, into active involvement; in 1164/559 he sent an army under his general Shīrkūh to support the candidacy of the vizier Shāwar. Shāwar's subsequent break with Shīrkūh brought the Crusaders back at Shāwar's invitation, and they returned again in 1167/563 to meet a new invasion by Shīrkūh. A third Crusader campaign, in 1168/564, was undertaken to reduce Egypt to a tributary state, but it withdrew in the face of yet another invasion by Shīrkūh, which unseated Shāwar. Shīrkūh became vizier to the last Fāṭimid Caliph, al-ᶜĀḍid, but died shortly thereafter. He was succeeded by his nephew Ṣalāḥ ad-Dīn, who brought Fāṭimid rule to an end two years later, in 1171/567, and restored Egypt to the Sunnī fold.

The rise and fall in the fortunes of the Fāṭimids were shaped by external factors, primarily the ascendancy of the Saljūqs and the arrival in the Islamic world of the Crusaders. With such strong challenges to their rule from outside Egypt the Fāṭimids were barely able to contain the establishment of various petty dynasties on their North African territories. Their decline was also severely affected by circumstances within Egypt, where the Fāṭimid rulers suffered a series of catastrophic famines that led to a breakdown of order and of discipline among the troops.

The first two Fāṭimid Caliphs, al-Muᶜizz and al-ᶜAzīz, ruled an expansive Fāṭimid state, aided by military skills of Jawhar aṣ-Ṣiqillī. The third Fāṭimid Caliph in Egypt, al-Ḥākim, with his remarkable policies and personality, has overshadowed and perhaps unfairly dominated consideration of the Fāṭimids as a dynasty. Much of what al-Ḥākim did in his twenty-five years in office seems inexplicable to later times, though some of his edicts have been defended as making economic (if not other) sense as Egypt slid into the cycle of famine and disease that marred the entire Fāṭimid period. By the time of al-Ḥākim's disappearance there is no doubt that he was thoroughly controversial, but he did manage to hold on to power in a country where rulers who went beyond what the court or the army could accept were very easily deposed. The Caliphs who followed increasingly lost power to their viziers and their courts. The fifty-eight-year reign of al-Mustanṣir (1036-94/427-87) coincided with a level of misery and anarchy (through famine and army rebellions) that was to change the character of the Fāṭimid regime. The court was eventually required to recall its Armenian general, Badr al-Jamālī, from Syria to restore the situation, which he did in 1074/466. It was too late to stop the decline outside Egypt, however. Badr's campaigns in Syria in 1078/471 were ineffective, and by 1080/473 the Fāṭimid Caliph's name had ceased to be mentioned in prayers at Mecca. From the time of Badr al-Jamālī onward the Fāṭimid Caliphs were under the control of their military chiefs and viziers, who could only gain in power as the arrival of the Crusaders gave new importance to the defending armies of the Islamic world. The Fāṭimid military commanders proved, however, less able to meet the Crusaders in battle than they were capable of regularly deposing each other. The divisions among them, starting with the competition among the Berber, Sūdān, and Turkish regiments and developing into open factional fighting, gave scope for both the Crusaders and the Fāṭimids' Muslim opponents to expand their power and territory at the Fāṭimids' expense.

The Fāṭimid dynasty did not succeed in converting the majority of Egyptians to Shīʿa Islam. Disputes over succession to the Fāṭimid Caliphate gave rise to a number of breakaway Shīʿa groups, which are found today in India and Yemen though not in the country of their origin. The Druze in Syria revere al-Ḥākim, declared a holy being by their founder, ad-Dārāzi. Each of these movements had the effect of splitting the Dāʿī, the religious missionaries who were the support of the Caliph and the supervisors of his administration. In turn, the falling off of the backing of the Dāʿī was one more factor in the decline in position of the Caliphs which, acting in tandem with the external and military threats they faced, hastened the end of the Fāṭimid period in Egypt.

The Fāṭimids enjoyed the services of some extremely competent viziers, especially in the early decades of their rule. In later years the vizierate became a powerful and contested office in Egypt. However, the Fāṭimids' taxation and rural policies led to the neglect of irrigation and repair works to existing canals and a consequent agricultural decline that did much to destabilize their regime. The Fāṭimids gave every encouragement to trade, which flourished with a number of countries during this period almost in spite of the chaos. The Fāṭimids left Egypt a wealth of art and architecture whose delicacy and style were seldom matched by succeeding regimes. Poetry, science, historiography, and theological writings were all encouraged by the court. The first major mosque founded by the Fāṭimids, al-Azhar, subsequently became a center for training Shīʿa missionaries but went on to become, under later Sunnī dynasties, the foremost Sunnī religious university in the Muslim world.

The Fāṭimid court, built around the glorification and mystical authority of the Caliph, has come down in the sources as a place of overwhelming luxury and high culture, set in an increasingly anarchic Egypt. The unique character of the Fāṭimids in Egypt was shaped as much by their Shīʿa faith as by their Egyptian setting.

<u>Fāṭimid Caliphs in Egypt:</u>

953/341	Al-Muʿizz
975/365	Al-ʿAzīz
996/386	Al-Ḥākim
1021/411	Aẓ-Ẓāhir
1036/427	Al-Mustanṣir
1094/487	Al-Mustaʿlī
1101/495	Al-Āmir
1130/524	Al-Ḥāfiz (first year as regent)
1149/544	Aẓ-Ẓāfir
1154/549	Al-Fā'iz
1160-71/555-67	Al-ʿĀḍid

FAWZI, MAHMUD (1900-80). Egyptian diplomat and politician, Mahmud Fawzi, Egypt's first permanent UN representative, served twenty-six years in various diplomatic posts before being appointed Foreign Minister of Egypt after the 1952 Revolution, a post he held until 1958. Following the formation of the UAR Fawzi served as Minister of Foreign Affairs. Throughout this period he led occasional delegations to the United Nations to make special representations on matters of concern to Egypt, most notably the 1956 Security Council debate over the Suez Canal nationalization. In 1962-64 Fawzi was appointed to serve on the Presidential Council. He was made Deputy Prime Minister for Foreign Affairs in 1965, during the period of difficult diplomatic relations with Britain and Saudi Arabia over Yemen. In 1967 Fawzi became Nasser's Special Presidential Adviser on Foreign Affairs and served as Vice-President in 1967-68.

In October 1970, after Nasser's death, Fawzi was chosen Prime Minister and served President Sadat in that post until 1972, when he again became Vice-President. He remained Vice-President and Adviser on Political Affairs until his retirement in 1974.

FAWZI, GENERAL MUHAMMAD (1915-). Minister of Defense from 1968 to 1971, Fawzi was dismissed by President Sadat for involvement in an alleged plot to overthrow the government. Fawzi had been Commander-in-Chief since the dismissal of General Amer in June 1967. He had previously commanded the Egyptian Expeditionary Force to the Yemen in 1962 and was made General and Armed Forces Chief of Staff in 1964. In recognition of his past services to the army, Fawzi's fifteen-year prison sentence was terminated by a pardon in January 1974.

FEDDAN. Unit of land measurement in Egypt and the Sudan, equivalent to 1.038 acres or 4,201 square meters.

FEDERATION/CONFEDERATION OF ARAB REPUBLICS. Concluded in April 1971 between Libya, Syria, and Egypt, the Agreement was intended as the basis for creation of a federal union of these states. The involvement of Sadat in the negotiations came shortly after his election as president of Egypt and was viewed by some observers as an attempt to identify himself with Nasser's pan-Arab legacy. The following month a political shake-up in Egypt led to the arrest of several powerful figures associated with the Nasser regime.

A draft constitution for the Confederation was signed on August 1971 and approved by all three countries in referendums.

Sadat was chosen to be the Federation's first president, with Cairo as the capital. It was also announced the name "United Arab Republic" (used by Egypt since the breakup of the UAR in 1961) would be dropped in favor of "Egypt." Various economic, political and military areas were to be examined to determine where coordination or unification could best be attempted.

Momentum for the union faded in the following year, and by the outbreak of the 1973 Arab-Israeli War the federation had been shelved due to President Sadat's alienation from the Libyan leader Colonel Gaddafi, after the latter sent 30,000 Libyans to march on Egypt to express support for the federation.

FEDERATION OF ARAB STATES see UNITED ARAB STATES

FELLAH, FELLAHIN. The peasant cultivators of Egypt; the word derives from the Arabic "fallāḥ," meaning "tiller of the soil."

FIVE-FEDDAN LAW. Introduced in 1912 at the instigation of the new High Commissioner, Lord Kitchener, the Five-Feddan Law sought to relieve the growing problem of rural indebtedness. Agricultural holdings of individuals who did not own more than five feddans of land in toto could not be seized for indebtedness. The Agricultural Bank, established in 1902, was encouraged to assist these smallholders with the provision of credit. The Five-Feddan Law had little actual impact, as the necessity for raising annual loans remained, and land represented, for most small farmers, their only collateral.

FIVE-YEAR PLANS. Beginning in 1957 the Egyptian government sought to introduce systematic economic planning through five-year plans (which have generally been put forward as two segments of an overall ten-year plan). The first five-year plan was initiated in January 1958, following the establishment of a National Planning Committee and Economic Agency and discussions on the relative merits of public and private sector investment in development. The 1958 plan was replaced in 1960, following its failure to spur private investment in the economy, by a new five-year plan, with a targeted increase in the national income of 40 percent. Government investment in industry aimed at a 2/3 rise in the GNP, with greater emphasis on heavy industry rather than consumer-goods production. The second part of this five-year plan (1965-69) aimed at a further generous expansion in Egypt's industrial base to cope with the economic and employment problems caused by Egypt's burgeoning population. This plan was replaced in 1967 by the more modest Accomplishment Plan, which toned down many of the earlier plan's ambitious goals.

In the post-Nasser period a series of yearly budgetary allocations and an eighteen month transition plan (June 1974 to December 1975) were replaced, in 1976, by a new five-year plan, once again with the emphasis on industrial development. In 1978 a reappraisal of the overall plan led to the creation of a transitional five-year plan covering the period 1978-82. This plan put greater emphasis on industrial performance rather than expansion per se, and on private, including foreign, investment. Under the combination of past plans the growth rate in the GNP has averaged about 5.6 percent per annum. The latest five-year (development) plan scheduled to run 1980-84, targets a 10-percent annual growth rate, greater decentralization, and continued private-sector growth. (See also TEN-YEAR PLANS.)

FREE NATIONAL PARTY see HIZB AL-WATANI AL-HURR

FREE OFFICERS. Name given by themselves to the military officers who engineered the 1952 coup d'état in Egypt, the Free Officers were in the main drawn from the 1938 graduates of the Military Academy. This was the first class admitted after entrance criteria for the academy had been liberalized with regard to the students' social background.

The Free Officers were from 1942 under the influence, if not the formal leadership, of Gamal Abdal Nasser, who by 1944 was holding irregular meetings with sympathetic young officers. By 1949 they were planning the takeover of the government. Other groupings of like-minded young officers kept in touch, and contacts were made with the mass parties, such as the Ikhwan al-

Muslimun (Muslim Brethren) and Misr al-Fatat. Although the facts are far from fully known, the Free Officers appear to have given some military training, and possibly equipment as well, to the paramilitary wing of the Ikhwan al-Muslimun in the pre-Revolutionary period.

The antagonism felt by the Free Officers toward the Egyptian government was sharpened as a result of their experiences in the 1948 fighting in Palestine, when the lack of equipment and the poor leadership of their senior officers led them to one defeat after another. The Free Officers began distributing anti-regime material after the war, and during this period they forged stronger links with groups like the Ikhwan. It is possible that some of the Free Officers were envisaging a cooperative movement with the Ikhwan whereby the latter would provide a mass following under Free Officer leadership. This was a serious miscalculation, whose full impact did not reveal itself until after the Revolution.

In 1950 Gamal Abdal Nasser was formally elected president of the Free Officers Executive Committee, and at this time it was planned that there would be a coup in 1954 or 1955. The burning of Cairo on Black Saturday (26 January 1952) convinced the Free Officers that they would have to act sooner. They had earlier decided to use General Muhammad Naguib as a figurehead, Naguib having incurred the Palace's disfavor by winning, with the support of the Free Officers, the presidency of the Officers' Club over Faruq's candidate. He was also one of the few senior military figures with a respectable record in the 1948 Palestine War.

Contacts were made between the Free Officers and the American Embassy in Cairo. It was apparently made clear to them the United States would not oppose a reformist coup. Potential sympathizers in the military and among Egypt's journalists were also approached.

On 22 July, the Free Officers were alerted by a friend in the Egyptian royal court that the Palace had learned of their plans and was intending to move against them. They decided to act immediately, and in the early-morning hours of 23 July 1952 the Free Officers seized power in Egypt virtually without bloodshed and resistance, and named Naguib Commander-in-Chief. Faruq abdicated three days later in favor of his infant son and departed the country unharmed and largely unregretted.

The Free Officers asked veteran politician Ali Mahir to form a government and announced a moderate six-point program of social and political reform. The Free Officers tried until September 1952 to work within the country's existing political structure, but the resistance they encountered led to their decision to install Naguib as Prime Minister. That December the Constitution was suspended, and in January 1953 Naguib announced the commencement of a three-year transitional period during which executive and legislative power would be vested in the Revolutionary Command Council, composed of the thirteen member Free Officer Executive, and the cabinet. Activity by politicians from the pre-Revolutionary period was banned.

At the time of the announcement of the monarchy's abolition in June 1953 several of the Free Officers now on the RCC took up key ministerial portfolios in the Naguib government. The Free Officers, particularly Abdal Hakim Amer and Baghdadi, formed a strong core of support for Nasser; the promotion of Amer to Commander-in-Chief (replacing Naguib in this post) ensured that Nasser had the crucial backing of the army for his coming confrontation with Naguib.

The term "Free Officer" became one of tremendous political importance in Egypt; the original Free Officers Committee and their supporters (whose composition and number vary according to sources) occupied prominent positions (albeit some for rather short times) in post-Revolutionary Egypt. A few of the Free Officers soon split off from the RCC over policy disagreements, but others, the bulwark of Nasser's strength, took ministerial and bureaucratic posts.

Free Officers Committee:

1. Lt. Col. Gamal Abdal Nasser

2. Major Abdal Hakim Amer
3. Lt. Col. Abdal Latif al-Baghdadi
4. Major Kamal Addin Husayn
5. Major Hassan Ibrahim
6. Major Khalid Muhiaddin
7. Lt. Col. Zakaria Muhiaddin
8. Maj. Gen. Muhammad Naguib
9. Col. Anwar al-Sadat
10. Lt. Col. Gamal Salim
11. Major Salah Salim
12. Lt. Col. Husayn al-Shafi
13. Col. Yusuf Sadik

FRENCH INVASION OF EGYPT. Napoleon Bonaparte landed in Alexandria in July 1798 at the head of a French Expeditionary Force, accompanied by a group of scientists and scholars who were to conduct a major study of the country. He justified his invasion as an attempt to support the Ottomans in Egypt (without, however, informing the Ottoman Sultan) against the anarchy inflicted by the Mamluks, two of whom, Murād and Ibrāhīm Bey, were in power in Cairo. The French army marched inland from the coast, met, and defeated the Mamluks in battle at Gaza on 21 July, and entered Cairo. Napoleon, who obviously envisaged French control of the country as permanent, established a series of Diwāns (consultative councils on the Ottoman mode) in the cities held by the French. Egypt was divided into sixteen military districts with French military governors working through local officials.

The British responded to the French advance by sending a fleet under Nelson to Abu Qir in August 1798, which sank the French fleet. The Ottomans declared war the next month. Napoleon's attempt to extend his conquest to Syria in 1799 was halted at Acre by the Ottoman commander Jazzar Pasha, with British assistance. Napoleon also had to confront the active hostility of the Mamluks, in bitter exile in Upper Egypt, and a revolt by Muslims in Cairo, which was brutally suppressed. The

French meanwhile were facing administrative and financial difficulties with their occupation.

Napoleon left Egypt just over a year after his arrival, turning power over to General J. A. Kléber. Faced with an impossible military situation, Kléber attempted to negotiate a convention with the British in January 1800, but the rejection of this convention by the British, communicated to him by Admiral Keith, led Kléber reluctantly to reopen hostilities. He was assassinated in June 1800, whereupon General Menou was put in charge.

Menou advanced north to meet an Ottoman army, which was supported by British reinforcements in March 1801, leaving General Compte A. D. Belliard in Cairo. Beset by a widespread outbreak of plague and local resistance, General Belliard was forced to capitulate, and eventually Menou, defending Alexandria, accepted terms. The French departed from Egypt by October.

Despite the brevity and unpopularity of the French occupation of Egypt (and their nearly continuous involvement in military challenges to their rule) the French made a strong impact there. The organization and equipment of their troops and their training, artillery, and general level of performance were noted by the more astute Mamluk and Ottoman officers, one of whom, the Albanian Muhammad Ali, took power in Egypt four years later, deeply committed to the modernization of the Egyptian army on European lines. The cultural impact produced during this short invasion was also considerable. The scholars accompanying the expedition staffed the Institut de l'Égypte, giving Egyptian scholars for the first time a broad exposure to all aspects of European culture while the French collected information on Egypt. The Institut also set up the first Arabic-language printing press, removed from the Vatican by Napoleon. The French invasion in every sense marked the beginning of a period of revolutionary change in Egypt, with the rejoining of Egypt to the world outside its borders and the awakening of European interest in the country.

FUAD I (r. 1917-36). King of Egypt, Fuad ruled the country as it made the transition from a British Protectorate to the nominal independence granted under the 1922 Declaration. Fuad was educated in Europe and spoke little Arabic at the time he took power as Sultan in 1917, following the death of Husayn Kamil. His title changed to that of "King" at the time of the 1922 Declaration.

Fuad spent most of his reign in largely successful attempts to increase and enlarge his powers vis-à-vis Egypt's Parliament and to limit the effectiveness of the country's representative institutions. He actively sowed intrigue among the nationalist parties and politicians and managed to get the 1923 Constitution abrogated in 1930, after six years of suspending Parliament and parts of the Constitution when it suited him.

Fuad resented the advocacy of constitutional government by Allenby, High Commissioner at the time of the first Constitution's promulgation in 1923. He felt that the British, and Allenby in particular, did not understand the need for Egypt to be governed with a strong hand. His implacable hostility to parliamentary government doomed it from the start, because the 1923 Constitution, however Fuad viewed it, gave the King broad powers to dissolve parliament. The British, particularly Allenby's successor, Lord Lloyd, were not as unsympathetic toward Fuad's position as he believed, but they saw parliament as one of the few restraints on his desire to rule autocratically. Between October 1930 and November 1934 Fuad ruled under a revised Constitution, drafted at his direction, which reduced the powers of the Parliament. The 1923 Constitution was eventually restored when the King's illness made him incapable of offering further opposition.

Fuad was a major patron of higher education in Egypt, and the opening of the Egyptian state university at Cairo in 1925 owed much to his strong support. It is unfortunate that his antagonism toward the nationalist movement has tended to dominate memories of Fuad's reign, rather than the valuable contributions he made to education and scholarship in Egypt.

Fuad was involved in the controversies during the 1920s over the fate of the Islamic Caliphate, following the abolition of that title by the Turkish government in 1924. His claims to the office were rejected by other Arab leaders, and his attempts to hold an international Islamic Congress to discuss the Caliphate were superceded by the establishment of Ibn Saud in Arabia and consequent lapse of the title.

FUAD II (AHMAD FUAD II) (1951-). Last ruler in Egypt of the Muhammad Ali dynasty, Fuad was proclaimed following the abdication of his father, Faruq, in July 1952. A Regency Council was established for the infant king with the participation (until October 1952) of Free Officer Rashid Mehanna and under the direction of Prince Abdal Munaym, son of the ex-Khedive Abbas II. The gradual consolidation of the revolutionary government's power led to the decision to dispense with the monarchy and declare Egypt a republic in June 1953. Fuad lives quietly in Europe.

AL-FUSṬĀṬ (MIṢR AL-ᶜATĪQA, MIṢR AL-QADĪMA). First city to be established in Egypt following the Muslim conquest, al-Fusṭāṭ was founded by the general ᶜAmr b. al-ᶜĀs in 640/19, near the Roman city of Babylon on the East Bank of the Nile and to the south of the present-day city of Cairo. The exact origin of the name is disputed, but probably derives from the Latin and Greek words for "camp." By tradition, al-Fusṭāṭ was the site where ᶜAmr and his army pitched their tents prior to the conquest of Babylon. The first mosque in Egypt was constructed here and survives until now (although vastly altered and rebuilt).

Despite the construction of new residential quarters by later dynasties and the foundation of a palace city, al-Qāhira, by the Fāṭimids in 969/358, al-Fusṭāṭ maintained its importance as a center of commerce. In time the quarters of succeeding dynasties, such as al-ᶜAskar and al-Qaṭā'iᶜ, were incorporated into al-Fusṭāṭ; only al-Qāhira maintained its separate identity over a long period.

The Umayyad Caliph Marwān and the Fāṭimid Caliph al-Ḥākim both ordered the burning of sections of al-Fusṭāṭ. The Fāṭimid vizier Shāwar set al-Fusṭāṭ on fire in 1168/564 during a Crusader invasion; this last fire burned for fifty-four days, according to the sources. The city was rebuilt after this, and in the Ayyūbid period (1171-1250/567-648) Ṣalāḥ ad-Dīn fortified al-Fusṭāṭ and al-Qāhira, as well as the new residential and administrative complex, the Citadel, which he built on the hills overlooking the two centers. Al-Fusṭāṭ, despite the reverses it suffered, continued to be important for both trade and manufacturing and was also helped by its closeness to the island of Roda (ar-Rawḍa), headquarters of the Baḥrī Mamluk regiments founded by the Ayyūbid Sultan aṣ-Ṣāliḥ.

The Mamluk Sultans (1250-1517/648-922) used al-Fusṭāṭ as the administrative capital for Upper Egypt, with Cairo used for the administration of Lower Egypt, but from the fourteenth century onward the city lost ground in all areas to Cairo, as the shops, merchants, and traders moved north. The city kept a small population, though the newer sections of Cairo, built northward and closer to the East Bank of the Nile (which was expanding as the Nile moved westward), gradually replaced it in importance. The ruins of al-Fusṭāṭ are today nearly obscured by the debris of later generations. The archaeological site is gradually being covered over by modern building developments in this last open section near central Cairo.

-G-

GAMAAT (prop. JAMA^{c}AT) ISLAMIYYA (ISLAMIC SOCIETIES). University-campus-based Islamic political grouping active since 1973, the Gamaat Islamiyya is in informal or formal control of many of the student unions in Egyptian universities. The Gamaat preaches a mixture of personal religious reform and social action, as well as extremely conservative behavior and dress for members. The group combines its religious preaching with the operation of social-welfare and medical clinics and the provision of inexpensive textbooks for students. The amount of centralized control and/or coordination between these groups on a campus-by-campus basis is uncertain, but a major figure linking them, Sayyid Sabiq, regularly circulated (until 1981) among the campuses, speaking on Islamic and socio-political topics. The Gamaat have been extremely active in expressing religious opposition to certain university policies and government programs. Along with a number of other religious revivalist groups the Gamaat Islamiyya was the subject of an extensive government crackdown in September 1981, with many of its known leaders and organizers arrested.

GAMASSY, GENERAL ABDAL GHANI AL- (1921-). Prominent Egyptian military figure, Field Marshal Gamassy distinguished himself as Head of Operations during the 1973 Arab-Israeli War and in the subsequent negotiations with General Yaariv of the Israeli army over the disengagement of forces. From 1955 to 1964, Gamassy was involved with the Armored Brigade, and in 1966 became Chief of Army Operations. He had overall supervision of the military zones in 1967-68. Gamassy was made Chief-of-Staff of the Egyptian army in November 1973 and Minister of War and War Production, as well as Commander-in-Chief, in December 1974. In Mamduh Salim's 1976 cabinet he was appointed Deputy Prime Minister and Minister of War, serving until 1978. Since 1978 Gamassy has been retired from active service, and named presidential military adviser.

GAZA INCIDENT. After the 1952 Revolution the Nasser regime had fairly quiet "nonrelations" with Israel, being rather more preoccupied with domestic issues. The Lavon Incident in 1954 did not cause an especially sharp reaction from the Egyptian government; the agents and personnel involved were tried and sentenced. This moderation may be linked to the arms deal that Egypt was hoping to secure from the West; nevertheless, before the Gaza Incident Egypt was not making hostile gestures toward the Israelis. Secret contacts had, in fact, been maintained between Nasser and the Israeli premier, Sharett.

Israel was later to claim its actions in Gaza were triggered by concern about threats from Palestinian fighters operating from the Gaza Strip, which was then in Egyptian hands. This concern became a decision to act with the reentry of hardliner David Ben-Gurion into the Israeli cabinet. On 28 February 1955 Israeli forces attacked Egyptian army headquarters in Gaza, ambushing a relief convoy. There was a loss of thirty-eight Egyptian lives, with thirty military and civilian personnel injured. Rather than dampen the level of activity in Gaza, however, the attack provoked Nasser into giving the Palestinian fighters his full support. The Security Council condemned Israel in March for the attack, and both sides were instructed to refrain from further provocative acts. No evidence was subsequently found by General Burns, the UNEF Commander, to back up Israeli claims that Gaza was being used as a base against them. Palestinian raids did not begin until April 1955.

The Gaza Incident raised fears in Egypt about Israeli intentions; border incidents between the two countries in March 1955, along with the difficulties in negotiations, led to further military clashes. Serious fighting in August-November 1955 resulted in 109 Egyptian deaths; indirect negotiations brought active hostilities to a halt, and the status quo was maintained until the outbreak of the Suez War in the following year.

GENERAL AGRICULTURAL SYNDICATE. Set up in January 1921, the General Agricultural Syndicate was established to protect the interests of large Egyptian landowners and to enable them to bypass the system of middlemen who had dominated commodity-trading in Egypt, particularly cotton. The cotton policy pursued by the government during World War I had favored exporters, not growers, and revealed inequities in the trading system's distribution of profits. The crisis in the cotton market following the post-war downturn in world demand heightened the feeling of many cotton producers that they were being victimized by market forces. The syndicate was able to exert its influence to correct this inequity in the cotton market through legislation, market intervention, and the formation of cooperative societies of commodity-growers. The syndicate remained identified with the larger landowners, however, and was unable to attract the medium landowners it needed to broaden its rural support. During the Depression in the 1930s the Syndicate was successful in pressuring the Sidqi and Wafd governments to provide various agricultural relief measures, including price supports and limitations on cotton acreage.

GENERAL ASSEMBLY (1883) see LEGISLATIVE ASSEMBLY

GENERAL CONFEDERATION OF LABOR. Trade-union grouping founded in February 1921 with the strong backing of Egypt's Socialist Party, the General Confederation's leadership seemed to overlap at points with that of the Socialists. Headquartered in Cairo, the group had 3,000 trade-union members. The involvement of the General Confederation in the labor unrest of the 1920s, and its vigorous and left-wing leadership outside the control of the main political parties led to efforts by the Wafd to form a labor grouping of less radical stripe. The General Confederation, along with the Socialist Party, were both subject to vigorous suppression following serious labor disturbances in 1924.

GENERAL FEDERATION OF TRADE UNIONS. Founded in January 1952 during the rapid decline in national political life and a particularly tense period in Anglo-Egyptian relations, the General Federation represented a group of labor activists unhappy with the past conservative line of most of the Egyptian trade-union leadership. Trade unionists were among those involved in the civil disturbances of 26 January 1952 (Black Saturday), which culminated in the burning of sections of Cairo, and the GFTU may have been formed to capitalize on the political feelings of these workers. The federation was very supportive of the Revolution, and profited from the Free Officers' initially pro-union line. The labor movement also backed Nasser in his 1954 power struggle with Naguib. Legislation passed in 1956 favored trade-union formation and membership, and at the time the legislation was introduced there were over 1,200 unions with nearly half a million members under the umbrella of the GFTU, whose president, Anwar Salama, was strongly pro-Nasser. The group was restructured in 1957, when it changed its name to the Egyptian Trade Union Federation.

The campaign against the left wing in Egypt that began in the late 1950s ultimately affected the federation, which did have some communist participation. In April 1959 a series of restrictions on union activity were introduced prior to its being banned altogether a few months later. In May 1960 the country's labor representation system was reorganized into sixty-four occupationally defined unions, and Anwar Salama was elected president of the new federation in elections held in January 1961. Subsequent reorganization of the unions under the federation reduced their number to twenty-seven, and they were placed under stricter government control.

With strikes banned in Egypt (though unofficial industrial action still occurs), the effectiveness of the unions is rather circumscribed. Despite these restrictions some of the industrial unions have maintained power on the shop-floor level, especially in the textile industry. The ETUF is affiliated with the International Confederation of Arab Trade Unions. Its twenty-seven affiliated unions have a combined membership of some 2.5 million; the federation is currently (1980) headed by Saad Ahmad. A weekly journal of information about the union, its activities, and relevant legislation is published by the federation for its members.

GENERAL ORGANIZATIONS see ECONOMIC ORGANIZATIONS

GENERAL UNION OF LABOR SYNDICATES OF EGYPT. Founded in 1930, the General Union consisted of three labor syndicates headed by Liberal Constitutional Party member Daud Ratib, whose support the government of Sidqi Pasha tried to gain. At the end of 1930 the membership replaced him with Prince Abbas Halim, who was to figure prominently in labor-union activity in Egypt and internationally throughout the 1930s. Although Halim had Wafdist sympathies, he steered the General Union on an independent courst that led to uneasy relations with the Wafd, especially after Halim sponsored a short-lived labor party. When Halim was under threat of repression by the Sidqi government, relations with the Wafd improved, but when the Wafd tried to gain influence (1931-32) over the General Union, relations deteriorated. The General Union participated in the political efforts mounted in the early 1930s to gain the restoration of the 1923 Constitution and free political life, and also staged industrial action in support of this goal. Following the formation of a Wafd government, the Wafd pressed Halim to assume the presidency of the Wafdist High Labor Council, in exchange for a promise by the General Union as a whole not to interfere in politics. Halim accepted the presidency only to see the Wafd try to gain full control of the labor-union movement. In August 1937 Halim rejoined the General Union, which in 1938 changed its name to the General Union of Worker's Syndicates, gaining the affiliation of a number of new unions. The General Union worked actively for reforms in the labor law and workers' conditions. It was suspended at the outbreak of World War II. After the war, the General Union was involved with other trade unions in the popular protests of 1946-47 against government policies.

GENERAL UNION OF WORKERS' SYNDICATES see GENERAL UNION OF LABOR SYNDICATES

GENEVA CONFERENCE. In an effort to resolve the Arab-Israeli conflict after the 1973 war a Geneva Conference, attended by Egypt, Israel, and Jordan, met briefly in December 1973. The conference was jointly chaired by the United States and Russia, and its reconvening was a major plank in Egypt's foreign policy prior to President Sadat's visit to Jerusalem in November 1977. The potential use of the conference in Geneva to resolve the Arab-Israeli dispute was stalled by Syria's boycott of its proceedings and by the Israeli refusal to negotiate in any form with the PLO, whose participation was demanded by all the Arab parties to the conflict. An Egyptian-Israeli military committee was set up.

Russia's role in the settlement of the Middle East conflict was largely obscured during the period of "shuttle" diplomacy carried on by U.S. Secretary of State Henry Kissinger prior to January 1977. Momentum for a reconvening of the Geneva Conference, with superpower involvement, increased in October 1977, with the issuance of a joint U.S.-Soviet statement on the Middle East. However, Israel had announced its intention of increasing the number of new West Bank settlements and continued to strike heavily at Palestinian camps in southern Lebanon in retaliatory raids. The peace initiative by President Sadat later that month compromised the Geneva Conference as the main potential negotiating forum; at the time of his initiative President Sadat invited all interested parties in the region to attend a conference in Cairo that December, an invitation accepted by the United States, Israel, and the UN in an observer capacity.

GENIZA DOCUMENTS. The Geniza documents take their name from the store-room, or geniza, of a Jewish synagogue in al-Fusṭāṭ, where they were found when the Synagogue was undergoing reconstruction in 1890. The documents span the Fāṭimid through to the Ottoman periods (though with gaps in the Mamluk era) and provide a wealth of material on the Jewish community in Egypt during this time, as well as many general and specific details about other aspects of popular and official life. From the material, scholars have been able to form a picture of a community with extensive trading interests in the Mediterranean and with active links to their co-religionists in the Levant, Iraq, and North Africa. Most of the documents are written in Hebrew, but using Arabic characters, and demonstrate a certain linguistic fusion going on between the two languages.

GHAZALI, SHAYKH MUHAMMAD. Prominent Islamic leader and a prolific modern writer on Islamic revivalism, Ghazali has been associated since the early 1950s with the activist wing of the Ikhwan al-Muslimun (Muslim Brethren), becoming a leading voice in the Ikhwan in the post-Revolutionary period. He supported the Ikhwan's radical faction that between 1952 and 1954 sought veto power without compromise over the legislative acts of the Revolutionary Command Council, a demand that was to lead to an utter breakdown in relations between the two groups. Following the suppression of the Ikhwan in 1954 Ghazali continued to write; he rose to prominence by leading the opposition to the Charter of National Action in 1962 on the grounds of its failure to accord Islam its proper place in Egyptian society. He came close at that time to leading a popular revolt of sentiment against Nasser, as Egyptians of widely varying political and religious views rallied behind his Islamic opposition. Ghazali was subject to official censure after the new crackdown on the Ikhwan in the mid-1960s and became politically inactive. He held a number of positions in the Ministry of Waqfs (religious endowments) in the 1970s, before leaving Egypt in the aftermath of the disturbances of January 1977.

GODE see GULF ORGANIZATION FOR DEVELOPMENT

GORDON, CHARLES (1833-1885). Governor-General of the Sudan from 1877 to 1880 under the Khedives Ismail and Tawfiq, Gordon was selected by the British government to lead the evacuation of Egyptian troops from the Sudan in 1884. The activities of the Mahdist forces in Sudan made the maintenance of a British or Egyptian presence there impossible, though the British decision to withdraw Egypt's troops was not universally accepted within the Egyptian government, whose province the Sudan was. Contrary to his instructions, Gordon held Khartoum, waiting for reinforcements that did not arrive in time. Gordon and his troops were killed during the Mahdist attack on Khartoum in January 1885. The events surrounding Gordon's last days in the capital, the massacre of the troops, and his own rather flamboyant personality and military record became popular topics in the press in Britain and undoubtedly played some role in shaping later British actions in the province, reconquered from Mahdist forces in 1896-98.

GORST, SIR ELDON (1861-1911). British Agent and Consul-General in Egypt from 1907 until his death in 1911, Gorst was originally appointed to the British Agency in Cairo in 1886. He was made controller of taxes in 1890 and in 1894 became adviser to the Minister of the Interior. In 1898 Gorst succeeded Palmer as the Egyptian government's chief financial adviser.

In the years prior to his takeover from Lord Cromer, Gorst, who spoke Arabic, acquired a genuine sympathy for some of the demands of the Egyptian nationalists, influenced by the friendship he formed with the Khedive, Abbas II. He negotiated the Entente Cordiale in 1904, which finally defined Britain's place in Egypt with regard to French claims, and spent the next three years in England before returning to Egypt to replace Cromer.

At the time Gorst took up his post Egyptian attitudes toward Britain had been badly marred by the Dinshaway Incident. His efforts to repair Egyptian-British relations did not meet with much success. The nationalists rejected him, as did most British opinion in Egypt and in the Foreign Office, for diametrically opposed reasons. His attempts at constitutional reform and greater Egyptian involvement in government were undercut when the death of Mustafa Kamil left the Nationalist Party with a divided leadership. Egypt's Copts were politically alienated by the assassination of the first Coptic Prime Minister, Butrus Ghali Pasha, in 1910. Their religious opposed his decision not to have Sunday as a day of rest. Gorst's good relationship with Abbas earned him the mistrust of many of the elite and some elements within the British Foreign Office.

Gorst gave his support, in 1907, to the campaign to raise funds for the national university, thus reversing a major policy of his predecessor, Cromer, as did his encouragement of Egyptians in the bureaucracy. Gorst came to his post charged with a mission to introduce reforms. He tried to do so within the moderate lines envisaged by the Foreign Office but ended with a series of half-measures that pleased no one. He persuaded Abbas, whom he treated with a great deal of respect and kindness, to revitalize the Legislative Assembly and permit the greater participation of ministers in decision-making, but Gorst's last years in office were handicapped by a painful and fatal disease that greatly debilitated him. Gorst returned to England in April 1911. Abbas journeyed there to visit Gorst in July, shortly before his death; an adequate testimony to the personal bonds of friendship which the two men formed in the course of their official relationship.

GREAT INSURRECTION. The weakening of the Ottoman government's control of Egypt in the last century of its rule was a product of competition within the Ottoman garrison for dominance, and of the struggles within the beylicate of individuals and factions. The Ottoman garrison was divided between the Janissaries and ᶜAzeban (with the Janissaries themselves divided between supporters and opponents of the commander Afranj Aḥmad); the beylicate was split between the Faqāriyya, with their military allies, the Qāzdughliyya, and the Qāsimiyya. To complicate the situation, the alliance that was effected between the Janissaries and the Faqāriyya came at a time when the Janissaries and the Qāzdughliyya military household were having uneven relations.

Troubles within the Janissary corps early in 1711/1123 brought the Faqāriyya, under Ayyūb Bey and Muḥammad Bey, to the side of their ally Afranj Aḥmad, who prevailed. The other Ottoman corps, now ranged against Afranj Aḥmad, received the support of the Qāsimiyya (under Iwāẓ Bey and Abū Shanab Bey). The Ottoman Viceroy, under Janissary guard, had little option but to throw his backing to them. A period of fierce street fighting and general chaos followed, as these factions and their allies fought it out in Cairo. The conflict continued for nearly seventy days in April, May, and June, during which time one of the Qāsimiyya leaders, Iwāẓ Bey, was killed and the Viceroy's palace attacked. The Viceroy was declared deposed by the Qāsimiyya, and the Faqāriyya were eventually put to flight, with the Janissary leader Afranj Aḥmad killed. A Qāsimiyya Qā'im Maqām (acting Viceroy) ruled until the arrival of a new Ottoman governor, though the latter found his office stripped of almost all pretensions to power and control.

The Qāsimiyya, who emerged as victors from this encounter, were able to keep their pre-eminence for only thirteen years. Following the death of the Qāsimiyya leader Ismā^{c}īl Bey in 1724/1137 the Faqāriyya and Qāzdughliyya reentered the competition for supremacy in the beylicate.

GREEN SHIRTS (Ar. AL-QAMĪS AL-AKHDĀR). Paramilitary political group, the Green Shirts were the activist wing of the "Young Egypt" (Misr al-Fatat) Party, founded in October 1933 by Ahmad Husayn. The Green Shirts were influenced by the ideas and successes of the National Socialist movement in Germany and Italy. They preached a message of ardent nationalism and social discipline, but their violence and hostility toward the mainstream political parties aroused great official opposition. At the same time their idealism and spirit stood in contrast to the increasingly self-seeking nature of many of the national political parties and earned them support among students and young nationalists in the cities.

Students supporting the Wafd Party established the Blue Shirts in 1935 as a rival youth group, and the two shirt organizations quickly fell into open hostility. The Green Shirts' rejection of the Wafd-negotiated 1936 Anglo-Egyptian Treaty led to violent street clashes between the two groups. Both shirt organizations were restricted in December 1936 by the Wafd government of Nahhas Pasha. The Green Shirts were subsequently accused of involvement in an assassination attempt on Nahhas in November 1937. Paramilitary organizations were officially proscribed by the government of Mahmud Pasha in March 1938. Many Green Shirt members became affiliated with the Ikhwan al-Muslimun, which propagandized actively among them.

GULF ORGANIZATION FOR THE DEVELOPMENT OF EGYPT (GODE). Set up in 1976 after the Arab-Israeli War, by Saudi Arabia, Kuwait, the United Arab Emirates, and Qatar, GODE funded Egyptian development projects. The group was formed in response to an earlier call by President Anwar Sadat for the establishment of an OAPEC-based fund to relieve Egypt of its international debt and balance-of-payments problems caused by Egypt's position as a front-line state with heavy defense responsibilities. GODE funding in 1976 was devoted to helping Egypt meet its budget allocations, and following the January 1977 riots GODE was asked to provide a $1.5 billion program loan, at 5-percent interest, a three-to-five-year grace period, and a ten-year repayment scheme. Further GODE loans were suspended after the Arab Boycott of May 1979, though the countries involved have continued to meet commitments made prior to that date.

GUMAA, SHARAWI (1920-). Deputy Prime Minister and Minister of the Interior after the death of Nasser in September 1970 and the accession of Sadat, Gumaa was a powerful figure under Nasser. Along with Sami Sharaf and Ali Sabri, he was arrested and tried for conspiracy by the Sadat government in May 1971.

Gumaa was an instructor at the military academy prior to 1961, when he was appointed governor of the Suez District. In 1964 he was made a minister in the joint Iraqi-Egyptian Council meant to supervise the proposed Federation between the two countries. Gumaa became Minister of State in the Prime Minister's office in 1965, charged with coordinating relations between the government and the Arab Socialist Union. He was linked with the establishment of a special section within the ASU and was active in all the party's affairs. In September 1966 Gumaa was made Minister of the Interior, an extremely important post in Nasser's Egypt, and following Nasser's death was named Deputy Prime Minister for the Services Sector in addition to the Interior Ministry.

Following his trial Gumaa was sentenced to life imprisonment, and his property was confiscated. He was released for health reasons in 1976.

-H-

HADI PASHA, IBRAHIM ABDAL (1901-). Prime Minister of Egypt from December 1948 to July 1949, Hadi was one of the founders of the Saadist Party in 1938. He served in a number of finance and foreign-affairs posts in the prewar cabinets of Ali Mahir and Hassan Sabri and was Foreign Minister in the government of Sidqi Pasha in 1946, resigning to serve as Chief of the Royal Cabinet in 1947.

Hadi's first task as Prime Minister was to restore order both internally and externally, with regard to the high level of civil disturbance in Egypt and the conclusion of the 1948 fighting with Israel.

Hadi continued and intensified the antiterrorist campaign started by his predecessor Nuqrashi Pasha, whose assassination in December 1948 by an Ikhwan member protesting the group's proscription had led to the formation of Hadi's government. Hasan al-Banna, head of the Ikhwan al-Muslimun, was killed, probably by a police agent, in February 1949, which hurt the unity of the Ikhwan; action overt and covert was taken against left- and right-wing groups, and those organizations implicated in the street violence of the past two years.

The fighting with Israel in Palestine was ended by a truce signed in February 1949 after negotiations by Ralph Bunche on behalf of the UN. Hadi's involvement with these negotiations did not add luster to his reputation, already tarnished through association with the government and the fiasco over the supply of weapons to Egyptian troops. His government fell when the King finally withdrew his support from Hadi in the summer of 1949.

In September 1953 Hadi was arrested on conspiracy charges by the revolutionary regime and sentenced to death that October. His sentence was commuted to life imprisonment, though he was later released for health reasons. Hadi's political rights were restored in 1960.

AL-ḤĀFIZ (r. 1130-49/524-44). Fāṭimid Caliph, al-Ḥāfiz was the cousin and successor to al-Āmir. Al-Ḥāfiz originally came to power as regent for the unborn child of al-Āmir and was deposed by the vizier Kutayfāt, a grandson of Badr al-Jamālī. Kutayfāt imprisoned al-Ḥāfiz and declared himself Imām, or representative of the hidden Imām, expected by some sects of the Shīᶜa. With the help of a court chamberlain, the Armenian Yānis, al-Ḥāfiz escaped in 1131/526, Kutayfāt having been murdered by Yānis and his supporters. Al-Ḥāfiz then laid claim to the Caliphate, overriding the opposition of the court. When Yānis showed signs of becoming too powerful, however, al-Ḥāfiz had him poisoned.

Thereafter, al-Ḥāfiz tried ruling with his sons. The first, Sulaymān, died shortly after his appointment, to be replaced by a second son, Ḥaydara. A third son, al-Ḥasan, distressed by his exclusion from power, mounted a minor rebellion and was eventually poisoned on his father's orders.

A Christian, Bahrām, was then appointed vizier in 1135/530, but this proved an unpopular choice both with the army and the people, and al-Ḥāfiz was forced to appeal to Riḍwān, governor of Ascalon, to depose Bahrām. Riḍwān organized his supporters and took power when Bahrām was driven from Cairo by elements opposed to his rule. In the event Riḍwān proved no happier a choice than Bahrām and ended by trying to depose al-Ḥāfiz, presumably to take power in his own name.

In addition to his problems with his viziers al-Ḥāfiz also had to face the opposition of some Shīᶜa inside and outside Egypt who felt that the succession to the Fāṭimid Caliphate should have remained in al-Āmir's direct line. His promotion of the Christian Bahrām aroused strong resistance in Egypt, not only for his religion but for the large army of his fellow Armenians that he raised. These controversies surrounding the court, religious and political, dominated al-Ḥāfiz' reign and were a cause of unrest in Egypt, as was the continuing disunity and competition within the Fāṭimid army.

ḤĀFIZIYYA (MĀJIDIYYA). Sect within Ismāᶜīlī Shiᶜism, the Ḥāfiziyya believe that Ḥāfiz (see above) was the legitimate successor to the Imamate of the Fāṭimids in Egypt after his cousin al-Āmir, and in preference to al-Āmir's infant son, aṭ-Ṭayyib. There is some uncertainty about whether aṭ-Ṭayyib, born around the time of his father's death and al-Ḥāfiẓ' accession, did in fact exist, with some, pro-Ḥāfiẓ, sources claiming that a daughter had been born to al-Āmir's widow, or that aṭ-Ṭayyib had died.

After the Fāṭimid dynasty came to an end in 1171/567 Dā'ūd, son of the last Caliph, al-ᶜĀḍid, was recognized by the Ḥāfiziyya as Imām. Dā'ūd was kept imprisoned by the Ayyūbids, but conspiracies surrounding him forced Ṣalāḥ ad-Dīn to move his supporters from Cairo to Upper Egypt, which subsequently became a center of the Ḥāfiziyya movement. Dā'ūd died in 1207 or 1208/604 and his son and successor, Sulaymān, died in 1248/645. The Ḥāfiziyya died out thereafter.

HAIKAL see HEYKAL

ḤĀJJĪ I (AL-MUẒAFFAR SAYF AD-DĪN ḤĀJJI Ī) (r. 1346-47/747-48). Baḥrī Mamluk Sultan, Ḥājjī I was the sixth son of an-Nāṣir Muḥammad to hold power in Egypt. Like his predecessors and successors he was soon deposed. A faction of Circassian Mamluks favoring the candidacy of his brother Ḥasan speeded his exit. Ḥājjī's brief reign was dominated by his absolute disloyalty to friend and foe alike, according to the sources, and by his unchecked generosity toward his harīm at a time when the state funds were running low.

ḤĀJJĪ II (AṢ-ṢĀLIḤ ṢALĀḤ AD-DĪN ḤĀJJĪ II) (r. 1382/783-84 and 1389-90/791-92). Baḥrī Mamluk Sultan, Ḥājjī II succeeded his brother ᶜAlī at the age of eight. His first reign of a few months was ended by the first Burjī Mamluk Sultan, Barqūq, who was himself subsequently displaced, and Ḥājjī returned to power, in 1389/791. Real power during his reign was in the hands of the Atabeg, Yilbughā an-Naṣirī. Yilbughā was overturned by his former ally, Mintash, during Ḥājjī's second reign; Mintash was in turn challenged by Barqūq, who was in exile. The two men met in battle in 1390/792; Ḥājjī accompanied his minister and was captured in camp by Barqūq in the course of the battle. Barqūq's honorable treatment of the young Sultan helped win much support for him. Ḥājjī II was confined to his apartments in the Citadel by Barqūq and apparently died a natural death.

AL-ḤĀKIM (r. 996-1021/386-411). Fāṭimid Caliph, al-Ḥākim is the most enigmatic and controversial ruler of that dynasty. Al-Ḥākim was only eleven at the time of his accession; the early years of his reign saw the struggle between Ibn ᶜAmmār, chief of the Kutāma Berbers, and the Caliph's tutor, Barjawān. Barjawān eventually displaced Ibn ᶜAmmār in 997/387 before himself falling victim to the resentment and jealousies of al-Ḥākim in 1000/390.

Discontent among the Bedouin over the fate of Ibn ᶜAmmār may have lay behind a rebellion in Cyrenaica (eastern Libya) in 1005-06/396; the Berbers initially defeated a Fāṭimid force sent to suppress them, though they were finally overcome. He later faced challenges to his power in Palestine (1012/403).

Egypt was struck by a disastrous famine in 1007-08/398-99 due to a failure of the Nile. It was at this time that al-Ḥākim, whose previous decrees had imposed dress codes on Christians and Jews, began to issue the more extraordinary decrees that have led later historians to question his sanity. He banned the consumption of certain foodstuffs, including the popular vegetable, mulukhiyya; mounted a campaign against dogs; forbade the playing of chess and the manufacture of ladies' shoes; and towards the end of his life, ordered shops to remain open late into the night while he wandered the street incognito. It should be pointed out that these eccentricities were well publicized by his Sunnī and ᶜAbbāsid opponents and tend to obscure the fact that his court was also a center of high cultural and scientific endeavor, and that, more importantly, he held power for a considerable time in view of his alleged insanity. More problematical is the movement which arose toward the end of his reign, led by ad-Darazī among others, which proclaimed his divinity. Al-Ḥākim's involvement in this is not fully clear, but most of his own Dāᶜī (Ismāᶜīlī missionaries) condemned ad-Darazī. Whether divine or divinely mad, or, as is more likely, greatly misunderstood, al-Ḥākim was murdered under mysterious circumstances and his body was never recovered. His sister, Sitt al-Mulk, is accused in some sources of complicity in his demise;

she assumed de facto power after his death as regent for his son and successor, aẓ-Ẓāhir. Al-Ḥākim is revered by members of the Druze sect.

AL-HAKIM, TAWFIQ (b. c.1898). Leading twentieth-century Egyptian writer, Tawfiq al-Hakim initially trained as a lawyer and received part of his education in France. Early in his career he worked as a government prosecutor, which gave him the deep knowledge of the lives of rural Egyptians that he used to great effect in his novels and plays. Al-Hakim is considered a seminal force in the development of Egypt's modern theater. His work is widely read throughout the Arab world and has been translated into several European languages. Aside from his writing, Al-Hakim occupied various government posts, being director of the National Library in 1951-56 and Under-Secretary for the Higher Council for Arts, Letters, and Social Science in 1956-59 and again in 1960. He also served as director of the semiofficial Al-Ahram newspaper and was a member of the Arabic Academy. In 1974 Al-Hakim was appointed to the National Council for Services and Social Affairs. Until the mid-1970s, Tawfiq al-Hakim continued to write on politics and led the scholarly reappraisal of Nasser's role.

ḤAMZA b. ᶜALI see DARAZĪ

HARAD CONFERENCE. Held in the Yemen in November 1965 the Harad Conference sought to mend the opposition between Saudi Arabia and Egypt over the Yemen War and to seek a way to end the fighting there. A proposal was made at a meeting between Nasser and King Faysal in Jedda (August 1965) that a transitional government be formed until a national plebiscite could be held. As a diplomatic initiative Egypt announced before the conference a withdrawal of 10,000 troops, to begin that December and proceed on a monthly basis until all had been withdrawn in seven months' time. But the conference failed to end the fighting, as neither side could fully agree--or, more importantly, get their respective protégés in the conflict to agree--to a negotiated solution especially on the issues of holding a plebiscite or providing for a transitional regime until a postplebiscite government was elected and established. A second meeting at Harad, scheduled for February 1966 never took place.

HARB, TALAT (1876-1941). Egyptian nationalist and lawyer, Talat Harb was a major force behind Egypt's twentieth-century industrial development. Talat Harb first attracted public notice when he wrote a rejoinder to Qasim Amin on women's rights. In 1907, he joined the Umma Party, which represented the moderate wing of the nationalist movement. He became involved with efforts to make Egypt more independent financially and, with a group of like-minded individuals, founded Bank Misr in 1920 as a source of capital for Egypt's industrial expansion.

Politically Talat Harb was more concerned with economic development than party politics. He viewed the growth of industry and a diversified economy as prerequisites for Egypt, and he actively supported a greater voice for Egypt's industrialists and the establishment of a healthy private sector in Egyptian hands. He worked with the Egyptian Federation of Industries to secure greater government protection for, and promotion of, Egypt's industrial sector. Despite his insistence that industrialization formed a necessary complement to, not a substitute for, agriculture, Harb was not entirely successful in convincing Egypt's large landowners to invest in the Bank and, through it, in Egypt's nonagricultural development. He eventually secured European financing for some of his development plans, and the group of companies built up under his leadership made Bank Misr one of the leading Egyptian financial and industrial establishments at the time of the Revolution.

HARĪM. The women of, or the women's quarters in, a royal or nonroyal household. The term derives from the Arabic for "inviolable."

HĀRŪN (r. 896-905/283-92). Fourth Ṭūlūnid ruler of Egypt, Hārūn ruled under the regency of Muḥammad b. ᶜAbba (Abū Jaᶜfar). His reign saw the gradual disintegration of the Ṭūlūnid's hold on the territories in Syria and Mesopotamia granted them by the ᶜAbbāsid Caliph. The Qaramatians in Syria, a Shīᶜa sect, gained strength from the resentment in that province at the high rate of taxation, and the Ṭūlūnid armies in Syria showed slight enthusiasm for fighting the local population. Hārūn's surrender to the pleasures of court life made him incapable of providing the strong leadership necessary in a situation where a small foreign ruling elite and army had to control a large and relatively restless population. The ᶜAbbāsid Caliph al-Muᶜtaḍid, as a reflection on the Ṭūlūnids' declining position, reduced their territorial grants and increased their tribute in 899/286. A major revolt took place in Syria in 901-03/288-89 and proved difficult to suppress; these disturbances, plus the increasing power of the Qaramatians, led the ᶜAbbāsid Caliph to decide to reimpose direct ᶜAbbāsid rule in Egypt. The ᶜAbbāsids launched a joint land and sea attack; Hārūn was murdered, and his uncle Shaybān succeeded him briefly before being conquered by the ᶜAbbāsid forces.

AL-ḤASAN (AN-NĀṢIR NĀṢIR AD-DĪN AL-ḤASAN) (r. 1347-51/748-52 and 1354-61/755-62). Baḥrī Mamluk Sultan, al-Ḥasan was a son of an-Nāṣir Muḥammad. His first reign was marred by a catastrophic outbreak of Black Death, which followed its usual course in Egypt, starting a cycle of famine. Only eleven at the time of his accession, he was without real power during his first reign, though he apparently managed or approved of the disposal of a number of potential antagonists. His first reign was brought to an end by a faction of Mamluks supporting the candidacy of his brother aṣ-Ṣāliḥ. Upon his restoration al-Ḥasan was under the control of the viziers Shaykhū (d. 1357/759) and Ṣarghatmish (d. 1358/760). After the death of the former and imprisonment of the latter al-Ḥasan made a brief bid for independence, which was terminated by the Amīr Yilbughā, who had him murdered and replaced as Sultan by Muḥammad.

Al-Ḥasan's second reign was given largely over to a life of hedonism, while his Mamluks held real power and murdered each other with regularity, which probably aided his removal by Yilbughā. He left behind a madrasa and mosque complex whose construction was begun during his reign and is still extant.

AL-ḤASAN b. UBAYD ALLĀH (r. 968/357). Briefly ruler of Egypt in the closing days of the Ikhshīdid dynasty, al-Ḥasan returned to Egypt from Syria to depose his cousin Aḥmad and restore some order to Cairo, where the Ikhshīdid armies were engaged in fighting each other. He imprisoned the vizier Ibn al-Furāt for a short time but was himself later deposed and Aḥmad restored to power.

ḤASAN AṢ-ṢABĀḤ see NIZĀRĪ

HAWWĀRA. Important Berber tribe, the Hawwāra were among the tribes coming to Egypt at the time of the Fāṭimid conquest. They were invited to settle in Upper Egypt by the Mamluk Sultan Barqūq (d. 1399/801) and quickly gained dominance in the area, attacking the Banī Kanz/Kenuz, a local tribe, at Aswan in 1412-13/815 and establishing their hegemony. They were recognized as de facto governors of Upper Egypt by the Ottoman conqueror Selīm I in 1517/922.

Increasing clashes between the Ottoman Viceroys and the Hawwāra led to the tribe being stripped of its governing privileges and subjected to the rule of an appointed governor in 1576/984, though how effective these Ottoman nominees were against the tribe is unclear. The Hawwāra profited from the ascendancy of the beylicate and the increase in fighting among its factions. The Hawwāra were allied with the Qāsimiyya faction and following the final defeat of that group in 1730/1142-43 offered refuge to its beys and supporters in exile from Cairo. The Hawwāra rose against a former ally, the Shaykh al-Balad, ᶜAlī Bey, in 1769/1183, after rejecting a candidate he posted to their area as governor, but were defeated in the ensuing battle.

The power that the Hawwāra lost at this time was partially regained in the subsequent power struggles in Cairo, the fighting between the Mamluk Duumvir Murād and Ibrāhīm Bey and their local and Ottoman opponents, and the disturbances attendant on the French invasion of Egypt in 1798. But this renewed position was challenged by Muḥammad ᶜAlī, who took power in 1805. He stripped the Hawwāra of their major source of revenue, tax-farming, in 1812, and in 1813 his son, Ibrāhīm Pasha, defeated the Hawwāra in battle. The tribe thereafter gradually was absorbed into the local population.

HAYKAL see HEYKAL

HEALTH CARE. The development of public health care in Egypt benefited from the encouragement of works for the public good under Islam. Aḥmad b. Ṭūlūn established a hospital for civilians in 872-73/259. Other rulers and Sultans, such as Ṣalāḥ ad-Dīn, Qalā'ūn, and Mu'ayyad Shaykh, attended public health care through construction and grants, but Qalā'ūn's hospital complex, built in his reign (1280-89/678-88), was the most extensive and famous.

The existence of such facilities led to an efflorescence of medical work by medieval scholars, attracting to Egypt such men as Ibn Maymūn (d. 1204/600) and Ibn Nafīs (d. 1288/687). These scholars were of Christian and Jewish as well as Muslim origin, but down to the time of Muhammad Ali medical training in Egypt, as with other higher education, was closely tied to Arabic-Islamic scholarship.

It was Muhammad Ali (r. 1805-48) who introduced to Egypt the concept of secular education in medicine, specifically Western medicine. He hired a French physician, A. B. Clot (Clot Bey), who founded the first modern teaching hospital in Egypt. Though Clot Bey's career suffered a brief interruption during the reign of Abbas I (1848-54), the teaching institution he established helped to make Egypt's reputation as the foremost center for medical training in the Near East. The hospital also carried out research on endemic diseases, such as Bilharzia (named for the German physician at Qasr al-Aini hospital who identified the parasite that caused it), and on other public health problems. The teaching hospitals in Cairo and Alexandria were at the center of the pre-1952 health-care system. The cities also had Egyptian- and European-trained doctors practicing privately.

Despite this early introduction of modern medical training the standard of health care in rural areas remained poor, as doctors were concentrated in the cities and larger towns. To remedy this, private benevolent associations were started in the early twentieth century, usually with religious affiliation, to operate clinics and small hospitals. The operation of these private clinics was limited, however, and an early priority of the Free Officers after the 1952 Revolution was the establishment of more comprehensive health care in rural areas.

The post-Revolutionary government updated a 1942 plan that had called for the construction of 840 health-care centers; only a quarter of these had been completed by 1952. Despite government encouragement for doctors to work in rural areas only 15 percent of Egypt's physicians were working in such areas at the time of the Revolution. The government combined elements of the 1942 plan with parts of a 1946 plan that called for the creation of social-service centers in rural areas, and proposed a "combined units" scheme whereby health and social-welfare services would be offered together in one facility. In 1955 the government announced plans to build 864 combined units, but due to the lack of available financing by 1965 only 300 combined units had been constructed. The combined-units plan was supplemented by the more modest "rural units" scheme, offering a limited range of medical treatment. The distribution of these centers, both the combined and rural units, still remains uneven despite government efforts to spread the benefits of health care as broadly as possible. Aside from force majeure the government has not enjoyed great success in convincing young doctors to settle permanently in rural areas, though doctors completing their training at the national universities are required to serve a certain time in rural areas.

The operation of the various health units has from time to time, and especially in the Nasser period, raised political questions that have sometimes gained a national forum. Criticisms of the overly political criteria that were on occasion used to assess the performance and assignment of doctors in these rural clinics, and allegations of mismanagement of resources and money have constantly plagued the program. Despite this, available health facilities have been increasing at the rate of 11 percent per annum since the Revolution.

On the national level the large number of doctors graduated from the universities has been achieved at the cost of intense pressure on medical training facilities in the country. As with other disciplines the enormous class sizes have led to charges that the overall quality of the graduates, save those who are able to afford private and small-scale tutoring, has declined. Many of the graduate doctors are now employed in the labor-importing OAPEC (Arab oil-producing) countries, where their services, like those of Egypt's teachers, are still much needed. Current government policy is to maintain this trend of training for the export market, while continuing to use a combination of professional and financial inducements to encourage doctors to work in Egypt's rural areas as well.

HELWAN (ḤULWĀN). Ancient city to the south of the new capital, al-Fusṭāṭ, established by the Muslims when they conquered Egypt, Helwan did not assume importance until the reign of the Umayyad governor ᶜAbd al-ᶜAzīz b. Marwān, who was forced to relocate there during a serious flood in al-Fusṭāṭ in 690/70. The city, possessing health springs and gardens, enjoyed some popularity with later governors as a retreat from al-Fusṭāṭ and Cairo, but it declined under the Mamluks, like much else in Egypt. The rulers of the Muhammad Ali dynasty revived the city as a health resort.

In the mid-1950s Helwan also began to increase substantially its industrial role. An iron and steel complex was opened with Russian assistance between 1958 and 1960, and since then numerous other factories have opened, mostly for heavy industry and related manufacturing enterprises. Helwan is now a major industrial area in Egypt, linked by railway line to modern Cairo 27 kilometers to the north.

HENATICON (ACT OF UNION). Issued by the Emperor Zeno in 482, the Henaticon was a religious treatise intended as a compromise between the Monophysites in Egypt and the position of the Chalcedonians and supporters of the orthodox in Constantinople. Though some commentators felt that the Henaticon made substantial concessions to Monophysite beliefs, it failed to gain acceptance among Egypt's Coptic Christians, largely because its acceptance by the Bishop of Rome, a Nestorian, compromised it in the eyes of the anti-Nestorian Christians of Egypt.

The promulgation of the Henaticon underlines how important religious controversies continued to be, especially where, as in Egypt, they affected the political position of the Byzantine state. Evidence of this is found in the murder of the Byzantine-appointed Patriarch of Alexandria in 452, and the continued restlessness of the population before the proclamation of the Henaticon and following its rejection. The existence of a strong national church in Egypt opposed to the Byzantine state was a problem the edict did not, or could not, really solve.

HEYKAL (prop. HAIKAL), MUHAMMAD HASANAYN (1924-). Egyptian editor and journalist, Heykal was one of the most influential writers in the latter half of the Nasser era. Heykal began his career writing for the weekly journal Rus al-Yusuf. He joined the newspaper Akhair Sa^c^a in 1945 as a war correspondent and covered both the Greek Civil War and the 1948 Arab-Israeli war over Palestine, including the fighting in Faluja where Nasser was based with his unit. Heykal reported on the Korean War and upon his return to Egypt was made editor of Akhair Sa^c^a (1953-56), Akhbar al-Yawm (1956-57), and finally editor of Al-Ahram, a post he held from 1957 until his dismissal by President Anwar Sadat in 1974.

Heykal's weekly column in Al-Ahram was considered to reflect Nasser's own thinking and sentiments fairly closely, and he worked with Nasser in formulating some of the ideology and policies of the government in the 1960s. How much Heykal deserves to be considered Nasser's eminence grise is a matter of dispute, but his influence within Egyptian journalism was unrivaled prior to the presidency of Sadat.

Heykal's identification with government policy and his influence on its thinking declined after 1973, a decline that may have been hastened by his giving the impression that he no longer felt Sadat a worthy or full successor to the Nasser legacy. His criticism of the new government led Sadat to encourage Al-Ahram's rival, Akhbar al-Yawm. Heykal was finally removed from the editorship of Al-Ahram in February 1974, following a series of sharply critical articles on government policy.

In addition to his activities as a journalist Heykal also served as a member of the ASU Central Committee from 1968 to 1974 and in 1965 was made head of the ASU's Press Section, replacing the controversial Khalid Muhiaddin. In 1970 Heykal was made Minister for National Guidance but resigned after Nasser's death. Since Heykal's dismissal in 1974 he has worked independently as an author and journalist in Egypt and abroad. Heykal was briefly detained in the wave of arrests which preceded the assassination of President Sadat in October 1981, but was released shortly thereafter with a full pardon under an amnesty granted by Egypt's new president, Mubarak.

HEYKAL, MUHAMMAD HUSAYN (1888-1956). Egyptian writer, journalist, and politician, Heykal received his education in law in both Egypt and France. He was associated with the Umma Party and its newspaper, Al-Jarida, before becoming involved with the founding of the Liberal Constitutionalist Party in 1922, serving as editor of its newspaper, Al-Siyasa. Heykal was Minister of Education in the 1940-42 Sirri government.

In 1941 Heykal became head of the Liberal Constitutionalist Party following the death of its founder, Muhammad Mahmud, and served as Minister of Education and Social Affairs in the 1944-45 governments of Ahmad Mahir and Nuqrashi Pasha. He played an important role in the development of education. Like all pre-Revolutionary politicians Heykal was banned from involvement in politics under the January 1953 Party Law.

Heykal's major work, Zaynab, was published during World War I and is considered a major influence in the shaping of the modern Egyptian novel, most especially in its realistic portrayal of life in an Egyptian village. Heykal's political and fictional works have stressed the need for Egypt to return to its unique, pharaonic roots within a revitalized Islamic setting. This commitment to the virtues of the past did not compromise his commitment to modernization and the need to reform aspects of Egyptian society, particularly with regard to the role of women. His concentration on his own society's problems and prospects sometimes gave a rather Egypt-centered cast to Heykal's outlook on the country's political future and represented a move away from the more pan-Arab thinking of the prewar political parties, particularly the nationalists. Heykal's life of the Prophet Muḥammad is considered a key work of Islamic reformist literature and thinking; Heykal himself was often criticized for his active defense of other modernist writers whose work offended the conservative religious establishment.

HIGAZI (prop. HIJAZI), DR. ABDAL AZIZ AL- (1923-). Prime Minister of Egypt from September 1974, Higazi resigned in April 1975 following a cabinet re-shuffle. Higazi, an economist, was known for his advocacy of liberal economics during his tenure as dean of the Faculty of Commerce at ᶜAyn Shams University. He was appointed Minister of Finance by Nasser in 1968 and served in that post until 1973. Higazi was also elected to the National Assembly in 1969. He was first Deputy Prime Minister from April to September 1974.

As Prime Minister, Higazi supervised and fostered the transition from state capitalism to the encouragement of private enterprise under the Open Door Policy. He came to office pledged to reverse the weakness of Egypt's currency and to relieve the problems of her international indebtedness. Approaches were made in November 1974 to the Arab oil-exporting (OAPEC) states to help fund Egypt's economic recovery. But Egypt's deteriorating economic situation was in need of stronger and more immediate remedy. Discontent with economic conditions resulted in violence and industrial action (especially among textile-workers) in January and March 1975, which required military intervention. Sadat replaced Higazi in April, while announcing changes in some domestic economic policies and a restructuring of elements of the Open Door policy.

HIGHER COMMITTEE FOR AGRARIAN REFORM. The Higher Committee for Agrarian Reform, established after the introduction of the 1952 Agrarian Reform Law by the Free Officers, was charged with superintending the implementation of the law's provisions. Chaired by Sayyid Marei, the HCAR was composed of high-level technocrats and bureaucrats but was at first administratively autonomous from the rest of the Egyptian bureaucracy. The HCAR established the administrative and procedural guidelines for the early stages of agrarian reform and was eventually incorporated into a new Ministry of Agrarian Reform created in 1956, when some 13 percent of arable land had been redistributed.

The HCAR was highly regarded by outside observers in terms of its personnel and efficiency in the four years of its operation, and the success of this special autonomous body, removed from bureaucratic interference and delay, may have influenced the government's decision to establish similar groupings to superintend the Suez Canal and High Dam project.

HILALI, NAGUIB AL- (1891-1958). One of the last Prime Ministers before the Revolution, Hilali Pasha was a moderate reformist. Before joining the Wafd Party in 1937 Hilali served as Royal Counsellor, then as Minister of Education in the 1934 Nassim government. The Wafd government of Nahhas Pasha named him Minister of Education, a post he held for only two months, until the dismissal of that government in December 1937. He rejoined the wartime Wafdist ministry from 1942 to 1944 as Minister of Education. In 1951, following a policy disagreement, Hilali was dismissed from the Wafd Party.

Hilali was extremely influential in the shaping of the high quality and character of the Ministry of Education in the pre-Revolutionary period. His reputation for effectiveness and honesty led him to be asked twice to form a government in the troubled period between the burning of Cairo in January 1952 and the Revolution that July. His first government lasted three months, March-June 1952, and fell because of his inability to gain support among other politicians or the Palace, which turned against him when it appeared that his investigations into corruption might involve them. Parliament was dissolved in March.

Following Hilali's dismissal Husayn Sirri tried unsuccessfully to form a government, whereupon Hilali was returned in July, with Faruq's brother-in-law forceably installed in his cabinet. Within a day of his taking office the Revolution was proclaimed.

Hilali was widely respected outside Egypt and regarded, prior to the Revolution, as the last chance Egypt had of maintaining civilian government and conducting necessary reforms. For this reason Hilali met with more success in his early dealings with the British than many of his predecessors. Britain made further concessions on the Sterling Reserves agreement to prop up his government. Hilali also enjoyed the friendship of Hudaybi, leader of the Ikhwan al-Muslimun, with the result that the group's activities were somewhat restrained during Hilali's first tenure in office. Though his government could have profited from these positive factors, Hilali lacked a popular base and, ultimately, Palace support.

Despite Hilali's reputation his association with the former regime led to a short detention after the 1952 coup, and he was deprived of his political rights. Many of the reforms he introduced at the Ministry of Education did not survive the Revolution.

AL-ḤIZB AL-WAṬANĪ AL-ḤURR (FREE NATIONAL PARTY). An early Egyptian nationalist political grouping, founded in 1879, the Hizb al-Watani drew its membership from nationalists of moderate stripe, such as Muhammad Abduh; politicians opposed to the government of the new Khedive, Tawfiq; and the military movement, which centered on Colonel Arabi. The party, based in Helwan, presented its program in April 1879; its pan-Islamic, anticolonialist policies included the loosening of European financial controls and political involvement in Egypt and the establishment of constitutional government. A manifesto based on the party's demands and advocating Egyptian autonomy was drafted in November 1879. The Free National Party, with the help of

Colonel Arabi and his supporters in the army, pressed for the dismissal of Riyad Pasha as Prime Minister; following pressure from the group Tawfiq was forced to ask Sharif Pasha, one of its politician members, to form a government in September 1881. The party benefited from the active support of Wilfred Blunt, who publicized its goals, and a modified version of its manifesto in the British press in December 1881, and defended its political ambitions. The Free National Party was dissolved after the British invasion of 1882. (See also NATIONAL FREE PARTY.)

AL-HUDAYBI, HASAN ISMAIL (d. 1973). Supreme Guide of the Ikhwan al-Muslimun following the death of its founder, Hasan al-Banna, Hudaybi led the organization from his election in 1951 until the group was banned in 1954. Hudaybi, a senior jurist, was chosen as a compromise candidate for the Ikhwan leadership after in-fighting between several candidates had failed to produce a clear favorite. But the two-year struggle for the succession that preceded Hudaybi's election had left much dissension and bitterness within the Ikhwan hierarchy, and Hudaybi, an outsider, lacked the strong support of any of the various factions. This made his job as Supreme Guide difficult and made it impossible for him to control all elements of the Ikhwan.

Hudaybi brought to his position a conservative attitude toward the Ikhwan's involvement in politics, which was out of line with many members' expectations. His connections (through marriage) with the Palace and his repudiation of the paramilitary Special Section aroused unfavorable comment within the Ikhwan, as did his toning down of the Ikhwan's more popular anti-British activities.

By 1952 there was a gap between Hudaybi's statements and the programs and activities of the Ikhwan membership under more radical leaders in its hierarchy. The Liberation Squads fighting the British at the Canal Zone, and the burning of Cairo in January 1952, captured the public's imagination. Hudaybi's slow, patient negotiating through the morass of Egyptian politics seemed out of step with a greater political reality.

Hudaybi continued the link established by the Ikhwan's founder, Al-Banna, with the Free Officers, though he apparently felt ambivalent about Nasser. Both this and the divisions within the Ikhwan hierarchy about how to come to terms with the Free Officers after the July 1952 Revolution led to a rapid deterioration in relations between the Ikhwan and the Free Officers from 1953 onward. The conflict between the Revolutionary Command Council and the Ikhwan, and within the Ikhwan itself, over the issue of how much or how little power the Ikhwan should have in a new government was never resolved; Hudaybi accepted an offer of three ministries made by the RCC, only to have the rest of the leadership reject it. In November 1953, following a bitter row among the Ikhwan leadership, Hudaybi secured the dissolution of the paramilitary Secret Section, but by now, real control of the Ikhwan had fallen into more radical hands. The attempt by the RCC to ban the group in January 1954 heightened the activism of those who feared for the Ikhwan's survival. Hudaybi was arrested but released two months later. Shortly afterwards, Hudaybi left Egypt and the Ikhwan for a few weeks to enable the group to form a clear direction, but this was unsuccessful. The Ikhwan was allowed to resume its activities in March 1954, but the growing eclipse of General Naguib, the only member of the RCC to give them some open backing, boded ill for the organization's future. They gravely antagonized Nasser by opposing his recently concluded treaty with the British.

Hudaybi did not control much of the Ikhwan's day-to-day activities, particularly those of the Special Section, and it is difficult to know how much he agreed to, or approved of, the plan to assassinate Nasser that was nearly carried off in October 1954. The attempt enabled Nasser to ban the organization and crush its leadership; following a trial of those involved in the assassination attempt Hudaybi was sentenced to death, later commuted to life imprisonment at hard labor. He was released in 1966, but a new wave of Ikhwan activity resulted in yet another official crackdown, with Hudaybi's rearrest and imprisonment. He died in 1973.

HUSAYN, AHMAD (d. 1982). Founder of Misr al-Fatat (Young Egypt Party) in 1933, Ahmad Husayn originally trained as a lawyer before becoming involved in the nationalist movement. Like Hasan al-Banna, founder of the Ikhwan, Ahmad Husayn led a group that was outside the mainstream of Egyptian political life, though unlike Al-Banna's his group was suspected, at least initially, of enjoying the support of the Palace. His slogan, "God, Country, and King," was combined with a program of industrial and social development and reform. He established a paramilitary organization of his followers and an ideology similar to that of the pre-1919 Nationalist Party. His paramilitary youth groups resembled those of the National Socialists in Germany and Italy. His writings on the problems facing Egypt enjoyed an audience among the young and, more particularly, among the younger army officers, such as Gamal Abdal Nasser and his contemporaries in the military academy.

The Young Egypt Party did not have the same sizable membership as the Ikhwan, but it did have an extremely activist public image, thanks to its "Green Shirt" organization, which conducted marches and demonstrations before its proscription in 1938.

At the outbreak of the Second World War Husayn altered the name of his party to the National Islamic Party, possibly to give it a more Islamic character and gain supporters from the Ikhwan. Husayn's internment during the war put a temporary halt to his political activities. After his release Husayn sought affiliation with some of the antigovernment fronts and changed the party's name once more to the National Socialist Party, advocating a combination of socialist economic planning in the setting of a strong nationalist state, a program that was to find an echo in the policy statements of the Free Officers after the July 1952 Revolution.

Following the burning of Cairo in January 1952 Husayn was

arrested for his alleged involvement. His trial adjourned without a conviction at the time of the 1952 Revolution. Deprived of his right to participate in politics by the 1953 Party Law, Husayn nonetheless maintained a personal following. He was active in the anti-government protests in 1954 and was arrested. Following his release in 1956, he withdrew from public life but did occasionally contribute articles to the press.

HUSAYN KAMIL (r. 1914-17). Sultan of Egypt, Husayn Kamil was named by the British to replace his nephew, the Khedive Abbas, deposed by the British when a Protectorate was established in Egypt in December 1914, after Turkey entered World War I. The declaration of this Protectorate brought to an end the nominal sovereignty of the Ottoman Sultan over Egypt, and accordingly Husayn Kamil was given this title (as opposed to his predecessors' title of Khedive). A son of the Khedive Ismail, Kamil had served before the war as president of the Legislative Council. His popularity within Egypt was strongly affected by the course of the war and Britain's successes and failures. Two attempts on his life were made in 1915 by disgruntled nationalists.

During Husayn Kamil's reign the British were in effective control of Egypt, directing the country's economy and production to meet the British war effort, at a very high cost to most Egyptians. Husayn devoted himself to the promotion of agriculture and protection of Egypt's landed classes, and gave his support to improvements in higher education and technical training. In declining health, he died in 1917.

HUSAYN, TAHA (1889-1976). One of the major literary figures of modern Egypt, Taha Husayn's literary criticism was considered revolutionary by his contemporaries. Husayn, blind from childhood, was educated in France, returning to Egypt in 1919 to begin a lifetime involvement with education and administration in addition to his writing. He was actively assisted by his wife and a number of other colleagues.

Husayn's most controversial work, a study of Arab poetry in the pre-Islamic period, was published in 1926 and resulted in his condemnation by religious authorities in Egypt. A committed supporter of humanitarian liberalism, Husayn devoted himself to writing and educational reform thereafter. His autobiography, *Al-Ayyam*, which details his personal struggles and those he faced in his professional life, is considered a major example of modern literary Arabic prose. He went on to serve as a dean at King Fu'ād University in Cairo and later was appointed rector of King Fārūq University.

Husayn was made Minister of Education by the Wafd government in 1950 and was one of the few individuals involved with pre-Revolutionary government in Egypt whose career thereafter was not unduly handicapped. He continued until his death to be the dominant man of letters in Egypt; the full implications of much of his literary criticism are still being studied in Egypt and elsewhere, as are his works on Egypt's Mediterranean heritage.

-I-

IBN AL-^{c}ASSĀL. Coptic family of administrators and scholars, the Bani'l-^{c}Assāl flourished during the Ayyūbid period (1171-1250/567-648). In addition to achieving high positions in the Ayyūbid bureaucracy several members of the family wrote extensively on all areas of Coptic exegesis and theology, philology, and poetry. The numerous manuscripts left by the Bani'l-^{c}Assāl have great value in Coptic studies. The rise and position of this family in Ayyūbid Egypt, at a time when that dynasty was actively fighting the Christian Crusaders abroad and eventually in Egypt itself, evidence the continued importance of Copts in the administration.

IBN AYĀS see IBN IYĀS

IBN AL-DĀYA (AḤMAD b. YŪSUF b. IBRĀHĪM) (d. mid-tenth century/mid-third century). Historian of the Ṭūlūnid dynasty in Egypt. Aḥmad's father originally served at the ^{c}Abbāsid court in Baghdad before coming to Egypt following the death of his patron at court in 839/224. This association with the ᶜAbbāsids, and his father's subsequent friendship with the vizier Ibn al-Mudabbir, earned the family the enmity of Aḥmad b. Ṭūlūn (r. 868-84/254-70), who came to power determined to establish his autonomy vis-à-vis the former and to gain ascendancy over the latter. Ibn al-Dāya was arrested after his father's death but was shortly released. His history of Ibn Ṭūlūn and his heirs has survived as summaries in the works of later historians, and he also wrote on philosophy and compiled biographical studies of the leading scientific figures of his day.

IBN AL-FURĀT (ABŪ'L FAḌL JAᶜFAR b. AL-FAḌL) (d. 1001/391). Ikhshīdid vizier, Ibn al-Furāt oversaw the administration of Egypt during the reigns of Ūnūjūr (d. 961/349), ᶜAlī (d. 966/355), and Kāfūr (d. 968/357), the latter having held de facto power in Egypt since Ūnūjūr's accession. Following Kāfūr's death Ibn al-Furāt engineered the succession of the young Aḥmad Abu'l-Fawāris, whose rule was then challenged by his cousin al-Ḥasan. During Al-Ḥasan's brief time in power he imprisoned the vizier but was compelled to retreat. As acting governor of Egypt, Ibn al-Furāt was unable to offer any resistance to the steady advance of the Fāṭimid armies under Jawhar aṣ-Ṣiqillī. Not only was his treasury empty but Ibn al-Furāt could not suppress the frequent clashes between the divisions of the Ikhshīdid army, which were more interested in gaining supremacy over each other than in meeting the Fāṭimid threat. He was himself in competition at court with Yaᶜqūb b. Killis, who had risen under Kāfūr. Yaᶜqūb b. Killis was briefly imprisoned, after which he left Egypt to join the Fāṭimids. His subsequent prominence in the Fāṭimid court was to be at Ibn al-Furāt's expense.

Ibn al-Furāt supervised the handover of Egypt to the Fāṭimids but declined the offer of the vizierate made by Jawhar aṣ-Ṣiqillī. Ibn al-Furāt's son accepted a similar offer made by the Caliph al-Ḥākim, but served only a few days before being executed.

IBN ḤAJAR. Name of two prominent scholars of Islamic studies in

Egypt. The first Ibn Hajar, AL-ᶜASQALĀNĪ (1372-1449/773-852), was a renowned scholar of Ḥadīth, a professor and judge in the religious courts. He served as rector of the theological school originally established by the Sultan Baybars from 1410/813 to 1445/849 and preached at the teaching institutions of al-Azhar and the Mosque of ᶜAmr in al-Fusṭāṭ. He also served as Chief Qāḍī (judge) for over twenty years, though he seems to have been subject to frequent dismissal. Ibn Ḥajar al-ᶜAsqalānī's writings on theology gained popularity in his lifetime. In addition to his voluminous studies on Ḥadīth he wrote biographical dictionaries and handbooks that are still used as reference works by historians.

The second Ibn Ḥajar, AL-HAYTAMĪ (1504-67/909-74), was a leading Shāfiᶜī jurist, born in Egypt, whose writings form an important part of the corpus of legal works of this school, which, with the Hanafi, is the dominant legal school in Egypt.

IBN AL-HAYTHAM (ABŪ ᶜALĪ AL-ḤASAN b. AL-ḤASAN b. AL-HAYTHAM) (965-1039/354-431). Iraqi-born scientist who was a major figure at the court of the Fāṭimid Caliph al-Ḥākim, al-Haytham's researches covered a broad field of scientific inquiry. Al-Ḥākim charged him with the investigation of ways to control the Nile to ensure a more dependable flow, but his lack of success in this forced him to retreat from the court to escape the Caliph's wrath. Ibn al-Haytham published over 100 books on scientific topics, largely dealing with mathematics, astronomy, and physics. Known as Alhazen in Latin, Ibn al-Haytham gained a wide audience in medieval Europe for his work on optics, being a seminal work in this field, the implications of which can be found in the researches of da Vinci, Bacon, and others. His work in pure geometry made a similar impact on European scholars.

IBN IYĀS/AYĀS (ABŪ'L-BARAKĀT MUḤAMMAD b. AḤMAD) (1448-c.1524/852-930). Historian of Mamluk Egypt, Ibn Iyās came from a well-connected Mamluk family. His chronicles concentrate on the fall of the Mamluks from power and the transition in Egypt to Ottoman rule. A student of as-Siyūṭī, Ibn Iyas provided much detail of life in Egypt during the Mamluk period, both in the court and among the people, dealing with the effects of the plagues and natural disasters that occurred during this period and that helped hasten the Mamluks' end.

IBN KHALDŪN (WALĪ AD-DĪN ᶜABD AR-RAḤMĀN b. MUḤAMMAD) (1332-1406/732-809). The best-known medieval Muslim historian in the Islamic world and the West, Ibn Khaldūn's innovative approach to historiography places him well above his contemporaries.

Ibn Khaldūn's view of Islamic history was enriched by his own experiences in various courts of the western Islamic world, at a time when that world was undergoing a transformation following the withdrawal of the Crusaders and with the continued pressure from the Mongols and Turkic tribes in the east. He served in the North African and Spanish courts, enjoying periods of both favor and exile, before coming to Egypt in 1382/784.

In Egypt, Ibn Khaldūn gained the support of the Mamluk Sultan Barqūq, who first appointed him Chief Qāḍī (judge) of the Malikite school of Islamic law in 1384/786. Ibn Khaldūn also served as head of Baybars' Khanqah, or teaching institution. Ibn Khaldūn traveled in company with Barquq's son and successor, Faraj, when that Sultan went to Syria to meet Tīmūr in 1401/804. He was apparently much taken with Tīmūr and wrote for him a brief history of North Africa.

Ibn Khaldūn's most famous work is a three-volume history of the Islamic Arab world, drawn from his own experience in the higher positions of the Muslim courts and based on his particular approach of blending critical examination with a form of sociological analysis. His identification of ᶜaṣabiyya, a group feeling or spirit that motivated the early conquerors of a dynasty and was diluted in time until that dynasty was replaced by a new group with greater ᶜaṣabiyya, was used by Ibn Khaldūn to explain the changeover in Islamic dynasties. He also provided fair and thorough criticism of what he felt were the less scientific approaches to the history of his time. His appreciation for the multiple factors affecting and shaping historical events and his search for the social meaning of those events are without parallel among his contemporaries in the field of historiography.

IBN KILLIS see YA^cQŪB b. KILLIS

IBN MAMMĀTĪ. Patronym of three prominent viziers who served the Fāṭimid and Ayyūbid rulers of Egypt. The first, ABU'L-MALIḤ (d. c.1100/493), was an administrator of the diwān under the vizier Badr al-Jamālī in the reign of the Fāṭimid Caliph al-Mustanṣir (1036-94/427-87). AL-MUHADHDHAB (d. c.1182/577) served in the court of the last Fāṭimid Caliph, al-^cĀḍid. The beginning of formal Ayyūbid control in Egypt then began, and the Christians in Egypt faced less generous official favor than they had under the Fāṭimids, something that may have contributed to al-Muhadhdhab's decision to convert to Islam. AL-AS^cAD, his son, served in the Dīwan as secretary under Ṣalāḥ ad-Dīn and al-^cAzīz but fell into disfavor after the death of his patron, the vizier al-Qāḍī al-Fāḍl, and was forced to flee to Syria, where he died in 1209/606. Among the works attributed to al-As^cad is a valuable cadastral survey of Egypt in the early Ayyūbid period, though much of his other literary production is lost.

IBN MAṢAL (NAJM AD-DĪN ABŪ'L-FATḤ SALĪM) (d.1149/544). Acting vizier in the last five years of the reign of the Fāṭimid Caliph al-Ḥāfiz, Ibn Maṣal was appointed vizier and Commander-in-Chief in the reign of al-Ḥāfiz' successor, aẓ-Ẓāfir, in 1149/544. He worked to restore order to the army, split by quarrels between the various regiments, but his vizierate was soon ended by the successful challenge of Sallār, the governor of Alexandria. Ibn Maṣal and his army were pursued to Upper Egypt, where they were defeated by Sallār and the vizier was executed by his successor. Aẓ-Ẓāfir was forced to accept this fait accompli, though the sources indicate Ibn Maṣal enjoyed the young Caliph's support.

IBN MAYMŪN/MOSES MAIMONIDES (ABŪ ^cIMRĀN MŪSĀ b. ^cUBAYD

ALLĀH AL-QURṬUBĪ) (d.1204/600). Jewish scholar of law, medicine, and philosophy, Ibn Maymūn was born in Spain. His family were compelled to flee in 1149/544 after a persecution of minorities, and Ibn Maymūn spent several years in North Africa before coming to Egypt in 1166/562. He became linked with the Ayyūbids as a court physician, and he and his family were later invested with the right to speak on behalf of Egypt's Jewish communities. Ibn Maymūn's extensive writings on Jewish law, medicine, and rationalist philosophy were informed by his tolerant and distanced approach to religion. His scholarly work gained an audience not only in Egypt, but even beyond the Islamic world.

IBN AL-MUDABBIR see AL-MUDABBIR

IBN AL-MUQAFFA[c] see SEVERUS

IBN AN-NAFĪS ([c]ALĀ' AD-DĪN ABU'L [c]ALĀ' [c]ALĪ b. ABU'L ḤARAM) (d.1288/687). Court Physician to the Mamluk Sultan Baybars I and Chief Physician of Egypt, Ibn an-Nafīs was instrumental in the development of medicine in medieval Egypt through his teaching at the hospitals built by Baybars and his successor, Qalā'ūn, and by his authorship of a number of theoretical medical treatises, including an encyclopedia, a study of ophthalmology, and several commentaries on the work of earlier physicians. His best-known work was a compilation of the diagnoses and treatment for various diseases, drawing on the work of Ibn Sīnā, which was used in Egypt until recent times. In addition to his philosophical and theological writings, Ibn an-Nafīs wrote a famous study on the circulation of blood, which anticipated many subsequent discoveries.

IBN AS-SALLĀR see AS-SALLĀR

IBN TAGHRĪ-BIRDĪ (ABU'L MAḤĀSIN JAMĀL AD DĪN YŪSUF) (d. 1469-70/874). Medieval Islamic historian, Ibn Taghrī-Birdī was the son of a high-ranking Mamluk official of Barqūq and was himself connected with the court. In 1401/804 his father accompanied the Sultan Faraj and the historian Ibn Khaldūn to

Syria, where he met Tīmūr, and Ibn Taghrī-Birdī himself took part in the Syrian campaign of the Sultan Barsbāy in 1432/836.

Ibn Taghrī-Birdī wrote a history of Egypt from the Arab Conquest to his own day, and also compiled a biographical work on the Mamluk Sultans and important figures associated with their courts. He produced several other works drawing on his biographical and historical researches.

IBN ṬŪLŪN (AḤMAD IBN ṬŪLŪN) (r. 868-84/254-70). Founder of the Ṭūlūnid dynasty, which ruled Egypt for thirty-seven years, Ibn Ṭūlūn came to Egypt originally as governor on behalf of Bāykbāk, a powerful figure in the ᶜAbbāsid court at Baghdad. Bāykbāk had been granted Egypt as an iqṭāᶜ by the Caliph al-Muᶜtazz (866-69/252-55), and after Bāykbāk's death the iqṭāᶜ passed to Yarujūkh, father-in-law of Ṭūlūn. In 873/259 the iqṭāᶜ of Egypt was transferred to the Caliph's son Jaᶜfar (al-Mufawwaḍ), in whose name Ibn Ṭūlūn ruled Egypt thereafter.

It took Ibn Ṭūlūn nearly four years to rid himself of al-Mudabbir, who had been placed in charge of Egypt's finances and communications prior to Ibn Ṭūlūn's appointment; he finally managed to have al-Mudabbir transferred to Syria. He soon tried to enlarge the territory under his control by offering to invade Syria, in the name of the Caliph, ostensibly to put down a rebellion there. He was permitted to expand his army, and his quest for power was assisted thereafter by the dislocations caused in Iraq by the Zanj rebellion and by the clash developing in Baghdad between the powerful courtier al-Muwaffaq and his own iqṭāᶜ holder, al-Mufawwaḍ. Approached by Muwaffaq for funds for military expenses (and asked secretly by the Caliph and al-Mufawwaḍ not to provide them), Ibn Ṭūlūn sent a part of the sum, responding curtly when al-Muwaffaq then castigated him. Al-Muwaffaq retaliated by sending troops to depose him. Ibn Ṭūlūn defeated this attempt to unseat him and shortly afterward, in 878/265-66, took advantage of the confused situation in Iraq and Syria to seize the latter. A final crisis came in 882/269, when Ibn Ṭūlūn invited the ᶜAbbāsid Caliph to reestablish himself in Egypt to escape the court intrigues in Baghdad; this began a new round of hostilities with al-Muwaffaq, which were only beginning to be resolved at the time of Ibn Ṭūlūn's death.

In Egypt, Ibn Ṭūlūn had to face the rebellion of his son ᶜAbbās, who broke with him over the issue of the military strategy to be taken in the Ṭūlūnid's planned expansion westward, and with his commander Luᶜluᶜ over the fighting with the Zanj for control of Egypt's border regions. He eventually resolved his dispute with ᶜAbbās, though the succession passed to another son, Khumārawayh. Ibn Ṭūlūn constructed a residential complex for himself, al-Qaṭā'iᶜ, and used some of the revenues formerly sent to Baghdad to improve public works in Egypt, including an aqueduct and repairs to the Nilometer on Roda (ar-Rawḍa) Island near al-Fusṭāṭ. The mosque he built in Cairo, with its distinctive Samarra-influenced minaret, albeit reconstructed, is among the most famous of the early Islamic architectural treasures in Egypt. Ibn Ṭūlūn was the first governor of Egypt in the Islamic period to realize the country's potential as an independent power base for an ambitious ruler. In this, he was undoubtedly helped by the troubles facing the ᶜAbbāsids in Iraq. But credit must also be given to his political and diplomatic maneuvering in his dealings with the ᶜAbbāsid court.

IBRĀHĪM BEY (d.1695/1107). Ibrāhīm Bey was a leader of the Faqāriyya Mamluk faction in its struggle with the Qāsimiyya at the end of the seventeenth century/twelfth century for supremacy within the Egyptian beylicate. The Faqāriyya had been eclipsed for over three decades, from the 1660s/1070s, after the decision of the Ottoman governor to favor their Qāsimiyya rivals (though the Qāsimiyya leader, Aḥmad Bey, was put to death shortly thereafter, rendering both factions quiescent).

Ibrāhīm effected an alliance with the Janissary leader, Küçük Mehmed, who had deposed the former, pro-Qāsimiyya, leadership of his regiment, and also with the Qāzdughliyya, an emergent military grouping not yet in the beylicate. This combination permitted Ibrāhīm to gain paramountcy in the beylicate and the office of Shaykh al-Balad in 1692/1104. The assassination of Küçük Mehmed in 1694/1106 and Ibrāhīm's death the year afterward once again left the beylicate in a confused and fractious condition.

IBRĀHĪM BEY (d. 1816/1232). With Murād Bey, Ibrāhīm was Shaykh al-Balad and co-ruler of the de facto Mamluk government of Egypt from c. 1775/1189, after serving as Amīr al-Ḥajj in 1772-73/1186-87. The two men inherited the power and position of Abu'dh-Dhahab, whose Mamluks they were and who had raised them to the beylicate, but their establishment in power was far from easy. Wanting to consolidate their initially fragile base, Murād decided they should try to depose Ismā^cīl Bey, a commander of the forces of the late ^cAlī Bey. However, this caused enough discontent for the plan to be abandoned. Even so, Ibrāhīm and Murād were forced to flee to Upper Egypt in 1777/1191. Fortunately for them, Ismā^cīl proved incapable of maintaining his supremacy over his supporters and one year after their exile, Ibrāhīm and Murād returned, deposed Ismā^cīl, and drove him and many of ^cAlī Bey's Mamluks out of Cairo. After failing to defeat these forces, the Duumvir decided to recognize the control of Upper Egypt by Ismā^cīl and his backers.

Ibrāhīm was briefly deposed as Shaykh al-Balad by his partner in 1784/1198. Whatever the reasons, the two were soon reconciled. Ibrāhīm and Murād were once more forced to retreat to Upper Egypt when an Ottoman army arrived to depose them in 1786/1201. Their rival, Ismā^cīl Bey, was restored as Shaykh al-Balad by the Ottomans. He died of plague in 1791/1205, whereupon the Duumvir took power again. The situation in Egypt remained highly unstable and provided the justification used by Napoleon to invade Egypt, claiming that he was helping to restore Ottoman power from the usurpation of the Mamluks.

During the French invasion the Duumvir was broken. Murād was defeated by the French at the Battle of Imbaba, and Ibrāhīm fled to Syria, where he apparently sought the help of the British in ridding Egypt of the French. After Murād's death in 1802/1217, Ibrāhīm joined forces with ^cUthmān al-Bardīsī to overturn the forces of the newly appointed Ottoman governor, Khusrau Pasha. They gained the support of Muḥammad ᶜAlī, with whose help Khusrau was defeated and imprisoned and al-Bardīsī named governor. Muḥammad ᶜAlī then broke with al-Bardīsī over a pay dispute, and he and Ibrāhīm were forced to flee to the south. Ibrāhīm escaped the first and second massacres of Mamluks by Muḥammad ᶜAlī and died in retirement in Nubia in 1816.

IBRĀHĪM KĀHYA (d.1754/1168). Leader of the Qāzdughliyya military faction in the period of its ascendancy in Ottoman Egypt, Ibrāhīm was initially allied with the Faqāriyya faction of the beylicate and with its two leaders, Dhu'l Faqār (assassinated in 1730/1143) and ᶜUthmān Bey. He helped the Faqāriyya gain ascendancy over the divided Qāsimiyya faction under Sharkas Bay in 1730/1143. This period of cooperation ended in 1739/1152, when Ibrāhīm Kahya turned against ᶜUthmān and defeated him in battle after the latter had fled to Upper Egypt. In the next ten years Ibrāhīm managed to suppress his opposition and gained control of the beylicate in alliance with Riḍwān Kahya, head of a minor Mamluk faction, the Julfiyya. Riḍwān interfered little with Ibrāhīm's rule, and the latter gradually filled the ranks of the beylicate with his own nominees. Following Ibrāhīm's death Riḍwān was assassinated, and a six-year struggle ensued for control of the beylicate, which was eventually gained by ᶜAlī Bey.

IBRĀHĪM PASHA (d.1536/943). Grand vizier of Sulaymān the Magnificent, Ibrāhīm was sent to Egypt by the Ottoman Sultan in 1524/930 to put down a rebellion involving the Viceroy, Aḥmad Pasha. Ibrāhīm and Aḥmad had a longstanding rivalry, and the latter had been bitterly disappointed when Ibrāhīm had been made vizier; Aḥmad accepted the appointment as Viceroy of Egypt, seeing in it a chance to use the province to create an independent base for himself. Following Aḥmad's defeat and death at the hands of the Ottoman army under Ayās Pasha, Ibrāhīm set about reforming the country's administrative, financial, and judicial systems and reshaping the government along the lines it would retain for almost three centuries. He reorganized Egypt's naval defenses and promulgated the Ottoman legal and administrative code, the Qānūn nāme during his one year stay in Egypt.

Ibrāhīm tried to create a balance within the power structure of the administration to prevent the coalescence of power around either the Viceroy, the military, or the Mamluk households and beylicate, while maintaining the overall supremacy of the Viceroy. The system worked well enough until the last decades of the sixteenth/tenth centuries, when the Mamluks began to regain their cohesion and the regiments became increasingly restive.

IBRĀHĪM PASHA "AL-ḤAJJĪ" (r. 1603-04/1012-13). Ottoman Viceroy of Egypt, Ibrāhīm was sent to the province to restore order after nearly thirty years of unrest, five major army revolts, and several highly corrupt predecessors. He got off to a bad start by being mobbed and robbed by the Ottoman troops before he even reached Cairo. He was assassinated by the Sipahis, the cavalry corps that had been in revolt against Ottoman governors since the 1580s/990s. His death marked a new low in the relations between the governor and the Ottoman military establishment in Egypt.

IBRAHIM PASHA (d. 1848). Son of Muhammad Ali, founder of the last dynasty to rule Egypt, Ibrahim Pasha had a distinguished career as leader of his father's armies in some of their major victories.

Ibrahim's first campaign, in 1811, was against the refugee Mamluks in Upper Egypt, and at its conclusion he was made governor of Upper Egypt, charged with implementing the administrative and fiscal reforms introduced by his father. He left this post in 1816 to lead the conquest of Najd in central Arabia on behalf of the Ottoman Sultan, driving the Wahhabi and Al Saud forces back to al-Dariyya, where they were defeated. In 1819 Ibrahim was named governor of Jeddah by the Ottoman Sultan. He was then sent in 1821 to northern Sudan as Commander-in-Chief of the Egyptian expeditionary force there but was forced to retire because of illness.

His next major campaign, in Greece and Crete, involved him

in successful but difficult fighting from 1824 to 1827 on behalf of the Ottoman Porte, until most of the Ottoman and Egyptian navy was sunk at Navarino in 1827. But the broader territorial ambitions of Muhammad Ali, carried out under his son Ibrahim's skillful command, made conflict with the Ottomans inevitable. In 1831 Ibrahim invaded Palestine and Syria and in 1832 met the forces of the Ottoman Sultan, inflicting three separate defeats on them and reaching far into Anatolia itself. Syria was eventually ceded to Muhammad Ali by the 1833 Convention of Kutahiya, and he nominated Ibrahim to rule it on his behalf. Ibrahim, though advised by his major local ally, the Amir of Lebanon, Bashir II Shihab, was unable to make Egyptian rule acceptable to the Syrians, who resented the introduction of conscription, higher taxes, and other administrative measures. Uprisings against Ibrahim's government began in 1834, with a major rebellion by the Druze community in 1838. Whatever ambitions Ibrahim may have had to initiate reforms, he was fully involved in meeting and containing local resistance.

The Ottomans decided to use the unrest in Syria to attack Ibrahim, but they were soundly trounced in the Battle of Nezib in June 1839. With the surrender of the Ottoman fleet to Muhammad Ali a few days later the dissolution of the Ottoman Empire seemed certain. This brought an immediate response from the European powers, which did not wish a weak Ottoman state to be replaced by a vigorous, Egyptian-based regional power. British and French warships attacked Ibrahim's positions in Syria. Undermined by the guerrilla activity of local rebels, Ibrahim was forced to withdraw in the winter of 1840, under conditions negotiated between his father and the British Admiral, Napier.

Ibrahim had worked closely with the French military adviser Colonel Sèves (Sulayman Pasha) and General Boyer on the reorganization of the Egyptian army and shared many of his father's ideas on reform. Upon his return to Egypt, Ibrahim devoted himself to preparing for his eventual takeover from his father. He studied Egypt's administration, agriculture, and development potential. Ibrahim was nominated governor of Egypt in 1848, due to his father's advancing illness, but served only two months before his own death in November 1848.

IBRAHIM, MUHAMMAD HAFIZ (d. 1932). Egyptian poet, Hafiz Ibrahim was associated with the leaders of the nationalist movement in the early twentieth century and with the Islamic reformer Muhammad Abduh.

Like Sami al-Barudi, an earlier and similarly innovative poet, Hafiz Ibrahim had his early career as an officer in the Egyptian army and served in the Sudan. After this posting he retired from the army, in 1906, and devoted himself to his writing and to his contacts with such individuals as Sa^{c}d Zaghlul and Mustafa Kamil among the nationalists. In 1911 he was made director of the literature section of the National Library, which gave him the position and time to pursue his writing and translating work. Ibrahim's poetic images were based on the lives and the material and spiritual concerns of ordinary Egyptians, representing a distinct break with older and more formal themes and styles. His poetry gained a wide and appreciative audience in Egypt before his death, both for its high moral themes and for the beauty and style of his Arabic.

IBRAHIM PASHA, YAHYA (d. 1936). Prime Minister of Egypt from March 1923 until the elections of January 1924, Ibrahim Pasha took power from Nassim Pasha, whose government had been unable to control the wave of anti-British violence in Egypt. The new Egyptian Constitution was promulgated during his term in office, which also saw the termination of martial law and a slightly calmer internal situation. Zaghlul was released from exile in April 1923 and continued to dominate national political life. Ibrahim had previously served as President of the Court of Appeals. He was Minister of Justice in Wahba's government.

Ibrahim was closely identified with the Palace, and after his resignation became president of the Ittihad Party, a political grouping built around support for the Palace. Despite these links, Ibrahim joined the 1934-35 campaign by Egypt's political parties to restore constitutional government.

AL-IKHSHĪD (MUḤAMMAD b. ṬUGHJ AL-IKHSHĪD) (r. 935-46/323-34). Ruler of Egypt, Muḥammad b. Ṭughj was the founder of the Ikhshīdid dynasty. The increasing importance of Egypt as a buffer between the Fāṭimids in North Africa and the Levant decided the ᶜAbbāsid Caliph in Baghdad on the appointment of a strong, semi-independent governor in the area to counter this threat. Muḥammad b. Ṭughj, who had served with the Ṭūlūnids and was governor of Damascus, arrived in Egypt in 935/323. He made good use of his own troops to restore order, and was given the title of the "Ikhshīd" (used by the ruling family in Farghāna in Central Asia, from whom Muḥammad b. Ṭughj claimed descent) in 937/325.

The regional situation was disturbed. After an inconclusive battle with Ibn Rā'iq the Ikhshīd in 939/328 took Palestine and southern Syria which he placed under control of his brother ᶜAbdallāh. The Qaramatian rebels troubling this region were apparently bought off with a hefty subsidy of 300,000 dinars. The Ikhshīd added Aleppo (in Syria) and the Hijazi cities of Mecca and Medina to his territories. More Syrian territory was added following the death in 942/330 of Ibn Rā'iq. The ᶜAbbāsid Caliph confirmed the Ikhshīd's position in Syria in 944/333, the same year the Ḥamdānids, an emerging power, took Aleppo and Homs from the Ikhshīd and challenged him elsewhere in Syria.

Unlike the Ikhshīd's predecessor, Ibn Ṭūlūn, Muḥammad b. Ṭughj had the Caliph's support and that of his finance minister, Abū Bakr al-Madhārā'ī in his efforts to bring strong government to the area. But as with Ibn Tulun, his sons and heirs were incapable of taking over the role he established for himself in Egypt and Syria. He was succeeded in all but name by his slave, Kāfūr.

IKHSHĪDID EGYPT (935-69/323-58). Short-lived dynasty founded by the ᶜAbbāsid general Muḥammad b. Ṭughj, the dynasty takes its name from the Central Asian title granted to Ṭughj, "The Ikhshīd," in 937/325. The Ikhshīdid dynasty was in power during a major transition in the Islamic world, when the Fāṭimid dynasty in North Africa, the Ḥamdānids in Syria and the Qaramatians in Arabia and the Levant, all Shīʿa groups, were challenging the power and authority of the Sunnī Caliph in Baghdad. Though the founder of the dynasty, Muḥammad b. Ṭughj, managed to avert the immediate danger posed by the Fāṭimids, his successors steadily lost ground to them as they lost firm control of Egypt.

During his eleven years in power the Ikhshīd added Syria, Palestine, Mecca, and Medina to his territories, though Aleppo and Homs were lost to the Ḥamdanids in 944/333. The Qaramatians were pacified with a generous subsidy. The Ikhshīd was succeeded in power by his sons Ūnūjūr and ʿAlī, but during their reign real power was in the hands of Abu'l-Misk Kāfūr, a former slave of the Ikhshīd, who had served as general in his army before being appointed regent to his heirs. Local sentiment against the regime was sufficiently strong for the first in a series of civil disturbances to be reported in 954/343, shortly before a major earthquake and attendant plague brought misery to Egypt. In the south of the country the Nubians were also restive, having attacked the oases in 949/337, demanding improvements in the trade routes. They launched a major attack on Aswan in 955/344 and put up strong resistance to the Ikhshīdid army sent to suppress them. During the reign of ʿAlī there were several further outbreaks of famine.

In the twenty years Kāfūr acted as regent for the Ikhshīdid princes he gained a reputation for patronage of the arts and culture, as well as for a fairly indulgent life. Even with the assistance of the able vizier Ibn al-Furāt, the serious problems of the country defied solution. After the death of Kāfūr, who ruled briefly in his own name from 966/355 to 968/357, the struggle for the succession soon drew the attention of the Fāṭimids. Toward the end of Aḥmad Abu'l-Fawāris' reign Ibn al-Furāt was acting as governor of the country, and it was he who surrendered to the Fāṭimid general Jawhar aṣ-Ṣiqillī when the latter entered al-Fusṭāṭ in 969/358.

Ikhshīdid Rulers:

935/323	Muḥammad b. Ṭughj
946/334	Ūnūjūr
961/349	ᶜAlī
966/355	Kāfūr
968-69/357-58	Aḥmad Abu'l-Fawāris

IKHWAN AL-MUSLIMUN (IKHWĀN AL-MUSLIMŪN)/("The Muslim Brethren"). The major organized Islamic revivalist group in Egypt, the Ikhwan al-Muslimun was founded by Hasan al-Banna and was active from 1928 until it was banned at the end of 1954 following the attempted assassination of Gamal Abdal Nasser by an Ikhwan member. The group continued to exist unofficially after that time and emerged in the mid-1960s in opposition to the Nasser regime. The Ikhwan's exact relationship to many of the current radical Islamic revivalist groups in Egypt is uncertain, but it was surely a seminal influence in their formation and ideology.

From its foundation the Ikhwan was closely identified with Al-Banna's personality and ideas and with the link he emphasized between Islam as a religious and a social force. Starting in Ismailiyya, and from 1932 in Cairo, the Ikhwan as an organization offered a number of social-welfare institutions that helped familiarize and popularize the group among many segments of Egyptian society. Schools, clinics, and even small factories were started, and the level of involvement of the Ikhwan with the betterment of its members and supporters stood in favorable contrast to the more self-seeking attitudes of the major political parties, at a time when Egypt was facing great economic difficulties. This increased the number of Ikhwan supporters, as did the power of Al-Banna's message and personality. He preached the need for Muslims to follow an Islam that returned to the original pure state of the religion in its dawning years in Arabia. Such a religion, rigorously adhered to, could provide the solution to the personal, social, and, indeed, political problems faced by Islamic societies. His message also contained a rejection of Western, and particularly British, involvement in these Islamic societies, enabling the Ikhwan to draw supporters from the deeply religious as well as from the nationalist elements in the population. This message of Islamic revival and renewal was preached in mosques, coffee-houses, classes, and clinics. The platform and approach was thus broader and deeper than that of the major Egyptian political parties, including the Wafd.

The Ikhwan began acquiring journals, including the popular Islamic magazine Al-Manar, and publishing its ideas and programs in pamphlets, easily available in urban areas, and making skilled use of Western techniques of propaganda and journalism. Al-Banna made a political statement at the national level in 1936, in an open letter addressed to the new King, Faruq, in which he discussed the role of a monarch in Islamic society. As the group continued to gain supporters, it increasingly became more active politically, casting itself in the role of the defender of Islamic values in a political system in which secularism had played a large role. As a counterweight to the secular political parties, the Ikhwan had supporters even at the level of the Palace.

By the Second World War the Ikhwan was acknowledged nationally as a group whose favor should be sought, though approaches by the major political parties were less successful than those by a young group of disaffected army officers who were later to lead the Revolution of 1952 as the Free Officers. From these initial contacts a pattern of cooperation and influence was established. The Ikhwan leader, Al-Banna, was briefly imprisoned early in the war for his opposition to Egyptian involvement in Britain's war effort, which did his reputation with more ardent nationalists no harm. But despite his own growing prestige the expansion of the Ikhwan membership and hierarchy was creating subgroupings and ideological controversies within the Ikhwan that were difficult for Al-Banna to control fully.

One grouping created in this period was the Special, or Secret, Section, a paramilitary group organized in the early 1940s, which eventually received training and probably equipment from the Free Officers. Other groups, which disapproved of what they saw as the "moderation" and apolitical quality of Al-Banna's leadership or which found some of the individuals around him unsavory, broke away from the Ikhwan. The pyramidic leadership structure notwithstanding, as the membership approached several hundred thousand the organization had to reflect the needs and demands of its members and became unwieldy to manage. It was largely thanks to Al-Banna's charisma that the group's overall cohesion was maintained.

This membership became actively involved in the civil disturbances that swept Egypt after the war and until the end of 1948. Demonstrations, strikes, and assassinations had the involvement of groups on the extreme left and right of the political spectrum. However much Al-Banna knew of the activities of the Special Section during this time, the Ikhwan drew a large portion of blame from the government for the internal disorders. The assassination of the Cairo Chief of Police in 1948, following accusations from the Ikhwan that he had been involved in setting them up for arrest for terrorist offenses, led Nuqrashi Pasha to ban the organization in December 1948. He was himself assassinated shortly thereafter by an Ikhwan member, and in retaliation Al-Banna was assassinated in February 1949. A large number of Ikhwan members were arrested in April 1949, only to be exonerated of most charges in trials held in 1951.

The Ikhwan as an organization gained from its active support for Palestinian rights, and at the outbreak of the 1948 fighting in Palestine it sent special commando units that participated in several battles. The effectiveness of these units, in stark contrast to the performance of the rest of the army, boosted the Ikhwan's prestige in Egypt still further. But the advantage was lost after Al-Banna's death, with the leadership locked in a power struggle that took two years--and the election of Hasan al-Hudaybi--to paper over. The election of Hudaybi in 1951 in fact resolved nothing, for beneath his nominal leadership the division between the extremist and more conservative elements continued. Among the activists such as Salah al-Ashmawi and the powerful Abdal Qadir Awda was a growing tendency to act autonomously from the leadership. The Ikhwan was able to resume their public activities in December 1951, when the ban imposed by Nuqrashi was finally lifted.

The Ikhwan cooperated with the Wafd government of Nahhas in anti-British activities in the Canal Zone in the autumn of 1951. Their involvement in the burning of Cairo on Black Saturday has never been satisfactorily settled.

By the time of the Free Officers' coup of 23 July 1952 many in the Ikhwan leadership were expecting to be brought into the government as full partners. The Ikhwan was the only pre-Revolutionary grouping excluded from the ban on political parties introduced in January 1953, an exemption gained by the group's established popularity and influence. The Free Officers needed the support of the Ikhwan (or thought they did) if only to gain the acceptance of its many members. The Ikhwan viewed the 1952 coup as the first stage toward power-sharing, but the Free Officers did not want its leadership, and the Ikhwan's demands for veto power over the legislation introduced by the Revolutionary Command Council were rejected.

Instead, and as a limited concession, the RCC in September 1953 offered the Ikhwan three ministerial posts. Following the RCC offer a wrangle ensued among the leadership over its acceptability. The offer was finally rejected. Increasingly frustrated with the direction of the Revolution and their exclusion from power, Ikhwan members took to the street in protest in late 1953-early 1954, leading to an RCC decision to proscribe the group. Some 450 members were arrested and a state of emergency declared by the government, which charged the Ikhwan with planning a coup. Hudaybi appealed to General Naguib following his dismissal and reinstatement in February 1954; while this appeal did not directly touch on broader issues, in the leadership struggle between Naguib and Nasser thereafter the

Ikhwan made no secret of its preference for the former. The group was allowed to resume its peaceful activities in March, but took to the streets later in protest at the agreement concluded by the RCC and the British over the evacuation of Suez, which the Ikhwan portrayed as a capitulation to the British. The assassination attempt on Nasser in October 1954 gave him the excuse he needed to institute a thorough crackdown on the Ikhwan. Some 500 members were arrested immediately and imprisoned, and a further 4,000 arrests followed. At the trial of the Ikhwan leadership in November 1954, six of the high command were sentenced to death (Hudaybi's sentence was commuted to life imprisonment at hard labor) and several thousand were interned in camps.

In the late 1950s, as part of its suppression of the Left, the Nasser government permitted the publishing house specializing in Ikhwan works to resume its activities. Many Ikhwan members imprisoned in 1954 were released in the early 1960s, and by the mid-1960s they were active in urban and rural areas. They were linked by the government with a series of strikes and civil disturbances in 1964-65. In 1966, claiming it had discovered an Ikhwan-led plot to overthrow it, the government instituted another crackdown on the group. A trial that year resulted in three executions and 200 imprisonments and was protested by other Arab governments sympathetic to the Ikhwan.

The reemergence of the Ikhwan as a threat to the government in the mid-1960s may be linked to the failures of some programs and policies of the Nasser regime, the lack of an alternative political voice, and the anger aroused by some of the regime's more repressive characteristics. Similarly, its renewed strength in the early 1970s (initially with some official encouragement) came at a time when Egyptian society was in the throes of the transition from Nasserism to the new approaches offered by President Sadat, and when left-wing, secular opposition to the regime was high. Umar Tilmasanni headed the Ikhwan in the mid-1970s.

The Ikhwan has never lost its credibility among those elements of the population prepared to support a social/political program based on Islamic revival and renewal. The group has also profited from the fact that it is easier for the government to suppress its secular and leftist critics than to move against a religious grouping, however political its voice. As the most comprehensive and successful of the Islamic revivalist groups in Egypt the Ikhwan has continued to enjoy the affiliation, however clandestine, of many Egyptians. The years since its foundation have, to some degree, sharpened the conflicts between the religious and politically drawn supporters of the Ikhwan. The formation of more politicized and activist offshoots gives certain evidence that the longstanding problems of the Ikhwan with regard to its religious versus political role have been resolved by the creation of separate organizations, though with certain ideological principles in common.

IMĀM. Imām is the leader of the Muslim community and also the title taken by the person who leads Friday prayers. The title was understood very differently by the Sunnī and the Shīʿa, with strongly conflicting ideas on how Imāma (or leadership) was acquired. The essentially spiritual nature of this office can be contrasted with Sulṭān, Malik (king), and Amīr, all secular posts.

IMAM PARTY see ABDUH, UMMA PARTY

ILTIZĀM. Tax farms established by the Ottomans as a means of collecting revenue from Egypt. Revenue sources were divided into units for auction. The tax-farmer (multāzim) would bid for a certain area from the central government, from which he was expected to collect taxes plus an amount for his own, not inconsiderable, profits. The iltizām system and the tax-farmers associated with it were important figures in Ottoman Egypt. They were often the local rulers in the areas where they collected tax and frequently ruthless in the manner they exacted the sums due from their area. Certain Ottoman regiments in Egypt were also granted revenue-collecting privileges, which were deeply unpopular in rural areas.

The office of tax-farmer tended to become hereditary, thanks to the bestowal of large and frequent gifts on the central authorities from the multāzim. The privilege was, however, technically revokable. Muḥammad ᶜAlī had abolished the system by about 1816, once the Mamluks, who then formed the majority of important multāzim, had been suppressed and the opposition of the ᶜulamā' (religious) who held many iltizām, had been overcome. Yet the system was maintained in urban areas until the 1870s although multāzim were subjected to regulation that removed most of the potential for abuse of the office.

INĀL (AL-ASHRAF SAYF AD-DĪN INĀL) (r. 1453-61/857-65). Burjī Mamluk Sultan, Ināl was a Mamluk of Barqūq; his career was advanced in the reign of Barsbay. In 1446/850 he was made Amīr al-Kabīr, having earlier led the Mamluk fleet unsuccessfully against Rhodes. In 1453/857 Ināl led a street rebellion against the Sultan's successor, ᶜUthmān, and was himself proclaimed Sultan. A brief rebellion against Ināl, involving the shadow Caliph al-Qā'im, was suppressed by Ināl in 1455/859 and the Caliph in question deposed.

In 1458-60/862-64 Ināl became involved with the succession to the throne in Cyprus, but his intervention there ended, in 1460/864, with his defeat. Aside from this episode Ināl's relations with the other states under Mamluk influence were reasonably peaceful. He also exchanged friendly embassies with the Ottoman Sultan Mehmed.

Although Ināl is claimed to have been illiterate by some sources, he was an extremely pious man and favored Egypt's Ṣūfī community. Inal's reign was efficient and prosperous. He tried to associate his son Aḥmad in power with him and promoted him to high office. He secured the succession in favor of Ahmad, but his son did not remain long in power.

INDIAN-EGYPTIAN FRIENDSHIP TREATY. Concluded in April 1955, the signing of the treaty between Egypt and India followed three visits by Jawaharlal Nehru to the country. The treaty marked the official acceptance in Egypt of Nehru's Five Principles, which centered on peaceful relations between all states, territorial integrity, national self-determination, equality among nations, and autonomy in the conduct of internal affairs. The Egyptians saw in these bridges to India (and later to other Third World states) a means to counter continued Western influence in the area and in Egypt, at a time when the West was actively seeking to build defensive alliances (e.g., the Baghdad Pact) with the cooperation of states in the region. At the same time the treaty represented a considerable diplomatic achievement for India, anxious to build links to the Arab and Islamic world as support for her territorial and political differences with Pakistan.

INDUSTRIALIZATION. Modern industrial development in Egypt had its beginning in the reign of Muhammad Ali, though the country had well-established artisans. Part of the impetus for industrialization came from the need to supply the army with basic equipment, particularly during its enormous expansion in the 1820s and 1830s. Muhammad Ali's early ventures thus centered on military goods production and were badly affected by the reduction in the size of his army following his agreements with the Ottoman Sultan in 1841. Aside from this, however, Egypt still lacked the infrastructure to proceed with large scale industrialization, and it was projects to improve Egypt's internal communications by rail and water-borne transport that received much of his successors' attentions. The attempts of the Khedive Ismail to revive some of these industrialization plans were without much success.

The primary processing of commodities, such as tobacco and cotton, developed prior to the First World War, and Egypt was fortunate in having in its urban areas a large number of skilled and semi-skilled artisans on which industrial development could draw. The labor-force potential expanded due to the growing influx of people from rural areas to the cities.

Given the availability of labor and raw materials, the establishment of Bank Misr in 1920 was intended to use these elements, in combination with Egyptian capital, to found Egyptian-owned and -directed industries and to help the country make the transition away from its marked dependence on agriculture. The start was slow, however, for the Bank was not very successful in attracting capital from Egypt's landed classes. Finally, with public and foreign help, it began a program of industrial development that really took off in the 1930s. Between 1938 and 1951 industrial production in Egypt rose 138 percent. Given its low starting base, however, at the time of the Revolution it still contributed only 15 percent to the GNP and employed only 10 percent of the work force. Nonetheless, it was clear enough that Egypt's industrial sector had great potential for expansion, both in terms of production and to relieve the problem of growing urban unemployment.

After the 1952 Revolution the Revolutionary Command Council and its economic advisers targeted industrialization as a basic necessity to create employment opportunities for Egypt's fast-growing population. Overall planning was faulty, however, and on occasion Egypt's precious reserves of foreign capital (released under the Sterling Reserves Agreement with England) were wasted on projects with small returns. The Soviet Union provided capital for Egypt's industrialization plans in 1958 and helped with the design and construction of the iron and steel works at Helwan. The Aswan Dam, with its massive hydroelectric generating power, was also meant to help with the drive for industrial development.

Prior to 1961 it had been hoped that some of Egypt's private capital would flow into industrialization and investment in the development of industry. This hope proved as overly optimistic as the schemes of Bank Misr in the 1920s for attracting private capital to its development plans. Nasser responded by nationalizing many of the larger private companies and interests in Egypt in 1961 and in the following year nationalized the remainder of Egyptian industry. The association of these nationalizations with the regime's shift to socialist political policies made an unfortunate association of industrialization with political rather than economic criteria for success and performance. Under the 1962 Charter of National Action nine corporations were established to supervise the activities of the nationalized companies, within the structure of the Five- and Ten-Year Plans. Few of these plans were actually carried to completion because they were so often out of line with the productive capacity of industry and had to be redrawn. Thus, the political and overly ambitious criteria established for the industrial sector led to frequent shortfalls between planning targets and realization.

The managers of Egypt's public-sector industries were initially recruited on the basis of technological skill and qualifications, but this did not exempt them from bureaucratic control or political judgment for tenure and success. In time the gradual infiltration of bureaucrats into the administration of national industries produced, inevitably, bureaucratic attitudes about procedures and formalities at the expense of efficiency and production. Nasser attempted an ideological and policy correction to this in the Production Congress, which met in March 1967, answering some of the political critiques advanced by bureaucrats against the industrial managers. It was promised at the time that there would be greater decentralization in industrial decision-making, though, as with past attempts, the promise remained largely unfulfilled. Productivity and appropriate investment problems continued to trouble the public sector.

With the deregulation of Egypt's economic life started in 1974 by President Anwar Sadat, private investment, particularly foreign investment, in Egypt's industrialization was once again encouraged. However, the advent of private industry and imports since the Open Door Policy was introduced has badly affected Egypt's domestic industries, which are unable to compete in finish, quality, and, sometimes, price. The higher salaries offered in the new and expanding private sector, especially by foreign companies, can be expected to have a predictably negative effect on personnel recruitment for the state industries. Current plans envisage the public-sector industries, which employ 50 percent of Egypt's 1.4 million industrial workers, remaining dominant in a few critical and basic fields, with private industry (35 percent of the work force) taking an ever-larger share of the other sectors of the economy. Under the latest five year plan, public sector industry will receive only 9 percent of government investment.

In addition to the private and public sectors Egypt has an extremely large informal sector and small-scale light industries that function to this day much as they did in earlier times. Small enterprises have been promised a higher level of government investment, but the survival of small-scale industry in Egypt may in the long run be affected by a rising level of cheaper imports able to compete with them for the urban market. In the meantime the informal sector continues to serve its traditional role of providing a pool of potential skilled and unskilled labor for Egypt's industrial development, as well as locally made and inexpensive goods affordable by most Egyptians.

INDUSTRIALIZATION PLAN. In January 1958, after two years of discussions, Dr. Aziz Sidqi announced Egypt's first comprehensive economic plan, with an enormous concentration of capital in industrialization, £E250 million over five years. Nasser later announced that he expected the plan to be accomplished in three years, and the Soviet Union provided assistance with the financing, through a 700-million-ruble loan repayable on easy terms (2.5 percent interest) over twelve years. The plan did not succeed in attracting the level of private-sector investment in industrialization that had been hoped and was eventually replaced with a Five-Year Plan in 1960.

INFITAH see OPEN DOOR POLICY

INTERIM AGREEMENT see EGYPTIAN-ISRAELI INTERIM AGREEMENT

INTERNATIONAL COMMISSION. The establishment of Dual Control over Egypt's finances in 1876 was based on estimates of Egypt's revenues of £9.5 million per annum. The first two years of the Caisse de la Dette Publique's operations showed the country's revenues nowhere near this figure, in part because of a particularly poor Nile in 1877, but also because of irregular bureaucratic practices, much used in the past, which enabled many

Egyptians to escape tax assessments and payment through the enrichment of selected local officials. The inability of Egypt's new European financial controllers to directly intervene in this situation and to bring actual revenues in line with expectations led to the convening in 1878 of a commission, in which the major creditor countries participated. It was agreed in the commission's interim report of August, 1878, that a number of Europeans should be appointed to ministerial posts to safeguard the creditors' interests. This "European" cabinet was confirmed by a rescript (the Rescript of 1878) issued by Ismail. The cabinet was headed by Nubar Pasha and proved to be immediately and deeply unpopular in Egypt.

The commission's final report of March, 1879, recommended alterations in Egypt's tax and debt repayment systems. The opposition to these proposals and the verdict of bankruptcy enlarged the already active hostility to the European cabinet which was dismissed that April.

IQṬĀ^{c}. A grant of state land revenues made by Muslim rulers to viziers and military personnel, iqṭā^{c} was also awarded for services to the Caliph. Iqṭā^{c} of land in Egypt became important in ^{c}Abbāsid times; the Caliph al-Mu^{c}tazz (866-69/252-55) granted iqṭā^{c} over his lands to generals appointed as governors. Each general then sent one of his officers as his representative, plus troops for his support. Aḥmad b. Ṭūlūn came to Egypt in this capacity in 868/254, as deputy for Bāykbāk. Financial control was to remain in the hands of an autonomous individual answerable to Baghdad.

The iqṭā^{c} holder was required to pay a tithe, or portion of his revenues, to the Caliph, and to cover his administrative expenses. When used by a wise ruler, the system allowed for a greater amount of Egypt's revenues to be invested within the country. The nature of the Ṭūlūnid iqṭā^{c} changed when in 884/770, Ibn Ṭūlūn's son, Khumārawayh, was granted hereditary control of Egypt and wide areas of Syria. Twelve years later, the Caliph raised the sum due him from Egypt as Ṭūlūnid power was in decline. Thus, the precise character of the iqṭā^c to a certain extent turned on the power balance between the center and the holder.

In the thirty-year interregnum between the fall of the Ṭūlūnids in 905/292 and the rise of the Ikhshīdids, the revenues from Egypt were sent directly to Baghdad to pay for the ^{c}Abbāsid armies. However, the rising threat to Egypt posed by the Fāṭimids, along with the general disorder of the ^{c}Abbāsid state in the east, led to the decision to grant Muḥammad b. Ṭughj the same form of military-administrative iqṭā^c in Egypt as was held by his predecessor Ibn Ṭūlūn.

Under Fāṭimid rule (969-1171/358-567) all land in Egypt was considered the Caliph's property. Some individuals were granted ownership rights, but the revenues due to the Caliph were collected by individuals from set areas they bid for at auction. In time, the right to collect such revenues tended to become hereditary, and to this extent bore some relation to the iqṭā^c of the preceding period.

Ṣalāḥ ad-Dīn (r. 1169-93/564-89), founder of the Ayyūbid dynasty, used iqṭā^c to pay his amīrs. The iqṭā^c-holder, unlike his predecessors in the ^{c}Abbāsid period, did not possess any administrative jurisdiction but merely received an annual payment from his iqṭā^c. The Ayyūbid iqṭā^c were revokable and, technically, nonhereditary; they were also on a much smaller scale than the overall grants or fiefs Ṣalāḥ ad-Dīn made to his sons and relations from the vast territory he had conquered.

This form of iqṭā^c continued through Mamluk times, with the nonhereditary iqṭā^c granted to military officers (in lieu of pay) in exchange for their maintaining a certain number of men under arms. They usually did not live in the area they were granted. Revenue was in money and in kind, and its size was calculated by the central government not the iqṭā^c-holder. Iqṭā^c in Egypt probably accounted for half the country's agricultural lands, with the rest being controlled directly by the government. See also ILTIZĀM.

ISLAMIC CONGRESS. Established in 1954 by the Revolutionary Command Council, the Islamic Congress was formed to spread the message of Egypt's revolution in terms of Islamic culture and promote active cooperation among the Islamic countries. The regime emphasized this involvement in Islam to link Egypt more closely with the region and with the more conservative Islamic countries whose support it sought. It was also intended to counter the appeal of the Ikhwan al-Muslimun as a group devoted to the protection of Islam. Anwar Sadat was the first Secretary-General of the organization, charged with maintaining and improving relationships with the Gulf states. The congress published widely on the subject of Islam's role in the Arab world and elsewhere and was also used by the regime as a forum of communication with Islamic states in Africa and Asia.

The first Islamic Congress met in Mecca in 1955, but as Egypt's role within the region changed, and especially after the formation of the UAR, Egypt's use of the organization became an increasingly political one. Kamal Husayn, a former Free Officer, became president of the Islamic Congress in 1961. The congress' political importance steadily eroded from the mid-1960s.

The Yemen War in 1962, which saw Saudi Arabia and Egypt supporting the opposing sides, caused a major rupture between Egypt and that country; Egypt's relations with the other Gulf states had been deteriorating even before this time, thanks to her involvement in their political and labor situation. These political tensions inevitably led to the creation of new forums independent of Egyptian control. King Faysal of Saudi Arabia called for the establishment of a new Islamic Congress headquartered in Mecca. This Islamic Congress, with a pan-Islamic focus, was established in May 1971 after preparatory conferences in Rabat and other Arab capitals in 1969-71.

ISLAMIC MODERNISM/REFORMISM. One of the two main philosophical movements of modern Islam, Islamic modernism, like Islamic revivalism, developed from the work of Muhammad Abduh.

The Islamic modernists, or reformists, picked up on the trend in Abduh's thought that sought a reconciliation between the teachings of Islam and the technological, scientific, political and philosophical developments of the West. The thinkers and writers of this school have argued for alterations in the religious and cultural patterns of Egyptian Islamic society, in such areas as the position and role of women, family law, and social planning, as well as for a simpler and less legalistic view of Islam able to respond to the changes of a developing society. Their attitudes toward Western or European values vary widely within the movement. It may be generally observed, however, that many reformists seek a stronger yet more open Islam capable of thriving in a world where Western values are widely disseminated. Thus, while some thinkers of this school have been strongly influenced by Western humanist philosophies, a good many writers past and present have based their arguments for reform on the strength of Islam itself. Islam, stripped of the pre- and non-Islamic social and cultural practices that have accrued to it through the centuries, was felt by them to be a far more flexible system of beliefs than is currently found. Many modernists have also sought ways of harmonizing Islam with the intellectual and scientific developments of the West or with the needs of developing societies. The progressive attitude of the modernists toward social reform and development harmonized well with the moderate secularism of past Egyptian governments, but, overall, Islamic modernism has remained a movement whose attractiveness has less appeal among ordinary Egyptian Muslims than Islamic revivalism. The rejection of Islamic reformism by some among Egypt's religious community has influenced popular attitudes. Such writers as Qasim Amin, Taha Husayn, and Ali Abdal Rizzik have had their writings condemned by the religious authorities, though these writings usually gained more acceptability later. Among the recent modernists, Khalid Muhammad Khalid enjoyed a broad popular audience in the 1960s.

ISLAMIC REVIVALISM. Developed in and from the writings of Muhammad Abduh, Islamic revivalism has become in time the dominant trend in Islamic theology in Egypt and elsewhere in the Islamic world. Revivalists stress the need for a return to the pure Islam found at the time of the Prophet Muḥammad, and in this their arguments are similar to those of the modernists. The revivalists go one step farther from this point to argue that an ideal Islamic life is modeled on the revelations and precepts of this early Islam, with minimal (if any) references to non-Islamic influences. Similarly, the revivalists feel that an ideal Islamic social order should be built on this pattern of early Islam; they differ from the modernists in their rejection or modification of Western social and cultural influences that may be allowed to act within an Islamic society.

The scripturalist or Salafiyya movement in Islam owes its strength in Egypt to a number of distinguished and charismatic successors to Abduh, such as Rashid Rida, Hasan al-Banna, and Sayyid Qutb, as well as to the success of revivalist movements in other Islamic countries. Often requiring none of the complex intellectual arguments used by the modernists and reformists in the defense of their views, the relative simplicity and appeal of Islamic revivalism's basic tenets, and the image it presents of a just and holy society freed of negative foreign influences or interference, have won it a wide following in Egypt. Supporters of Islamic revivalism have been grouped into such organizations as the Ikhwan al-Muslimun, and more radical modern groupings. Using their considerable popular strength, they have pressed the Egyptian government in the past and the present (with increasing success) to bring the country's laws in line with the precepts of Islam.

ISLAMIC SOCIETIES see GAMAAT ISLAMIYYA

ISMĀʿĪL (AṢ-ṢĀLIḤ ʿIMĀD AD-DĪN ISMĀʿĪL) (r. 1342-45/743-46). Baḥrī Mamluk Sultan, Ismāʿīl was the son and fourth successor of the Sultan an-Nāṣir Muḥammad. He displaced his brother Aḥmad and managed to hold office for nearly three years, a record for Nāṣir Muḥammad's sons to that date. Aḥmad fled to Kerak, where he mounted a campaign to regain the throne, enjoying the covert support of Ismā^cīl's own vizier. In 1344/745 Ismā^cīl launched an attack on Aḥmad and his supporters, which resulted in the former Sultan's being captured at Kerak and executed in 1345/746. Ismā^cīl himself died shortly thereafter.

ISMĀ^cĪL BEY (d. 1724/1137). Leader of the Qāsimiyya faction of Mamluks, Ismā^cīl Bey became Shaykh al-Balad in 1711/1123. His father, Īwāz Bey, and Īwāz' allies in the Ottoman garrison in Egypt emerged as victors after the Great Rebellion of 1711/1123, successfully countering a challenge from the Faqāriyya faction and their Janissary allies. Īwāz was killed during the fighting, and his son inherited his position; Ismā^cīl initially shared power with his father's partner, Abū Shanab, but soon established his own supremacy within the Qāsimiyya, especially following Abū Shanab's death in 1118/1130.

During Ismā^cīl's period of supremacy, which lasted until his death, the beylicate was filled with members of his faction. Ismā^cīl also enjoyed the support of the chief of the Hawwāra tribe, Humām b. Yūsuf, which helped keep Upper Egypt peaceful during his tenure in office. The Faqāriyya were far from absolutely crushed, however, despite Ismā^cīl's organization of the assassination of their chief, Qayṭās Bay, in 1714/1126. A group of Faqāriyya effected an alliance with the followers of Abū Shanab, restive after their exclusion from power by Ismā^cīl; though Ismā^cīl managed to keep this alliance from threatening him before his death, following his assassination this allied group seized power, only to be overturned in 1730/1143 by a Faqāriyya group allied with the Qāzdughliyya faction.

ISMĀ^cĪL BEY (d. 1791/1205). Shaykh al-Balad and de facto ruler of Egypt in the troubled closing decades of Ottoman rule, Ismā^cīl was a Mamluk of ^cAlī Bey. After the death of Abū'dh-Dhahab in 1775/1189 Ismā^cīl and the ^cAlawiyya faction (composed of the Mamluks of ^cAlī Bey) stood opposed to the new Duumvir of Ibrāhīm and Murād Bey. The latter planned to have Ismā^cīl killed to reduce any threats to their power, but the ^{c}Alawiyya rose against them and the Duumvir were forced to leave Cairo. Ismā^{c}īl became Shaykh al-Balad in 1777/1191 but was unable to control the situation within the beylicate; he withdrew when Ibrāhīm and Murād returned to Cairo one year later.

The Duumvir expelled many of the ^{c}Alawiyya from Cairo, but the faction regrouped in the south of Egypt and Ismā^{c}īl joined them. The ^{c}Alawiyya gained control of the region and were given territorial concessions there by the Duumvir in 1781/1195, after an unsuccessful attempt to defeat them. With the arrival of the Ottoman forces in Egypt in 1786/1200 the Duumvir was forced to withdraw to the south, and Ismā^{c}īl was once again installed as Shaykh al-Balad by the Ottoman commander Ḥasan Pasha. Ismā^{c}īl's time in office was troubled by a rebellion in the south, led by the Duumvir, a rapidly deteriorating economy, and his inability to control the Mamluks. The entire situation was greatly worsened by an outbreak of plague, which first struck in 1786/1200; by 1790/1205 Cairo was in active rebellion as the plague became endemic in Egypt, claiming Ismā^{c}īl among its victims and permitting the restoration of the Duumvir.

ISMAIL (r. 1863-79). Khedive of Egypt, Ismail was the son of Ibrahim Pasha; his reign saw the greatest transformation of Egypt since that of his grandfather, Muhammad Ali. It was, however, a transformation that led to Egypt's international bankruptcy and its eventual takeover by the British in 1882. Ismail's vision of Egypt's development matched that of his grandfather, and he was equally anxious to preserve his autonomy and extend his territory.

Ismail was in exile during the reign of Abbas, returning to hold official and diplomatic posts before his accession. He secured both hereditary and territorial concessions from the Porte. In 1865 he obtained the return of the ports of Sawakin and Massawa, held by the Ottomans for sixteen years, as well as the right of primogeniture in his own line in 1866. Ismail's title was changed from Viceroy to Khedive in 1867 (the latter being a princely title of Turco-Persian origin), and he was granted certain increased rights in political and financial dealings with foreign powers. In 1873 the Sultan recognized Ismail's autonomy within Egypt, following a period of difficult relations between the two. Each of these decrees Ismail secured or rewarded with generous contributions to the Porte.

Ismail had territorial ambitions in Africa, and Samuel Baker and other explorers conducted expeditions on his behalf to the Sudan and Equatorial Africa. In 1870 Egyptian troops occupied Zaila on the Red Sea coast; Ismail laid claim to the Somali coast down to Ras Assir. By 1873 Samuel Baker had annexed huge territories around the Equatorial lakes in the name of the Khedive. Dafur was taken in 1874 by a private army led by Zubayr Pasha, and in 1875 Harar was annexed. Thereafter the Egyptian expansion southward ran into difficulties. The British objected to Egypt's attempt to take land claimed by Zanzibar, and the Egyptian army was defeated in 1875 in a battle with the Ethiopians at Gundet. Gordon withdrew from parts of the Equatorial Province in that year, and the army also experienced reverses in Nubia. The Mahdist movement, which became active in the Sudan after Ismail's deposition, was to challenge Egyptian control of that province, granted to the Egyptian rulers by an 1841 Ottoman decree.

Within Egypt, Ismail's reign witnessed a tremendous expansive phase in the country's development. A postal service was started in 1867. Two years later the Suez Canal was opened, municipal government granted to Alexandria, and the National Library founded. A Khedival Mail Line began operation on the Nile in 1870, taking over from a private European concession. In 1875 a new reform of the legal system was introduced and the mixed courts established. The Ismailiyya quarter of Cairo was constructed, based on European city plans, and necessary municipal services, such as sewage, were installed in several areas of Cairo and Alexandria. Ismail also tried to revive some of Muhammad Ali's plans for industrialization by privately funding a few government factories. He expanded his grandfather's system of sending promising students abroad for their education. Through his sponsorship and active support the National Library, Museum, Geographical Society, and Opera were founded and greatly enriched the level of learning and culture in Egypt. Administrative reform was also introduced at the provincial level and a national assembly was formed.

Ismail's tenure as Khedive was profoundly affected by events in which Egypt gradually lost ground to the colonizing powers. The opening of the Suez Canal in 1869 dramatically increased Egypt's strategic importance to Europe. The canal halved the journey between England and its most important colony, India, and for that reason alone Egypt's future was to be linked with the expansion of European colonialism. Ismail's ambitious development projects were put into effect with little regard for the country's actual income. The enormous revenue earned by Egypt from European purchases of Egyptian cotton during the American Civil War were not long-lived, though the Khedive's spending policies were. Ismail obtained loans from the major European banks and the spending (and lending) continued. Though Ismail doubtless received poor advice from his financial experts, the country's growing indebtedness also stemmed from his vision of an Egypt modernized on a European model. By 1875 Ismail was unable to meet the interest payments on his debts and was forced to sell his, i.e. Egypt's, shares in the Suez Canal to Britain. Britain and Egypt's other creditors established the Caisse de la Dette Publique, and control over the country's finances, in 1876. To strengthen their control of the Egyptian government the British and French forced the formation of a "European Ministry" under Nubar Pasha in 1878, with Europeans placed in key ministerial posts. In the same year a civil list was created for Ismail, under European supervision.

The outrage caused in Egypt by the European cabinet led directly to the founding of the first nationalist grouping, the Hizb al-Watani; popular and military agitation against the cabinet grew so vehement that Ismail dismissed the "European" cabinet in April 1879. The European powers thereupon applied great pressure to the Ottoman Sultan to dismiss Ismail and appoint his son, Muhammad Tawfiq Pasha, as Khedive, which was done in June 1879. Ismail died in exile in Istanbul in 1895, having never reconciled himself to his loss of power.

ISMĀ^{c}ĪLIYYA. Ismā^{c}īliyya was the official sect of Shī^{c}a Islam in Egypt during the Fāṭimid period (969-1171/358-567). Ismā^{c}īl (d. 760/143) was the son of the Imām (head of the Islamic community among the Shī^{c}a) Ja^{c}far aṣ-Ṣādiq (a descendant of the fourth Caliph, ^{c}Alī); he predeceased his father. The early Ismā^{c}īliyya believed that Ismā^{c}īl (or, sometimes, his son Muḥammad) had disappeared, not died, and that the Imāma, or leadership of the Shī^{c}a community rested with him (other Shī^{c}a acknowledge different lines of descent from Ja^{c}far). Some Ismā^{c}īlis believed Ismā^{c}īl would return to his faithful followers as a Mahdī, or savior/restorer of the community of believers.

In 899/286 ^{c}Abdallāh (also known as ^{c}Ubayd Allāh) al-Mahdī declared that he and his line were the holders of the Imāma of Ismā^{c}īl and that his family were descended from the Prophet Muḥammad through his daughter Fāṭima. Many Ismā^{c}īliyya in Iran, Iraq, and Bahrain refused to recognize his claims, however. ^{c}Abdallāh, founder of the Fāṭimid dynasty, left Syria and eventually settled in Tunisia, achieving power there and establishing the Fāṭimid Ismā^{c}īlī Caliphate in 909/297.

During the Fāṭimid Caliphate in Egypt the Ismā^{c}īliyya split into the Nizāriyya, Ḥāfiziyya, and Āmiriyya factions over disputes regarding succession to the Caliphate.

ITTIHAD (UNION) PARTY. Pre-Revolutionary political party, the Ittihad was founded after a falling out between King Fuad and his former Prime Minister, Tharwat Pasha, of the Liberal Constitutionalist Party. The King was deeply unhappy about what he saw as the loss of his privileges under the 1923 Constitution, in whose drafting Tharwat Pasha had been involved. The Ittihad was formed late in 1924, and announced its leadership that January. King Fuad intended the party to represent the Palace viewpoint and draw support away from whichever party was in

Fuad's disfavor. The party had representatives in the non-Wafdist ministries and acted at various times with the Liberal Constitutionalists when the Wafd was in the ascendant, and against the Liberal Constitutionalists when the Palace felt the latter were gaining too much power. Headed by former Egyptian Prime Minister Yahya Ibrahim, the Ittihad Party was also directed by Nashat Pasha, Deputy Chief of the Royal Cabinet and a powerful political figure in the court. The party declined after 1936 and eventually merged with the Sha^cb Party under the presidency of Muhammad Hilmi Isa, a former president of the Ittihad. Its political role thereafter was minor, being largely the politically organized expression of the Palace's views.

IZBAK (EZBEK) AT-TUTUSH (d. 1499/904). Amīr in the reign of Qā'it Bay (1468-96/872-901), Izbak was originally a Mamluk of Barsbāy, purchased and manumitted by the Sultan Jaqmaq (1438-53/842-57), who gave Izbak two of his daughters in marriage. Izbak rose to a position of power fairly quickly and became governor of Syria. Under Qā'it Bay he was made Commander-in-Chief (Amīr al-Juyūsh) and acting Sultan in Qā'it Bay's absence. Izbak distinguished himself militarily in several campaigns against the Bedouin in Egypt and against Ottoman supporters in Asia Minor. He had periods of being in disfavor and suffered a brief imprisonment, but this was fairly unremarkable for Mamluks in his time. Izbak led the Mamluk army to victory over the Ottomans in 1490/895, shortly before a peace was concluded.

Izbak gained renown for a series of public works he instituted in Cairo, including a resort and landscaped lake in Cairo itself. Despite his building activities he managed to leave a great fortune that historical sources have described in glowing if probably inflated terms. In the dispute among his heirs for control of his estate, the Sultan intervened and decided to keep the estate for himself. The lake that Izbak had dug was filled in by Muḥammad ^cAlī in 1824 and became the site of a populous quarter in modern Cairo that still bears Izbak's name.

-J-

AL-JABĀRTĪ, ᶜABD AR-RAḤMĀN (1756-1825). Historian of Egypt, al-Jabārti came from a family of religious scholars and held a post teaching astronomy at al-Azhar. This position earned him an appointment to the Diwān (council) established by Napoleon during the period of French control of Egypt (1798-1801).

Al-Jabārtī's historical study of Islamic Egypt began when he served as an apprentice to the Syrian biographer al-Murādī. In his writings al-Jabārtī gave many details on the personalities and status of the ᶜulamā' and on the decline in Egypt's urban and rural intellectual and social life as the country suffered political instability in the seventeenth and eighteenth centuries. His unfavorable attitude towards Muḥammad ᶜAlī (which prevented publication of his work for many years) can probably be traced to the restrictions on, and downgrading of, religious figures during Muḥammad ᶜAlī's reign as he sought to remove much of their autonomy.

JĀNBALĀT (AL-ASHRAF JĀNBALĀT) (r.1500-01/905-06). Burjī Mamluk Sultan, Jānbalāt was originally a Mamluk of Qā'it Bay. He held several posts of importance before assuming power: Amīr al-Ḥājj, ambassador to the Ottomans, chief purchaser of Mamluks, governor of Aleppo. In 1499/904 the army rose in rebellion against the Sultan Qānṣūḥ al-Ashrafī and named Jānbalāt as Sultan, though not all Mamluks recognized him as such. His rise to power was greatly helped, according to some sources, by his marriage to Assilbai, a former concubine of Qā'it Bay whose wealth helped fund his ambitions. Jānbalāt was eventually overthrown and imprisoned after a successful challenge by Tūmān Bay, who used Syria as a base from which to attack him.

JANISSARIES. Infantry corps established by the Ottoman rulers, the Janissaries (from the Turkish Yeñi Cheri, "new troops") enjoyed preeminence in the Ottoman garrison in Egypt over the other regiments. At their foundation the Janissaries were responsible for local secutiry. They were intended to be directly answerable to the Ottoman Sultan himself and were drawn from a levy on the Sultan's Balkan Christian subjects. This system was replaced at the end of the sixteenth/tenth centuries by an open recruitment system that did much harm to the corps' discipline and unity. The Janissaries featured prominently in the struggles within the Egyptian beylicate during the last century of Ottoman control. Their leaders Küçük Mehmed (d.1694/1105) and Afranj Aḥmad (d.1711/1123) allied themselves with the Faqāriyya faction of the beylicate.

During Küçük's ascendancy he carried out coups against senior corps commanders (supporters of the Faqāriyya's opponents, the Qāsimiyya) with the support of the Faqāriyya, who were to gain strength during his first tenure in office (1674-80/1084-91) and supremacy during his second (1692-94/1103-05). Following Küçük's assassination in 1694/1105, the Janissaries were extremely restive and their leadership was divided. They participated in civil disturbances in 1698/1110 and in 1706/1118 and were for part of this time under the leadership of Afranj Aḥmad, though his supremacy in the corps was challenged by other members of the Janissary command. The Janissaries and their Faqāriyya allies were bested in the Great Rebellion of 1711/1123 by the Qāsimiyya faction and the ᶜAzaban infantry corps of the Ottoman garrison, the Janissaries' traditional opponents. The defeat only temporarily eclipsed the losers, as the political and military situation remained fluid in the face of a weak Ottoman governor and a contentious beylicate that dominated the divided army.

JANUARY RIOTS. After an attempt by the government of President Anwar Sadat to remove price subsidies on basic foodstuffs following negotiations with the IMF, a series of antigovernment riots broke out in January 1977 over the sudden sharp rise in prices. The demonstrations in Cairo resulted in seventy-nine deaths over a two-day period. Removal of the subsidies had been demanded by the IMF as a precondition for further lending to Egypt.

The removal of the subsidies was presented to the People's Assembly on 17 January 1977 as a revenue bill cutting government spending and subsidies by £E200 million, representing rises of between 10 and 60 percent in the prices of such commodities as bread, tea, sugar, and gas. On 19 January, following two days of street violence, the government announced the reintroduction of the subsidies.

The seriousness of Egypt's domestic economic problems and the relationship these problems had to the country's worsening international debt were underlined by the riots and resulted in the extension of another tranche of aid from GODE, the OAPEC group formed to assist Egypt's development efforts. A cabinet reshuffle took place in May 1977, and in the following year a group of communists was put on trial, charged with instigating the disturbances.

JAQMAQ (AẒ-ẒĀHIR SAYF AD-DĪN JAQMAQ) (r. 1438-53/842-57). Burjī Mamluk Sultan, Jaqmaq displaced Barsbāy's son Yūsuf, who had reigned briefly under Jaqmaq's regency. A revolt at court in the early days of Jaqmaq's reign was quickly suppressed, but his invasion of Rhodes in 1444/848 was unsuccessful. Jaqmaq maintained very cordial relations with the other Muslim rulers. During his reign, Jaqmaq removed certain state offices from Christians and Jews and imposed restrictions on European merchants. The lavishness of Jaqmaq's court came at a time when the Egyptian economy could barely support it. The country's internal situation was dominated by the increasingly uncontrolled and rapacious behavior of the Mamluks. Jaqmaq's attempt to secure the succession of his son ᶜUthmān were without success; ᶜUthmān was deposed shortly after Jaqmaq's death.

AL-JARJARĀ'Ī (AḤMAD) (r. 1027-45/415-36). Vizier and virtual ruler of Egypt during the reign of the Fāṭimid Caliph aẓ-Ẓāhir (r. 1021-36/411-27), al-Jarjarā'ī continued to be influential during the early years of the reign of aẓ-Ẓāhir's successor, al-Mustanṣir. Earlier in his career al-Jarjarā'ī served in the court of the Caliph al-Ḥākim and succeeded al-Ḥākim's sister, Sitt al-Mulk, at the court of al-Ḥākim's heir, aẓ-Ẓāhir.

During his eighteen years in the vizierate al-Jarjarā'ī controlled both court life and the government policy of Egypt, with the Caliph reduced to little more than a figurehead. In 1027/418 there were disturbances in Egypt over a famine caused by the failure of the Nile. This was suppressed, but later in al-Jarjarā'ī's career he had difficulty in countering trouble in Syria (1037/429), and in 1041/433 the Zīrids in North Africa broke away from Fāṭimid control. Balanced against this were the sometimes quite harmonious relations established with the Byzantines in the middle years of Jarjarā'ī's vizierate.

Al-Jarjarā'ī was eventually displaced by the Caliph al-Mustanṣir's mother and the vizier aṭ-Ṭustarī.

JARRING MISSION see ROGERS PLAN

JAWHAR AṢ-ṢIQILLĪ (d. 991/381). Fāṭimid general who conquered Egypt on behalf of the Caliph Mu^cizz, Jawhar was probably a Christian in origin, brought to the Fāṭimid capital of Qayrawān as a youth. His military skills gained him rapid advancement in the Fāṭimid army. In 958/347 Jawhar led Fāṭimid supporters in a pacification campaign in North Africa. Jawhar gained distinction in these campaigns and was placed in charge of the long-planned conquest of Egypt, which the Fāṭimid armies had previously raided in 913-14/301-02 and 919-21/307-09 and again in 935/323.

Jawhar defeated the disorganized Ikhshidid forces and entered al-Fusṭāṭ in July 969/358; shortly afterward he laid the foundations for a new capital city, Cairo, or al-Qāhira ("The Victorious"), and founded, in 970/359, the al-Azhar Mosque. Jawhar defeated an attack by the Qaramatians on Egypt and Syria in 971/360.

The Caliph al-Mu^cizz finally joined his general in Egypt in 973/362, the year Jawhar defeated another Qaramatian attack on Cairo itself. Jawhar had, early on, sent a deputy of his to establish a foothold in Syria, but this met with resistance. Following the arrival of al-Mu^cizz, Jawhar was sent to confront the forces of the Turkish commander Alptakīn, who was beseiging

Damascus. This campaign, whose prosecution was apparently not fully supported by the vizier Ya^cqūb b. Killis, ended badly when Alptakīn allied himself with the Qaramatians, compelling Jawhar to withdraw to Ascalon and negotiate the full withdrawal of his armies from Syria. In retreat Jawhar was met by the new Caliph, al-ᶜAzīz, and an army of reinforcements; the two combined forces and launched an attack in which they defeated Alptakīn and his Qaramatian allies at Ramlah in 977/367. Through this victory the Fāṭimids gained a presence in southern Syria, though they still had to contend with the ambitions of the Byzantines for control of the rest of the province, a situation not resolved until 997/387, when treaty negotiations commenced between the two over their Syrian territories.

In addition to his skill as a general Jawhar brought to Egypt a high level of administrative ability, demonstrated in the four years he ruled the country before the arrival of the Caliph. He restored the workings of the government and calmed an internal situation disturbed during the declining years of the Ikhshīdid dynasty. After his Syrian campaigns Jawhar retired from active military service, though he continued to serve the Caliph al-ᶜAzīz until his death. His son Ḥusayn succeeded him as a military commander at the court of al-Ḥākim.

JAYSH (r. 896/282-83). Ṭūlūnid ruler of Egypt, Jaysh was quickly displaced by his brother Hārūn after a reign of only nine months. Jaysh seemed unable to command the support of the troops of his father, Khumārawayh, many of whose generals and administrators returned to Baghdad.

JEWS IN EGYPT. A community of Jews was first settled in Alexandria in Ptolemaic times, and by the early years of the Christian period were well established there. However, relations between the Jews in Alexandria and the Hellenic-Roman and, later, the Christian community of that city were not good. Both groups engaged in mutual denunciations, violent clashes with high casualties occurred and few links were established between Alexandria's disunited populace. The dislocation of the Jews following the fall of Jerusalem in AD 70 affected the attitudes of the Jews in Egypt toward Rome, a hostility that developed into sporadic open rebellion. The Jews of Alexandria were subjected to a persecution by the Patriarch Cyril in AD 413-14, when many of their synagogues were destroyed, and under Justinian (r. AD 527-64) and Heraclius in AD 628-29.

Syrian Jews were in the armies of the Muslim general ᶜAmr b. al-ᶜĀṣ during his conquest of Egypt in 639-41/18-20. They were settled in al-Fusṭāṭ, the new capital of Egypt founded by ᶜAmr, and presumably integrated with their co-religionists in Egypt. During the Islamic period, there were a number of important Jewish viziers (generally converts to Islam), scholars, and physicians at the courts of the governors and rulers of Egypt. As "people of the book" (a term given in the Qur'ān to those religions possessing a holy scripture) Jews and Christians were given the protection of Islam. Both groups were subject to a special communal tax, but in exchange their communities functioned autonomously. Relations with the ruler were regulated by the head of the community, which among Egyptian Jews was the Naqib, appointed by the ruler of the country.

The Geniza documents have provided scholars with a fairly comprehensive source on the activities of the Jews in Egypt down to the Ottoman period. The Jewish community, largely concentrated in Egypt's cities, had extensive trade interests in the Mediterranean and active links with their co-religionists throughout the Arab world. They maintained the use of Hebrew, written in Arabic characters, and developed a Judeo-Arabic dialect and literary form. Egypt became a refuge for many Jews from Spain, who had flourished in that country under Islamic rule down to the twelfth/sixth century. Of these later Jewish immigrants to Egypt, mention must be made of Moses Maimonides (Ibn Maymūn, see entry) who was not only a physician and author of distinction, but whose family assumed the leadership of the Jewish community for two centuries following his death in 1204/600.

Both Jews and Christians in Egypt were subjected to occasional persecutions, which took the form of their being proscribed from holding certain state offices. These prohibitions were usually overcome by some form of bribe, which in this case amounted to a tax on their assumption of office. More serious persecutions, such as the imposition of sumptuary regulations of Christians and Jews, were found on occasion. In the Fāṭimid period, these were usually associated with a reaction to policies of tolerance. When compared to the treatment of the Jews in Europe, however, the Islamic world and Egypt in particular were free of the violent and bloody persecutions found there.

In the nineteenth and twentieth centuries, Jewish Egyptians participated in all aspects of national life, though they were generally not well represented among the political elite. However, individuals like James Sanua (see entry) made an important contribution to the nationalist movement, and to the development of the modern Arabic theater and satire. Joseph Rosenthal was instrumental in the establishment of Egypt's first socialist party. European Jewish financial interests had a heavy stake in Egypt. Many of the loans raised by the Khedive Ismail were funded through Oppenheim and Bischoffsheim & Goldsmidt banks. After the British occupation of Egypt in 1882, European Jewish companies and individuals made substantial investments in Egypt. There was at this time an immigration of European Jews to Egypt, largely individuals escaping persecution in their own countries, but also those involved in the nascent Zionist movement.

It was the development of Zionism as a force in the region which was to change absolutely the position of Egypt's Jews. A Zionist plan in the first decade of the twentieth century to establish a Jewish state in Sinai was rejected by the British, but the British government's subsequent guarantee of a Jewish homeland in Palestine under the Balfour Declaration was greeted with hostility by almost all Arabs, including the Egyptians. The injustice of giving Palestinian Arab land to settlers who were at that time largely European in origin provoked a reaction in Egypt that was to build in intensity throughout the 1920s, 30s, and 40s. With the crises attending the establishment of Israel in Palestine in 1948, and the subsequent war, anti-Zionism reached a peak, both officially and popularly. Though many of Egypt's Jews had a longstanding relation with the country, resentment mounted against those Jews who had lived in Egypt without acquiring Egyptian nationality. Questions about their loyalty were raised, and, with the agitation by Zionists outside Egypt urging Jews to leave the country, many decided to emigrate.

The Lavon incident in 1954, in which a group of foreign Jews in Egypt (working with Israeli intelligence) were arrested and convicted on spying charges, did not help attitudes toward the indigenous Jewish community in Egypt, but the real spur to Jewish migration from Egypt to Israel came after the 1956 Suez War. In consequence of Israel's involvement, foreign Jewish business interests, along with those of the British and French, were nationalized. Only a small Jewish community remains in Egypt today.

AL-JIHAD. A post-1970 radical Islamic political grouping, Al-Jihad has been accused of fomenting communal strife in Egypt and been implicated in several bombings of churches. Al-Jihad, a militant breakaway faction of the Takfir wa'l-Hijra group (itself implicated in the assassination of a former Minister of Waqfs), first came to official attention in August 1977, following the seizure of an arms cache of the group by the police. Its known leader, Ali Mustafa al-Maghrabi, was killed in a shootout with the police in January 1978. The group (along with other radical offshoots) has continued to operate clandestinely and has been the target of a number of antiterrorist campaigns by the government.

JOINT NOTE(S). The first joint note delivered to Egypt by France and Britain was drafted on the initiative of the new French Premier, Gambetta, and presented to the Egyptian legislature in

January 1882. The note was meant to caution the Assembly that Britain and France would oppose any action that would impair the Khedive Tawfiq's position or challenge foreign interests in Egypt. Coming at a time when nationalist sentiment in Egypt was high, the note created a furious reaction among all segments of the nationalist movement. Following delivery of the note Sami al-Barudi formed a government that included Colonel Arabi; both men had a strong commitment to the nationalist cause and no intention of yielding to foreign pressure.

The spring of 1882 saw a number of actions by Arabi, in particular signaling the Egyptian government's determination to push an independent line against the European interests in the country. An open challenge was presented to Tawfiq by Arabi, and, faced with a reversal in their positions, the Europeans delivered a second joint note in May, demanding the dismissal of the Sami government and the exile of Arabi and his supporters. The cabinet was reformed under the nominal government of Raghib Pasha; Arabi and his supporters then faced a confrontation with the Europeans over the fortification of Alexandria.

JOINT PRESIDENTIAL COUNCIL. Established on the basis of an accord between President Nasser and President Abdal Salim Arif of Iraq in May 1964, the Joint Presidential Council was meant to explore the basis for a future constitutional union of the two countries, set for 1966. Under the accord Egypt and Iraq were also to form a joint military command. The accord brought to an end five years of diplomatic and verbal hostilities between the two countries. The proposed union was not implemented, though Iraq during this time adopted a constitution drawing heavily on the constitution of the UAR, with relations between Iraq and Egypt continuing generally cordial through the 1967 Arab-Israeli War. Iraq also announced its recognition of Kuwait (an Arab League member with whom it had a longstanding territorial dispute). However, the death of General Arif in March 1966 removed from the Iraqi government the strongest backer of the union.

JUMEL (L. A.) see COTTON

JUNE WAR see ARAB-ISRAELI WAR (1967)

-K-

KĀFŪR (ABU'L-MISK KĀFŪR) (r. 966-68/355-57). Ikhshīdid ruler of Egypt, Kāfūr was originally a slave of the founder of the Ikhshīdid dynasty, Muḥammad b. Ṭughj. As commander, Kafur conducted highly successful campaigns in the Hijaz and Syria for the Ikhshīd. After the Ikhshīd's death Kāfūr became the de facto ruler of Egypt during the reigns of Muḥammad b. Ṭughj's two sons, for whom he was appointed tutor (ustādh). Ūnūjūr (946-61/334-49) and ᶜAlī (961-66/349-55) were apparently little involved in the administration of the country.

Shortly after the Ikhshīd's death in 946/334 Kāfūr forcefully put down a local rebellion, but his dealings with the Nubians who attacked the oases and Aswan in 949/337 and 955/344 were less conclusive. Civil disturbances against the regime reemerged in 954/343, when Kāfūr was faced with an attempted coup against him in which Ūnūjūr appears to have been implicated; order was restored only to be shattered one year later by a major earthquake and plague.

During Kāfūr's reign the Ikhshīdid forces held southern Syria as a buffer against the advance of the stronger Ḥamdānid forces to the north, with whom a treaty was concluded in 947/335. To help stabilize the south, Kāfūr stationed garrisons in the Nubian border areas. These essentially defensive and protective actions came at a time when Egypt was being threatened on a third, western, front by the Fāṭimids. Kāfūr secured power in his own name on the death of ᶜAlī in 966/355; his own death two years later was a signal to the Fāṭimids to commence their invasion of the country.

Kāfūr's colorful reputation in Islamic history is due in part to his association with the poet al-Mutanabbī, who began by praising Kāfūr's achievements and ended by bitterly and satirically attacking the ambitions of the black slave who came to rule Egypt. Kāfūr's lavish court stood in poor contrast to the parlous condition of the rest of Egypt, rent by plague, famine, and other natural catastrophes.

KAISSUNI, ABDAL MONAYM (1916-). Egyptian economist who has served in the governments of Presidents Nasser and Sadat, Kaissuni joined the cabinet as Minister of Finance in 1954, a post he held until 1966. Dr. Kaissuni also held a number of positions in planning, the Economic Agency, and the Treasury. He was a member of the Egyptian delegation which sought finance for the High Dam project in 1955-56. Kaissuni served on the ASU Executive 1962-64, and in 1964-66 was Deputy Prime Minister for Economic Affairs and Finance.

In addition to his formal appointments in ministerial capacities Kaissuni was an important economic adviser to both Presidents. After the 1973 war he assisted the government drive to arrange a capital transfer from the OAPEC states to Egypt to help in the country's postwar recovery. President Sadat created a strong ministerial portfolio for Kaissuni in November 1976, when he was appointed Deputy Prime Minister for Financial and Economic Affairs. As one of President Sadat's chief economic strategists Kaissuni was charged with the redirection of Egypt's economy toward the free-market strategy envisaged by the Open Door Policy. He was given the Planning portfolio in 1977, and placed in charge of a cabinet-level group reexamining Egypt's internal economy.

Kaissuni was involved in the readjustment of Egypt's subsidy program in response to IMF demands prior to the outbreak of the January 1977 rioting, after which he was charged with finding a revenue base for these subsidies. He resigned from his posts in May 1978 following a cabinet reshuffle, and rejoined the Arab International Bank, where he had previously served as chairman from 1972 to 1976.

KAMCHICHE AFFAIR. The murder in May 1966 of an official of the Arab Socialist Union (the government's official political party) in the village of Kamchiche was blamed on a large landowning family there who were angered at the investigation the official was conducting into abuses of the Agrarian Reform Law. The murder was cited by Ali Sabri and the ASU as evidence of the continuation of feudal and reactionary relationships in rural areas; to investigate this a Committee for the Liquidation of Feudalism was set up under the chairmanship of General Amer. The subsequent campaign against the big landlords, spearheaded by the ASU, may have been intended to counter at least partially the unpopularity of the government's campaign against the Ikhwan al-Muslimun, who had reemerged as a political power in the urban and rural areas in the mid-1960s.

AL-KĀMIL (AL-KĀMIL I NĀṢIR AD-DĪN) (r. 1218-38/615-35). Ayyūbid ruler of Egypt, al-Kāmil was the son, viceroy, and successor of al-ᶜĀdil and the nephew of Ṣalāḥ ad-Dīn. A vigorous and successful ruler, al-Kāmil defeated a Crusader invasion of Egypt in 1221/618. He initially offered generous terms to the Crusader commander, Pelagius, but these were refused, and after their defeat and retreat back to Damietta the Crusaders were forced to accept merely a free withdrawal from that city and an eight-year peace treaty.

The treaty was to be suspended if a new Crusade was launched by a Christian king, and the arrival of Frederick II of Sicily in the Middle East met these terms. However, contacts between al-Kāmil and Frederick antedated the latter's Crusade, and the understanding between these sovereigns was sufficiently good for al-Kāmil to sign a treaty with Frederick in 1229/626 by which Nazareth, Bethlehem, and Jerusalem (with a land corridor linking that city to Acre) were ceded to Frederick for a ten-year period. Al-Kāmil's son aṣ-Ṣāliḥ campaigned on his behalf in Syria and Iraq in the 1230s/630s.

Al-Kāmil continued his father's sound domestic policies, combining religious tolerance with a concern for social welfare and education. Al-Kāmil had, however, great difficulties in Syria, where his leadership was contested by other members of his family. These difficulties continued throughout his reign and to a certain extent hampered his military scope of action.

KAMIL, MUSTAFA (1874-1908). A leader of the modern Egyptian nationalist movement, Mustafa Kamil was, until his death and even thereafter, the most charismatic nationalist figure until the emergence of Zaghlul in the post-World War I period. Kamil first attracted notice for leading the demonstrations against the pro-British newspaper Al-Muqattam in 1893, the same year he founded a nationalist magazine for students. He was himself a student of law in France, and on his return to Egypt in 1895 he was introduced to the young Khedive, Abbas, and the circle of nationalists around his court. Abbas dispatched Kamil back to France for a year to gain greater European support for the nationalists; Kamil came under the patronage in Paris of the French parliamentarian François Deloncle and journalist Juliette Adams. The latter proved more supportive, but neither was able to secure for Kamil the widespread support for Egyptian nationalism in France that he and the Khedive were hoping for. He returned to Egypt in January 1896 and continued his nationalist campaign in Egypt. Kamil's initially good relations with the Khedive and Shaykh Ali Yusuf, editor of the pro-Palace newspaper Al-Muayyad, appeared to turn sour toward the end of the century; it is alleged that Kamil's increasing popularity within Egypt was at fault.

Kamil's popularity grew from his skills as an orator and publicist; when he found his access to Shaykh Ali's newspaper was being restricted, he founded his own nationalist journal, Al-Liwa (funded by his colleague Farid), which soon gained a wide circulation and eventually a French and English edition. Kamil's pan-Islamic interests took on a more distinctly pro-Turkish character after his break in relations with the Khedive in 1904. But his main political ambition was and remained the securing of Egypt's full independence from all forms of British control. It may be argued that his support for the Ottoman Sultan grew less out of a desire to revive Ottoman sovereignty in Egypt than to use the Ottomans as a lever against the British.

The Dinshaway Incident in 1906 gave an enormous boost to both the nationalist movement and to Kamil's own position and led to a brief but unsustained attempt at rapprochement between Kamil and the Khedive. Kamil traveled to London that summer and through the efforts of Wilfred Blunt met with the new British Prime Minister, Campbell Bannerman; from him Kamil extracted a promise of greater autonomy for the Egyptian government and an increase in political rights and participation.

In the summer of 1907 Kamil announced the formation of the Nationalist Party, in association with his colleague Muhammad Farid, with whom he had worked since the 1890s. The first congress of the party, held in November 1907, elected Kamil to lead the group. His premature death a few months later, in February 1908, was to deprive the party of its most unifying leader. Such was the force of Kamil's appeal within Egypt that the Khedive himself did not choose to affiliate with the pro-Palace Constitutional Reform Party until after the death of Kamil.

KANUZ (BANŪ KANZ). Nubian-speaking tribe that is a dominant power in the region, the Kanuz acted as protectors of claimants to the Fāṭimid Caliphate during the early Ayyūbid period, as well as of other refugees from the regular power struggles in Egypt. They were attacked by the forces of Ṣalāḥ ad-Dīn under the command of Tūrān Shāh in 1172-73/568 for sheltering Fāṭimid refugees and continued to be restive throughout the Ayyūbid period.

With the rise of the Mamluks, and especially under the reign of Baybars I (1260-77/658-76) and Qalā'ūn (1280-90/678-89), there was increasing Arab Bedouin immigration into the area and a more rapid spread of Islam among the Kanuz; by the sixteenth/tenth century the region had been Islamicized and there were strong links through marriage among the Kanuz, other Nubians, and the Arabs. The Kanuz maintained their distinct tribal identity down to modern times, though they were suppressed politically during the Nubian campaigns of Ibrāhīm Pasha in 1820-21. There were migrations of the Kanuz in 1912, the early 1930s, and the 1960s, as successive raisings of the Aswan

Dam flooded their traditional homelands. Today they are intermixed with other tribal Nubian groups in resettlement areas.

KĀRIMĪ. Guild of merchants established in Egypt and Aden during the Fāṭimid period, with their Egyptian headquarters in Cairo and Qūṣ, the Kārimī grew in importance during Ayyūbid and Mamluk times thanks to their control of Red Sea and Indian Ocean trade. The Kārimī commercial network included banking facilities, which permitted their commerce to be carried on a larger scale than that of their competitors, and they came to control the valuable trade in pepper and spices. The Kārimī acted both as bankers and government financiers. By Burjī Mamluk times, however, and especially in the fifteenth/ninth century, the Kārimī were eclipsed by gradual encroachment of the Mamluk Sultans on the spice and pepper trade, beginning with Barsbāy's imposition of a pepper monopoly in 1429/830. By the mid-fifteenth/ninth century, the Kārimī had been ruined by the taxation, tariff, and monopolies policies of the Mamluk Sultans.

KĀSHIF. Provincial administrators in the provinces of Egypt during Ottoman times, the Kāshifs were equivalent to local governors, but eclipsed in time by the Mamluk beys. Their duties and their actual involvement in the tax-collection process varied but were more usually done through a locally appointed lower-level official acting on the Kāshif's behalf. The Kāshifs were also charged with overseeing the maintenance of irrigation works in rural areas, although by the eighteenth century village shaykhs had largely taken over this role.

KATHKUDA ("Commander"). Ottoman title used by Ottoman military chiefs in Egypt, and also by some of the higher-ranking Mamluks in the beylicate, with supervisory administrative roles.

KHĀ'IR BAY (KHAYRĪ BEG) (d. 1522/928). First Ottoman governor of Egypt, Khā'ir Bay was originally Burjī Mamluk governor of Aleppo. He defected to the Ottoman side when their army under Selīm was attacking the Mamluk positions in Syria, taking with him a group of Mamluks who had decided to quit the defense mounted by the Burjī Mamluk Sultan. Following the death of the Sultan Qānṣūḥ al-Ghawrī at the battle of Marj Dābiq (1516/921), the Mamluk Sultanate in Egypt passed into the reluctant hands of Tūmān Bay. Despite the affiliation of Khā'ir Bay and his faction Selīm seemed to wish to avoid a campaign in Egypt and offered to allow Tūmān Bay to remain ruler of Egypt if he acknowledged Selīm as Sultan. The Mamluks around the Egyptian Sultan resisted this idea, and Selīm, his army, and Khā'ir Bay and his supporters entered Cairo in January 1517/922. Tūmān Bay and his army retreated to the north, where they led a spirited defense of the country that had some popular support. Though Selīm emerged victorious, he was apparently prepared to be generous to the vanquished; it was Khā'ir Bay who pressed for the execution of Tūmān Bay. Khā'ir Bay was then named by Selīm governor of Egypt, ensuring for the Mamluks a continued role in the country's government. His appointment pacified the Mamluks, who were fearful for their future after the Ottoman conquest. These fears reappeared upon the death of Khā'ir Bay, and gained expression as a series of disturbances which were not calmed until the arrival of the Ottoman governor Aḥmad Pasha. He subsequently led his own revolt against the Sultan.

KHALĪL (AL-ASHRAF ṢALĀḤ AD-DĪN KHALĪL) (r. 1290-94/689-93). Baḥrī Mamluk Sultan, Khalīl was associated with his father, Qalā'ūn, in the last two years of Qalā'ūn's reign following the death of his brother and predecessor, Mūsā, whom he was later suspected of poisoning. Qalā'ūn died while preparing to meet the Crusaders in battle at Acre, a campaign Khalīl successfully prosecuted, taking Acre and expelling the Crusaders from the Levantine coast in 1291/690. Thereafter he completed his father's plans for the fortification of the Syrian border towns.

Khalīl had an uneasy relationship with his court, having removed most of the officials associated with his father. He was murdered after intervening in a dispute between the members of his court. At the time of his death he was rebuilding the Egyptian fleet in preparation for an attack on Cyprus.

KHALIL, MUSTAFA (1920-). Prime Minister of Egypt from October 1978 to May 1980 and Foreign Minister from February 1979 until May 1980, Khalil was a leading negotiator for the Egyptian side at Camp David and throughout the peace-treaty discussions. Trained as a civil engineer, Khalil first came to political prominence as one of the few civilian members of the Supreme Executive of the Arab Socialist Union in 1962-64, having served from 1956 as Minister of Communications and Transport and on the board of the Permanent Council for National Production from 1955.

Khalil served as Deputy Prime Minister for Broadcasting and Television in 1964-65 and as Deputy Prime Minister for Industry, Mineral Resources, and Electrification in 1965-66. Khalil's technological background provided a basis for his rapid advancement under a regime that constantly stressed the role of the technocrat in national development, though policy disputes led him to resign from the cabinet in September 1966. He became head of the Broadcasting Corporation in 1970 and, from 1970 to 1976, was Secretary-General of the Arab Socialist Union. Since November 1977 Khalil has been a member of Egypt's National Security Council. Following the cabinet reshuffle of May 1980 he assumed the post of deputy chairman for Foreign Affairs in the National Democratic Party.

KHARTOUM CONFERENCE. Held in Khartoum, Sudan, in August-September 1967, the conference was the first major meeting of Arab leaders after the 1967 Arab-Israeli War (though it was boycotted by Syria, Algeria, and Tunisia). The Khartoum Conference marked the beginning of a rapprochement between King Faysal of Saudi Arabia and President Nasser and helped bring to an end Egypt's involvement in the Yemen. The conference outlined financial arrangements to be funded by the oil-producing states that would compensate Egypt and the other front-line states for losses caused by the war. In Egypt's case the economic consequences of the war had included the loss of her revenues from the Suez Canal, for which she was compensated with a $280 million annual subvention. The conference also lifted the Arab oil embargo and pledged a continuation of the struggle against Israel by nonmilitary means, despite the objections of some hard-line states.

KHEDIVAL AGRICULTURAL SOCIETY see AGRICULTURAL SOCIETY

KHAYRĪ BEG see KHĀ'IR BEY

KHEDIVE. Perso-Turkish title meaning "Lord," the title was granted to the rulers of the Muhammad Ali dynasty in Egypt in 1867 by the Ottoman Sultan Abdal Aziz, in exchange for a large contribution to the Ottoman treasury from the newly entitled Khedive, Ismail. Previously rulers of the dynasty were entitled Pasha and Viceroys of the Sultan, although Muhammad Ali and his sons had long unofficially used the Khedival title.

At the time the British imposed a Protectorate on Egypt in 1914 they changed the title from "Khedive" to "Sultan" to signify Egypt's break with the Ottoman Porte, and "Sultan" was in turn replaced by "King" following the Unilateral Declaration of Independence in 1922.

KHUMĀRAWAYH (r. 884-96/270-82). Second Ṭūlūnid ruler of Egypt, Khumārawayh was the younger son of Ibn Ṭūlūn, gaining his father's favor after his elder brother ^{c}Abbās had led a short-lived rebellion in Ibn Ṭūlūn's reign. Soon after he came to power Khumārawayh resisted an attempt by the Caliph in Baghdad to re-exert control of Egypt. He met a force of ^{c}Abbāsid troops in Syria in 884/270; after three years of campaigns a compromise was struck, with Khumārawayh given control of Damascus and Palestine.

Khumārawayh's court has been described in fantastic terms by Islamic historians--a quicksilver pool with inflated cushions to cure his insomnia, tame lions to guard his sleep, trees fashioned of precious metals, and stones to adorn his garden. Upon the marriage of his daughter to the ^{c}Abbāsid Caliph al-Mu^{c}taḍid, he reputedly bestowed on her a dowry of a million dirhams, which may have partially influenced al-Mu^{c}taḍid's decision to grant Khumārawayh, in 892/279, a thirty-year iqṭā^{c} in Egypt.

Outside of the court Egypt's administration was deteriorating during Khumārawayh's reign, and there were outbursts of insubordination among the troops, such as the uprising of the Sūdān in 887/273. Khumārawayh inherited enough of his father's force of character to maintain ultimate control of Egypt and most of the Ṭūlūnid territories, but he was eventually murdered by his own slaves, who put his fourteen-year-old son Jaysh in power.

KHURSHID PASHA (r. c. 1804-05). Last Ottoman governor of Egypt, Khurshid was called from his post as governor of Alexandria after his predecessor, Khusrau Pasha, had been driven from Cairo by Muḥammad ᶜAlī and the new Ottoman governor, ᶜAlī Pasha Jazarli, murdered by the Mamluks. He displaced al-Bardīsī and Ibrāhīm Bey, who had seized power, but Khurshid proved no more successful than his predecessors at bringing the Mamluks and beys under control and had to rely on the support of Muḥammad ᶜAlī to maintain himself in office. But he lacked the military strength to control Muḥammad ᶜAlī, who headed a strong, loyal Albanian regiment. When Khurshid arrived in Cairo, the city had already been cleared of many Mamluks, whom Muḥammad ᶜAlī was busy subjugating in Upper Egypt. Yet they remained a dangerous and destabilizing force. Khurshid's poor treatment of the Cairenes and his inability to suppress the civil chaos led the people to send a delegation of ᶜulamā' to Muḥammad ᶜAlī asking him to depose Khurshid and assume the governorship. Khurshid was beseiged in the Citadel by Muḥammad ᶜAlī and his troops and was finally forced to surrender. He left Egypt in the summer of 1805.

KHŪSHQADAM (AẒ-ẒĀHIR SAYF AD-DĪN KHŪSHQADAM) (r. 1461-67/865-72). Burjī Mamluk ruler of Egypt, Khūshqadam displaced the Sultan Ināl's son Aḥmad from power. Supported by the Ẓāhiriyya Mamluk faction formed by the Sultan Barqūq, Khūshqadam was the first ruler of Greek origins in Egypt since Ptolemaic times. During his reign there was sporadic fighting in the provinces that bordered Mamluk and Ottoman territory, a reflection of the expansive and dynamic Ottoman presence in regions the Mamluks had always claimed as their own.

Shortly after his accession Khūshqadam turned against Jāni Bay (Beg), who had been instrumental in his climb to power, and also successfully countered the threat posed by Janīm, who from his base in Syria was plotting to gain the Sultanate. Throughout his reign Khūshqadam profited from the factional fighting of the Mamluks, which kept his enemies divided and which he did everything to encourage. In line with many other Burjī Mamluk Sultans, Khūshqadam tried to establish trade monopolies, with varying success; his harsh taxes contributed to a climate of domestic unrest not only in the cities but also among Egypt's Bedouin communities. Discriminatory policies against Christians and Jews were instituted, and many non-Muslims were dismissed from their administrative posts.

KHUSRAU PASHA (r. c. 1802-03). Ottoman governor of Egypt, Khusrau was appointed by the head of the Ottoman forces, Yūsuf Pasha, before his withdrawal from Egypt following the French defeat. Khusrau was soon overtaken by the internecine struggle for power by the beys. Muḥammad Bey al-Alfī defeated Khusrau's troops in 1802, before departing for England to seek British support for the Mamluks. Khusrau was also unable to suppress the revolt of ᶜUthmān and Ibrāhīm Bey and was deserted by his own commander, Ṭāhir Pasha, after a pay dispute. Although Khusrau managed to get Ṭāhir assassinated after he had attempted a brief coup, Ṭāhir had sent a message to Istanbul requesting the appointment of a more effective governor. Ṭāhir was succeeded as head of the Albanian regiment by Muḥammad ᶜAlī, who supported the Mamluk ᶜUthmān al-Bardīsī against Khusrau. Muḥammad ᶜAlī pursued and captured Khusrau in the Delta, but the former governor was later released and returned to Istanbul.

KILLEARN, LORD (SIR MILES LAMPSON) (1880-1964). British High Commissioner (1933-36) and ambassador (1936-46) in Egypt, Lord Killearn served as a diplomat and administrator in the Far East before his appointment to Egypt in 1933. When the office of

High Commissioner was abolished after the 1936 Anglo-Egyptian Treaty, Lampson's title changed to that of ambassador.

During his tenure in office Lampson exercised an influence over political life in Egypt that came close to matching that of his predecessor Cromer, in the pre-Independence period. He seemed at times to realize only imperfectly that the Egyptian political scene had changed profoundly since 1922, with divisions and factions within the major political party, the Wafd, and the emergence of such mass groupings as the Ikhwan al-Muslimun and Misr al-Fatat. While the Wafd government of 1936-37 was pressing Lampson and the British government for concessions on the Suez Canal Company agreements, it was being attacked by younger, more radical groupings (including on occasion its own youth wing) for not being nationalistic enough. The other political parties were becoming progressively less representative of anything other than the interests of their immediate leadership or backers, and the Palace was able to play a small but significant role through its representatives in some of these parties.

Lampson's difficulties in coming to terms with the changing nationalist movement contributed to the increasingly poor relationship he had with the young King, Faruq. He sought to influence Faruq's domestic political policies, particularly after the outbreak of the Second World War. Lampson was concerned about the number of Italians in Faruq's inner circle and made several attempts to have them removed. Following a period of intense pressure on Faruq to allow the Wafd to form a government (on the grounds that the Wafd would support more enthusiastically, and gain greater popular support for, the British war effort), Lampson decided in February 1942 to apply force majeure. He had Abdin Palace surrounded with tanks and presented Faruq with an ultimatum either to abdicate or to call in the Wafd. Faruq capitulated, but the Palace Incident earned Lampson and the British and to some extent, the Wafd itself, the enmity of many ardent Egyptian nationalists. Lampson's actions proved beneficial to Britain however, as the Wafd kept

Egypt under control in the difficult days in 1942 when a German invasion of Alexandria seemed imminent. In his last years in office he saw the formation of the Arab League (which had British support) and the reemergence of Egyptian official demands for new negotiations on the Sudan.

AL-KINDĪ (ABŪ ᶜUMAR MUḤAMMAD b. YŪSUF) (897-961/283-350). Historian of Egypt in pre-Fāṭimid times, al-Kindī compiled a biographical listing of Egypt's Umayyad and ᶜAbbāsid governors and judges, covering the history of Egypt until the death of Muḥammad b. Ṭughj, founder of the Ikhshīdid dynasty, in 946/335. His work also contained a valuable record of the legal decisions taken during this time, enabling the study of the evolution of the Islamic legal system in practice. After his death an unknown scholar updated the listing of governors and judges to the beginning of the Fāṭimid era, in 969/358.

KIRĀ see IQṬĀᶜ

KITBUGHĀ (AL-ᶜĀDIL ZAYN AD-DĪN KITBUGHĀ) (r. 1295-97/694-96). Baḥrī Mamluk ruler of Egypt, Kitbughā, of Mongol origin, was originally a Mamluk of the Sultan Khalīl. He emerged victorious in the struggle within the Regency Council of an-Nāṣir Muḥammad, where he originally shared power with ᶜĀlim ad-Dīn Sanjar ash-Shudjai; his pardon of the murderers of Khalīl earned him the support of the powerful court elements who had been involved. Kitbughā's two-year reign witnessed a devastating outbreak of plague and famine, with consequent social dislocations. During his absence from Cairo power was seized by Lājīn.

KITCHENER, HORATIO HUBERT, EARL (1850-1916). High Commissioner in Egypt from 1911 to 1914, Kitchener had previously served as Sirdar (Governor-General and Commander-in-Chief of the army) in the Sudan.

Kitchener tried to keep the situation in Egypt calm, continuing the moderate reforms of his predecessor, Gorst, and worked for legislative improvement of the welfare of the fellahin, the smallholder or sometimes landless laborer who made up the bulk of the rural workforce. During Kitchener's time in office, in

1912, the Five-Feddan Law was passed to protect the rights of smallholders, and a model-village program was started. A new ministry, Agriculture, was created to encourage development. An Organic Law was promulgated in 1913, creating a single legislative assembly to replace the dual legislature established under the 1883 Organic Law. But Kitchener was hampered by his bad relations with the Khedive Abbas, which stemmed from an incident in 1894, early in Abbas' reign, when the two men had exchanged words during a review of the Egyptian and British troops; Abbas had been forced to apologize, a fact he had neither forgotten nor forgiven. A Ministry of Awqaf (religious endowments) was formed to remove from the Khedive some of the revenues he controlled. The Khedive's right to bestow honorific titles was also curtailed.

Kitchener was called back to England at the outbreak of the First World War; he was, at that time, advocating the formal annexation of Egypt and deposition of Abbas by the British but was overruled in London, where the Foreign Office decided to limit itself to the establishment of a Protectorate and the replacement of Abbas with the more amenable Husayn Kamil.

KLÉBER, GENERAL J. B. (d. 1800). Appointed governor of Egypt in 1799 by Napoleon Bonaparte, Kléber spent most of the year prior to his assassination in suppressing the many revolts against French rule. At the same time he negotiated with Sir Sidney Smith for the withdrawal of French troops from the country. The convention that the two men concluded was subsequently rejected by the British, who decided to maintain their formal intervention on behalf of the Ottomans. Kléber met this challenge and defeated an Ottoman army advancing on Cairo in March 1800. He restored order in much of Cairo, and benefited from the decision of Murād Bey to accept the governorship of Upper Egypt on behalf of the French. But opposition to French control continued and in June 1800 Kléber was assassinated by a member of the Janissary corps. He was succeeded by Baron Menou.

KÜÇÜK MEHMED (d. 1694/1105). A leader of the Janissary corps at the time of its alliance with the Faqāriyya faction of the beylicate in Ottoman Egypt, Küçük had difficulty in his initial attempts to establish his leadership within the contentious Janissary command. He first held power in 1674-80/1085-91, when he secured the removal of some of his senior officers, but this proved unpopular and he was forced to leave Egypt.

His next period of ascendancy began in 1687/1099, when he was removed from the Janissary officer corps after regaining his commission a short time before; he joined a regiment commanded by Ḥasan Agha Balfiyya hoping to exploit the latter's links with the Faqāriyya under Ibrāhīm Bey to restore himself to power within the Janissary corps.

The Faqāriyya were at this time seeking an alliance with the Janissaries, the most powerful of the Ottoman regiments, in their own bid to gain supremacy in the beylicate, but the Janissary leadership favored their rivals, the Qāsimiyya. Thus both Küçük Mehmed and Ibrāhīm Bey had an interest in cooperating; with their backing Küçük pulled off a coup of the Janissary leadership in 1692/1104, and sent many of his former commanders into exile.

Küçük's period of control prior to his death had a number of interesting populist characteristics, which were not that surprising in view of the often quite humble background of the Janissary recruits and the links they formed on occasion with the local population. Küçük's removal of some of the tax-collecting privileges of the regiment and his efforts to stabilize food supplies and prices during the 1694/1105 famine show a concern for the public welfare that was rare in Ottoman Egypt. He eventually attracted the hostility of Muṣṭafā al-Qāzdughlī and the Janissary corps; whether because of his popularity or power is unclear. Despite their alliance with the Faqāriyya, who strongly supported Küçük, al-Qāzdughlī arranged for his assassination in 1694/1105.

KŪJŪK (AL-ASHRAF ᶜALĀ AD-DĪN KŪJŪK) (r. 1341-42/742-43).

Baḥrī Mamluk Sultan, son and second successor of an-Nāṣir Muḥammad, Kūjūk, placed in power by the Mamluk Qūsūn, was six years old at the time of his accession. His reign of a few months was dominated by Qūsūn, whose gradual fall from grace among the other Mamluks at court opened the way for Kūjūk's brother Aḥmad. Qūsūn had exiled Aḥmad to Kerak at the beginning of Kūjūk's reign, and the opponents of Qūsūn used his exile to build support for Aḥmad at court. Kūjūk was deposed and imprisoned and was later strangled under orders of the Sultan Sha^{c}bān I, another of an-Nāṣir Muḥammad's undistinguished sons and heirs.

KURA (SINGULAR, KARIYYA). Administrative units of Umayyad Egypt, the kura were modeled on the Byzantine system of administration, the pagarchies, and largely run by cooperative Egyptian personnel. The head of each kariyya reported directly to the governor of Egypt, with groups of kuras under a single name occasionally being formed, though they remained discrete for actual administration. The geographical boundaries of the kuras (which numbered between fifty and seventy), were flexible.

KUSHAF. Powerful clan in Nubia, the Kushaf claim descent from the Mamluk, Ottoman, and Bosnian governors of Nubia and still possess a great deal of social power. A major influx of Bosnians (known locally as Ghuzz) came to Nubia at the time of the Ottoman conquest of Egypt (1517/922), when the Gharbiyya tribe approached the Ottoman Sultan for assistance against its local enemies and was sent a detachment of Bosnians under Hasan Koosy. The regiment settled in the area and after a time intermarried with local groups. Like many of the near-autonomous and powerful tribes and clans in Upper Egypt their position was greatly reduced by Muhammad Ali.

KUTAYFĀT (d. 1131/526). Grandson of the vizier Badr al-Jamālī, Kutayfāt was the last of his line to hold power in Egypt. His father, al-Afḍal, had been assassinated on orders of the Fāṭimid Caliph al-Āmir. When that Caliph was himself assassinated in

1130/525, his cousin al-Ḥāfiz was declared regent for the unborn child of al-Āmir by two powerful courtiers, Hazāmard and Barghash. Almost immediately the two fell out and a military faction supporting Barghash installed Kutayfāt as vizier. With their support Kutayfāt deposed and imprisoned al-Ḥāfiz; he then declared the Fāṭimid dynasty ended and announced himself as representative of the hidden Imām of the Shīᶜa. One year later Kutayfāt was assassinated by Yānis, chamberlain to al-Ḥāfiz, who resumed power as regent and shortly thereafter took the title of Caliph.

-L-

LABOR. Egypt's trade unions began to form after World War I with the involvement of both Egyptian and foreign organizers. Remnants of the guild system that preceded the trade unions were limited to the more traditional crafts, though in some of the larger indigenous industries, especially tobacco, transport, and cotton, associations of workers long antedated formal organizations. Disputes in these industries led to the establishment of labor-conciliation procedures under a Labor Board as early as 1919, but the effectiveness of these measures may be gauged from the eighty-one strikes that took place in Egypt between 1919 and 1922; by 1922 there were some ninety-eight unions in operation.

The Socialist Party was from its beginnings closely linked with the trade unions in Egypt, but every political grouping that had any pretensions to being a mass party (particularly the Wafd) courted the labor movement. The Wafd benefited from the government's suppression of the socialist movement in Egypt in the mid-1920s and carefully placed its advisers wherever possible on the boards of the major unions and syndicates. Even the Ittihad Party, founded to support the political position of the Palace, sought support among the unions, probably in an attempt to weaken the Wafd's acknowledged appeal. However, the Wafd's General Union of Industrial Workers (established in 1924), as well as the numerous union leaders who gave their support to the Wafd, ensured that the labor movement in Egypt was largely identified, at least officially, with the Wafd. The unions joined the Wafd in boycotting the 1931 elections.

For all their organization, the labor unions did not have the political power to force the government to pass essential legislation to protect industrial workers. The Rida Commission Report (1929) and the less radical Butler Commission Report (1932) strongly recommended such legislation. A High Labor Council, without much power or influence, was formed by the government, following completion of the Butler Report. Egypt's first labor legislation was passed in 1933 but was too general to be effective. The year 1934 saw Egyptian workers involved in industrial and political action in protest over the country's deteriorating economic position and the absence of political liberties. These protests were widespread, and in concert with various groups they eventually forced the government to reinstate the 1923 Constitution and free political life.

Leadership of Egypt's trade-union movement in the vital pre-World War II period was actively contested, though largely dominated by Abbas Halim. After some negotiations with the Wafd, which organized its own High Labor Council in February 1935, Halim assumed the leadership of the new organization. Pressure from his own supporters forced him to quit the council. In 1937 he rejoined the General Union of Labor Syndicates which he helped found in 1930, and whose name he changed to the General Union of Workers' Syndicates in 1937.

The Wafd introduced the first Workmens' Compensation Legislation in 1936; the General Union and Abbas Halim pressed for this legislation to be expanded and made compulsory. After heavy union pressure, draft legislation was prepared in 1939 but not enacted.

The Wafd formed a wartime ministry in February 1942 and subsequently introduced the compulsory workmen's compensation that the General Union had been demanding as well as legal recognition of their negotiating rights. The trade unions' leadership, forced into quiescence by the war were in the meantime becoming radicalized; propaganda from the left and the Young Egypt parties gained a wide audience. Egyptian trade unions were represented in a World Trade Union Congress held in Paris in 1945, and they affiliated themselves with radical students in the National Committee of Workers and Students, which operated from 1945 to 1946. Through the National Committee the trade unions became more involved with demands for social reform outside the field of labor; their mass demonstrations drew public attention to their platform. In 1947 labor legislation was introduced to protect local workers, requiring foreign companies to give 90 percent of their jobs, and 80 percent of their wages, to Egyptian workers.

The failure of the governments of the day to meet the workers' demands kept the level of strikes high; in 1951 there were forty-nine violent strikes with economic and political motives. A newer and more politicized trade-union grouping, the General Federation of Trade Unions, was formed after the January 1952 burning of Cairo. (For the history of the labor-union movement since the Revolution of 1952, see GENERAL FEDERATION OF TRADE UNIONS.) Labor legislation introduced after the Revolution includes a Social Insurance Law (passed 1953) and a Social Security Law (passed 1959). Nongovernment trade unions were banned in 1959.

LĀJĪN (AL-MANṢŪR ḤUSĀM AD-DĪN LĀJĪN) (r. 1297-99/696-98). Baḥrī Mamluk Sultan, Lājīn was a Mamluk of the Sultan Qalā'ūn and was implicated in the murder of Qalā'ūn's successor, Khalīl. He was appointed governor of Syria by the Regency Council for Khalīl's successor, an-Nāṣir Muḥammad, in 1294/693; in the subsequent rise to power of, and coup by, the regent Kitbughā, Lājīn lent his support. He then changed sides or ambitions, at first remitting the unpopular taxes introduced by Kitbughā in Syria and finally deposing and murdering Kitbughā in 1297/696.

Lājīn was unable to keep the Mamluk factions sufficiently divided to preserve his own position, and his promotion of one of his favorites, Mankutimur, within the court alienated established

Mamluk interests there. He was eventually displaced when an-Nāṣir Muḥammad was returned to power a second time.

LAMPSON, SIR MILES see LORD KILLEARN

LAND RECLAMATION. The enormous pressure of population on Egypt's available agricultural land prompted the introduction of land-reclamation schemes in the post-Revolutionary period, in an effort to create more land for the production of food. The Liberation Province development (begun in 1953) and the New Valley Land Reclamation Project (begun in 1959 under the Egyptian General Desert Development Organization) as well as reclamation projects begun with the assistance of the Egyptian American Rural Improvement Service in the early 1950s, all aimed to increase the amount of Egypt's arable land.

In all these cases the ambitious nature of the early goals set, as well as instances of maladministration, produced results that fell far short of the objectives. The most serious problems arose with the Liberation Province scheme, which, in addition to land reclamation, was also designed as a social experiment. Its dimensions proved out of line with what Egyptian farmers were prepared to accept: dress codes, regimented living patterns, socialist cultural mores. The enormous costs, which tended to be underestimated in the initial funding, also acted as a brake on the progress of the land-reclamation component of the project. A separate bureaucratic unit, the Organization for Land Improvement and Desert Development, was established in 1958 to supervise and direct the reclamation projects more efficiently.

By the 1970s the various land-reclamation schemes had generated 400,000 new feddans (one-quarter of which were marginal) on an investment of £E350 million. Since the introduction of the Infitah ("Open Door") policy, there has been a revival of some of the older schemes, particularly the New Valley project, which has adequate artesian water for a potential land reclamation of some 500,000 feddans. The French government has become involved with reclamation in Liberation Province, and foreign business interests have also begun to participate in land reclamation on a commercial basis. At the time of the conclusion of the peace treaty with Israel, President Sadat announced plans to build a canal to divert water from the Nile to the Sinai peninsula as part of a major new land reclamation scheme there.

LANE, WILLIAM EDWARD (1801-1876). British writer on Egypt. Lane's book An Account of the Manners and Customs of the Modern Egyptians, first published in 1836, was one of the most widely read books on Egypt in English. The book was frequently reprinted in the nineteenth and twentieth centuries, though its real impact was in the first decades after its initial publication. Lane's other works, on the Arabic language and Islam, were not as highly popular as the vivid and fascinating picture he presented in his first book on Egypt in the early nineteenth century. Lane spent nearly twelve years there, traveling, studying, and living with the Egyptians, giving him a rich insight into their life and culture. His great-nephew Stanley Lane-Poole (1854-1931) continued Lane's work on Arabic lexicography and contributed his own study of medieval Egypt.

LAVON INCIDENT. In July 1954 an Israeli agent was arrested in an Alexandrian cinema following the premature explosion of a bomb he was intending to plant. The agent was part of a team headed by Colonel Bentsur of the Israeli intelligence service, Mossad, that had made several attacks on U.S. and British government offices and agencies in the guise of "Egyptian extremists." The aims of the Bentsur group appear to have been to destabilize the Nasser regime internally and weaken the links between the regime and Western governments. The arrest of the agent was followed by the arrest of fourteen other suspects, and led to the resignation of the Israeli Defense Minister, Lavon, though whether he had given his approval for the bombings in advance was not clear. Within Egypt the incident led to a hardening of attitudes toward Israel by the RCC, particularly with the revelation of an extensive Israeli espionage campaign at a time when Egypt was not engaged in any provocative acts politically or militarily. Two foreign Arab Jews were subsequently executed for their involvement in the bombing campaign, with eleven others given long prison sentences.

LEGAL SYSTEM see TANZIMAT

LEGISLATIVE ASSEMBLY/GENERAL ASSEMBLY (AL-JAM^{c}IYYA AL-^{c}UMUMIYYA) (1883). Formed after the introduction of the Organic Law of May 1883, the Legislative Assembly had virtually no power. Its eighty-two members were drawn from the ministers, the thirty members of the Legislative Council, and forty-six indirectly elected representatives each serving a six-year term. Potential representatives were bound by property, age, and literacy qualifications which were extremely limiting. Given the composition of the Assembly and the tight control on political activity in Egypt, it is not surprising that the Assembly offered little opposition to the government's plans. The Assembly was required, however, to approve new direct taxes and advise on major public works and irrigation projects. Unlike the Council, the Assembly was entitled to an answer or explanation when its advice was refused by the government. The Assembly was required to meet at least once every other year; its sessions were closed to the public.

LEGISLATIVE ASSEMBLY (AL-JAM^{c}IYYA AT-TASHRĪ^{c}IYYA) (1913). Established on the urging of Kitchener, the 1913 Legislative Assembly combined the Legislative Council and Assembly of 1883 but had slightly more power than its predecessors, and its procedures were open to the public. The 1913 Legislative Assembly actually met for the first time in January 1914 and managed to function briefly before being suspended after Egypt became a British protectorate. It was composed of sixty-six members elected by an indirect vote from a pool of 2,000 electors, and seventeen appointed members were drawn from government ministers and minorities, as well as special-interest groups. Members served for six years, with one-third of the members being replaced every two years. The Legislative Assembly had veto power over the imposition of new taxes and was entitled to introduce and delay legislation. Kitchener intended the Assembly to be a more effective check on the Khedive Abbas rather than a nationalist forum (which despite its dissolution in 1915, it became). The president and one of the two vice-presidents of the Legislative Assembly were appointed; Muhammad Mazlum Pasha and Adli Pasha were appointed to the presidency and vice-presidency respectively. The second vice-president was elected, and this post was won by Sa^{c}d Zaghlul, future leader of the Wafd Party. The Legislative Assembly was not convened after the Protectorate was announced in December 1914, though some of its members, particularly those associated with Zaghlul, met informally during the war and formed the delegation organized by Zaghlul in 1918 to press for Egypt's independence.

LEGISLATIVE COUNCIL (MAJLIS SHŪRĀ'L-QAWANĪN). The second legislative body created under the 1883 Organic Law, the Legislative Council had a more restricted membership than the Assembly. It was composed of fourteen permanent members appointed by the Khedive with the remainder selected for six-year terms by each of the fourteen provinces of Egypt, plus Cairo and Alexandria. They had the right to examine all bills, regulations, and the annual budget. The Council had no veto power, and the government was not bound by its advice. The Council was to meet on five days spread throughout the year. As with the Assembly, the composition of its membership precluded its acting as an effective opposition to government policy.

LESSEPS, FERDINAND, DE (1805-1894). The driving force behind the excavation of the Suez Canal, de Lesseps began his career in Egypt as French Vice-Consul in Alexandria. In the 1830s he became convinced of the economic desirability of cutting a canal across the strip of land linking Sinai with the Egyptian mainland, even though the project had been judged technically unfeasible by the scientists who accompanied Napoleon's invasion of Egypt in 1798. The trade advantages of linking the Mediterranean and Red seas attracted the support of the Viceroy, Muhammad Ali, as well as European financial backing, but the project was temporarily halted during the reign of Abbas I (1848-54), who opposed it along with most of the innovations favored by his father.

Abbas' successor, Sa^{c}id, was a boyhood friend of de Lesseps, and under him, the project was revived. An initial concession was granted in 1854 but was actively blocked by the British government and its representatives at the Ottoman Porte. Despite this, de Lesseps was able to gather support for the project in Europe, largely through his personal lobbying for the canal. In 1856, an international commission (set up largely on de Lesseps' urging) discussed the engineering and technical aspects of the project. De Lesseps' funding came from many sources, but the Khedive of Egypt and several European banks provided the bulk of it. When Sa^{c}id showed signs of wavering on the project (largely because of the hostility of the Ottoman Sultan) de Lesseps pressed on regardless, and work began in 1859. The terms arranged between de Lesseps and the Khedive were extremely favorable to the canal's European investors, with a substantial part of the capitalization and labor costs borne by the Egyptian government.

De Lesseps' connections with Egypt remained strong, and in 1878 the Khedive Ismail requested his appointment to the commission charged with investigating Egypt's finances. The Suez Canal made de Lesseps' name, fame, and fortune and changed utterly Egypt's strategic position in the Middle East.

LIBERAL CONSTITUTIONALIST PARTY (ḤIZB AL-AḤRĀR AD-DUSTŪRIYYĪN). Moderate nationalist political grouping, the Liberal Constitutionalist Party was founded in October 1922 by the former Egyptian Prime Minister Adli Pasha and other politicians to support the government of Tharwat Pasha. This government fell shortly afterward, however, and the Liberal Constitutionalists went on to defend the 1922 Declaration of Independence granted Egypt by Britain (rejected by more ardent nationalists as inadequate) and to urge continued negotiations with the British and the use of moderation and conciliation to secure nationalist goals. The party also started its own paper, Al-Siyasa.

In many respects the Liberal Constitutionalists strongly resembled the old Umma Party, also an extremely conservative and moderate nationalist grouping. It drew its supporters from those groups within the nationalist movement opposed to the Wafd Party or to Zaghlul, the Wafd leader, and from the better-off landowning elements, as well as from political moderates, such as Muhammad Heykal. The party had no organization at the local level; its only permanent governing body was its Board of Directors. Much of the party's ideological focus was provided by Lutfi al-Sayyid, who wrote widely on the need for education and the gradual advancement of the electorate in a democratic system. Support for constitutional government and the strengthening of Egypt's national identity and independence were part of the party's general goals.

In the period 1923-30, when King Fuad gave his support to his own party, the Ittihad, the Liberal Constitutionalists and the Wafd tended to draw together, though during the government of Sidqi Pasha, which the Liberal Constitutionalists and Wafd boycotted, some members defected to join the Palace government. The Liberal Constitutionalists twice formed a government: the 1928 government under Mahmud Pasha lasted fifteen months, and Mahmud's 1937 government lasted twenty months. Both of these governments were actually in violation of their own party principles, which opposed the formation of governments without elections, and both followed the peremptory dismissal of a Wafd government by the Palace.

Support for the Liberal Constitutionalists declined in the 1940s, and it was, with all other pre-Revolutionary parties, banned under the Party Law of January 1953.

LIBERAL SOCIALIST PARTY. Initially created as a right-wing platform within the Arab Socialist Union following the political liberalizations of 1976, the Liberal Socialists have enjoyed limited electoral success. The party was formally constituted under the terms of the Party Law of 1977, under the chairmanship of Mustafa Kamil Murad. The party published its own paper, Al Ahrar. The Liberal Socialists advocate the decontrol of the economy, reintroduction of capitalist economic measures, and greater political liberalizations. Its representation in the People's Assembly dropped from twelve to seven in the 1978 parliamentary reshuffle and to three following the 1979 elections. The Liberal Socialists were originally supportive of President Sadat's domestic and foreign policies, although they have increasingly distanced themselves from the peace process.

LIBERATION PROVINCE. Large land-reclamation scheme based in the Western Desert fifty kilometers northwest of Cairo, Liberation Province was among the most ambitious projects attempted during the Nasser period. The original goal of the planners was to create 600,000 feddans of arable land to be settled on and farmed by a selected group of cultivators whose social and economic role would be based on a "modern" (as opposed to traditional) model with elements of socialism and nationalism. The entire Liberation Province scheme was meant as a pilot project for comprehensive economic and social planning.

Work in Liberation Province began in May 1953, but it quickly drew criticism for its enormous cost overruns and unrealistic goals. Allegations of fiscal mismanagement finally halted the more ambitious elements of the project. The Ministry of Agriculture took over in 1957 from the project's director, Magdi Hasanayn, and Liberation Province was placed under the management of the Organization for Land Improvement and Desert Development. Land reclaimed in the 1950s and 1960s (about 200,000 feddans) was not highly productive, and in the 1970s the French government undertook to rehabilitate the originally reclaimed land and increase its fertility. A British plan is also going ahead in the province, and it is expected that the two projects could eventually reclaim some 400,000 feddans at a cost of $440 million.

LIBERATION RALLY. Political group formed by the Revolutionary Command Council following the January 1953 ban on political activity by the pre-Revolutionary political parties, the Liberation Rally was intended to gain a popular base of support for the

RCC. As a government-sponsored "People's Movement," the Liberation Rally was a combination of mass political party, official "claque" for the regime's programs, and informal security network to detect opponents of the regime and/or the Revolution.

In creating the Liberation Rally, the RCC was also seeking to draw support away from the Ikhwan al-Muslimun (Muslim Brethren), which was the sole political force still officially active in Egypt. The Rally's political appeal was pitched to labor and youth elements in urban areas, and under the leadership of its Secretary-General, Gamal Abdal Nasser, the Liberation Rally played an active role in the anti-Naguib movement during the struggle between Nasser and Naguib in 1954.

The political platform of the Liberation Rally was a fair reflection of RCC policy in the 1953-56 period, calling for an unconditional British withdrawal from the Canal Zone, Sudanese self-determination, the creation of a socialist welfare state, pan-Arabism, and the introduction of a Constitution with appropriate guarantees of civil liberties. The Liberation Rally was replaced by the National Union in 1956.

LIBERATION SQUADS/BATTALIONS. Paramilitary bands formed under the direction of the Wafd government late in 1951, and active until late January 1952, the Liberation Squads were intended to combat the continued British presence in the Canal Zone by various acts of sabotage. The Liberation Squads drew their members from the existing paramilitary groups in Egypt such as those of the Ikhwan al-Muslimun, with the cooperation of the auxiliary police. Actions were taken by these squads autonomously and with varying success. Though exact figures are not agreed, it would appear several hundred squad members were involved and casualty levels were high. The squads' activities created much tension and unrest in the Canal Zone.

The step-up in attacks by the Liberation Squads in the Canal Zone in January 1952 led to a British decision to occupy forcibly areas where the attacks had occurred and to arrest guerrilla suspects, including the auxiliary police. On 25 January

1952 a strong force of British troops surrounded police headquarters in Ismailiyya and issued an ultimatum for the police to surrender within the hour. The police fought back, it is said on government orders, with heavy casualties. The following day Cairo was the scene of anti-British rioting and the burning of sections of the European quarters.

LLOYD, GEORGE LORD. British Consul-General and High Commissioner of Egypt from October 1925 until July 1929, Lord Lloyd did not enjoy an easy relationship with either the Palace or the nationalists. In the year after Lloyd took office the two Wafdist defendants in the Lee Stack assassination case were acquitted, in what the British viewed as a travesty of justice and what many Egyptian nationalists, especially in the Wafd Party, saw as a fair trial. Though the trial failed to disclose any links between the Wafd leadership and the assassination, it nonetheless resolved the British and Lord Lloyd on opposing any future Wafd involvement in an Egyptian government.

Following the elections of 1926, which returned a Wafd majority to the Parliament, the Wafd leader Zaghlul was placed under strong British pressure to refuse to form a government. He made way for Adli, who found himself unable to control the Wafd-dominated Parliament and resigned one year later, in April 1927.

Attempts by the Egyptian government under Adli and Tharwat, his successor, to gain more control of the army were resisted by Lord Lloyd, who demanded the continued command of the army by the British and the retention of all serving British officers, leading to the Army Crisis of 1927. A Wafd government formed in March 1928 did not last three months, during which time the Egyptian legislature was forced to withdraw a Wafd-supported Assemblies Bill under pressure from Lloyd, who opposed the liberalization of political life and association it offered.

To counterbalance this Lloyd encouraged the legislature to stand up to the Palace whenever it appeared that the King was gaining too much power. He pressed Fuad to reinstate the 1924 electoral law before the 1926 elections and to remove the powerful Nashat Pasha from the court by posting him overseas. Nashat, the King's main domestic adviser, had been actively manipulating the political parties to the King's advantage, and Lloyd apparently felt the situation had gotten out of hand. In the area of bilateral relations Lloyd was unable to popularize the Tharwat-Chamberlain treaty in government political circles in Egypt, a setback for British efforts to secure a new treaty relationship on its own terms.

Lloyd's skill at manipulating the cleavages existing between the nationalist parties and the Palace, as well as among the nationalist parties themselves, permitted him to have an influence on Egyptian political affairs far in excess of his diplomatically defined position. This skill was backed up by his readiness to use force if his decisions were not implemented. The domestic opposition against Lloyd, on occasion massive, was never sufficiently cohesive to be effective.

LORRAINE, SIR PERCY. British Consul-General and High Commissioner of Egypt from August 1929 until mid-1933, Sir Percy Lorraine's appointment by the newly elected Labor government in Britain aroused hopes among Egypt's nationalists for a more sympathetic hearing from England. In this Sir Percy proved disappointing, being a firm supporter of Britain's imperial position. He treated the Sidqi regime installed by the Palace favorably despite his initial support for the 1930 Wafd government. His initial profile was vastly lower than that of his predecessors, though he became more interventionist in time, especially with regard to what he viewed as England's declining share in areas of Egypt's economic life. This decline can be traced to a determined campaign by many Egyptian industrialists to develop and protect Egypt's nascent manufacturing sector. Both Lorraine and the British government attempted to combat this by encouraging cooperative ventures and direct investment.

LUTFI AL-SAYYID, AHMAD (1872-1963). Egyptian intellectual and political figure, Ahmad Lutfi al-Sayyid made a substantial contribution to education in Egypt, both as an administrator and writer. His involvement with the nationalist movement began in 1896, when the young law-school graduate was invited to join the Society for the Revival of the Nation, a select grouping of nationalists around the leadership of Latif Salim and headed by the Khedive, Abbas.

Lutfi al-Sayyid was sent to Geneva in 1897 by the Khedive Abbas to acquire Swiss citizenship, which would gain him immunity from the penal codes of Egypt (under the capitulations, foreign nationals had extraterritorial legal status), and enable him more freely to publish a proposed nationalist newspaper. The newspaper idea was subsequently abandoned. Lutfi al-Sayyid became increasingly interested in the work of Shaykh Muhammad Abduh and other conservative nationalist figures and this, as well as the shift in Palace support away from the more ardent nationalists, led to a tempering of Lutfi al-Sayyid's own political stance. He joined the government judiciary following his return from Switzerland, and after the formation of the Umma Party in 1907 he became editor of its newspaper, Al Jarida, until 1915. In this position he was to become the best-known advocate of moderate constitutional government in Egypt.

Though the gradualist political reforms Lutfi al-Sayyid sought may strike modern observers (as it did some of his contemporaries) as excessively cautious, at the time they represented a commitment to the development of the electorate through education that was a distinct advance on political thinking within the more conservative groupings of the nationalist movement. His eminence within the nationalist movement led to his inclusion in the delegation formed by Zaghlul to press for Egypt's independence in 1918. Lutfi al-Sayyid later broke with Zaghlul over the latter's attitude towards the 1921 Adli ministry.

As with many others in the more conservative wing of the nationalist movement, Lutfi al-Sayyid was dismayed by the fragmentation of Egyptian political life in the years after the First World War; he joined the moderate Liberal Constitutionalist Party at its foundation, and became increasingly involved with his directorship of the National Library and with the foundation of Egypt's first national university, which he served as rector. In this post Lutfi al-Sayyid was to have enormous impact on the development of intellectual life in Egypt.

Among other official posts, Lutfi al-Sayyid served as Minister of Education in the governments of Mahmud Pasha. Lutfi al-Sayyid was widely acknowledged as the originator of much of Egypt's mainstream nationalist thought.

-M-

McMAHON, SIR HENRY (1862-1949). High Commissioner of Egypt in 1915-1916, McMahon handled foreign and domestic affairs while General Maxwell directed the war effort. McMahon was responsible for obtaining from the Egyptians the massive requisitions of material required for the armed forces. As with General Maxwell's conscription of Egyptians for the Labor Corps, this program aroused bitter feelings, especially in rural areas. Sir Henry, who had previously served in India, was involved in extremely important negotiations with the Sherif of Mecca, Husayn, to encourage him to lead a rebellion against the Turks in exchange for certain territorial guarantees. In Egyptian affairs, McMahon tended to defer to the judgment of Lord Cecil, the financial adviser, and Sir Willaim Brunyate, the judicial adviser. Internally, Egyptian political life was effectively silenced by the operation of martial law, strict censorship, and a ban on assemblies.

MADHĀRĀ'Ī. Family of administrators of Persian origin, the Madhārā'ī controlled the finances and effectively the government of Egypt in the thirty-year period of direct ᶜAbbāsid control of the country between the overthrow of the Ṭūlūnids and the rise of the Ikhshīdids (905-35/292-323). The family first came to prominence in Ṭūlūnid times and were able, with the support of the center in Baghdad, to gain control of Egypt's financial administration under the ᶜAbbāsid-appointed governors.

MAGLIS (prop. MAJLIS) AL-MASHWARRA. Consultative council established in 1829 by the Ottoman Viceroy Muhammad Ali, the Maglis was an advisory council meant to deal with administrative matters. The 156 individuals chosen to serve consisted of thirty-three senior government officials, twenty-four district-level supervisors, and ninety-nine notables (local and religious leaders). The Maglis provided advice only in matters of general administration and public welfare, agricultural policy, and public works; it met once a year. The Maglis was a short-lived grouping though individual advisers continued to play a role in the government in a non-formalized capacity.

MAGLIS (prop. MAJLIS) AL-MILLĪ. The General Council of Orthodox Copts, the Maglis is an elected assembly of prominent Coptic laymen, first formed in 1874 to assist in the supervision of the Coptic Church's financial and civil affairs. The constitution and responsibilities of the Maglis underwent substantive changes during the ensuing years. Butrus Ghali Pasha (d.1910) secured the assent of the Khedive Ismail for the formation of the Council and was instrumental in its development. The Maglis gained control of most Coptic waqfs in 1883.

Despite the formation of the Maglis, or possibly because of it, relations between the Coptic lay community and the Patriarchate remained generally distant, particularly because of the Patriarchs' fears that the Council was an attempt to limit their autonomy. Political developments outside the Coptic community have helped support the demands of the laity for an active role in Church management. In 1960 Coptic Waqfs (religious endowments) were placed under control of a special, government-appointed committee of Copts.

MAGLIS (MAJLIS) AN-NUWWĀB see ASSEMBLY OF DELEGATES

MAHFUZ, NAGUIB (prop. NAJIB) (1911-). One of the leading Egyptian novelists of the twentieth century, Mahfuz has revolutionized the novel form in Arabic by the extensive use of colloquial language in the dialogue of his characters, as well as by the directness of his story lines and characterizations. Such novels as <u>Midaq Alley</u> presented a realistic and yet sympathetic portrayal of the life of ordinary Egyptians. Mahfuz, who has written more than forty novels, has developed a distinctly somber and politically complex tone in later years. Mahfuz is among the most popular modern Arabic authors. His work has been translated into a number of other languages.

MAHIR PASHA, AHMAD (1886-1945). Prime Minister of Egypt at the time of his assassination in February 1945, Ahmad Mahir was associated with the Egyptian nationalist movement from its earliest days.

Ahmad Mahir (brother of Ali; see below) was the son of a government official; he held a doctorate in law and economics, and taught in Egypt's first graduate faculty of economics. He was an early member of the Nationalist Party. In the post-World War I period Mahir was involved with the nationalist leader Zaghlul in the formation of the Wafd and especially of the Wafd Secret Apparatus. It was this latter link that led to his arrest in 1924 following the assassination of Sir Lee Stack, the British Sirdar; at the time he was serving as Minister of Education in the first Wafd cabinet. He was acquitted in June 1926, but this failed to convince the British, and Mahir was kept from active involvement in national politics for a while. He joined the Wafd executive in 1927 as secretary to its parliamentary group.

Within the Wafd leadership Mahir came to be allied with Nuqrashi, and after an initial period of cooperation and support the two men increasingly opposed the control of the party by Zaghlul's successor, Nahhas. Nuqrashi was voted out of the Wafd leadership in September 1937, and Mahir followed him four months later. The two men formed the Saadist Party in 1938. The Saadists joined the government of Ali Mahir in 1939. Ahmad Mahir was strongly critical of the Palace's and government's refusal to become involved in World War II on the Allies' side, and resigned along with four Saadist ministers in September 1940.

In October 1944 Ahmad Mahir was invited to form a government following the dismissal of Nahhas and the wartime Wafd government forced on King Faruq in February 1942. He included in his cabinet Makram Ubaid, the former Wafdist minister who was the last of the old-guard Wafd hierarchy to break with Nahhas. Elections held in January 1945 were boycotted by the Wafd, and Ahmad Mahir again formed the government.

It had been decided at the Yalta Conference that attendance at the Peace Conference following the close of the war would be limited to those countries that had declared war against Germany and her allies as of March 1945; accordingly on 24 February 1945 Mahir announced Egypt's intention to do so. He was assassinated in parliament the following day by a fascist sympathizer.

MAHIR PASHA, ALI (1883-1960). Egyptian Prime Minister and prominent political figure, Ali Mahir served in many ministerial and government appointments prior to the 1952 Revolution, after which he was for a short time Prime Minister under the Free Officers. Involved in the nationalist movement in the pre- and post-World War II period, Ali Mahir broke with Zaghlul over policy issues in 1921, while serving on the Wafd Central Committee. In 1922 he was appointed to serve on the Constitutional Commission. When the pro-Palace Ittihad party was founded in 1925, he became its vice-president. Mahir served as Minister of Justice in the Sidqi government (1930-1933).

Ali Mahir enjoyed good relations with the Palace and in 1935 was appointed Chief of the Royal Cabinet; he formed a caretaker government in January 1936 and appointed the delegates, headed by the Wafd party leader Nahhas, to commence treaty negotiations with the British that February. Following the elections in 1936 and the formation of a Wafdist government that June, Mahir resumed his duties as Chief of the Royal Cabinet. He was active in marshaling the palace and political forces that led to the fall of the Wafd government in 1937.

Ali Mahir again formed a government in August 1939, with the help of a breakaway Wafdist faction, the Saadists, but his cabinet fell under British pressure in June 1940, following his government's failure to affiliate clearly with the British. He was kept out of the government and under house arrest during the Wafdist war ministry, falling under British suspicion as possibly having pro-German sympathies. Following the war Mahir founded the Egypt Front, a platform for political moderates.

In the aftermath of the burning of Cairo in January 1952 Mahir formed a government that fell soon afterward, in March 1952. After the Revolution he was again called on to form a government. His lack of sympathy with some of the aims of the Free Officers, and disagreements over Agrarian Reform, led to his resignation in September 1952. Along with other pre-Revolutionary political figures he was eventually prohibited from participating in political activities, although in January 1953 he served on a Constitutional Commission formed by the RCC.

In addition to his ministerial and palace posts Ali Mahir was instrumental in the establishment and development of the Egyptian Ministry of Social Affairs. He enjoyed close links with Shaykh al-Maraghi of al-Azhar, with whom he worked in the 1930s on the formation of a religiously based, pan-Arabist and anti-Wafdist movement. Mahir acted as a liaison from time to time between the Palace and other Arab countries, notably Saudi Arabia, and kept his contacts with Misr al-Fatat and the Ikhwan. A skilled political survivor, he maintained a public profile until 1954, the only prominent politician of the pre-Revolutionary period to do so.

MAḤMAL. The Maḥmal was for many centuries an important feature of the annual pilgrimage of Muslims to Mecca. The sending of a Maḥmal, or decorated litter mounted on a camel, and a covering for the Ka^{c}ba, symbolized a ruler's dominance in and his claims to act as a protector of Islam's holiest cities. The Egyptian Mamluk Sultans started a tradition of sending extremely lavish and splendid Maḥmals; it is indicative of the political significance attached to the Maḥmal that at the time of the emergence of Tīmūrid power in Persia they approached the Mamluks for permission to send their own covering in procession to Mecca.

The Egyptian processing traveling with the Maḥmal, with its elaborate decor and accompanying musicians, continued to be a feature of the annual pilgrimage until the reconquest of the Hijaz in 1926 by the forces of the Najdi ruler Ibn Saud. His strict Wahhabi followers objected to the Maḥmal itself, and to the music accompanying it as un-Islamic. When the Maḥmal procession entered the Holy Cities in 1926, an incident between the Egyptians and the Wahhabis resulted in the loss of several lives. Relations between Saudi Arabia and Egypt were broken for a ten-year period over the incident, during which time the kiswa (covering for the Ka^{c}ba), traditionally made in and presented by Egypt, was woven in the Hijaz.

MAHMUD PASHA, MUHAMMAD (1884-1940). Prime Minister of Egypt and one of the founders of the Liberal Constitutionalist Party, Muhammad Mahmud began his career in politics as an associate of Zaghlul and was deported to Malta with him in 1919. In 1920-1921 however, Mahmud became allied with the more moderate and anti-Zaghlul nationalist faction, which coalesced into the Liberal Constitutional Party in 1922, of which Mahmud became vice-president. He joined the government of Adli Pasha in June 1926 as Minister of Communications and was appointed Minister of Finance in the government of Tharwat Pasha in April 1927. When the Wafd returned to power in March 1928, Nahhas made him Minister of Finance. Following the dismissal of the Nahhas government that June, Mahmud formed his first government, with royal permission to suspend electoral procedures and parliament for three years.

During his first tenure as Prime Minister, Mahmud worked actively to resolve the outstanding differences between Egypt and Britain; the negotiations stalled after agreements had been reached on the presence of British troops and the replacement of the High Commissioner with an ambassador. The new Labor government in England came to feel that only a Wafd government had the popular backing in Egypt to negotiate and sign such an agreement. Mahmud stepped down, elections were held in December

1929, and the Wafd returned to power. Earlier that year, Mahmud was elected president of the Liberal Constitutionalists, and he led his party in a cooperative movement with the Wafd to oppose the 1930-1933 Sidqi government.

In December 1937 Mahmud was once more asked by the Palace to form a government to replace a dismissed Wafdist cabinet. He remained in office until August 1939 in the face of increasingly fierce opposition. He was forced to reshuffle his cabinet twice following elections held in April 1938, to maintain a semblance of distance between himself and the Palace. Mahmud's last year in office was dominated by the growing threat of war in Europe and in North Africa and domestic political agitation over Palestine. He was criticized by some of his own party for agreeing to form a government without elections, a violation of the party's political principles. This heightened the vulnerability of his own hold on the Prime Ministership. Mahmud finally made way for a new government headed by Ali Mahir in August 1939.

MAKRAM, UMAR (d. 1811). Dean of Notables (Naqib al-Ashraf, or leader of those who claim descent from the Prophet Muhammad) during the French occupation of Egypt (1798-1801), Umar Makram later presented the popular petition to Muhammad Ali that resulted in the latter's installation as Viceroy of Egypt.

Makram led popular opposition to the French invasion of Egypt. Following the withdrawal of the French, complete chaos descended on Egypt and in Cairo as contenders for the Viceroy's position among the Ottoman nominees and Mamluk aspirants fought each other. The installation of the Ottoman nominee, Khurshid Pasha, in 1804 was unacceptable to the Cairenes, and, acting on their behalf, Umar requested Muhammad Ali to return to Cairo (he was on campaign in Upper Egypt) and depose Khurshid. His relationship with Muhammad Ali subsequently deteriorated as the latter made clear his intention of gaining full control over the activities of both the Mamluks and the religious in Egypt. Makram disputed Muhammad Ali's plan to tax the previously exempt landholdings of the religious, and he was ousted from office in 1809. His role during the transitional period before Muhammad Ali took power was illustrative of the way the Muslim religious in Egypt had gained a role as defenders and representatives of popular interests in the last, troubled century of Ottoman control in Egypt. As such, Makram was praised by later generations of Egyptian nationalists.

MALET, SIR EDWARD (1837-1908). British Agent and Consul-General in Egypt from 1879 to 1883, Malet was witness to the rise of Colonel Arabi and the nationalist movement in the period prior to the Arabi Revolt of 1882. Although Malet appreciated some of the grievances of the Egyptian officers, like most European observers he appeared to have little understanding of the true dimensions of the nationalist movement. He regarded Colonel Arabi, leader of the nationalist officers, as a fanatic; to meet his military threat Malet acquired ascendancy over the indecisive Khedive, Tawfiq, appointed to office in 1879. Working with the financial adviser Colvin, Malet helped shape British policy in Egypt toward its ultimate interventionist form.

Despite his influence with Tawfiq, Malet was unable to prevent or counter the military upheaval in 1881 that saw Riyad Pasha, the Prime Minister, dismissed and the more moderate Sharif Pasha installed in his stead. The rising tide of nationalism proved less acceptable to the French, and especially to the new French Prime Minister, Gambetta; at his urging the British and French governments dispatched a joint note in early 1882, cautioning the Egyptian Parliament and the nationalists to do nothing to impair Tawfiq's position. Malet and some in the British government found the wording inflammatory, and Wilfred Blunt, the British Orientalist who was working with the nationalists, was approached by Malet to try and soften the effects of the note's delivery.

Sharif Pasha had resigned early in 1882 over the joint note and his own policy disagreements with the Palace. In his wake the more nationalist Muhammad Sami al-Barudi Pasha formed a government, with Arabi as Minister of War. Malet gave ever stronger support to Tawfiq in the face of Arabi's demands and encouraged Tawfiq not to countersign an order exiling fifty anti-nationalist military plotters against Arabi. Tawfiq's encounter with Arabi over this in May 1882 ended acrimoniously and strengthened Malet's own resolve that something had to be done about Arabi.

The Arabi Revolt that summer was directly sparked by the decision of the British to place a fleet off Alexandria, a decision in which Malet participated. By the time the fighting started Malet acknowledged the popular character of the resistance and cautioned restraint on the British invaders, though he continued to perceive Arabi as hostile to British interests in Egypt and to urge his removal.

MAMLUKS (Ar., MAMLŪK). Soldiers of slave origin. The word "Mamlūk" means "owned" or "belonging to," but the concept behind the term in practice was rather different from what its English translations suggest. The Mamluks were purchased as young children, given a superb military education, and manumitted upon completion of that training. Though they continued to owe absolute fealty to their master, with the growing importance of military figures in the various Islamic courts, for defense and protection, the Mamluks frequently ended with far more real power than the masters they were meant to serve. Mamluk status was nonhereditary. The children of the majority of Mamluks (Awlād an-Nās) inherited none of their fathers' position or power. They traditionally either joined the regular army corps or pursued a religious life; a few of these sons, such as the historian Ibn Taghrī-Birdī, did remain important in Mamluk court life, but this was exceptional. The sons of Sultans, however, often inherited their father's throne. The Baḥrī Mamluks were virtually the dynasty of Qalā'ūn, although in Burjī times the success of these sons in maintaining their father's power was generally quite ephemeral. The Mamluks were, in ethnic origin, drawn from the eastern Islamic lands and southern Russia. The source of supply of Mamluks altered in time, with Turkic tribes eventually supplanted in favor of Circassians.

During Ayyūbid times (1171-1250/567-648) Mamluks were imported in ever increasing numbers. The elite unit, the ḥalqa, established by the dynasty's founder Ṣalāḥ ad-Dīn, came in time to be largely composed of Mamluks. However, the major impetus behind the development of the Mamluks as a force in Egypt was provided by the Ayyūbid Sultan, aṣ-Ṣāliḥ (1240-49/637-47) who headquartered his Mamluks on the island of Roda (ar-Rawḍa). It was this group of Mamluks, known as the Baḥrīs, who were to take power in their own right following their murder of aṣ-Ṣāliḥ's son and successor, Tūrān Shāh. Although aṣ-Ṣāliḥ attracted criticism from his own family for his reliance on his Turkish Mamluks rather than on the Kurds who had formed the traditional backbone of the Ayyūbid armies, it was the divided and contentious nature of the Ayyūbid clan which made the possession of a loyal, ethnically neutral force so attractive.

The Mamluk Sultans who succeeded the Ayyūbids used the establishment of the ᶜAbbāsid Caliphate in Cairo in 1261/659 to legitimize themselves as rulers and defenders of Islam. They were, until the rise of the Ottomans, the dominant power of medieval Islam. During the Baḥrī and Burjī (or Circassian) Mamluk dynasties the importation of Mamluks by the regime continued, and the more important of the Sultans tended to leave behind a well-organized faction of Mamluks. It was the fighting among these factions that made life in Cairo such a torment in later Mamluk times.

The Mamluks enthusiastically drew revenues not only from taxes but also through their eventual control of the trade with India and the East. During Burjī times efforts were made to extend this control to a virtual monopoly on trade in various valuable commodities, such as pepper, and in basic foodstuffs, such as sugar. Such policies brought hardships and shortages to Egypt and may have acted to encourage European traders to investigate other routes to the sources of the merchandise passing through Mamluk ports. As the Mamluk period advanced, the rulers and their courts did not hesitate to seize wealth wherever it was found, be it in the treasury, in private hands, or through extorting the poor.

The role of the Mamluks in Egypt was not entirely negative; in 1260/658 they saved Egypt from much destruction by the Mongols, when they defeated them at the Battle of ^{c}Ayn Jālūt, and the Mamluks completed the defeat of the Crusaders begun under their predecessors, the Ayyūbids. Many Mamluk Sultans contributed to the welfare and educational facilities of Egypt, particularly during the Baḥrī Mamluk period.

In political terms, however, the presence of such a large group of military men concentrated around the Sultan, many with their own ambitions to rule the country, created a condition of sustained political instability toward the end of the Mamluk period. The rise of the Ottomans in the north (who had adopted the use of artillery disdained by the majority of Mamluks as unmanly), the rise of the Portuguese as a mercantile naval power in the Indian Ocean, and the internal discontent in Egypt caused by the Mamluks' increasingly heavy demands for revenue, all helped the eventual Ottoman triumph.

The Ottoman conquest of Egypt in 1517/922 did not really resolve the problems of instability associated with the Mamluks. The first Ottoman governor of Egypt was the Mamluk deserter Khā'ir Bay, and from the beginning of their rule the Ottomans associated the Mamluks with the government of Egypt and the beylicate. After a period of adjustment the formation of Mamluk households continued, though these were now grouped into two (eventually three) major factions, which continually vied for power in the last century and a half of Ottoman rule.

The century before the rise of Muhammad Ali in 1805 saw the regular rise and fall of Mamluk aspirants to de facto control of Egypt. The Mamluks who held the offices of Shaykh al-Balad or Amīr al-Ḥajj, though technically subordinate to the Ottoman Viceroy, had in fact long since ceased to be so. ^{c}Alī Bey, who held independent power as Shaykh al-Balad in Egypt in the 1760/1170s, even had coins minted in his own name.

Proper Ottoman control was never reestablished prior to the arrival of the French in Egypt in 1798, despite a short-lived Ottoman restoration in 1786/1200.

The French used the Mamluk threat to Ottoman control in Egypt as a pretext for their invasion of the country; whatever their justification, they had to meet a spirited defense of Egypt by the Mamluks. They, with Ottoman and British military assistance, finally defeated the French in 1801. There followed nearly four years of absolute chaos as Ottoman and Mamluk candidates for the governorship fought each other. By 1805 Muhammad Ali was able to profit from the disarray among the Mamluks, the discontent with the Ottoman alternative, and the desire of the Egyptians for the restoration of order to gain control of the country for himself. He conducted two great purges of Mamluks in 1805 and 1811 and pursued them during his campaigns in Nubia and Dongola where many of the survivors of these massacres had fled.

AL-MA'MŪN (r. 813-33/198-218). The first ᶜAbbāsid Caliph to visit Egypt, al-Ma'mūn's presence there in 831/216 was required by the widespread revolts among both the ᶜAbbāsid troops and the population. The army dissensions mirrored the larger conflict going on in the ᶜAbbāsid center in Iraq and were easily suppressed by the superior military forces under the command of his general, Afshīn, who accompanied al-Ma'mūn. The popular revolts against the high level of taxes, both the older land taxes and the newer and harsher taxes introduced by al-Ma'mūn's governors, were quelled when these taxes were revised. A new system of collecting taxes, the qabāla, was initiated, with one member of each community liable to taxation, guaranteeing and paying his community's assessment. During his stay in the country al-Ma'mūn renewed relations with the Christian Nubian kingdom to the south. The difficult internal situation in Egypt and among the troops there was undoubtedly affected by the instability of the ᶜAbbāsid government in the country under the former Caliph Hārūn ar-Rashīd, who had appointed some twenty-four governors to Egypt in the twenty-three years of his reign.

AL-MANAR ("The Lighthouse"). Journal founded in 1897 by Shaykh Rashid Rida, a disciple of Muhammad Abduh, *Al-Manar* was among the most influential of the contemporary journals dealing with Islamic themes. Rida continued after his master's death in 1905 to develop the conservative themes of Abduh's work in his own writings. The journal focused its articles on the need for a return to the purity of early Islam and early Islamic society, through which the modern Muslim states would be able to survive the challenges of modernism and the West. The journal also served as a forum for some of the pan-Islamic political issues of the day. Rida, as editor, gave the journal's support to the claims of Fuad to the Caliphate, though this had scant support outside Egypt. Many of the political, social, and religious issues which came to dominate the Islamic revivalist movement in Egypt were initially examined in the pages of the journal, which enjoyed great popularity in Egypt and elsewhere in the Islamic world. *Al-Manar* was eventually taken over in the 1930s by the Ikhwan al-Muslimun.

MANIFESTO OF 30 MARCH. A restatement of the Nasser regime's commitment to its socialist programs and policies, the manifesto was issued by the government in March 1968, following a wave of internal disturbances against the regime. The manifesto maintained the necessity of one-party rule while promising a cabinet reshuffle, reform of the ASU, and a constitution of a permanent nature once Egypt had been secured against the Israelis. The ASU would be restructured and supervise new elections, a supreme court would be established, and new laws would be promulgated offering greater protection for civil liberties. The Parliament would ultimately be given control over the executive branch. The manifesto was given an overwhelming vote of approval in a referendum that May, but antigovernment disturbances continued to plague the regime.

AL-MANṢŪR (AL-MANṢŪR NASĪR AD-DĪN) (r. 1198-1200/595-96). Third Ayyūbid ruler of Egypt, al-Manṣūr was the son of al-^{c}Azīz and great-nephew of al-^{c}Ādil. Al-^{c}Ādil was ruling Damascus on behalf of al-ᶜAzīz at the time of the latter's death, having deposed al-ᶜAzīz' brother and bitter rival, al-Afḍal, as ruler of Damascus in 1196/592. As al-Manṣūr took power, al-Afḍal's supporters in Syria and Egypt began to demand his reinstatement; al-ᶜĀdil, who was regent to the young Sultan, met them in battle in Syria, then in Egypt, where he deposed al-Manṣūr from power. This act brought to a halt for a time the factionalism that had beset the family of Ṣalāḥ ad-Dīn since his death, restoring the unity of Egypt and Syria under al-ᶜĀdil.

AL-MAQRĪZĪ (TAQĪ AD-DĪN AḤMAD) (1364-1442/766-845). Among the most eminent of the Mamluk historiographers of Egypt, al-Maqrīzī dealt with all areas of Egypt's history since the coming of Islam. The Islamicization and Arabization of the population, the position of Egypt's Copts, the impact of the immigration of Arab tribes into Egypt, the evolution of the Egyptian administration, and the changes within the country with the rise and fall of Muslim dynasties were all considered in his extensive works.

In addition to his writings al-Maqrīzī held several high offices as a judge and teacher in both Egypt and Syria. Though al-Maqrīzī was educated in the Ḥanafī school of Islamic law, he later affiliated himself with the more liberal Shāfiᶜī school. His period of public service came to an end in about 1418/821, when he retired to Egypt to compile his historical studies.

AL-MARAGHI, SHAYKH MUSTAFA (1881-1945). Rector of al-Azhar and an active figure in the Egyptian nationalist movement, Shaykh al-Maraghi was appointed Qāḍī (religious judge) in 1925 and served as rector in 1928-29. He resigned in 1929 because of political pressure but was restored to his post in 1935, following popular agitation for his reinstatement; he served until his death ten years later. Shaykh al-Maraghi was a supporter of the ideas of Muhammad Abduh and a member of the pan-Islamic movement within the nationalist camp, forming a Committee for the Defense of Islam in 1933. He gave his support to Kings Fuad and Faruq, as leaders of an Islamic state, against the more secular perspectives of the majority of nationalist leaders.

Shaykh al-Maraghi participated actively in the 1938 electoral campaigns on behalf of the non-Wafd parties, alleging Coptic control of the Wafd through its secretary William Makram Ubaid. His attacks on the Copts were unpopular, and eventually Maraghi had to be restrained by Muhammad Mahmud, the Liberal Constitutionalist leader.

The influence Al-Maraghi exerted on Faruq when the young king came to power declined as Faruq's personal life became indulgent. Al-Maraghi joined Ali Mahir in an anti-Wafd, pan-Arab, pan-Islamic front shortly before the Second World War and went on to support the Ikhwan al-Muslimun in their efforts to promote a revitalized Islamic polity. Al-Maraghi's anti-British stance and opposition to Egypt joining the British war effort aroused the antagonism of Sir Miles Lampson. With the formation of a Wafd government in 1942 Al-Maraghi lost direct influence on the government, though he remained influential in religious affairs and in political circles opposed to the Wafd.

MARAI, SAYYID (1913-). Director from its inception of the Agrarian Reform program in post-Revolutionary Egypt, Sayyid Marai initially trained as an agricultural engineer. In 1945, as a member of the Egyptian legislature, he introduced agrarian reform legislation that proposed a rent ceiling for small farmers. The Free Officers chose Marai to be Director of the Higher Committee for Agrarian Reform from 1952 until the Higher Committee was absorbed by the Ministry of Agriculture in 1956, whereupon Marai assumed that ministerial post in the 1957 cabinet. He was also made president of the Agricultural Credit and Cooperative Bank.

Following the formation of the United Arab Republic, Marai served as Minister of Agriculture and Agrarian Reform until the breakup of the UAR in 1961. He was then replaced by Major Muhsan Abdal Nur amid rumors of policy disagreements between himself and Nasser. Allegations of financial misdealing were proven unfounded and Marai returned to the government in 1964 as Deputy Speaker.

Marai was named Secretary for National Capitalism in the Arab Socialist Union in 1964, Minister of Agriculture again in 1967, and Deputy Prime Minister in 1970. He was elected to the People's Assembly in 1971 and became first Secretary of the ASU in 1972. President Sadat made Marai Presidential Assistant in 1973, and from 1975 to 1978 he served as Speaker of the People's Assembly. Marai was a close and important confidante of Sadat during the latter's presidency. He retired from public life in 1982.

MARJ DĀBIQ (1516/922). The decisive military engagement between the Mamluks and Ottomans, Marj Dābiq was the last battle fought by the Ottomans before their invasion of Egypt itself. The Ottomans, led by their Sultan, Selīm, were fresh from victory over the Persians in the Battle of Chāldirān when they began advancing on Mamluk territory in the spring of 1516/921. Though the Mamluks were reluctant to meet the Ottomans in battle, Qānṣūḥ al-Ghawrī set out with his army from Egypt. The two forces met at Marj Dābiq, near Aleppo in Syria on 24 August 1516/922; the Mamluks were utterly vanquished and al-Ghawrī died during the fighting.

The Mamluk defeat was the end of a lengthy process of decline in their ability to govern and defend Egypt. The Mamluks had not mastered the use of artillery, which the Ottomans employed to great effect, and their cause was also not helped by the defection of Khā'ir Bay and a number of prominent Mamluks to the Ottoman cause. Within five months Selīm and his army entered Cairo.

MARJ AṢ-ṢUFFĀR. The final encounter between the Mamluks and the Mongol forces of the Il Khān Ghazan, fought at Marj aṣ-Ṣuffār in 1303/702, forced the Mongols to relinquish their bid to control Syria.

The Il Khān Ghazan had crossed the Euphrates into Mamluk territory in 1299/699, occupying Aleppo and Damascus and defeating the Mamluks in battle near Homs. Il Khān Ghazan's temporary withdrawal to Iran allowed the Mamluks to recover most of their Syrian territory before the Il Khān launched a new offensive in 1302/701. The following year the Mongol armies once more crossed the Euphrates to be met by the Mamluks under the command of Baybars II, who inflicted total defeat on them. The unity of this last wave of Mongol attackers was broken by the death of the Il Khān shortly after the battle, and although hostility long persisted between the Mamluks in Egypt and the Mongols in Iran, there were no further threats to Mamluk territories from the East for several decades.

MARWAN II (r. 744-50/127-32). Last Umayyad Caliph, Marwān II ("al-Ḥimār") was assassinated by his own soldiers while seeking refuge in the Fayyum oasis of Egypt. His persecution of the Copts during his reign was seen by them as justifying his fate, and an account of his defeat at the hands of the ᶜAbbāsid general Ṣāliḥ b. ᶜAlī found its way into the Coptic apocalyptic writings and in the work of Severus of Ashmunayn, a Coptic historian. During his transit through Egypt, Marwān is said to have instigated the burning of parts of al-Fusṭāṭ.

MASĪḤ PASHA (r. 1574-80/982-88). Ottoman governor of Egypt, Masīḥ Pasha was sent by the Porte to restore order after an outbreak of civil disturbances in the cities and towns. He acted swiftly to remedy the situation, with widespread execution of malcontents. During his second year in office Upper Egypt was placed under direct Ottoman control, removing the autonomy granted the tribes there at the time of the Ottoman conquest of Egypt; this was not a positive move, as it created one more group in Egypt ranged against the Ottoman center. Masīḥ Pasha was an extremely pious man and gave much support to religious establishments in Egypt, believing these were the best means to exert influence on the people. Despite his crackdown on malcontents, troubles in Egypt began again within six years of his leaving the governorship.

AL-MASRI, AZIZ ALI (1878-1965). Military figure associated with the Egyptian nationalist movement, Masri studied at the Military Academy in Istanbul, where he was influenced by the pan-Islamic and nationalist ideas current in Turkey at the time. After the 1908 Young Turk uprising in that country Masri's hope that they would encourage Arab autonomy was disappointed. He participated in the Ottoman army's campaign in Libya against the Italians in 1911-12, organizing local resistance forces after the army withdrew. About this time he became associated with several clandestine groupings of Arab officers in the Ottoman army and eventually founded his own group, the Ahd, which planned an anti-Ottoman pan-Arab revolt in the Levant and Arabia.

This latter involvement led to his arrest by the Turkish authorities in 1914. Masri was tried and threatened with execution, causing a widespread outcry in Egypt and the development of strongly anti-Ottoman feelings there, a sentiment encouraged by the British. Anxious to secure Egyptian cooperation with the British war effort, the British exploited any wedge that could be driven between the Egyptians and their nominal suzerain, the Ottoman Sultan. Masri was finally released after the intervention of the Egyptian government.

After his departure from Turkey, Masri participated with the forces of the Sharif of Mecca in the Arab Revolt of 1916. He then returned to Egypt, and pursued his army career, being promoted to Inspector-General of the Egyptian army in 1938. By 1939, when he was appointed by the Prime Minister Ali Mahir as Chief of Staff, his commitment to ridding Egypt of British influence gave him distinctly pro-German sentiments. Alarmed, the British pressed for his dismissal but were resisted by the Palace and the government. He lost his post as Chief of Staff when the Mahir government fell in 1940.

As the British gained firmer control of the Egyptian government in the early years of the war, while the Germans and Italians were advancing, Masri decided to defect. In May 1941, with the assistance of some nationalists (among whom was Anwar Sadat), he borrowed an army plane and flew toward the German lines in the Western Desert. The plane, short of fuel, failed to reach the front and Masri was forced to go into hiding;

he was captured shortly afterwards and was tried and imprisoned until his pardon by the newly elected Wafd government in March 1942. This gesture by the Wafd may have been intended to counter the fact that its installation in power was a direct result of British pressure on the Palace, for others in Egypt with less demonstrable pro-German sympathies than Masri were imprisoned during the Wafd ministry.

Though Masri had a certain influence and popularity with the Free Officers, he declined to act as the figurehead leader of their planned coup. Masri lived quietly in Egypt until his death.

MAXWELL, GENERAL SIR JOHN GRENFELL (1859-1929). General Commanding Officer of Egyptian troops in World War I, Maxwell brought to his post lengthy experience with Egypt and its administration. He was a sympathetic and effective commanding officer, and with Milne Cheetham, a strong opponent of British annexation of the country. Maxwell introduced martial law, while allowing certain civilian institutions to remain functioning, but this move was unpopular with the nationalists and with many ordinary Egyptians whose lives it affected. Despite Maxwell's assurances to the contrary Egyptian soldiers were eventually drafted for the labor corps supporting the British war effort, which by 1916 had succeeded in repulsing two major Ottoman attacks on Egypt. Conscription and the forcible seizure of draught animals caused great disruption in rural areas, as the men needed to farm and the animals needed to run agricultural machinery were taken. Sir Archibald Murray replaced him in 1916. He returned to Egypt in 1919 as a member of the Milner Mission.

MEHANNA, RASHID (Ar. Mahanna) (1918-82). Rashid Mehanna was appointed by Naguib to the Regency Council of Ahmad Fuad II, formed after the Revolution of July 1952, which had deposed the infant monarch's father, Faruq. Mehanna, who was associated with the Ikhwan al-Muslimun, was a powerful artillery officer who had earlier declined the leadership of the Free Officers' coup. He soon attempted to use his position on the Regency Council to increase his power over the Free Officers' Executive, whereupon he was dismissed from the Council in October. However, this attempt led to accusations by some Free Officers that he had political ambitions out of line with the Revolution. Mehanna maintained his opposition to RCC policies thereafter. He was arrested, court-martialed, and sentenced to a long imprisonment in January 1953, coincident with a more general purge of army officers conducted by the RCC. He served a few years of this sentence before his release for health reasons, and lived quietly in Egypt until his death.

MEHMED (MUḤAMMAD) PASHA (r. 1607-11/1016-20). Ottoman Viceroy, Mehmed was sent to Egypt to bring an end to the wave of disturbances that had beset the country since 1586/994. The Mamluks had succeeded in removing or compromising four Viceroys and in killing a fifth, Ibrāhīm Pasha, in 1604/1013, partially in revolt over Ottoman fiscal measures, but also over administrative reforms that threatened their power. Mehmed Pasha, known as "Kul Kuran" ("Breaker of Mamluks"), suppressed a revolt of the sipahis in 1607/1016 and brought to an end a major revolt by Ottoman troops in the Delta in 1609/1018, caused by his stopping the exactions made by some of the Ottoman corps in rural areas. Shortly before his term came to an end in 1610/1019 Mehmed promulgated in Egypt a new Ottoman administrative code.

MELKITE. Theological school that stressed the dual, divine and human, nature of Christ, the Melkite position was adopted at the Council of Chalcedon in 451 and became the theology of the Byzantine state. The Melkite school was opposed by the majority of Egypt's Christians, who were Monophysites, though the Melkites did have some supporters in the south of the country and in Nubia.

MENOU, GENERAL ABDULLAH. Successor in July 1800 to General Kléber as governor of Egypt on behalf of Napoleon Bonaparte, Menou was a Muslim convert who declared Egypt to be a French colony. His conversion did not endear him to the French, nor his declaration of Egypt's colonial status to the Egyptians. As an administrator and general he was unable to restore order fully or to meet the British and Ottoman challenge. This began in March 1801 and resulted in the British and Ottoman capture of Rosetta, followed by an advance on the Delta. Meantime, an Ottoman force advanced against the French overland from Syria. To meet this two-pronged attack the defense of Cairo was left in the hands of General Belliard, while Menou himself advanced with his troops to Alexandria and the coast. Belliard, faced with the spread of plague to Cairo, local resistance and the prospect of heavy fighting, surrendered. Menou was then left isolated in Alexandria. His own surrender followed, and by October 1801 the French had withdrawn from Egypt.

MILITARY. (For the period before 1800, see also MAMLUKS, SŪDĀN.) From the time of the Muslim conquest until the ascendancy of Muhammad Ali, the military in Egypt was composed of foreign troops whose ethnic origin altered through the centuries and with the shifts in dynasties. As with all the other Arab states, the passage of time saw the increased dominance within the military of groups from the more easterly lands of the central Islamic world.

The military structure of Egypt, like those of many other Arab and Islamic states, was also transformed by the growing reliance on, and importance of, Mamluks, soldiers of slave origin prized for their fealty to their master and trained to a high level of martial skill. The use of Mamluks helped to free the Islamic armies of some of the ethnic and tribal rivalries that had marred, for instance, the Fāṭimid dynasty in Egypt prior to the reign of the vizier Badr al-Jamālī. The appearance of the Crusaders to the Islamic world during this time gave importance to the role of the military and the need for military preparedness in the face of the Crusader ambitions in the Islamic states of the region.

During the reign of the Ayyūbid Sultan aṣ-Ṣāliḥ a Mamluk regiment was formed by him and housed on the island of Roda (ar-Rawḍa) near al-Fusṭāṭ. This regiment, the Baḥrī, represented a structural expansion of the Ḥalqa, or guard, formed by the founder of the Ayyūbids, Ṣalāḥ ad-Dīn, but the close link it created between the ruler and the elite of the military started a process that had parallels in many other Islamic states, ending in the ultimate assumption of political power by this military elite. The Baḥrī and their Burjī Mamluk successors combined military and political leadership of Egypt, but, as many Mamluks regarded themselves as potential Sultans, the possibility for political instability was considerable and became manifest given any opportunity for the seizure of power.

The conquest of Egypt by the Ottomans in 1517/922 resulted in the establishment of their own troops in the country; the seven corps of the Ottoman garrison and the Mamluk beys coexisted and on occasion, collaborated, as factions formed within the garrison and among the Mamluks. The involvement of the Mamluks in the administration of the country permitted them to maintain their positions, and with the decline in Ottoman control of Egypt in the eighteenth/twelfth centuries the Mamluks made a concerted and successful bid to regain their political power.

Mamluk challenges against Ottoman control of Egypt eased the way for Napoleon's invasion of the country in 1798; Muhammad Ali, who seized power in 1805 during the chaos that followed the French withdrawal, decided that the ability of the Mamluks to present such a strong challenge to the government had to be ended. A large group of Mamluks were massacred in 1811 after being invited to a banquet in the Citadel by Muhammad Ali, and those who fled to the south were pursued during campaigns in Nubia in the next two years.

Impressed by what he had seen of the performance of European soldiers, and borrowing the example of the Ottoman Sultan, Muhammad Ali hired European instructors to train his army in modern techniques of warfare. Sulayman Pasha, Boyer, de Cerisy, and Besson from France instructed this "new model army," along with Muhammad Ali's son Ibrahim Pasha. The Viceroy intended to change the composition of the regular army corps through the use of Sudanese as soldiers. These Sudanese, captured when Nubia was conquered in 1820-21, had such appalling mortality rates, however, that Muhammad Ali decided in the early 1820s to introduce the conscription of Egyptians. The officer corps remained dominated by the Viceroy's own Albanian Mamluks and officers of Turco-Circassian origin.

Recruiting Egyptian soldiers proved difficult. In rural areas the loss of a son was critical for farmers who depended on their labor, and almost anything was tried to escape service. Neither force, inducement, nor threat produced willing recruits, but the recruits that were pressed into service were gradually shaped into the regular soldiery of an army of some 100,000 men. The officer corps benefited from several new schools of training opened in the mid-1820s, and throughout the army European methods dominated. Cavalry regiments were recruited from among the bedouin.

After the Treaty of London in 1840 the Ottoman Porte reduced the size of the Egyptian army to 18,000 men. Abbas I (r.1848-54) and Sa^{c}id (r.1854-63) sent Egyptian troops to fight with the Ottomans in the Crimea, and possibly the use of the Egyptian soldiers there contributed to the Sultan's decision to allow a slight expansion of the Egyptian army. Ismail secured from the Sultan a total waiver on the size of the army in 1873, but this waiver did not survive his deposition.

During Sa^{c}id's reign native Egyptians had been allowed to join the officer corps; once there, and under the Khedive Ismail and his successor, Tawfiq, these officers found their progress blocked by the favoritism still shown officers of Turco-Circassian background. The demands of the Egyptian officers, under the leadership of Colonel Arabi, resulted in near-coups in 1881 and 1882 and the dismissal of the War Minister, Rifqi Pasha, in February 1881.

Recruitment procedures for the army were changed in 1880, with the establishment of a lottery system and the removal of communal restrictions, which meant that Christians and Jews could serve in the army for the first time since the Muslim conquest of Egypt. In 1881 Colonel Arabi and the Egyptian officers secured from the Khedive, after considerable agitation, a promise that Egyptians and Turco-Circassians would receive equal promotion opportunites after the expiry of the conscripts' four-year service.

The Egyptian army was disbanded after the British invasion of Egypt in September 1882 and the defeat of the nationalist forces under Colonel Arabi. The army was replaced by a British-trained and -led force of 10,000 men, which saw service under British command in the Sudan. The soldiery were recruited by lottery but were allowed to buy their way out; however, forced enlistment continued to be used in some rural areas.

The Declaration of 1922, which granted Egypt limited independence from British control, maintained British de facto control of the army. The struggle by successive governments in the 1920s to reduce this British role in the Egyptian army was unsuccessful; the Army Crisis of 1927 demonstrated the British commitment to the maintenance of its military control in Egypt. It was not until the 1936 Anglo-Egyptian Treaty was concluded that Egypt finally gained autonomy over its own military forces. Among the most significant outcomes of this treaty was the decision by the government to open the Military Academy to a broader class of students. The government hoped by this to build up an Egyptian officer corps loyal to the nationalist movement, the Palace hoped for a broader base in the military: both proved a serious miscalculation. The first graduating classes after the more relaxed admissions criteria produced the Free Officers, who were to take power in Egypt in 1952.

During the Second World War the Egyptian army, like the majority of Egyptian civilians, was affected by the rise in nationalist sentiment as Britain reimposed its presence and control on the country. Large numbers of British troops were stationed in the major Egyptian cities, where their presence aroused resentment. The Egyptian army, angered over the forced imposition of a Wafd government by Britain, became a fertile ground for the more politicized younger officers. They used the war years to build up their support and to make contacts with other nationalists and the Islamic revivalist movement in Egypt. The 1948 fighting in Palestine, which revealed the higher command's lack of ability to lead or direct, and the army's unpreparedness in terms of materiel, was for these same younger officers a further radicalizing experience. The disappearance of money meant to buy arms, the failure of supplies to reach the front, the lack of clear government policy, all reflected badly, in these officers' eyes, on the country's civilian government. The formation of a Free Officer executive, composed of younger nationalist officers, grew directly from this experience. The shaping of the political goals of the Free Officers was subsequently directed by the deterioration of Egypt's domestic political life. The burning of Cairo in 1952, as well as government suspicions about the Free Officers, finally forced them to decide on an active intervention in Egypt's politics in July 1952.

With the Revolution of 1952 the role of the military in Egypt changed substantially. As was perhaps inevitable given that the Revolution was led by military officers, the top positions in the government tended to be filled by military men for many years thereafter. Following a purge of nearly 450 senior officers in the six months after the Revolution, the Free Officers moved to place their own men in the military command. Power in the government was ultimately balanced between Nasser, who was in charge of the civilian apparatus, and Amer, who commanded the army. As it was the main backing of his regime, Nasser was extremely attentive to the needs of the military, whose power and importance were also underlined by the longstanding confrontation with Israel and by the 1956 Suez War, when Egypt had to be defended against a combined Israeli, British, and French invasion. Tensions did develop between Nasser and Amer in the 1960s, in consequence of personal differences and Amer's own near-autonomy. The country's civilian government took political turns not always in accord with the attitudes of the military high command and development budgets had to compete with military budgets for scarce resources, but until the 1967

Arab-Israeli War this tension was not allowed to affect overly the civilian-military cooperation characteristic of Egypt in the post-Revolutionary period.

The devastating defeat suffered by Egypt in the 1967 war cast a long shadow over the military high command. General Amer committed suicide in September 1967, during a purge of senior army officers charged with plotting against the government. Despite this defeat the critical relationship between the military and the civilian government brought the army only a temporary eclipse in its central role. The new high command lacked the public profile of Amer but maintained key, if less political, positions in the hierarchy of the civilian government.

The rebuilding of military capability and morale, post-1967, had to go on simultaneously with the War of Attrition. This conflict with Israel saw Egypt clearly losing the war through lack of sophisticated weaponry capable of matching that used by Israel. Nasser was finally successful in getting the Russians to supply him with their latest SAM missiles, and Russian pilots participated in training their Egyptian counterparts and flying in some missions. The War of Attrition, which finally ended in the Summer of 1970, gave a new technological emphasis to military training.

Egypt's military is the largest in the Arab world, some 395,000 troops with massive potential reserves. President Sadat no less than Nasser was cautious in his handling of it. The dismissals of General Sadek in 1972 and General Shazli in 1973, both individuals with some potential political impact, were followed by the bringing into the government of Air Marshal Husni Mubarak as Vice-President. Mubarak's position in the administration, second only to that of Sadat, gave the military a strong voice within the civilian government, as did the promotion of General Kamal Hasan Ali to the post of Deputy Prime Minister. The Egyptian army was under the command of General Ahmad Badawi until his death in a 1981 helicopter crash that also claimed the lives of several senior Egyptian officers. He was succeeded by General Abu Ghazzali. The military is under the overall control of the President, who holds the office of Supreme Commander-in-Chief.

MILNER MISSION. Following the Rebellion of 1919 the Milner Mission was formed to examine the causes of the Rebellion and make recommendations. Under the chairmanship of Alfred, Lord Milner, Secretary of State for the Colonies, the six-man mission arrived in Egypt on 7 December 1919. There it faced a Wafd-organized boycott on formal contacts by many Egyptian nationalists, though a variety of informal meetings took place before the mission's departure in March. The Wafd leader Zaghlul finally met with the mission in London in the summer of 1920. Milner's recommendations at this time--independence for Egypt with certain areas reserved for Britain (troop stationing, minority rights, communications, the capitulations)--split the nationalists. Zaghlul and most nationalist sentiment in Egypt were against the proposals, but Adli and his supporters were prepared to accept them and negotiate further concessions in future.

The Milner Mission report was presented late in 1920, with its recommendations made public in February 1921. These included the termination of the British Protectorate and its replacement by a treaty between an independent Egypt and Britain, in which Britain would guarantee Egypt's defense and would, in exchange, be granted special status and rights, most prominent of which was the right to maintain an army and bases in Egypt. The British government would also have the authority to protect foreigners and minorities and their interests; there would be co-ordination between Egyptian and British foreign policy.

Following the publication of the report the moderate nationalist Adli Pasha formed a government in March 1922, preparatory to organizing a negotiating team to discuss the Milner Report that summer with the British government. Adli had to contend with the strong opposition of Zaghlul, who had returned from exile in April 1922 and who strictly opposed any compromise with the British in these negotiations. Adli Pasha and his delegation (which included no representatives from the Wafd) traveled to London in June; talks broke down over the issue of the presence of British troops in Egypt, though they were also gravely compromised by domestic opposition within Egypt to the Adli negotiations organized by Zaghlul and the Wafdists. Adli resigned at the end of 1921 and Zaghlul was returned to exile; further progress on ending the Protectorate was not achieved until the High Commissioner, Allenby, threatened to resign unless the British government took action. In February 1922, a year after the publication of the Milner Report, the British government issued a unilateral declaration of independence, terminating the Protectorate and affirming many of the principles of future British participation in Egypt contained in the Milner Report.

MINTASH (d. 1393/795). Briefly de facto ruler of Egypt as regent for the last Baḥrī Mamluk Sultan, Ḥājjī II, Mintash was in power during Ḥājjī's second reign (1389-90/791-92). Formerly an Amīr of Malatya, he was allied with Yilbughā Nāṣirī, the powerful governor of Aleppo. Yilbughā had led the defeat of Barqūq in 1388/790, which enabled the two Amīrs to reinstate the young Ḥājjī in power. Mintash soon turned against Yilbughā and his other allies, while in Cairo civil disorder reigned. Barqūq escaped from exile at Kerak, gathered his supporters, and met Mintash in battle at Gaza. Ḥājjī, whom Barqūq deposed, was unharmed and Mintash managed to flee. Barqūq resumed power in 1390/792, and finally captured Mintash and had him executed in 1393/795.

MIṢR. The Arabic name for Egypt and Cairo, Miṣr was originally the name of an unfortified town near the walls of Babylon, the Greco-Roman city conquered by the Muslim general ᶜAmr in 640/19. As the town founded by Egypt's Muslim conquerors, al-Fuṣṭāṭ, expanded, the two names became linked as Miṣr al-Fuṣṭāṭ. Some Arabic sources identify Miṣr with Amṣar, "camp" (a reference to the camp of the Arab armies), though the name Miṣr was applied to Egypt in pre-Islamic times by the Arabs.

MISR AL-FATAT (MIṢR AL-FATĀT) ("Young Egypt Society"). Founded in October 1933 by Ahmad Husayn, Misr al-Fatat was the first Egyptian political party to adopt a truly radical ideology and mass organization. The party slogan, "God, King, and Country," was combined with a political program of nationalism and national socialism, unity of the Nile Valley, and industrial and social development. Misr al-Fatat's extreme nationalism and militancy resembled aspects of the fascist ideology prevalent in Germany and Italy, just as its paramilitary group, the "Green Shirts," drew their inspiration from the fascist shirt organizations in Europe.

The appeal of the party lay in its readiness to defend more ardently than the political mainstream the nationalist demands of Egypt. In 1936 Misr al-Fatat demonstrated against the Anglo-Egyptian treaty negotiated by the Wafd government on the grounds that it gave insufficient protection to Egyptian interests. They continued extremely active throughout that year and came to a clash with the Blue Shirts, a group formed by the Wafd to counter Misr al-Fatat's appeal among young people. Both shirt organizations were proscribed in March 1938, when the level of their violence became unacceptable. Despite this, it appears Misr al-Fatat itself maintained some links with the Palace.

As the Ikhwan al-Muslimun gained power and supporters in the late 1930s, including members of Misr al-Fatat, the leadership brought more religious elements and themes into the party program and changed its name to the National Islamic Party. In 1948 the party underwent yet another transformation, becoming the Egyptian Socialist Party, hoping possibly to capitalize on the growing appeal of left-wing ideologies in the post-World War II era. But during this period it was somewhat overshadowed by the vastly larger membership and more visible leadership of the Ikhwan al-Muslimun.

Despite the seemingly inconsistent swings in name and ideology, the Misr al-Fatat party was always dominated by its strongly nationalist, antiforeign character and had a great deal of influence on some of the Free Officers.

The Party was accused of involvement in the burning of Cairo in January 1952, and its leader, Ahmad Husayn, was then imprisoned, though his trial adjourned without conviction at the time of the 1952 Revolution. Along with all other pre-Revolutionary political parties, the group was banned from further involvement in politics in January 1953, though there is evidence it maintained a loyal core of supporters until Husayn's rearrest in 1954.

Two earlier political formations took the name Young Egypt: a radical nationalist grouping in 1879, with which the Egyptian journalist and author Abdullah Nadim was associated, and a small pre-World War I faction party headed by Idris Raghib and modeled on the Young Turks. The former faded from existence in 1880, eclipsed by the more powerful Hizb al-Watani of Arabi, Sharif Pasha, and their political supporters, the latter joined the Nationalist Party of Farid. In both cases these earlier Young Egypt parties enjoyed only a very short existence independent of larger political groupings.

MIXED COURTS/TRIBUNALS. Established in 1875-76 after prolonged negotiations between Egypt and the capitulatory powers the mixed courts, with European and Egyptian judges, superseded the consular courts, in which Europeans accused of legal and criminal violations had previously been tried. The success of the negotiations to establish these courts came after the adoption by Egypt in 1873 of a new criminal and civil code, which was in turn based strongly on the French legal code; this contained what the negotiators felt were adequate guarantees of due process. With the advent of British control in Egypt, changes in the judiciary were inevitable. Even the national court system was affected; the number of European judges was increased following a report by a former judge of the mixed courts, Sir John Scott, in 1889. Despite agreements between Egypt and the capitulatory powers, criminal cases continued to be heard in the consular courts until 1917.

The mixed-court system was abolished under the Montreux Convention in 1937; the courts themselves were to be closed in 1949, and prior to that point all cases brought before the mixed court would be tried under Egyptian law.

MONASTICISM. Christianity had, early in its spread through Egypt, seen the development of hermeticism, the voluntary retreat of religious men and women into the desert. The monastic tradition in fact antedated Christianity in Egypt; there were Jewish monks, the Therapeutai, who lived in seclusion in the Nile Delta near Lake Mariotis, and also pagan recluses. The Christian anchorites were distinguished from these by the extremes of asceticism they pursued. Such individuals as Anthony (252-357) and Paul (235-341) led lives of total deprivation, cut off as much as possible from all human contact (although in the latter they were hampered by becoming objects of pilgrimage by devout Christians).

Monasticism as an organized movement developed under the direction of Pachomius in the fourth century, who gathered monks into religious communities under strict discipline and the direction of a spiritual head. These communities, located in both urban and rural settings, were in two forms: monasteries, where the monks lived together as a group, and lauras, cells isolated from the main monastery physically but under its jurisdiction. There was also a form of urban monasticism, remoboth, where the monks lived together in twos and threes and attended to each other's welfare. Monasticism played an important role in shaping the character of Egyptian Christianity, though many of the Christian monks did choose to live independent of monastic discipline. The unyielding religious fervor of some monks and monastic communities, and their determination to suppress by force what they regarded as heretical, on occasion led them to descend on cities and towns with the spirit of an avenging mob. Their rejection of all evidences of Egypt's pre-Christian past was bound to create problems in such places as Alexandria, which had long been a major center of Hellenism.

Aside from their theological role, the monasteries became in time a part of the pre-Islamic Egyptian economy, producing among other items linen and leather goods whose quality was highly prized. The exemption granted monks from military service became an abused privilege by the fourth century, with entire villages taking monastic vows to avoid conscription. The Emperor Valens (r. 364-78) sent troops to Egypt to revoke by force some of the privileges enjoyed by monks, but they were not successful despite some occasionally brutal attacks on the monasteries. The monks had become too important a social force among Egypt's Christians. By the time of the Muslim Conquest, the monasteries had also assumed a role in local administration, as tax-collectors and overseers of government policy in rural areas. The early Muslim rulers of Egypt left this status quo where appropriate until the ninth century/third century, when the decline in the number of monks through conversion of the population to Islam, and the increase in lay administrators--Muslim, Christian, and Jewish--made reliance on the monasteries unnecessary, and for some rulers, undesirable.

Coptic monasteries survived down to modern times as places of contemplation, learning, scholarship, and retreat, though in the twentieth century far fewer young men have been drawn into the monastic life. Theologically the Coptic Church maintains the superiority of the religious vocation over married life, and there are still individuals who elect to follow the Church's tradition of monasticism and high valuation of celibacy.

MONOPHYSITISM. The theological definition of Christ's nature accepted by the Coptic Church, Monophysitism denies or downplays Christ's human nature and upholds His one, divine nature. The condemnation of this view at the Council of Chalcedon in 451 led to the official break between the Coptic Church and the Orthodox Church of Byzantium. The murder of the newly appointed Orthodox Patriarch of Alexandria, Proterus, in 457 by a Monophysite mob led to the total breakdown of relations with Constantinople. The Emperor Zeno tried in 482 to resolve the dispute between the Monophysites and their opponents with the Henaticon, a compromise theological position, but his efforts failed.

MONTREUX CONVENTION. In May 1937 a conference was concluded at Montreux, Switzerland, by Egypt and the twelve European powers that had enjoyed capitulatory rights in Egypt. In return for an undertaking that Egypt would apply laws to foreigners that were in line with the principles of modern legislation and were not discriminatory, the capitulations (which had given consular courts criminal jurisdiction over their own citizens) were abolished. During the twelve years before their abolition in 1949 the mixed courts would adjucate disputes between Egyptian and foreign parties and handle criminal cases affecting foreigners, while the consular courts would be limited to handling matters relating to personal status. Only Egyptian law would prevail in the mixed courts, and Egypt obtained full rights of taxation over foreigners living in the country. The agreement was approved by the Egyptian parliament two months later. The Caisse de la Dette Publique, still hanging on in vestigial form, was wound up in 1940.

AL-MU'AYYAD SHAYKH (AL-MU'AYYAD SAYF AD-DĪN SHAYKH) (1412-21/815-24). Burjī Mamluk Sultan, al-Mu'ayyad Shaykh was a Mamluk of Barqūq. Shaykh was sent to Syria by Faraj, Barqūq's son and successor, to depose the Amīr Nawrūz; in an earlier revolt (1407/809) Nawrūz had gained control of much of Syria. Instead of deposing him Shaykh allied himself with Nawrūz and the two eventually defeated Faraj in 1412/815. The Caliph al-Musta^{c}īn acted as Sultan in the interregnum before Shaykh, having broken with Nawrūz, assumed power in his own name.

Al-Mu'ayyad Shaykh was a vigorous ruler as Burjī Mamluks went and was able, through the campaign of his son Ibrāhīm in 1419/822, to keep the Tīmūrid tribes of Central Asia in check after they had retreated to the borders of Mamluk territory following their withdrawal from Syria in 1405/808. In Egypt a widespread famine marred his reign. The Mamluks continued to be a fearsome, troublesome, and destabilizing force in the cities and towns; a short-lived attempt by the Sultan to place some restraints on them ended in defeat. Mu'ayyad Shaykh hoped to pass power to his son, Ibrāhīm, but the latter died while on campaign in the year before the Sultan's own death, following which another period of anarchy descended.

MUBARAK, ALI (1823-1893). Prominent government official during the reigns of Abbas I and Ismail, Ali Mubarak was also the author of a voluminous study of nineteenth-century Egypt. Mubarak was sent to France for his education by Muhammad Ali; he entered the service of Abbas and became director of the Military Academy. Mubarak also saw service with the Ottoman army during the Crimean War. His career advanced further under Ismail, who appointed him to many ministries during his tenure in office. Mubarak founded a teacher's training college, supervised many public-works projects, and assisted in the foundation of the Dar al-Kutub, the Egyptian National Library. His study of Egypt, the Khiṭāṭ (published between 1888 and 1889 during his tenure as Minister of Education) was written with the help of several assistants; its twenty volumes are a compilation of a wide variety of information about Egypt, drawing on his own experiences and the writings of Arabic and European authors.

MUBARAK, MUHAMMAD HUSNI (1928-). President of Egypt since October 1981, Mubarak formerly was Vice-President and a prominent military figure in the Sadat government. Air Marshal Mubarak had a distinguished record in the 1973 Arab-Israeli War, having led the first air strikes across the canal. Mubarak was made Vice-President in 1975 and held that post until the assassination of President Sadat on 6 October 1981. Mubarak's appointment to the vice-presidency was taken as a signal of the continuing close cooperation between the government and military in Egypt, and he had frequently deputized for President Sadat on important state occasions, giving evidence of the great trust placed in him by Sadat.

During the presidency of Gamal Abdal Nasser, Mubarak served as an instructor in the Air Force Academy until 1959, when he was sent on training missions to the Soviet Union. These missions culminated in a higher studies course there in 1964-65. Returning to Egypt, Mubarak held the post of Base Commander at a number of different Air Force installations. He was appointed Director-General of the Air Force Academy in 1967, a particularly important position following the devastation of the Air Force in the 1967 fighting. Mubarak maintained a tightly disciplined schedule for himself and his students to speed through the graduates needed for Egypt's decimated air command. In 1969, Nasser made Mubarak Chief of Staff of the Air Forces and Air Vice Marshal. Under President Sadat, Mubarak became Commander-in-Chief of the Air Force in 1972 and Air Marshal in 1974. Prior to the assassination, Mubarak was elected Secretary-General of the National Democratic Party, becoming Chairman of the party in January, 1982. One of Mubarak's first acts as president was to release many of the political and religious opponents and activists imprisoned during the preceding two months. He has made clear his commitment to the Camp David Process though negotiations have been stalled in consequence of recent Israeli actions in Lebanon. His government has promised certain domestic economic adjustments.

AL-MUDABBIR (ABU'L-ḤASAN AḤMAD) (d. 883 or 884/270 or 271). Financial administrator sent to Egypt in 861/247, during the reign of the ᶜAbbāsid Caliph al-Muntaṣir, al-Mudabbir completely reorganized the country's system of taxation, modifying the qabāla system introduced by al-Ma'mūn (r. 813-33/198-218). He reintroduced elements of the pre-Islamic tax system, establishing state monopolies on items like fodder and introducing measures for stricter control of, and greater revenue from, Egypt's agriculture. Al-Mudabbir remained in control of the country until the arrival of Aḥmad b. Ṭūlūn in 868/254, whereupon a struggle began between the two men for control of the country's administrative structure. Initially supported by Baghdad, al-Mudabbir gradually lost ground to Ibn Ṭūlūn; in 871/258 al-Mudabbir was transferred to a new post at Damascus, having suffered a brief imprisonment by Ibn Ṭūlūn. When Ibn Ṭūlūn invaded Syria in 878/265, he again arrested al-Mudabbir, who was returned to Egypt and died there in prison.

MUḤAMMAD (AL-MANṢŪR ṢALĀḤ AD-DĪN MUḤAMMAD (r. 1361-63/762-64). Baḥrī Mamluk Sultan, Muḥammad was the son of Sultan Ḥājjī I. Muḥammad was completely under the control of the court and reigned until the Amīr Yilbughā (who had murdered his predecessor, Hasan) replaced Muḥammad with Sha^cban II.

MUḤAMMAD (Baḥrī Mamluk Sultan, d. 1340/741) see AN-NĀṢIR MUḤAMMAD

MUḤAMMAD (AṢ-ṢĀLIḤ NĀṢIR AD-DĪN MUḤAMMAD) (r. 1421-22/824-25). Burjī Mamluk Sultan, Muḥammad's three-month reign was really an interregnum while the interested candidates for the Sultanate fought each other. He was only ten at the time he succeeded his father, Ṭaṭār. His co-regents (and, inevitably, enemies) were Barsbāy, an Atabeg, and Jānī (Gāhī) Bay, who was meant to be chief regent. Muḥammad died unexpectedly, and after a brief struggle Barsbāy emerged as his successor.

MUḤAMMAD BEY see ABU'DH-DHAHAB

MUḤAMMAD AL-KARALĀNJĪ see ṬŪLŪNID EGYPT

MUḤAMMAD b. SULAYMĀN (d. 917/314). ^cAbbāsid general who overthrew the Ṭūlūnid dynasty in Egypt in 905/292, Muḥammad b. Sulaymān reestablished direct ^cAbbāsid control of the country. Muḥammad had previously served in the Sūdān regiment in Ibn Ṭūlūn's army before defecting to Baghdad and was aided in his conquest of Egypt by his personal knowledge of the country. In this Egyptian campaign he moved against all the power bases that possessed the potential for an independent or rebellious movement: the Sūdān regiments, the remaining Ṭūlūnid forces, and the Ṭūlūnid general Badr (who had earlier defected to the ^cAbbāsid cause). After his victory Muḥammad reorganized the country's administrative structure and the Madhārā'īs were installed as financial administrators of Egypt on behalf of the ^cAbbāsid Caliphs.

MUḤAMMAD b. ṬUGHJ see THE IKHSHĪD

MUHAMMAD ALI PASHA (r. 1805-48). Ruler of Egypt as Viceroy/ Wālī for the Ottoman Sultan, Muhammad Ali founded a dynasty that ruled the country until the Revolution of 1952. Born in Macedonia in 1769, Muhammad Ali came to Egypt with his regiment to support the installation of the Ottoman governor Khusrau Pasha in 1802. His commander Tahir Pasha was assassinated after deposing Khusrau. Muhammad Ali succeeded him. His control of the large, loyal, and efficient Albanian regiment permitted Muhammad Ali quickly to gain influence in the chaotic situation following the departure of the French from Egypt in 1801. Muhammad Ali initially gave his support to the Mamluk challengers Uthman al-Bardisi and Ibrahim Bey. He captured the Citadel and in 1803 advanced toward the coast, where he defeated and captured Khusrau. Late in 1803 al-Bardisi took power in Cairo after a new Ottoman governor was assassinated on his orders. Muhammad Ali then turned against al-Bardisi, demanding heavy taxes to meet the expense of the Albanian regiment. He used popular sentiment to unseat al-Bardisi in 1804 and installed Khurshid Pasha, governor of Alexandria.

Muhammad Ali was on a successful campaign in Nubia while the Mamluks and Khurshid Pasha were fighting for control in Cairo. Khurshid finally gained ascendancy, but he was so unpopular with the Cairenes that they deputed Umar Makram and a number of other citizens to approach Muhammad Ali and request him to take power. He returned to Cairo and brought order to the city. He gained the recognition of the Porte from an envoy of the Sultan then in Cairo, and enjoyed popular support, if only because he was perceived as being able to bring peace to the capital and countryside after several years of complete anarchy. His strength in Egypt led to the failure of a British bid to restore the Mamluks to power in 1807. In March 1811 Muhammad Ali himself removed the Mamluk threat to him by arranging a large-scale massacre of the Mamluks who had proved so problematic to the stability of past governments. He invited them to the Citadel to celebrate the investiture of his son Tusun, locked the gates, and had his own Mamluks slaughter a reputed 470 of their number. Though brutal, this act broke the power of the Mamluks in Egypt. The survivors of the massacre fled to the south of the country to join Mamluks already there. Many of these Mamluks later died during the Nubian campaign of Muhammad Ali's son Ibrahim Pasha.

Muhammad Ali's reign revolutionized Egypt both externally and internally. His military campaigns in Arabia, Nubia, Syria, and Greece pushed Egyptian power to the Ottoman heartlands and nearly brought the Ottoman Empire to an end before the European powers moved against him. Within Egypt he introduced a number of educational and administrative reforms that, if not always successful, set the country irrevocably on the path of modernization.

Muhammad Ali's military conquests were directed by his sons Tusun, Ismail, and Ibrahim, though the latter quickly overtook his brothers and became his father's leading commander. Ibrahim finished Tusun's campaign in Arabia, where the Viceroy had been requested to intervene by the Ottoman Porte. The Al Saud with their Wahhabi forces were defeated at their capital, al-Diriyya, in 1818. Campaigns in Nubia (1820-21), Crete (1822), and Morea (1824) followed, but whatever ambitions Muhammad Ali may have had in the Mediterranean at that time were terminated by the crushing defeat of his navy at the Battle of Navarino in October 1827 at the hands of a combined European force.

Muhammad Ali then turned his attentions to Syria, traditionally an area in which Egypt held, or tried to hold, power. Late in 1831 Ibrahim began his campaign and by 1832 had secured the region and launched attacks against the Ottomans in Anatolian territory. In 1833, with his son only 150 miles from the Ottoman capital, Muhammad Ali was ceded a large territory in Greater Syria by the Sultan under the Convention of Kutahiya. Ibrahim governed Syria on his father's behalf, while Muhammad Ali's territorial expansion continued. There were campaigns in Arabia and Yemen was attacked in 1839; at the same time Ibrahim inflicted a major defeat on the Ottomans at the Battle of

Nizib in Anatolia. Shortly after, the Ottoman fleet surrendered to Egypt. In the face of the almost certain collapse of the Ottoman Empire, the European powers intervened. Ibrahim, whose control of Syria was under increasing challenge from local rebels, was compelled to withdraw from Syria in late 1840-41 after an allied naval blockade had been imposed and Acre seized. By the Treaty of London (1840), Muhammad Ali's territories were restricted, with Crete and Syria removed from his control. However, in 1841 the Ottoman Sultan formally added Sudan to his territories and made the governorship of Egypt hereditary in his family. It should be emphasized that the restrictions imposed on Muhammad Ali at this point in his career were the result of European action and not the capacities of the Ottoman Porte.

The numerous reforms introduced under Muhammad Ali touched every aspect of Egyptian life. Education was improved, both by sending qualified students abroad and by raising indigenous standards with the import of European instructors and techniques and the founding of training institutes in several disciplines. A government printing press, established in 1821, helped keep the country's administration in touch with the Viceroy's decisions through the official Gazette. A modern medical school, as well as modern techniques for the training and equipment of the army, were started, and Egyptians were recruited to the regular army for the first time. An institute of translation made available to the educated public the works of a variety of European authors. A canal was dug in 1819-20 to shorten the travel time between Alexandria and Cairo, and the Viceroy supported research into the improvement of agricultural techniques. His interest in developing Egypt's cash-crop economy got an unexpected boost when, in 1820, Louis Alex Jumel developed a long-staple cotton plant that was to transform Egypt's agricultural exports. Less successful were Muhammad Ali's industrialization projects to provide basic stores and equipment for his army. His ambitions were handicapped by the lack of indigenous trained manpower and technical expertise, but they also suffered a collapse in demand following the reduction in the size of the Egyptian army after the agreements of 1841. Administratively Egypt was reorganized; the structure of the country's bureaucracy was centralized, and by 1840 a pyramidic structure was established, which was answerable to the central government. The Ottoman system of tax-farming, the iltizām, was abolished in rural areas and with it the power of many traditional elites was diminished.

Muhammad Ali's successors (his son Ibrahim having predeceased him) did not fully share the comprehensive vision of Egypt's future and power held by him, with the exception of his grandson Ismail. Unfortunately Ismail's programs for modernization and economic development were fiscally ill advised and so overambitious that Egypt ended in receivership to her creditors at the end of his reign. With the advent of British control late in 1882 the rulers of the Muhammad Ali dynasty were only partly masters in their own country.

The titles used by the rulers of the Muhammad Ali dynasty changed; Muhammad Ali was the Viceroy, technically the governor of Egypt on behalf of the Ottoman Sultan, but in reality virtually an independent ruler. His grandson Ismail was granted the princely title "Khedive" in 1867 after negotiations and the presenting of a large payment to the treasuries of the Ottoman Sultan. Upon the establishment of the British Protectorate in 1914 the new ruler, Husayn Kamil, was given the title "Sultan" to reflect the break between Egypt and the Ottoman Sultanate. Following the Declaration of 1922, by which Britain granted Egypt a limited independence, Fuad took the title of "King."

Muhammad Ali Dynasty:

1805	Muhammad Ali (Viceroy)
1848	Ibrahim Pasha
1848	Abbas I
1854	Sa^{c}id
1863	Ismail (Khedive, 1867)
1879	Tawfiq
1892	Abbas II Hilmi
1914	Husayn Kamil (Sultan)

1917	Fuad I (King, 1922)
1936	Faruq
1952-53	Ahmad Fuad II

MUḤAMMAD PASHA (Viceroy) see MEHMED PASHA

MUHIADDIN, KHALID (1923-). One of the original Free Officers and member of the Revolutionary Command Council, Muhiaddin broke early with Nasser over the struggle with Naguib for control of the government. In February 1954 he led a Cavalry Officers' rebellion demanding Naguib's reinstatement after the latter had been demoted by Nasser. He was temporarily successful in having Naguib reinstated as President, and then Premier. But as Nasser began to win the power struggle, Muhiaddin was sent on an enforced holiday abroad, in April 1954.

In 1956, following the easing of relations between Egypt and the USSR, Muhiaddin was allowed to return from Europe and became editor of the journal, Al-Missa; under him, the journal became a forum for socialist and radical political and economic viewpoints. This brief liberalization in political attitudes by the regime did not long survive the establishment of the United Arab Republic and the Iraqi Revolution. Muhiaddin was relieved of his post in 1959 during a government crackdown on the Left.

Muhiaddin rejoined the government in 1964 as head of the Press Section of the Arab Socialist Union and in 1965 became Chairman of the Press Council as well as of the mass-circulation newspaper Akhbar al-Yawm, but he was out of office by 1966. In 1968 he was elected to the ASU Central Committee.

Muhiaddin has served in the Egyptian Parliament, and in the 1976 elections led the "left" platform of the ASU. Following the political liberalizations of June 1977 he formed the National Progressive Unionist Party, which became the most vocal opponent of the Sadat government. The party subsequently suffered from the restrictions on political activity introduced in 1978, though Muhiaddin remains active in his opposition to the Camp David Accords and to the reintroduction of capitalism in Egypt via the Open Door Policy. He is still an influential voice among the left-wing politicians in Egypt.

MUHIADDIN, ZAQARIA (1918-). A cousin of Khalid Muhiaddin, Zaqaria was also a Free Officer and member of the Revolutionary Command Council, though his political views were more conservative than Khalid's. Zaqaria became involved with Nasser from the beginning of their military careers. After the revolution, he oversaw the establishment and administration of the country's security services and held a number of posts, including Minister of the Interior (1953-62), member of the National Union Executive (1957-58), Vice-President (1961), and Vice-President and Deputy Prime Minister (1964-65). He was appointed Prime Minister and Minister of the Interior in September 1965.

Muhiaddin's tenure in this last office came to an end the following year over policy disagreements in connection with the economic retrenchments necessary in view of Egypt's foreign-exchange shortages. Despite his split with the government on this issue he remained a member of the National Defense Committee from 1962-69 and Vice-President from 1966-68.

Following the Arab-Israeli War in 1967 Muhiaddin's position with the government was restored: he was appointed Vice-President and successor to Nasser when the latter made his decision (subsequently revoked) to resign in June 1967. Muhiaddin was named to serve as Deputy Premier in Nasser's 1967-68 cabinet, but he retired from public life in March 1968.

AL-MU^{c}IZZ (r. 953-75/341-65). Fourth Fāṭimid Caliph and the first to rule in Egypt, al-Mu^{c}izz spent only two years in Egypt before his death. Most of the initial work in the establishment of the Fāṭimid state there was effected by his trusted general Jawhar aṣ-Ṣiqillī, whose administration was organized with the assistance of the equally capable Ya^{c}qūb b. Killis. At the time of his departure for Egypt, al-Mu^{c}izz distributed the Fāṭimid's North African and Sicilian territories to local allies.

Before undertaking the conquest of Egypt al-Mu^{c}izz worked to consolidate the Fāṭimids' position in North Africa and carefully cultivated and expanded the tribal alliances developed by the dynasty there. The Fāṭimid military advance was preceded by the activity of their missionaries, who could observe and report on a country suffering a shortage of food and of effective leadership. Doubtless from these missionaries, and also from friends at the Ikshīdid court, al-Mu^{c}izz was able to keep close watch on the situation in Egypt to appraise when the right time had come for the Fāṭimid advance there. During his brief reign in Egypt, military activity continued in Syria, though the Fāṭimid position in Syria was not established until several years later.

MUKHTAR PASHA, GHAZI. Turkish Commissioner for Egypt, Mukhtar Pasha was appointed by the Ottoman Sultan Abdal Hamid II in 1885. Mukhtar Pasha negotiated with Sir Henry Drummond Wolfe over the future British position in Egypt and the definition of Turkey's future role in the country. Following these negotiations Mukhtar went to Egypt as representative of the Ottoman Sultan. The presence of a resident Turkish Commissioner in Egypt created certain legal and diplomatic ambiguities for the British Consul-General, but in practice Lord Cromer never let it affect him greatly. Mukhtar Pasha participated in the activities of the leading pan-Ottoman, pan-Islamic nationalist groupings. He was suspected by Cromer of encouraging the independence of the young Khedive, Abbas II. Mukhtar later became involved in the foundation of the Nationalist Party in 1907.

MULTAZIM see ILTIẒĀM

MUQABALA LAW OF 1871. Passed during the Khedive Ismail's reign, the Muqabala Law was designed to ease some of the financial difficulties caused by revenue shortages faced by the government. The law offered Egyptian taxpayers an opportunity to gain a perpetual 50-percent reduction in their land-tax bills in future if they paid immediately into the Egyptian Treasury a sum equivalent to six years' tax. A similar reduction could be gained if this sum was paid in twelve annual installments. Like many of Ismail's fiscal measures this was ill advised and damaging in its consequences, as expenditures rose to meet the new revenue levels and the government was faced with the prospect of much lower revenues at the end of the six-year period. The Khedive's attempts to get the law repealed subsequently were opposed by the Assembly. The Muqabala was finally abolished in October 1879 by Egypt's European financial controllers, largely because of the ease with which falsified documents showing payment of the lump-sum tax were available, and used, to the great detriment to the country's annual tax revenues.

MURĀD BEY (d. 1801/1216). With Ibrāhīm Bey, Murād Bey ruled Egypt from the death of their master, Abū'dh-Dhahab, in 1775/1189. Ibrāhīm took the title of "Shaykh al-Balad," which conferred nominal superiority on him within the Duumvir, but Murād's character more than balanced this. Murād and Ibrāhīm's control of Egypt depended on their ability to keep the other Mamluk factions in line; Murād wished to assassinate Ismā^{c}īl Bey, a Mamluk of ^{c}Alī Bey and the strongest of their potential challengers. His plans were discovered, and the other Mamluk factions, including the ^{c}Alawīyya (of the late ^{c}Alī Bey) forced the Duumvir to leave Cairo in 1777/1189. They managed to restore themselves the next year, and drove the ^{c}Alawīyya and Ismā^{c}īl from Cairo; the ^{c}Alawīyya retreated to Upper Egypt.

Murād and Ibrāhīm proved unable to defeat the ^{c}Alawīyya in a series of campaigns, and in 1781/1195 Murād ceded to them a large area in Upper Egypt. He then turned against Ibrāhīm and expelled him from his office and from Cairo in 1784/1198, though the two were reconciled and jointly ruling again the next year. Murād led the unsuccessful defense of Egypt against the Ottoman army in 1786/1200 and with Ibrāhīm was in exile during the rule of Ismā^{c}īl. The Duumvir regained power in 1791/1205 following Ismā^{c}īl's death.

Murād was twice defeated by the French during their invasion of Egypt in 1798/1213 and was forced to retreat while Ibrāhīm fled to Syria. However, he eventually joined forces with the French when it became obvious the Ottomans were determined to re-exert control. He became governor of Upper Egypt in the

Spring of 1800 and defeated the Ottoman forces under Dervish (Ar., Darwīsh) Pasha operating in the region. Murād died one year later during a widespread outbreak of plague.

MŪSĀ PASHA (r. 1630-31/1040). Ottoman governor of Egypt, Musa Pasha was the first governor to be effectively thrown out of office by a coup d'etat of the Mamluk beys with Ottoman support, and as such his term in office can be seen as the start of the political as well as the military ascendancy of the beylicate. One of Mūsā's predecessors, Muṣṭafā Pasha had been retained in office an additional three years through the agitation of the Mamluks, who refused to accept the new governor, ᶜAlī Pasha, when he was sent in 1623/1032. Mūsā alienated the Mamluks through his mistreatment of Qayṭas Bey, who had been granted a military appointment, then had had it revoked by the governor, and finally had been killed on the governor's orders. Mūsā refused to prosecute the assassins of Qayṭas, whereupon the Mamluk beys exercised their (acquired) privilege of nominating one of their number as Qāᶜim maqām, or acting Viceroy, and petitioning the Sultan for a replacement for Mūsā Pasha. This action was to alter permanently the power balance between the governor and the other elements (the garrison and the beys) in Egypt, effectively establishing the precedence of the latter two when they acted in tandem against the former.

MUṢĀDARA. An irregular tax applied particularly in Burjī Mamluk times, the Muṣādara affected every form and type of property. It was not set at any fixed level but rather on what the Sultan thought he could exact. The amount and arbitrariness of the tax were a fair measure of the degree of financial trouble it was meant to remedy, or in some cases, the offensiveness of the person it was meant to penalize.

MUSLIM BRETHREN see IKHWAN AL-MUSLIMUN

AL-MUSTAᶜĪN (AL-ᶜĀDIL AL-MUSTAᶜĪN) (r. 1412/815). The only member of the ᶜAbbāsid Caliphate in Egypt to hold power as Sultan (although a successor, al-Qā'im, tried unsuccessfully in 1455/859), al-Musta^{c}īn was selected in 1412/815 as a figurehead Sultan by the Mamluk factions contending for power. His appointment, favored by the strongest candidate, Mu'ayyad Shaykh, came to an end when the latter emerged as victor, whereupon al-Musta^{c}īn was stripped of both title and Caliphal role. Though he had been promised when he took power that he could resume his Caliphal office when a candidate among the Mamluks emerged, al-Musta^{c}īn was instead imprisoned in Alexandria by Mu'ayyad Shaykh. A successor, al-Mu^{c}tadid II was appointed Caliph in 1414/816.

AL-MUSTA^{C}LĪ (r. 1094-1101/487-95). Youngest son and successor to the Fāṭimid Caliph al-Mustanṣir, al-Musta^{c}lī was placed in power by the powerful vizier al-Afḍal over his three elder brothers. The partisans of al-Musta^{c}lī's eldest brother, Nizār, were deeply unhappy with this succession; under the leadership of the Persian missionary, Ḥasan b. aṣ-Ṣabbāḥ, who had supported Nizār's candidacy, these partisans formed themselves into a breakaway sect, the Nīzārī, that gained fame as the Assassins. This split also affected the unity of the Dā^{c}ī, some of whom supported Nizār and rejected al-Musta^{c}lī, weakening the latter's position.

Al-Musta^{c}lī's reign coincided with the arrival of the Crusaders in Syria. The Crusaders and Fāṭimids met and negotiated at Antioch in 1098/491, the same year that al-Afḍal took Jerusalem from the Saljūq Turks. Jerusalem was lost the next year to the Crusaders, and al-Afḍal was defeated by them at Ascalon. The Caliph al-Musta^{c}lī, who was twenty at the time of his accession, was largely confined to his palace by al-Afḍal. Al-Musta^{c}lī's premature death is blamed on the Assassins, whose activities in Egypt were to increase during the reign of his successor, al-Āmir.

AL-MUSTANṢIR (r. 1036-94/427-87). Longest-reigning Fāṭimid Caliph, al-Mustanṣir was the son of aẓ-Ẓāhir. Al-Mustanṣir's reign, faced by grave internal and external problems (largely outside his control), marked the beginning of a period of decline lasting nearly a century.

Al-Mustanṣir was only seven when he came to power, and he was under the direction of various figures in the court, beginning with his mother and her former owner (she had been a slave before her marriage to al-Mustanṣir's father). The latter, at-Tustarī, displaced the vizier al-Jajarā'ī in 1045/436 and was murdered two years later. A period of instability followed until the emergence of the vizier al-Yazūrī in 1050/442. Yazūrī held power for eight years and was able to bring some measure of order to the country and administration, although he proved unable to restrain the extravagances of the court. Between his death and the vizierate of Badr al-Jamālī, there was a continual changeover of viziers.

In the period prior to 1050/442 Fāṭimid control over its provinces greatly weakened. There were great difficulties in Syria in 1037/429, and in 1041/433 the Fāṭimids' allies in North Africa broke with them. The Fāṭimids profited from the decision of the Ṣulayḥids in the Yemen to ally themselves with Cairo and recognize Fāṭimid supremacy; in 1057-59/448-51 Mosul and Baghdad were very briefly added to Fāṭimid control by the actions of a rebel Būyid general, al-Basāsīrī.

It was the situation within Egypt that brought the greatest problems for al-Mustanṣir and his court. In 1054/442 the shortage of food in Egypt was so acute that the Byzantine Emperor had to be approached for emergency supplies. Another serious famine struck the following year, and a disastrous seven-year famine began in 1065/457. Accounts of conditions in Egypt during this time describe a level of misery that reduced people to cannibalism. These famines were partly due to successive failures of the Nile and also to the almost utter neglect of agriculture in the preceding decades, with canals and vital irrigation works falling into disrepair.

By 1072/464 Egypt was in complete civil and military chaos. The army regiments, which had been fighting for supremacy among themselves since 1062/454, contributed greatly to the level of anarchy in Cairo; one army leader, the Turkish commander Nāṣir al-Dawlā, virtually toppled the government, burning and plundering the city, including the Treasury. It was at this critical juncture, it is said, that the Harīm, or female household of the Caliph, sent an appeal to Badr al-Jamālī, the Fāṭimid governor and commander in Syria, to return to Egypt and restore order. Badr entered Cairo in 1074/466 and with a great deal of force put down the army rebellions, organized relief measures, and suppressed the rebel leaders.

Despite a campaign by Badr in 1078/471 and two further campaigns between 1085/478 and 1090/482 Syria was largely lost to the Saljūqs, though Egypt, through his efforts in that country, was saved from the irrevocable breakdown of its government and military forces. Nāṣir-i-Khusraw, the Persian traveler, visited Egypt during al-Mustanṣir's reign and provided one of the few eye-witness accounts of the Fāṭimid Caliphate in public ceremonial.

AL-MUSTANṢIR (d. 1261/659). First of the ᶜAbbāsid Caliphs in Egypt, al-Mustanṣir was installed in office by the Mamluk Sultan Baybars in 1261/659. Baybars had reestablished the ᶜAbbāsid Caliphate in Cairo following the sacking of Baghdad in 1258/656 by the Mongols. A distant relation of al-Mustaᶜṣim, the last ᶜAbbāsid Caliph in Baghdad, managed to escape the general destruction of the city and of his family.

This relation took the title al-Mustanṣir billāh Abu'l-Qāsim Aḥmad in 1261/659. The Sultan Baybars sent letters to all Muslim capitals announcing that Egypt was the new home of the Caliph of Islam. Al-Mustanṣir wished to retake Baghdad, an enterprise that did not have the fullest support of Baybars, who had no desire to create a rival center of power. Nonetheless he equipped al-Mustanṣir with a small, inadequate army to defend him on his journey to Baghdad, but the Caliph died shortly after the beginning of his march.

AL-MUᶜTAṢIM (d. 842/227). A governor of Egypt during the reign of his brother, the ᶜAbbāsid Caliph al-Ma'mūn (r. 813-33/198-218), al-Muᶜtaṣim took his post in 829/214 after several years of revolts in Egypt over extremely high taxes. His failure to resolve the population's discontent with these taxes brought new disturbances against the ^c^Abbāsids, peaking in 831/216 and forcing his brother to intervene militarily to restore order. Al-Ma'mūn thereupon reformed the taxation system, and by the time of al-Mu^c^taṣim's succession to the Caliphate in 833/218 the situation in Egypt had been pacified.

-N-

NADIM, ABDALLAH (1845-1896). Egyptian nationalist writer, Nadim was a member of several early Islamic benevolent groupings and political associations before becoming involved with the nationalist movement of Colonel Arabi in 1879-82. He was forced to go into hiding during the British occupation of the country, where he worked to keep alive the memory of the Arabi Revolt. Discovered and exiled in 1891, Nadim was permitted to return to Egypt in 1892 under a pardon granted by the new Khedive, Abbas, who was anxious to secure his links with the nationalists against the British. In August 1892 Nadim founded Al-Ustadh, a satirical journal that frequently attacked Lord Cromer, the British Consul-General who was deeply unpopular with the nationalists. Cromer responded to these attacks by demanding Nadim's re-exile; this request was refused by Abbas, though official support for the publication was dropped and its printing stopped in June 1893. Nadim was among the earliest advisers of the young nationalist leader Mustafa Kamil, as well as of other young members of the nationalist movement for whom he acted as a bridge between the Arabi period and the reemergence of the nationalist movement in the 1890s. He encouraged Kamil to adopt a conciliatory attitude toward the Palace, thus avoiding Arabi's mistake of alienating the Khedive and dividing him from the nationalist movement from the Palace. He was a strong advocate of an Islam-based political movement, with an emphasis on reform and the securing of personal and political liberty.

NAGUIB (NAJIB), GENERAL MUHAMMAD (1901-). Prime Minister of Egypt from September 1952 and President from the declaration of the Republic in June 1953, General Naguib was ousted from both posts by Nasser and the Revolutionary Command Council in February 1954. He was reinstated in both offices after a near-coup by Khalid Muhiaddin but was once more dismissed from the Prime Ministership in April 1954. He lost the presidency following his final ouster by Nasser in November 1954.

Born in the Sudan, Naguib graduated from the Military Academy in 1921. He steadily advanced through the officer ranks, serving in the General Staff during the Second World War. Naguib was one of the few senior officers to distinguish himself in the 1948 fighting in Palestine, where he served as Brigadier and Second-in-Command of the Egyptian troops and was twice wounded in the fighting. Because of his role in Palestine he had a certain public popularity and was respected by the younger officers, including the Free Officers. Naguib was promoted to the rank of General in 1950. The timing of the approach made to Naguib by the Free Officers is not agreed upon by the participants, but Naguib enjoyed their support in his successful bid for the presidency of the Officers' Club. Though Faruq tried to delay the elections to help his own candidate, Naguib won easily when the voting was finally held in late December 1951.

At the time of the Revolution of 23 July 1952 Naguib was presented as leader of the Free Officers. As the only member of the Free Officer Executive known nationally, Naguib naturally dominated the regime's initial public profile. Though Naguib was doubtless in sympathy with the Free Officers, he seems from the outset to have been more conservative in approach and policy. In July 1952 Naguib was made Commander-in-Chief of the armed forces, and following the resignation of the Ali Mahir government in September 1952 he became Prime Minister and Minister of War. There were reports of disagreements between Naguib and the Revolutionary Command Council early in 1953, as Egypt was being forced into austerity measures to cope with its foreign-exchange and balance-of-payments difficulties. These disagreements were sufficiently resolved for Naguib to be declared President and Prime Minister in June 1953, when Egypt was made a Republic. However, he lost his post as Commander-in-Chief of the armed forces to Abdel Hakim Amer at that time. In fact, from June 1953 onward Naguib's position in the RCC hierarchy was being slowly but inexorably challenged by Nasser and the Free Officers backing him, who had taken most of the major ministerial portfolios in Naguib's government.

Naguib's popular and paternalistic public image won him wide support in Egypt, and, more importantly, his half-Sudanese background helped ease relations between Egypt and its southern neighbor. An agreement between Egypt and the British over the political future of the Sudan was concluded early in 1953, with Naguib enjoying long and fruitful negotiations with the Sudan's political leaders throughout 1953, though he was reluctant to surrender Egypt's claims there. Naguib also enjoyed support among the Ikhwan al-Muslimun, the last organized religious-cum-political grouping in Egypt following the disbanding of the pre-Revolutionary political parties in January 1953. The decision of the RCC to ban the Ikhwan in January 1954, following the group's involvement in antiregime street demonstrations, led factions within the Ikhwan to appeal to Naguib for support. At the same time bitter disputes were occurring within the RCC over a return to free political life, which Naguib advocated. On 25 February 1954 the RCC announced the resignation of Naguib from the presidency, Prime Ministership, and chairmanship of the RCC. A near-coup by Free Officer Khalid Muhiaddin resulted in Naguib's full reinstatement by March 1953, when he announced there would be complete political liberalization in Egypt, elections, and the lifting of censorship. Naguib lost his post of Prime Minister and Chairman of the RCC the next month, and the RCC announced delays in the scheduling of the promised elections. He was replaced by Nasser as head of the Liberation Rally in May, though the latter organization had always been more Nasser's power base than his own. Nasser managed Naguib's March-April unseating through the organization of large demonstrations by Liberation Rally members, trade unionists, etc., in support of the RCC. Once Nasser assumed the Prime

Ministership in April 1954, he rapidly exerted his control of the country's political life.

Naguib was ousted as President of Egypt in November 1954, following an assassination attempt on Nasser in the preceding month, an attempt in which Naguib was alleged to have been involved. The would-be assassin was a member of the Ikhwan al-Muslimun, and connections were drawn between the group and Naguib as the member of the RCC to whom it had given their support. Naguib was placed under house arrest, which was eased in 1961 and officially terminated in 1974, though he has taken no public role at any time since his deposition.

NAHHAS PASHA, MUSTAFA AL- (1879-1965). One of the founders of the Wafd Party, Mustafa al-Nahhas was elected to head the party following the death of Zaghlul in August 1927. Nahhas was originally a member of the Nationalist Party, and was in vited to join the delegation (wafd) formed by Zaghlul in 1918 to press Britain for Egyptian independence and a voice at the Versailles Peace Conference. The Wafd Party formed after this and Nahhas became active in its Central Committee operations; Nahhas left the Nationalists to join forces with Zaghlul and the new party. He shared Zaghlul's second exile in 1921-23.

After his election as president of the Wafd, Nahhas formed a government in March 1928, but it fell three months later in the face of difficult relations with the Palace and the British, as well as after the publication in an Egyptian newspaper of documents alleging financial misdealings between members of the Wafd leadership and the royal family. Nahhas then led his party to victory in the elections of December 1929. Nahhas' 1930 ministry originally enjoyed the support of the British, who wanted to renegotiate their relationship with Egypt and felt that they would have more success with the Wafd than with Nahhas' predecessor, Mahmud, in gaining the support of popular opinion for any new treaty. The government he formed lasted six months, until the collapse of his negotiations with the British in April-May 1930.

Normal parliamentary life in Egypt was suspended from June 1930 until the restoration of the 1923 constitution in December 1935. During this time, Nahhas worked with other Egyptian political leaders to oppose the pro-Palace governments. The parties formed a united front, and finally prevailed upon Nasim Pasha to restore the constitution. Elections in May 1936 again returned the Wafd and Nahhas to power. Successful negotiations with the British led to the signing of a new Anglo-Egyptian Treaty in August 1936 and the normalization of Egypt's international status as a sovereign state in the following year. Egypt's internal situation, however, was deteriorating, with the rise in civil violence and increased activism by paramilitary groups and radical political parties, the latter opposed to the government's policies and (in the case of Misr al-Fatat) to the Anglo-Egyptian Treaty. Nahhas did not enjoy good relations with the new King, Faruq; following an assassination attempt on Nahhas in November 1937 the King dismissed his government that December.

In the critical period that followed Nahhas proved unable to contain the factionalism growing within the Wafd leadership. A number of Wafd leaders were unhappy with Nahhas' presidency and joined either the other political parties or formed factional groupings. The Saadist (Sa^{c}dist) Party was constituted shortly after the dismissal of the Wafd government in January 1938; it participated in several governments thereafter down to the 1952 Revolution. Within the Wafd itself Nahhas' (accurate) feeling that his party had been on every occasion wrongfully deprived of power did not translate itself into a particularly vigorous leadership. In the period between the fall of his government and the formation of a wartime ministry in 1942 Nahhas saw the Wafd lose power and support at the popular level to the newer and more active parties, especially the Ikhwan al-Muslimun but also Misr al-Fatat.

Nahhas formed his next government in February 1942, after the British had forced King Faruq to accept a Wafd government by presenting him with the alternative of abdication. The Wafd and Nahhas damaged their position politically by accepting to form a government under such circumstances, and their behavior while in office was disappointing. Political opponents were detained as Axis sympathizers; the government was unable fully to provide medical and welfare services during a devastating outbreak of malaria in rural areas. More damaging, accusations of corruption were published by the dismissed Wafd leader Makram Ubayd, accusations that echoed the charges that brought down Nahhas' government in the 1920s. His government kept Egypt calm in the face of an extremely difficult military situation but at some cost to the country's political life and the Wafd's reputation.

Nahhas was a major force behind the formation of the Arab League, through his leadership at the meeting of Arab states in Alexandria in October 1944, which produced the Alexandria Protocol, the Arab League's initial charter. Though his participation in these negotiations was also motivated by Nahhas' unwillingness to let the Iraqi Prime Minister Nuri al-Sa^{c}id gain leadership of the pan-Arab movement, his participation and support were active and enthusiastic. Shortly after the Alexandria Protocol was issued Faruq dismissed Nahhas.

Nahhas did not form another government until January 1950, when the Wafd was once more returned in new, relatively free, elections. The government lifted press censorship and ended martial law, imposed during the Palestine fighting and continued by its predecessors, and took a strongly nationalist line with regard to the presence of British troops in Egypt. The aging Nahhas, increasingly assisted by the Secretary-General of the Wafd, Fuad Siragaddin, introduced some extremely moderate socioeconomic reforms. He made approaches to the British in March 1951 for new treaty negotiations. However, British troop levels in Egypt and uncertainty over British intentions in the Sudan kept relations between the Wafd government and the British uneasy. Nahhas finally acted unilaterally in October 1951 and announced the suspension of the 1936 Anglo-Egyptian Treaty and the sovereignty of King Faruq over both Egypt and the Sudan.

The government later announced the start of a campaign, aided by paramilitary groups, to drive the British from the Canal Zone. During this last ministry of Nahhas, an increasing number of charges of corruption were leveled at the government.

The violence between the paramilitary groups and the Egyptian police on the one side and the British on the other was to have repercussions in Egypt domestically. A British attack on the Ismailiyya police station on 25 January 1952 (whose defenders were apparently under government instructions to hold their positions) resulted in a great loss of life among the police; the next day, in a move that caught the government unprepared and unaware, an anti-British mob descended on the European quarters of Cairo and burned them. The fires of Black Saturday brought down the Nahhas government.

Nahhas expected to be asked by the RCC to form a Wafd government after the 1952 Revolution, though the accusations of corruption that surrounded him may have encouraged the RCC to look elsewhere. Nahhas was forced to dismiss Siragaddin and two other important deputies in September 1952, and the Wafd Party was compelled to accept the resignation of Nahhas as its leader the next month. He and his wife were subsequently tried for conspiracy and corruption in September 1953. Nahhas was not sentenced and his wife was fined but not imprisoned. Nahhas' political rights were restored in 1960.

NASIM PASHA, TAWFIQ (1875-1938). Prime Minister of Egypt in 1920-21, for three months in 1922-23, and in 1934 to the beginning of 1936, Nasim Pasha was associated with the Royal Cabinet and was a strong defender of Palace interests while in power.

Before forming his first government in May 1920, Nasim had served as Public Prosecutor. He narrowly escaped an assassination attempt in June 1920. He resigned in March 1921 to make way for the moderate nationalist ministry of Adli and was named Chief of the Royal Cabinet in April 1922. His second term as Prime Minister, from December 1922 until February 1923, ended when he resigned in protest over the British refusal to recognize King Fuad's claims to the Sudan and his failure to reconcile the two positions. Zaghlul named him to serve in his first government (1924) as Minister of Finance; after the fall of the Zaghlul government Nasim resumed his activities with the Royal Cabinet. He was associated with the founding of the pro-Palace Ittihad Party.

Nasim was brought back to form a government in November 1934, at a time when the abrogation of the 1923 Constitution under his predecessors, the King's declining health, and the Wafd Party's popularity while out of office had created a variety of destabilizing political problems. British opposition to the restoration of the 1923 Constitution made its popularity swell, and Nasim was eventually forced to negotiate with the Wafd and the other opposition parties. Following anti-British riots in November 1935 and a general strike in support of the Constitution Nasim announced the reinstatement of the 1923 Constitution in December 1935. He resigned in January 1936 to make way for a caretaker government headed by Ali Mahir.

NĀṢIR AD-DĪN (Ayyūbid Sultan) see AL-MANṢŪR

AN-NĀṢIR MUḤAMMAD (AN-NĀṢIR NĀṢIR AD-DĪN MUḤAMMAD) (r. 1294-95, 1299-1309, and 1309-40/693-94, 698-708, and 709-41). Longest-reigning Sultan of the Baḥrī Mamluk dynasty founded by Qalā'ūn, an-Nāṣir Muḥammad's reign was twice interrupted by Mamluk challenges. His first year in power was brought to an end by the coup of Kitbughā. Four years of instability followed, and the Regency Cabinet that had ruled during his first reign decided to reinstall the young Sultan. An-Nāṣir Muḥammad's second reign was dominated by the arrival in Syria of the Mongols, who seized Homs and Damascus in the year of his accession, 1299/698, but withdrew the next year. A series of desultory military encounters between the Mongols under the Il Khan Ghazan and the Mamluk forces under Baybars al-Jāshankīr followed, and a peace initiative in 1301/700 was unsuccessful. Finally a decisive battle was joined at Marj aṣ-Ṣuffār in 1303/702; an-Nāṣir Muḥammad and the Caliph, al-Mustakfī, were in the Mamluk forces.

During an-Nāṣir Muḥammad's second reign real power was in the hands of his vizier, Sallār al-Manṣūri, and his commander, Baybars al-Jāshankīr. The external threats faced by the Mamluk state led to a decline in internal control, with Bedouin uprisings over taxes, communal difficulties, and a state of general discontent. Such a situation favored the military, and Baybars soon began vying with Sallār for absolute control within the court. Lacking support or power, an-Nāṣir Muḥammad announced his intention of going on Ḥajj, or pilgrimage to Mecca, in 1309/708; instead he left Egypt and retired to Kerak, while his vizier and commander-in-chief struggled for the throne. Baybars emerged victorious, whereupon Sallār helped an-Nāṣir Muḥammad gather support. An-Nāṣir Muḥammad marched on Egypt in 1309/709, forcing Baybars to flee, though he was later captured and executed.

The third reign of an-Nāṣir Muḥammad saw the introduction of many reform measures that reversed previous policies: the sumptuary regulations affecting Christians and Jews were abolished, the tax burden was alleviated, and more state revenues were devoted to much-needed irrigation repairs. A short-lived Coptic revolt was suppressed in 1320/720. Freed from the control of his court, an-Nāṣir Muḥammad proved, in his third reign, to be a strong and capable ruler, building monuments, patronizing the arts, and setting the country back on course after a lengthy period of instability. He left behind eight undistinguished sons, who ruled in the eleven years following his death, recommencing the cycle of instability that brought the Baḥrī Mamluk line to its end.

AN-NĀṢIR MUḤAMMAD II (r. 1496-98/901-03). Burjī Mamluk Sultan, an-Nāṣir Muḥammad II was the son and successor of Qā'it Bay. His reign was dominated in its early days by Qānṣūh Khamsmiyya, leader of the dominant Mamluk faction, whose rule was challenged and overturned by Akbirdī, then by another court official. The Sultan, given over to hedonism, was unconcerned with the internal anarchy of the country and, in any case, powerless to do anything about it. The Mamluks were completely out of control, with no person considered safe or sacred in the streets, houses, or mosques of Cairo. An-Nāṣir Muḥammad II's biggest problem appears to have been paying the Mamluks, something he managed, it is said, by torturing whomever seemed to have available capital. He was eventually murdered, unregretted, by the chamberlain Tūmān Bay.

NASSER, GAMAL ABDAL (NĀṢIR, JAMĀL ᶜABD AL-) (1918-1970). President of Egypt from 1956 until his death in 1970, Nasser was one of the most important Arab leaders of the twentieth century. As head of the Free Officers he planned and led the revolution that toppled the monarchy in Egypt on 23 July 1952, though for the first year and a half he operated very much behind the scenes. During 1954 he became premier when he challenged, then defeated, General Muhammad Naguib, who had been installed by the Free Officers after the Revolution as the head of the government.

The son of a postmaster, Nasser was among the first graduates of the Military Academy under the liberalized admissions scheme introduced after the 1936 Anglo-Egyptian Treaty, although his initial application was delayed because of his past involvement with nationalist politics. After his graduation Nasser made steady progress through the ranks while keeping in touch with a group of his fellow graduates from the 1938 class who were to form the nucleus of the Free Officers. During the 1940s he had several postings in Egypt and taught for a time at the Military Academy, which afforded him valuable contact with younger officers. He was heavily involved in the fighting in Palestine at Faluja in 1948. With other young officers, he witnessed the lack of leadership and planning of his commanders.

Nasser appears to have always had strongly nationalist ideology and sentiments, and he had read the writings of Ahmad Husayn, founder of the Misr al-Fatat party, as well as nationalist writings from many other sources. He was also in contact with the Islamic revivalist group Ikhwan al-Muslimun, either directly or through such Free Officers as Anwar Sadat and Kamal Husayn.

The Free Officers under Nasser's leadership did not really become activists until 1949-50; Nasser was elected president of the Free Officers Executive in December 1950. He was suspected of political activism but managed to escape detection by the authorities. The exact political goals of the Free Officers prior to 1952 were not well defined; they appear to have contemplated taking action sometime in the mid-1950s, until the burning of Cairo on 26 January 1952 emphasized the need to act. But it was not until the existence of the Free Officers as a group of antigovernment plotters became known to the Palace, and the Free Officers were warned by a sympathizer at court, that Nasser decided to act. In the early morning hours of 23 July 1952 the Free Officers secured the entire military and communications network without violence. They then named General Naguib Commander-in-Chief. Three days later King Faruq abdicated in favor of his son and a Regency Council was established with Free Officer representation. The "Six Principles" given by the Free Officers made clear their commitment to agrarian reform, but did not provide much of a guide to their long-term goals.

Naguib, the leader of the Revolution to the outside world, replaced Ali Mahir as Prime Minister in September 1952, while Nasser served as de facto chairman of the Free Officers Executive. Nasser became Deputy Prime Minister and Minister of the Interior in Naguib's June 1953 government, a government that also contained many of Nasser's supporters in the Free Officers Executive, now renamed the Revolutionary Command Council. Nasser was Secretary-General of the Liberation Rally (formed in 1953 to support the regime), which was to be used by Nasser in his own coming power struggle with Naguib. At the same time the regime began cracking down on supporters of the old regime.

Nasser and Naguib had a critical falling-out in January 1954, over both the RCC's decision to ban the Ikhwan al-Muslimun (the sole remaining popular grouping still outside direct government control) and the future political development of Egypt. Nasser used his support within the RCC to secure the removal of Naguib from all of his posts--Prime Minister, President of the Republic, Chairman of the RCC--in February 1954. Nasser took the title of Prime Minister and RCC Chairman, leaving the presidency of the Republic vacant, but was forced to reinstate Naguib as President of the Republic following the threat of a coup by another Free Officer, Khalid Muhiaddin. Naguib then regained his posts as Prime Minister and RCC Chairman until Nasser once again took these two titles in April. During his brief spell back in power, Naguib tried to introduce political liberalizations, but these were gradually rescinded when Nasser reasserted his supremacy. Nasser made good use of his following among members of the Liberation Rally and the trade unions to mount popular demonstrations in his own support during 1954; his international profile was helped by his success in negotiating an Anglo-Egyptian Evacuation Agreement that summer. The agreement was opposed by the Ikhwan al-Muslimun, which had been allowed to resume public life that spring. The assassination attempt on Nasser in October by an Ikhwan member gave him the chance he needed both to suppress the Ikhwan and to remove Naguib, tainted by his past support for and by the group. Naguib was placed under house arrest in November 1954. Thereafter Nasser assumed full leadership of the Revolution, with his presidency confirmed in a referendum held in June 1956.

Nasser made an early impact on international politics. His staunch opposition to the Baghdad Pact (January 1955), a Western-organized military alliance, earned him the support of countries as diverse as Saudi Arabia and Syria: it did not earn him the friendship of the U.S. or Britain.

The Bandung Conference, which he attended in April 1955, made an enormous impression on Nasser; the emphasis placed by the countries attending the conference on Third World unity, neutralism, and anticolonialism came at a time when Egypt's relations with the West were cooling. The Israeli attack on the Egyptian army in Gaza that February, and renewed tension along the border between the two states, led Nasser to seek arms from the West. When his requests were refused, Nasser turned to the Eastern Bloc for supplies in September 1955. This move, as much as Nasser's bitter attack on the Baghdad Pact, caused grievous damage to Egypt's reputation in the West. However much Nasser's Bandung neutralism might try to avoid it, the Cold War was to play a considerable role in shaping Egypt's foreign policy and Nasser's international role.

The American and British decision in July 1956 not to go ahead with funding support for the Aswan Dam project, after the International Bank for Reconstruction and Development had given its approval in February, may have been intended as a punishment for Egypt's new links with the East. In retaliation, however, Nasser nationalized the Suez Canal in a masterly public speech that signaled his rejection of Western pressure and a determination to pursue his own course. The subsequent war over Suez in October 1956 pitted Egypt against the Israelis, acting in conjunction with the French and British. The war helped create an image of Nasser in the Arab world as a strong Arab nationalist leader under siege from the West and Israel. But the conspiracy which lay behind the attack had the unfortunate consequence of creating a permanent suspicion of the West in Nasser's mind.

The Soviet Union announced its willingness to fund the Dam project and in the late 1950s participated actively in various Egyptian development schemes. Nasser's political relations with Russia were less clear-cut. Seeing in his links with the Soviet Union a balance to the far stronger U.S. presence in the region (via Israel), his policy actions at home and abroad betrayed on occasion a strong disquiet about Russia. This was especially marked after his 1958 trip to the Soviet Union, which was followed by a purge of leftist elements in the government and among Egyptian intellectuals.

Nasser as a domestic leader demonstrated a commitment to reform Egypt socially and economically, while resisting all pressure for a return to the "free" political life that had made pre-

Revolutionary Egypt so unstable. His charismatic oratory and personality compensated in part for this, but little effort was made on the local level to involve ordinary people in the political process. Decision- and policy-making were extremely centralized, and the bureaucracy was set the task of implementation. Moreover, prior to 1958 Nasser did not appear to devote as much time to making his domestic programs cohesive and acceptable as he did to making his foreign policy active.

Early in 1958 Nasser was approached by a group of Syrian politicians and military officers who strongly argued for the formation of a unified state of Syria and Egypt, headed by Nasser. This union was intended to bring stability to Syria's internal political situation and a greater role within the Arab world for both countries. The United Arab Republic was officially proclaimed on 1 February 1958, and Nasser was elected its president by a referendum on 21 February. Nasser, the dominant personality in the region, came to dominate the Union as well, which was soon largely run by Egyptian bureaucrats implementing Egyptian policy. The Syrians also objected to the increasingly left-wing drift of the government's policies, and following Nasser's introduction of the Socialist Laws the Syrians formally withdrew from the Union in September 1961.

Nasser's voice was by this time no longer unchallenged in the Arab world. In 1958 a revolution in Iraq had brought to power another group of officers with their own political views competing with Egypt's. Nasser's economic and social policies alienated the more conservative regimes of the area, as did his sometimes active intervention in their internal political affairs. Though the breakup of the union with Syria was a grave disappointment to Nasser, it did not produce a change in his government's economic or political direction. In 1962 Egypt became involved in the Yemen War supporting the revolutionaries there against the Saudi-backed royalists. From that point until the outbreak of the 1967 Arab-Israeli War, Egypt and some of the other Arab states underwent a constantly changing relationship: friends one year, enemies the next. Other Arab states merely stayed enemies. At the heart of these uneven relationships lay the strength of sentiment felt by many other Arab leaders toward Nasser personally and toward what they felt was his desire to dominate the region. Similar charges were leveled against him in Africa following Egypt's abortive involvement in the 1960-61 Congo dispute. Faced with overwhelming Western backing for the rebel Kasavubu, Nasser withdrew the Egyptian contingent of the UN force meant to back Lamumba's government; it subsequently fell and Lamumba was assassinated. Nasser then changed his mind, deciding to give arms to the pro-Lamumba government-in-exile. By this time it was too late; the arms more often than not never reached the Congo on their overland passage via Sudan. Nasser was seen by African leaders as attempting to act as power-broker in Africa, which in a sense he was but on a vastly smaller scale than Western powers whose influence he tried to combat.

Domestically the Nasser regime again moved sharply against its critics on both the left and right during the 1960s, especially against the religiously based opposition that had become active again in the mid-1960s. Political life in Egypt was limited to the Arab Socialist Union, which Nasser headed and controlled, and an elected legislature, all of whose members were from the ASU. The nationalizations and related government hiring and education policies created a vast army of bureaucrats who depended on the regime for survival and advancement and who considerably expanded Nasser's power base in the government.

Ideologically the period between the breakup of the union with Syria and the 1967 war was dominated by the close relationship between Nasser and Muhammad Heykal, the editor of Al Ahram. Heykal's column was felt by most observers to represent Nasser's thinking of specific issues, and Nasser's thinking in turn was held to be influenced by Heykal. State capitalism, Arab nationalism, nationalism, and Third World issues were woven for the first time into a reasonably cohesive whole in the Charter of National Action, which was the major ideological statement of the last decade of the Nasser regime.

This period also marked the ascendancy of Ali Sabri, who was to use his power base in the ASU to build up a considerable network of his own supporters. The mid-1960s saw most of the remaining Free Officers leave the government for personal or political reasons. Nasser had by this point assumed a thoroughgoing and intensely personal control of the mechanisms of government and the levers of executive power within Egypt. Only the military, under the control of General Amer, maintained a semblance of autonomy within the government structure. This political and governmental introversion resulted, conversely, in a distancing of Nasser from his critics, who were usually excluded from his circle. It also created a set of misapprehensions about regional realities, the most telling of which would become manifest in the 1967 Arab-Israeli war.

The time leading up to that war was filled with mixed signals in Egypt. At home, the suppression of dissent was combined with the espousal of high social and socialist principles. Abroad, Nasser's relations with the Saudi government were poisoned by Egypt's involvement in Yemen. The Gulf Arab states resented Egypt's sometimes heavy-handed attempts to propagandize against them. Nasser was opposed by Bourgiba in Tunisia on ideological grounds. The potential alliances of the 1964 rapprochement with Iraq and Syria were always drawn on Nasser's terms and tended to confirm his certainty of his own role as "the" Arab leader of the region. Still, the strength of his personality and his rhetoric helped him maintain a dominant role in the Middle East. He seemed then to have an ideological certainty that even his most fluent opponents lacked.

Nasser mended his relations with Syria sufficiently for the two countries to sign a defense treaty in 1966. This was put into effect after a series of provocative attacks by Israel on Syria. It has been suggested that Israel was trying to lure Nasser into making an attack, to bring the confrontation he had been threatening rhetorically to reality. If so, it was a trap Nasser walked into. Despite Nasser's efforts in May 1967 to manage the escalating confrontation with Israel, his closure of the Straits of Tiran was fatal. A lightning Israeli air and ground attack on 6 June 1967 left the Egyptian air force bombed and destroyed on the ground in a preemptive strike and the Israelis in control of Sinai, all within four days. After asking sacrifices of the Egyptian people for years to meet the Israeli threat, Nasser offered his resignation. A widespread and genuine popular protest forced him to reconsider, and, after dismissing General Amer as Deputy Supreme Commander and Chief-of-Staff and purging the army, the regime took stock.

From the autumn of 1967 until his death Nasser redirected Egyptian policy in several areas. Domestically, a series of economic and political readjustments were promised. The internal situation was unsettled, however, and Nasser had to cope with widespread unrest on Egypt's campuses. A reexamination of some aspects of Egypt's industrial and investment strategy was carried out, and reforms were promised in the public sector. Tensions with Israel remained high and led to an outbreak of hostilities in the 1969 War of Attrition. Israel's own strategic and military strength forced an increasing dependence by Egypt on Russia for arms and assistance in this conflict. Russian assistance helped bring the War of Attrition to an end, and American efforts produced the Rogers Peace Plan, accepted by Nasser in August 1970.

Nasser's relations with the Arab world were partially mended after the 1967 war. Egypt withdrew from the Yemen by December 1967, allowing a reconciliation with Saudi Arabia and the Gulf states. At the time of his death, Nasser was participating in negotiations to resolve the dispute between Jordan and the Palestine Liberation Organization. A truce between Jordan and the PLO was signed in Cairo on 27 September 1970, the day before Nasser's death. He was deeply, sincerely, and widely mourned in Egypt.

Nasser's political impact has been felt both inside and outside Egypt; the feelings he aroused among contemporary and later observers were never cool and seldom completely objective. Historical events and the force of Nasser's personality and rhetoric obtained for him a position in the Arab world that was largely unequaled by any other Arab leader of the time and that gained for him a following in many of the Arab states. A school of political thought, Nasserism, has flourished outside Egypt and is as much a part of Nasser's legacy as the corporate state that survived him in Egypt. A final assessment of his role must take several factors into account. Although Nasser was genuinely committed to a reform of Egyptian society, he resisted giving that society free voice. An advocate of Arab Nationalism, Nasser could not apparently accept the political heterogeneity of the Arab nation. International, regional, and domestic forces prevented Nasser from realizing his early commitment to a neutral, non-aligned Egypt.

NATIONAL ASSEMBLY (1957). Established by the Electoral Law of 1957, which followed the introduction of the 1956 Constitution, the National Assembly was to have 350 members, with elections to be held in July 1957. The newly formed National Union, a political grouping whose leadership was dominated by the Free Officers, was to select the candidates, ensuring that the Assembly would be tightly controlled by the government. Elections were held on 3 and 14 July 1957. Abdal Latif al-Baghdadi was elected the first president of the National Assembly, which despite its tame selection process managed to generate some heated debate on Egyptian domestic issues, such as the position of political detainees, education, and land reform. Deprived of the right to appoint or dismiss ministers, the National Assembly had, apart from speechmaking, little effective power. It was dissolved following the formation of the UAR and replaced with a joint National Assembly (UAR).

NATIONAL ASSEMBLY (UAR)/COUNCIL OF THE NATION (1960). Following the February 1958 referendum approving the establishment of the United Arab Republic a new provisional constitution was proclaimed that March creating a combined National Assembly of 600 members, appointed by President Nasser from Egypt (400 members) and Syria (200 members).

Most of the important organizational features of the UAR were established even before the National Assembly met in July 1960. Main tasks set before the Assembly were to approve the UAR joint economic program and select members for the Constitutional Committee. Anwar Sadat was elected its president. The Assembly conflicted with Nasser over plans to increase taxes and promulgate the Socialist Laws. The National Assembly was dissolved in 1961 following the withdrawal of the Syrians from the UAR that September.

NATIONAL ASSEMBLY (1964). Established by the 1962 Charter of National Action, the National Assembly was to have 360 members, ten of whom were appointed by the President, with elections in March 1964. Half its seats were reserved for workers and peasants. The 1964 National Assembly was charged with drafting a new Constitution, under the guidance of the Arab Socialist Union, nominating a president, organizing plebiscites and setting the broad outlines of government policy with regard to legislation. Anwar Sadat was the first Speaker of the National Assembly. Tight control of the Assembly was maintained by the ASU: all candidates for Assembly seats were drawn from the ASU membership and selected by the ASU Higher Executive Committee. Shortly before the National Assembly convened (26 March), Nasser reorganized the government, with a new cabinet headed by Ali Sabri.

NATIONAL BANK OF EGYPT. Founded in 1898 with European and British capital, the National Bank had its unofficial role as a central bank confirmed by laws in 1951 and 1957, though it had issued bank notes and acted as the government's banker since its foundation. It was nationalized in February 1960, and in January 1961 divided into two separate institutions, the Central Bank and the National Bank, the latter acquiring the former foreign-owned banks, and continuing the commercial activities of the parent institution and the former limited to normal central-banking tasks. Free Officer Sarwat Okasha was appointed Chairman in 1962. Under the 1964 reorganization of banking the National Bank was given responsibility for managing the import-export sector, which the regime was attempting to keep under stricter controls.

NATIONAL COMMITTEE OF WORKERS AND STUDENTS. Popular front organization formed in February 1946, the National Committee represented a broad section of political activists opposed to the government. The committee was formed after violent demonstrations at Cairo University and elsewhere resulted in the death of twenty students and the injury of many others. It operated at a time when Egypt's national political life was becoming dominated by populist groupings, as the postwar governments and political parties were felt to be increasingly out of touch with popular demands. These included social and economic changes, withdrawal of British troops, negotiations on the Sudan, and political reform. In September 1947 fifteen of the more active opposition groups formed a more structured alliance, building from the National Committee but broadening its membership. The Union of Political Party Youth and Groups contested specific aspects of British policy toward, and British influence in, Egypt. The group enjoyed a measure of public support and had the backing of the politically important Lawyer's Union, but neither the National Committee nor the Union was able completely to overcome the conflicting aims and goals of its constituent groups, nor provide clear and precise leadership against the political establishment.

NATIONAL CONGRESS OF POPULAR FORCES. The National Congress of Popular Forces was a 1,750-member assembly composed of 1,500 members elected in February 1962 from the five chief occupational groupings (intellectuals, workers, peasants, national capitalists, and military, plus the 250-member Preparatory Committee). It was to this congress, held in May 1962, that Nasser presented and defended the Charter of National Action, the regime's first definitive ideological statement since the breakup of the union with Syria. The National Congress as a representative grouping of the Egyptian people was meant to hold the only official national debate on the charter, and following such discussion elections for the local committees of the Arab Socialist Union would be held. In practice, however, debate about the charter took place inside and outside the government, in religious and intellectual circles, and the charter itself provoked demonstrations of opposition to itself and to the government.

NATIONAL DEMOCRATIC PARTY. Government party created in July 1978, the National Democratic Party was headed by President Anwar Sadat until his death. It was formed after government displeasure at the consequences of the political liberalizations of 1977 had led, in May 1978, to restrictions on political-party activity. The Arab Socialist Party merged with the NDP in October 1978. Its first Secretary-General, Makram Ubayd was replaced by Husni Mubarak in May 1980, when former Prime Minister Mustafa Khalil became Deputy Chairman for Foreign Relations of the party. In 1980 the NDP controlled 326 out of 367 contested seats in the June 1979 election and enjoyed the passive support of most of the opposition parties in Parliament. The NDP nominated Vice-President Husni Mubarak as successor to President Sadat following the latter's assassination in October 1981. Mubarak's Prime Minister, Fuad Muhiaddin became Secretary-General of the party in January 1982 when President Mubarak was elected NDP Chairman.

NATIONAL FREE PARTY (AL-ḤIZB AL-WAṬANĪ AL-ḤURR). Founded in 1907, it was the only political party in pre-World War I Egypt actively to favor the continuation of a strong British presence in Egypt. The party drew its limited support from the many Levantine immigrants in Egypt, who had prospered in the relatively free atmosphere in Egypt compared with that in their home countries. These immigrants viewed the British presence in a favorable light and saw Egypt's development as being best furthered under a guiding British hand. The National Free Party ceased to be active after 1910, having no audience among Egyptian nationalists.

NATIONAL FRONT. Formed on 10 December 1935 by a group of Egyptian politicians from several parties, the National Front pressed for the reinstatement of the 1923 Constitution and made approaches to the British government with a view toward renegotiating Egyptian-British relations so as to normalize Egypt's domestic and international position. The actions of the Front followed a long period of resistance by all Egypt's political parties to the suspension of the 1923 Constitution in 1930. This resistance was joined by many Egyptians and by the trade union movement. Though not fully coordinated, these groups had mounted demonstrations and strikes, and an anti-British boycott was organized, enjoying wide popular and political support. The 1923 Constitution was reinstated two days after the formation of the Front, and the British, worried as much by Italian colonial ambitions in Africa as impressed with the National Front demands, agreed to renegotiate Anglo-Egyptian relations on 20 January 1936.

NATIONAL ISLAMIC PARTY see MISR AL-FATAT

NATIONAL MOVEMENT OF 1882 see ARABI REVOLT

NATIONAL PARTY OF EGYPT see ḤIZB AL-WAṬANĪ AL-ḤURR

NATIONAL PROGRESSIVE UNIONIST PARTY. Created in 1977 following the introduction of Party Law that May, and headed by Khalid Muhiaddin, the National Progressive Unionists had two representatives in the People's Assembly at the time the party formed. The activities of the NPUP paper, Al-Ahli, in criticizing the Sadat government contributed to the government's decision to impose limitations on the political parties in May 1978, and the party lost its seats in Parliament following the 1979 elections. Pan-Arabist and left-wing in policy, the NPUP strongly opposed the Camp David Agreements and the economics of the Open Door Policy, and it was among the groups leading opposition to the Egyptian-Israeli peace treaty.

NATIONAL UNION. Political party formed by the regime after a referendum in June 1956, the National Union replaced the Liberation Rally. Like its predecessor the National Union never succeeded in becoming an effective political party in the true sense of the word, but was, rather, a support organization for the regime.

By a presidential decree issued in May 1957 the National Union Executive (appointed and headed by Nasser) was to select candidates for the first elections to the newly created National Assembly that July. In June the Union presented the list of 1,188 candidates for 350 seats. The constitution of the group, issued later in the year, defined its goals as the creation of a socialist democratic and cooperative state. An elaborate hierarchy was established, with Anwar Sadat as Secretary-General of the Union and a number of prominent Free Officers in its leadership. Final power over the National Union rested with President Nasser, who was entitled by his office to form it, pick the members of its Executive, and supervise its activities. Following the establishment of the United Arab Republic in February 1958 all political activity was placed under the control of the National Union, and the Egyptian Communist Party was persuaded to merge with the Union. The National Union assumed control of Egypt's newspapers and journals following the nationalization of the press in 1960. After the breakup of the union with Syria in 1961 the regime replaced the National Union with the Arab Socialist Union, officially constituted in February 1962.

NATIONALIST PARTY/NATIONAL PARTY (1907-53) (ḤIZB AL-WAṬANĪ). Origin dates to the early years of the reign of the Khedive Abbas II, as a semiclandestine grouping organized by the court and formally headed by the Khedive himself. This group, The Society for the Defense/Revival of the Nation, had as its goal ridding Egypt of European, and particularly British, influence. The circle around Abbas came to include Mustafa Kamil, whose initially cordial relations with Abbas cooled toward the end of the 1890s. Financed by his colleagues Kamil founded his own newspaper, Al-Liwa (The Standard). Through it, he had an open platform to preach his message of national renewal, firm opposition to the British presence in Egypt, support for pan-Islamicism and the Ottoman Sultan and advocacy of a broadening of national political life. Kamil was also an impressive orator, and built a personal following among younger and more ardent nationalists.

In the early 1900s, and particularly after the Dinshaway Incident of 1906, popular support for the nationalist message presented by Kamil grew. The Nationalist Party was officially constituted in 1907, and the party's first congress met that November to draft a platform and establish an organizational structure. By the time of Mustafa Kamil's premature death in February 1908 no such structure had been organized, however, and the death of Kamil created serious reverses for the new party. The Khedive, who had been cautious in his criticism of the Nationalist Party during Kamil's lifetime, withdrew funding he had provided from the foreign editions of Al-Liwa (The Egyptian Standard, L'Etendard Egyptien). Kamil's elected successor, Muhammad Farid, was not popular with some elements in the party leadership or with Kamil's family. A breakaway faction, the Party of Notables, gained the support of pro-Palace Nationalists opposed to Farid.

Under Farid's leadership the party took a more aggressive tone in its attacks on the Palace and government, and Prime Minister Butrus Ghali barred the publication of the party newspaper in 1909. The implication of a Nationalist Party member in the assassination of Butrus Ghali in 1910 led to a sharp fall in party fortunes, and Farid himself was sentenced to prison for sedition in 1912. Farid's self-imposed exile during the First World War kept him isolated from political developments in Egypt, and he was not invited to join the wafd (delegation) formed by Zaghlul in 1918 to press the case for Egypt's independence. Instead Mustafa Nahhas unofficially represented the Nationalists in Zaghlul's delegation.

After Farid's death in 1919 the leadership of the party eventually passed to Hafiz Bey Ramadan; the party became divided, after the formation of the Wafd Party from Zaghlul's original delegation, between those who wished to cooperate with the Wafd and those who refused any dealings with it because of its policies or personnel. The party lost many active members, including Nahhas, to the Wafd. The Nationalist Party survived until 1953, but was never a major political force after 1922; its members seldom held ministerial office, and it had only a small number of parliamentarians in the legislature.

NDP see NATIONAL DEMOCRATIC PARTY

NEWSPAPERS. The role of the press in the national life of modern Egypt had its beginnings in 1866 with the publication of Wadi al-Nil. This paper had quite a small circulation, however. The Taqla brothers, Lebanese immigrants, founded Al-Ahram in 1876. In the course of its development it became the leading newspaper in Arabic down to the present day. Though many early newspapers espoused a nationalist view, not all the newspapers of the pre-twentieth-century period opposed the British presence; Al-Muqattam, founded in 1885 by Lebanese immigrants, was a supporter of the British. The paper aroused strong feelings among Egyptian nationalists, and in 1893 its offices were attacked. A journal with religious and political themes, Al-Muayyad, was started in 1890 by Shaykh Ali Yusuf; it was meant as an alternative to Al-Muqattam and soon became an important nationalist forum, especially for the young lawyer Mustafa Kamil. In 1899 he in turn formed his own newspaper, Al-Liwa, which eventually published French and English editions, and became the forum of the Nationalist Party. The Umma published Al-Jarida.

Aside from these major political journals the period prior to 1910 saw a tremendous expansion in all forms of other publications, dealing with literary, religious, and general topics. Among these must be mentioned Al-Manar, founded by Shaykh Rashid Rida in 1897 and soon dominant in religious journalism. The Copts had a specialized newspaper, Al-Watan, founded in 1877, the same year the satirical nationalist magazine, Abu Naddara, was founded.

Political topics still tended to dominate national journalism, however, and following the formation of new political parties in the 1920s newspapers published by them began circulation. The Wafd had Al-Misri and two other papers; the Liberal Constitutionalists started Al-Siyasa. The Ikhwan al-Muslimun, which trained some of its followers in Western journalistic techniques, was active in publishing magazines such as Al-Dawaa and mass-circulation pamphlets. In the period after the Second World War Akhbar al-Yawm, a weekly news review, was started; by this time, in addition to the newspapers mentioned above, practically every Egyptian political party had some publication on a daily or weekly basis. Enormous press syndicates, such as the Al-Ahram group and the Dar al-Hilal publishing house, controlled an extensive range of publications.

Following the Revolution of 1952 the newspapers strictly identified with the pre-Revolutionary political parties ceased publishing as legislation came into effect, in January 1953, against these parties. The regime had its "official" newspapers, Al-Gumhuriyya (edited by Anwar Sadat) and Al-Missa. The government had its sympathizers on the remaining national newspapers, of which Al-Ahram continued to be extremely influential, particularly after the appointment of Muhammad Hasanayn Heykal as editor. Al-Ahram became virtually the official voice of the government executive, and Heykal's weekly column was actively consulted as a guide to the regime's thinking and future policy. This was especially so after the press nationalizations of May 1960, when all remaining newspapers and journals were placed under the control of the government's political party, the National Union, with their supervision then transferred to the Press Council of the Arab Socialist Union when that body was formed in 1962.

Until the political liberalizations of 1974, the newspapers in Egypt tended to be quite restrained in their criticism of the government; in the mid-1970s all of the national newspapers, including Al-Ahram, published much franker analyses of government programs and policies, particularly of the pre-1970 period. Some government constraints have to a certain extent been reimposed since 1978, though Egypt still enjoys one of the most extensive press establishments in the region.

NEW TOWNS PROGRAM. After the 1973 Arab-Israeli War a New Towns Program was launched to rehouse Egyptians displaced in the 1967 and 1973 wars and to provide accommodation for the urban population away from the overly congested cities of Cairo and Alexandria. Partially funded through OAPEC, the New Towns scheme envisaged the creation of five self-contained cities that would offer housing, employment opportunities, and a full range of services. Only two of these cities have been established: the Tenth of Ramadan, outside Cairo, and Sadat City, between Cairo and Alexandria. Although the program has encountered planning and funding problems, its implementation, even if on a slower schedule, is expected to continue to help solve Egypt's critical housing shortage and relieve population pressure in the urban centers.

NEW WAFD PARTY. Formed as a political party in February 1978 under the terms of the 1977 Party Law, the New Wafd was headed by Fuad Siragaddin and had twenty-four parliamentary members. The party suprised some observers by acquiring such a sizable representation among the opposition. A referendum in May 1978, prohibiting political activity by certain categories of individuals, including those associated with the pre-Revolutionary political parties, was agreed upon by the electorate. The New Wafd, whose leader, Siragaddin, was Secretary-General of the Wafd prior to 1952, decided to disband. The party's popularity and potential as a strong base of opposition was felt to have underlain the government's decision to proscribe its leadership.

NILE WATERS AGREEMENTS. The first Nile Waters Agreement, signed in 1929, followed nearly a decade of dispute between Egypt and Great Britain over how much water should be allocated to Egypt and the Sudan (and to the planned Gezira Agricultural project in the Sudan). Britain had unilaterally implemented its own redistribution scheme in 1925. The first agreement abandoned the principle of a fixed allotment for each country on set units but made Egypt's share of the Nile waters nineteen-twentieths that of the Sudan's. Although Britain negotiated on behalf of the Sudan, the Sudanese had no voice as such in this agreement, which made future irrigation and development works along the length of the Nile subject to the approval of the Egyptian government. On gaining independence in 1956, the Sudanese government refused to accept the agreement.

With the announcement of the High Dam Project in Egypt by the Nasser government in the mid-1950s, the Egyptian and Sudanese governments were both anxious to renegotiate the terms of the first agreement. The lake that would develop behind the dam would eventually reach Sudanese territory, but, more importantly, the distribution of water from a thoroughly harnessed Nile had to be reconsidered in the light of growing Sudanese needs. A new agreement was eventually reached in November 1959; it provided the Sudan with £E15 million compensation for the territory that would be flooded by Lake Nasser, a one-third share of total Nile flow once the dam was fully operational, and a program of technical cooperation. This 1959 agreement, which took one year to negotiate, is meant to last until 2059.

Recent negotiations among Sudan, Ethiopia, and Egypt have gone less smoothly, as the needs of the first two countries for water have increased sharply, and as Egypt has raised objections to Ethiopian plans for damming the Nile in its own territory.

NILOMETER see RAWḌA ISLAND

NIZĀRĪ. The first major split in the Ismā[c]īlī Shī[c]a Islam of Egypt's Fāṭimid dynasty (969-1171/358-567) occurred over a contest for the Caliphate following the death of al-Mustanṣir in 1094/487. The two candidates were Nizār, supported by the Persian Ismā[c]īlī leader Ḥasan aṣ-Ṣabbāḥ, and Aḥmad, Nizār's younger, weaker brother, who nonetheless was the candidate of al-Afḍal, the powerful vizier. Al-Afḍal forced the succession of Aḥmad, whereupon Nizār fled and attempted to organize a rebellion; he was seized in 1095/488 while trying to raise an army in Alexandria and was never seen again. Aḥmad became Caliph, taking the name al-Mustaᶜlī.

Soon after Nizār's disappearance Ḥasan aṣ-Ṣabbāḥ began preaching that Nizār was not dead but in hiding, in the tradition of the Hidden Imāms of Shīᶜa Islam. Thereafter, he was autonomous in Persia; his preaching was spread widely by Nizārī missionaries and became the foundation for the notorious Assassin cult in Syria. The activities of the Syrian Nizārīs were, thanks to the reports of Marco Polo and other European travellers, much misunderstood. It is unlikely that, as was believed in the Middle Ages, the Nizārī were drugged with hashish before commission of the political and religious murders of which they stand accused. However this story was popular in Europe and the word ḥashīshīyīn (or user of hashish) made its entry into literature as "assassin."

The Nizārīs are blamed for the murder of the vizier al-Afḍal in 1121/515, though the Caliph al-Āmir was also suspected of complicity in al-Afḍal's death. Al-Āmir himself fell victim to Nizārī assassins in 1130/524. More active outside Egypt than within its borders, the Syrian Nizārī were finally subdued, then suppressed by Ṣalāḥ ad-Dīn in 1176/571 and Baybars in 1272-73/670-71. The Nizārīs are today largely concentrated in India and Pakistan.

NONALIGNMENT. Following Nasser's 1959 visit to the Soviet Union, and with the increasingly complex political situation in Arab countries and the Third World, the Egyptian government decided to adopt a more "balanced" position with regard to the Great Power conflict and to tone down some of its rhetoric against the West. This was partially to counter the impression in the West that Nasser had gone over completely to the Eastern Bloc but was also affected by Nasser's own determination not to rely exclusively on any one power.

At the 1961 Belgrade Conference, Presidents Nasser and Tito outlined the principles of nonalignment as being based on the desire to pursue an independent and peaceful national policy and give support to popular liberation movements and other Third World issues. What was particularly stressed, however, was the need for a nonaligned country to refrain from any form of military arrangement with either of the big-power blocs, whether through military pacts, mutual defense arrangements, or the granting of bases.

The evolution of this policy won for Egypt promised financial benefits from Western governments, including the new U.S. administration under President Kennedy. It appeared to have little effect on Egypt's regional position: in the following year its involvement in the Yemen War created a new climate of hostility in its relations with the Arab Gulf states. The nonaligned movement has continued important in the foreign policy approaches of a number of developing countries. Egypt's participation after 1977 was criticized on the basis of her close identification with the United States in the aftermath of the Camp David Accords, just as Nasser was castigated by the nonaligned leaders (particularly Tito) for his over-reliance on the Soviet Union in the late 1960s.

NORTHBROOK COMMISSION. Set up by the British government of Gladstone in 1884, the Northbrook Commission was meant to put forth policy suggestions for the British Agent and Consul-General, Sir Evelyn Baring (Lord Cromer). Lord Northbrook traveled to Egypt in September and in November he recommended action in several areas: irrigation, the corvée (forced labor), taxation of foreigners, reformation of the tax system in agriculture, and Egypt's loan structure. Areas in which the Caisse interfered with the easy management of the country's finances and should be limited were also discussed. The extensive nature of the reforms and programs suggested that, if solely implemented by the British, they would have effectively altered the international control of Egypt's finances, and therefore the commission's suggestions brought immediate objections from France and other interested European parties. Egypt's financial position was finally clarified in the Convention of London (1885), with many of the reform suggestions of the Northbrook Commission report informally implemented by the Egyptian government during Cromer's consulship.

NUBAR PASHA (1825-1899). Egyptian politician and Prime Minister, Nubar Pasha served several Egyptian rulers in the course of his long involvement with the government. Born in Smyrna, Nubar came to Egypt in the last days of Muhammad Ali's reign and went to work for Ibrahim Pasha in 1844. Nubar was involved in the negotiations over the Suez Canal lease under the reign of Sa^{c}id Pasha, entering the service of Ismail Pasha when the latter became Viceroy in 1863. His relations with Ismail were not entirely smooth; he twice left Egypt when he had incurred the Khedive's disfavor. Nubar Pasha worked for the reshaping and reform of the Egyptian legal system from 1866, and he was responsible for the introduction of mixed courts in 1876. His involvement with the negotiations on Egypt's debt with her European creditors alienated Ismail; however, upon the insistence of the European managers of Egypt's debt Nubar was brought back in August 1878 to form a government that included, for the first time, Europeans serving in ministerial posts.

The formation of a European ministry was meant to ensure greater direct European management of Egypt's finances, in line with the system of Dual Control established in 1876. The move was profoundly unpopular in Egypt, and Nubar and the Khedive came in for sharp criticism. Ismail was forced to dismiss Nubar in February 1879, after Nubar had been attacked in a speech by Latif Salim, his own nominee as head of the military academy. Salim's denunciation of the European ministry nearly touched off a revolt among the Egyptian officers, who were already restive over being put on half-pay (thanks to Egypt's financial difficulties) and over promotion inequalities between themselves and the Turco-Circassian officers. Ismail's dismissal of Nubar led to protests by his European officials rejecting Ismail's privileges to hire and fire ministers and resulted in the British-engineered dismissal of Ismail by the Ottoman Sultan later that year, after Ismail turned the European cabinet out of office.

Following the establishment of a British presence in Egypt in 1882-83 Nubar was asked to form a second ministry early in 1884, to superintend Egypt's withdrawal from the Sudan. His conflicts with the British Agent, Sir Evelyn Baring (Lord Cromer), over Egyptian interests in the Sudan created difficulties, but the Egyptian withdrawal took place eventually in 1885. Nubar managed, with the support of Cromer, to abolish the corvée or forced-labor system for all but vital emergency repairs. As president of the Council of Ministers, Nubar had to strike a fine balance between pressures from the British on the one hand and from the Palace and political élite on the other; he managed largely by his policy of restrained cooperation, but when the British appeared to be considering withdrawing from Egypt in 1886-87, he built some hasty bridges to the nationalists and made an ill-considered attack on Cromer that was to damage their relations somewhat.

In 1887 Nubar proposed the reintroduction of a strong Egyptian police force and greater Egyptian control over domestic policy; his appeals to the British government over Cromer's head were rebuffed. Nubar lost the struggle to have Valentine Baker, the retiring British police commander in Egypt, succeeded by an Egyptian. When the Khedive Tawfiq realized that Nubar was no longer able to protect him against the British, he dismissed him.

Nubar formed a ministry in April 1894 under the new Khedive, Abbas II, but was retired in favor of Fahmi Pasha after a year. Nubar was never a popular figure with Egyptian nationalists, who saw in his policy of cooperation a capitulation to the British. As an Armenian Christian, Nubar was perceived by many Egyptians as insufficiently committed to their national interests. Following his retirement from political life Nubar became involved with the Armenian national delegation to the Porte, a diplomatic and political pressure group that represented Armenian interests to the Ottoman Sultan.

NUBIA. The area straddling the common border between the present-day states of Sudan and Egypt (though largely falling within Egypt) Nubia's boundaries run approximately from Aswan in Egypt to Dongola in the Sudan. Nubia is more a distinctive ethnic and cultural rather than geographic area, and its history has been linked since about 2500 BC with the Egyptian state to the north. The Nubians were not converted to Islam until the fourteenth century/eighth century; until then they had been Monophysite Christians, with their rulers in tributary and/or cooperative relations with the Muslim governors and rulers of Egypt. The second governor of Egypt, ᶜAbdallāh b. Saᶜd, campaigned in Nubia in 651-52/31-32, shortly after the Muslim conquest of Egypt. During ᶜAbbāsid times in 858/244, a revolt in Nubia involving the Beja tribe from the Eastern Desert was suppressed. With the coming to power of Aḥmad b. Ṭūlūn (r. 868-84/254-70) the King of Nubia appointed a representative at al-Fusṭāṭ, and Aswan became a mutual trade depot. Nubia provided an annual tribute of men, some of whom were incorporated into his army by Ibn Ṭūlūn and played an important, if destabilizing role, within the Egyptian military down to Ayyūbid times.

Nubia's Classical Christian phase (850-1100/236-493) was a time of prosperity and autonomy for the region; Nubia's association with the trade in gold and precious stones from pharaonic times had expanded into a trade in other commodities from more remote regions in Africa in demand in the Muslim courts. Disputes over trade brought the Nubians into conflict with the Ikhshīdids in 949/337 and again in 955/344, when they briefly seized Aswan.

Until the reign of the Mamluk Sultan Baybars (r. 1260-77/658-76) the rulers of Egypt did not do more than assert their hegemony, or claim thereto, over the region. The trade and soldiers provided by Nubia did not need military conquest to be provided. Baybars, however, was faced with the need to re-establish a strong state at a time when Nubia was undergoing a period of instability. He conducted a series of campaigns in

Nubia between 1272/671 and 1276/675, installing his own candidate as King and making the region more dependent on the goodwill of the Egyptian Sultans; he also increased their tribute. The expansion of the Mamluks' commercial interests also affected their attitude toward the trade monopolies of the Nubians. His successor, Qala'un (r. 1280-90/678-89), also used disputes over the succession to the throne to intervene militarily in Nubia.

Aside from these military incursions the Egyptian Muslims who came to Nubia through settlement, intermarriage and proselytization were gradually transforming Nubia into a Muslim state. The bitter succession disputes in Nubia in the fourteenth century/eighth century gave further military entrée to the Egyptians. Nubia was invaded several times during this period by Egyptian forces, usually invited by Nubian factions anxious to see order imposed and their candidate installed in power.

Early in the Ottoman period (1517-1798/922-1213), northern Nubia was annexed, but the granting of autonomy to the tribes of the regions bordering Nubia led to a far from stable situation. Nubia itself maintained its relative isolation, broken only by the activities of the slave traders who were to continue their activities down to the time of the Khedive Ismail (1863-78). Politically, the region was beyond Egypt's ability to control: the periodic instability at the center in Cairo made any long-term and consistent management of Nubia impossible. The region maintained its traditional position as a place of refuge for unsuccessful candidates for power in Egypt. It was to Nubia that many of the Mamluks fled following the establishment of the French in Cairo in 1798/1213, and after the slaughter of Mamluks by Muhammad Ali in 1811.

Muhammad Ali, the Viceroy of Egypt, finally brought Nubia under Egyptian rule with a major campaign in 1820-21 that extended southward into the Sudan. He was given control by the Ottoman Sultan of both Egypt and the Sudan, including Nubia, in 1841. The economic development of Egypt in the nineteenth and twentieth centuries weakened the cultural and physical separation between Nubia and the rest of Egypt, as growing numbers of Nubians migrated northward for work in Cairo or Alexandria. Their traditional occupations as major-domos, bawabs (door-keepers and guards), and servants in the cities and in the great households of the countryside altered as education and new opportunities became available both in Nubia and in the cities where they settled. The Nubians have been physically and culturally affected by the successive raisings of the Aswan Dam in the twentieth century, which had by 1970 flooded all but a small area of their original homeland and forced their progressive resettlement northward throughout this period.

NUQRASHI PASHA, MAHMUD FAHMI (1888-1948). Egyptian Prime Minister and one of the founding members of the Wafd Party, Nuqrashi was, until his resignation from the Wafd in 1937, regarded as the likely heir of the Wafd leader, Nahhas.

Nuqrashi was involved with the Secret Section of the Wafd during the early 1920s and because of this was brought to trial with fellow Wafdist Ahmad Mahir in 1926, for involvement in terrorist activities and the assassination of the British Sirdar, Sir Lee Stack. The subsequent acquittal of both men failed to convince the British of their innocence, however, and Nuqrashi did not assume a ministerial post until (over British objections) he joined the short-lived 1930 government of Nahhas, when he served as Minister of Communications. He regained the Communications post, and became Minister of Transport, in the 1936-37 Wafd government. Nuqrashi and some of the Wafd leadership in Nahhas' cabinet resigned in August 1937, following a dispute with Nahhas over the allocation of contracts for public works, but the dispute was additionally between Nahhas and his more able lieutenants over the issue of power-sharing.

After their resignation from the Wafd, Nuqrashi and Ahmad Mahir formed the Saadist Party, in 1938, and joined the 1939-40 governments of Ali Mahir and Hasan Sabri until both men decided to resign in September 1940 over Egypt's failure to declare war. Nuqrashi formed his first government in February 1945, following the assassination of Ahmad Mahir, whom he had served as Foreign Minister, and led the Egyptian attempts to force a renegotiation of the 1936 Anglo-Egyptian Treaty. He resigned in February 1946 following the deaths of some twenty student demonstrators protesting the British military presence, drowned when a bridge on which they were marching was raised. Nuqrashi returned to power in December as the level of civil disturbances in Egypt was rising to unprecedented levels and as popular protests against the government's inactivity over domestic and economic reforms turned violent.

With the Wafd exploiting the government's failures to extract concessions from Britain on the Sudan, Nuqrashi brought the Egyptian case over its claims to the Sudan before the United Nations Security Council in August 1947; the Council did not accept the Egyptian arguments, and the following year Britain announced unilateral measures for Sudanese autonomy. The outbreak of the fighting in Palestine in May 1948 brought Egypt reluctantly into the conflict; Nuqrashi, though realizing the state of the army and its equipment, could not resist domestic and regional pressures to become involved. The Palestine War did Nuqrashi's reputation domestically considerable harm, highlighting both the government's inability to organize the delivery of supplies and material and the levels of corruption as money for arms purchases was diverted to private hands. At home the Nuqrashi government faced a restive population, angered by the lack of solution to the economic and social problems facing Egypt and ready to translate that anger into street demonstrations and violence. The antiterrorist campaign initiated by Nuqrashi claimed the Prime Minister as its most prominent victim; his decision to outlaw the Ikhwan al-Muslimun in December 1948 led to his own assassination later that month at the hands of an Ikhwan member.

AN-NUWAIRĪ (SHIHĀB AD-DĪN AḤMAD) (1279-1332/677-732). Administrator and companion of Qalā'ūn's son an-Nāṣir Muḥammad, an-Nuwairī filled several offices during an-Nāṣir Muḥammad's three reigns. He related his experiences in an encyclopedia, a work that covered a range of subjects, including the history of Egypt from the Arab Conquest to the author's lifetime, which also provided a fascinating glimpse into "unofficial" courtly life in the Islamic period and aspects of a wealth of other subjects.

-O-

OCTOBER PAPER. The Sadat government's first program of political and economic reforms, the 1974 October Paper stressed the necessity of development based on the opening of investment in Egypt to the outside world and a gradual de-emphasis in reliance on the public sector. In foreign policy Egypt's long-term goal of Arab unity would be combined with a more moderate approach to the West. Censorship was lifted (but reimposed after the January 1977 riots), as were certain political restrictions. A number of sentences meted out to political prisoners during the Nasser period were commuted. The October Paper took a liberal position with regard to internal politics, promising the removal of some of the arbitrary practices instituted by Nasser's security services.

Although the October Paper represented a restatement of some aspects of the Nasserist position in the post-1967 period, it did so with a more pronouncedly right-wing bias, especially in the area of economic reforms. The changes, particularly in the economy, made in the October Paper were largely possible because of the strengthening in Sadat's domestic position after the October 1973 war with Israel.

OCTOBER WAR see ARAB-ISRAELI WAR (1973)

OPEN DOOR POLICY (INFITAH). The Open Door Policy is a series of economic liberalization measures, first announced in April 1974 and implemented thereafter in a series of laws removing restrictions on the investment of foreign capital in Egypt. Dr. Abdal Aziz Higazi, former Minister of Finance under Nasser and Prime Minister after the 1973 war, was made responsible for implementation of the Open Door Policy, elements of which he had been advocating before the 1973 war. From 1976 to 1978, Dr. Abdal Monaym Kaissuni assumed the direction of government strategy.

Law 43 (1974) was the legal basis for the investment of foreign capital in Egypt under the Open Door Policy. Foreign companies were deregulated and Free Zones were created as havens for industrial-investment projects. All foreign investment was placed under the supervision of a central body, the General Authority for Arab and Foreign Investment and Free Zones (GAAFIZ). Though the Open Door program brought a strong foreign response with regard to the banking sector, the takeoff in industrial investment was much slower than expected, and in 1977 new laws were introduced to make investment in industrialization more attractive. Foreign industrial companies are given substantial tax breaks, and exchange controls liberalized in 1977-79.

The Open Door Policy has not been without its critics in Egypt and abroad, who have seen it as increasing Egypt's dependence on the West and promoting unbalanced economic growth. The high and constant inflation rate since the 1973 war has been partially attributed to the decentralization and import policies adopted under the Open Door program, and Egyptian manufacturers have complained of their inability to meet the competition posed by cheaper foreign imports. The economic benefits of the Open Door Policy have not spread widely or deeply enough to counter strong public resentment at price rises affecting consumer products, an outgrowth of recent steep inflation.

OPERATION SUSANNAH see LAVON INCIDENT

ORGANIC LAWS. The first Organic Law after the British invasion of Egypt was introduced in 1883 and followed the completion of the Dufferin Report, on which it was based. It reorganized Egypt's administrative and constitutional framework on the provincial and national levels. Each province was to have a consultative council for the management of local affairs. On the national level a bicameral legislature was created. The Legislative Council would have thirty members, fourteen of whom were appointed and the rest elected by the provincial councils. The Legislative Assembly would have eighty-two members, forty-six of whom would be elected and the remainder drawn from the Council and the ministers. In fact, none of these institutions functioned effectively or independently until 1906 when, under the wave of reaction from the Dinshaway Incident, the British decided to increase the responsibility and participation of Egyptian political bodies.

The 1913 Organic Law replaced the two legislative chambers of the Egyptian Parliament with an eighty-three member unicameral legislature having sixty-six indirectly elected and seventeen appointed members including minorities. This Legislative Assembly had far more power than its predecessors to examine and delay bills presented for its consideration. It could also initiate some legislative action, though its powers fell far short of nationalist demands. Members of the Assembly served six-year terms, one-third of their number being replaced every two years. The Assembly was suspended at the outbreak of World War I.

OTTOMAN EGYPT (1517-1798/922-1213). The emergence of the Ottomans as a power in Anatolia coincided with the decline and internecine division in the ranks of the Burjī Mamluk Sultans of Egypt. The Burjīs, who for two centuries had dominated a Muslim world shattered by the Mongol invasions, found their territorial and political claims increasingly challenged by the Ottomans, among whom there was a vitality and martial spirit unmatched by these later Mamluks.

The Mamluks incurred the hostility of the Ottoman Sultan Bāyazīd II (r.1481-1512/886-918) when the Mamluk Sultan Qā'it Bay sheltered Jem, rival claimant to the Ottoman throne, in 1481/886. Six years of indecisive hostilities between the Mamluks and Ottomans came to an end in 1491/896, with neither party prepared to make a decisive move. Bāyazīd was succeeded in 1512/918 by Selīm I Yavuz ("the Grim"), who resolved to continue the campaign against the Mamluks. His defeat of the

Persians at Chaldiran (1514/920) freed him to act against the Mamluks, who had suffered a naval defeat at the hands of the Portuguese in 1509/915 and were still under threat from them. Selīm was also able to exploit the rivalry between the Mamluk Sultan in Cairo and his governors in Syria, particularly the ambitious Khā'ir Bay, who eventually defected to the Ottomans with a faction of supporters.

The Mamluk and Ottoman armies met in battle at Marj Dābiq in Syria in 1516/921, and the better-equipped and -trained Ottomans carried the day with their modern artillery. Factional feeling among the Mamluks prevented a compromise being effected between Selīm I and the last Mamluk Sultan, Tūmān Bay; Selīm advanced on Egypt, and in January 1517/922 he entered Cairo. A campaign against Tūmān Bay and his supporters, who had fled to the Delta region, was successfully prosecuted and Khā'ir Bay installed as governor. Upper Egypt was placed in the hands of strong tribes like the Hawwāra.

The defection of Khā'ir Bay and a number of prominent Mamluks to the Ottoman cause was instrumental in ensuring their survival in Egypt after the establishment of Ottoman control. Their involvement in the revolt of the Ottoman governor Aḥmad Pasha Khā'in in 1524/930 is evidence of their continued strength at this time but also demonstrated to the Ottoman Porte the need for firm control of Egypt's administration. A series of administrative and legal reforms were introduced in 1525/931. A cadastral survey for taxation purposes was carried out in Egypt in 1526/932 (and revised in 1550/957). Egypt was placed under the Ottoman system of capitulations in 1528/934, when the existing treaties covering European trading privileges in Egypt were renewed. During this time Egypt was also used by the Ottomans as a base for their territorial expansion along the coasts of Arabia and North Africa, provoking an unsuccessful Portuguese attempt on Suez in 1541/948.

The relative tranquility of the early period of Ottoman rule in Egypt was broken in the seventeenth/eleventh century, with military revolts from 1586/994 onward. The Ottoman Viceroy was killed in 1604/1013; several of his predecessors and successors were deposed or rejected. Ottoman troops garrisoned in the Delta again revolted in 1609/1017, and Egypt's internal stability was further harmed by two devastating plagues in 1619/1027-28 and 1643/1052. The administration of the country at this time was in the hands of salaried employees of the Porte, under the supervision of the governors, but in fact the Mamluks were creating an increasingly important role for themselves in the power structure and as governors of the Sanjaqs, or provinces. It was in this time that the two great factions of beys emerged, the Qāsimiyya and Faqāriyya, whose rivalry and feuding were gradually to undermine Ottoman power structures at the end of the seventeenth/eleventh century. Though the Ottoman governors tried to exploit this factional rivalry to keep the beys in balance, even the assassination of the head of the Qāsimiyya faction in 1662/1072 on orders from the governor and the suppression two years prior to that of the Faqāriyya faction brought only a temporary pause to their struggles.

The involvement of the Mamluks in the beylicate was meant to link them structurally to the Ottoman governate. Instead the beys or high officers of the Ottoman state in Egypt used their position to work against the governor, shaping the decision-making process at court and using the revenue they collected from taxes to build up their own household of Mamluks and their own power bases independent of the center. Factional feuding among the Mamluks certainly did not diminish their appetite for wealth or power. The lot of ordinary Egyptians trapped between governor and Mamluk bey could not have been a happy one. The Ottoman capacity to intervene in this situation was limited by their military involvements elsewhere.

The last phase of Ottoman rule during the eighteenth/twelfth century saw power in Egypt effectively shifted from the governor to the beylicate. The beys, in addition to controlling various important offices, such as those of Shaykh al-Balad and Amīr al-Ḥajj, had succeeded by the early 1700s/1100s in gaining control of most of the tax-collecting offices of the state. They effected alliances with both the powerful tribes in Upper Egypt and the Ottoman garrison. The beys exploited the divisions within the garrison, particularly that between the Janissaries and the ^{c}Azabān, more effectively than the governors had succeeded in exploiting the divisions among the beys themselves, and by 1711/1123 full-scale fighting broke out. This "Great Insurrection" lasted over two months, at the end of which time the Faqāriyya faction and their Janissary corps allies had been defeated. The insurrection also marks the beginning of the end of Ottoman "control" of the country, as several beys assumed the office of Shaykh al-Balad and, de facto, the governorship of the country from the nominal Ottoman governor. The Ottomans tried to restore the situation in 1786/1200 but in this enjoyed only temporary success. The beys who ruled Egypt during this time--^{c}Alī Bey, Abu'dh-Dhahab (Muḥammad Bey), Ibrāhīm Bey, Murād Bey, and Ismā^{c}īl Bey--were little more successful than their Ottoman predecessors at keeping their fellow Mamluks in line. ^{c}Alī Bey pursued an ambitious program of internal pacification and territorial conquest in Syria before being betrayed by his commander Abu'dh-Dhahab in 1772/1186. The other Shaykhs al-Balad had to face similar displays of disloyalty from their immediate circle, a situation that created chronic instability in Egypt and eased the French conquest of the country in 1798/1213. Though the Ottomans tried to place a governor in Egypt following the French withdrawal, two of their candidates were deposed, one died, and a fourth was murdered by the Mamluks. After he had deposed the Ottoman governor Khurshid Pasha, Muhammad Ali, commander of the Ottomans' Albanian regiment, took power as Viceroy.

The French invasion marks the effective end of direct Ottoman control of Egypt, although the country was under nominal Ottoman suzerainty until the outbreak of the First World War and the formal establishment of a British Protectorate. During this time the dynasty of Muhammad Ali secured virtual autonomy for itself. Muhammad Ali nearly toppled the Ottomans from their premier position in the Islamic world by virtue of his military activities in the 1830s, and his grandson Ismail obtained great concessions from the Ottoman Porte through the distribution of Egyptian largesse there.

At its establishment Ottoman administrative practice in Egypt envisaged the creation of three powers--the governor, garrison and beylicate--who would ideally balance out and hence preserve the overall interests of the Ottomans in Egypt. The Wālī (Vālī) or governor was appointed from Istanbul with the backing of the Sultan and his vizier and supported in Egypt by the Ottoman garrison. In practice the ease with which the governors were deposed or recalled (there were 106 in the Ottoman period) did much to undermine their position. The backing the garrison was meant to provide often proved ephemeral or, on occasion, openly hostile. The beylicate had its focus and its base in Egypt, which it successfully used in the eighteenth/twelfth century to overturn the power of the governors.

Ottoman Pashas of Egypt

(list adapted from Eduard von Zimbaur's Manuel de gênéalogie et de chronologie pour l'histoire de l'Islam, Hanover, 1927)

1517/923	Khā'ir Bey
1522/928	Muṣṭafā
1523/929	Qāsim (Guzelje) (deposed after one month)
1523/929	Aḥmad (killed after trying to gain autonomy)
1524/930	Qāsim (second term)
1525/931	Ibrāhīm
1025/931	Sulaymān (Khādim)
1535/941	Khusru
1536/943	Sulaymān (second term)
1538/945	Dā'ūd
1549/956	ᶜAlī Sāmiz (Semiz)
1553/961	Muḥammad (Dukagin)
1556/963	Iskandar (Iskender)
1559/966	ᶜAlī (Khādim)
1560/967	Lala Shāhīn
1564/971	ᶜAlī Ṣūfī

1566/973	Maḥmūd
1567/975	Sinān (in Yemen 1568/976)
1568/976	Iskandar (Tsherkes Iskender)
1571/979	Sinān
1573/980	Ḥusayn
1574/982	Masīḥ (Khādim)
1580/988	Ḥasan (Khādim)
1583/991	Ibrāhīm
1585/993	Sinān (Defter)
1587/995	Uways
1591/999	Ḥāfiẓ Aḥmad
1595/1003	Kurd
1596/1004	Sayyid Muḥammad
1598/1006	Khiḍr
1601/1010	Yāwuz ʿAlī
1603/1012	Ibrāhīm (al-Ḥajj) (killed)
1604/1013	Muḥammad (Gurjī)
1605/1014	Ḥasan b. Ḥusayn
1607/1016	Muḥammad (Oghuz)
1611/1020	Muḥammad (Ṣūfī)
1615/1024	Aḥmad
1618/1027	Muṣṭafā (Lefkelī)
1618/1027	Jaʿfar
1619/1028	Muṣṭafā
1620/1029	Ḥusayn (Mirī)
1622/1031	Muḥammad (Babar)
1622/1031	Ibrāhīm
1623/1032	Muṣṭafā (Qara)
1623/1032	ʿAlī (Tshetshedjī)
1624/1033	Muṣṭafā (second term)
1626/1035	Bayram
1628/1038	Muḥammad (Ṭabāny-Yaṣy)
1630/1040	Mūsā
1631/1040	Khalīl
1633/1042	Aḥmad (Baqīrdjy)
1635/1045	Ḥusayn (Delī)

1637/1047	Muḥammad (Juwān Qapījy Sulṭānzādé)
1640/1050	Muṣṭafā (Naqqāsh)
1642/1052	Maqṣūd
1644/1054	Ayyūb
1646/1056	Muḥammad (Ḥaydar Agha Zādé)
1647/1057	Muṣṭafā (Mustarī)
1647/1057	Muḥammad (Sharaf)
1649/1059	Aḥmad (Tarkhunjī)
1651/1061	ᶜAbd ar-Raḥmān (Khadīm)
1652/1062	Muḥammad (Khāṣṣeki)
1656/1066	Muṣṭafā (Khalījī-zādé Damad)
1657/1067	Muḥammad (Shahsuwār-zādé Ghāzī) (killed)
1660/1070	Muṣṭafā (Gurjī)
1660/1071	Ibrāhīm (Defterdār)
1663/1074	ᶜUmar (Silaḥdār)
1667/1077	Ibrāhīm (Ṣūfī)
1668/1079	ᶜAlī (Qaraqash)
1669/1080	Ibrāhīm
1673/1084	Ḥusayn (Jāmbalāt-zādé)
1675/1086	Aḥmad (Defterdār)
1676/1087	ᶜAbd ar-Raḥmān
1680/1091	ᶜUthmān
1683/1094	Ḥamza
1687/1098	Ḥasan
1687/1099	Ḥasan (Damad)
1689/1101	Aḥmad (Mufattish Kiaya)
1691/1102	ᶜAlī (Khaznadar)
1695/1106	Ismāᶜīl
1697/1109	Ḥusayn (Firārī)
1699/1111	Muḥammad (Qara)
1704/1116	Sulaymān
1704/1116	Muḥammad (Rāmī)
1706/1118	ᶜAlī
1707/1119	Ḥasan (Damad) (second term)
1709/1121	Ibrāhīm
1710/1122	Khalīl (Kosej)

1711/1123	Walī
1714/1126	^{c}Abdī
1717/1129	^{c}Alī (Kiaya) (second term)
1720/1132	Rajab
1721/1133	Muḥammad (Nishanjī)
1725/1138	^{c}Alī Muraly (six months, then Muhammad again)
1727/1140	Abū Bakr
1729/1141	^{c}Abdallāh (Keupruluzādé)
1733/1146	Muḥammad (Silaḥdār) then ^{c}Uthmān
1734/1147	Abū Bakr (second term)
1734/1147	^{c}Alī (Ḥakīmzadé)
1741/1154	Yaḥyā
1743/1156	Muḥammad Sa^{c}īd
1744/1157	Muḥammad (Rāghib)
1748/1161	Aḥmad (al-Ḥajj)
1751-52/1165	Muḥammad (Melek)
1752-53/1166	Ḥasan ash-Sha'rāwī
1755/1169	^{c}Alī (Ḥakīmzādé) (second term)
1756/1170	Sa^{c}d ad-Dīn
1757/1170	Muḥammad Sa^{c}īd (second term), then Muṣṭafā (Bāhir Keusé)
1762-63/1176	Bakr
1764-65/1178	Aḥmad
1765-66/1179	Ḥamza (Silaḥdār Māhir)
1766-67/1180	Muḥammad (Melek) (second term)
1767/1180	Muḥammad (Rāqim)
1768/1182	Muḥammad (Diwitdār)
1768/1182	^{c}Ali Bey al-Kabīr (from Beylicate)
1773/1187	Abu'dh-Dhahāb (from Beylicate)

Power passes to the Beylicate; series of Ottoman candidates for the office of Pasha following the withdrawal of the French in 1801 (see Chronology, 1802 to 1805, also KHURSHĪD PASHA, KHUSRAU PASHA, MUHAMMAD ALĪ)

OTTOMAN BRITISH TREATY see DRUMMOND WOLFE CONVENTION

OTTOMAN PORTE. An expression frequently used as a synonym for the Ottoman government in Istanbul, the phrase comes from the name of the Grand Vizier's palace, the Bab Ali, or Sublime Porte. The Sublime Porte housed the important ministries of state in addition to the office of the Grand Vizier, the most powerful official at court.

-P-

PACHOMIUS (d. c. 342). Founder of the first organized community of monks in Egypt, Pachomius was a soldier before his adoption of a religious life. He developed the idea of a community of monks with the structure, discipline, and regimentation of a military group, building on the well-established tradition of religious seclusion found among Egypt's Christians from the early days of Christianity in the country. The strict disciplinary codes established by Pachomius were combined with the formation of the monks into a productive work force. Within the community monks were graded on the basis of their mastery of theology and religious achievement. The rigid hierarchy and administrative structure of the monastic communities devised by Pachomius permitted them eventually to assume some secular administrative work in rural areas of Egypt, where they were often the most powerful and organized element in local life. The extended monastic community established by Pachomius at Tebannisi in Upper Egypt had at its peak a population of 50, 000 monks.

PALACE INCIDENT. Following a ministerial crisis in February 1942, the British government, through its ambassador, Sir Miles Lampson, pressed Faruq to have a Wafd or Wafd-coalition government replace Sirri's government. This reversal of longstanding opposition to the Wafd came from the British belief that the Wafd, still the most popular of the Egyptian political parties, would be more effective in gaining public support in Egypt for the British war effort than any of the other parties. It was also hoped that a Wafd government would weaken the influence of the pro-Axis elements around King Faruq. Lampson eventually decided to force this choice on Faruq by insisting that he abdicate unless he agreed to ask the Wafd leader, Mustafa al-Nahhas, to form a government. Lampson sought and finally gained the support of Oliver Littleton in the British cabinet to apply pressure on the Egyptian King.

On the night of 4 February 1942 General Stone surrounded Abdin Palace in Cairo with troops and tanks, and Lampson presented Faruq with an abdication decree drafted by Sir William Monckton. Faruq capitulated, and Nahhas formed a government shortly thereafter. But the humiliation meted out to Faruq, and the actions of the Wafd in cooperating with the British and taking power, lost support for both the British and the Wafd among both civilians and, more importantly, the military.

PALESTINE WAR see ARAB-ISRAELI WAR (1948)

PARTY LAW. In June 1977 the Egyptian People's Assembly passed a law that allowed, within strictly set criteria, the formation of new political parties. This party law followed a presidential decision the previous year diversifying the ASU. The ASU was split into left, center, and right platforms, and the elections of 1976 were held on that basis. These platforms represented the first broadening of the ASU since its establishment as the country's sole political party in 1962.

After the passage of the law a number of parties were formed, ranging from the National Progressive Unionist Party under Khalid Muhiaddin on the left to the right-wing Liberal Socialist Party. Fuad Siragaddin participated in the formation of a New Wafd Party in February 1978, which, unlike the other political groupings established at this time, had no former associations with the ASU. These new parties also started newspapers to publicize their platforms and leadership. The activities of one of these newspapers, the NPUP's Al-Ahli, with its trenchant criticisms of the government, soon drew official censure, as did the activities of some of the political parties within the legislature.

In May 1978 a referendum was passed forbidding political participation by any pre-1952 politicians (with a few stated exemptions), atheists, and those accused of corrupting political life before or after 1952. Organizing in factories or universities was not permitted. Each party was to have the authorization of the ASU and have at least twenty representatives in the People's Assembly, and it could not have been in existence before 1952. The subsequent dissolution of the New Wafd Party, and the decision of the Arab Socialist Party to merge with President Sadat's newly formed National Democratic Party, left the NDP in control of the People's Assembly.

PARTY OF INDEPENDENT EGYPTIANS see COPTIC CONGRESS

PARTY OF NOTABLES see NATIONALIST PARTY

PASHA (in Arabic, Bāshā). A word of disputed origin, "Pasha" was the title given to the Sultan's representative in Cairo during Ottoman times, as well as being awarded to individuals of certain administrative rank or at certain levels in the Ottoman hierarchy. The title was originally given to the governors of the Ottoman pashaliks (provinces). After the time of Muhammad Ali this title was more widely awarded to Egyptians of merit or to those who had performed certain services for the Khedive or Sultan. Though the title as given by the Sultan came to an end with the Protectorate established by the British in 1914 (terminating Ottoman suzerainty), it was widely used in Egypt down to the 1952 Revolution (and in some cases afterward) by those individuals who personally or through their families had been granted it, as well as being more generally applied as a casual honorific. The title was formally abolished after the Revolution.

PATRIARCHATE. The Patriarch of Alexandria held one of the most important posts in the early Christian Church. Alexandria ranked immediately after Rome, both for its Apostolic foundation and for the size of the Christian community that the Archbishop headed, as well as for its historic importance and the role it played in the doctrinal disputes that split Christianity in the early centuries of its growth. The Patriarch, as a representative of the theological doctrine accepted at Rome (and later Constantinople), was often at odds with the Christianity accepted by the majority of Egyptians. Under the Patriarch Dioscorus, conflicts among the bishops over Monophysite theology led to the breaking away of the (Egyptian) Coptic Church in 451. Thereafter the office of the Orthodox Patriarch in Alexandria (the Copts elected their own Patriarch) was one of considerable controversy. The first appointee after the secession of the Coptic Church was murdered, and incumbents of the office had an uneasy relationship with the Coptic community.

The Emperor Justinian (r. 527-64) completely altered the character of the bishopric in 550 when he granted the Patriarch Apollinarius the office of Prefect, or head of the civil administration; this meant that the Patriarch had to have soldiers on hand to enforce his decisions on, and collect revenues from, the people. The defensive character of the move may have been occasioned by the fate of Apollinarius' predecessor, Paul, who had been attacked and driven from Alexandria by a Coptic mob. The new Patriarch signaled his arrival and his new position by banishing the Coptic clergy from Alexandria and persecuting the Monophysite Christian community. Apollinarius' successors down to the time of Cyrus (who surrendered Egypt to the Arab conquerors) concentrated the exercise of their power in temporal areas; they had little influence, despite their office, over religious matters affecting the majority of Egyptians, and the Patriarch probably performed a minimum of purely religious public functions.

PEACE INITIATIVE (1977). After the breakdown of American efforts to resolve the impasse in Israeli and Egyptian positions following the 1973 Arab-Israeli War, and the failure of an October 1977 move by America and Russia to revive the Geneva Conference, President Anwar Sadat of Egypt decided to make a direct approach. Taking up Israel's past offer that they would be willing to talk to any Arab leader who approached them for peace discussions, President Sadat announced, in the course of an address to the Egyptian parliament on 9 November 1977, that he would be willing to go to Israel to discuss peace. The full implications of his statement were not immediately realized, but when they were, the Israeli government extended an invitation that Sadat made a pre-condition of his visit. Sadat's arrival in Israel on 19 November was without doubt one of the most highly charged moments in recent Arab-Israeli history, and he followed it up with a strong speech to Israel's parliament. In this speech, Sadat outlined Egypt's conditions for peace: a return to the 1967 borders and justice for the Palestinians. The cool response of Israel's leaders during the speech was, in its own way, ample forewarning of the difficulties to come. The Israeli Prime Minister, Menachem Begin, presented what amounted to Israel's counterproposals at a summit in Ismailiyya that December--extremely limited Palestinian autonomy in exchange for full Israeli control of security and order in the occupied Palestinian territories of the West Bank and Gaza.

Though the peace initiative signaled a new era in Egyptian-Israeli relations, it was an era fraught with problems for Egypt. The lack of consultation with Arab leaders prior to the visit (other than a brief, hostile meeting with President Assad of Syria) aroused the antagonism of Egypt's former allies and renewed the hostility of her longstanding opponents. The subsequent peace talks never caught the enthusiasm or generosity of Sadat's initial offer. They have been continued only with the greatest difficulty and with the active intervention of various U.S. negotiators and of former U.S. President Jimmy Carter, who brought President Sadat and Israeli Premier Menachem Begin together at Camp David in September 1978, after the breakdown of bilateral talks and of the Leeds Castle Summit in July.

The peace initiative initially gained broad acceptance in Egypt, which was tired of war and of the high personal and economic costs that confrontation with Israel had brought. However, opposition to a bilateral peace treaty and to normalization of relations has grown (1980-81) among political activists and religious groups, especially as negotiations between Israel and Egypt stalled through what many Egyptians viewed as Israeli intransigence on the issues of settlements, Jerusalem, and the Palestinian issue.

PEACE TREATY (1979) see CAMP DAVID ACCORDS; EGYPTIAN-ISRAELI PEACE TREATY

PEOPLE'S ASSEMBLY. Established under the 1971 Constitution, the People's Assembly replaced the National Assembly. The 350 (currently [1981] 386) members of the Assembly (half of whom must be workers or farmers) are elected by universal suffrage and represent 171 electorates. The President is empowered to appoint up to ten additional members. The composition of the People's Assembly was altered politically in 1976, when elections were held for the first time under a system whereby the Arab Socialist Union, formerly the only official political party, was divided into platforms representing the left, center, and right. The center took 280 seats, the right eighteen, the left two, with fifty independents. Following the introduction of the Party Law in June 1977 (and the formation of the New Wafd eight months later), the Arab Socialist Party still had an overwhelming majority in the Assembly. The New Wafd gained twenty-four legislators, the Liberal Socialists seven, and the National Progressive Unionists three, with eighteen parliamentarians declaring themselves independent. By a referendum of May 1978 limitations were placed on party activity and the New Wafd was dissolved. The Arab Socialist Party subsequently merged with President Sadat's National Democratic Party.

In June 1979, after the approval of the Peace Treaty in a referendum, new elections were held for the People's Assembly. Of 367 contested seats the National Democratic Party of President Sadat won 326, the Socialist Labor Party gained twenty-nine, and the Liberal Socialists held three, with nine independents. Despite the shifts in government policy toward the Assembly, it has on occasion provided a forum for expressing opposition to some government policies.

Fikhri Makram Ubayd was appointed Deputy Prime Minister for People's Assembly Affairs in May 1980. Dr. Sufi Abu Talib is currently (1980) speaker of the People's Assembly, having replaced Sayyid Marai in this post in 1978.

PERSIAN (SASSANIAN) CONQUEST OF EGYPT. The Persian armies of Khosrau II (d. 628) entered Egyptian territory in c. 616 following a successful sweep across Byzantine Syria and Palestine. The Persians took Alexandria in 619. Aside from the weak resistance of that city, they seem to have experienced little difficulty in imposing themselves on Egypt administratively. The Persians effected no major changes in the country's government or religion. During their time in Egypt taxes were raised and strictly collected. The Persians appointed their own candidate to the Patriarchate, Benjamin, who was removed when they were defeated. Upon the death of Khosrau II in 628 the Byzantines under Heraclius gradually regained their territory, with Egypt and other provinces restored to Byzantine control by 629.

POINT FOUR AGREEMENT. Negotiated in 1950 between the Nahhas government of Egypt and the United States, Point Four was a general treaty of friendship, cooperation, and financial assistance between the two governments, giving the United States trade and navigation rights. The treaty signed in May 1950 signaled a shift in the regional balance of power away from Great Britain, formerly dominant in the region, to the United States. The Point Four Agreement gave Egypt some added diplomatic leverage in its dealings with the British, at a time when Egypt was anxious to renegotiate its 1936 Treaty with the UK.

However, following the 1952 American elections and the appointment of John Foster Dulles as Secretary of State, the attempts by Dulles to expand the U.S. role within the Middle East and Egypt encountered resistance, and the Point Four Agreement was widely denounced by demonstrators during Dulles' May 1953 visit to Egypt. Sentiment against Point Four was also influenced by the slow appearance of substantial development aid from the U.S. (though Egypt did benefit from a $40 million loan to improve its infrastructure in 1954) and, more especially, from the U.S. refusal to supply Egypt with the arms it needed for its military.

POPULATION. Before the introduction of modern methods of disease control and the improvement in agricultural productivity and storage techniques, plague and famine acted to keep Egypt's population growth rate within manageable levels. Major outbreaks of plague and famine occurred in every century, with the sources often claiming that two-thirds of the population had been killed. While these figures are doubtless an exaggeration, it is clear that the effects of some of these plagues were devastating in the extreme, particularly when large numbers of farmers in rural areas perished, hampering the country's ability to provide food for the survivors and prolonging the plague and famine cycle. Even during Muhammad Ali's time a terrible plague struck in 1835, and during the Second World War an outbreak of dysentery in rural areas brought a massive death toll. The net effect of this recurring disease worsened in those years when its outbreak coincided with a failed Nile. Be it the resultant food shortages or the death rates in rural areas from disease, famine was the consequence, and both disease and famine kept the population level in equilibrium with the food supply in the years when the Nile was at its proper level.

Egypt's population-to-food ratio did not begin to unbalance until the last years of Cromer's tenure as Consul-General. Improvements in medical care and irrigation, combined with a high birth rate, created a surplus rural population. The first waves of this population were absorbed by the cities, as the modern twentieth-century migration from rural to urban areas got underway. The Second World War, which provided many job opportunities in the cities, also was a time of heightened migration, but in fact all through the twentieth century Egypt's cities have been absorbing the surplus population of the country at a phenomenal rate. In just thirteen years (1967-80) Cairo's population grew from 4 million to nearly 14 million.

Although Egypt's population growth rate has slowed somewhat of late, its exact rate is a matter of dispute. Official estimates of current (1980) levels are approximately 2.5 in a scale where 0 is zero population growth and 4 represents a doubling of the population in about twenty years. Other estimates put Egypt's population growth rate at closer to 4 than 2. Whatever its true level, the current rate of population growth has stretched Egypt's absorptive and productive capacities to the limit and given Cairo some of the highest population densities in the world. The country's population, which was approximately 42 million in 1980, will reach 60-80 million by the end of this century, based on current estimates.

Population pressure in Egypt in the 1970s was experienced in two areas: the disappearance of agricultural land as towns and villages expanded and the increase in population density in the urban areas. The need to house, feed, and find employment for this population continues and will continue to be a constant problem facing the government of Egypt.

Since the 1960s various population-planning measures have been introduced, and in 1965 a Supreme Council for Family Planning was created to supervise these planning programs. The government was careful to secure the approval of the leaders of all of Egypt's religious communities, and a variety of popular incentives and media campaigns have been tried. The mismanagement of some programs and ministerial rivalry over who should control the larger projects has frequently hampered the effectiveness of some family-planning programs. Though Islam has a generally pro-birth attitude, the Islamic authorities in Egypt have given their support to family planning. However there are strong cultural and social pressures still which encourage large families, and in many areas popular resistance by both Copts and Muslims to the whole idea continues strong.

Population growth has had serious effects on Egypt's economy, with rapidly rising levels of food imports spurred by a population that currently grows at the rate of 1.2 million per annum, rising yearly. Imports of wheat and flour, for example, supply 70 percent of domestic requirements. Plans to increase food production through land-reclamation schemes will still leave a substantive gap before this new food supply can be produced, when imports will play an ever more important (and expensive) role. The pressure that Egypt's population brings to bear on the economy has in part dictated that the country's economic priorities move away from reliance on agriculture (whose capacity to absorb spare labor is limited) and toward employment-creating industrialization. Controlling Egypt's population growth will remain an urgent priority of the government for the foreseeable future.

PORTE see OTTOMAN PORTE

POSITIVE NEUTRALISM. Following the Brioni meeting of July 1956 between President Nasser and President Tito of Yugoslavia, the two leaders formulated the tenets of Positive Neutralism, which were adopted by Egypt as part of her foreign policy. Positive Neutralism rejected alignment with any of the Great Power blocs, advocating peace through collective security, anti-imperialism in foreign relations, and disarmament. Development of the South was also seen as a precondition to a balanced and peaceful world order. In terms of active policy, Positive Neutralism committed its adherents to (1) defense of national independence against Big Power imperialism; (2) a stand on international issues based on Third World needs; (3) economic cooperation among the countries of the South; and (4) support of all liberation movements in colonial countries.

This Brioni meeting and the Bandung Conference that preceded it followed Egypt's initial attempts to evolve a foreign-policy stance. The relationship of Egypt after the 1952 Revolution to the two Great Power blocs was cautious, and early on Egypt demonstrated its involvement with Third World issues through the sponsorship of a conference of African and Asian leaders in Cairo in December 1952. Consultations between Nasser and Nehru, and Nasser and Tito, helped define Egypt's dedication to neutrality toward East and West. At the same time the continuing Western colonial presence in many Third World countries gave Egypt certain more active commitments that were outlined in the discussions on Positive Neutralism at Brioni.

However, because the colonial presence that Egypt and many

other independent states were pledged to fight was a Western one, it was inevitable that the rhetoric of Positive Neutralism took on an anti-Western tone. The Cold War also induced the United States and many European countries to feel that those countries who were not with them fully were automatically on the Soviet side. Both Positive Neutralism itself and Western attitudes toward this foreign-policy approach combined to leave the impression in the West of Nasser's hostility to them.

PRESIDENTIAL COUNCIL. Set up in September 1962 by President Nasser, the Presidential Council was meant to share the executive responsibilities of government with Nasser, who was one of its twelve members. The Presidential Council gave an executive platform to the military establishment, and was meant as well to diffuse executive power and responsibility more broadly within the government. The formation of the Council also saw the emergence of Ali Sabri as a power within the government; his appointment was made by Nasser over the strong objections of some of his colleagues and signaled his rise in the President's favor. The Presidential Council was abolished in 1964, when many of its functions were subsumed under the twenty-five-member Executive of the Arab Socialist Union, which Sabri headed.

PROGRAM FOR NATIONAL ACTION see TEN-YEAR PLAN

PROGRESSIVE UNIONIST PARTY (PUP) see NATIONAL PROGRESSIVE UNIONIST PARTY

PROTECTORATE. The imposition of direct and formal British control of Egypt was effected by a declaration of a British Protectorate over the country early in the First World War, in December 1914. The British felt such a measure was necessary to ensure full Egyptian cooperation with the requisitions and other measures necessary to the success of the British war effort. Full annexation would have reduced Egypt to a colony and likely made such cooperation more difficult to achieve.

The Protectorate formally ended Egypt's nominal status as a province of the Ottoman Porte. It was followed by an order deposing the ruler of Egypt, the Khedive Abbas Hilmi II, on the grounds that he supported the Ottoman Sultan; he was replaced with his uncle, Husayn Kamil, who was accorded the title Sultan to signify Egypt's new independence from the Porte.

The termination of Egypt's Protectorate status became a major issue in Egypt after the First World War, with Egyptian nationalists demanding, through the delegation (wafd) organized by Zaghlul, permission to present Egypt's case for ending the Protectorate to British and international official opinion. These nationalist demands were influenced not only by the desire for a fully independent Egypt but also by the support the nationalists felt was expressed in the American doctrine favoring self-determination of peoples, put forth by U.S. President Wilson. There was also a feeling that Egypt's contribution to the British war effort had gone largely unnoted and certainly unrewarded, while the participants in the Arab Revolt in Arabia had received both land and the promise of independence. The recognition of the British Protectorate over Egypt by the United States in April 1917 was a bitter blow to many of the nationalists; at the time Egypt was in the midst of a popular rebellion against both the Protectorate and the deportation of the nationalist leader Zaghlul.

The Milner Report, made public in 1921, recommended termination of the Protectorate, which was ended formally one year later, in February 1922. The declaration of Egyptian independence, however, was far short of a full grant of autonomy, as it still maintained a strong British control over many aspects of Egypt's national and international life.

-Q-

QABĀLA. Introduced in Egypt in ᶜAbbāsid times by the Caliph al-Ma'mūn (r. 813-33/198-218), the qabāla was basically a system of tax collection where one individual took responsibility for a tax unit (however that was determined) and agreed to raise and pay its tax assessment. Various refinements of the qabāla were a) the amount the tax collector was allowed to keep back for his own expenses; b) the extent of his responsibilities in the tax collection area; c) the tenure of the office; and d) whether it was appointed or auctioned.

The operation of the qabāla took place side by side with grant of revenues from state lands to individuals, the Iqṭā^c; in Egypt, the entire country was at points given as Iqṭā^c. This did not affect the need to collect other, non-land-based taxes. The dividing line between the qabāla system and tax-farming is really the acceptance of personal responsibility under the former. This divide widened when the qabāla system also entailed such things as the maintenance of irrigation systems or infrastructure in an area. However, the separation between the qabāla and tax farming can and did frequently disappear, particularly under the Fāṭimids when the offices were auctioned, carried no general responsibilities, became hereditary and made ever larger profits for their holders. But these problems were not limited to the Fāṭimids and were bound to arise whenever the government decided that selling or auctioning (rather than appointing) the offices was a speedy way to raise revenue. In Ayyūbid and Mamluk times, the centralization of many forms of revenue collection did not necessarily guarantee that stricter state supervision would preclude the problems mentioned. The collecting of taxes throughout the Islamic period in Egypt betrayed a tendency to become out-and-out tax farming, with all the abuses associated with it. Muhammad Ali's tax reforms went some way toward arresting this, and in the nineteenth century one finds the assignment of individuals to collect the taxes due from an area rather than the sale of the tax-collecting office. However, it was not really until the taxable units were broken down into their individual components that responsibility, whether in the paying or collecting of taxes, could be fully readjusted.

AL-QĀḌĪ AL-FĀḌL (1135-1200/528-96). Counsellor and head of Chancery to Ṣalāḥ ad-Dīn and his son al-^cAzīz, al-Qāḍī al-Fāḍl was one of the most prominent figures in the court of the early Ayyūbid rulers of Egypt. Al-Qāḍī al-Fāḍl had originally joined the Fāṭimid court in 1153/548, managing to survive the internal turmoils that preceded the final arrival of Shīrkūh and his nephew Ṣalāḥ ad-Dīn in 1169/564. He was closely associated with Ṣalāḥ ad-Dīn and with his brother, al-ᶜĀdil, in reforms and reorganizations introduced in the early years of Ayyūbid rule in Egypt. In 1189-90/585-86 al-Qāḍī al-Fāḍl was Ṣalāḥ ad-Dīn's administrator in Egypt while al-ᶜĀdil served as regent for al-ᶜAzīz. He joined Ṣalāḥ ad-Dīn in Syria the next year, serving there until the latter's death in 1193/589. He then joined the service of al-ᶜAzīz and tried to mediate in the dispute between the Egyptian Sultan and his brother al-Afḍal in Damascus.

Al-Qāḍī al-Fāḍl is praised in the Arabic sources for his learning and for the elegance of his court prose, an especially prized distinction. His enormous library of 120,000 books reputedly became the basis for a new state library in Cairo established by the Ayyūbid Sultan al-Kāmil (r. 1218-38/615-35).

QA'IM MAQĀM. Ottoman official, often drawn from the ranks of the beylicate, the Qa'im Maqām acted as governor during the interregnums between the death, dismissal, assassination, or rejection of one Ottoman governor and appointment and arrival of his successor.

QAISSUNI see KAISSUNI

QĀ'IT BAY (AL-ASHRAF SAYF AD-DĪN QĀ'IT BAY) (r. 1468-96/872-901). Burji Mamluk Sultan, Qā'it Bay's reign marks the beginning of the closing era of the Mamluks in Egypt. The rise of the Ottomans as a threat to continued Mamluk power occurred during his rule, and Qā'it Bay became involved in the struggle for succession between the Ottoman Sultan Bāyazīd II and his brother Jem. Qā'it Bay sheltered Jem in 1481/886, when the latter was unsuccessful in his bid for power, an act that did not endear him to the Ottomans. In 1485/891 a series of military encounters along the borders of Mamluk and Ottoman territory took place; though they continued for six years, nothing was resolved. However, the drain on Egypt's Treasury from both the campaigns, the need to keep a large body of men under arms and the Mamluks' usual rapaciousness for wealth led Qā'it Bay to impose a capital levy in 1490/895. Aware of Egypt's relatively weaker position, Qā'it Bay made approaches to Bāyazīd in the hopes of resolving their conflicts peacefully, but these were without success. The conflict was not resolved, nor was it prosecuted, for the remainder of Qā'it Bay's reign.

Internally Qā'it Bay concentrated on the collection of as much revenue from trade as possible and despite the parlous condition of the Treasury, he built extensively in Egypt, Palestine and the Hijaz. However, an outbreak of plague in 1492/897 devastated the population and reduced the state revenues; in the closing years of the Sultan's reign there were desperate struggles among the Mamluks for power and control of what resources remained in the Treasury, which was nearly empty through the military and construction activities of the ruler. Qā'it Bay finally secured the succession of his son, which he had sought, but his death was followed by five years of instability in the succession.

QAL^cĀ see CITADEL

QALĀ'ŪN (QALĀWŪN) (AL-MANṢŪR SAYF AD-DĪN QALĀ'ŪN AL-ALFĪ) (r. 1280-90/678-89). Baḥrī Mamluk Sultan and founder of the longest ruling Mamluk dynasty, Qalā'ūn and his successors held Egypt for a hundred years. Qalā'ūn was early in his career (1254/652) implicated with Baybars in the assassination attempt on the first Mamluk Sultan, Aybak, and went into exile with a number of his co-conspirators. Captured and imprisoned in 1257/655, Qalā'ūn escaped and made his way back to Kerak. He was eventually pardoned by the Sultan Qutuz in 1259/657; his career advanced rapidly under the reign of Qutuz' murderer and successor, Baybars. Qalā'ūn arranged the exile of Baybars' son and successor, his son-in-law Baraka Khan, in 1280/678, after a two-year reign during which Qalā'ūn campaigned in Armenia. He then deposed his ward, Baybars' second son, Salāmish, after he had succeeded his brother for three months.

At the beginning of his reign in 1280/678 Qalā'ūn had to meet a challenge for the throne by Sunqur al-Ashqār, who received some unmanageable help from the Mongols after his defeat and whose candidacy enjoyed the support of Baybars' other Amirs and their supporters in Syria. He defeated this opposition and quickly established his position. Qalā'ūn faced two major challenges, from the Mongols and from the remains of the Crusader states, which he wished to expel from Palestine completely. He inflicted a major defeat on the Mongols at the Battle of Homs in 1281/1680. He then renewed a truce with the Knights Templar in 1282/680. The fort of al-Maqab was taken after a siege in 1285/683. When the Mongol threat had receded somewhat, he broke the truce in 1289/688 and seized Tripoli from the Crusaders. At the same time he mounted a campaign in Nubia (1288-89/686-88), which had been restive over a dispute concerning the succession to power there and which created problems of stability along Egypt's southern border. At the time of his death, he was embarking on a campaign against Acre.

Qalā'ūn built a hospital in Cairo, the Māristān, which was among the most modern of its time. Its generous endowment attracted the best physicians and medical writers of the day. The hospital, along with a mosque and school, formed a large complex and was only part of the public-welfare activities that Qalā'ūn funded. He actively promoted Egypt's share in the eastern trade, and he helped the economy through reasonable management of its finances, a course that few of his successors chose to follow. His son Khalīl completed the campaign his father had started against the Crusaders at Acre, although the Mongols were to return to Mamluk lands within a decade of Qalā'ūn's death.

QĀNṢŪḤ AL-ASHRAF (AẒ-ẒĀHIR QĀNṢŪḤ AL-ASHRAF) (r. 1498-1500/903-05). Burjī Mamluk Sultan, Qānṣūḥ was the uncle of his predecessor, an-Nāṣir Muḥammad II. Qānṣūḥ was more literate than his predecessors but not strong enough to restore order among the warring Mamluk factions. Though initially supported by Tūmān Bay, one of the more powerful Mamluks at court, he was finally forced to flee the capital for Alexandria, where he was imprisoned and died.

QANṢŪḤ AL-GHAWRĪ (AL-ASHRAF SAYF AD-DĪN QANṢŪḤ AL-GHAWRĪ) (r. 1501-16/906-22). Burjī Mamluk Sultan, Qanṣūḥ al-Ghawrī led the Mamluk armies in the decisive battle of Marj Dābiq in Syria in 1516/921, where their defeat by the Ottomans was a prelude to the Ottoman conquest of Egypt in the next year.

Qanṣūḥ al-Ghawrī came to power after a five-year period of great instability in Egypt. Faced with declining revenues as a result of the European discovery of routes between Europe and the East giving direct access to the spice trade, and confronted with an expansive Portuguese naval presence in the seas where Muslim traders once dominated, the Sultan decided to make war on the Portuguese, who were increasingly challenging the Mamluk fleet. The Mamluks were defeated in a series of naval battles between 1505/911 and 1509/914 that left most of their fleet destroyed.

Within Egypt taxes were high and inflation worsened by al-Ghawrī's habit of coining money as needed. His Mamluks' resistance to the introduction of necessary modernizations in the artillery were to bear negative returns at Marj Dābiq, where the superior Ottoman artillery greatly helped their troops. Al-Ghawrī's taxation policy, following long years of financial chaos, was bitterly resented by the people. Al-Ghawrī died of a seizure during the battle with the Ottomans and was succeeded after a delay by his commander Ṭūmān Bay. Many of the buildings he had constructed during his reign survive him, including a mosque in Cairo.

QĀNŪN NĀME ("Book of Laws"). The Qānūn Nāme, the Ottoman legal and administrative code, was introduced in Egypt by the Grand Vizier Ibrāhīm Pasha during his brief rule of Egypt (1524-25/930-31). The revolt of Khā'in Pasha in the previous year had demonstrated to the Porte the necessity of imposing firmer order on their governors in the country, and on the Mamluks. The administrative provisions drawn up by Ibrāhīm were designed to balance some of the potential for regional power-building by the Mamluks by linking in the provincial chiefs more closely with the governor. Certain local responsibilities were deputed to the kāshifs (district chief), but their overall supervision was vested firmly with the central government. The Viceroy was to head a diwān, or council, meeting four times each week. The Qānūn Nāme also outlined certain military provisions for Egypt. The code was eventually replaced in 1610/1019 by a new administrative decree.

QARĀMIṬA, QARMĀTI, QARMĀTIYYŪN (QARAMATIANS, CARMATIANS). A Shī^{c}a group based in Bahrain and Syria, the Qarāmiṭa were active in Syria from the Ṭūlūnid through to the early Fāṭimid period. These were in essence a populist movement, though in common with most Shī^{c}a sects there were esoteric elements both in their religious practices and leadership. Strongly opposed to the ^{c}Abbāsids, the Qarāmiṭa caused a good deal of unrest in Syria. Bahrain became the base and final center of the movement.

QARĀQŪSH (BAHĀ' AD-DĪN b. ^{c}ABDALLĀH) (d.1201/597). Eunuch and Amīr of Shīrkūh, Qarāqūsh became a trusted minister of Shīrkūh's nephew Ṣalāḥ ad-Dīn, founder of the Ayyūbid dynasty. During the initial Ayyūbid period in Egypt prior to the death of the last Fāṭimid Caliph, al-^{c}Āḍid, in 1171/566 Qarāqūsh served as commander of the Palace guards, suppressing the disturbances which followed al-^{c}Āḍid's death. In 1175/570 he was charged by Ṣalāḥ ad-Dīn with the construction and fortification of the Citadel and the defenses of Cairo. In 1176/572 he became governor of Acre after it had been seized by Ṣalāḥ ad-Dīn from the Crusaders. Qarāqūsh was captured when the city was retaken by the Crusaders in 1191/587, and ransomed by Ṣalāḥ ad-Dīn. He returned to Egypt thereafter. In 1194/590 Qarāqūsh was nominated regent governing Cairo in the absence of the Sultan al-^{c}Azīz, who had succeeded to power in Egypt the year previously. Appointed Atabeg to al-^{c}Azīz's son and successor, Manṣūr, Qarāqūsh was opposed by other members of the Ayyūbid court on account of his age. Another Qarāqūsh, Sharaf ad-Dīn (d.1212/609), was an important Ayyūbid military figure who campaigned in North Africa from 1172/568 until his death.

QĀSIMIYYA. With the Faqāriyya, the Qāsimiyya was one of the leading houses of the Mamluk beylicate in Ottoman Egypt. It was associated with the Niṣf Haram local faction of merchants and artisans, as well as having links with the Hawwāra tribe in Upper Egypt. The Qāsimiyya were overshadowed by their rivals, the Faqāriyya, from 1630/1039 to 1660-1070, when they effected an alliance with the Ottoman Viceroy against the Faqāriyya. This ascendancy was terminated in 1662/1072, when the governor had the Qāsimiyya leader, Aḥmad Bay, assassinated, and both Mamluk factions entered a thirty-year period of quiescence.

At the end of the seventeenth/eleventh century, the Qāsimiyya were dominated once again by the Faqāriyya, who in tandem with the Janissaries and a newly emergent military household, the Qāzdughliyya, achieved supremacy among the Mamluks. However, the alliance formed by the Qāsimiyya under Īwāz and Ibrāhīm Bey (Abū Shanab) with the ᶜAzāban and the other Ottoman regiments opposed to the Janissaries led them to victory during the fighting of the Great Insurrection of 1711/1123. Internal divisions following the death of the Qāsimiyya leader Ismāᶜīl Bey in 1724/1137 permitted the Faqāriyya to gain control of the powerful offices of the beylicate and to crush the Qāsimiyya in 1730/1143, whereupon many of the faction members fled to Upper Egypt and joined the service of their former allies, the Hawwāra.

AL-QAṬĀ'Iᶜ. Residential quarter of the Ṭūlūnid rulers of Egypt, the original foundation of al-Qaṭā'iᶜ was completed in 877/263-64 by Aḥmad b. Ṭūlūn. The city, a square mile in area, was located to the northeast of the original foundation city of al-Fusṭāṭ. It contained a hospital and the Ṭūlūnid residences. Ibn Ṭūlūn's son Khumarawayh expanded and enriched the city until its wealth and beauty assumed legendary proportions in the historical sources of the period. Revenues for construction of the city, like many of the other public-works projects initiated by Ibn Ṭūlūn, came from the increased proportion of Egypt's revenues he retained in the country rather than remitting back to Baghdad. The city was heavily destroyed during the ᶜAbbāsid reoccupation of Egypt in 905/292. Al-Qaṭā'i^c was subsequently eclipsed by the construction of the Fāṭimid royal city of al-Qāhira to the north, and al-Qaṭā'i^c was eventually incorporated into al-Fusṭāṭ.

QAYS. The Banū Qays, the major North Arabian tribe and an important force in the northward expansion of Islam out of the Ḥijaz, became dominant in the Umayyad period (661-750/41-132). They were settled in the Jazīra province (adjoining Syria) early in the Umayyad period. The Caliph Hishām (724-43/105-25) encouraged them to relocate to Egypt. Population pressures in the Jazīra and the contentious nature of the Qays themselves may have prompted this decision of the Caliph.

The initial group of 400 families who migrated to Egypt were granted stipends, land, and resettlement subsidies from Damascus and from Cairo; they were eventually joined by other tribesmen. In all some 3,000 Qays families relocated to Egypt, settling in the Eastern Delta. This was among the most organized of the Arab settlements in Egypt, though the process of tribes migrating to the country had occurred in the past and was to continue for the next two centuries, especially as their density increased in Islamic lands to the east. The relocation of these tribes helped speed the process of Arabization and Islamicization in Egypt, through their contacts and intermarriage with the local population.

QĀZDUGHLIYYA. The last major faction of the beylicate to form in Ottoman Egypt, the Qāzdughliyya were originally a purely military grouping until the last sixty years of Ottoman rule. The ultimate victors in the power struggle between the Qāsimiyya and Faqāriyya, the Qāzdughliyya were formed by Muṣṭafā al-Qāzdughlī, a Turkish officer, in the 1690s/1100s during his service with a senior military leader, Ḥasan Balfiyya. They originally allied with the Faqāriyya faction, which enjoyed supremacy in the ranks of the beylicate until 1695/1106, though the Qāzdughliyya were in opposition to the leader of the Faqāriyya's other ally, the Janissary Küçük Mehmed.

The tripartite alliance reformed in the early 1700s/1120s,

when the allies stood against the challenge of the Qāsimiyya and their allies in the Ottoman corps in the Great Insurrection of 1711/1123. As the losers in this encounter the Faqāriyya and Qāzdughliyya had to suffer the ascendancy of the Qāsimiyya until the death of the Qāsimiyya leader in 1724/1137. By 1730/1143, taking advantage of factional rivalry among the Qāsimiyya, the Faqāriyya had again emerged triumphant. However, they proved as vulnerable to factionalism as their opponents, and the Qāzdughliyya under Ibrāhīm Bey acting in alliance with a small household, the Julfiyya, gained ground steadily from 1743/1156. The Qāzdughliyya were fully dominant from 1748/1161 onward, placing their candidates in the beylicate and fairly united until the death of Ibrāhīm in 1754/1168. A period of confusion followed until the emergence of ᶜAlī Bey, originally a Mamluk of Ibrāhīm, in 1763/1176-77. With sometimes rapidly changing fortunes, ᶜAlī Bey ruled the country until his ouster by his son-in-law Abu'dh-Dhahab in 1772/1186. Thereafter factions formed within the Qāzdughliyya, particularly among the former Mamluks of ᶜAlī Bey, who resisted the joint rule of Abu'dh Dhahab's successors, Murād and Ibrāhīm Bey. The Qāzdughliyya Duumvir of Murād and Ibrāhīm Bey held power at the time of the French invasion of 1798/1213. The eventual seizure of power by Muḥammad ᶜAlī in 1805 was followed by the permanent removal of these factions and groups from the political situation in Egypt.

AL QIMṢĀN AZ-ZARQĀ'/AL-KHAḌRĀ' see BLUE SHIRTS/GREEN SHIRTS

QURRA b. SHARĪK AL-QAYSĪ (d. 714/96). Umayyad governor of Egypt from 709/90 until his death. The correspondence of Qurra with the Prefect of Upper Egypt survived in the Aphrodito Paprii, excavated in 1901 near Sohag. Qurra's communications with the Prefect Basilius reveal the extent to which the early Umayyad governors of Egypt took over existing administrative forms. Qurra seems to have devoted much of his time as governor to increasing Egypt's agricultural strength after a serious famine had weakened the country during the reign of his predecessor, ᶜAbdallāh b. ᶜAbd al-Malik.

QŪSŪN (d. 1342/743). Vizier, Atabeg, and de facto ruler of Egypt from the death of an-Nāṣir Muḥammad in 1340/741 until he himself was deposed in 1342/743, Qūsūn was originally a member of the court of an-Nāṣir Muḥammad and in alliance with another court figure, the Amīr Bishtāk. The two installed Abū Bakr, an-Nāṣir Muḥammad's son, in power, but shortly afterward Qūsūn had Bishtāk killed, Abū Bakr deposed and exiled, and Kūjūk installed in power. He then dispatched an expedition to Kerak to kill Aḥmad, one of an-Nāṣir Muḥammad's elder sons who had been passed over in the succession and was in exile. The expedition was won over by Aḥmad, however, largely because Qūsūn was not a Mamluk and enjoyed little support among them. He had also earned the enmity of some powerful court elements when he arranged for Abū Bakr to be strangled during his exile in Qūṣ. Aḥmad and his supporters captured and imprisoned Qūsūn when they retook Egypt and deposed Kūjūk; the vizier died in prison.

QUTB, SAYYID (1902-1966). One of the chief spokesmen for, and writer on, Islamic revivalism in Egypt after the dissolution of the Ikhwan al-Muslimun in 1954, Qutb was associated with Shaykh Al-Ghazzali of al-Azhar in the Dar al-Uraba publishing house. Qutb was known for a variety of books and articles he wrote on the attitudes of revivalists toward the social, economic, and political issues facing modern Islamic societies. His best-known work was Social Justice in Islam, a major study that was translated into English and in its original Arabic version enjoyed wide circulation throughout the Islamic world. The work highlighted the social responsibility of the Islamic community and the path offered by Islam to meet this.

Sayyid Qutb's relationship with the Ikhwan was not always smooth; in 1947-48, as editor of a competing journal, Al-Fikr al-Jadīd ("The New Idea"), he was regarded by Al-Banna as a threat to the unity of the revivalist movement. His views on Islam's role in contemporary Egyptian society and on the problems and poverty of its rural areas were also more activist than those of the Ikhwan's founder, Al-Banna, at that time. Qutb's writings became an important influence with the Ikhwan, giving the Ikhwan ideology greater depth and relevance to the immediate problems facing Egypt and heightening the group's appeal to politically active Muslims.

Following a period of unrest in urban and rural areas in the mid-1960s, in which the government believed Islamic activists were involved, Sayyid Qutb was arrested and brought to trial in 1966. He was found guilty of involvement in an alleged antigovernment plot developed by the Ikhwan, and executed, despite protests from other Islamic countries.

QUTUZ (AL-MUẒAFFAR SAYF AD-DĪN QUTUZ) (r. 1259-60/657-58). Baḥrī Mamluk Sultan, Qutuz was originally a Mamluk of the first Baḥrī Sultan, Aybak. In 1257/655 Qutuz campaigned against the exiled Mamluks involved in plotting the assassination of Aybak, then served as regent for Aybak's son, ᶜAlī. He deposed ᶜAlī after two years and, after securing the throne for himself, began to welcome back from exile the Mamluk commanders whom he wished to use as the backbone of a massive army needed to confront the Mongols. At the time Qutuz assumed power the Mongol hordes of the Il Khanid, Hülegü, had already devastated Iraq and much of Syria. The Mongol commander, Kitbughā Noyon, sent an ambassador to Qutuz in the spring of 1260/658, demanding his submission. Qutuz put the ambassador to death and prepared for battle, which was joined at ᶜAyn Jālūt ("The Spring of Goliath"), Syria, in September 1260/658. On 25 September the Mamluks defeated the Mongols and thereby saved Egypt from the destruction suffered by the central and eastern Islamic lands.

Qutuz' heavy taxes, caused by the burden of his high military expenditures, were unpopular. His welcoming back of his patron's assassins, while it helped boost the quality of the Mamluk high command who met the Mongols, placed rather too many ambitious Mamluks close to the center of power. In December 1260/658 Qutuz was assassinated by one of his commanders, Baybars, who then assumed power.

-R-

RCC see REVOLUTIONARY COMMAND COUNCIL

RABAT CONFERENCE. In November 1969 President Nasser asked for a meeting of Arab heads of state to discuss the consequences of the 1967 Arab-Israeli War and the War of Attrition on the Egyptian economy. At the conference convened that December in Rabat, Morocco, the Egyptian government submitted a plan prepared by War Minister Muhammad Fawzi. The nonconfrontation states were asked to make more substantial contributions in money and materials to enable Egypt to meet the continued Israeli threat and to rebuild Egypt and its army. The conference broke down when Nasser and the other Arab leaders failed to agree about strategy toward Israel and on the financing and scheduling of future aid, though Egypt received an increased subvention from the new revolutionary regime in Libya.

RAMADAN WAR see ARAB-ISRAELI WAR (1973)

AR-RAWḌA/RODA. Island in the Nile at Cairo, Rawḍa was used since Roman times as a military barracks, as a resort, and as the site of one of the important Nilometers to measure the river's annual rise and fall. It was first known to the Muslims as Jazīra, or island.

The southern half of the island was originally connected by a bridge to Babylon (Bābalyūn), the pre-Muslim city on the site of present-day Cairo's southern boundary. This link with the mainland was sometimes unnecessary, as the silting up of the Nile would create a natural land-bridge between the island and the mainland. The Fāṭimid vizier, al-Afḍal (1066-1121/458-515), built a resort on the island which he named al-Rawḍa, a name which came to be applied to the island as a whole. Its population and commercial importance expanded throughout this period.

Under the Ayyūbids (1171-1250/567-648) the island became a waqf, or religious endowment, acquired by the Sultan aṣ-Ṣāliḥ (r. 2140-49/637-47). Following the example of Ibn Ṭūlūn, he constructed a fortress there to house his Mamluks, who took their name, the Baḥrīs, from their location on the Nile (baḥr = river), deepening the channel between the island and the mainland to limit access to his stronghold.

At the beginning of the Baḥrī Mamluk period (1250-1382/648-784) the Sultan Aybak destroyed the fort. Baybars built a new castle on Rawḍa which was used for a short time. The island lost its importance, however, and the Burjī Mamluk successors to the Baḥrīs looted the structures on the island for stone to use in their own building works on the mainland.

Rawḍa was also the site of the Nilometer (miqyas), a deep shaft sunk into the earth from which the Nile water level was measured. The Umayyad governor ᶜAbd al-ᶜAzīz built the first Nilometer in Helwan; the Rawḍa Nilometer was completed by Usāma, the Minister of Finance for Egypt, in 715/99. This Nilometer was replaced in 861/247 by the administrator al-Mudabbir. The annual reading of the Nilometer in August was the time of a grand festival marking the opening of the irrigation canals; the country's tax assessment was also set dependent on the state of the Nile. Rawḍa is a heavily settled residential area of modern Cairo, containing a fine palace of the Muhammad Ali dynasty, currently used as a resort.

REBELLION OF 1919. The first mass uprising against British rule in Egypt since the British came in force to Egypt in 1882 to suppress the Arabi Rebellion. The 1919 Rebellion was sparked by the British decision in March of that year to deport the nationalist leader Zaghlul, who had led a delegation (wafd) of supporters in their efforts to secure from Britain a termination of the Protectorate Britain had established in Egypt at the start of the first world war. The four months preceding Zaghlul's deportation had seen a nationwide campaign of petitions and telegrams in support of the wafd, a campaign that greatly heightened political consciousness in all areas of Egypt.

Zaghlul and some of his associates were deported in March, touching off a month of anti-British, antiforeign demonstrations and violence throughout Egypt. Railway and telegraph lines were cut, street demonstrations were held (with the participation of women for the first time), and boycotts of British goods were organized. Confrontations between crowds of Egyptians and British travelers and officials resulted in the loss of forty British and several hundred (some sources say 1,000) Egyptian lives. There was vigorous use of British military force by General Bulfin to put down the rebellion, in which virtually every class and every group in Egypt save the Palace itself participated. Allenby was appointed by the British as Special High Commissioner late in March in an attempt to pacify the situation. He released Zaghlul from exile and permitted him to travel to Paris, an action that immediately quieted the violence.

The rebellion was also spurred by the long-term privations suffered by Egypt as a result of its Protectorate status during the war, when the British were empowered to corvée for troops, seize draught animals and goods, and repress normal political life in Egypt. Ending the Protectorate was thus a major demand of the nationalists. The Wafd, in leading the fight against the Protectorate, guaranteed itself a wide and sympathetic audience. The persecution of Zaghlul and the subsequent Rebellion were to link firmly the Wafd with strong advocacy of Egypt's national cause in the mind of most Egyptians. At the end of 1919, the British dispatched the Milner Mission to Cairo to investigate the causes of the Rebellion.

RESCRIPT OF 1878. Forced from the Khedive Ismail in August 1878 by the British and European members of the Commission established to investigate Egypt's finances, the rescript established a "responsible" ministry in which Europeans were officially included for the first time. The cabinet was nominally headed by Nubar Pasha but in fact was controlled by the British Finance Minister, Rivers Wilson, and the French Public Works Minister, de Beligniers. The ministries concerned had no direct responsibility to the Khedive; they were in fact primarily concerned with the implementation of economic policies acceptable to the Caisse de la Dette Publique. The deep unpopularity of the European ministry among the army and the people led to political agitation in the officer corps and to pressure being applied to Ismail by nationalist leaders. He was finally forced to dismiss the European Ministry in April 1879, shortly before he himself was deposed, at British urging, by the Ottoman Sultan.

RESERVED SUBJECTS/POINTS. The Reserved Points were four areas of action reserved for themselves by the British government when it granted Egypt independence under the Declaration of 22 February 1922. The Reserved Points effectively set limits on the Egyptian government's freedom of action in the following areas: (1) security of British imperial communications in Egypt, (2) defense of Egypt against direct or indirect aggression, (3) protection of foreign interests and those of the national minorities, and (4) the Sudan. The nationalists' appreciation that the reserved points severely constrained Egypt's independence led them to demand renegotiation of these four areas virtually from the time the Declaration was issued. The first three areas were generally covered under, and ameliorated by, the 1936 Anglo-Egyptian Treaty, though the Sudan remained an issue between Egypt and Britain until the 1953 Anglo-Egyptian Sudan Agreement.

REVOLUTION OF 1952. Although the Free Officers had been planning some form of intervention in the government since 1949, it appears that most of the young officers involved were not intending to make a move until the mid-1950s. The burning of Cairo on 26 January 1952, Black Saturday, made manifest the imminent collapse of social and political order. Even then the Free Officers' decision to initiate a coup d'état was not apparently finalized until shortly before the Revolution, when they were warned by a sympathizer at the Palace that their existence as an active group of plotters had been uncovered and that action was being planned against them.

The Free Officers, led by Gamal Abdal Nasser and headed by General Muhammad Naguib, seized power in Egypt in the early morning hours of 23 July 1952, after six months of chronic governmental instability following the burning of Cairo. The Free Officers and their supporters easily took over Egypt's military installations, radio station, airport, and communications. General Muhammad Naguib was named Commander-in-Chief. At 7 a.m. Colonel Anwar Sadat broadcast news of the coup over national radio. Three days later, on 26 July, the King yielded to the Free Officers' demand that he abdicate in favor of his son, Ahmad Fuad; he was allowed to depart unharmed. Ali Mahir, a respected politician of the old regime, formed a government and a Regency Council was created for the infant king.

The immediate goals of the Revolution, the "Six Principles"--including agrarian reform, social justice, sound democratic life, and a strong army--were vague enough to earn the Free Officers initial support. Aside from General Naguib most of the Free Officers' Executive Committee were unknown to Egyptians, but the promise of a release from the chaos that had kept any Egyptian government from effective action since the Cairo fires was welcomed. The Free Officers lifted press censorship and promised to restore free political life. But uncertainty about the Revolution's ultimate political direction occurred when the Free Officers suppressed an industrial strike at Kafr al-Dawa on 13 August and executed the union leaders involved, despite the strike leaders' enthusiastic support for the Revolution and their linkage of their own industrial action with it.

The early days of the Revolution, with Ali Mahir in power as Prime Minister and most government functions continuing normally, did not involve any major reordering of either social or economic structures. It was only with the resignation of Ali Mahir in September over the regime's proposals on land reform that the country's new leaders began to put forth policies and rhetoric that were substantially different to those of its predecessors. Thereafter the pace of changes increased: a Party Law was promulgated in September, censorship reimposed in

October after two months of press freedom, the 1923 Constitution suspended in December, and political parties outlawed in January 1953.

The initial caution of the Free Officers in introducing policy and the nature of their early reforms have raised questions as to whether the actions of 23 July could be termed a revolution, or whether they more precisely constituted a coup d'état. Whatever the initial nature of the Free Officers' actions, from the mid-1950s onward, their leader, Gamal Abdal Nasser, committed his government to a profound and revolutionary reordering of Egypt's socioeconomic structures.

REVOLUTIONARY COMMAND COUNCIL. The Revolutionary Command Council was the name taken by the thirteen member Free Officer Executive following the revolution of July 1952. In January 1953 the RCC and the cabinet (increasingly composed of RCC members) were constituted as the executive arm of the Egyptian government. The RCC was under the leadership of General Muhammad Naguib, though real power in its daily and decision-making functioning was in the hands of its first chairman, Gamal Abdal Nasser. The RCC was intended to have full legislative and executive power during a three-year period (1953-56) before the promised reintroduction of parliamentary life.

The other Egyptian political parties having been barred from activity, the Ikhwan al-Muslimun remained the only surviving link between the RCC and an organized group of supporters and hence was able to present itself as representing a body of popular sentiment. During 1953 discussions of increasing acrimony took place between the two groups over the issue of power-sharing, with the Ikhwan demanding veto power (in view of its religious-guidance role), which the RCC was unwilling to grant. At the same time the RCC formed the Liberation Rally to provide it with its own base of political supporters.

In June 1953 Nasser and three of his closest RCC supporters joined General Naguib's government as Vice-Premier and Minister of the Interior (Nasser), Minister of War (Baghdadi), and

Minister of Culture and National Guidance (Salim). General Naguib also appointed Abdal Hakim Amer, another Nasser confidante, Commander-in-Chief of the army in his stead. The involvement of these supporters of Nasser in Naguib's government gave evidence of Nasser's increasingly public emergence as the dominant figure in the government, and certainly within the RCC.

It was the RCC that, in the aftermath of the leadership struggle between Nasser and Naguib in February-March 1954, announced the appointment of Gamal Abdal Nasser as Premier and Chairman of the RCC, as well as the delay in elections for the planned Constituent Assembly. The RCC finally stripped General Naguib of his functions as President of the Republic that November and ordered his house arrest. It also announced the proscription of the Ikhwan al-Muslimun, involved in an assassination attempt on Nasser the previous month.

Though the RCC was meant, with the cabinet, to be vested with authority for the governance of Egypt, apart from supervising overall policy in line with the RCC's demands, it exercised little direct executive power because most of its members did not occupy posts so much as form bases of support within various ministries for the new regime. Its power base ultimately remained the military, though in time it built up a network of supporters and clients in the civilian sector. The RCC was disbanded in 1956 following the promulgation of a Constitution approved by referendum and the election of Gamal Abdal Nasser as President. (See also FREE OFFICERS)

RI'ĀSA/RA'ĪS AL-BALAD. Ri'āsa, supreme influence or supremacy, was the goal of the leaders of the factions within the beylicate in eighteenth/twelfth century Ottoman Egypt and was expressed through holding one of the powerful offices (particularly the post of Shaykh al-Balad) reserved for them. Ri'āsa was partially gained through control of the revenues from iltizām, or tax-farming grants (awarded by the Ottoman government), which provided the funds to build up a sizable household of Mamluks; alliance with one of the Ottoman regiments was also used, particularly until the time of the Great Rebellion in 1711/1123. Essentially, however, ri'āsa depended on the number of supporters an individual Mamluk could claim within the beylicate; and those beys whose iltizāms enabled them to maintain large numbers of their own Mamluks (such as ᶜAlī Bey in the 1750s-60s/1160s-70s) had a proportionally greater influence in official councils. The flexible nature of the power structure within the beylicate made the composition of forces necessary to gain or lose ri'āsa vary widely.

RIDA, SHAYKH MUHAMMAD RASHID (1865-1935). Syrian-born writer who was a major influence on the development of Islamic revivalism in Egypt, Shaykh Rashid Rida was the founder of *Al-Manar*, an important journal that represented the thinking of its editor and of Shaykh Muhammad Abduh on the role of Islam in modern Egypt and other Islamic states. He was also involved with a number of clandestine pan-Islamic political movements, particularly in the 1910-20 period.

Shaykh Rida became a pupil of Abduh's in 1894, finding in his writings a message in sympathy with his own commitment to religious renewal in Islam. He came to Cairo in 1897 and quickly became Abduh's most vocal exponent and defender. *Al-Manar*, which he founded in 1897, became the major forum for writings about Abduh's ideas on Islamic revival. In its pages he developed the trend in Abduh's thinking that called for salāf, or return to the social models and teachings of the Prophet Muḥammad and early Islam as a model for modern life. Rida was active in the discussions about the status of the Islamic caliphate after that office was abolished by the Ataturk government in Turkey in 1924, and gave his support to the claims of Egypt's King Fuad in the latter's call for an Islamic congress to elect a new caliph. Rida's relations with the Egyptian nationalist movement were mixed. Though he supported the abolition of British influence in Egypt, he believed that Islam must be revitalized to enable Islamic societies to face the threat posed by the West. Like many individuals involved in the Islamic movement he possibly found the issues and personalities involved in Egypt's political competition irrelevant to what he felt were the more important issues surrounding Islam's survival as a social and political power. In addition to his editorship of Al-Manar Shaykh Rida also compiled and edited several volumes of Abduh's writings and wrote a biography of Abduh.

RIAZ PASHA see RIYAD PASHA

RIḌWĀN b. WALAKHASHĪ (r. 1137-39/531-33). Fāṭimid governor of Qus and Ikhmim, Riḍwān was called back to Egypt by the Fāṭimid Caliph al-Ḥāfiz (1130-49/524-44) to rid him of his Armenian vizier Bahrām. Bahrām uncovered the plot and managed to avert his deposition by arranging for Riḍwān to be posted to another governorship before he could act against him. The unpopularity of the Christian vizier made Riḍwān's efforts to build a group of supporters in Egypt easier, and he eventually displaced Bahrām in the vizierate after the latter had been driven from Cairo.

Once in office Riḍwān, who was a Sunnī, proved as dangerous to the Caliph as his predecessor and was unpopular with Egypt's Shīʿa Muslims. Riḍwān was deposed after two years in office in 1139/534, shortly before the restoration of Bahrām. He either fled to, or went on campaign in, Syria. Riḍwān returned to Egypt following the death of Bahrām in 1140/535. He is next reported as leading some disturbances in 1147/542, during which he was killed.

RIḌWĀN BEY AL-FAQĀRĪ (d. 1656/1067). Founder of the Faqāriyya faction of the Ottoman beylicate, Riḍwān Bey was the dominant power in Egypt from the deposition of the governor Mūsā Pasha in 1631/1040 until his own death. At the time of Mūsā Pasha's deposition Riḍwān was leading the pilgrimage caravan to Mecca in his office as Amīr al-Ḥajj; his colleague ʿAlī Bey acted for him on behalf of the Faqāriyya faction and in the subsequent negotiations between the Ottoman Porte and the beylicate.

The powerless Ottoman Viceroys of this period sought to rid themselves of Riḍwān by appointing him to head various military expeditions to Persia, which he avoided; and at one point the

Ottoman Viceroy nominated him for the governorship of the Red Sea province of Habash, equivalent to exile. His refusal of this last post led him to leave Egypt and seek refuge with an unsympathetic Ottoman court in 1640/1050, though he was soon reinstated in Egypt in his position as Amīr al-Ḥajj. From 1640/1050 until 1648/1058 Riḍwān enjoyed the support of the new Ottoman Sultan, Ibrāhīm, support that enabled him to defeat an attempt by the Qāsimiyya chief and the Ottoman governor to unseat him in 1647/1057.

When the Sultan Ibrāhīm fell from power in 1648/1058, the Ottoman governor Muhammad attempted to split the Faqāriyya leadership by appointing ᶜAlī Bey as Amīr al-Ḥajj in lieu of Riḍwān, but this was unsuccessful. However, ᶜAlī Bey's death in 1652/1062 and Riḍwān's death three years later greatly weakened the Faqāriyya leadership. Unable to offer a united opposition to the Qāsimiyya and the Ottoman Viceroy, the Faqāriyya found themselves politically and militarily overwhelmed. A campaign was mounted against them in 1659/1070, and they were proscribed a year later.

RIYAD PASHA, MAHMUD (1835-1911). Prime Minister of Egypt in 1879-81, 1888-91 and 1893, Riyad Pasha entered the service of the Khedive Ismail as an agricultural adviser. He served on the 1878 Commission investigating Egypt's finances, and as Minister of the Interior in the deeply unpopular European cabinet of Nubar Pasha. Ismail disliked Riyad's growing power, and tried to move him to the ministry of foreign affairs, a move resisted by Riyad with European backing. With the dismissal of the European cabinet in April 1879, Riyad went into exile until his recall that August by the new Khedive Tawfiq.

During his first term in office Riyad stood in active opposition to the rising nationalist movement and to Colonel Arabi; though he espoused the principle that Egypt should be ruled by the Egyptians, he interpreted this as meaning Egyptians like himself ruling largely on behalf of the Europeans. He was dismissed in September 1881, after intense pressure from the nationalists and a near-coup by the army, to make way for the more moderate

Sharif Pasha. His ministry had seen the effective stifling of nationalist debate at every level, and his appointment of Rifqi Pasha to the War ministry insured Riyad Pasha's unpopularity with the army.

Riyad's second term in office came during the consolidation of British control of the country, and though he occasionally attempted an independent line against the wishes of the British Agent, Lord Cromer, his independence was tempered with the realization that the British could at any time force his resignation. It was in this term that Riyad introduced a ban on the kurbash, or flogging. He resigned in 1891 over his failure to prevent increased European supervision of the Egyptian law courts, something recommended by a British jurist, Sir John Scott, and favored by Cromer.

Riyad Pasha was brought back in 1893 to replace Husayn Fakhri, after the latter had aroused Cromer's hostility. Riyad's appointment ended over his objections to continued British control of the army and his inability to protect Abbas, the new Khedive, from having to make a humiliating apology to the British Sirdar, Kitchener, after the two men had exchanged remarks during a troop review. Riyad appears to have encouraged the nationalist sentiments and anti-Cromer feelings of Abbas and claimed links with some of the informal salons of nationalists that arose in Cairo in the first decade of Abbas' rule. He was replaced by Nubar Pasha following his resignation in April 1895. By 1904 Riyad was again defending the British position in Egypt, serving shortly before his death as president of the Legislative Assembly and head of a congress of Muslims formed to defend their communal rights.

RODA see RAWḌA

ROGERS PLAN. Following the October 1967 war between the Arab states and Israel, Swedish diplomat Gunnar Jarring was charged that November with the conduct of talks between the Arab and Israeli leaders on the basis of United Nations resolution 242. These talks proved unsuccessful, and in March 1969 hostilities resumed between Egypt and Israel in the War of Attrition. By January 1970, Nasser was making public and private approaches to the United States for a resumption of the Jarring negotiations. To make use of a lull in the War of Attrition and initiate a peace process, U.S. Secretary of State William Rogers put forward to the Egyptian and Israeli governments a three-point plan for the normalization of relations between them, and between the United States and Egypt. The plan was accepted for consideration by Nasser in July 1970, shortly before his death.

The Rogers Plan called on Egypt and Israel to accept a ninety-day cease-fire along the Suez Canal, beginning 7 August 1970, with talks to be conducted by UN mediator Gunnar Jarring on the following points: (1) withdrawal of Israel to the Sinai passes, (2) restoration of full Egyptian-American relations following completion of the Israeli withdrawal, and (3) an eventual peace treaty with Israel, based on UN Resolution 242, which called for an Israeli withdrawal to its pre-1967 territory in exchange for secure and recognized borders.

Talks were begun by Jarring in August 1970, but following allegations of cease-fire violations by both sides Israel and the United States withdrew from the negotiations in September 1970. The cease-fire itself was twice extended by the Egyptian government, though upon its expiry in March 1971 it was not renewed. President Sadat, the new ruler of Egypt, made a counterproposal to the Rogers Plan in February 1971 in which he offered to reopen the Canal in exchange for a limited Israeli withdrawal to the Sinai passes.

ROSETTA STONE see CHAMPOLLION, JEAN FRANÇOIS

RUSHDI PASHA, HUSAYN (1864-1928). Prime Minister of Egypt from 1914 to 1919, Rushdi Pasha formed a government after Sa^{c}id Pasha was forced to resign in May 1914. Prior to that, Rushdi had served as Minister of Justice (1908-1910) and Foreign Affairs (1910-1912). Before the Khedive Abbas was deposed following the establishment of a British Protectorate in December of that year, Rushdi briefly served as acting Regent until the investiture of Husayn Kamil. In consultation with Zaghlul, Rushdi decided not to protest the imposition of the Protectorate, which both men felt was preferable to full incorporation as a British colony.

During Rushdi's wartime ministry the country was under virtually direct British management, with numerous and unpopular sequestrations of animals and crops in the countryside, the eventual conscription of men, and the imposition of martial law in the cities, with the attendant suppression of free political activity. The deep unpopularity of the British military presence led to an assassination attempt on Rushdi in 1915.

In November 1918 a delegation, or wafd, was formed by the Egyptian nationalist Zaghlul and approached the High Commissioner, Sir Reginald Wingate, for permission to present the case for the termination of the Protectorate to the British government. This move had Rushdi's tacit approval, but the British not only rejected Zaghlul's request but would initially not even receive a delegation headed by Rushdi himself (despite the support of Wingate). This insult to the head of Egypt's government was built by Zaghlul into a popular protest; by the time Balfour relented the atmosphere was too highly charged for Rushdi to accept an invitation without being accompanied by Zaghlul, which Balfour again rejected. Rushdi and his cabinet resigned in January 1919, though this was not accepted by the Palace, and for a second time in March 1919 with the approval and permission of the Palace, as Zaghlul was being deported and massive public demonstrations were being mounted in his support.

Rushdi returned to form a government in April 1919 at the request of the new High Commissioner, Allenby, during the anti-British disturbances associated with the Rebellion; he was unable to restore order and resigned two weeks later. Rushdi served in the 1921 Adli government and chaired the 1922 Constitutional Commission. He joined the new Egyptian Parliament in 1924 as an appointee of King Fuad.

AR-RUZZĪK b. AṢ-ṢĀLIḤ ṬALĀ'I^{c} (d. 1163/558). Vizier to the last Fāṭimid Caliph, al-^{c}Āḍid, ar-Ruzzīk succeeded his father, aṣ-

Ṣāliḥ Ṭalā'i, to power upon the latter's death in 1161/556. He quickly met with opposition from Shāwar, a former Mamluk of his father's who had been appointed governor of Upper Egypt. Ruzzīk attempted to have Shāwar deposed by naming a new governor, but the latter merely took advantage of his removal from office to gather an army of supporters to topple Ruzzīk, whom he then had put to death.

-S-

SAADIST (SA^c^DIST) PARTY. Formed in January 1938 by Ahmad Mahir and Mahmud Nuqrashi, the Saadists presented themselves as the true heirs to the Wafd leader Saad (Sa^c^d) Zaghlul, from whom they took their party name. The origins of the party lay in the leadership struggle within the Wafd hierarchy, which plagued Wafd leader Nahhas virtually from the formation of his 1936 government. The struggle ended with the resignation or dismissal of his two chief lieutenants and some of their supporters over the awarding of some public-works contracts and other matters connected with power-sharing.

The Saadists became one of the small anti-Wafd groupings relied on to join non-Wafdist governments. Saadist ministers joined in two cabinets, resigning in September 1940 over Egypt's failure to declare war. Saadist Ahmad Mahir served as Prime Minister from October 1944 until his assassination in February 1945; Nuqrashi served as Prime Minister from February 1945 for one year, and again from December 1946 until his assassination in December 1948. Ibrahim Abdal Hadi, who succeeded Nuqrashi as head of the Saadist Party, then formed a government that remained in office until July 1949. The Saadists had their own weekly newspaper, Biladi ("My Country"), but their organization at the local level was scant compared with the Wafd's. The party was proscribed in January 1953, along with all other pre-Revolutionary political parties.

Another grouping that took the name Saadist was formed in 1932 by Hamid al-Basil, an early member of the Wafd leadership, but this party had no significant political impact.

SABRI, ALI (1920-). One of the most influential and powerful figures in the left wing of the Arab Socialist Union in the closing years of Nasser's rule, Sabri was a member of Nasser's inner circle and Vice-President at the time of Nasser's death. He became associated with the Free Officers early on and acted as a liaison with the U.S. Embassy prior to the 1952 Revolution. He was appointed to be Director of the President's Office, and was subsequently made Minister for Presidential Affairs (1957-62), both offices giving him close access to Nasser.

Sabri was a member of the Presidency Council (1962-64), Prime Minister (1964-65), Vice-President (1965-67), Deputy Prime Minister and Resident Minister of the Canal Zone (1967-68) at a time when tensions in the Zone between Egypt and Israel were leading to increasingly heavy fighting. Sabri was appointed Deputy Premier in 1969 and Presidential Adviser in 1970 until Nasser's death that September, when he became Vice-President. Sabri's rise to power in the early and mid-1960s took place as many members of the original Free Officers were losing their position and influence in the government. Sabri himself suffered a reverse to his career in the summer of 1969 when, following a trip to the Soviet Union, he was removed from his post at the ASU and thereafter assigned to a relatively minor position in the government.

In fact, Sabri's real power base was the Arab Socialist Union, and his use of the ASU was eventually to antagonize Nasser and lead to his downfall. Sabri served as a member of the ASU Supreme Executive from 1962 to 1965, and was appointed Secretary-General of the ASU in 1965, a post he held with one interruption (June 1967-January 1968) until his dismissal in September 1969. He remained a member of the ASU Executive. As head of the ASU Sabri is credited with having organized the demonstrations of support that convinced Nasser to change his mind after he had offered his resignation following Egypt's defeat in the 1967 war. He was a prime mover in placing Anwar Sadat in the presidency following Nasser's death, believing Sadat would be under his control (he took the post of Vice-President) and that of his associates. In May 1971 Sabri, Shaarawi Gumaa, and Sami Sharaf, among others, broke publicly with Sadat over policy issues. They were subsequently arrested for participation in an alleged coup against Sadat, for which Sabri was sentenced to twenty-five years imprisonment at a trial later in the year. He was released in 1981.

SABRI PASHA, HASAN (1875-1940). Prime Minister of Egypt from July 1940 until his death that November, Hasan Sabri was a political moderate and independent. He first joined the government as Minister of Finance in the 1933 Yahya cabinet, then joined the Liberal Constitutionalist government of Mahmud in January 1938 as Minister of War. Sabri resigned one year later following a cabinet dispute over control of the army. Sabri was backed by a powerful court official in the June 1940 cabinet crisis. Following the resignation of Mahir, Sabri was asked to form a government; he served as both Prime Minister and Minister of Foreign Affairs during his few months in office.

SADAT, MUHAMMAD ANWAR AL- (1918-1981). President of Egypt from the death of Gamal Abdal Nasser in 1970 until his assassination on 6 October 1981, Sadat was among the original Free Officers involved in the 1952 Revolution. Nasser and Sadat became friendly in 1939, but the two men apparently pursued independent involvement in the nationalist movement prior to the formal establishment of the Free Officers in 1949.

After graduating from the Military Academy in 1938 Sadat was associated with many nationalist groupings, including the Ikhwan al-Muslimun (the Muslim Brethren), with whom he acted as a link for one group of Free Officers in 1940-42. But his contacts were more wide-ranging than the Ikhwan and must have been known or suspected; he was approached--or, rather, the group of officers he was working with was approached, by General Aziz Ali al-Masri in the spring of 1941 for help with the organization of Masri's intended defection to the Germans.

Involvement in anti-British activities with German agents or sympathizers led to Sadat's eventual arrest in June 1942 and his dismissal from the army. Detained by the martial-law authorities, he finally escaped in October 1944 and remained a fugitive until September 1945, when he emerged to form a group of nationalist supporters who were to attack selected pro-British targets. The subsequent assassination in January 1946 of Amin Osman, the Finance Minister, led to Sadat's second arrest, though he was acquitted at trial in August 1948.

During the 1940s Sadat had brief careers as a businessman and as a journalist. His former fellow officers convinced Sadat after his release in 1948 to try to regain his army commission (lost upon his arrest in 1942) and he succeeded in this in 1950, becoming active in the Free Officers under Nasser. At the time of the Revolution, he had regained his rank and was a colonel in the infantry. Sadat broadcast the news of the revolution by radio on the morning of 23 July. He was a member of the Revolutionary Command Council and served as a member of the Revolutionary Tribunal, which in 1953-54 heard a number of cases against political figures of the old regime.

Sadat was made Secretary-General of the Islamic Congress when that group was formed in 1954, becoming President later that year. He chaired the first meeting of the Congress in Mecca in 1955. Sadat was Secretary-General of the National Union, the government party, in 1957 and served in that post until the National Union was replaced with the ASU in 1962. Sadat served as Deputy Speaker of the Egyptian National Assembly in 1957-58 and following the formation of the United Arab Republic became president of its combined National Assembly, which met in 1961. During the 1950s Sadat was editor-in-chief of Al-Gumhuriyya, a government newspaper founded in 1953. Aside from his official appointments Sadat was responsible for relations with the Arab Gulf states and the Afro-Asian People's Solidarity Congress. Sadat was active in the government's efforts to mute the left-wing, particularly the communists, and negotiated with the latter to ensure its affiliation with the National Union, the government's political grouping. But Sadat's role in the government at this time appears to have been remote from the administration's real power centers.

Following the breakup of the union with Syria, Sadat served as Joint Chairman of the 200-member Constituent Assembly that drafted the Charter of National Action (presented in May 1962) and joined the Supreme Executive of the Arab Socialist Union in 1962. Sadat served on the Presidential Council (1962-64), was Minister for Yemeni Affairs (1963), Vice-President (1964-67), and Speaker of the National Assembly (1964-69).

In December 1969 Nasser named Anwar Sadat as his Vice-President and Deputy; upon Nasser's death in September 1970 Sadat emerged as a compromise candidate, as members of Nasser's inner circle prepared to press their individual claims to the leadership. However, Sadat in power proved less amenable to the direction of these factions than was expected, and a plot to overthrow him in May 1971 gave Sadat a chance to purge the government of his political opponents.

While it is too early to offer a definitive verdict on Sadat's presidency, it did mark a major shift in direction for Egypt in the 1970s, economically, politically, and diplomatically. Having led his country to victory (albeit militarily a rather fragile one) in the 1973 Arab-Israeli War, he was able to trade on his new-found popularity to press forward with a series of economic liberalizations known as the Open Door Policy, which returned elements of capitalism to the Egyptian economy. The 1973 war, even if it produced only a partial correction to the regional imbalance caused by the Israeli victory in 1967, gave Sadat enough diplomatic leeway to ease Egypt out of its longstanding relationship with the Soviet Union (already partially severed by Sadat's 1972 expulsion of Soviet technicians) and toward a renewed relationship with the United States, which by the end of the 1970s had become Egypt's major ally.

Sadat greatly altered Egypt's relations with the other Arab states during this period. At the beginning of his presidency he affirmed his commitment to Nasser's plans for Arab unity by agreeing to a federation with Libya and Syria and by discussing a possible union with the Sudan. His support for all save the Sudanese union faded in time, and following the 1973 war his relations with some of the more hard-line states, notably Syria and Libya, deteriorated over what they felt was his too-accommodating position to the West and his over-readiness to abandon the 1973 war in favor of a truce. On the positive side, the period after the 1973 fighting marked a clear improvement in Egypt's relations with the Gulf states and Saudi Arabia, with Egypt gaining both economic and political benefit from their support. Yet by 1977, Sadat was becoming displeased over what he saw as the oil-producing states' unwillingness to fund freely Egypt's development of its troubled economy. These states in turn were concerned that much of the aid they did advance was not always reaching its target.

The problem of Egypt's relationship with Israel remained unsolved, despite two disengagement agreements. The election of the extremist Likud leader Menachem Begin in May 1977 boded ill for Israeli moderation toward their Arab neighbors in future. The ever-present threat of a military confrontation may have abated somewhat since the 1973 war, but the need to maintain the army affected Egypt's economic development, and the lack of a peace complicated, in Sadat's view, Egypt's international position. The Egyptian people themselves were also weary of a struggle that had brought them to battle four times in twenty-five years, with all the costs this involved, personal, social, economic. Following a long period of American and international mediation efforts between the two parties Sadat decided to treat directly with the Israelis. In November 1977, following a sudden, dramatic announcement, Sadat went to Jerusalem and addressed the Israeli Parliament on Egypt's terms for peace. This peace initiative by Sadat, taken apparently without prior consultation with the other Arab states, resulted in his almost total official isolation within the Arab world and a consequently heavier dependence on the United States. The difficulties encountered in negotiations between Egypt and Israel in the aftermath of Sadat's visit have demonstrated the size of the gap that remains between these two major antagonists in the Middle East conflict.

Internally Sadat's presidency was marked by a mixture of liberalization and a retreat from newly awarded freedoms. Sadat made clear in his May 1971 "Corrective Revolution" speech his lack of sympathy with the more repressive police-state tactics found under Nasser. His initially cautious approach was shaped by the fact he was not very well known among Egyptians, despite his long association with Nasser. His popularity fell during 1972, following his announced "Year of Decision" vis-à-vis Israel; when nothing happened, there were disturbances on the campuses. To counter left-wing strength on the campuses, the government encouraged the re-emergence of the Ikhwan al-Muslimun. In March 1973 Sadat took over the office of Prime Minister and had to cope later that year with a march by 30,000 Libyans on Egypt in support of a planned merger of the two countries.

This hesitation and unclear public profile changed with the 1973 war, which made Sadat "Hero of the Suez Crossing." However limited Egypt's real gains were, most Egyptians viewed the 1973 war as a victory. It also brought Sadat a new international role, at a time when the domestic economy was rapidly deteriorating and international help increasingly needed.

Sadat introduced the Open Door Policy in April 1974, hoping to benefit from the stasis in Egypt's relations with Israel and from the attractiveness of Egypt as a place for the investment of foreign capital. Political constraints were also eased in 1974, with the promise of more protection for civil liberties.

The Open Door Policy, despite the intentions of Egypt's economic planners, proved no immediate panacea to Egypt's economic ills; in January and March 1975 serious industrial disturbances and rioting occurred in several textile-producing areas. Despite this evidence of discontent Sadat allowed the liberalization program to continue, and a new government was formed under Mamduh Salim in April 1975. In the elections in the autumn of 1976 the ASU was split into platforms representing the left, center, and right, and the elections were contested on that basis; Sadat was also returned for a second six-year term in this ballot.

Also in September 1976 negotiations with the IMF resulted in an Egyptian government decision to alter the subsidy structure affecting basic foodstuffs and a host of other items. The decision was announced in January 1977 and touched off several days of violent street demonstrations in Cairo and Alexandria, leading to the recension of the order and the formation later that year of a new government. Under a law passed in June of that year political parties properly constituted as such were allowed to form.

Internal discontent was not satisfied by either the replacement of the subsidies or the liberalized political climate. The activities of extreme Islamic fundamentalist groups were growing beyond what the government had anticipated or could control. In July 1977 a former minister of Waqfs (religious endowments) was kidnapped and assassinated by a group of Islamic extremists, and the religious groups brought in to counter left-wing criticism of the regime were by this point leading opposition to the government. Sadat's peace initiative in November 1977 was received with enthusiasm by many Egyptians, especially in view of the glowing picture painted by the government of the benefits of peace. Reaction to the subsequent enormous difficulties in the negotiations with Israel was given voice by some politicians and by the Islamic groups, who were also able to capitalize on the soaring inflation affecting Egypt in 1978-79. In May 1978 Sadat presented a referendum barring from political activity a broad category of individuals. Simultaneous with the tightening of political activity came further liberalizations in the economic sphere.

Sadat formed his own political party in July 1978, which had the effect of largely reversing the political reforms made earlier. In April 1979, a referendum gave overwhelming approval to the peace treaty, which was already being overshadowed by the imposition of an Arab boycott on Egypt and the steady deterioration in Sadat's relations with other Arab leaders. There is no doubt that, to outside observers, Sadat's presidency as a whole is now identified with the peace initiative and subsequent agreements he made with Israel. But the dramatic nature of Sadat's foreign policy must be balanced against the equally complex domestic issues--the economy, population, food supplies, employment--that his government had to face and by which it was judged in Egypt. This judgment tended to be, on the whole, unfavorable and despite government efforts to suppress it, the unofficial opposition in Egypt, spearheaded by a variety of Islamic groups and some left-wingers, was escalating in the two years prior to his assassination. A "Law of Shame" passed in the same May 1980 referendum that voted Sadat the presidency for life, gave his government sweeping powers to define and detain the opposition. In response to rising communal violence, the Sadat government mounted a massive campaign of arrests, both of Coptic and Islamic figures, and political opponents. Sadat was assassinated on 6 October 1981 by a group of soldiers affiliated to the Islamic opposition groups.

SA^{c}DIST PARTY see SAADIST PARTY

SAFADIN see AL-^{c}ĀDIL I

SA^{c}ID (r. 1854-63). Viceroy of Egypt, Sa^{c}id came to power after the murder of his nephew Abbas. He reestablished the modernization and Westernization policies of his father, Muhammad Ali, interrupted during the reign of Abbas.

The year of his accession saw the formal introduction of the new Ottoman legal code, whose implementation in Egypt had been the subject of prolonged negotiations between the two parties. Sa^{c}id also renewed Egypt's troop commitments to the Ottoman side in the Crimea. However, Sa^{c}id's reign was more noted for the beginnings of alterations in Egypt's domestic economy, which were to gain further momentum during the reign of his successor, Ismail. In 1855 a rail link was completed between Cairo and Alexandria, greatly aiding Egypt's internal communications. In the following year work was begun on extensions to the rail network, and, more importantly, a concession was granted to the Frenchman Ferdinand de Lesseps (a childhood friend of Sa^{c}id's) for a canal through the Isthmus of Suez. Concessions for a Nile steamship company and telegraph service were granted in 1857, when further ministries under the supervision of the Privy Council were created. Sa^{c}id renewed his father's attempts at Egyptianizing the local government, giving Arabic preference over Turkish in official communications. He also recruited the sons of village Shaykhs to the officer corps, removing for the first time their exemption from military duty. Landholding privileges were improved and extended and the Bank of Egypt was founded in 1855. In 1858 full rail service between Cairo, Alexandria, and Suez was opened. Sa^{c}id was assisted by a nine-man Council with representatives from the Palace, administration, and bureaucracy.

The negative consequence of Sa^{c}id's programs, the Egyptian national debt, was to worsen under Ismail. When Sa^{c}id came to power, the Treasury was in the black; at his death the country had already accumulated £11 million in foreign debts.

SA^{C}ID PASHA, MUHAMMAD (d. 1928). Prime Minister of Egypt following the assassination of Butrus Ghali in 1910, Sa^{c}id Pasha served in that office until he resigned in May 1914. Sa^{c}id was Minister of the Interior in Butrus Ghali's government from 1908 to 1910, which may have contributed to his intense unpopularity with nationalists once he was in the prime ministership. The nearly continual attacks on him led to his dismissal by Abbas.

Sa^{c}id participated in an alternate delegation formed by Prince Umar Tusun in November 1918 to counter the appeal of Zaghlul and his delegation of nationalists. The involvement of Umar Tusun had the unanticipated consequence of forcing the Sultan, Fuad, to give his support to Zaghlul against the ambitions of his cousin. Thereafter, however, Sa^{c}id acted as a liaison between the Palace and the Wafd.

Sa^{c}id formed a government in May 1919 after Rushdi Pasha

had failed to form a cabinet. An assassination attempt was made against Sa^{c}id in September, and he resigned that November when the Milner Mission was announced. Sa^{c}id served as acting Premier and was in Sa^{c}d Zaghlul's 1924 cabinet before breaking with the Wafd in 1925.

SALAFIYYA. An Arabic term applied to the Islamic revivalist movement as a whole, the term derives from the expression "Salaf as-Ṣāliḥ" and as such indicates an adherence to the religious faith and social mores of the early Muslim community. By implication, salafiyya accept this early community as a model for their own practices and beliefs, rejecting latter accretions to, or elaborations of, Islam.

ṢALĀḤ AD-DĪN (ṢALĀḤ AD-DĪN YŪSUF IBN AYYŪB) SALADIN (r. 1171-93/567-89). Founder of the Ayyūbid dynasty, which ruled Egypt from 1171/567 until 1250/648, Ṣalāḥ ad-Dīn is one of the most famous and popular military figures in Islam, both for his victories over the Crusaders and for his exemplary life and conduct. "Saladin" is the name by which this ruler was known to the Crusaders, and the model of chivalry and honor in battle that he presented deeply impressed European as well as Muslim observers.

Ṣalāḥ ad-Dīn, of Kurdish origin, was associated with his uncle Shīrkūh in the service of the Zangid ruler of Damascus, Nūr ad-Dīn. He accompanied his uncle on the latter's expeditions to Egypt at the behest of the Fāṭimid vizier Shāwar (see entry SHĪRKŪH). During Shīrkūh's second invasion (1167/563) Ṣalāḥ ad-Dīn served briefly as governor of Alexandria, where he was forced to meet a siege by Shāwar and his Crusader ally Amalric. Shīrkūh's third attempt, in 1168/564, had the active support of the court and the people, anxious to be rid of Shāwar and his Crusader alliances. Shīrkūh's advance put the Crusaders (in process of invading Egypt after sacking Bilbays) to flight. He entered Cairo and seized and killed Shāwar shortly afterward. Still in the service of Nūr ad-Dīn, Shīrkūh succeeded to the vizierate of the last Fāṭimid Caliph, al-^{c}Āḍid, and upon his death two months later Ṣalāḥ ad-Dīn succeeded his uncle by popular acclaim of the army.

Ṣalāḥ ad-Dīn was an extremely pious Sunnī Muslim, and shortly before the death of al-ᶜĀḍid in 1171/567 he oversaw the restoration of Egypt to the Sunnī Islamic fold after two centuries of Shīᶜa rule. In the early years of his control of Egypt, Ṣalāḥ ad-Dīn was under the suzerainty of Nūr ad-Dīn in Damascus and did not really gain autonomous power until the latter's death in 1174/569. He then embarked on nearly twelve years of fighting to reunite Egypt and Syria preparatory to a move against the Crusaders. The supporters of the Fāṭimid dynasty were suppressed after a two-year campaign by Tūrān Shāh near Aswan in 1173/568. In the next year Ṣalāḥ ad-Dīn had to meet an invasion by the Norman fleet at Alexandria in support of the Fāṭimids.

In 1175/570, at the battle of Hama, Ṣalāḥ ad-Dīn met and defeated the Zangid armies of Nūr ad-Dīn's son and successor, Ismāᶜīl, a young boy completely under control of the eunuch Gūmūshtakīn. He thereupon received from the ᶜAbbāsid Caliph in Baghdad large though then somewhat theoretical land grants in Egypt, Syria, Palestine, North Africa, Nubia, and the Hijaz.

Ṣalāḥ ad-Dīn's next major campaign was against both the Zangids and the Assassins in Syria in 1176/571. He then had to face the challenge of the Crusader Raynald de Chatillon, who began a series of attacks on shipping and the pilgrimage caravans in 1182-83/581. Raynald's navy was sunk at Qulzum on the Red Sea coast in 1185/581. Crusader and Ayyūbid forces met in battle at Ḥaṭṭīn in 1187/583, followed by a great Ayyūbid sweep across Crusader territory. The Crusaders were driven from Acre and Jerusalem. Raynald, for his great barbarity toward the civilian population of the area, was personally put to death by Ṣalāḥ ad-Dīn. His treatment of Raynald is especially noteworthy in view of the honor and compassion he displayed toward other captured Crusader chiefs.

The Crusaders tried to regain their position, and in 1191/587 they managed to recapture Acre and attempted to retake Jerusalem. A period of fierce fighting between the two sides ended in a treaty in 1192/588 that formally recognized most of Ṣalāḥ ad-Dīn's gains in Palestine, which, save for a tiny coastal strip, was completely in Ayyūbid hands. At the time of Ṣalāḥ ad-Dīn's death in 1193/589 he had formed through conquest a sizable empire within the Islamic world. He began the process, completed by his successors, of expelling the Crusaders from Muslim lands. In Egypt, though the economy and finances were far from healthy during Ṣalāḥ ad-Dīn's reign, he began reform of the country's administration and tax system, which in the declining years of Fāṭimid rule was in a shambles. In particular, Ṣalāḥ ad-Dīn removed many of the taxes he felt were in conflict with Sunnī Islam. In 1176/572 he initiated work on an enormous fortified complex on the Citadel overlooking Cairo; this was to become the seat of government in Egypt down to the time of Muḥammad ᶜAlī.

SALĀMISH (AL-ᶜĀDIL BADR AD-DĪN SALĀMISH) (r. 1280/678). Baḥrī Mamluk Sultan, Salāmish was the brother and successor (at the age of seven) to his predecessor, Baraka Khan. His appointment was never more than a stopgap; Qalā'ūn, his atabeg (commander-in-chief) and guardian, deposed him after just three months.

AṢ-ṢĀLIḤ ṬALĀ'Iᶜ b. RUZZĪK (d. 1161/556). Powerful vizier in the closing days of the Fāṭimid dynasty in Egypt, aṣ-Ṣāliḥ Ṭalā'iᶜ was de facto ruler of Egypt for nearly seven years before his death.

Aṣ-Ṣāliḥ, an Armenian by birth, was governor of the important Egyptian province of Ashmunayn at the time he was recalled to Cairo following the murder of the Fāṭimid Caliph aẓ-Ẓāfir in 1154/549; he captured and executed aẓ-Ẓāfir's assassins. The new Caliph, al-Fā'iz, was only six at the time, giving his guardian aṣ-Ṣāliḥ ample scope for his ambitions. In 1158/553 aṣ-Ṣāliḥ campaigned against the Crusaders in Palestine and managed to take Hebron and Gaza. He lacked the support of the powerful Zangid ruler of Damascus, Nūr ad-Dīn, and so was unable to press his campaign northward.

Upon the death of al-Fā'iz in 1160/555 aṣ-Ṣāliḥ Ṭalā'i^c tried to ensure his own succession to the vizierate under the new Caliph, al-^cĀḍid, by marrying the latter to his daughter. A threatened invasion of Egypt in the year of al-^cĀḍid's succession by the Crusader King Baldwin was averted by the promise of tribute, which was not, in fact, delivered. Egypt shortly afterward suffered two invasions by Amalric, who did obtain tribute from the Caliph. Al-^cĀḍid proved less amenable to aṣ-Ṣāliḥ's control than his predecessor; the court and harīm were also unhappy with the restrictions on their expenditure imposed by the vizier. The Caliph, with the assistance of the court and the backing of his aunt, arranged for aṣ-Ṣāliḥ's execution in 1161/556; he was succeeded in the vizierate by his son ar-Ruzzīk.

During aṣ-Ṣāliḥ's vizierate Egypt suffered from a period of harsh and efficient tax-collection. Aṣ-Ṣāliḥ himself does not appear to have been especially effective as a ruler, delaying the purchase of necessary provisions for the army and artificially raising prices. An equally unpopular revenue-raising technique he employed was the periodic execution of members of the court and seizure of their estates. Part of the revenue he accumulated was spent in patronage of the arts, including a splendid and still-extant mosque. He acquired a number of Mamluks during his years in power, starting a tradition that was to increase in popularity under the Fāṭimid's Ayyūbid successors.

AṢ-ṢĀLIḤ (AṢ-ṢĀLIḤ NAJM AD-DĪN AYYŪB) (r. 1240-49/637-47). Ayyūbid ruler of Egypt, aṣ-Ṣāliḥ came to power after deposing his brother al-^cĀdil II, the latter having been raised to the throne over his brother by their father, al-Kāmil, in 1238/635. Aṣ-Ṣāliḥ had served as his father's deputy in Egypt before the latter's death; during his brother's reign, he embarked on a series of military campaigns in Mesopotamia while preparing to challenge his brother's control of Egypt. Al-^cĀdil II tried to placate his brother by offering him the governorship of a Syrian province of the Ayyūbids in exchange for certain territorial concessions and presumably an abandonment of aṣ-Ṣāliḥ's ambitions toward the Egyptian throne. Aṣ-Ṣāliḥ, for a time detained by al-ᶜĀdil, effected an alliance with the Ayyūbid Amīr of Kerak, Dā'ūd, and deposed his brother.

Shortly after his accession aṣ-Ṣāliḥ defeated a Crusader advance under Tibald in battle at Gaza, though for a few years the Crusaders were able to maintain themselves in the area through exploiting the rivalry between aṣ-Ṣāliḥ and his cousin Ismāᶜīl in Damascus. The Khwārazmian Turks, who retook Jerusalem from the Crusaders in 1244/642, joined the army of aṣ-Ṣāliḥ in the second battle of Gaza (1244/642), where the Crusader position in Palestine was completely reversed. This defeat followed a period of Crusader gains by locally based Christian princes, after the expiry of the treaty concluded by Frederick II with the Ayyūbids in 1229/626.

The Khwārazmians proved difficult allies, however. Following the successful Ayyūbid attack on Damascus in 1245/643, in which aṣ-Ṣāliḥ triumphed over Ismāᶜīl, these troops revolted over pay and conditions. They were crushed in a battle near Homs in 1246/644. Aṣ-Ṣāliḥ's forces took Tiberias and Ascalon the next year; in 1248/646 a new campaign was launched in Syria and Mesopotamia by his son Tūrān Shāh.

In 1248/646, alarmed by the growing power of aṣ-Ṣāliḥ and the success of his campaigns against Crusader territory, the Christian powers of Europe launched a new Crusade under Louix IX, which reached Egypt in 1249/647. Aṣ-Ṣāliḥ died while preparing to meet these Crusaders in battle at Mansura, but his wife and eventual successor, Shajar ad-Durr, managed to conceal his death from the Christians and summoned Tūrān Shāh from campaign.

In addition to restoring some of the unity and vigor of the original Ayyūbid state aṣ-Ṣāliḥ helped establish the supremacy of the Mamluks in Egypt. From his early career as his father's deputy he gave preference to the Turkish slave soldiers he purchased, imported, and trained, rather than to the Kurdish and regular forces his predecessors had employed. He continued this policy in his military alliance with the Khwārazmians, and within Egypt he housed his own Mamluk regiment in a special garrison on the island of Rawḍa (Roda). His military campaigns featured many Mamluks in positions of high command, including Baybars, who eventually took power in Egypt. During his reign all four legal schools of Sunnī Islam established themselves in Cairo in a madrasa (school) he constructed especially for them. Aṣ-Ṣāliḥ was effectively the last of the Ayyūbid Sultans; his son and successor Tūrān Shāh, held office but briefly before his deposition and murder by his father's Mamluks.

AṢ-ṢĀLIḤ (AṢ-ṢĀLIḤ ṢALĀḤ AD-DĪN ṢĀLIḤ) (r. 1351-54/752-55). Baḥrī Mamluk Sultan, aṣ-Ṣāliḥ was the brother of Sultan Ḥasan, installed after the latter was deposed for the first time. He was placed in power by the Mamluks Taz and Minkāli, who proceeded to fight among themselves and with the Mamluks in Syria, as well as with the Egyptian court as a whole. These quarrels continued throughout his reign, while aṣ-Ṣāliḥ, powerless, gave himself up almost entirely to the pursuit of pleasure. The presence at court of an unpopular vizier, a Christian convert to Islam, aroused antagonisms in Egypt, and the weakness of the center gave scope to the rebelliousness of the Bedouin. Aṣ-Ṣāliḥ was deposed by a faction of Mamluks favoring the restoration of Sultan Ḥasan. He died while in prison.

SALIM, MAMDUH MUHAMMAD (1918-). Prime Minister of Egypt from 1975 to 1978 and, with a new cabinet, from May 1978 until October of that year, Salim was in office as Egypt experienced major internal changes. His background prior to the 1970s was with the Egyptian security services and local administration. In the 1960s he served as governor of Alexandria (1964-67), Assyut (1967-70), and Gharbiyya (1970, for six months) before returning to Alexandria as governor in 1970-71. President Sadat made him Minister of the Interior in 1971, as well as a member of the ASU Central Committee. In 1973 Salim became Deputy Prime Minister, in addition to maintaining his Interior portfolio.

Following the fall of the Higazi government and in the aftermath of the January 1975 riots Salim was asked to form a government in April 1975. In the autumn of the next year he led the center platform of the ASU to victory in the first elections contested on a multiparty basis since the Revolution. He headed the Arab Socialist Union when that body was stripped of its political activities and made into a supervisory body for the new political parties formed after the June 1977 Party Law was introduced. Salim then became leader of the Arab Socialist Party, which had the majority of seats in the People's Assembly until it merged in October 1978 with the National Democratic Party newly formed by President Sadat.

After the January 1977 riots Salim resumed his Interior portfolio. When restrictions were introduced on the activities of political parties in May 1978, Salim was instructed by President Sadat to re-form his cabinet, but in October 1978 he was replaced as Prime Minister by Mustafa Khalil. Salim has been a Presidential Adviser since October 1978.

AS-SALLĀR (SAYF AD-DĪN ABU'L-ḤASAN AL-ᶜADIL b. AS-SALLĀR) (d. 1153/548). Fāṭimid vizier who rose to power at the beginning of the reign of the Caliph aẓ-Ẓāfir, as-Sallār had to first defeat his predecessor in office, the general Ibn Maṣāl, in what amounted to a virtual coup d'état in 1149/544. During Sallār's first year in office the Crusaders began making preparations for an attack on the Fāṭimid fortress at Ascalon. As-Sallār sent the Amīr Usāma to the court of Nūr ad-Dīn, Zangid chief of Syria, in 1150/545 to suggest that Egypt and Syria combine forces in attacking the Crusaders, but Nūr ad-Dīn had no interest in the scheme. The Egyptians proceeded to raid the Frankish coast in 1151/546; Ascalon was used in the following year by Usāma as a base for further raids on the Franks.

Unpopular with the court and the Caliph, Sallār was murdered by Naṣr, the son of his own step-son ᶜAbbās, the latter desiring his position and fortune.

SALLĀR AL-MANṢŪRĪ (d. 1310/709). Vizier of Egypt during the second reign of an-Nāṣir Muḥammad (1299-1309/698-708), Sallār shared power with the Amīr Baybars II in the de facto rule of Egypt. Though Sallār was vizier, he was ultimately overshadowed by Baybars, who had the backing of the army that he had led to victory against the Mongols in 1303/702. Baybars defeated Sallār in a lengthy power struggle in 1308-09/707-08, whereupon an-Nāṣir Muḥammad decided to leave the country. When Baybars claimed power in his own name, he unwisely retained Sallār as vizier; Sallār soon began intriguing against Baybars with the exiled an-Nāṣir Muḥammad. He helped build up forces and supporters to reinstall the deposed Sultan, who resumed power in 1310/709. Baybars II fled Cairo but was captured and strangled. Sallār was himself executed shortly thereafter under orders of the Sultan.

SAMI AL-BARUDI PASHA, MAHMUD (d. 1904). Prime Minister of the first nationalist ministry formed under Tawfiq, Mahmud Sami was allied with Colonel Arabi, who led the nationalist revolt against European influence in Egypt in 1882. Sami al-Barudi, of distinguished Mamluk ancestry, had a varied and successful career in the military and in diplomacy in both Istanbul and Egypt. He was recruited by the Khedive Ismail to continue his diplomatic career on the Khedive's behalf, and during Ismail's reign Sami headed an important military mission to France and served with great distinction in the Ottoman army. Under Tawfiq, Sami al-Barudi was involved both with waqf (religious endowment) reform and the reorganization of the army. Throughout this time, Sami al-Barudi maintained his deep interest in Arabic poetry, from its earliest sources through its later development, and studied it both intrinsically and in comparison with European poetic forms.

By 1881, the situation in Egypt was far from stable. Protests by the Egyptian officer corps, angry at discrimination in the areas of pay and promotion, forced the Prime Minister, Riyad, to name Sami to replace the deeply unpopular Rifqi Pasha as

Minister of War (February-July). He was then brought in to head a cabinet (which included Arabi Pasha as Deputy Minister of War) after the fall of the Sharif ministry in January 1882. Sami's government coincided with the opening phase of the Arabi movement in Egypt, which he was sometimes accused of guiding. A decree was issued in February 1882 establishing a Council of Deputies to serve a five-year term, creating a constitutional commission, and making Arabic the official language of government, rather than Turkish. Sami resigned in May 1882 after a confrontation with the Khedive. An Anglo-French Joint Note followed, demanding the dismissal of his cabinet.

The Arabi Rebellion that spring and summer brought the British to Egypt in September 1882. Sami al-Barudi was deported to Ceylon, where he spent the next eighteen years researching a collection of Arabic poetry and writing his own verse. He was pardoned in 1900. Most of Sami al-Barudi's works were not published until after his death.

SANUA, JAMES (YA^{c}QŪB ṢANŪ^{c}) (1839-1912). Egyptian nationalist playwright and satirist, Sanua is considered a founder of modern Arabic satire and had an important influence on the development of theatrical forms. Sanua's satirical articles and plays placed this Egyptian Jewish writer among the forerunners of the nineteenth century Egyptian nationalist movement. He began publication of his journal, Abu Naddara Zarga ("the man with blue eyeglasses") in 1877, but was shortly afterwards obliged to leave Egypt for causing offense to the court. He continued his work in Paris, attacking the political establishment and colonial powers in Egypt, as well as all those he felt betrayed the Egyptian cause. His journal was smuggled into Egypt and enjoyed a small circulation elsewhere, but little survives of his other writings.

SARWAT PASHA see THARWAT PASHA

SAYF AD-DĪN/SAFADIN see AL-^{c}ĀDIL I

ṢAWT AL-^{c}ARAB see VOICE OF THE ARABS

SELĪM I YAVUZ ("The Grim") (r. 1512-20/918-26). Ottoman Sultan and conqueror of Egypt, Selīm brought to an end two and a half centuries of Mamluk rule in Egypt.

Prior to his attack on the Mamluks in 1516/922 Selīm and his predecessor, Bāyazīd, had on occasion supplied the Mamluks with artillery, gunpowder, and materials for their navy, which had suffered a major defeat by the Portuguese in 1509/915. This Ottoman help for the Mamluks came because the Portuguese were threatening the Mamluks at the same time as Shah Ismā^{c}īl of Persia, the latter also being an enemy of the Ottomans. With the defeat of Shah Ismā^{c}īl by Selīm in 1514/920 the need to maintain the Mamluks against either enemy vanished. Selim's expansion southward from Anatolia meant inevitable encroachment on Mamluk territory. This occurred in 1516/922, when Selīm captured Diyar Bakr, which straddled territory claimed by the Mamluks.

The Mamluk Sultan Qānṣūḥ al-Ghawrī had no alternative but to answer this challenge; leading the Mamluk army, he met Selīm in battle at Marj Dābiq, near Aleppo in Syria, in August 1516/922. Helped by his artillery, a superior army, and the defection of some prominent Mamluks, including the governor of Aleppo, Khā'ir Bay, Selīm carried the day. After the battle (in which al-Ghawrī died), Selīm received the homage of the last Egyptian Caliph, al-Mutawakkil III, who handed over to him some religious relics associated with his office, an act that symbolized as much as the battle itself the transfer of power in the central Islamic world from the Mamluks to the Ottomans. After Selīm had consolidated his position in Syria, he advanced on Egypt, defeating the Mamluks in battle outside Cairo in January 1517/923.

Tūmān Bay had succeeded Qānṣūḥ al-Ghawrī following the latter's death at the Battle of Marj Dābiq. Urged on by his fellow Mamluks, he rejected peace terms made by Selīm in which he was offered what amounted to the governorship of Egypt on Selīm's behalf. The risk of not accepting this offer was the promised destruction of the Mamluks. In defiance of this Tūmān Bay declared himself Sultan in October 1516/922. Upon Selīm's entry into Cairo, Tūmān Bay and the Mamluk defenders moved northward into the Delta. Despite Selīm's efforts to compromise on the one hand, and to use the Caliph al-Mutawakkil to calm popular fears on the other, the people of Cairo rose in support of a still-defiant Tūmān Bay, or possibly a reluctant Tūmān Bay with a defiant court of Mamluks around him. It was not until March 1517/923 that the Mamluks were finally defeated. Selīm's impulse to be generous in victory to Tūmān Bay was opposed by the Mamluk defector Khā'ir Bay, who feared Tūmān's retribution if allowed to live. Tūmān Bay was therefore executed. Selīm finally left Egypt in September 1517/923, after appointing Khā'ir Bay as governor.

SEPARATION OF FORCES AGREEMENT. Signed by the chiefs of staff of the Israeli and Egyptian armies on 18 January 1974, the Agreement defined the final position of the combatants following the Arab-Israeli war in October 1973. The Israelis were required to withdraw from the forward positions they occupied after the cease-fire. A ten-kilometer buffer zone between the two armies was established, under United Nations supervision. Beyond this, "thinned out" zones were defined, where each side was to reduce the number of its troops to parity with the other--eight infantry battalions, thirty tanks and thirty-six cannons. The signatories were given four weeks to reduce their troop levels in the "thinned out" zones. Behind the thinned out zones, Egypt and Israel were allowed to station any number of troops, but Egypt was forbidden to install antiaircraft missile batteries in this area. The parties were given seven weeks to position their forces, subject to UN supervision. The agreement followed the mediation of U.S. Secretary of State Henry Kissinger and direct talks between the military chiefs of both sides. A second disengagement agreement between Egypt and Israel was concluded one year later.

SEVERUS (IBN AL-MUQAFFA^{c}) (c. tenth century/fourth century). Bishop of Ashmunayn, Severus was an illustrious figure both in the Coptic Church and in the court of the Fāṭimid Caliph al-^{c}Aziz. His discussions and debates about Christian Coptic theology with representatives of other Christian schools, in which the Caliph was on occasion involved, were well known in their own day and may have influenced the general esteem in which many of the Fāṭimid Caliphs were held by Egypt's Copts. Severus developed the use of Arabic as a language for Coptic ecclesiastical purposes. His history of the Patriarchs of the Coptic Church not only deals with biographical matters but also discusses the rise and development of Coptic Christianity in Egypt and its spread to Nubia and Abyssinia. It is still consulted by historians, as it also provides useful information on many aspects of early life in Islamic Egypt.

SHA^{c}B (PEOPLE) PARTY. Formed by Prime Minister Ismail Sidqi in November 1930 to support his ministry, the Sha^{c}b was, with the Ittihad Party, the main pro-Palace political grouping in pre-Revolutionary Egypt. The Sha^{c}b was meant to provide Sidqi with an official base from which to contest the 1931 elections and to balance his over-reliance on the Palace for political support. The Sha^{c}b was therefore never more than a faction group supporting his government and was not a political party properly speaking. When Sidqi lost his prime ministership in September 1933, he also lost the leadership of the party to the new Prime Minister, Yahya Pasha, as he had no more political favors to dispense.

Sidqi regained the presidency of the Sha^{c}b in 1935, but the party remained largely dormant in the prewar years. In 1938 Sidqi himself became an independent, and Muhammad Hilmi Isa of the Ittihad became president when the Sha^{c}b and Ittihad Party united under his leadership.

SHA^{c}BĀN (AL-KĀMIL SAYF AD-DĪN SHA^{c}BĀN I) (r. 1345-46/746-47). Baḥrī Mamluk Sultan, Sha^{c}bān was the son and fifth successor to an-Nāṣir Muḥammad. Sha^{c}bān gathered support among the Mamluks for his candidacy during the illness of his predecessor and brother Ismā^{c}īl, following whose death he succeeded to power, after forcing Ismā^{c}īl's widow to marry him. He led a thoroughly indulgent life, while corruption and chaos raged through the country. His murder of two of his brothers and several senior Mamluks finally led the Syrian Mamluk Amīrs to demand his deposition. The harīm and Sha^c^bān's mother intervened to put a halt to the killings, and it was with his mother that Sha^c^bān sought refuge when finally toppled. He was discovered and executed shortly thereafter.

SHA^c^BĀN II (AL-ASHRAF NĀṢIR AD-DĪN SHA^c^BĀN II) (r. 1363-76/764-78). Baḥrī Mamluk Sultan, Sha^c^bān II's succession at the age of ten was engineered by the atabeg Yilbughā, who thought the young Sultan would be easier to control than his father, Ḥusayn, the other candidate for the post. Two years after he took power Egypt was attacked by the last group of Crusaders to land in the country, under the command of King Peter of Cyprus. The sack of Alexandria in 1365/766 resulted in a heavy loss of lives and property among the Christian, Jewish, and Muslim communities. Yilbughā's subsequent decision to attempt to retake Cyprus was unsuccessful, and a treaty was subsequently signed in 1370/772. The viciousness of the Crusader attack on Alexandria led to a cooling of relations with Europe, both diplomatically and in the precious goods trade for which Alexandria served as an entrepôt. Nubia was also turbulent during Sha^c^bān's reign. In 1375/777 Armenia fell to the Mamluks.

In 1367/768 a revolt against Yilbughā forced him to flee; he returned to Cairo shortly thereafter and tried to depose Sha^c^bān in a coup, naming his brother Unuk as Sultan. Sha^c^bān was forced to resist by a Mamluk faction opposed to Yilbughā, and the latter was finally executed after escaping his captors. In the struggle for the regency of Sha^c^bān, Aktimūr as-Sahābi emerged victorious but proved no more popular than his predecessor, as relations with the court and with Nubia continued to decline. Sha^c^bān was finally murdered by his own Mamluks while on pilgrimage to Mecca.

SHADOW (EGYPTIAN) CALIPHATE see CALIPHATE

SHAFI, HUSAYN AL- (1918-). One of the Free Officers directly involved in the 1952 Revolution, Shafi was a member of the Council of the Revolution/Revolutionary Command Council and served in the Egyptian government until 1975.

For a few months in 1954 Shafi held the Ministry of War, becoming Minister of Social Affairs later that year. He continued in the latter post after the formation of the United Arab Republic in 1958. He was made a Vice-President of the UAR in 1961, shortly before its breakup, following which he became Vice-President and Minister for Waqfs and Social Affairs (1961-62).

Shafi was appointed to the Higher Executive of the Arab Socialist Union after its formation in 1962, and from 1964 to 1967 served as Vice-President. After the 1967 war Shafi presided over the Revolutionary Court trying the military officers charged with plotting against the government. From 1967 to 1970 Shafi was Deputy Prime Minister and Minister of Waqfs. Upon Nasser's death in September 1970 Shafi was one of two Vice-Presidents appointed to serve under President Sadat; he was succeeded in this post by Husni Mubarak in 1975.

SHAJAR AD-DURR (r.1250-57/648-55). The only woman to rule Egypt in her own name during the Muslim period, Shajar ad-Durr was the widow of aṣ-Ṣāliḥ, the last major Ayyūbid Sultan. Originally a courtesan, Shajar ad-Durr must have been a fairly remarkable woman for the Sultan to have married her and for her to have achieved some prominence in annals of that period. At the time of her husband's death in 1250/647, he was preparing to meet the Crusaders in a crucial battle at Mansura. His son and successor Tūrān Shāh was on campaign in Iraq; Shajar ad-Durr's role in keeping her husband's death a secret until Tūrān Shāh could arrive and take charge of the army was invaluable. After leading the army to victory in this battle Tūrān Shāh proved incapable of satisfying the Mamluks; when he began to displace aṣ-Ṣāliḥ's commanders with his own Mamluks, he was assassinated.

Shajar ad-Durr, who was carrying aṣ-Ṣāliḥ's child (which died after birth), was proclaimed by the Mamluks, but the Caliph al-

Musta^csim in Baghdad refused to accept a woman as ruler. To satisfy him and elements of her own court she married one of her husband's Mamluks, Aybak. The relationship was far from easy; though Shajar ad-Durr controlled the Treasury, Aybak began to assume royal prerogatives that she felt were rightly hers. At one point (1253/651) he tried to gain ascendancy by declaring Egypt a province of the ᶜAbbāsid Caliphate in Baghdad and himself the Caliph's Viceroy. His decision to take another wife (Shajar ad-Durr had forced him to divorce his first wife at the time of their marriage) led Shajar ad-Durr to have him murdered in 1257/655. Shajar ad-Durr was in turn imprisoned by Aybak's Mamluks and finally handed over to Aybak's ex-wife and harīm for execution.

SHANUDA III ANBA (1923-). Patriarch of the Coptic Orthodox Church of Egypt from October 1971 to September 1981, Shanuda is the Pope of Alexandria and Patriarch of the See of St. Mark in All Africa and the Near East. Shanuda became a monk in 1954 and was ordained in 1955. Before his elevation he was a professor of theology and patrology. Since becoming Patriarch he has been a vigorous defender of the religious and political rights of Egypt's Copts. In 1979-80 he experienced some difficulties over political statements he made about Egypt's Copts during an overseas visit and went into a lengthy retreat. The worsening communal tensions in Egypt in 1981 led to a major government crackdown on both Muslims and Copts; in consequence of this crackdown Shanuda was dismissed from office by President Sadat in September 1981.

SHARAF, SAMI ABDAL RAᶜUF (1929-). Nasser's aide at the time of his death in September 1970 Sharaf was a powerful member of Nasser's inner circle. He first joined Nasser's office after the 1952 Revolution, occupying several staff positions. Following his revelation of an army plot against the new regime in 1954, he was appointed to the Ministry of the Interior. He also headed Nasser's Information Office until 1961, when he was appointed Chef de Cabinet. Sharaf gained considerable power in this post, though he operated largely behind the scenes. Through his control of access to Nasser, and his own alliance with Ali Sabri, Sharaf helped shape the character of the last years of Nasser's presidency. In April 1970 Sharaf was appointed Minister of State for the Presidency of the Republic, a post he continued to hold until he broke with Sadat in May 1971. Along with Ali Sabri, Sharawi Gumaa, and others, Sharaf was arrested and tried for plotting against Sadat. Convicted at a trial late in 1971 he was sentenced to a long prison term and the confiscation of his property. Sharaf was eventually released in the summer of 1981.

SHARAWI, HODA. Egyptian feminist leader, Hoda Sharawi was actively involved in the nationalist movement. The wife of Ali Sharawi, one of the original members of the delegation ("wafd") formed by Zaghlul in 1918 (which later became the basis of the political party of the same name), Hoda Sharawi participated in the anti-British demonstrations of the 1919 Rebellion, organizing women protestors. At the time of the Milner Mission in 1919-20 she organized demonstrations by women opposed to a continuation of the British Protectorate. In 1920 Hoda Sharawi founded the Wafdist Women's Central Committee, which among other activities led a boycott of British goods in 1922. With Ceza Nabarawi and other Egyptian feminists, she and the Central Committee also fought actively for the rights of women and for greater protections for working women. In 1938 Hoda Sharawi chaired the First Arab Women's Congress in Cairo. As editor of L'Egyptienne, 1925-40, she wrote about, and campaigned for, a more enlightened attitude about women's role in Egyptian society. She founded the Eyptian Feminist Union in 1925.

SHARIF PASHA (1823-1887). Prime Minister of Egypt three times--in 1879, 1881-82, and 1882-84--Sharif's political career was strongly tied to the development and collapse of the nationalist movement in Egypt. He formed his first cabinet in April 1879, under the Khedive Ismail; no Europeans were included in it, a response to the nationalists whose pressure had caused the collapse of the government of his predecessor. He resigned his post four months later, shortly after the Khedive Ismail was deposed, over his desire to introduce certain legislative reforms. These were resisted by the new Khedive, Tawfiq, and Egypt's European Controllers. Sharif drew closer to the nationalists at this time, and was a founder of Egypt's first nationalist party.

He was brought back to form a government by Tawfiq in September 1881, again after intense nationalist pressure had resulted in the dismissal of his predecessor, Riyad Pasha. Colonel Arabi, who was to play a role in the nationalist rebellion that took his name, eventually joined the cabinet as Deputy Minister of War. Sharif, who was strongly pro-Turkish, nonetheless sympathized with the nationalists' rejection of European domination of Egypt. Additionally, the nationalists had, through Arabi and the army, the power to force their views forward and enormous popular support among many Egyptians. But his difficulties in his relationship with Tawfiq, and the delivery of a joint note by the French and British governments that directly threatened Egypt's elected Parliament, led to his decision to step down in January 1882.

After the arrival of the British in Egypt and the failure of the Arabi Revolt, Sharif formed a new government in September 1882. His conflicts with the British over their actions in Egypt and in the Sudan caused him twice to attempt to step down. He finally resigned in January 1884 over the British decision to withdraw from the Sudan. During his last ministry he was forced to become a passive spectator while the outlines of future British control of Egypt and the Sudan were being sketched through the Dufferin Report, with increased British participation on the Suez Canal Board and the reassertion of British and European control of Egypt's finances.

SHĀWAR (d. 1169/564). Last vizier of Fāṭimid Egypt before the Ayyūbid conquest and the end of Fāṭimid rule, Shāwar was a Mamluk originally in the service of aṣ-Ṣāliḥ Ṭalā'i[c]. The latter appointed him governor of Upper Egypt, where he was serving in

1163/561 when summoned back to Cairo by the last Fāṭimid Caliph, al-ᶜĀḍid, to rid him of the vizier ar-Ruzzīk, who had succeeded his father, aṣ-Ṣāliḥ Ṭalā'iᶜ.

Upon seizing the vizierate he immediately had a falling out with his chancellor, Dirgham. Dirgham gained ascendancy, and Shāwar was forced to flee Egypt in 1163/561. Shāwar made his way to the court of the powerful Zangid prince of Damascus, Nūr ad-Dīn; he offered Nūr ad-Dīn tribute and certain territorial concessions if Nūr ad-Dīn would provide an army (which Shāwar would pay for) to install him back in power. Nūr ad-Dīn sent his general Shīrkūh, who restored Shāwar to the vizierate in 1164/559, whereupon the ungrateful Shāwar ordered Shīrkūh to leave Egypt. Shīrkūh resisted and seized Bilbays in the Eastern Delta; Shāwar then asked the Crusader chief Amalric (already in Egypt seeking to extract promised tribute) to intervene and rid him of Shīrkūh. Both Shīrkūh and Amalric were anxious, for different reasons, to return to Syria, and managed to negotiate a parallel withdrawal that left Shāwar in control of Egypt.

Shāwar's betrayal did not sit well with Shīrkūh, and in 1167/563 he sought and received from Nūr ad-Dīn and the Caliph permission to invade Egypt. He reached Cairo, where his army was met by that of Amalric's, facing each other on opposite banks of the Nile. Battle was eventually joined downriver at Ashmunayn, where the Crusaders were defeated. Shīrkūh proceeded to Alexandria; there opposition to Shāwar was strong enough for the city to welcome him openly. Installing his nephew Ṣālaḥ ad-Dīn as governor, Shīrkūh went on campaign. On the insistence of Shāwar, Amalric laid siege to Alexandria, and Ṣalāḥ ad-Dīn had to request his uncle's return.

The two opponents once again negotiated a withdrawal, but Egypt was made a tributary of Amalric. Shāwar came to resent, as did the Egyptian people, the relationship with the Crusaders and the presence of Frankish troops in Cairo, and payments of tribute were soon delayed. News reached Amalric in Syria that Shāwar had made friendly approaches to Shīrkūh, and the Crusader chief decided to act. Amalric's army descended on Bilbays in 1168/564, sacking and plundering the city after the brave but unsuccessful negotiations of Shāwar's son Taiy. The slaughter of Bilbays' population, regardless of religion, lost the Crusaders support among those Egyptian Christians who had favored them and stiffened the resistance of Cairo. Shāwar himself set fire to al-Fusṭāṭ, the section of Cairo founded by the Muslim conqueror ᶜAmr, and told Amalric he would burn Cairo itself to the ground before surrendering it.

Faced with such a desperate future the Caliph al-ᶜĀḍid wrote to Nūr ad-Dīn, pleading with him to intervene. Shīrkūh was dispatched from Aleppo with a large and well-equipped army; in the face of his advance the Crusaders withdrew, leaving Shīrkūh to enter Cairo in 1169/564. With advance planning by the Caliph and Shīrkūh, Shāwar was at first treated civilly but then was suddenly arrested and executed upon the order of the Caliph barely two weeks after Shīrkūh's entry into Cairo.

SHAWISH, ABDAL AZIZ see DAWISH, ABDAL AZIZ

SHAYBĀN (r. 905/292). Last Ṭūlūnid ruler of Egypt, Shaybān was a son of Ibn Ṭūlūn and the uncle of his predecessor, Hārūn. The ᶜAbbāsid court at Baghdad was anxious to restore direct control of the country, which since 868/254 had been in the hands of Ibn Ṭūlūn and his descendants. Shaybān had to confront an invasion by the ᶜAbbāsid general Muḥammad b. Sulaymān, aimed at toppling him from power; the two men had formerly been allied in military campaigns against the Qaramatians before Muḥammad defected to the ᶜAbbāsids, but Shaybān found that his armies, divided after years of internal quarrels, did not have the resources or enthusiasm of their erstwhile allies. The defection of the Ṭūlūnid general Badr deprived Shaybān of one of his more able commanders; a few months after his accession to power Shaybān was deposed by Sulaymān when the latter seized al-Fusṭāṭ.

SHAYKH (Burjī Mamluk Sultan) see MU'AYYAD SHAYKH, AL-

SHAYKH AL-BALAD. One of the two leading offices held by Mamluks during Ottoman times (1517-1798/922-1213), the position was equivalent to the governorship of Cairo, giving control over the city's complex internal affairs. In the last century of Ottoman rule the office virtually, and at times completely, supplanted that of the Ottoman Viceroy himself, as the Mamluks steadily acquired more power vis-à-vis the Viceroy. The office was sometimes known as "Amīr Miṣr" (Commander of Cairo), "Kabīr al-Qawm" (Senior of the People), or "Kabīr al-Balad" (Senior of the country).

"Shaykh al-Balad" was also the title given to village headmen in Ottoman times. The local Shaykh al-Balad was responsible for ensuring his community's fulfillment of its tax bill under iltizām and for supervising tenure and redistribution of farmlands. These functions of the Shaykh al-Balad were eroded in the nineteenth century, as the government administration became more centralized and began to assume more direct control of village administration. The title was eventually replaced by that of "ᶜUmda," or mayor.

SHAYKH OF AL-AZHAR. The office of Shaykh of Al-Azhar (equivalent to the position of rector) represents control of the largest and one of the most influential teaching establishments in the Islamic world and is one of the premier positions open to leading Egyptian ᶜulamā' (religious scholars). The Shaykh of Al-Azhar has enormous influence and prestige within Egypt and the post was and is usually actively sought after. The Shaykh played an important role in the nineteenth- and twentieth-century movement to reform Al-Azhar, a campaign spearheaded by Muhammad Abduh and opposed by conservative elements within the university. The Shaykhs of Al-Azhar were also involved with, and affected by, the development of the nationalist movement in Egypt.

Since the 1952 revolution, the post of Shaykh of Al-Azhar has been filled by appointment of the president of Egypt. Over the past three decades, the Shaykhs of Al-Azhar have therefore tended to support government policy in such sensitive areas as family planning. In fact, this link with the government does not represent such a radical departure from past policy, as shaykhs in the pre-revolutionary period who did not support the general lines of palace policy were subject to dismissal. The current (1980) Shaykh of Al-Azhar is Dr. Muhammad Abdur-Rahman Bisar, appointed by President Sadat in 1978.

SHAZLI, Lieutenant General SAAD MUHAMMAD (1922-). Military officer who held a number of posts in the army high command and diplomatic service, Shazli was a commander in the Parachute Brigade at the time of his appointment as Commander of Egyptian forces in the Congo (1960-61). Following some diplomatic postings, Shazli served as Brigade Commander in the Yemen (1965-66) before becoming head of the Special Forces from 1967 to 1969. Shazli was appointed Chief of Staff of the Egyptian armed forces in 1970, serving until 1973. Following a policy disagreement with Sadat after the 1973 war, Shazli was given diplomatic postings in Britain (1974) and Portugal (1975-78). He broke with the government over the peace initiative with Israel, and formed an opposition group in March 1980 based in Algeria, where he is currently (1981) in self-imposed exile.

SHĪ^{c}A/^{c}ALĪD. The term "^{c}Alīd" was originally applied to supporters of the Caliph ^{c}Alī (r. 656-61/35-40), fourth successor to the Prophet Muḥammad, in his struggle against the founder of the Umayyad dynasty, Mu^{c}āwiya (661-80/41-60). After ^{c}Alī's defeat and death the ^{c}Alīds argued that the Caliphate, or leadership of Islam, should be vested in his sons and descendants. The Shī^{c}a, or party, of ^{c}Alī became the major opposition to the rule of the Umayyads (the descendants of Mu^{c}āwiya) and later, to that of the ^{c}Abbāsids, contesting the legitimacy of these Sunnī, orthodox, rulers' control of the Caliphate of Islam. The ^{c}Alīds enjoyed a small following in Egypt prior to the conquest of Egypt by the Shī^{c}a Fāṭimid dynasty in 969/358. Shī^{c}a Islam has produced numerous offshoots whose beliefs vary widely.

The position of Egypt's Shī^{c}a varied from grudging toleration to persecution during Umayyad and ^{c}Abbāsid times. The ^{c}Abbāsid Caliph al-Mutawakkil called for the deportation of Egypt's

Shīᶜa in 850/236. Aḥmad b. Ṭūlūn (r.868-84/254-70), founder of the Ṭūlūnid dynasty in Egypt, fought several battles with Egypt's ᶜAlīds in the early years of his reign. The decline of the ᶜAbbāsid power in the post-Ṭūlūnid period, and the rise of several ᶜAlīd dynasties in the Middle East, led to a renaissance in the Egyptian ᶜAlīd movement immediately prior to the conquest of the Fāṭimids. However, though the Fāṭimids held power for two centuries as a Shīᶜa dynasty (969-1171/358-567), Egypt remained largely a Sunnī country. (See also ISMĀᶜĪLIYYA.)

With the reestablishment of Sunnī orthodoxy in Egypt under the Ayyūbids in 1171/567 the ᶜAlīd movement in Egypt began the period of its eclipse. Though Shīᶜa were found in the south of Egypt, throughout this time and in the subsequent Mamluk era there was a general emigration of ᶜAlīds of various factions out of Egypt to the more religiously heterogeneous Levant and to the Yemen.

Although Egypt today has a tiny population of nonindigenous Shīᶜa, its Muslim population is one of the most homogeneously Sunnī in the Islamic world.

SHĪRKŪH (d.1169/564). Kurdish general in the service of the Zangid prince of Damascus Nūr ad-Dīn, Shīrkūh was the uncle of Ṣalāḥ ad-Dīn, founder of the Ayyūbid dynasty in Egypt and Syria. Shīrkūh was sent to Egypt by Nūr ad-Dīn following the request of Shāwar, from the Fāṭimid court of al-ᶜAḍīd, for assistance in restoring him to power after he had been deposed as vizier by Dirgham in 1163/561. Shāwar was restored with Shīrkūh's aid in 1164/562 but he then demanded that Shirkuh leave Egypt, breaking his agreement with Nūr ad-Dīn to provide revenues for Shīrkūh's troops as well as tribute for Damascus. Shīrkūh responded by seizing the fortified Delta town of Bilbays. Shāwar appealed to the Crusader chief Amalric for help in dislodging him. Shīrkūh and Amalric negotiated their mutual withdrawal. The Crusaders were extremely impressed with Shīrkūh's character and military capabilities, as they were to be with those of his nephew Ṣalāḥ ad-Dīn, who accompanied his uncle on this campaign.

Three years after his first withdrawal from Egypt, Shīrkūh asked the ʿAbbāsid Caliph in Baghdad, and Nūr ad-Dīn, for permission to conquer Egypt, on the grounds the country was in the hands of heretical Shīʿa; the request was doubtless also spurred by his own anger at Shāwar's treatment of him. He entered Egypt in 1167/563, eventually settling his army in Giza on the West Bank of the Nile opposite Cairo. He was met by the army of Amalric, which set up opposite them, and for several weeks neither side moved. The two armies finally met in battle at Ashmunayn, downriver from Cairo, where Shīrkūh defeated the Crusaders. He then marched on Alexandria, which welcomed him, as Shāwar was not especially popular in the city. He installed Ṣalāḥ ad-Dīn in Alexandria with some troops and took the main body of his army southward. With Shīrkūh out of Alexandria, Shāwar pressed Amalric to besiege the city. Ṣalāḥ ad-Dīn, realizing that his troops were inadequate for the defense, had to call his uncle back from his campaign in the south. Once again Amalric and Shīrkūh negotiated an amicable withdrawal. Egypt, however, was made a tributary of the Crusaders.

Shīrkūh was sent back to Egypt in 1168/564 after his chief, Nūr ad-Dīn, received a request from the Fāṭimid Caliph for help in expelling a new wave of Crusaders from Egypt. This Crusader assault began when Amalric suspected contacts by Shāwar with Shīrkūh and Nūr ad-Dīn. Once more Shīrkūh, supplied this time with additional troops and transport, was able to threaten the Crusaders sufficiently for them to make a withdrawal in advance of his arrival, their eagerness to withdraw encouraged by the resistance they faced from the local population after they had plundered and massacred at Bilbays shortly before Shīrkūh's arrival.

Shīrkūh entered Cairo in January 1169/564 and carefully arranged the execution of the unsuspecting Shāwar shortly thereafter. Shīrkūh died just two months after taking the office of vizier to al-ʿĀḍid, and power passed to his nephew Ṣalāḥ ad-Dīn.

SIBAʿI, YUSUF AL- (d. 1978). Former cavalry officer and associate of the Free Officers, Siba^{c}i became a writer of popular fiction during the regimes of Nasser and Sadat and was known in Egypt especially for his newspaper serials and plays. He served as Chairman of the High Council for Arts, Letters, and Social Sciences from 1956 to 1961 and also as President (1958) and Permanent Secretary-General (1958-64) of the Afro-Asian People's Solidarity Conference. Siba^{c}i became a managing director of the Rose al-Yusuf publishing house following the press reorganization in 1960.

Siba^{c}i was closely associated with President Sadat and accompanied him on his visit to Israel in November 1977. His assassination in Cyprus the following spring was blamed on opponents of the Peace Initiative, and led to a brief and unsuccessful assault in Cyprus by Egyptian army commandos.

SIDQI, DR. AZIZ (1920-). Prime Minister in 1971-72, Sidqi served as an adviser to President Sadat from March 1973 onward. An engineer by training, Sidqi joined the government under Nasser as Minister of Industry in 1956 (he served until 1961). In this position he was directly involved in formulating Egypt's economic policy. Sidqi was made a member of the Higher Executive Committee of the Arab Socialist Union in 1962. In 1964 Sidqi became Deputy Prime Minister for Oil, Development, Light Industry, and Natural Resources and a member of the Ministerial Committee for Science. He was out of public office for the duration of 1965 after a split between himself and Ali Sabri of the ASU, but in 1966 he was appointed Presidential Adviser for Production and Industrial Development, regaining the Industry portfolio (1967-71). After the expulsion of the Sabri faction from the ASU in May 1971 Sidqi briefly served as its Secretary-General. In the 1971-72 government of Mahmud Fawzi, Sidqi was Deputy Prime Minister and Minister of the Economy. He formed a government in January 1972 and held office as Prime Minister until President Sadat assumed that post in March 1973.

SIDQI PASHA, ISMAIL (1875-1948). Egyptian politician and Prime Minister, Sidqi served in several ministerial roles prior to the

1922 Declaration granting Egypt independence from the British Protectorate. Though he had been a supporter of Zaghlul and a member of the delegation, or wafd, formed by him to press the case for Egypt's independence in 1918, and was exiled with him in 1919, Sidqi soon distanced himself from Zaghlul. He joined the government of Ziwar Pasha formed in December 1924 after the dismissal of the Wafd, becoming Minister of the Interior and Chairman of the Electoral Law Commission in 1925. Sidqi joined the Liberal Constitutionalist Party in 1924.

The King dismissed the Wafd government of Nahhas in June 1930, whereupon Sidqi was invited to form a non-Wafdist government. Sidqi dismissed Parliament, introduced press censorship, and promulgated a more conservative constitution to replace the 1923 Constitution, which he suspended. In December of that year he founded a political party to support his government, the Sha^{c}b, and used it as his platform to contest the May 1931 elections, which were held with a restricted franchise and the nonparticipation of the Wafd and a coalition of liberal nationalists. Sidqi's autocratic rule was not popular, and during his three years in office there were protests by all nationalist politicians, and demonstrations against his government and in favor of a restoration of the 1923 Constitution. He was helped, however, by the in-fighting of the Wafd and other parties, which kept any powerful opposition divided.

Sidqi enjoyed the support of the Palace until 1933, when the King felt his hold on the country was sufficiently strong after what he hoped had been a short-lived experiment with democracy (1923-30), followed by a period of restoration of his power. Sidqi's government nearly fell early in 1933 but he managed to re-form his cabinet. He stepped down in September to make way for Yahya Pasha and then joined the National Front pressing for reinstatement of the 1923 Constitution which he had been instrumental in abrogating. In January 1936 Sidqi was appointed a member of the team charged with negotiating a new treaty relationship with Britain. Sidqi served as Minister of Finance in the 1938 Mahmud government. Thereafter he joined the opposition to the 1940-41 pro-Palace governments.

Following the war, there were massive popular protests against a continued British military presence in Cairo, and official uncertainty about British intentions in the Sudan. The death of several students and the injury of many others during a demonstration in Cairo led to the resignation of the Nuqrashi government in February 1946, when Sidqi was invited to form a government. He became involved with attempts to restore law and order to Egypt, whose internal situation had become highly charged and violent in the postwar years. Sidqi also led the Egyptian negotiating team in their discussions with the British government over troop withdrawals. The negotiations between Sidqi and the British Foreign Ministry officials took place in May-July 1946. That October Sidqi went to London to finalize the agreements reached. Though he had managed to resolve many points with the British (including evacuation of their troops), both sides had different interpretations of clauses on the future of Egypt in the Sudan.

The internal situation of Egypt did not much improve during this time, despite a campaign of suppression and arrests, and Sidqi nearly resigned in October. He finally stepped down on the grounds of ill health in December 1946, a decision influenced by the failure of negotiations with the British. These negotiations, particularly the threat to Egypt's position in the Sudan, were widely condemned in Egypt by most of the nationalist parties, the strength of these condemnations making his stay in office extremely difficult.

SIDQI-BEVIN AGREEMENT. The British had been pressed by the Egyptian government since 1945 for a renegotiation of the 1936 Anglo-Egyptian Treaty and for negotiations on British troop withdrawals from Egypt. Following the British government's announcement in May 1946 that it was willing to withdraw troops from Egypt on a mutually-agreed-upon basis, Sidqi Pasha, the Egyptian Prime Minister, went to London in October 1946 to hold talks with Foreign Minister Aneurin Bevin over the proposed new treaty and troop levels. These negotiations were unpopular in Egypt and there were widespread demonstrations as Sidqi left for London.

As many of the details had been pre-negotiated in Egypt, a draft treaty was quickly agreed on. This provided for the withdrawal of British troops from Cairo and Alexandria by the end of March 1947 and from the whole country by September 1949. A joint defense board would be set up for military cooperation if Egypt was attacked or if Britain became involved in a war with any of Egypt's neighbors. The treaty gave Egypt's nationalists what they wanted with regard to troop withdrawals, but the joint-defense scheme was found by many to be unacceptable. Nationalist reaction was also mixed over the proposed continuation of the Anglo-Egyptian alliance. More seriously, the draft treaty glossed over the Sudan issue by saying that the 1899 Condominium would remain in effect until consultations with the Sudanese over the Sudan's future in the framework of a proposed unity of the two countries under the Egyptian crown. Sidqi interpreted this as meaning that the British recognised the Egyptian King, Faruq, as King of Egypt and the Sudan; the British had a completely different interpretation of this clause, their policy, and their intent. They finally defined the situation by promising self-determination for the Sudan.

Sidqi resigned following a general outbreak of anti-British demonstrations, strikes, boycotts, and book-burnings, and the Sidqi-Bevin Agreement was shelved. His successor, Nuqrashi, brought the Sudan issue before the UN without gaining satisfaction. The British unilaterally fulfilled part of the Sidqi-Bevin Agreement by withdrawing their troops from the Delta to the Canal Zone, but their troop levels in the Canal Zone were still seven times those permitted under the 1936 Anglo-Egyptian Treaty.

SINAI. Peninsula 23,600 square miles in area, the Sinai adjoins Egypt's major land mass on the northeast. It was variously incorporated and administered by successive Egyptian dynasties but was of little agricultural significance. Its major strategic importance prior to the digging of the Suez Canal lay in the land bridge it afforded between Egypt and the rest of the Levant. In Islamic times this bridge was used by several rulers and invaders, beginning with ᶜAmr b. al-ᶜĀṣ, who used the peninsula as his route into Egypt, and ending with Napoleon, who used it as his route into Syria, only to meet the Ottoman army there with its Mamluk allies. The area in the southeast corner of the peninsula is the site of the major Coptic monastery of St. Catherine.

The opening of the Suez Canal in 1869 greatly increased the strategic importance of the peninsula and of Egypt itself; Sinai's actual juridical status internationally was not settled, however, until 1906, when the British government, after the Tabah incident forced Turkey to recognize Egypt's de jure control of the peninsula, in exchange for a fixed border sought by the Ottomans.

The settled population of Sinai is concentrated along its shores, with a population of Bedouin who, before 1948, moved between Palestine and the peninsula. The vulnerability of Sinai to attacks from the East was demonstrated in the 1956 Suez War, when the Israelis swept across it to attack Egyptian positions at the Canal, and again in 1967, when the Israelis once more seized the entire peninsula and were in a good position to mount an assault on the Egyptian mainland. In the 1973 fighting the Egyptians crossed the Canal and managed to drive the Israelis back from the Sinai's western edge, only to be trapped themselves in Sinai in an Israeli counteroffensive.

Under the terms of the Camp David Accords the peninsula was returned to Egyptian sovereignty by April 1982, in three segments linked to advances in the overall negotiations. In June 1979 there was an Israeli withdrawal behind Al-ᶜArish.

Egyptian plans for the peninsula include a massive irrigation project, the Al-Salaam Canal, which will bring large areas of the Sinai under cultivation. The Sinai has good mineral resources and contains several of Egypt's major oilfields. The

SUMED Pipeline, in which Egypt has a quarter share, has given a Mediterranean outlet for oil pipelines from Sinai, though plans to link it with the Saudi TAPline at Yanbu were suspended after the Arab boycott.

SINAN PASHA (r. 1567-73/975-80). Ottoman governor of Egypt, Sinan Pasha took office after a successful campaign in North Africa on behalf of the Sultan, including the capture of Tripolitania (western Libya) in 1551/958. During his tenure in Egypt, Sinan used the country as a base for further Ottoman expansion, this time against Yemen, in 1568/976. While he was in Yemen, Iskandar Pasha held the post of governor until Sinan returned to Egypt in 1572/979.

SIPAHIS. The cavalry corps of Ottoman Egypt, the Sipahis were drawn largely from the Circassian areas under Ottoman control. The troops, funded through land grants (timār) made to their commanders, were traditionally paid in silver. As large quantities of this metal became available from the Americas, its value declined, with predictable consequences for the Sipahis' salaries. The Sipahis participated in several major revolts against the Ottoman governors in the period 1586-1601/994-1009 before murdering the governor Ibrāhīm Pasha in 1604/1013. Two other serious revolts followed, in 1607/1015 and 1609/1017, before the new governor, Mehmed Pasha, vigorously suppressed them and removed many of their privileges. The last Sipahi revolt, which raised its forces at the Ahmadiyya Sufi shrine in Tanta, Egypt, acquired a separatist character indicative of deep-seated discontent of the mamluks, but was quickly crushed.

SIRAGADDIN, FUAD (1906-). Egyptian politician, Fuad Siragaddin was Secretary-General of the Wafd Party at the time of the 1952 Revolution. He also headed the New Wafd Party from its formation in 1977 until its dissolution in June 1978.

Siragaddin, who comes from a large land-owning family, rose in the Wafd hierarchy in the 1945-50 period, restoring some of the vitality of the party leadership, which was then headed by the old and ailing Nahhas. Siragaddin became Minister of the

Interior in Nahhas' 1950 government. He sought a linkage with the Ikhwan al-Muslimun that would give the Wafd support among the revivalist group's followers.

Siragaddin organized the formation of the Liberation Squads late in 1951 to combat the British in the Canal Zone. The activities of these squads (who often had the participation of the auxiliary police) was soon to provoke a strong British response in the form of an attack on the Ismailiyya police station, where some of the Liberation Squad members were believed to be hiding. The attack, on 25 January 1952, caused a heavy loss of Egyptian lives; Siragaddin was blamed in some quarters for encouraging the police involved to continue their resistance to the British attack despite the latter's overwhelming superiority in men and equipment.

The attack on the Ismailiyya police station touched off a massive anti-European riot in Cairo the next day (26 January), with the destruction of British and European property and the loss of several lives. The Wafd government fell, and Siragaddin was later arrested and briefly detained, in March 1952, after an investigation into the causes of the rioting.

Following the July 1952 Revolution and after the Wafd had been forced to dismiss him from his leadership posts, Siragaddin was twice detained. A brief arrest in September 1952 ended in his unconditional release, but four months later, in January 1953, Siragaddin was arrested on serious charges of conspiracy and of opposition to the government's programs and policies. He was given a fifteen-year jail sentence that September. The severity of the sentence aroused much comment. Siragaddin was released several years later on health grounds, but his political rights were not restored until 1974.

In February 1978, after the passage of a Party Law permitting political groupings to form, Siragaddin helped found the New Wafd Party. The subsequent popularity of the New Wafd, combined with the active opposition to the government of another independent political party, the National Progressive Unionists, caused the government some concern. Under a referendum approved in May 1978 certain categories of individuals were excluded from political participation. Siragaddin's 1952 and 1953 arrests disbarred him from acting as the New Wafd Party leader, and the party dissolved itself in June 1978.

Siragaddin was arrested in the September 1981 campaign by the Sadat government against its domestic political and religious opponents, but released shortly after President Mubarak took office.

SIRDAR. Persian title used during the period of British control of Egypt (1882-1936) for the British Commander-in-Chief of the Anglo-Egyptian army.

SIRRI PASHA, HUSAYN (1892-1960). Egyptian politician and Prime Minister, Husayn Sirri headed a government of National Unity from November 1940 until the formation of a British-imposed Wafd government in February 1942. He previously served in the 1938 Mahmud government and in Ali Mahir's 1939 cabinet. Sirri's first term in office was far from smooth, as pressures built within Egypt and from Britain for the country to link itself formally with the British war effort, a move Sirri resisted. The economic strains of Egypt's increasing if unofficial involvement in this war effort were partly offset during Sirri's first months in office by the British decision to buy Egypt's entire cotton crop. Sirri was not uncooperative with the British, despite his government's nonbelligerent status. His cabinet re-shuffle in July 1941 brought in some saadist ministers. But the deteriorating economic, political, and military situation, exacerbated by food shortages in Egypt, led to mass demonstrations against Sirri and the British in the last months of his rule. A bitter confrontation between Sirri and the Palace over the government's decision to break relations with France (under the Petain regime) made Sirri's resignation inevitable. Following the fall of the Sirri government, the British presented an ultimatum to the King in February 1942, forcing him to call the Wafd in to form a new government.

In the summer of 1949, Sirri was invited to form a government with the Wafd but this proposed coalition did not work out. Instead, Sirri formed a caretaker government in November 1949. Sirri resigned when the Wafd won the elections of January 1950 and became Chief of the Royal Cabinet, a post he held until forming a government in June 1952. His last ministry came at a time when the nation's political decline had become terminal. Three weeks after taking office, on 20 July, he stepped down in favor of Hilali Pasha after Faruq refused his suggestion of bringing General Naguib into the government. Along with other pre-Revolutionary politicians Sirri was banned from further participation in political activities in January 1953.

SITT AL-MULK (d. 1027/418). Regent for her nephew, the Fāṭimid Caliph aẓ-Ẓāhir, Sitt al-Mulk was the sister of his predecessor, al-Ḥākim. She had a serious falling out with her brother prior to his disappearance and supposed death in 1021/411, and was suspected of some involvement in his vanishing. Her nephew was a boy of sixteen at the time of his elevation to the Caliphate and appeared to show little inclination to become involved in the politics of the Fāṭimid court. Sitt al-Mulk therefore acted as de facto ruler of Egypt until her death, after disposing of the main challenger to her rule, the governor of Damascus ᶜAbd ar-Raḥmān, whom her brother had appointed. During her period in power Aleppo broke away from Fāṭimid control (1023/414). Sitt al-Mulk also had to cope with a severe two-year famine in 1024-25/415-16.

SIX DAY WAR see ARAB-ISRAELI WAR (1967)

SIX-POINT AGREEMENT (1973 CEASE-FIRE AGREEMENT). Following the passage of UN Security Council Resolution 338, calling for a cease-fire to end the 1973 Arab-Israeli War, Egyptian and Israeli officers met at Kilometer 101 on the Ismailiyya-Cairo road. On 11 November 1973 the cease-fire agreement was signed; it took its name from the six points agreed to during the negotiations. These included (1) observance of the UN-sponsored cease-fire; (2) discussions on positions held by each side as of 22 October (the Israeli forces had advanced beyond these at the time of the first cease-fire); (3) the provision of food, water, and supplies daily to troops trapped in the Sinai, and the evacuation of the Egyptian wounded; (4) the lifting of restrictions on the delivery of nonmilitary supplies to the Egyptian army in Sinai; (5) the maintenance by UN Emergency Force troops of checkpoints on the Cairo-Suez Road; and (6) the exchange of prisoners.

Following the conclusion of this agreement both sides negotiated a further Separation of Forces Agreement, signed in January 1974.

SIX PRINCIPLES. The first formulation of the political objectives of the Free Officers, the Six Principles were announced after the Revolution of July 1952 and became the basis of the Provisional Constitution of 1953. The Six Principles were (1) the destruction of colonialism and its Egyptian collaborators, (2) the eradication of feudalism, (3) the ending of monopolies and the control of the state by private financial interests, (4) the establishment of social justice, (5) the construction of a strong national army, and (6) the abolition of censorship and creation of a sound democratic life. The deliberate vagueness of the principles was doubtless intended to secure the broadest possible popular backing for the Free Officers. Aside from Agrarian Reform, which was introduced in September 1952, little indication was given by the Free Officers Executive of how these principles were to be implemented or incorporated into a legislative program under Egypt's then-existing political system. The Six Principles were eventually included in the preamble to the 1956 Constitution. Censorship was reimposed in October 1952 and in January 1953 pre-revolutionary political parties were banned.

AS-SIYŪTĪ, JALĀL AD-DĪN (1445-1505/849-911). Writer, scholar and encyclopaedist of Islamic Egypt, as-Siyūtī is credited with 560 books on a wide variety of subjects, ranging from religion and law through grammar and history. As-Siyūtī, from a Hijazi family, traveled in Egypt and the Hijaz and briefly worked in academia and the legal profession before retiring to pursue his writing. His encyclopedia, considered to be his major work, is divided into fourteen general subjects, discussing the life and character of the Prophet Muḥammad and the traditions associated with him, general world history, Egyptian and Islamic history as well as the sciences, law, and philology. His work was largely a compilation of the writings of previous scholars, remarkable for the sheer volume and breadth of the topics he covered.

SOCIALIST LABOR PARTY. The largest of Egypt's official opposition parties, the Socialist Labor Party was formed following the introduction of the Party Law of June 1977, which permitted the formation of political parties in Egypt. It survived the government's restrictions on party activity introduced and approved in a referendum the following year. The Socialist Labor Party, headed by Ibrahim Shukri, has a right-wing platform with regard to economics and foreign affairs, supporting the Infitah, or Open Door Policy, and the Peace Initiative. In the June 1979 elections the party won twenty-nine seats.

SOCIALIST LAWS. Series of economic decrees introduced in the late spring and early summer of 1961, the Socialist Laws began the process of nationalizing Egypt's banking and major industrial enterprises still in private hands, and the sequestration of the private wealth of certain Egyptians. The Socialist Laws signaled the Nasser government's commitment to a thorough restructuring of the Egyptian economy and, to a certain extent, Egyptian society itself. The first Socialist Laws aroused great antagonism in Syria and contributed to that country's decision to break away from its union with Egypt.

After the breakup of the United Arab Republic the Egyptian government in October 1961 introduced new Socialist Laws, placing large sections of private commercial activity, such as cotton-trading, under government control, set limits on personal income and shareholding, increased the progressive income tax, reduced the ceiling on permissible landholding from 200 to 100 feddans, and introduced stricter controls on imports and exports.

The owners of capital nationalized under the laws were to be indemnified with 4-percent government bonds. Further nationalizations took place in 1963.

The Socialist Laws aimed at a redistribution of national wealth to ensure the predominance of the public sector (and with it the government) in the economy. They effected the transformation of Egypt from a mixed economy with strong capitalist representation to a state economy with centralized economic planning and management. Many of the more restrictive economic aspects of the Socialist Laws passed in this period were abrogated by the People's Assembly in 1975.

SOCIALIST PARTY. The first Egyptian Socialist Party was formed late in 1920 in Alexandria by labor organizer Joseph Rosenthal and a group of Egyptian intellectuals led by Antun Marun and Salama Musa. The party attempted to organize the industrial workers in Alexandria and in the textile centers of the Delta region. The Socialist Party eventually changed its name to the Communist Party in 1923, but it had already moved sharply to the left following its formation and sought affiliation with the Communist International. Unlike the other Egyptian nationalist parties it had a large proportion of foreigners in its leadership; it in fact gave little support to the nationalist movement as such, preferring to concentrate on industrial issues. The Tharwat government suppressed the party in Cairo in July 1922, though it continued active in Alexandria. The involvement of the Wafd Party in the Egyptian labor movement caused a split in the previous pattern of cautious cooperation between the Wafd and the Socialists; Zaghlul's government arrested many of the leaders of the Socialist Party when it came to power in 1924. The party took on a new platform, calling for the unity of workers and peasants against the government, but was almost totally silenced by government repression in 1925 and 1926.

The Socialist Party of the post-World War II period was a quite different organization, being the renamed Misr al-Fatat (Young Egypt) party of Ahmad Husayn.

SOCIETY OF INDEPENDENT EGYPT (JAM^{c}IYA MISR AL-MUSTAQILLA). A grouping of Egyptian politicians founded in August 1921, the Society of Independent Egypt did not differ greatly from the pre-World War I Umma Party and was a base for those moderate nationalists who opposed the Wafd. Its guiding light was Adli Pasha, who together with a group of dissident Wafdists founded it and formed its leadership. The Society was formed to support the official delegation, headed by Adli, that went to London in the summer of 1921 to discuss, with the British Foreign Secretary Curzon, Egypt's continued status as a Protectorate, against claims by Zaghlul and the Wafd that Adli's delegation was unrepresentative of Egyptian nationalist sentiment. Many of the leaders of the Society later joined the Liberal Constitutionalist Party when that group was founded in 1922.

SOCIETY FOR THE REVIVAL OF THE NATION. Clandestine anti-British grouping under the informal leadership of the Khedive Abbas II, the Society was active in the first decade of Abbas' reign (1892-1902). The exact activities of the Society, aside from gatherings for discussions on political topics, are not known, but it included in its membership practically every significant nationalist leader of the day: Mustafa Kamil, Muhammad Farid, Lutfi al-Sayyid, and others. Some of this group found an outlet for expressing their ideas in Al-Muayyad, edited by Shaykh Ali Yusuf. The group was undoubtedly affected by the growing rift between Abbas and Mustafa Kamil, the most dynamic and radical among this group of nationalists, which led to a split between the two in about 1904. Other personalities associated with the Society were instrumental in the formation of the major pre-World War I political parties.

SOVIET-EGYPTIAN AGREEMENT. Signed between the Egyptian and Soviet governments in March 1968, the agreement provided naval facilities for the Soviet's Mediterranean fleet at Alexandria. In return Russia was to supply Egypt with materiel lost during the 1967 Arab-Israeli War. The agreement was extended for a further five years by negotiations held in February 1973, in exchange for a new and much higher level of Russian weapons supplies. The agreement came to an end when Egypt unilaterally canceled Soviet docking rights at Alexandria in 1976.

SOVIET-EGYPTIAN TREATY OF FRIENDSHIP. Fifteen-year friendship treaty concluded in May 1971 between Soviet President Podgorny and President Sadat of Egypt, the Treaty of Friendship pledged mutual support and the supply of weapons to Egypt from Russia on a regular basis. The Egyptians asked at the time of the negotiations that the Russians make certain approaches to the U.S. on its behalf with regard to Israel, possibly seeking a negotiated settlement to the impasse caused by the 1967 Arab-Israeli War.

The failure of the Russians to keep up a supply of weapons steady enough to satisfy the Egyptian government and to present effectively Egypt's case in the Arab-Israeli dispute, led to a rapid cooling of relations. President Sadat expelled 6,000 Soviet military advisers in July 1972 and took over their equipment. The treaty was unilaterally abrogated by President Sadat in March 1976.

The shift in Egypt's relationship with the Soviet Union was not a smooth process. The signing of the treaty with Russia came during the same month as the crackdown on the left-wing Ali Sabri faction. At the time of the expulsion of the Soviet technicians Prime Minister Aziz Sidqi had just returned from a visit to Moscow; six months later, however, Egypt concluded its biggest-ever arms deal with the Soviet Union. Whatever Sadat's long-range intentions towards Russia were, Egypt was still heavily dependent on the Soviet Union for supplies and spare parts. Only a complete restocking of the Egyptian armed forces with Western weapons would end this dependence.

STACK, SIR LEE (1868-1924). Sirdar and Governor-General of the Sudan, Sir Lee Stack had been in office for eight years at the time of his assassination in Cairo in 1924. His death had enormous impact on the political future of Egypt, both internally and with regard to its claims in the Sudan.

The status of the Sudan had been vigorously and at times acrimoniously discussed and debated between Egypt and Britain in the early 1920s. Egyptian resentment and the British unwillingness to yield its position in the Sudan probably helped create the poisoned atmosphere in which the assassination took place. Demonstrations in the Sudan also helped to arouse popular Egyptian sentiment about the issue. Stack was shot on 19 November, and a young nationalist was immediately seized and arrested. Further arrests occurred, including those of two prominent members of the Wafd leadership, Ahmad Mahir and Nuqrashi, though they were subsequently acquitted after a controversial trial.

Stack's death provoked a public outcry in Britain, and stiff penalties were demanded by Britain's High Commissioner, Allenby, from Egypt, including the immediate evacuation of Egyptian troops in the Sudan and the Egyptian acquiescence to Sudanese use of the Nile for large-scale irrigation. Though the Egyptian government of Zaghlul Pasha accepted some of the ultimatum demands, such as the prosecution of Stack's assassins, prohibition of political demonstrations, and payment of a £500,000 indemnity, they rejected out of hand the demands relating to the maintenance of British military advisers and to the Sudan. Britain seized the Alexandria customs post, and Zaghlul's government fell.

In the aftermath of the assassination the British for several years blocked any inclusion of the Wafd in an Egyptian government, accusing it of involvement, direct or indirect, in the assassination. The British also put into effect an irrigation scheme for the Sudan that raised its share of the Nile waters, without prior consultation with Egypt.

STERLING RESERVES AGREEMENT. The political involvement and economic links between Egypt and Great Britain, particularly the latter's purchase of Egyptian commodities during the Second World War, led Egypt to accumulate enormous sterling reserves. Egyptian estimates of these reserves were about £600 million, British estimates somewhat nearer the final agreed sum of £405 million. Egypt left the sterling area in 1947, whereupon these reserves were blocked by the Bank of England and only released to Egypt in small, gradually paid sums to prevent a run on sterling. Reserve repayment agreements were negotiated in 1947, 1948, and 1949.

The Sterling Reserves Agreement, concluded in July 1951, provided that Egypt's sterling reserves could be drawn entirely over a thirteen-year period, and allowed £14 million equivalent to be drawn in U.S. dollars. Further concessions were made by the British in 1952 over the reserves to prop up the government of Hilali. In 1955 a new agreement with Britain increased Egypt's annual drawing entitlements, but these were blocked after the Suez Canal nationalization. In 1959 a final agreement on the sterling reserves was reached with the British, settling their outstanding financial obligations; this settlement came at a time when strained relations over the Suez War were being repaired. Under this final agreement £90 million in sterling-reserve balances were released.

SŪDĀN. Name applied to the regiments of troops of Nubian and Sudanese origin, from the time of Ibn Ṭūlūn (868/254). Ibn Ṭūlūn formed a regiment of Nubians recruited from the tribute furnished by the Kingdom of Nubia and from other tribes in the southern regions. Though the regiments were formed to help the ᶜAbbāsid Caliph suppress a rebellion in Palestine, the Sūdān gave Ibn Ṭūlūn a military force under his direct control, a crucial factor in his subsequent bid for autonomy. The regiments participated in several important campaigns during Ibn Ṭūlūn's reign. During Fāṭimid times (969-1171/358-567) the Sūdān regiments and the Turkish troops, along with the Berber supporters of the Fāṭimids, engaged in constant struggles for position within the military hierarchy, which deteriorated into bitter factional fighting between the ethnic regiments in 1067-73/459-65. The resultant chaos in Egypt was not quelled until the arrival from Syria in 1074/466 of Badr al-Jamālī, who suppressed this dissension at the request of the Fāṭimid court. But the Sūdān remained important throughout the Fāṭimid period.

When Ṣalāḥ ad-Dīn took power in Egypt as vizier for the last Fāṭimid Caliph in 1169/564, there were entrenched regiments of Sūdān troops in the country. Their influence may have diminished vis-à-vis the Turkish troops, but their numbers were still substantial. Ṣalāḥ ad-Dīn drove many thousands of these troops from the country, and they were thereafter a much smaller component of the Egyptian army.

At the time of the French invasion of Egypt in 1798 Napoleon apparently considered reviving the Sūdān regiments. The idea was picked up by Muhammad Ali, who attempted to form regiments of Nubians following his conquests in the region in 1820-21. Training and adaptation difficulties experienced by these forced recruits led him to abandon the idea shortly afterward.

SUDAN. Egyptian claims to the Sudan in modern times date from the initial conquest of Nubia and the Sudan in 1820-24 by Muhammad Ali's army under the command of his son Ismail. Following Ismail's assassination in 1822, Muhammad Bey took charge and continued the campaign. Muhammad Ali's initial goals, slaves for his army and gold, were unfulfilled. The slaves taken proved unsuccessful as soldiers, and the fabled gold failed to materialize. The Egyptian ruler received land grants for the area from the Ottoman Sultan (under whose nominal sovereignty the regions and kingdoms to the south of Egypt were) hereditarily in 1841 when it was formally added to Egypt by a decree of the Sultan. Egyptian control of the area was limited at the time to a strong presence in the northern regions, divided at the time of Muhammad Ali's conquests into four governates, and a small military force in the south.

Sudan was given the beginnings of a bureaucratic system modeled on that of Egypt, and some investment was made to develop Sudan's infrastructure. However, the slave trade carried on under the Egyptians produced great unhappiness in Sudan and was not curbed until the reforms of Khedive Ismail (r. 1863-1879).

The involvement of Egypt in the Sudan increased markedly during the reign of Ismail, who pushed forward Egypt's expansion into Africa and in the process completed its control of the Sudan. Samuel Baker, the British explorer, was hired by Ismail to explore Africa toward the sources of the Nile, and served as Governor-General of the Equatorial Provinces in 1869-73. Another European, Charles Gordon, was Governor-General of the Sudan in 1877-79. Ismail succeeded in getting back from the Ottomans the Red Sea ports they had granted to his grandfather, Muhammad Ali but which had reverted to Ottoman control. His final conquest in the region, Dafur, was annexed in 1874.

Ismail was less successful in expanding and making effective Egypt's administration in the country; the many Europeans he hired for service in the Sudan were resented by the Sudanese, as indeed were most of the Egyptians who served there, usually with great reluctance. However, an anti-slavery campaign was pursued with some effect, if not total success.

A reaction was inevitable. In 1881 the Mahdist movement started; a religious and martial bid for independence from Egyptian control. The arrival of the British in Egypt late in 1882 brought them involvement with the Sudan, and the Mahdist movement as well. The British policy of a careful withdrawal of troops from the Sudan ended disastrously with the Khartoum massacre of Gordon (who had been sent by the British to lead the withdrawal there) and his troops in 1885. The Mahdists gained power in northern Sudan, and under the leadership of Abdallahi at-Ta'ishi established an independent state that held power until the British, using their own and Egyptian troops, reconquered the country between 1896 and 1898.

The British and Egyptians signed the Anglo-Egyptian Condominium Agreement in 1899, outlining the administration of the Sudan. Though the Sudan was under Egyptian sovereignty, it was run virtually as a British colony, with Egypt paying much in administrative costs but having little role in management of the Sudan. Despite this de facto control of the Sudan by the British, Egyptian nationalists and the Egyptian government in particular never abandoned Egypt's claims to the country. Its future status under an Egyptian government became a sticking point in all major negotiations between Egypt and Britain in the 1920s, 30s, 40s, and 50s. Egypt was also concerned with defining the allocations of Nile water it and the Sudan were entitled to; this topic assumed more critical character as the various projects for damming the Nile in Egypt and increasing land under irrigation in the Sudan made a common policy on river use of growing importance.

The 1924 assassination of the Governor-General of the Sudan, the Sirdar Sir Lee Stack, came at a time of strong popular sentiment in Egypt about who should control the Sudan. The "Unity of the Nile Valley" (the union of Egypt and the Sudan under the Egyptian crown) was a political theme of the Nationalist Party, strongly supported as well throughout the pre-Revolutionary period by all other Egyptian political parties. The failure of the 1936 Anglo-Egyptian Treaty to come to terms with the issue of the Sudan brought the Wafd government that negotiated the treaty its first wave of unpopularity, though under the circumstances Egypt had little power to reverse a British determination to maintain its presence in the Sudan.

In 1946 negotiations between the Egyptian Prime Minister, Sidqi Pasha, and his British counterpart, Aneurin Bevin, also failed to resolve the Sudan issue. Although the two ministers reached agreement on some issues, both parties presented conflicting interpretations of what they had agreed to regarding Sudan's future. At the end of 1946, the British made clear they favored self-determination for Sudan, and the Sidqi-Bevin agreement broke down. The government of Nuqrashi Pasha obtained Arab League backing for Egyptian claims over the Sudan in 1947. That August Nuqrashi presented Egypt's case for control of the Sudan to the Security Council of the UN. The Council responded by urging continued negotiations, a decision Nuqrashi found disappointing. Following these diplomatic and political moves the 1950 Wafd government of Nahhas Pasha, faced with its inability to obtain satisfaction from the British with regard to the Sudan, unilaterally abrogated the 1936 Anglo-Egyptian Treaty in October 1951 and declared Faruq King of Egypt and the Sudan. Egypt subsequently gained only limited recognition in the Arab world and Europe for its claims.

This unilateral abrogation of the treaty did not affect the course of events in the Sudan, where the British had been gradually laying the groundwork for autonomy and assuring the Sudanese of prior consultation with them before deciding on any long-term strategy. In April and October 1952 the British announced measures for Sudanese self-government. There were elements in the Sudan who did favor union with Egypt, though later events throw into question how much their advocacy of union was seen as a way of prising the British out of their country. In Egypt, both before and after the 1952 Revolution, popular and official attention focused on this pro-Union sentiment and its chief advocate, the National Union Party. After the Revolution, General Naguib held discussions with Sudanese political leaders, and Egypt and Britain managed to conclude a treaty over the Sudan in 1953. The treaty provided for the establishment of a freely elected parliament that would choose whether it wished to affiliate with Egypt. Egypt backed the National Unionist Party, which underwent a split at the time Sudanese independence was declared in 1956; the Sudanese government, to the great disappointment of the Egyptians, elected not to form a union with Egypt.

The decision of the Sudanese government to pursue its own course was influenced not only by internal political considerations but probably also by the desire for distance from its powerful northern neighbor; it may also have been somewhat affected by the fate suffered by the half-Sudanese President of Egypt, General Naguib, who was deposed in 1954 by Nasser. Postindependence relations between the countries were strained in 1958 by a border dispute and by the question of future distribution of Nile waters after completion of the proposed Aswan High Dam. The latter issue, and compensation for Sudanese land due to be flooded by the lake formed behind the dam, were settled in the 1959 Nile Waters Agreement. The Nile Valley Association, in which both countries participate, has become an important forum for their joint cooperation on a common policy toward the Nile.

Though the Sudan participated in inter-African affairs, the need to address its domestic and political problems led to its having a rather low international profile compared with that of Egypt prior to 1969, when the accession of President Numayri saw new links being formed by Sudan with both the Arab and African worlds; its links with the former had been growing since the 1967 Khartoum Summit. Sudan participated in federation talks with Egypt, Libya, and Syria at the beginning of the presidency of Anwar Sadat of Egypt, but when the Confederation was announced in 1971, Sudan opted not to participate. A similar currency and administrative union has been discussed since 1977, and both countries have made statements about intended cooperative measures throughout the 1971-77 period. The Sudan did not officially support the Camp David Accords, though it was restrained in its criticisms. Despite political disagreements the two countries are vitally linked by, and dependent on, the Nile and their cooperative use of it. There is little doubt that the deep and longstanding links between Egypt and Sudan will have much more impact on their future relationship than the temporary and political disputes which have occasionally arisen between them.

SUDAN AGREEMENT (1953) see ANGLO-EGYPTIAN SUDAN AGREEMENT

SUEZ CANAL. The Suez Canal is an artificial channel connecting the Mediterranean and Red Seas through the Isthmus of Suez, which lies between the mainland of Egypt and the Sinai peninsula. Its original dimensions were altered some eight times before 1980, when the Canal was again extensively widened and deepened. The northern outlet of the Canal is at the city of Port Sa^{c}id, and its southern outlet is the city of Suez, known in earlier times as Qulzum, and an ancient harbor.

The idea of a canal first occurred in pharaonic times, and the Nile Delta (rather than the Mediterranean) was linked to the

Red Sea via canals at several points in Egypt's history. In the early Islamic period, this canal was re-dug, then later filled. A direct link between the Mediterranean and the Red Sea was usually rejected on the belief that the sea levels of the two bodies of water to be joined were so different as to make the project impractical. French scientists who accompanied Napoleon's invasion of Egypt in 1798-1801 re-examined the possibility of a canal, but the first attempts at its construction were actually done by disciples of the French socialist Saint Simon during Muhammad Ali's time.

Ferdinand de Lesseps, a French engineer and entrepreneur, became the driving force behind the Suez Canal project. He not only recognized the canal's feasibility, but also the effect its construction would have on world shipping. His personal intervention with European governments and banks was largely responsible for the success of the project. In November 1854, de Lesseps secured the first concession to construct the canal from the new Viceroy, Sa^{c}id Pasha, who had been a longstanding friend of his. The concession entitled the Universal Suez Canal Company to dig the canal and operate it for ninety-nine years. Sa^{c}id also gave de Lesseps a number of undertakings about the supply of labor and purchase of shares which were to be financially disastrous for Egypt. The British government pressed the Ottoman Sultan to invalidate the concession (largely because it was under French direction) and a new concession had to be obtained in 1856; despite continuing opposition, work began in 1859. Ismail tried to modify the concession when he came to power in 1863, placing more responsibility on the company to provide the labor promised by Sa^{c}id. In the end Egypt paid over 70 percent of the £16-million cost of the Canal and received 15 percent of the profits.

The Suez Canal was opened in 1869, with the Egyptian government holding 44 percent of the shares. It dramatically changed Egypt's strategic importance, particularly for the British, to whom it offered a vastly shorter route to their major colony, India. When the increasing bankruptcy of the Khedive

Ismail forced him to sell his interest in the Canal in 1875, British banks pressed their government to acquire them, which it did, paying Ismail nearly £4 million. The protection of the Canal's shareholders was among the reasons used by the British to justify their military intervention during the Arabi Rebellion in 1882. After the establishment of British control they increased their power on the board of the Suez Canal Company in November 1883. In 1888 the British secured in the Convention of Constantinople the agreement of other maritime powers that the Canal would always remain open to shipping. The Canal's ownership by foreigners was distressing to many Egyptians; an attempt by Prime Minister Butrus Ghali Pasha in 1910 to extend the Company's concession was one factor leading to his assassination.

Though the Canal was a highly profitable enterprise for the Company, Egypt did not gain any revenue from it until 1938, because of her debt repayment obligations to the European banks who were Egypt's creditors in the 1870s. This situation was partially remedied by agreements in 1937 and 1948. The latter gave Egypt increased profits and representation on the Suez Canal Company Board.

The Canal continued to be operated as a private concession until its nationalization in July 1956, when annual profits were some £E16 million. Its operations were then transferred to the temporary supervision of a Council of Administration until the formation of the Egyptian government's Suez Canal Authority. The Canal was closed twice in recent times; for a brief period after the Suez War, and following the 1967 Arab-Israeli War until 1975.

Egypt currently (1980) earns $550 million per annum from the Canal, although recent improvements are expected to boost revenues to $1 billion, and plans for a second canal are under discussion.

SUEZ CANAL AUTHORITY. Established in 1957, one year after the nationalization of the Suez Canal, the Authority handles navigation and piloting on the Canal and operates it as a public corporation. Its first director, Mahmud Yunis, led the occupation of the Canal Company's headquarters when the Canal was nationalized. He was widely praised for his skill in managing the transition from private to national ownership while substantially increasing the Canal's profits. The Authority oversaw the dredging of the Canal in the aftermath of the Suez War in 1956, and after the 1973 Arab-Israeli War it appealed for international assistance in dredging and clearing the Canal of wrecked ships and mines. The Suez Canal Authority is currently (1980) headed by Mashur Ahmad Mashur. In addition to its supervisory functions of the Canal's physical operation the Authority also sets tariff rates and supervises related development projects in the areas adjoining the Canal.

SUEZ CANAL TREATY. In May 1949, following a prolonged period of negotiations, the Suez Canal Company agreed (1) that Egypt should receive a greater share of gross profits (reaching an eventual level of 7 percent); (2) that the two Egyptian directors (as against twenty-five foreign directors) on the board would be increased to seven by 1964; (3) that major expansion of the Canal should be investigated; and (4) that the Company should try to increase the number of its Egyptian employees, particularly pilots. This new agreement was meant to hold until the expiry of the original concession in 1968, after which it would not be renewed. At the time the Canal was nationalized, discussions were taking place between the Company and the government about increased investment by the Company. Subsequent events invalidated the treaty.

SUEZ WAR. In July 1956 the United States and Britain announced that they would not be going through with their commitment to finance a loan by the International Bank for Reconstruction and Development for construction of the Aswan High Dam. The two countries felt that it would be economically impossible for Egypt to repay the debt it would incur, in view of Egyptian resistance to certain fiscal controls sought by the U.S. and Britain. The decision by the two Western powers was partly based on their displeasure at Nasser's opposition to the Baghdad Pact and at his friendly moves toward the Eastern Bloc, including the purchase of arms from that source in the previous year (a deal concluded after Egypt had been unable to get arms from the Western states). On 26 July 1956 Nasser made a dramatic speech in Alexandria in which he announced that the Canal would be nationalized and its revenues used to pay for the dam. Egyptian troops moved in and took over the Canal's operation.

The response of the Europeans and Americans was to call on Nasser to observe past treaties and agreements and to observe the 1888 Maritime Convention (which had been negotiated by Britain and in which Egypt had no direct role). In this Convention signatory nations pledged to keep the Canal open to shipping. After a sharp attack on him by the British Prime Minister, Eden, Nasser refused a virtual summons from the British government to attend a Conference of twenty-four Maritime Powers in London that August, under the chairmanship of Australian Prime Minister Robert Menzies. The following month a scheme was proposed for international management of the Canal. Menzies made an unsuccessful trip to Cairo following this meeting to gain Egyptian approval for the idea.

The controversy over the nationalization of the Canal built up during the weeks preceding the Israeli invasion on 29 October. On the suggestion of the United States, the Western governments who used the Canal formed SCUA (Suez Canal Users Association) to protect their official and private interests. In the meantime the Canal was functioning smoothly under Egyptian operation, despite the withdrawal of nearly all foreign pilots by their governments. The performance of the Egyptian personnel appointed to oversee its operations rather muted a Security Council debate on the nationalization: by October 1956 Egypt had shown that it was fully capable of running the Canal alone. A Security Council resolution presented that month by the British and French was therefore vetoed by the USSR on the grounds that there was no need for international operation of the Canal as called for in the resolution. Egyptian concessions to Britain and France, presented to those countries' foreign ministers at a secret UN meeting in October, were subsequently rejected by the French and British Prime Ministers despite the generous terms Egypt offered to both countries. The reasons for the rejection of Egypt's offer were soon made manifest.

Since September 1956 the British, French, and Israelis had been developing a plan for the invasion of Egypt and seizure of the Canal. This involved an Israeli attack on Egypt, followed by the two European powers landing in the Canal Zone under pretext of separating the warring parties.

Israel launched an invasion on 29 October 1956, using the justification that it was acting in self-defense in moving against Palestinian bases in Egyptian territory, and under threat from a Joint Military Command established by the Arab states a few days previously. Britain and France then issued an ultimatum for an immediate cease-fire between Egypt and Israel and withdrawal of the parties to a line ten miles on either side of the Canal, threatening otherwise to invade Egypt and "restore" order. The ultimatum also required Egypt to permit British and French troops to move into key positions at Port Sa^{c}id, Suez, and Ismailiyya. Israel, not being within ten miles of the Canal, agreed, but Egypt rejected the ultimatum. Britain and France bombed the Canal cities from 31 October prior to landing troops on 5 November at Port Sa^{c}id, in violation of a UN resolution calling on Israel to withdraw to the 1949 armistice lines and on other states to refrain from involvement; the UN also voted to establish an Emergency Force.

Israel agreed to a cease-fire, but not a withdrawal, if Egypt surrendered or withdrew. On 7 November, following intense pressure from U.S. President Eisenhower, Britain, and then France, agreed to suspend hostilities if Egypt and Israel accepted a cease-fire and international forces took over the two countries' positions. A UN force was sent to Egypt in late November, and Britain and France withdrew from Egypt on 22 December 1956. David Ben Gurion, Premier of Israel, refused to withdraw completely after the cease-fire on the grounds that Gaza was a part of biblical Israel and Sharm al-Shaykh was vital for Israel's security. Following U.S. and UN pressure, including the threat of sanctions, Israel announced its decision to withdraw on 1 March 1957.

The Suez War produced profound shifts in Egyptian domestic and foreign policy. The country suffered the destruction of the large areas of Port Sa^cid; the inhabitants of the Canal Zone resented deeply the heavy loss of lives and property they had experienced. The Suez Canal was blocked and its revenue lost. The government nationalized or sequestered French, British, and foreign Jewish businesses in Egypt. The United Nations helped Egypt clear the Canal, and Russia and other Eastern Bloc countries helped replace lost weaponry. Former owners of shares in the Suez Canal Company were compensated in 1959, at the time when relations with Britain and France were being slowly mended. The war greatly enhanced Nasser's image in the Third World, as the clear victim of Israeli and European aggression, an image that helped overshadow the difficulties the Egyptian army had experienced in facing this invasion and defending the country.

SUFISM. Islamic fraternal movement, Sufism has special liturgical and communal religious practices that vary from group to group; these practices are generally based on the teachings of the orders' founders. Sufism and Sufi orders came to Egypt in a major way during Ayyūbid times (1171-1250/566-684), when they enjoyed the support of Ṣalāḥ ad-Dīn and his successors. Ṣalāḥ ad-Dīn built Ṣūfī khānqāhs, retreats or hostels for visiting Sufis. These were often attached to madrasas (schools), where orthodox Sunnī Islam was taught to counteract the effect of the long period in which Egypt had been under the control of the Shī^ca Fāṭimids. Ṣūfīs participated in many public rituals during the Ayyūbid period. An Egyptian Sufi order was started by the Moroccan mystic Aḥmad al-Badawī in the mid-thirteenth/seventh century. The Aḥmadiyya order founded by him continues popular to the present day and is, with the Burhāmiyya, Qādiriyya, and Rifa^ciyya, one of the leading Ṣūfī groups in Egypt. The Al-Bakrī family (claiming descent from the first Caliph, Abū Bakr, have traditionally held or claimed leadership (Shaykh ash-Shayūkh) of the Egyptian Sufi community.

Sufism has played an important part in the religious life of Egyptians at every level of society, but particularly among the poor. Public appearances by, and the rituals of, the Sufis were also part of many public ceremonies, such as the sending of the kiswa, or curtain, to Mecca at the time of the annual pilgrimage, and on the mawlids, or birthday celebrations, of early Islamic figures. In contemporary Egypt the Sufi orders continue to be a vital element in popular religious life, both in the cities and rural areas. The government exercises control of the orders through the Council of Sufi Brotherhoods. Sufi rituals occur after Friday prayers and at other times during the week. These rituals bring together the individual Sufis for worship and companionship. The deeply emotional level of religious sentiment found in the Sufi orders has influenced many Egyptian religious thinkers, such as Muhammad Abduh and Hasan al-Banna, founder of the Ikhwan al-Muslimun.

SULAYMĀN (ᶜAbbāsid general) see MUḤAMMAD b. SULAYMĀN

SULAYMĀN PASHA KHĀDIM (d. 1548/955). Twice Ottoman governor of Egypt (1525-35/931-41 and 1536-38/943-45) under Sulaymān the Magnificent, Sulaymān was sent to administer the country following the suppression of the revolt of his predecessor, Aḥmad Pasha Khā'in, by the Ottoman vizier Ibrāhīm Pasha in 1524/930. During his governorship Sulaymān Pasha instituted regular payments of Egyptian revenue to the Ottoman Treasury and implemented Ibrāhīm Pasha's plans for strict control by the central government of all aspects of Egypt's administration. The first cadastral survey was carried out during his governorship, permitting the application of the Ottoman iltizām system in Egypt. Egyptian trading treaties with the European powers were renewed in 1528/934, and Egypt was placed under the Ottoman system of capitulations. Renewed activity by corsairs and the strength of the Portuguese navy led Sulaymān Pasha to refurbish and restore the Egyptian fleet in 1530/936; it took part in Sulaymān's campaign against Aden and India in 1538/945.

SULAYMAN PASHA (D. J. A. SEVE) (1788-1860). Originally a French military officer, Sève was recruited by Muhammad Ali in 1819 to supervise the modernization of the Egyptian army. Training was begun in Cairo, but some of the Muslim recruits reacted against receiving their training and discipline from a Christian, and the nearness and distractions of Cairo made desertion easy. The instructor and his recruits were removed to a more isolated camp near Esna in 1820. Muhammad Ali's original idea of using Sudanese trainees captured and taken prisoner during his campaigns in the region in 1820-22 were unsuccessful, despite Sève's efforts, as they proved unable to stand the climate and local diseases and were doubtless deeply unhappy with their enforced conscription as well. Egyptian peasants, recruited for the first time into the army, proved successful and were used to form the bulk of the ordinary soldiery. Sève was soon joined by a number of other French officers who spread the use of European training methods. Special schools were established to offer instruction in specialized technical skills.

After his conversion to Islam Sève changed his name to Sulayman and was eventually awarded the title Pasha. He participated with Muhammad Ali's son Ibrahim in his campaigns in Greece and in the invasion of Syria in 1831. Sulayman Pasha remained in Egypt until his death, his family becoming linked with the Muhammad Ali line through marriage.

SULAYMAN, SIDQI (1919-). Prime Minister from September 1966 until June 1967, Sulayman was a Lieutenant-Colonel in the Engineering corps. He served on various economic planning boards before his appointment as Minister for the High Dam from 1962 to 1967. Following the 1967 Arab-Israeli War, Sulayman became Deputy Prime Minister and Minister of Industry, the High Dam, and Power in 1967-70. His role in the construction and development of the High Dam project is well regarded. Through his work on the High Dam, Sulayman became involved on an official level with the Soviet Union, which was providing the dam's funding. His relationship with the Russians led to a diminution in his political career following the fall of the Sabri faction in 1971. In addition to his appointments in connection with the High Dam project Sulayman also served for many years on the Executive Committee of the Arab Socialist Union.

SULTAN (SULṬĀN). Title used by the Ayyūbid and Mamluk rulers of Egypt (1171-1517/567-922). It was also adopted by Husayn Kamil when he took power under the British Protectorate in 1914 and by his successor, Fuad, from his accession in 1917 until the declaration of Egyptian independence in 1922, when his title changed to that of King. At an earlier date the title "Sultan" was used by the Saljūq Turks, in 1055/446, when they took over the protection of the ᶜAbbāsid Caliph from the Būyids, distinguishing their temporal power from the Caliph's spiritual position. "Sultan" derives from the Arabic word for authority, sulṭ.

SUMMIT CONFERENCES see ARAB SUMMITS

SUNNĪ. The vast majority of Egypt's Muslims have been Sunnī, a name that derives from the sunnah, or way, of the founder of Islam, the Prophet Muḥammad. The Sunnīs accept the succession of the first four Caliphs of Islam, Abū Bakr, ᶜUmar, ᶜUthmān, and ᶜAlī. Unlike the Shīᶜa they do not accept that ᶜAlī had any greater or lesser claim to succeed Muḥammad. The beliefs of Sunnī Muslims are drawn from the Qurān and the Ḥadīth, or traditions associated with the Prophet's life and times. In the course of its evolution Sunnī Islam gave rise to four legal schools, the Shāfiᶜī, Ḥanbalī, Malakī, and Ḥanafī, which are held in equal honor. One or two of these schools tend to dominate in each Islamic country; the Shāfiᶜī and Ḥanafī schools predominate in Egypt.

-T-

TABAH INCIDENT. When the Egyptian Khedive Abbas II formally ascended the throne in 1892, the firmān (decree) of investiture from the Ottoman Sultan Abdal Hamid II did not include Sinai on the list of territories recognized by the Sultan as being under Abbas' control. For the previous fifty years, Egypt had only maintained supervision of the northern area of the peninsula, which contained a pilgrimage route. The rest of the Sinai had virtually no formal administrative structures; save for the bedouin and the monks at St. Catherine's, the area was sparsely settled. In October 1906, the Ottoman Porte decided to press its claims on the peninsula, and a patrol was sent to occupy Tabah, a town on the eastern Sinai coast close to the port of Aqaba. The Ottomans claimed that Egyptian sovereignty had lapsed, something the Khedive seemed inclined to agree with. However the British wanted to secure the area under Egyptian (which amounted to British) control to protect the eastern approaches to the Suez Canal. Following a period of diplomatic pressure by Britain, the Ottomans withdrew their troops and agreed to demarcate a straight border between Rafah and Aqaba, and a treaty about respective areas of sovereignty was concluded between the two countries in October. The exact siting of this 1906 border has become a major issue between Egypt and Israel during their recent (1981) negotiation on Israel's withdrawal from Sinai.

TAHTAWI, RIFAA RAFI (1801-1873). Egyptian religious figure and scholar, Tahtawi was a member of the liberalizing element within the Egyptian ᶜulamā' (Islamic religious and legal scholars). Tahtawi studied with Shaykh Hasan al-Attar at al-Azhar and was influenced by Attar's description of his experiences with the French expedition to Egypt (1798-1801), when he had visited the French Institute and observed the work of the scholars there. Tahtawi's career served as an important link between the more traditional elements of religious and scholarly life in Egypt and the Westernizing trends of the country's leadership.

Tahtawi was appointed Imām (spiritual counselor or guide) to the new Egyptian army and spent five years in France, 1826-31, as Imām to the Egyptian educational mission sent there by Muhammad Ali. Upon his return in 1832 he became editor of the Official Gazette, in addition to translating many classics and works of philosophy from French into Arabic. He was appointed a member of a government secretariat on education in 1836. Tahtawi's career suffered a brief eclipse during the reign of Abbas I (r. 1848-54), but he was returned to favor by Sa^{c}id (r. 1854-63) and helped set up the new Egyptian educational system. He fell out with Sa^{c}id toward the end of the latter's reign but was again restored, this time by Ismail (r. 1863-79). Tahtawi became editor of an educational magazine, resumed his directorship of the Language School at the School of Artillery (a post he had first held in 1833) and became head of the Translation Office.

TAKFIR WA'L-HIJRA (JAMA^{c}A AT-TAKFĪR WA'L-ḤIJRĀ). Islamic political grouping that uses paramilitary tactics, Takfir wa'l-Hijra has been active in Egypt since 1971. The group first came to official attention in 1975, when a number of its members were arrested after the burning of some religious shrines in the Delta and for involvement in other incidents with communal and violent overtones. In July 1977 the group kidnapped the former Minister of Waqfs (religious endowments), claiming a large ransom and the release of some sixty group members from prison. Dr. Dhahabi, the former Minister, was executed by the group the next month. Police had already arrested the alleged leader of Takfir wa'l-Hijra in July 1977 and following the assassination instituted a crackdown on the organization. At a trial later that year five members of Takfir wa'l-Hijra were sentenced to death and many others given long prison terms. Despite this crackdown, the group was estimated (1979) to have several thousand members. Its activists were among the main targets of the Sadat government's mass arrests of religious and political opponents in September 1981.

TANẒĪMĀT (LEGAL REFORMS). A term applied to the revised Ottoman legal code, the second version of which was adopted in modified form during the early months of the reign of the Viceroy Sa^c^id Pasha in 1854. The Egyptian government had resisted the introduction of the first reformed Ottoman legal code ("The Noble Rescript" of 1839) despite an 1841 firmān from the Sultan to do so. Muhammad Ali continued to issue laws, including a general code for the prosecution of criminal cases promulgated in 1844, known as the Code of Abbas (Muhammad Ali's successor).

The Ottomans issued a new, more comprehensive legal code in 1851; the Egyptians raised immediate objections over its provisions in several areas, but particularly over the clause depriving the Egyptian Viceroy of final sanction in the case of executions. This would weaken the Viceroy's firm hand, it was argued, needed to bring order in rural and tribal areas. Some of the Ottoman penalties were found too mild, and the Tanẓīmāt missed many crimes common in such a strongly agricultural society as Egypt's. Finally the introduction of Ottoman legal supervisory institutions was resisted; the Viceroy had no intention of compromising his autonomy. A negotiating team was sent to Istanbul in May 1851, and by May 1852 all issues were resolved. Abbas gained final rights with regard to executions for seven years in exchange for a £30,000 increase in Egypt's yearly tribute.

Despite the prolonged negotiations and the concessions of the Porte the Ottoman code was not introduced until the reign of Abbas' successor, Sa^c^id (1854-63). The new code contained most of the lighter penalties of the original unnegotiated Ottoman code, though in practice these were largely disregarded in favor of the stiffer penalties of the Code of Abbas.

This code stayed in force in Egypt until the accession of Ismail in 1863, despite the adoption by the Porte in 1858 of a new legal code modeled on the French Code Napoleon. Ismail gave permission to one of his ministers, Nubar, to initiate a series of legal reforms and diplomatic contacts in an effort to establish a judiciary in Egypt which would have the authority to try foreigners for offenses committed there. The mixed-court system was established by a revised criminal and civil code that took six years to prepare and was finally introduced two years later, in 1875. Largely modeled on the 1858 Ottoman Code, the Egyptian version was more comprehensive; its references to the authority of the state and not the Ottoman Sultan reflected Ismail's nearly autonomous position since 1867. The Egyptian code also broke with legal tradition in Islamic countries by supplanting the Sharīᶜa (Islamic law) for some crimes. This code was revised following the 1882 British Occupation when the existing court system--mixed, consular, civil-criminal, and religious--was expanded and a Civil Code introduced.

ṬAṬĀR (AZ-ẒĀHIR SAYF AD-DĪN ṬAṬĀR) (r. 1421/824). Burjī Mamluk Sultan, Ṭaṭār was acting as regent for the infant Sultan Aḥmad at the beginning of the latter's reign on behalf of the actual regent, Altunbughā, who was out of the capital. He took the regency in his own name shortly afterward and then deposed Aḥmad. A Mamluk of Barqūq, Ṭaṭār had risen in rank during the reign of al-Mu'ayyad Shaykh, most of whose family he murdered before assuming the Sultanate. He died three months after taking office.

TAWFIQ (r. 1879-92). Khedive of Egypt, Tawfiq succeeded his father, Ismail, when the latter was deposed by the Ottoman Sultan under pressure from Egypt's European creditors. Tawfiq had to deal with the increasingly powerful nationalist movement headed by Colonel Arabi Pasha, which was to bring about the British occupation of Egypt in 1882. Tawfiq served as Prime Minister for one month before his government, the "European" cabinet, was dismissed by his father in April 1879.

After Tawfiq's accession the British and French reestablished more firmly their dual control of the Egyptian economy, which had been briefly interrupted in the closing months of Ismail's reign. The reemergence and presence of the British and French in the Egyptian economy and administration angered many Egyptians of every social level. Combined with the resentment of the junior and non-Turkish officers over barriers to their advancement in the army, and the general population's resentment against control of Egypt by outside Christian elements, the potential for a violent explosion was building. Tawfiq tried to gain control of the situation by exiling the Islamic political reformer, Al-Afghani, and dismissing the moderate Sharif Pasha from government. He replaced him as prime minister with Riyad Pasha, a reactionary who could be counted on to stifle domestic opposition to the regime and the Europeans. But Riyad's Minister of War, Rifqi Pasha, proved exceptionally unpopular with the army, and his own domestic policies succeeded in uniting Egyptians against him. After a near-coup in September 1881, Tawfiq was forced to reappoint Sharif Pasha. The growing popularity of the Egyptian Colonel Arabi was worrying to Tawfiq, who ordered his unit out of Cairo. By the end of 1881, however, the nationalist movement had grown enormously, especially after the elections in November. Having failed to control the nationalist movement, Tawfiq was in danger of being utterly eclipsed by it.

The credibility lost by Tawfiq through his lack of responsiveness to any of the nationalists' demands enhanced the appeal of the nationalists for many Egyptians. This appeal was heightened after the delivery of the Joint Note to the Egyptian Parliament by the French and British in January 1882. The note expressed support for the Khedive and threatened to take action against the legislature if they took any steps to undermine Tawfiq's position. The results were predictable: an expression of outrage on the part of the Parliament, a rise in popular feelings against the Europeans, and a further strengthening of the position of the nationalists. Tawfiq asked Sami al-Barudi Pasha, a distinguished soldier, nationalist, and diplomat, to form the next government; Sami was eclipsed in public notice, however, by his own Minister of War, Colonel Arabi, whom he actively supported and around whom the nationalist forces coalesced.

Conflict between Arabi and the Palace came in May 1882,

when the Khedive refused to countersign an order by Arabi banishing some forty military plotters against him. The confrontation between Tawfiq and Arabi betrayed Tawfiq's innate weakness: faced with defeat, he appealed to the European consuls for support. Fortunately for him, the British were sufficiently alarmed by Arabi's strength and nationalism to have decided on a course of military intervention. Tawfiq fled to Alexandria, where he remained until the British had secured control of the country from Arabi and his supporters in September 1882. Sharif was brought back to head a ministry, the leading nationalists were deported, and Tawfiq disbanded the army. Those Egyptians associated with the Arabi "rebellion" were exiled or harassed. Tawfiq was for the rest of his reign dependent on the British to decide what power remained to him. Beyond his control, the British were, with the Ottomans, the Europeans, and cooperative Egyptian politicians, shaping what their future role in Egypt would be. Tawfiq was succeeded on his death by his son, Abbas II.

TAWKILAT. A campaign conducted via petition and telegram beginning in November 1918, the Tawkilat declared support for Zaghlul and his wafd (delegation) as deputies or representatives of Egypt in negotiations over nationalist demands with the British. The campaign was started in response to British allegations that Zaghlul and the nationalists did not have the support of Egyptian public opinion. Though the campaign was extremely successful, the British were not persuaded. The widespread distribution of petitions however, contributed to raising popular consciousness about Zaghlul, the Wafd, and Egypt's postwar situation and probably contributed to the wide base of, and participation in, the 1919 Rebellion touched off by Zaghlul's deportation that March.

ṬAYYIBIYYA/AMRIYYA. Branch of the Fāṭimid Ismā^{c}īli doctrine, the Ṭayyibiyya believed that the Caliph al-Āmir's son, Ṭayyib, should have inherited the Imamate from his father upon the latter's death in 1130/524 (when al-Āmir's widow was still pregnant with Ṭayyib). Instead, Ṭayyib's uncle al-Ḥāfiz succeeded in 1131/526 after a period of confusion in which the vizier Kutayfāt had declared himself representative of the hidden Imām of a Shīʿa sect opposed to the Fāṭimids. Al-Ḥāfiz, regent for the unborn child, was in prison. He was finally released by supporters and declared himself Caliph, claiming that Al-Āmir's intention was that he, al-Ḥāfiz, should succeed him. It was also argued that al-Āmir's child was a girl, or had died, which was not accepted by the Ṭayyibiyya. The movement enjoyed some support in Egypt but, as with the Nizārī schism, picked up even more supporters outside the country. As with the Nizārī movement it led to a schism among the Dāʿī and a consequent reduction in their backing of the Fāṭimid Caliphate.

TEN-YEAR PLAN. Industrial and economic plan introduced in 1973, the Ten-Year Plan was meant to be implemented in two five-year stages, though its overall operation was altered by the introduction of the Open Door (Infitah) Policy in 1974. Under the terms of the plan, infrastructure would receive the largest share of government investment (40 percent) and transport the next largest (15 percent). Industry would receive 8.5 percent of investment and was expected to reach a targeted annual growth rate of 12 percent by 1976. The plan gave emphasis to the rehabilitation of existing plant, the completion of eighty-eight existing projects, and the introduction of forty-four new industrial schemes. Agriculture, with a targeted annual growth rate of 3 percent, was to receive 10 percent of total investment. Local services took a substantial share of the budget allocations, some 23 percent, with additional allocations for a contingency fund. In the social sphere, family planning was to be accorded a high priority.

The dislocations in the economy caused by the 1973 Arab-Israeli War resulted in the substitution of the first five-year part of the plan with an eighteen-month transition plan, which ended in December 1975. Since then a variable five-year plan was put into effect in 1976 and revised in 1978. (See also FIVE-YEAR PLAN.)

THARWAT PASHA, ABDAL KHALIQ (1873-1928). Egyptian Prime Minister, Tharwat formed Egypt's first government following the unilateral Declaration of 1922, granting Egypt its independence, and served again in 1927. Tharwat had been Procurator-General in the government of Butrus Ghali Pasha (1908-10) and prosecutor in the trial of Ghali's assassins. In 1921 Tharwat joined the government of Adli Pasha as Minister of the Interior. Following the breakdown in talks between Adli and Curzon the King asked Tharwat to form a Ministry in December 1921. Tharwat was insistent that the Protectorate be terminated. In this, he had the support of Allenby but not the British Foreign Office. In addition, the deportation of Zaghlul for the second time, as well as dismay in some quarters over the fall of the Adli government, made it impossible for Tharwat to form a ministry until March 1922. This followed Allenby's success in forcing the British government to unilaterally terminate the Protectorate.

Although Tharwat was not a firm supporter of all points in the 1922 Declaration, he gave his limited support to the Constitutional Commission formed to draft a postindependence constitution. The continuing domestic unrest led Tharwat to maintain martial law during his government. Fuad asked Tharwat to include in the Constitution provisions making ministers responsible to Parliament but then changed his mind. The Wafd and the British each raised objections to various articles. Tharwat was faced with a situation where to capitulate to one party brought him in instant disfavor with the other two. In the end the reduction of Fuad's role to that of a constitutional monarch sealed Tharwat's fate. The King began to ally himself with the Wafd to get rid of Tharwat and demanded that the Prime Minister recall Zaghlul from exile, even though Fuad had been a prime mover in getting Zaghlul exiled in the first place. He resigned in November 1922.

Tharwat formed a second ministry in April 1927, again following the resignation of Adli Pasha. During his year in office he negotiated a draft treaty with the British Foreign Secretary,

Austin Chamberlain. The Wafd, under the leadership of Mustafa Nahhas (who had succeeded to the presidency of the party following the death of Zaghlul in August 1927), opposed the draft on the grounds it did not meet the minimum expectations of the nationalists. Fuad objected to the Egyptian army remaining so strongly under British control, which the draft did not alter, an objection shared by the nationalists. Tharwat made a tactical error in not consulting with the other political parties following the conclusion of his negotiations, which doomed the acceptance of the draft treaty. When his cabinet refused to discuss the draft, in February 1928, Tharwat had no choice but to resign, which he did one month later.

THARWAT-CHAMBERLAIN DRAFT TREATY. A treaty was discussed by Foreign Secretary Austin Chamberlain and Egyptian Prime Minister Tharwat Pasha during the visit of King Fuad to London in July 1927. A draft treaty was concluded in November which provided that there be a strong alliance between the British and Egyptian governments and that Egypt be sponsored for membership in the League of Nations by Britain. However, the draft treaty failed to address the Sudan issue, British troop withdrawals from Egypt, or the future role of the British with regard to the command structure of the Egyptian army, all basic issues as far as the nationalists in Egypt were concerned. The unpopularity of the draft treaty among official and Palace circles doomed it in Egypt, and it was rejected by Tharwat's cabinet in February 1928.

THREE CIRCLES. A rhetorical image used in Nasser's Philosophy of the Revolution to describe Egypt's geopolitical position in the Third World, the three circles were those of the African, Arab, and Islamic worlds, which had their common meeting point in Egypt, and in all of which Egypt was an actor and could be viewed as a linchpin. The image was also meant to suggest the community of interests uniting all these Third World states: anticolonialism, anti-imperialism, and national and regional autonomy.

TIMURBUGHĀ (AẒ-ẒĀHIR TIMURBUGHĀ) (r. 1467-68/872). Burjī Mamluk Sultan of Greek origin, Timurbughā held office briefly before voluntarily stepping down in favor of his ally and Commander-in-Chief, Qā'it Bay. The Burjī Mamluks were in their final throes when Timurbughā assumed power, with an empty Treasury and a rapid turnover of Egypt's highest officeholders. His immediate predecessors had been unable to exercise power in any realistic or reasonable fashion, and they had let the Mamluks inflict complete anarchy and chaos on the country. Timurbughā eventually returned to residence in Damietta, where he had been serving before overthrowing Bilbay.

TRIPARTITE DECLARATION. In May 1950 the United States, France, and Britain announced that they would defend Egypt in the case of attack. The declaration, issued after discussions by the Foreign Ministers of these countries, promised intervention if any state violated the 1949 cease-fire lines. The signatories agreed to supply arms only for self-defense, internal security, and regional defensive alliances. No discussions were held with any state in the region prior to the announcement of the declaration, designed to counter potential Soviet activity in the Middle East while at the same time being an endorsement of the post-1948 status quo in the region.

TRIPARTITE TALKS. Held in March 1963 between Egypt, Syria, and Iraq, the Tripartite Talks considered various forms of union for the three states and aimed at easing past tensions in their relationship. The three agreed during these talks to disband their political parties in favor of an Arab Socialist Union and the Charter of National Action. The organizational agreements, announced 17 April 1963, provided for a president to be elected by a federal assembly with at least a two-thirds majority of the votes, to serve a four-year term, and to be empowered to appoint ministers and higher officials as well as serving as Commander-in-Chief of the combined armed forces. All three countries would be equally represented on an executive Presidential Council, drawn from the military and senior officials. The

Council would decide overall policy direction, and be responsible to the bicameral National Assembly. The lower house of the Assembly, the Chamber of Deputies, would be elected by universal suffrage. It would be balanced by an upper house or Federation Council, whose structure was modeled on the United States Senate--an equal number of representatives from each region. In line with Egyptian practice, half the members of the Assembly would be drawn from the "popular forces," i.e. workers and peasants. Each region would have a strong local government, with a legislature, cabinet and premier, echoing the structure of the federated government above it. A federal constitution would be submitted to referendum that September, and the federation itself was scheduled to come into operation in December 1964.

In the structure of the Federal and Presidential Councils, with the equal representation for the three states, it is possible to see that care had been taken to avoid giving Egypt the kind of overwhelming strength in numbers that helped fracture its previous union with Syria.

Political changes in Syria that July, and in Iraq in November, resulted in the Syrians losing interest in the federation and the Iraqis no longer being eager to link politically with Syria.

ṬŪLŪNID EGYPT (868/254-905/292). First dynasty to rule Egypt independently of the ᶜAbbāsid Caliph in Baghdad, the Ṭūlūnids were founded by Aḥmad b. Ṭūlūn, who came to Egypt in 868/254 initially as governor of the country for Bāykbāk, who was granted the iqṭāᶜ of Egypt by the ᶜAbbāsid Caliph. Ibn Ṭūlūn soon gained ascendancy over the financial administrator, al-Mudabbir, who had been sent to Egypt prior to Ibn Ṭūlūn's appointment to put its fiscal affairs in order. Al-Mudabbir's transfer in 872/258 gave Ibn Ṭūlūn a freer hand to give his own direction to Egypt's administration.

Ibn Ṭūlūn was helped in his search for autonomous power by the internal disorders in the Caliphal court at Baghdad, whose plans to overthrow this increasingly independent appointee failed, as it became involved in dealing with a major revolt in southern Iraq. Though his 870/256 campaign in Syria was stopped by Baghdad, eight years later Ibn Ṭūlūn succeeded in gaining control of this province, which was then united to Egypt under his rule. He also actively urged the ᶜAbbāsid Caliph to come to Cairo; he offered him protection and a chance to escape the factions and fighting of the Baghdad court.

Ibn Ṭūlūn's son, Khumārawayh, succeeded him by popular acclaim in 884/270. In the year of his accession he had to drive back a ᶜAbbasid attack on Syria. He experienced some difficulties with his armies, which he was able to bring into line in 887/273, and managed an effective piece of diplomacy by marrying his daughter to the new Caliph, al-Muᶜtaḍid, who came to power in 892/279. Khumārawayh settled an enormous dowry on his daughter; his tribute was set at 300, 000 dinars a year and he secured from the Caliph an extension for thirty years of the iqṭāᶜ by which the Ṭūlūnids now controlled Egypt and Syria. Khumārawayh was eventually killed by his own slaves and was succeeded by his fourteen-year-old son, Jaysh.

Jaysh managed to hold power a mere nine months, during which time he made himself thoroughly unpopular with the military and administrative establishment. After his murder his brother Hārūn succeeded under the regency of Muḥammad b. Abba. The new state of affairs in Egypt was reflected in a treaty signed with the ᶜAbbāsid Caliph in 899/286, by which Ṭūlūnid territories were decreased and their tribute increased.

The activities in Syria of the Qaramatians, a Shīᶜa group, brought severe dislocations to the province in 901-05/288-92. The weak Hārūn and his divided court and rebellious army were not able to counter this threat, which provided Baghdad with the chance of re-establishing direct ᶜAbbāsid control. Hārūn was murdered in 905/292 and was succeeded by his uncle Shaybān. Shaybān's efforts to rally his troops were futile. In 905/292 the ᶜAbbāsid troops entered al-Fusṭāṭ, and the remaining members of the family were sent back to Baghdad as prisoners. In

905-06/292-93 an adventurer who supported the Ṭūlūnids, Muḥammad al-Khalānjī, seized the government in Egypt for six months. The real heirs to the Ṭūlūnids, however, were the Ikhshīdids, who came to power in Egypt thirty years after the overthrow of the last Ṭūlūnid ruler.

Ibn Ṭūlūn built a palace city for himself, al-Qaṭā'i^{c}, with a splendid mosque partly in the Samarran style (of Iraq), which is still standing; the first hospital of its kind in Egypt; and a Nilometer on the island of Rawḍa (Roda). The court of his son, Khumārawayh, has few parallels in historic sources for descriptions of its luxury. Despite the building activities and indulgences of its rulers the Ṭūlūnids were reasonably competent, at least initially, in their administration of the country. Much of the founder's building activities were paid for by the increased revenues retained by him in Egypt under the iqṭā^{c} granted by the ^{c}Abbāsid Caliph. Ibn Ṭūlūn was also able to increase his revenues from land taxes by encouraging agricultural productivity through greater security of tenure, removal of abuses in administration, and expansion of the land area under cultivation. As with many other dynasties, the vigor of the founder was only imperfectly, if at all, reflected in his sons and heirs.

Tulunid Rulers in Egypt:

868/254	Aḥmad b. Ṭūlūn
884/270	Khumārawayh
896/282	Jaysh
896/283	Hārūn
905/292	Shaybān

TŪMĀN BAY I (AL-^{c}ADĪL SAYF AD-DĪN TŪMĀN BAY) (r. 1501/906). Burjī Mamluk Sultan who reigned for a few months between the fall of Jānbalāt and the rise of Qānṣūḥ al-Ghawrī, Tūmān Bay had previously been Chancellor to an-Nāṣir Muḥammad II, whom he assassinated in 1498/903. He was then protector of the equally short-reigning Qānṣūḥ al-Ashrafī, who ruled until 1500/905, after which he served the new Sultan, Jānbalāt, as Commander-in-Chief of the Mamluk forces in Syria. In 1501/

906 Tūmān Bay deposed and executed Jānbalāt, whose widow he then persecuted.

His character as Sultan is not highly rated by the sources, and when he went in pursuit of Bedouin dacoits in Upper Egypt he was himself pursued and ousted from power by Qānṣūḥ al-Ghawrī, who had much courtly support. Tūmān Bay was forced to go into hiding, but he was soon betrayed and executed by an Amīr with whom he was sheltering but whose friends he had killed during his brief time in office.

TŪMĀN BAY II (AL-ASHRAF TŪMĀN BAY II) (r.1516-17/922-23). Last of the Mamluk Sultans of Egypt, Tūmān Bay led (at times reluctantly) the Mamluk resistance to the Ottoman invasion of Egypt under Selīm. Selīm had defeated Tūmān Bay's predecessor, Qānṣūḥ al-Ghawrī, in battle at Marj Dābiq in 1516/922; al-Ghawrī died of a stroke during the battle, and Tūmān Bay managed to turn what could have been a rout into an orderly retreat.

Selīm was inclined to be lenient with the Mamluk commander and offered him the governorship of Egypt if Tūmān Bay would acknowledge Selīm's supremacy and have him mentioned in Friday prayers. There was great resistance to this among the Egyptian Mamluks, however, and Tūmān Bay was eventually prevailed upon to declare himself Sultan, which he did in October 1516/922, making an Ottoman invasion of Egypt inevitable.

After the Ottomans' entry into Cairo in January 1517/922 (following a battle in which 800 Mamluks died) Tūmān Bay led his forces to the Delta for a last stand against Selīm's army. There was some popular support for this resistance, and in the Ottoman camp Selīm still seemed prepared to compromise rather than risk a further battle. However, Selīm was being urged on by the Mamluk traitor Khā'ir Bay, and Tūmān Bay was being urged to fight by the Mamluks around him. The murder of Selīm's envoy by some of these Mamluks sealed Tūmān Bay's fate. Following a series of battles the Mamluks were defeated by the Ottomans in March 1517/923, after which Khā'ir Bay obtained Tūmān Bay's execution.

TŪRĀN SHĀH (r. 1249-50/647-48). Last of the Ayyūbid rulers of Egypt, Tūrān Shāh was the son of aṣ-Ṣāliḥ. In the ten years prior to his accession Tūrān Shāh had conducted many military campaigns and acted as governor on his father's behalf in Palestine, Syria, and Iraq. He was on campaign in Iraq when word reached him from his stepmother, Shajar ad-Durr, that his father had died while preparing to meet the Crusaders under Louis IX in battle at Mansura. She kept her husband's death a secret until Tūrān Shāh could arrive (which he did in February 1250/647) to lead the Ayyūbid troops in battle.

The Mamluk commanders of aṣ-Ṣāliḥ played a major role in the defeat of the Crusaders during this battle, particularly Qutuz and Baybars. Tūrān Shāh, who arrived at the battle with his own Mamluks, did not know how to handle these strong military commanders of his father's troops. The Mamluks of aṣ-Ṣāliḥ, for their part, feared that they would be ousted, and this fear seemed confirmed when Tūrān Shāh began putting his own Mamluks in high positions and threatening Shajar ad-Durr, to whom many of them had transferred their loyalty after her husband's death, as she was carrying his child. The Mamluks of aṣ-Ṣāliḥ, led by Baybars, arranged and participated in Tūrān Shāh's murder in 1250/1648, effectively ending the Ayyubid dynasty in Egypt.

TURCO-EGYPTIAN FRONTIER AGREEMENT see TABAH INCIDENT

AT-TUSTARĪ (ḤASAN b. IBRĀHĪM b. SAHL) (r. 1045-47/437-39). Vizier and co-ruler of Egypt during the reign of the Fāṭimid Caliph al-Mustanṣir, at-Tustarī shared power with the Caliph's mother, a former slave whom he had once owned. Tustarī was a Persian Jewish banker who had converted to Islam, but his deep unpopularity with the court resulted in his murder.

-U-

UBAID, FIKHRI MAKRAM. The son of Makram Ubaid and closely associated with the government of President Anwar Sadat, Ubaid served as chairman and Secretary-General of the National Democratic Party from its foundation in July 1978 until he was replaced as chairman by Husni Mubarak in the spring of 1980. He also served as Deputy Prime Minister and Minister for People's Assembly Affairs and deputized for President Sadat at the Nobel Peace Prize ceremonies. In the new cabinet named in May 1980 Ubaid was Deputy Prime Minister of People's Assembly Affairs. Following the assassination of President Sadat in October 1981, Ubaid was retained in the Mubarak cabinet in his post of Deputy Prime Minister. Ubaid is currently (1982) Chairman of the Permanent Secretariat of the NDP.

UBAID, WILLIAM MAKRAM (1889-1961). Egyptian nationalist politician, Makram Ubaid was associated with the Wafd Party from its earliest days in 1919 until he was dismissed from the Wafd government of Nahhas Pasha in July 1942. Ubaid was among the most prominent Copts associated with the nationalist movement, a companion-in-exile of the founder of the Wafd, Zaghlul. He was arrested in 1924 for suspected involvement in the assassination of the British Sirdar, Sir Lee Stack, but was soon released, serving in various ministerial capacities and as Secretary-General of the Wafd party for fifteen years prior to 1942. He gave his strong and unqualified support to the Anglo-Egyptian Treaty of 1936 and to the leader of the Wafd, Nahhas, when his leadership was being challenged during the 1938-40 period. Ubaid himself was subject to frequent attacks during this period for his religion, with allegations being made about Coptic control of the Wafd.

Ubaid joined the 1942 Nahhas government but shortly thereafter had a serious dispute with Nahhas. Ubaid then published the Black Book, containing detailed allegations of corruption involving the Wafd leadership. The government's ire at the publication of the book inevitably aroused public curiosity about its contents, which echoed the charges that had brought down the Nahhas government in the 1920s. In 1943 Ubaid was expelled from the Egyptian parliament and was arrested in 1944, although he continued to serve as leader of the National Wafdist Bloc Party (Al-Hizb al-Wafdiyya al-Mustaqilla), which he founded when Nahhas dismissed him. Ahmad Mahir brought Ubaid back into the government when he named him Minister of Finance in his 1944 cabinet.

Ubaid was one of the few pre-Revolutionary politicians to survive the Nasser period with an unscathed reputation, through his dissociation with the less honorable aspects of pre-Revolutionary political parties.

UMAYYAD EGYPT (661-750/41-132). The shift in the center of power in the Islamic world from Mecca and Medina to Damascus occurred with the triumph of Mu^{c}āwiya b. Abī Sufyān over the fourth Caliph, ^{c}Alī b. Abī Ṭālib, for leadership of the Muslim community. ^{c}Amr b. al-^{c}Āṣ, Arab conqueror of Egypt, returned to the country as Mu^{c}āwiya's governor, having been instrumental in the negotiations following the Battle of Ṣiffīn between Mu^{c}āwiya and ^{c}Alī.

The twenty-five governors of Egypt during the Umayyad period all seem, from their names, to have been Arabs. Islam as a religion made only indifferent progress in the country, whose Christian population grew restive after its initial welcome of the Arabs as liberators of Egypt from Byzantine control. Part of their discontent was due to the imposition of regularly applied and collected taxes. Widespread tax revolts, particularly in 725/107 and 733/116, were suppressed, but the source of discontent remained. Administrative policies seem to have varied from governor to governor, though aspects of the pre-Islamic Byzantine structures remained.

The Arabization of Egypt, or at least the intermingling of Arabic and indigenous culture, made progress in this early period of Islamic rule. The settlement of Arab tribes in Egypt commenced on a large scale in 727/109 (though there had been some movement of tribes into the area prior to this) and helped speed this infusion of Arabic and Egyptian cultures. At the same time, however, these tribes, such as the Qays, were far from a stabilizing influence. A reduction in their allotment of grain as a result of a decision by the government to send more grain outside Egypt for distribution caused resentment and restiveness among the tribes. The Caliph Hishām's refusal to compromise on the grain supply was not reversed until 742/124, when the whole grain allotment was restored to the tribes.

A contribution to the Arab presence in Egypt on the local level had come earlier under the governorship of ᶜAbd al-ᶜAzīz b. Marwān (r. 685-705/65-85), who disbanded the Arab garrison at al-Fusṭāṭ and dispersed it over various parts of Egypt. The country's administration, still largely in native hands, was supervised by these Arabs, who were paid stipends and who were expected to provide security services in the provinces.

Egypt's importance during the Umayyad period was twofold: it was an important source of grain for the holy cities of Mecca and Medina, brought by an ancient canal to the Red Sea (cleared by ᶜAmr), as well as a rich source of other revenue; and it served as a base for the expansion of Muslim power westward under ᶜAmr and his successors. Native Egyptians participated in the Umayyad naval forces, which were an important counterweight to the strong Byzantine naval presence in the Mediterranean.

Some of the unevenness of the later Umayyad Caliphs' relationships with their Egyptian subjects can be seen in the issue of the stipends awarded to these Egyptian naval personnel. The Caliph ᶜUmar II (r. 717-20/99-101) granted stipends to the Muslim converts among these sailors. ᶜUmar's successors first suspended the stipends, then, twenty-four years later, reinstated them briefly in the reign of Yazīd III (r. 744/126), only to withdraw the stipends once more in the reign of Marwān II (r. 744-50/127-32). This inconsistency of policy, which extended to other areas of administration, aroused opposition in Egypt; upon the accession of Marwān II the Egyptians revolted and briefly reinstalled the governor appointed by the wise but short-lived Yazīd III. Marwān sent an army to restore order; once the army was withdrawn, however, there were numerous uprisings all over the country, both by Copts in the Delta and Muslim converts elsewhere, with the Arab settlers in revolt over a decision to extend their military duties. Marwān II, the last Umayyad Caliph, was driven from Syria by the forces supporting the revolt, in 750/132, of Abū al-^{c}Abbās, who was to become the first ^{c}Abbāsid Caliph. Marwān was forced to flee to Egypt; he was killed by his own troops near the Fayyum, bringing the Umayyad period to an end.

Umayyad Governors of Egypt

(List adapted from Eduard von Zimbaur's Manuel de génêaologie et de chronologie pour l'histoire de l'Islam, Hanover, 1927)

658/38	^{c}Amr b. al-^{c}Āṣ
663/43	^{c}Utbah b. Abī Sufyān
667/47	Maslama b. Mukhlid
681/62	Muḥammad b. Maslama
682/62	Sa^{c}īd b. Yazīd Al-^{c}Azdī
684/64	^{c}Abd ar-Raḥmān b. ^{c}Utbah
685/65	^{c}Abd al-^{c}Azīz b. Marwān
704/84	^{c}Abdallāh b. ^{c}Abd al-Malik
709/90	Qurra b. Sharik
715/96	^{c}Abd al-Malik b. Rifā^{c}ī al-Fahmī
718/99	Ayyūb b. Shurabīl al-Asbuhī
720/101	Bishr b. Ṣafwān al-Kalbī
721/102	Usāma b. Zayd
721/102	Ḥanẓala b. Ṣafwān
723/105	Muḥammad b. ^{c}Abd al-Malik
724/105	Al-Ḥurr b. Yūsuf al-Ḥakam
727/108	Ḥafṣ b. al-Walīd
727/109	^{c}Abd al-Malik b. Rifā^{c}ī (second term)
727/109	Al-Walīd b. Rifā^{c}ī
729/111	^{c}Ubaydallāh b. al-Habhāb (on behalf of Al-Ḥakam b. Qays)
735/117	^{c}Abd ar-Raḥmān b. Khālid al-Fahmī
737/119	Ḥanẓala b. Safwān (second term)
742/124	Ḥafṣ b. al-Walīd (second term)
745/127	Ḥasan b. ^{c}Atāhiya at-Tujibī (for a few days only)
745/127	Ḥafṣ b. al-Walīd (third term)

745/128 Hawthara b. Suhayl al-Bāhilī
749/131 Al-Mughayra b. ᶜUbaydallāh al-Fazārī
750/132 ᶜAbd al-Malik b. Marwān al-Lakhmī

Beginning of ᶜAbbasid period

UMMA PARTY. Egyptian political party, the Umma was formed in September 1907. The party reflected the break between Mustafa Kamil, head of the Nationalist Party, and the Khedive Abbas over the question of the future role of the Khedive in an independent Egypt, as well as other issues of longstanding dispute between the Nationalists and the Palace.

The pan-Islamicism that pervaded much of Kamil's writings was unacceptable to some Egyptian nationalists, and the radical tone of his message lost him the support of those elements in the nationalist movement who favored a continuation of the position of the Khedive and of the general status quo with only minor modifications. Formation of the party was encouraged by Cromer before his retirement; the party was officially constituted in 1907, with the newspaper Al-Jarida, edited by Lutfi al-Sayyid, as its official voice. Its program was moderate; though it supported constitutionalism, it was oriented toward cooperation with the British, a rejection of pan-Islamicism, and a discreet low-level opposition to the continued dominance of the Khedive over all aspects of Egyptian political life. In 1908 the party sponsored the subscription campaign for the establishment of the first national university.

The party took a reformist line with regard to Islam, being much influenced by the writings of Muhammad Abduh. Elements of the Umma's leadership were, prior to 1907, found in the Imam Party, a grouping structured around Abduh's teachings.

The Umma Party's role in Egyptian politics was affected by the consulship of Eldon Gorst (1907-11) whose cordial relations with the Palace meant that the Umma, along with other nationalist parties, was largely excluded from gaining a hearing there. After the First World War many Umma members joined the Wafd when that party was formed under the leadership of Umma member Sa^c^d Zaghlul, or went on to affiliate with the more conservative Liberal Constitutionalist Party.

UNILATERAL DECLARATION OF EGYPTIAN INDEPENDENCE see DECLARATION OF EGYPTIAN INDEPENDENCE

UNION OF POLITICAL PARTY YOUTH AND GROUPS see NATIONAL COMMITTEE OF WORKERS AND STUDENTS

UNION PARTY see ITTIHAD (UNION) PARTY

UNITED ARAB REPUBLIC. Formed in February 1958, the United Arab Republic was a union of Egypt and Syria; this was the first time in the twentieth century that two Arab states had attempted a joint government.

The impetus for the formation of the UAR came largely from Syria, which in late 1957 had been experiencing internal political difficulties, including the increasing strength of the Syrian Communist Party, which seemed set to win a substantially increased vote in the June 1958 elections. Previous Syrian approaches to Egypt had been successful, yielding an economic-cooperation program in September 1957, shortly after Nasser had sent Egyptian troops to Syria to help support the government in the face of a threat from Turkey. In January 1958 the Syrian military made the initial approaches to Nasser. Afterwards Salah Bitar, the Ba^c^ath party leader, met with Nasser on behalf of his political colleagues and the President of Syria, Shukri al-Quwaitli. After intense discussions the Syrians secured Nasser's agreement to unify Egypt and Syria politically. The concessions Nasser gained in exchange, in addition to leadership of the new union, amounted to a virtual carte blanche with regard to the shape of the future government, and eventually proved the undoing of the UAR.

A referendum on the union was held in both countries in February 1958, following which Nasser went to Syria and received a tumultuous welcome there. In March a provisional constitution was announced in which Egypt and Syria were constituted as the Northern and Southern Regions of the Republic, though in all aspects of the administrative structure Egypt remained predominant. A National Assembly was formed from the parliaments of the two countries, and executive power was vested in a cabinet under the President, though exercised in fact by Nasser. A small central government dealt with defense, foreign affairs, education, and "national guidance," with two regional governments and four vice-presidents, two from each country. At the end of 1958 the cabinet was expanded to twenty-one ministers, of whom fourteen were Egyptian. The powers of the central government were increased by removing the distinction between regional and central-government areas of responsibility.

The 1958 Provisional Constitution abolished all political parties and placed their membership under the direction of the National Union. Under Article 13 of the Constitution, President Nasser was empowered to appoint the 600 members of the new National Assembly (which was to replace the parliamentary bodies in each country), 400 of whom were to be Egyptian. Nasser completed his appointments in July 1960, and Anwar Sadat was elected president of the Assembly. The Council of the Nation, as the Assembly was also known, was in fact constituted well after most of the important measures affecting internal policy had been put forth. Neither the Assembly nor the press (nationalized in 1960) was given much opportunity therefore to participate in and comment on the decision-making process.

The increasing control of Egyptian national life in 1960-61 by the regime also involved the removal of ever-larger portions of the economy to state management, something regarded with less than enthusiasm by the Syrian bourgeoisie, who were far better organized and politically active than their Egyptian counterparts. On 16 August 1961, following the first wave of socialist laws, the executive branch of the UAR was revised. There were no longer to be two regional executives under the central cabinet, but a single entity, consisting of a central cabinet assisted by seven vice-presidents, two of them Syrian, and all under the direction of President Nasser. A Syrian vice-president of the UAR, Colonel Siraj, resigned on 26 September 1961.

On 28 September 1961, responding to the increasingly vehement denunciations of recent policies by their own political leaders, Syrian army units garrisoned near Damascus began to move on the Syrian capital, where they seized control. General Amer, who served as the vice-president of the Northern Region (Syria), was arrested after rejecting an ultimatum presented by Syrian officers, whereupon fighting broke out between officers supporting and opposing union with Egypt. Nasser at first ordered the UAR troops to resist, then acceded to the obvious wishes of the Syrians for independence, withdrawing his troops and personnel.

The breakup of the union with Syria was felt among the leadership in Egypt to be a rejection of Egypt's good-hearted offer to help the Syrians survive a threatened period of anarchy; the collapse of the UAR was blamed on "reactionary" elements opposed to the regime's socializing trends. This latter cause probably contributed to the collapse of the union, but the breakup was also speeded by Syrian resentment at the growing dominance of Egypt in every aspect of Syrian national life. Additionally, the National Union was meant to take the place of all pre-UAR political parties but failed to take root in Syria, as its format--a series of pyramidic cadres with the President at the summit--was more suitable to Egyptian rather than Syrian political behavior. The Syrian bourgeoisie and its supporters in the political elite resented the leftward drift of the government, being taken without thorough consultations with them, and Syria's Ba^{c}ath Party, which had originally pressed for the union, found itself completely disregarded.

Relations between Egypt and Syria were not restored to a friendly basis until early 1963, when the two states, with Iraq, participated in tripartite talks for a new federation.

UNITED ARAB STATES/FEDERATION OF ARAB STATES. On 8 March 1958 the government of the Yemen combined with the United Arab Republic to form the United Arab States, a federation whose purpose was ostensibly to coordinate foreign policy and defense. The Yemen was not involved in the extensive restructuring of domestic political affairs found in the UAR proper, but hoped to derive added international and regional strength through its affiliation. Education and technical programs were discussed though these, when they were actually planned, tended to move bilaterally between Egypt and the Yemen rather than between the UAR and Yemen. After Syria seceded from the UAR in September 1961 Egypt dissolved the Federation that December. Imam Ahmad, the Yemeni ruler, had hoped the union would help his domestic position; but civil war broke out seven months later, and Egypt went to the aid of the rebel leader, Colonel Sallal.

"UNITY OF THE NILE VALLEY." Political slogan that featured prominently in Egyptian nationalist politics from the early 1900s, the "Unity of the Nile Valley" referred to the desirability of a union of the Sudan and Egypt under the Egyptian Crown, based on Egypt's historic and legal claims to the Sudan. The unity of the two countries was based also, in the eyes of the Egyptian nationalists and the Palace, on their common and critical dependence on the Nile as the sole source of water for their agriculture, and on the historical, cultural, and religious links that united the two countries.

ŪNŪJŪR (r. 946-61/334-49). Second Ikhshīdid ruler of Egypt, Ūnūjūr was the son of the founder of the dynasty, Muḥammad b. Ṭughj. Only fifteen at the time of his accession, Ūnūjūr was throughout his reign under the control of Kāfūr, a slave of his father's who had been appointed tutor to the young ruler and to his brother, ᶜAlī.

Three years after Ūnūjūr's accession the Nubians launched an attack against Aswan, demanding trade concessions. This attack was put down in 949/337, but the Egyptian forces failed to quell the troubled situation in the South. In Syria, Aleppo fell to the Ḥamdānids in 947/336. By 954/343 Egypt itself came near to a full-scale revolt. A particularly disastrous fire struck al-Fusṭāṭ, the capital, and there were outbreaks of civil disturbances throughout the country as the army and Ūnūjūr (probably chafing under the rule of Kāfūr) attempted a coup. The situation was barely restored when in 955/344 a disastrous earthquake struck Egypt, bringing plague and famine in its wake. The Nubians became restive again that year and briefly seized Aswan. Ūnūjūr himself resented his exclusion from power by Kāfūr, who is suspected of having poisoned Ūnūjūr to replace him with his more amenable younger brother, ᶜAlī.

ᶜURĀBĪ PASHA see ARABI, COLONEL AHMAD

AL-URWAT AL-WUTHQA ("The Indissoluble Bond"). Journal published during the joint exile of Muhammad Abduh and Jamal ad-Din Al-Afghani, Al-Urwat al-Wuthqa is considered to be among the first modern political journals of its kind in Arabic. Muhammad Abduh joined Al-Afghani in Paris in 1883, following the collapse of the Arabi Rebellion and Abduh's exile from Egypt. The two men used the paper to present a political platform drawing on pan-Islamicism, Islamic reformism, and a rejection of Western colonial and cultural dominance in the Islamic countries. The journal was almost immediately banned in the areas controlled by the European powers. Though it did not continue beyond eighteen issues, the journal enjoyed a wide circulation and had enormous impact on the emerging nationalist movement in Islamic countries and on religious reformism within Islam.

USTADHAR. "Ustadhar" was a title used with various meaning by both the Fāṭimids and Mamluks in Egypt. Under the Fāṭimids the Ustadhar was the master of the guard and in the second rank of the administration, but in time the office increased in power, particularly when occupied by a strong personality. On occasion the position approached that of the vizier.

In Mamluk times the title was given to one of the highest court figures, a individual charged with the internal organization of the court and the ordering of the Mamluk courtiers around the Sultan. The Ustadhar was also in charge of the pay of the Mamluks; a frequent cause of losing the post was the inability to deliver salaries on time, which happened with increasing regularity toward the end of the Mamluk era. In times of instability, chronic in the Mamluk period, the Ustadhar held a critical position by virtue of his centrality at the court, and he was often able to shift the power balance among the contenders for the Sultanate.

ᶜUTHMĀN (AL-MANṢŪR FAKHR AD-DĪN ᶜUTHMĀN) (r. 1453/857). Burjī Mamluk Sultan, ᶜUthmān was the son and successor to the Sultan Jaqmaq. His cruelty and tyranny brought his reign to an end six weeks after its commencement. ᶜUthmān's deposition was hastened by his inability to meet the financial demands of the Mamluks, as the Treasury was empty. After the revolt and succession of Ināl, ᶜUthmān was captured in his harīm, where he was in hiding. He was kept thereafter under house arrest, unmolested, in Alexandria.

ᶜUTHMĀN AL-BARDĪSĪ see AL-BARDĪSĪ

ᶜUTHMĀN BAY (d. 1776/1190). Last leader of the Faqāriyya faction of the beylicate before it was eclipsed by its former allies, the Qāzdughliyya. He succeeded Dhū'l-Faqār as Shaykh al-Balad after the latter was assassinated in 1730/1143. Dhū'l Faqār had, just before his death, secured the defeat of the Faqāriyya's traditional rivals, the Qāsimiyya under Sharkas Bay. ᶜUthmān used his own faction's longstanding alliance with the Qāzdughliyya to suppress the remnants of the Qāsimiyya. ᶜUthmān and the Qāzdughliyya leader, Ibrāhīm Kahya, fell out in 1739/1152. ᶜUthmān was forced to flee Cairo and take refuge with the Hawwāra tribe in Upper Egypt. He was defeated while attempting to lead a revolt from Upper Egypt and managed to flee the country. He then settled in Istanbul, where he died. The Faqāriyya's divided leadership proved no challenge to Ibrāhīm Kahya; within a decade Ibrāhīm and his own allies were in complete command of the beylicate.

-V-

VEILED PROTECTORATE. "Veiled Protectorate" was the term used to describe the political control of Egypt by Britain from 1883 until the outbreak of the First World War, when a formal protectorate was instituted. Under the Veiled Protectorate, England ruled in all but name against or with a series of Egyptian ministries and the Khedives Tawfiq and Abbas. The position of France in Egypt (France was still a major creditor) was resolved in 1904 when the Entente Cordiale was signed and France surrendered her position in Egypt to the British. Britain controlled Egypt's military, handled its foreign relations, and set its internal policy. It also took over from Egypt in the Sudan, which it ruled as a virtual colony under the ostensible joint control established by the 1899 Anglo-Egyptian Condominium.

VENGEANCE SOCIETY. Anti-British nationalist group, the Vengeance Society carried out a number of terrorist attacks in Egypt after the First World War, when the subject of Egypt's continued relationship with Britain under the Protectorate had become a controversial issue. Membership of the society was drawn largely from young town- and city-dwellers. In 1920 several members were brought to trial for a series of murders and assassinations of British government personnel in Egypt over the preceding two years. An attempt was made to link the society with the Wafd Party in the hopes of discrediting the latter, and the nationalist movement as a whole. The Wafd, however, had its own secret wing ("The Secret Apparatus") and disassociated itself from the activities of the Vengeance Society.

VIZIER see WAZĪR

VOICE OF THE ARABS (ṢAWT AL-ᶜARAB). After the 1952 coup d'état the new Egyptian government was anxious to have a platform or forum through which it could explain the revolution to other Arab countries. In July 1953 the Voice of the Arabs began broadcasts to the Arabic-speaking world, presenting news, propaganda, and speeches. The Voice became in time a powerful political weapon in the hands of the Egyptian government, largely but not exclusively because no other Arab state had at the time a similar broadcasting technique and coverage. It gave Nasser a chance to appeal to the Arabs over the heads of their governments, a chance he skillfully exploited.

The Voice of the Arabs was blamed for a variety of antigovernment movements in the Arab world. The broadcasts reflected the Nasser regime's increasingly negative attitude toward the more traditional governments of the area. It probably helped fuel the labor disputes in the Gulf region in the 1950s and 60s and is credited with speeding the demise of the Iraqi monarchy in the wake of the 1955 Baghdad Pact, to which Egypt strongly objected. Many Arab countries--particularly Iraq (pre- and post-revolution), Jordan, Saudia Arabia, and Tunisia--objected to what they saw as attempts to destabilize their governments by the Voice broadcasts. By 1970 Egypt's international service, broadcasting in twenty-four languages, was ranked fifth in the world in terms of geographical coverage and air time.

-W-

WAFD. After an informal meeting of the suspended Legislative Assembly at the close of World War I, Sa^{c}d Zaghlul, former vice-president of the Assembly, and other Egyptian nationalists formed a delegation (wafd) to present the case for Egypt's independence to the British government and to the forthcoming Versailles Peace Conference. It seems likely that the Sultan, Fuad, gave his approval to, or at least acquiesed in, this initiative, as did the Prime Minister at the time, Rushdi Pasha.

Two days after the Armistice, on 13 November 1918, Zaghlul and two other members of the wafd, Abdal Aziz Fahmi and Ali Sharaawi, called on the British High Commissioner, Sir Reginald Wingate, to ask permission to go to Britain. The British government refused to receive the wafd, arguing that it could not accept Zaghlul as a representative of the Egyptian people and as a spokesman for Egypt's national interests. The Foreign Office's refusal to receive a similar delegation headed by the Egyptian Prime Minister threw Egypt into turmoil; no nationalist wished to cooperate with the British against the wafd and his or her own government. Rushdi himself resigned in protest at this insult to his position; this was held up until Wingate failed to change the attitude of the Foreign Office. The original delegation became the foundation of the Wafd Party (see below). Among the members of the wafd or its close associates who were later to figure importantly in Egyptian politics were Ismail Sidqi, Muhammad Mahmud, and Mustafa al-Nahhas, though only the last of these remained affiliated with the Wafd Party and Zaghlul.

WAFD PARTY. The Wafd Party developed as an organization from the original delegation headed by Sa^{c}d Zaghlul, which he formed in 1918 with a group of other nationalists to press the case for Egypt's complete independence from Britain. Zaghlul led the Wafd Party until his death in 1927. He was succeeded by Mustafa al-Nahhas, who served until the Revolution of 1952. The Wafd Party, founded in 1919, is considered to be the premier Egyptian nationalist party, winning all freely contested Egyptian elections. It was never able to complete its term in office, however, always encountering the ire of the Palace and/or the British and being forced to resign or be dismissed.

Zaghlul and the delegation members responded to British charges that they were unrepresentative of the Egyptian people (allegations used to deny them permission to go to London or Versailles) by organizing the Tawkilat campaign. Petitions supporting the delegation were circulated throughout Egypt and received a strong public response. Popular agitation against the British was growing early in 1919, and in an effort to calm the situation the British deported Zaghlul. The 1919 Rebellion broke out instead. The Wafd Party and Zaghlul became identified with popular sentiments against the British and against British control of Egypt, a sentiment encouraged by the Wafd executive, organized in the spring of 1919.

Zaghlul was released from exile in April 1919 and traveled to Paris and eventually London to press the nationalist case. In the summer of 1920 in London, he and his supporters met the Milner Mission, which had been in Egypt early in 1920 to investigate the 1919 disturbances. The Wafd Party had organized an effective boycott of the Mission when it was in Egypt. The Mission's report concluded that the Protectorate in Egypt must be ended, but with certain conditions rejected by more ardent nationalists.

Zaghlul returned to Egypt--and a tumultuous welcome--in April 1921. He immediately began attacking the government of Adli Pasha. Adli, a moderate nationalist, had agreed to form a government in March 1921 and to lead the discussions with the British Minister, Curzon, on Egypt's future. Zaghlul's bitter attacks on Adli alienated many of the moderate nationalist leaders, though these denunciations did not seem to affect his own public popularity. Deported once more at the end of 1921, Zaghlul was again cast in the role of a nationalist martyr at the hands of the British by his supporters in the party.

Zaghlul was not able to return from exile until the summer of 1923, following the drafting and promulgation of the new Constitution. The Wafd Party had been carefully building its base of popular support during this time, and in the first free elections, in January 1924, the Wafd won an overwhelming victory. Zaghlul in power proved no easier for the British to manage or control than when he led the nationalist opposition. The Wafd government, for example, pressed for a resolution to the Sudan issue, that is, a definition of the Sudan's future relationship to Egypt. Negotiations with the British broke down in October 1924, one month after they started.

The Wafd was turned out of office in November 1924, following the assassination of Sir Lee Stack, Sirdar and Governor-General of the Sudan. It was held culpable for Stack's death by the British, not least for keeping the public mood in Egypt inflamed about the Sudan issue. Although the Wafd won the elections of May 1926, British opposition prevented Zaghlul from forming a government. Nahhas inherited the Wafd leadership upon Zaghlul's death in August 1927. He formed a government in March 1928 that lasted just three months before being brought down on charges of corruption; the government he formed in December 1929 lasted just six months before being turned out of office, having pleased neither the Palace nor the British.

The Wafd remained in opposition for six years. It formed an opposition coalition with the Liberal Constitutionalists and refused to participate in the 1931 elections, held on the basis of a restricted franchise and a new Constitution. A leadership purge took place in 1932, as some members grew restive during their time in opposition. The Wafd regained momentum in 1934, when Mahmud Nasim Pasha formed a government. A paramilitary youth organization, the Blue Shirts, was formed by students sympathetic to the Wafd in 1935. The Wafd held discussions with Nasim in June of that year and in November joined the National Front, a grouping of political parties pressing the government for the restoration of the 1923 Constitution and free political life. It used its links with the trade-union movement to organize strikes in support of the front's demands.

Elections were held in May 1936, following the restoration of the Constitution of 1923 in December 1935. The Wafd won its usual majority of the popular vote and formed a government that lasted until December 1937, when it was dismissed by King Faruq for its failure, among other things, to control the growing level of civil violence in Egypt (and in which its own paramilitary youth wing, the Blue Shirts, had been involved). This 1936 ministry was important for Egypt's international position; the Wafd government negotiated a new treaty with Britain in 1936, and the Montreux Convention in May 1937 brought to an end the capitulatory laws and mixed courts that had so unfairly favored the foreign community in Egypt. Egypt also became a member of the League of Nations.

At the end of 1937 another shakeup of the Wafd leadership occurred, this time over the award of contracts for public-works projects and possibly over allegations of corruption. There was also some unhappiness in the hierarchy over Nahhas' unwillingness to share power. The dissident Wafdists--among whom Nuqrashi Pasha and Ahmad Mahir (formerly involved with the Wafd's Secret Section in the 1920s and tried and acquitted of charges connected with the Lee Stack assassination) featured prominently --formed the Saadist (Sa^{c}dist) Party. Constituted in January 1938, the Saadists strongly challenged the Wafd's claim to be the heirs to the leadership of Sa^{c}d Zaghlul and went on to play an important role in several non-Wafd governments.

A curious reversal of British antagonism toward the Wafd took place in the early 1940s. In the 1920s the British had strongly opposed the Wafd and after 1924 had refused to countenance its forming a government. But at the beginning of 1942 they were encouraging the Palace to have the Wafd back in power. The British were partly influenced by the success they had enjoyed in negotiating the 1936 treaty with the Wafd, a success helped by the Wafd's popularity in Egypt. All other treaty negotiations prior to 1936 had stumbled on this point of popular and political acceptance. Now, faced with the necessity of broad popular participation in the war effort, the British felt that the Wafd, with its public support far in excess of any other party, was the ideal group to lead a wartime government.

Despite British urging Faruq refused to have the Wafd in power; in February 1942 Sir Miles Lampson threatened the King with enforced abdication if he did not ask the Wafd to form a government. This wartime ministry of Nahhas and the Wafd lasted until October 1944. Makram Ubaid Pasha, who had been associated with the Wafd leadership since the 1920s, was dismissed by Nahhas shortly after his appointment as Minister of Finance. He then published the Black Book, detailing the alleged corruption of the Wafd leadership; Ubaid's book did the Wafd no end of harm. The Nahhas government's inability to respond to a serious epidemic in rural areas in 1943-44 also did not help its standing, and its perceived cooperation with the British was unpopular. As with his 1936 ministry, however, Nahhas managed to pull off a foreign-policy coup for Egypt: in October 1944 a conference was convened in Alexandria that laid the groundwork for the formation of the Arab League, thus muting a potential Iraqi challenge to Egypt's leadership in the Arab world. (See ALEXANDRIA PROTOCOL.) Shortly after this conference Faruq dismissed Nahhas.

During its six years in opposition prior to winning the January 1950 elections the Wafd leadership took on a more anti-British, populist position, accusing each Egyptian government in turn of neglecting Egypt's national interests. This period also saw the emergence of Fuad Siragaddin as a powerful figure in the Wafd leadership and increasing attempts by the leadership to build bridges to mass political parties and groups, such as the Ikhwan al-Muslimun, which seemed to be gaining an ever-larger share of popular political support in Egypt during this time.

The Wafd government held power in Egypt from January 1950 until the burning of Cairo two years later; it seemed unable to move fast enough to meet the growing demands for change and a readjustment of national priorities. Though the Nahhas government successfully negotiated the Sterling Reserves Agreement with Britain in July 1951, there was great difficulty with the British over the issue of the Sudan. In October 1951 the Wafd government abrogated the 1936 treaty with Britain and declared Faruq King of Egypt and the Sudan. At the same time it was trying to control a domestic situation that was increasingly unsettled and to cope with a strong British presence in the Canal Zone. Anti-British and antigovernment demonstrations occurred throughout 1951, and a state of emergency had to be declared four times during that year. In November 1951, hoping to profit from this anti-British feeling, the Wafd called for the formation of Liberation Squads that would engage the British in fighting at the Canal.

The involvement of the police in these squads led to a British attack on the Ismailiyya police station on 25 January 1952. The government instructed the defenders to hold off the British at all costs, an order that resulted in heavy Egyptian casualties. The burning of Cairo took place the next day. The Wafd government was blamed for its instructions to the Ismailiyya police to defend what was certainly a hopeless situation and for its failure to bring the Cairo fires and the crowds under control soon enough to prevent the loss of lives and property. The Wafd government fell the next week and was never returned to power. Siragaddin was arrested during an investigation into the riots that March (1952) but was released. Following the 1952 Revolution, Siragaddin was twice arrested and Nahhas forced to step down from the party leadership. A concerted crackdown on the leadership left the Wafd hierarchy decimated by 1954. A further suppression of Wafdists occurred in July 1957, with the imprisonment that October of three more of its leaders. There were forty more arrests in October 1961.

The Wafd's role in Egyptian politics over the three decades prior to the Revolution changed markedly. The party worked hard at its beginning to gather a broad base of support among all segments of the Egyptian population. Of all the national political parties it certainly had the support of the majority of Egyptians prior to 1952. But its long periods in opposition from 1930 to 1942 led to increasing competition for power within the Wafd leadership. Nahhas did not have the desire to share his power, and he lacked the personal charisma and credibility of Zaghlul, which could have counteracted the centrifugal tendencies of this period.

The Wafd also came, in time, to reflect more of the attitudes and concerns of the wealthier segments of the Egyptian bourgeoisie. It was unable in its last term in office to take control of the popular demands for change and reform that were to destabilize the monarchy. The emergence of a left-wing trend within the Wafd is testimony to the increasingly right-wing drift of the leadership itself, a drift that was responsible for the Wafd losing some of its support to groups like the Ikhwan, which was closer to more Egyptians and their concerns.

Despite the sometimes clouded reputation the party leadership acquired, the association of the Wafd Party with Egypt's twentieth-century nationalist movement ensured that the party had a faithful body of supporters throughout the pre- and post-1952 period. The formation of the New Wafd in February 1977 demonstrated the continued appeal of the type of moderate nationalism that came to be identified with the Wafd Party in its closing years. The New Wafd quickly became the largest of the independent opposition parties prior to its dissolution in June 1978.

WAFDIST BLOC see UBAID, MAKRAM

WAFDIST GENERAL UNION OF INDUSTRIAL WORKERS. Formed in July 1924 to counter the growing influence of the Communist Party among industrial workers, the General Union was intended to serve as a link between the Wafd Party and the trade-union movement. The leadership of the General Union, drawn from the Wafdist Central Committee, acted as a moderating influence in worker-management relations in the 1920s for those unions affiliated with it. In 1935 the Wafd Party formed a Wafdist Higher Council of Labor, which sought a dominant voice among trade-union federations, but it enjoyed rather less success in this as the independent federations gained an autonomous political role for themselves.

WAFDIST WOMEN'S CENTRAL COMMITTEE. Founded in January 1920 by Hoda Sharawi on the suggestion of Sa^{c}d Zaghlul, the Central Committee sought to build consciousness among Egyptian women of the political demands of the Wafd Party, and to gain their support in a number of practical actions. The committee organized an anti-British boycott in 1922; its pamphlets urged people not to purchase British goods or patronize British businesses and emphasized the need to build national economic independence. The committee provided an outlet for the involvement of women in national politics, and it campaigned for social-welfare legislation for women and women workers, as well as for reforms in the family laws to improve the legal position of women.

WAHBA PASHA, YUSUF (d.1924). Egyptian Prime Minister, Wahba Pasha formed a government in November 1919, after the short-lived and unpopular ministry of Sa^{c}id Pasha. Wahba Pasha, a Copt, had served in the prewar ministry of Sa^{c}id as Minister of Foreign Affairs from 1912 to 1914 and held the Finance portfolio in Sa^{c}id's 1919 ministry. Soon after he took office the Milner Mission arrived in Egypt. Wahba had a difficult time in overriding the boycott of the Mission organized by the Wafd, which prevented many Egyptians from officially meeting with Milner and his colleagues. He was himself nearly assassinated shortly after taking office by nationalists protesting the Mission. Wahba Pasha resigned in May 1920 on the grounds of ill health.

WAQF. The origins of the waqf, or religious endowment, in Egypt can be traced to the Coptic practice, termed ahbas, by which the revenues of properties were assigned by their owners to support Church establishments and religious works. Management of these properties remained in private hands, and the disbursal of their tax-free income was at the owner's or his heirs' discretion. The practice greatly reduced state revenues, but government attempts to control or limit waqfs were always successfully resisted, especially when the creation of religious endowments was adopted by Egypt's Muslims for similar purposes. The ᶜAbbāsid Caliph al-Mahdī was among those Muslim rulers who tried unsuccessfully to put a halt to this practice.

Property dedicated as waqf is given in perpetuity and theoretically forbidden to be bought or sold once established. Income from waqfs were distributed either through the donor's family (ahli waqf) or assigned directly to the beneficiary (khairi waqf), the latter commonly used for the maintenance of religious buildings. Legislation to control the use of waqfs to escape the inheritance laws was passed in 1946.

Following the 1952 Revolution family waqfs were abolished in September 1952 and the administration of khairi waqfs subjected to outside controls by a law passed in 1953. The Ministry of Waqfs, formed in 1913, was authorized under this law to use waqf income for purposes other than those to which the property was dedicated. In 1957 the income from khairi waqfs was nationalized for investment in development projects. Agricultural properties were removed from waqf status and distributed for the Agrarian Reform program.

The Ministry of Waqfs oversees the several thousand mosques whose funding is drawn from religious endowments. A government-appointed committee of Coptic leaders supervises their religious endowments in line with government legislation.

WAR OF ATTRITION. The War of Attrition was a sporadic but damaging conflict between Egypt and Israel from March 1969 until a cease-fire was arranged by U.S. Secretary of State Rogers, with the assistance of UN mediator Gunnar Jarring, in August 1970. Attacks began with artillery bombardment of the Israeli positions in the Sinai, and Israeli deep-penetration attacks on Egypt. Whatever specific provocative act may have been committed by either Egypt or Israel before this, both sides blamed each other for initiating and/or continuing exchanges. Israeli commando operations, including the removal of a large radar installation, were generally successful. Egyptian commandos made two attacks on Israeli military positions in Sinai.

Israeli bomber strikes in civilian areas forced a pause in the War of Attrition until nonmilitary areas could be better defended. The effectiveness of Israeli deep-penetration bombing led Egypt to seek, and receive, the latest SAM antiaircraft missiles from the Soviet Union in March 1970.

The costs of the War of Attrition were high. The Israeli bombing of the Egyptian industrial complex at Abu Zaabal in February 1970, resulted in seventy deaths and scores of injuries, and forced President Nasser to seek increased Russian support. The Israelis largely controlled the military situation until Egypt received advanced Soviet weaponry and assistance. The War of Attrition brought the United States and the Soviet Union into an increased involvement with the Arab-Israeli conflict, the former seeking to balance the influence of the latter. The U.S., via the Rogers Peace Plan, finally succeeded in bringing hostilities to a halt.

WAZĪR/VIZIER. The wazīr was a court official with supervisory responsibilities over the administration and occasionally the army, the religious establishment, and finances of the government. In the Fāṭimid period in Egypt, when the Caliph was distanced physically and ritually from the day-to-day administration of the country, the vizier was able to assume wide powers for himself. From the time of al-Mustanṣir (r.1036-94/427-87) the vizier was often ruler of Egypt in all but name. Competition for the office was intense, and turnover frequent. The vizierate declined in importance during Ayyūbid and Mamluk times.

WINGATE, GENERAL SIR REGINALD (1861-1953). High Commissioner and British Agent in Egypt from 1916 to 1919, Wingate had lengthy experience of the Sudan and Egypt, serving as Governor-General of the Sudan for seventeen years prior to his appointment in Egypt. In this position Wingate was deeply involved in the coordination of the Arab Revolt in the Hijaz. His tenure in Egypt came at a time when the Egyptian nationalist movement was undergoing a radicalizing phase. At the close of the First World War, Wingate was approached by Zaghlul and the wafd (nationalist delegation) for permission to go to London to present the case for Egypt's independence. He tried to convince the British Foreign Office to receive Zaghlul and his delegation or, failing that, to receive a general Egyptian delegation headed by the country's Prime Minister and including Zaghlul. Wingate's advice was ignored, and when he went to London in January 1919 to press the case for receiving Rushdi and allowing Zaghlul to go to Versailles, it was two weeks before he received a hearing. His representations were refused and the Embassy in Cairo decided that the deportation of Zaghlul would ease the internal situation in Egypt. In the event this proved a serious miscalculation. Wingate was in London at the time of the outbreak of the 1919 Rebellion, which was sparked by the deportation. He was superseded, but not officially replaced, by the appointment of a Special High Commissioner, Allenby; Wingate was not returned to Egypt thereafter.

-Y-

YAGAN PASHA see ADLI PASHA YEGEN

YAHYA PASHA, ABDAL FATAH (1876-1951). Egyptian Prime Minister, Yahya served from September 1933 to November 1934 during the authoritarian closing phase of the rule of King Fuad, which only eased when Fuad fell ill late in 1934. Yahya, a vice-president of the Sha^{c}b Party (during his ministry he served as President) had previously been Minister of Foreign Affairs in the 1930-33 Sidqi government. He was asked to form a government when Sidqi resigned. Yahya's government nearly totally reflected Palace interests; the Palace representative, Zaki al-Ibrashi, had dominant influence in the cabinet. Yahya's cool relations with the British were instrumental in forcing him to step down in favor of Nasim Pasha. Yahya later served as Minister of Foreign Affairs in the 1938 Mahmud government.

YA^{c}QŪB b. KILLIS (930-91/318-80). Islamicized Iraqi Jew who was associated with the Ikhshīdid court from his arrival in Egypt in 942/331, Ya^{c}qūb b. Killis was the first holder of the vizierate under the Ikhshīdid's successors, the Fāṭimids.

Arrested after the death of the Ikhshīdid ruler Kāfūr in 968/357, Ibn Killis made his escape and fled to the court of the Fāṭimid Caliph, al-Mu^{c}izz, in North Africa. Following the Fāṭimid conquest of Egypt the next year Ya^{c}qūb b. Killis began his service as vizier to the Caliph and then to his successor, al-^{c}Azīz. He organized the fiscal and administrative system of Egypt, and his power increased greatly through the years, though he did suffer two periods of eclipse. During his time in office he also participated in the Fāṭimid's campaigns in Syria, in 977-78/367-68. In addition to his reforms of Egypt's administration Ibn Killis was a scholar of Ismā^{c}īlī theology and a patron of learning who founded a generously funded school for philosophical studies. According to the sources, he died a rich and much-mourned man, the latter an unusual achievement for a vizier.

AL-YĀZŪRĪ (ABŪ MUḤAMMAD ḤASAN) (d. 1058/450). Religious judge of Palestinian origin in the court of al-Mustanṣir, al-Yāzūrī emerged as vizier in 1050/442, following nearly three years of confusion after the murder of his predecessor in the office, at-Tustarī. A sincerely religious man, al-Yāzūrī sought to correct the abuses that had arisen at the Fāṭimid court during Tustarī's term in office. A serious famine in 1054-55/445-46 led al-Yāzūrī to make a successful appeal for food to the Byzantine Emperor, Constantine Monomachos. Thereafter he instituted a system of grain stores to improve Egypt's fragile food security.

The last years of al-Yāzūrī's career were strongly linked with the progress of the Buyid adventurer al-Basāsīrī, who proclaimed the Fāṭimid Caliph's control of Mosul in 1057/448 and who went on to proclaim him in Baghdad two years later. Al-Yāzūrī at first did not support al-Basāsīrī but then changed his mind and backed him generously. He was thereafter accused of bankrupting the Treasury and also suspected of taking bribes. Al-Yāzūrī was turned out of office in favor of Ibn al-Maghrabī (who had formerly worked with al-Basāsīrī) and executed by the Palace guards on charges of treason.

YEGEN/YEGHEN PASHA see ADLI PASHA

YEMEN WAR. On 27 September 1962 a coup brought Abdullah al-Sallal to power in Yemen when he deposed the country's ruler, the Imam Ahmad. The latter's heir, Muhammad al-Badr, decamped to the north of the country, where he mounted a resistance movement with the support of loyal tribesmen and the financial and material backing of the Saudi Arabians. Sallal requested aid from Egypt, which, anxious to recover lost pan-Arab ground after the breakup of the UAR, granted it in the form of troops and supplies. The U.S., USSR and several other governments recognized the Sallal government, but not the British, then in occupation of Aden in the south. In consequence of Egypt's involvement Yemen became a military and diplomatic battleground between Egypt and Saudi Arabia. Following the Egyptian bombing of a Saudi border town in November 1962 the Saudis broke relations with the Egyptians, and thereafter relations between the two states were acrimonious.

Despite their own poor relations both parties seemed to want an end to their involvement in the conflict. Yet neither UN efforts in 1963 nor the Egyptian-Saudi Armistice in 1964, nor the Jeddah and Harad Conference in 1965, could convince the Yemenis to stop fighting. Egypt's troop commitment grew from 8,000 in 1963 to 70,000 in 1965. A meeting between Nasser and King Faysal in August 1965 saw agreement between Egypt and Saudi Arabia on a schedule for the withdrawal of Egyptian troops, and new negotiating approaches at Harad were made that November. Neither meeting was effective in ending Egypt's involvement, which was adversely affecting its economy and draining troops and equipment from its army. At the same time Egypt had difficulty controlling the different revolutionary factions which proliferated during the fighting. Egypt used the Yemen War to mount a major attack on Saudi Arabia and other traditional governments in the area both physically (bombing) and through propaganda and infiltration. Thus, in between the periods when both parties were trying to negotiate an end to the fighting, their mutual hostility sharpened. Egyptian-Saudi relations hit an all-time low prior to the 1967 war, with Saudi charges of Egyptian poison-gas attacks on Yemeni villages and Saudi border towns.

Egyptian involvement in the Yemen War was officially brought to an end following the Khartoum Conference in the autumn of 1967, when relations between Egypt and Saudi were on the mend again. Egyptian troop withdrawals were agreed on, and a massive Saudi, Kuwaiti, and Libyan loan extended to Egypt to help pay the costs of the 1967 Arab-Israeli War. The partition of Yemen into North Yemen and the People's Democratic Republic of Yemen (Aden) took place in November 1967.

YILBUGHĀ AL-JAJAWĪ (d.1366/768). Ustadhar during the reign of the Baḥrī Mamluk Sultan Muḥammad (1361-63/762-64) and for the first few years of the reign of Sha^{c}bān II, Yilbughā was deeply unpopular in Egypt and among the Mamluks. Crusader activity in Cyprus caused Yilbughā to increase taxes massively to pay for military expenditure, never a popular measure. The Crusaders' brutal sacking of Alexandria in 1365/766, and their massacre of its inhabitants, further aroused popular discontent. Yilbughā's attempt to depose Sha^{c}bān resulted in a revolt of the Sultan's Mamluk guard, including Barqūq, future Burjī Sultan.

Though Yilbughā managed at first to suppress this revolt, the leaders of it arranged the Ustadhar's assassination shortly thereafter.

YILBUGHĀ AN-NĀSIRĪ (d. 1391/793). Mamluk Amīr of Aleppo (Syria), Yilbughā rose in revolt in 1389/791 against the first Burjī Mamluk Sultan, Barqūq. He succeeded, in tandem with the Mamluk Mintash, in restoring the child Sultan Ḥājjī II to power, with himself as regent.

Yilbughā's revolt against Barqūq had the strong backing of the Syrian and provincial Amīrs, who were increasingly perturbed at the presence of Tīmūr on their borders. With their support he easily defeated an army sent by Barqūq in 1389/791 and proceeded to march on Egypt. Barqūq was trapped in the Citadel with the remains of his army, and after a lengthy siege by Yilbughā and Mintash he was forced to capitulate. Yilbughā allowed Barqūq to go into exile and installed Ḥājjī in power.

Mintash and Yilbughā soon fell out over what Mintash felt was Yilbughā's assumption of nearly supreme power and the latter's mistake in granting clemency to Barqūq. Mintash managed to gain ascendancy over Yilbughā within the duumvirate but had to flee Egypt when Barqūq regained power in 1390/792. Barqūq made Yilbughā Commander-in-Chief of the Syrian Mamluks, but his undistinguished fighting against his former ally, Mintash, aroused Barqūq's suspicions; Yilbughā was put to death in 1391/793, along with many of his friends and supporters among the Syrian Mamluks.

YOM KIPPUR WAR see ARAB-ISRAELI WAR (1973)

YOUNG EGYPT CONGRESS. First held in Geneva in 1908, the Young Egypt Congress was formed by the more radical supporters of the Egyptian nationalist movement, led by Idris Raghib. At the congress the delegates attacked the British presence in Egypt, asked the Egyptian government to improve educational opportunities for Egyptians in their own country, and sought the creation of an activist and radical nationalist party modeled on the Young

Turks. Delegates from the British Labor Party attended the congress, which was under the presidency of Mahmud Fahmi. The congress held two more annual sessions, attracting public support in Egypt before being proscribed by the British in 1910 for the alleged involvement of Ibrahim Wardani, one of its delegates, in the assassination that year of the Egyptian Prime Minister, Butrus Ghali Pasha.

YOUNG EGYPT PARTY see MISR AL FATAT

YOUNG MEN'S MUSLIM ASSOCIATION. Founded in November 1927 by nationalist politician Dr. Abdal Hamid Sa^{c}id, a deputy of the Nationalist Party, the YMMA was strongly influenced by the prewar ideology of the Nationalist Party. The association was meant to inculcate Muslim ideas and values among Egyptian students and young people, specifically those young students most at risk of losing touch with their Islamic roots through exposure to Western or missionary education. The YMMA philosophy was a mixture of radical nationalism and Islam and the group supported a variety of pan-Islamic goals, including the defense of Palestine against Zionism. The YMMA participated in a number of demonstrations and campaigns against Jewish settlement in Palestine, and became more activist in line with the general rise in militancy by political groupings in the mid-1930s. The YMMA set up branches in many other Muslim countries. In Egypt, the group banded together with other parties in the National Union of Political Party Youth and Groups, which participated in antigovernment demonstrations in the post-World War Two period.

YŪSUF (AL-^{c}AZĪZ JAMĀL AD-DĪN YŪSUF) (r. 1437-38/841-42). Burjī Mamluk Sultan, Yūsuf was the son and successor of Barsbay. His regent, Jaqmaq, having gained support of the Ashrafiyya Mamluk faction, deposed his charge after Yūsuf had been in power only three months. Yūsuf was imprisoned in the Citadel, but shortly afterward a rebellion broke out in Syria and Egypt in support of his Sultanate, and he was smuggled out of the Citadel by his supporters in 1439/843. His brief taste of freedom ended when he was recaptured shortly afterward. He was more honorably treated by Jaqmaq thereafter and settled in a comfortable house arrest in Alexandria.

YUSUF, SHAYKH ALI see ALI YUSUF, SHAYKH

-Z-

AẒ-ẒĀFIR (r. 1149-54/544-49). Fāṭimid Caliph and the youngest son of al-Ḥāfiz, aẓ-Ẓāfir was a weak ruler whose tenure in office was brought to a close by his assassination at the hands of his favorite, Nāṣr, and his vizier, Nāṣr's father, ᶜAbbās. For the first four years of his reign the vizier Sallār was in office, but he fell victim to the ambitious ᶜAbbās and his son in 1153/548, the year the last Fāṭimid possession in Palestine fell to the Crusaders. Aẓ-Ẓāfir, who was personally involved with Nāṣr, then made ᶜAbbās (Sallār's adopted son) his vizier. The two decided to execute the Caliph to resolve their own insecure positions: ᶜAbbās worrying that the Caliph was encouraging Nāṣr to murder him and Nāṣr that his father was planning to have him killed. They committed the murder jointly in 1154/549 and placed aẓ-Ẓāfir's young son Fā'iz on the throne.

ZAGHLUL PASHA, SAᶜD (SAAD) (1854-1927). Founder of the Wafd Party and Egyptian Prime Minister, Saᶜd Zaghlul was the most important pre-Revolutionary nationalist figure. Zaghlul joined the Umma Party on its formation in 1907; he had been associated with the nationalists and with Muhammad Abduh since the 1890s. He served in the Fahmi and Butrus Ghali governments from 1906 to 1910 as Minister of Education. Following Ghali's assassination Zaghlul was Minister of Justice in the government of Saᶜid Pasha (1910-13) resigning over the prosecution of the Nationalist Party leader, Farid. Zaghlul was the first elected vice-president of the Legislative Assembly created by the Organic Law of 1913. Aside from his political involvements he was appointed to the Establishments Committee of the National University Fund in 1906.

Toward the end of the First World War, Zaghlul and a number of nationalists formed a delegation (wafd) to present the case for Egypt's independence. The Protectorate imposed by the British at the outbreak of the war had effectively stifled political life at the national level, and its abolition was sought by all parties in Egypt. Zaghlul apparently had the support of the Palace and of the pro-Palace politicians in forming this delegation.

Zaghlul and his colleagues went to Wingate, the British High Commissioner, two days after the signing of the Armistice, on 13 November 1918, to ask his permission to go to London, and eventually to the Versailles Peace Conference. The British government, despite Wingate's recommendations, refused to receive not only Zaghlul, but also a delegation headed by the Prime Minister, with Zaghlul travelling unofficially to Versailles to present the nationalist cause. This last act was badly received in Egypt but was justified by the British on the grounds that Zaghlul had no claim to be representative of opinion in Egypt, whether heading or participating in a delegation. They subsequently reluctantly agreed to receive Rushdi, provided Zaghlul remained in Egypt. This Rushdi refused and put into effect a resignation he presented at the time his original delegation was rejected.

In the meantime Zaghlul and his followers organized the Tawkilat, a campaign to gain signatures for a petition supporting Zaghlul; and the wafd, or delegation, became the nucleus of the Wafd Party. The situation in Egypt was growing tense, as it became apparent the British would not terminate the Protectorate at the end of the war, as many had thought. The British deported Zaghlul to Malta in March 1919, hoping that this would calm the discontent, but it produced the reverse effect. The Rebellion of March 1919 followed, and saw Wingate replaced with Allenby, and Zaghlul released from exile in April, whereupon he was given permission to go to Paris. He operated from his European exile for the next two years, keeping close control of the Wafd Party in Egypt.

Zaghlul instructed his supporters in Egypt to boycott the Milner Mission, which came to Egypt late in 1919 to investigate the causes of the Rebellion. The boycott was effective. Few Egyptians wished to disobey a man who had become a nationalist hero. Zaghlul finally consented to meet the Mission after its return to London, in the summer of 1920. The Milner Report, issued in February 1921, recommended termination of the Protectorate; in anticipation of the changes this presaged in Egyptian political life and in response to British approaches for an official Egyptian negotiating team, the King asked Adli Pasha, a moderate nationalist, to form a government.

Zaghlul's refusal to support the Adli government upon his return to Egypt in April 1921 marked the first great split in the nationalist movement, as the more moderate and conservative nationalists rallied to Adli's support, and the Society of Independent Egypt was established as a political grouping in opposition to the Wafd. Zaghlul traveled and spoke widely until his freedom of movement was restricted. Such was the effectiveness of his opposition that the Palace and the British again decided to deport him successively to Aden, the Seychelles, and Gibraltar. Zaghlul was not released until April 1923, though he continued once again to direct the party's activities from exile. After a period of recuperation in France, Zaghlul returned to Egypt in time to contest, and win, the first elections held in Egypt under the new Constitution. To the horror of the Palace, the British, and the moderates, the Wafd won by a landslide and Zaghlul formed a government in January 1924.

Zaghlul's year in office was dominated by the Sudan issue and his unsuccessful negotiations with the British. His failure to resolve the differences in the British and Egyptian views on the future of the Sudan caused him at one point to threaten resignation, in June 1924, following which there were nearly two months of anti-British disturbances. In September Zaghlul accepted a British offer of negotiations in London; these collapsed within a month. The assassination in November 1924 of Sir Lee Stack, Sirdar of the Egyptian army and Governor-General of the Sudan, produced a swift British reaction: an ultimatum demanding various Egyptian capitulations on the Sudan, a heavy fine, and the prosecution of the guilty. Zaghlul, who could not accept the terms of the ultimatum with regard to the Sudan, had no choice but to step down.

In the elections for Parliament in March 1925, under the government of Ziwar Pasha, the Wafd took half the seats and Zaghlul was elected its president. The Palace, displeased, ordered the Parliament dissolved in June 1925. The Wafd won the elections of May 1926, which were called in an attempt to reduce the Wafdist domination of the Parliament. The British refused to have Zaghlul as Prime Minister, blaming him and his party for involvement in the Lee Stack assassination (despite the acquittal of the two Wafdists charged). Adli Pasha was again asked to form a government, but a Wafd-controlled Parliament, with Zaghlul as its president, proved no easy group to rule against. Adli was eventually replaced with Tharwat Pasha in April 1927; four months later, Zaghlul died.

In his entire political career Zaghlul was actually in power just eleven months. Despite this he dominated Egyptian politics until his death. His first electoral victory was remarkable: the Wafd, under his leadership, won 190 out of 214 seats in the 1924 elections. His hold on the popular imagination was a product of his long period of mistreatment by the British, his image as a man of the people, his skills as an orator, and his impeccable nationalist record. With his colleagues, however, he was less successful. He did not seem able to share the power he acquired, nor was he generous to his opponents. His break with the moderate nationalists proved a grave error, splitting the nationalists in their dealings with the Palace, which enabled the King to gain the upper hand.

No other nationalist politician had quite the impact on the Egyptian people as Zaghlul. Whatever his flaws as the leader of a political party, he was effective in winning the support of the people and gaining their identification with him. He believed himself to be not the head of a political party but the leader of a nation.

AẒ-ẒĀHIR (r. 1021-36/411-27). Son of the Fāṭimid Caliph al-Ḥākim, az-Zāhir succeeded to power following the mysterious disappearance of his father. For the first four years of his reign he was under the strong regency of his aunt, Sitt al-Mulk. His aunt had secured az-Zāhir's succession in lieu of his cousin ᶜAbd ar-Raḥmān, who had been nominated by al-Ḥākim in preference to his own son. ᶜAbd ar-Raḥmān declared himself independent and seized Aleppo in 1023/414 but was defeated by a group of Fāṭimid supporters, captured, returned to Cairo, and imprisoned.

A disastrous famine struck Egypt in the last two years of Sitt al-Mulk's regency, with attendant civil disorders. After her death Aḥmad al-Jarjarā'ī seized power, but the situation both in Egypt and at the Fāṭimid court itself remained unstable in the aftermath of the famine and the decline in revenues. Az-Zāhir, whose major contribution seems to have been to block the negotiations with the Byzantines started by his aunt, was succeeded by his son, al-Mustanṣir.

ZIWAR PASHA, AHMAD (1864-1945). Egyptian Prime Minister, Ziwar Pasha served in several ministerial capacities before forming a government in November 1924 to replace that of Saᶜd Zaghlul. Ziwar joined the government of Rushdi Pasha in 1919 as Minister of Education and became Minister of Communications in the governments of Wahba Pasha and Nasim Pasha in 1920. Following the formation of the Adli government in 1921 Ziwar kept his Communications Ministry through to January 1924. After the elections that year Ziwar was voted president of the Senate.

The Lee Stack Affair, which brought down the government of Zaghlul in November 1924, resulted in the imposition of a heavy fine on the Egyptian government and several other provisions relating to both internal-security matters and the Sudan. It was Ziwar's task to ensure that the British were satisfied with Egyptian fulfillment of these provisions.

Ziwar Pasha was eclipsed as a leader within his own government by his extremely powerful Interior Minister, Sidqi Pasha, who led the government's efforts to change the electoral law and keep the Wafd out of office. His Justice Minister, Abdal Aziz Fahmi, became involved in a dispute with the religious community over its condemnation of a political work by the Islamic modernist Ali Abdur Raziq. The minister resigned, fatally weakening Ziwar's government.

Despite the efforts of Sidqi the Wafd made a strong showing in the May 1926 elections; Ziwar was forced to make way for a government headed by the more moderate Adli Pasha that June. Ziwar went on to serve as chief of the Royal Cabinet in 1934-35. He resigned his government posts in November 1935.

SELECTED BIBLIOGRAPHY

The number of books published on Egypt, both in Arabic and non-Arabic languages, is vast. In this bibliography, I have given the most recent titles wherever possible, particularly for Arabic language works published in Egypt. An attempt has also been made to list the most recent publishers and date of publication; many classic works on Egypt have been reprinted in paperback in the last few years.

Because this bibliography is limited to books and booklets, students and researchers interested in journal articles are asked to consult the sections on bibliography and reference works, both of which contain basic introductions to, or listings of, articles on different aspects of Egyptian history. There are special sections dealing with the arts, literature, the press, religious movements in Islam, and social and anthropological writings. Many studies have been done on Egypt's Copts; a selection of these is listed separately, as are some of the works which have been done on the Egyptian economy in both its industrial and agricultural aspects.

I should like to thank Manijeh Bayani and HRH Prince Turki b. Muhammad b. Saud al-Kabir for their help with the Arabic listings in this bibliography.

TABLE OF CONTENTS

SELECTED BIBLIOGRAPHY

General History

Non-Arabic Titles

Ball, John. Egypt in the Classical Geographies. Cairo, Government Press, 1942.

Becker, C. H. Beiträge zur Geschichte Ägyptens unter der Islam. repr. Philadelphia, Porcupine Press, 1977.

Birks, Walter A. A Short History of Islamic Egypt from the Arab Conquest to Muhammad Ali. Cairo, Anglo-Egyptian Bookstore, 1951.

Fisher, Sydney N. The Middle East: A History. London, Routledge Kegan Paul, 1971.

Hitti, Phillip K. A History of the Arabs from Earliest Times to the Present. London, MacMillan, 1970.

________. A Short History of the Near East. London, Van Nostrand, 1966.

Holt, P. M., ed. Studies in the History of the Middle East. London, Cass, 1973.

Hanotaux, Gabriel, ed. Histoire de la nation Egyptienne, Paris, 1931-40.

Kirk, George. A Short History of the Middle East. London, Metheun, 1964.

Lewis, Bernard. The Arabs in History. New York, Harper and Brothers, 1960.

Précis de l'histoire de l'Egypte, Cairo, Institut Français, 1932-35.

Shaban, M. A. Islamic History: A New Interpretation. Cambridge, Cambridge University Press, Vol. I, 1971; Vol. II, 1976.

Tawfiq, M. A Short History of Islam and Islamic Egypt. Cairo, Tsoumas Press, 1968.

Arabic Titles

Al-^{c}Adawī, Ibrāhīm Aḥmad. Miṣr al-Islāmīya, Muqawwimātuhā al-^{c}Arabīya wa Risālatuha al-Ḥaḍārīya. Cairo, Maktaba al-Anjlū al-Miṣrīya, 1976.

Ḥasan, ^{c}Alī Ibrāhīm. Miṣr fi'l-^{c}Uṣūr al-Wusṭā. Cairo, Maktaba an-Nahḍa al-^{c}Arabīya, 1963.

Ḥusayn, Aḥmad. Mawsū^{c}a Tārīkh Miṣr. Cairo, Dār ash-Sha^{c}b, 1972- .

Al-Ḥuwairī, Maḥmūd. *Aswān fi'l-^{c}Uṣūr al-Wusṭā.* Cairo, Dār al-Ma^{c}ārif, 1980.

Ar-Rāfi^{c}ī, ^{c}Abd ar-Raḥmān. *Miṣr fi'l-^{c}Uṣūr al-Wusṭā min al-Fatḥ al-^{c}Arabī ḥattā'l-Ghazw al-^{c}Uthmānī.* Cairo, Dār an-Naḥda al-^{c}Arabīya, 1970.

Sālim, As-Sayyid ^{c}Abd al-^{c}Azīz. *Tārīkh al-Iskandarīya wa Ḥaḍāratihā fi'l-^{c}Aṣr al-Islāmī.* Cairo, Dār al-Ma^{c}ārif, 1969.

Egypt Before the Muslim Conquest

Non-Arabic Titles

Bagnall, Roger S. and K. A. Worp. *Regnal Formulas in Byzantine Egypt.* Missoula, Montana Scholars Press, 1979.

Bell, H. I. *Egypt from Alexander the Great to the Arab Conquest: A Study in the Diffusion of Helenism.* repr. Westport (Conn.), Greenwood Press, 1977.

________. *Jews and Christians in Egypt: The Jewish Troubles in Alexandria and the Athanasian Controversy.* repr. Westport (Conn.), Greenwood Press, 1972.

Bernard, André. *Le Delta égyptien d'après les textes grecs.* Cairo, Institut Français, 1970.

Bowman, Alan K. *The Town Councils of Roman Egypt.* Toronto, A. M. Hakkert, 1971.

Chitty, Derwas James. *The Desert City: An Introduction to the Study of Egyptian and Palestinian Monasticism under the Christian Empire.* London, Mowbrays, 1977.

Demicheli, Anna Maria. *Rapporti di pace et di guerra dell' Egitto romano con le populazioni dei deserti africani.* Milano, A. Guiffr, 1976.

Hardy, E. R. *The Large Estates of Byzantine Egypt.* New York, AMS Press, 1968.

Johnson, Allan Chester. *Egypt and the Roman Empire.* Ann Arbor, University of Michigan Press, 1951.

Jouget, Pierre. *La vie municipale dans l'Égypte romaine.* repr. Paris, Éditions de Boccard, 1968.

Lefort, L. Th., ed. *Oeuvres de S. Pachôme et de ses disciples.* Louvain, Durbecq, 1956.

Lesquier, Jean. *L'Armée romaine d'Égypte d'Auguste à Diocletian.* Cairo, Institut Français, 1918.

Lindsay, Jack. *Daily Life in Roman Egypt.* London, Muller, 1963.

Maehler, Herwig. Urkunden römischer Zeit. Berlin, Hessling, 1966-68.

Marlowe, John. The Golden Age of Alexandria from Its Foundation by Alexander the Great in 331 BC to Its Capture by the Arabs in 642 AD. London, Gollancz, 1971.

Maspero, Jean. Organisation militaire de l'Égypte Byzantine. Cairo, Institut Français (et Bibliothèque de l'École des Hautes Études), 1912.

Milne, Joseph Grafton. A History of Egypt under Roman Rule. London, Methuen, 1898.

Persson, Axel W. Staat und Manufaktur im romischen Reiche. N.Y., Arno Press, 1979.

Reimuth, O. W. The Prefect of Egypt from Augustus to Diocletian. repr. Wiesbaden, Scientia Verlag Aalen, 1963.

Roberts, Colin Henderson. Manuscript, Society and Belief: Early Christian Egypt. London, Oxford University Press, 1979.

Rouillard, Germain. L'Administration civile de l'Égypte Byzantine. Paris, Guenther, 1928.

Simaika, Abdullah. Essai sur la Province romaine d'Égypte depuis la conquête jusqu'à Diocletian. Paris, 1892.

Arabic Titles

Al-ᶜAbbādī, Muṣṭafā. Miṣr min al-Iskandar al-Akbar ila'l-Fatḥ al-ᶜArabī. Cairo, Maktaba al-Anjlū al-Miṣrīya, 1966.

ᶜAlī, ᶜAbd al-Laṭīf Aḥmad. Miṣr wa'l-Imbaraṭūrīya ar-Rūmānīya fī Ḍaw' al-Awrāq al-Bardīya. Beirut, Dār an-Nahḍa al-ᶜArabīya, 1977.

Al-ᶜAyrīnī, As-Sayyid al-Bāz. Miṣr al-Byzanṭīya. Cairo, Dār an-Nahḍa al-ᶜArabīya, 1961.

Egypt from the Muslim Conquest Through the Fāṭimid Period

Non-Arabic Titles

Akram, A. I. The Muslim Conquest of Egypt and North Africa. Lahore, Feroz Sons, 1977.

Assad, Sadik A. The Reign of al-Ḥākim bi Amr Allah (386/996-411/1021) A Political Study. Beirut, Arab Institute for Research and Publication, 1974.

Butler, Alfred J. The Arab Conquest of Egypt and the Last Thirty Years of the Roman Dominion. repr. Oxford, Clarendon, 1978.

Cohen, Mark. Jewish Self-Government in Medieval Egypt: The Origins of the Office of Head of the Jews, c. 1065-1126 AD. Princeton, Princeton University Press, 1980.

Gottschalk, H. L. *Die Madara'iyyin: Ein Beitrag zur Geschichte Ägyptens unter der Islam*. Berlin and Leipzig, Walter Gruyter, 1931.

Hasan, Z. M. *Les Tulunides: Étude de l'Égypte musulmane à la fin du IXeme siècle 868-905*. Paris, Établisments Bussons, 1933.

Ivanov, Vladimir A. *Ismaili Tradition Concerning the Rise of the Fatimids*. London, Oxford University Press, 1942.

Al-Kindi (Abu Umar). *The Governors and Judges of Egypt* (translated and edited by R. Guest). Leiden, Brill, 1912.

________. *The History of the Governors of Egypt* (translated and edited by A. Koenig). New York, Columbia University Press, 1908.

Muller, C. Detlef Gustav. *Grundzüge des Christlich-Islamischen Ägypten*. Darmstadt, Wissenchaftliche Buchgesellschaft, 1969.

O'Leary, De Lacy. *A Short History of the Fatimid Caliphate*. repr. Wilmington (Del.), Scholarly Resources, 1975.

Stern, Samuel Miklos. *Fatimid Decrees: Original Documents from the Fatimid Chancery*. London, Faber and Faber, 1964.

Vatikiotis, P. J. *The Fatimid Theory of the State*. repr. Lahore, Orientalia Publishers, 1957.

Zaydan, Jurji. Umayyads and ^{c}Abbasids (Part IV of Zaydan's *History of Islamic Civilization*, translated by D. S. Margoliouth). Leiden, Brill, 1907.

Arabic Titles

Abū Sa^{c}dā, Muḥammad Jabr. Ibn ^{c}Abd al-Ḥākim, Al-Mu'arrikh wa Kitābuhu Futūḥ Miṣr wa Akhbāruhā. Cairo, Maṭba^{c}a al-Ḥusayn al-Jadīda, 1979.

^{c}Amārā, Muḥammad. ^{c}Indamā Aṣbaḥa Miṣr al-^{c}Arabīya: Dirāsa ^{c}an al-Mujtama^c al-Miṣrī fi'l-^{c}Aṣr al-Fāṭimī. Beirut, Al-Mu'assasa al-^{c}Arabīya li'd-Dirāsāt wa'n-Nashr, 1974.

Al-^{c}Asalī, Bassām. ^{c}Amr b. al-^{c}Āṣ. Beirut, Dār an-Nafā'is, 1979.

Barrī, ^{c}Abd Allāh Khurshīd. Al-Qur'ān wa ^{c}Ulūmihi fī Miṣr 20-358AH. Cairo, Dār al-Ma^{c}ārif, 1970.

Al-Bāshā, Ḥasan. Dirāsāt fī Tārīkh ad-Dawla al-^{c}Abbāsīya. Cairo, Dār an-Nahḍa al-^{c}Arabīya, 1975.

Diyab, Ṣābir Muḥammad. Dirāsāt fī Tārīkh Miṣr al-Islāmīya wa Ḥaḍāratuhā min al-Fatḥ al-Islāmī ḥattā Muntaṣaf al-Qarn ath-Thālith al-Hijrī. Cairo, Jāmi^{c}a al-Qāhira, 1976.

________. Siyāsa ad-Duwal al-Islāmīya fī Ḥawḍ al-Baḥr al-Mutawassiṭ min Awā'il al-Qarn ath-Thānī al-Hijrī ḥattā Nihīya al-^{c}Aṣr al-Fāṭimī. Cairo, ^{c}Ālam al-Kutub, 1976.

Ḥasan, ^{c}Alī Ibrāhīm. Istikhdām al-Maṣādir. Cairo, Maktaba an-Nahḍa al-^{c}Arabīya, 1963.

———. Tārīkh ad-Dawla al-Fāṭimīya. Cairo, Maktaba an-Nahḍa al-^{c}Arabīya, 1958.

———. Tārīkh Jawhar aṣ-Ṣiqillī. Cairo, 1933.

Ibn ^{c}Abd al-Ḥākim. Futūḥ Miṣr. Cairo, Maṭba^{c}a Majlis al-Ma^{c}ārif al-Faransawīya, 1914; repr. New Haven, 1974.

Al-Ibyārī, Ibrāhīm. Abū'l-Misk Kāfūr. Cairo, Dār al-Fikr al-^{c}Arabī, 1962.

Kāshif, Ṣayyīda Ismā^{c}īl and Ḥasan Aḥmad Maḥmūd. Miṣr fī ^{c}Aṣr aṭ-Ṭūlūnīyīn wa'l-Ikhshīdīyīn. Cairo, Maktaba al-Anjlū al-^{c}Arabīya, 1960.

Kāshif, Sayyīda Ismā^{c}īl. Miṣr fī ^{c}Aṣr aṭ-Ṭūlūnīyīn. Cairo, Maktaba an-Nahḍa al-^{c}Arabīya, 1959.

———. Miṣr fi ^{c}Asr al-Ikhshīdīyīn. Cairo, Maṭba^{c}a Jāmi^{c}a Fu'ād I, 1950.

———. Misr fī fajr al-Islam. Cairo, Dār al-Fikr al-^{c}Arabi, 1947.

Al-Kindī (Abū ^{c}Umar). Al-Mukhtār min Kitāb Wulāt Miṣr wa Qudātihā. Cairo, Dār al-Ma^{c}ārif, n.d.

Al-Madanī, ^{c}Abd Allāh b. Muḥammad. Sīra Aḥmad b. Ṭūlūn. Damascus, 1939.

Maḥmūd, Ḥasan Aḥmad. Ḥaḍāra Miṣr al-Islāmīya fi'l-^{c}Aṣr aṭ-Ṭūlūn. Cairo, 1900.

Majīd, ^{c}Abd al-Mun^{c}īm. Nuẓūm al-Fāṭimīyīn. Cairo, Maktaba al-Anjlū al-Miṣrīya, 1973.

———. Ẓuhūr Khalīfa al-Fāṭimīyīn. Alexandria, Dār al-Ma^{c}ārif, 1968.

———. Al-Imām al-Mustanṣir Billāh al-Fāṭimī. Cairo, Maktaba al-Anjlū al-Miṣrīya, 1960.

Al-Maqrīzī (Aḥmad b. ^{c}Alī). Itti^{c}āẓ al-Ḥunafā bi-Akhbār al-A'imma al-Fāṭimīyīn al-Khulafa'; Vol. I ed. Jamāl ad-Dīn ash-Shayyal, Vol. II and III ed. Muḥammad Hilmī Aḥmad. Cairo, Al-Majlis al-A^{c}lā li'sh-Shu'ūn al-Islāmīya, 1967-73.

Musharrafā, ^{c}Aṭīya Muṣṭafā. Nazm al-Ḥukm bi-Miṣr fī ^{c}Aṣr al-Fāṭimīyīn. Cairo, Dār al-Fikr al-^{c}Arabī, n.d.

Nazmī, Lūqā. ᶜAmr b. al-ᶜĀṣ. Cairo, Al-Hai'a al-Miṣrīya al-ᶜĀmma, 1970.

Surūr, Muḥammad. Miṣr fī ᶜAṣr ad-Dawla al-Fāṭimīya. Cairo, Maktaba an-Nahḍa al-ᶜArabīya, 1960.

Ayyūbids and Mamluks

Non-Arabic Titles

Atiya, A. S. Crusader Commerce and Culture. repr. Gloucester (Mass.), P. Smith, 1969.

________. The Crusade: Historiography and Bibliography. Bloomington, Indiana University Press, 1962.

Ayalon, David. The Mamluk Military Society. London, Variorum, 1979.

________. Studies on the Mamluks of Egypt 1250-1517. London, Variorum, 1977.

________. Gunpowder and Firearms in the Mamluk Kingdom: A Challenge to Medieval Society. London, Valentine, Mitchell, 1956.

________. L'Esclavage de Mamelouk. Jerusalem, Israel Oriental Society, 1951.

Cahen, Claude. La Syrie du Nord à l'époque des croisades. Paris, Institut Français de Damas, 1940.

Darraj, Ahmad. L'Egypte sous le règne de Barsbey 1422-38AD/825-41AH. Damascus, Institut Français, 1961.

Davis, Edwin John. The Invasion of Egypt in AD 1249(AH 647) by Louis IX of France and a History of the Contemporary Sultans of Egypt. London, S. Lowe Marston and Co., 1898.

Dols, Michael. The Black Death in the Middle East. Princeton, Princeton University Press, 1977.

Ehrenkreutz, Andrew. Saladin. Albany, SUNY Press, 1972.

Elbeheiry, Salah. Les institutions de l'Égypte au temps des Ayyubides. Lille, L'Université de Lille, 1972.

Elisséf, N. Nūr ad-Dīn, un grand prince musulman de Syrie au temps de Croisades (511-69/1118-74). Damascus, Institut Français, 1974.

Fischel, Walter Joseph. Ibn Khaldun in Egypt: His Public Functions and His Historical Research 1382-1406. Berkeley, University of California Press, 1967.

Gabrielli, Francesco. Arab Historians of the Crusades. Selected and Translated from the Arabic by F. Gabrielli (translated from the Italian by E. J. Costello). London, Routledge, Kegan Paul, 1969.

Gibb, H. A. R. The Life of Saladin from the Works of ᶜImād ad Dīn and Bāhā'ad Dīn. Oxford, Clarendon Press, 1973.

Glubb, John Bagot. Soldiers of Fortune: The Story of the Mamluks. London, Hodder and Stoughton, 1973.

Gottschalk, H. L. Al-Malik Al-Kamil von Ägypten und seine Zeit. Weisbaden, Harrassowitz, 1958.

Haarmon, Ulrich. Quellenstudien zur frühen Mamlukenzeit. Freiburg im Breisgau, Steiner Verlag, 1970.

Al Hajji, Haya Nasser. The Internal Affairs of Egypt During the Third Reign of the Sultan an-Nāṣir Muhammad b. Qalawun 709-41/1309-41. Kuwait, Kuwait University Press, 1978.

Halm, Heinz. Ägypten nach dem mamlukischen Lehensregistern. Weisbaden, Reichert, 1979.

Hindley, Geoffrey. Saladin. London, Constable, 1976.

Ibn Abil-Fadail. Histoire des Sultans Mamlouks. (French and Arabic texts, translated by E. Blochet.) Paris, Firman-Didot, 1920.

Ibn al-Furāt (Muḥammad b. ᶜAbd ar-Raḥmān). Ayyubids, Mamlukes and Crusaders: Selections from the Tārīkh ad-Duwal wa'l-Muluk of Ibn al-Furāt. (Text translated by U. and M. C. Lyons.) Cambridge, Hoffer, 1971.

Ibn Iyās (Ayas). Journal d'un Bourgeois du Cairo. (Translated and annotated by G. Wiet.) Paris, Bibliothèque Général de L'École Practique des Hautes Études, 1955-60.

________. Histoire des Mamlouks Circassiens. (Translated and arranged by G. Wiet.) Cairo, Institut Français, 1945.

Ibn Khaldūn. The Muqaddimah: An Introduction to History. (Translated by F. Rosenthal.) Princeton, Princeton University Press, 1979.

Ibn Taghrī-Birdī. An-Nujūm aẓ-Ẓāhira fī Mulūk Miṣr wa'l-Qāhira, History of Egypt 1382-1469AD. (Translated by W. Popper.) New York, AMS Press, 1976.

________. Extracts from Ḥawādith ad-Duhūr fī Madā'l Ayyām wa'sh-shuhūr. (Translated by W. Popper.) Berkeley, University of California Press, 1930.

Iman, Younis Bishr. Die Einwerkungen der mamlukischen Beziehungen zu Nubien und Begaland auf die historische Entwicklung dieser Gebiete. Hamburg, 1971.

Al Khowaiter, Abdul Aziz. Baybars I: His Endeavors and Achievements. London, Green Mountain Press, 1978.

Kortantamer, Samira. Ägypten und Syrien zwischen 1317 and 1341 in der Chronik des Mufaḍḍal b. Abī'l Fadāᶜil. Freiburg im Breisgau, Klaus Schwarz, 1973.

Lane-Poole, Stanley. Saladin and the Fall of Jerusalem. repr. N.Y., AMS, 1972.

________. A History of Egypt in the Middle Ages. repr. London, Frank Cass, 1968.

Lapidus, I. M. Muslim Cities in the Later Middle Ages. Cambridge (Mass.), Harvard University Press, 1967.

Lyons, Malcolm Cameron. Saladin, The Policies of Holy War. Cambridge, Cambridge University Press, 1979.

Al Maqrīzī (Aḥmad b. ᶜAlī). A History of the Ayyūbid Sultans of Egypt. (Translated by R. J. C. Broadhurst.) repr. Boston, Twayne Publishers, 1980.

________. Les Marchés du Caire. (Translated by G. Wiet and A. Raymond.) Cairo, Institut Français, 1979.

________. Le traite des famines de Maqrizi. (Translated by G. Wiet.) Leiden, Brill, 1962.

________. Le Livre des admonitions et de l'observation sur la histoire des quartiers et des monuments ou description historique et topographique de l'Égypte. (Translated by U. Bouriani.) repr. Cairo, Institut Français, 1920.

Margoliouth, David Samuel. Cairo, Jerusalem and Damascus: Three Chief Cities of the Egyptian Sultans. London, Chatto and Windus, 1907.

Mayer, Hans Eberhard. The Crusades. (Translated by J. Gillingham.) London, Oxford University Press, 1972.

Muir, Sir William. The Mameluke or Slave Dynasties of Egypt from the Fall of the Ayyubite Dynasties to the Conquest of the Ottomans, 1260-1517. repr. London, 1968.

Oldenburg, Zoé. The Crusaders. New York, Pantheon Books, 1966.

Paine, Lauren. Saladin, A Man for All Ages. London, Robert Hale, 1974.

Petry, Carl F. The Civilian Elite of Cairo in the Later Middle Ages. Princeton, Princeton University Press, 1981.

Pipes, Daniel. Slave Soldiers and Islam: The Genesis of a Military System. London, Yale University Press, 1981.

Popper, William. Egypt and Sudan under the Circassian Sultans 1382-1468: Systematic Notes to Ibn Taghrī-Birdī's Chronicles of Egypt. repr. N.Y., AMS, 1977.

________. The Cairo Nilometer: Studies in Ibn Taghrī-Birdī's Chronicles of Egypt. Berkeley, University of California Press, 1951.

Richard, Jean. Orient et Occident au Moyen Age: Contacts et relations 12e-15e. repr. London, Variorum, 1976.

Runciman, Steven. A History of the Crusades. Harmondsworth, Penguin, 1971.

Saratain, E. M. Jalāl ad Dīn as Siyūṭī. Cambridge, Cambridge University Press, 1975.

Saunders, J. J. Aspects of the Crusades. Christchurch, Whitecombe and Tombs, 1962.

Setton, Kenneth Meyer, ed. A History of the Crusades. Madison, University of Wisconsin, 1969- .

Ash-Shujā^{c}ī, Shams ad-Dīn. Die Chronik aš-Šugā^{c}īs. (Translated and arranged by B. Schäfer.) Weisbaden, Steiner Verlag, 1977.

Wiet, Gaston. Les marchands d'épices sous les sultans Mamelouks. Cairo, Institut Français, 1955.

Ziadeh, N. A. Urban Life in Syria under the Early Mamluks. Beirut, Libraire du Liban, 1963.

Arabic Titles

Aḥmad, Ḥamad ^{c}Abd ar-Razīq. Dirāsāt fi'l-Maṣādir al-Mamlūkīya al-Mubakkira. Cairo, Maktaba Sa^{c}īd Ra'fat, 1974.

Amīn, Muḥammad. Al-Awqāf wa'l-ḥayāt al-Ijtimā^{c}īya fī Miṣr 648-923H/1250-1517M. Cairo, Dār an-Nahḍa al-^{c}Arabīya, 1980.

Al-^{c}Asalī, Bassām. Ṣalāḥ ad-Dīn al-Ayyūbī. Beirut, Dār an Nafā'is, 1980.

^{c}Āshūr, Sa^{c}īd ^{c}Abd al-Fattāḥ, ed. Nuṣūṣ Tārīkhīya wa Qā^{c}a Baḥth ^{c}Aṣr al-Ayyūbīyīn wa'l-Mamālīk. Beirut, Dār an-Nahḍa al-^{c}Arabīya, 1972.

_______. Al-Ayyūbīyūn wa'l-Mamālīk fī Miṣr wa'sh-Shām. Cairo, Dār an-Nahḍa al-^{c}Arabīya, 1970.

_______. Aḥmad al-Badawī, Shaykh wa Tarīqa. Cairo, Dār al-Kātib al-^{c}Arabī, 1967.

_______. Al-Ḥaraka aṣ-Ṣalībīya: Ṣafḥa Mushriqa fī Tārīkh al-Jihād al-^{c}Arabī fi'l-^{c}Uṣūr al-Wusṭā. Cairo, Maktaba al-Anjlū al-Miṣrīya, 1963-71.

Al-^{c}Aynī, Badr ad-Dīn Maḥmūd. Ar-Rawḍ aẓ-Ẓāhir fī Sīra al-Malik aẓ-Ẓāhir. Cairo, 1950.

^{c}Azzam, ^{c}Abd al-Wahhāb. Majālis as-Sulṭān al-Ghawrī. Cairo, 1941.

Daraj, Aḥmad. Al-Mamālīk wa'l-Ifranj. Cairo, Dār al-Fikr al-^{c}Arabī, 1961.

Ghānim, Ḥāmid Zayyān. Ṣafḥa min Tārīkh al-Khilāfa al-^{c}Abbāsīya fī Ḍill Dawla al-Mamālīk. Cairo, Dār ath-Thaqāfa, 1978.

Ḥamādā, Muḥammad Māhir, ed. Wathā'iq al-Ḥurūb aṣ-Ṣalībīya wa'l-Ghazw al-Mughūlī li'l-ᶜĀlam al-Islāmī 489-806h/1096-1404m. Beirut, Mu'assasa ar-Risāla, 1979.

Ḥasan, ᶜAlī Ibrāhīm. Dirāsāt fī Tārīkh al-Mamālīk al-Baḥrīya. Cairo, 1944.

Ibn Āghā (Muḥammad b. Maḥmūd). Al-Amīr Yashbak aẓ-Ẓāhirī. (Edited by ᶜAbd al-Qādir Ṭulaymāt.) Cairo, Dār al-Fikr al-ᶜArabī, 1974.

Ibn Ḥajar al-ᶜAsqalānī. Inbā' al-Ghumr fī Anbā' al-ᶜUmr. (Edited by Ḥasan Ḥabashī.) Cairo, Al-Majlis al-Aᶜlā li'sh-Shu'ūn al-Islāmīya, Vols. 1-3, 1971-76.

Ibn Mammātī (Asᶜad b. Muhadhdhab). Kitāb Qawānīn al-Dawāwīn. (Edited by ᶜAṭiya ᶜAzīz Suryāl.) Cairo, Maṭbaᶜa Miṣr, 1943.

Ibn Qāḍī Shuhbā (Shams ad-Dīn). Tārīkh. (Edited by ᶜAdnān Darwīsh.) Damascus, Institut Français, Vol. 1, 1977.

ᶜIzzat Allāh, Aḥmad, ed. Ibn Iyās: Dirāsāt wa Buḥūth. Cairo, Al-Hai'a al-Miṣrīya al-ᶜĀmma, 1977.

Jirjīs, Fawẓī. Dirāsa fī Tārīkh Miṣr as-Siyāsī Mundhu al-ᶜAṣr al-Mamlūkī. Cairo, 1958.

Al-Kinānī (Aḥmad b. Ibrāhīm). Shifāᶜ al-Qulūb fī Manāqib Banī Ayyūb. (Edited by Nāẓim Rashīd.) Baghdad, Wizāra ath-Thaqāfa wa'l-Funūn, 1978.

Majīd, ᶜAbd al-Munᶜīm. Nuẓum Dawla Salāṭīn al-Mamālīk. Cairo, Maktaba al-Anjlū al-Miṣrīya, 1964.

Al-Maqrīzī (Aḥmad b. ᶜAlī). Kitāb as-Sulūk. (Vols. 1-2 edited by Muḥammed Muṣṭafā Ziyāda; Vols. 3-4 edited by Saᶜīd ᶜAbd al-Fattāḥ ᶜĀshūr.) Cairo, Lajna at-Ta'līf, 1933-73.

Nūrī, Durayd ᶜAbd al-Qādir. Siyāsa Ṣalāḥ ad-Dīn al-Ayyūbī fī Bilād al-Miṣr wa'sh-Shām wa'l-Jazīra 570-89h/1174-93m. Baghdad, Maṭbaᶜa al-Irshād, 1976.

Qalᶜajī, Qadrī. Ṣalāḥ ad-Dīn al-Ayyūbī: Qiṣṣa aṣ-Ṣirāᶜ bain ash-Sharq wa'l-Gharb Khilāl al-Qarnain ath-Thānī ᶜAshar wa'th-Thālith ᶜAshar. (Cairo?), Dār al-Kātib al-ᶜArabī, 1979.

Saᶜdāwī, Naẓīr Ḥasan. Al-Ḥarb wa's-Salām Zamān al-ᶜUdwān aṣ-Ṣalībī. Cairo, Dār al-Maᶜārif, 1961.

Ash-Sharqāwī, Maḥmūd. Miṣr fi'l-Qarn ath-Thāmin ᶜAshar. Cairo, Maktaba al-Anjlū al-Miṣrīya, 1957.

As-Siyūṭī (Jalāl ad-Dīn). Ḥusn al-Muḥāḍara fī Tārīkh Miṣr wa'l-Qāhira. (Edited by Ibrāhīm Muḥammad Abū'l-Faḍl.) Cairo, 1968.

Surūr, Muḥammad Jamāl ad-Dīn. Dawla Banī Qalā'ūn fī Miṣr. Cairo, Dār al-Fikr al-ᶜArabī, 1947.

Tarkhān, Ibrāhīm. Miṣr fī Dawla al-Mamālik ash-Sharākisīya. Cairo, Maktaba an-Nahḍa al-Miṣrīya, 1960.

Al-Yūsuf, ᶜAbd al-Qādir Aḥmad. ᶜAlāqāt bain ash-Sharq wa'l-Gharb bain al-Qarnain al-Ḥādī ᶜAshar wa'l-Khāmis ᶜAshar. Beirut, Maktaba al-ᶜAṣrīya, 1969.

Zakkār, Suhayl. Madkhal ilā Tārīkh al-Ḥurūb aṣ-Ṣalībīya. Damascus, Dār al-Fikr, 1973.

Ottoman Egypt

Non-Arabic Titles

Clement, Raoul. Les Français d'Égypte au XVIIème et XVIIIème siècles. Cairo, Institut Français, 1960.

Holt, P. M., ed. Egypt and the Fertile Crescent 1516-1922. Ithaca, Cornell University Press, 1966.

Humbsch, Robert. Beiträge zur Geschichte des osmanischen Ägyptens. Freiburg im Breisgau, Schwarz, 1976.

Husayn Effendi. Ottoman Egypt in the Age of the French Revolution. (Translated by S. Shaw.) Cambridge (Mass.), Harvard University Press, 1964.

Ibn Iyās. An Account of the Ottoman Conquest of Egypt in the Year AH 922 (AD 1516). (Translated by W. H. Salmon.) repr. Westport (Conn.), Hyperion Press.

Livingstone, John William. Ali Bey al Kabir and the Mamluk Resurgence in Ottoman Egypt. Ann Arbor, University of Michigan Press, 1970.

El Nahhal, Galal H. The Judicial Administration of Ottoman Egypt in the 17th Century. Minneapolis, Bibliotheqa Islamica, 1979.

Shaw, Stanford. The Budget of Ottoman Egypt 1005-6AH/1596-7AD. The Hague, Mouton, 1968.

________. Ottoman Egypt in the 18th Century: The Nizâmnâme Misr of Cezzar Pasha. Cambridge, Harvard University Press, 1963.

________. The Financial and Administrative Organization and Development of Ottoman Egypt 1517-1798. Princeton, Princeton University Press, 1962.

Tietze, Andreas. Mustafa Ali's Description of Cairo of 1599. Vienna, Verlag Österreich, 1975.

Winter, Michael. Society and Religion in Early Ottoman Egypt: Studies in the Writings of cAbd al-Wahhab al-Sharani. New Brunswick (New Jersey), Transaction Books, 1981.

Arabic Titles

Mutawallī, Ahmad Fu'ād. Al-Fatḥ al-cUthmānī li'sh-Shām wa Miṣr. Cairo, Dār an-Nahḍa al-cArabīya, 1976.

Rāfiq, cAbd al-Karīm. Al-cArab wa'l-cUthmāniyūn 1516-1916. Damascus, Matābic Alif-Bā', 1974.

________. Bilād ash-Shām wa Miṣr. Damascus, Matābic Alif-Bā', 1968.

Ar-Rāqid, Muḥammad cAbd al-Muncīm. Al-Ghazw al-cUthmānī li-Miṣr wa Natā'ijuhu calā'l-Waṭan al-cArabī. Alexandria, Mu'assasa Shabāb al-Jāmica, 1972.

The French Invasion (1798AD) to the Fall of the Khedive Ismācīl (1779)

Non-Arabic Titles

cAbd al-Karīm, Ahmad cIzzat. A Collection of Articles by Various Hands on the Historian al-Jabārtī. (Arabic, French and English texts.) Cairo, Al-Hai'a al-Miṣrīya al-cĀmma, 1976.

Benoist-Mêchin, Jacques. Bonaparte en Égypte ou le rêve inassouvi. Paris, Perrin, 1978.

Bernoyer, François. Avec Bonaparte en Égypte et en Syrie 1798-1800. (Letters transcribed and presented by C. Fortel.) Abbeville, Les Presses Français, 1976.

Carré, Jean Marie. Voyageurs et écrivains français en Égypte. Cairo, Institut Français, 1932.

Cattaui, René and Georges Cattaui. Mohamed-Aly et l'Europe. Paris, Guenther, 1950.

Charles-Roux, François. Bonaparte: Gouverneur d'Égypte. Paris, 1936; printed in English as: Bonaparte: Governor of Egypt. (Translated by E. W. Dickes.) London, Metheun, 1937.

________. L'Angleterre et l'éxpedition français en Égypte. Cairo, Institut Français, 1925.

Clot-Bey, Antoine. Aperçu général de l'Égypte. Paris, Méline, Cans et Compagnie, 1840.

Crabitès, Pierre. Ibrahim of Egypt. London, Routledge, 1935.

________. Ismael, the Maligned Khedive. London, Routledge, 1933.

Dodwell, Henri Herbert. The Founder of Modern Egypt: A Study of Muhammad Ali. repr. Cambridge, Cambridge University Press, 1967.

Douin, Georges. Histoire du règne du Khedive Ismail. Cairo, Institut Français, 1933.

_______. La première guerre de Syrie. Cairo, Institut Français, 1931.

_______. Mohammed Aly et l'expédition d'Alger (1829-30). Cairo, Société Royale de Géographie d'Égypte, 1930.

_______. L'Angleterre et l'Égypte (Vol. 1, 1801-03; Vol. 2, 1803-07). Cairo, Société Royale de Géographie d'Égypte, 1930.

_______. Mohammad Aly Pacha du Caire (1805-07): Correspondance des consuls de France en Égypte. Cairo, Société Royale de Géographie d'Égypte, 1926.

_______ and E. C. Fawtier-Jones. La Compagne de 1807. Institut Français, 1928.

Driault, Edouard. L'Égypte et l'Europe, la crise de 1839-41. Cairo, Société Royale de Géographie d'Égypte, 1930.

_______. La formation de l'empire de Mohammed Aly de l'Arabie au Soudan (1814-23). Cairo, Institut Français, 1927.

Elgood, Percival George. Bonaparte's Adventure in Egypt. London, Humphrey Melford, 1931.

Flaubert, Gustave. Sensibility on Tour: A Narrative Drawn from Gustave Flaubert's Travel Notes and Letters. (Translated and edited by F. Steegmuller.) London, Bodley Head, 1972.

Girgis, Samir. The Predominance of the Islamic Tradition of Leadership in Egypt During Bonaparte's Expedition. Frankfurt, Peter Lang, 1975.

Gordon, General Sir Charles. Equatoria under Egyptian Rule. Gordon's Unpublished Correspondence with the Khedive Ismail, with introduction and notes by M. F. Shoukry. Cairo, Cairo University Press, 1953.

Herold, J. Christopher. Bonaparte in Egypt. New York, Harper and Row, 1962.

Hill, Richard Leslie. Egypt in the Sudan 1820-81. London, Oxford University Press, 1959.

Hofmann, Inge. Der Sudan als Ägyptische Kolonie im Altertum. Vienna, Institut für Afrikanistik, Afro Publications, 1979.

Al-Jabārtī (ᶜAbd al-Rahmān). Merveilles biographiques et historiques. (Translated by Chefik Mansour Baye, et al.). Cairo, Imprimerie Nationale, repr. Nedeln, 1970.

de Jong, F. Ṭuruq and Ṭuruq-linked Institutions in Nineteenth Century Egypt: An Historical Study in Organisational Dimensions of Islamic Mysticism. Leiden, Brill, 1978.

Kinross, John Patrick Douglas Balfour, Baron. Between Two Seas: The Creation of the Suez Canal. London, John Murray, 1968.

Lloyd, Christopher. The Nile Campaign: Nelson and Napoleon in Egypt. Newton Abbot, David and Charles, 1973.

Louca, Anouar. Voyageurs et écrivains égyptiens en France au XIXe siècle. Paris, Didier, 1970.

Marlowe, John. Anglo-Egyptian Relations 1800-1956. Hamden (Conn.), Archon Books, 1965.

Motzi, Harold. Dimma und Égalité: die nichtmuslimischen Minderheiten Ägyptens in der zweiten Häfte des 18. Jahrhunderts und die Expedition Bonapartes (1798-1801). Bonn, Selbstverlag des Orientalischen Seminars der Universität, 1979.

Niqula, Ibn Yusuf al-Turki. Chronique d'Égypte 1798-1804. (Translated by G. Wiet). Cairo, Institut Français, 1950.

Politis, Athanase G. Les rapports de la Grèce et de l'Égypte pendant la règne de Mohamed Aly. Cairo, Société Royale de Géographie d'Egypte, 1935.

Pudney, John. De Lessep's Canal. London, J. M. Dent, 1968.

Puryear, Vernon. Kleber and Menou: Egypt Enters World Politics. Davis (Cal.), n.p., 1968.

Riaux, François. L'Égypte et la France. Paris, Librairie Internationale, 1870.

Sabry, Muhammad. L'Empire égyptien sous Ismail et l'ingérence anglo-français. Paris, Guenther, 1933.

Sammario, Angelo, ed. Il regno de Mohammed Ali nei documenti diplomatici italiani inediti. Cairo, Société Royale de Géographie, 1930.

Shukri, M. F. The Khedive Ismail and Slavery in the Sudan (1863-1879). Cairo, Anglo-Egyptian Bookstore, 1937.

Talami, Ghada Hashem. Suakin and Massawa under Egyptian Rule, 1865-85. Washington, D.C., University Presses of America, 1979.

At-Tahṭāwī, Rifā'ā Rāfi^{c}. The Awakening of Modern Egypt. repr. Lahore, Premier Book House, 1964.

Volney, Constantine F. C. Voyage en Égypte et en Syrie. repr. Paris, 1957.

Wegand, Maxime. Histoire militaire de Mohammed Aly et de ses fils. Paris, Imprimerie Nationale, 1936.

Arabic Titles

Abu'l-Majd, Ṣabrī. Ar-Rajīya al-^{c}Arabīya. Cairo, Dār al-Qawmīya aṭ-Ṭabā^{c}ī wa'n-Nashr, 1963.

Al-Baqlī, Muḥammad Qandīl. Abṭāl al-Muqawama ash-Sha^{c}bīya. Cairo, Dār al-Isnāwī aṭ-Ṭabā^{c}ī wa'n-Nashr, 1963.

Faraj, Muḥammad. An-Niḍāl ash-Sha^{c}bī ḍidda al-Ḥamla al Fāransīya. Cairo, Dār al-Qawmīya aṭ-Ṭabā^{c}ī wa'n Nashr, 1962.

Al-Jabārtī (^{c}Abd ar-Raḥmān). Al-Mukhtār min Tārīkh al-Jabārtī. (Edited by Muḥammad Qandīl al-Baqlī.) Cairo, Maṭābi^{c} ash-Sha^{c}b, 1958-59.

________. ^{c}Ajā'ib al-Āthār fi'l Tarājīm wa'l-Akhbār. Cairo, 1908 repr. Beirut, Dār Ibn Khaldūn, 1970.

Mansī, Maḥmūd Ḥasan Ṣāliḥ. Mashrū^{c} Qanāt as-Suwīs bain ittibā^{c} Sān Sīmūn wa Firdīnān dī Lisibs. Cairo, Dār al-Ittihād al-^{c}Arabī, n.p., 1971.

Mubārak Bāshā, ^{c}Alī. Al-Khiṭāṭ at-Tawfīqqīya al-Jadīda. repr. Cairo, Maṭba^{c}a Dār al-Kutub, 1969.

Qarqūt, Dhūqān. Taṭawwur al-Fikra al-^{c}Arabīya fī Miṣr 1805-36. Beirut, Al-Mu'assasa al-^{c}Arabīya, 1972.

The British Invasion of Egypt and the Early Nationalist Movement

---

Non-Arabic Titles

Ahmed, Leila. Edward W. Lane: A Study of His Life and Works and of British Ideas of the Middle East in the 19th Century. London, Longmans, 1978.

Barker, John. Syria and Egypt under the Last Five Sultans of Turkey. repr. New York, Arno Press, 1973.

Blunt, Wilfred Scawen. The Secret History of the English Occupation of Egypt. repr. New York, Howard Fertig, 1967.

________. My Diaries, Being a Personal Narrative of Events in 1888-1914. London, Secker, 1932.

Bourget, Alfred. La France et l'Angleterre en Égypte. Paris, Plon, 1897.

Brinton, Jasper Yates. The American Effort in Egypt: A Chapter in the Diplomatic History of the Nineteenth Century. Alexandria, 1972.

________. The Mixed Courts of Egypt. repr. London, Oxford University Press, 1968.

Burns, Elinor. British Imperialism in Egypt. London, Labour Research Department, 1928.

Charles-Roux, François. L'Angleterre, L'Isthme de Suez et L'Égypte. Paris, 1922.

Chenevix Trench, Charles P. The Road to Khartoum: A Life of General Gordon. New York, W. W. Norton, 1979.

Colvin, Sir Auckland. The Making of Modern Egypt. London, T. Nelson and Sons, 1909.

Crabitès, Pierre. Gordon, the Sudan and Slavery. repr. New York, Negro Universities Press, 1969.

Cromer, Lord. ᶜAbbas II. London, Macmillan, 1915.

________. Modern Egypt. London, Macmillan, 1908.

Dust, Mohammed. In the Land of the Pharaohs, a Short History of Egypt from the Fall of Ismail to the Assassination of Butrus Ghali. Cairo, n.p., n.d.

Dye, William McEntyre. Moslem Egypt and Christian Abyssinia or Military Service under the Khedive and Beyond. repr. New York, Negro Universities Press, 1969.

Farwell, Byron. Prisoners of the Mahdi. repr. New York, Harper and Row, 1967.

Frederickson, Børge. Slavery and Its Abolition in 19th Century Egypt. Bergern, Hivedoppegave i Historie Høsten, 1977.

Ghurbal, Shafik. The Beginnings of the Egyptian Question and the Rise of Muhammad Ali. repr. New York, AMS, 1977.

Landau, Jacob. Jews in Nineteenth Century Egypt. New York, New York University Press, 1971.

Longford, Elizabeth. A Pilgrimage of Passion: The Life of Wilfred Scawen Blunt. London, Weidenfeld and Nicholson, 1979.

Lytton, Noel Anthony Scawen, 4th Earl of Lytton. Wilfred Scawen Blunt, a Memoir by His Grandson. London, MacDonald, 1961.

Malet, Sir E. B. Egypt 1879-83. (Ed. Lord Sanderson.) London, John Murray, 1909.

Mansfield, Peter. The British in Egypt. London, Weidenfield and Nicholson, 1972.

Marlowe, John. Cromer in Egypt. London, Elek, 1970.

Meyer, Gail E. Egypt and the United States: The Formative Years. London, Associated University Presses, 1980.

Milner, Alfred Lord. England in Egypt. repr. New York, Fertig, 1970.

Ritchie, William Kidd. The British in Egypt. Harlow, Longmans, 1973.

Rowlatt, Mary. Founders of Modern Egypt. New York, Asia Publishing House, 1962.

Al Sayyid-Marsot, Afaf Lutfi. Egypt and Cromer: A Study in Anglo-Egyptian Relations. London, Murray, 1968.

Schölch, Alex. Ägypten den Ägyptern: die politische und gesellschaftliche Krise der Jahre 1878-82. Zurich, Atlantis, n.d.

Tignor, Robert. Modernization and British Colonial Rule in Egypt 1882-1914. Princeton, Princeton University Press, 1966.

Wright, Lenoir. U.S. Policy Towards Egypt 1830-1914. New York, Exposition Press, 1969.

Arabic Titles

^{c}Amr, ^{c}Abd ar-Ra'ūf Aḥmad. Qanāt as-Suwīs fi'l-^{c}Alāqāt ad-Duwalīya 1869-83. Cairo, Al-Hai'a al-Miṣrīya al-^{c}Āmma, 1978.

Dhuhnī, Ṣalāḥ ad-Dīn. Miṣr bain al-Ihtilāl wa'th Thawra. Cairo, 1939.

Ḥāfiẓ, Ḥasan. Ath-Thawra al-^{c}Urābīya fi'l-Mīzān. Cairo, Dār al-Qawmīya aṭ-Ṭabā^{c}ī wa'n-Nashr, 1962.

Shafīq, Aḥmad. A^{c}mālī Ba^{c}d Mudhakkirātī. Cairo, Maṭbā^{c}a Miṣr, 1941.

Twentieth Century Egypt Before the Revolution of 1952

Non-Arabic Titles

Abbas, Mekki. The Sudan Question. London, Faber and Faber, 1952.

Ahmad, Jamal Muhammad. The Intellectual Origins of Egyptian Nationalism. London, Oxford University Press, 1968.

Ali Shah, Iqbal. Fuad: King of Egypt. London, Jenkins, 1936.

Antonius, George. The Arab Awakening: The Story of the Arab Nationalist Movement. repr. Beirut, Librairie du Liban, 1970.

Badawi, Zaki. The Reformers of Egypt. London, Croom Helm, 1978.

Al Barawi, Rashid. Egypt, Britain and the Sudan. Cairo, Renaissance Books, 1952.

Bernard-Deroane, Jean. Farouk, la déchéance d'un roi. Paris, Éditions Françaises d'Amsterdam, 1953.

Bourgeois, Albert. La formation de l'Égypte moderne; le traite Anglo-Égyptien de 26 Août 1936 et la convention de Montreux du 8 Mai 1937. Paris, Librairie Générale de Droit et Jurisprudence, 1939.

Boutrus-Ghali, Mirrit. The Policy of Tomorrow. Washington, American Council of Learned Societies, 1953.

Colombe, Marcel. L'évolution de L'Égypte, 1924-50. Paris, Maison-Neuve, 1951.

Darwin, John. Britain, Egypt and the Middle East: Imperial Policy in the Aftermath of War 1918-22. London, Macmillan, 1981.

Deeb, Marius. Party Politics in Egypt: The Wafd and Its Rivals 1919-39. London, Ithaca Press, 1979.

Evans, Trefor Ellis. Mission to Egypt, 1934-46, Lord Killearn, High Commissioner and Ambassador. Cardiff, University of Wales Press, 1971.

Fabunmi, L. A. The Sudan in Anglo-Egyptian Relations: A Case Study in Power Politics. repr. Westport (Conn.), Greenwood Press, 1973.

Fitzgerald, Percy. The Great Canal at Suez: Its Political, Engineering and Financial History. repr. N.Y., AMS Press, 1978.

Galatoli, Anthony M. Egypt in Mid-Passage. Cairo, Urwomd and Sons, 1950.

Georges-Picot, Jacques. The Real Suez Crisis: The End of a Great Nineteenth Century Work. (Translated by W. G. Rogers.) N.Y., Harcourt, Brace, Jovanovich, 1978.

Ghali, Ibrahim Amin. L'Égypte nationaliste et libérale de Moustapha Kamel à Saad Zaghloul 1892-1927. Hague, Martinus Nijhoff, 1969.

Grafferty-Smith, L. Bright Levant. London, John Murray, 1970.

Grant, Samuel Becker. Modern Egypt and the New Turco-Circassian Autocracy. Ann Arbor, University of Michigan Press, 1968.

Hallberg, Charles William. The Suez Canal, Its History and Diplomatic Importance. repr. New York, Octagon Press, 1974.

Harris, Murray. Egypt under the Egyptians. London, Chapman and Hall, 1925.

Holt, P. M., ed. Political and Social Change in Modern Egypt. London, Oxford University Press, 1968.

Hourani, Albert. Arabic Thought in the Liberal Age, 1798-1939. London, Oxford University Press, 1970.

Jankowski, James. Egypt's Young Rebels: Young Egypt, 1933-52. Stanford, Hoover Institution, 1975.

Johansen, Baber. Muhammad Husain Haikal: Europa und der Orient im Weltbild eines Ägyptischen Liberalen. Beirut, Hans Steiner Verlag, 1967.

Kamil, Mustafa. Lettres égyptiennes-françaises addressées à Mme. Juliette Adams, 1895-1908. Cairo, 1909.

Killearn, Baron. The Killearn Diaries 1934-46: The Diplomatic and Personal Record of Lord Killearn. Edited by Trefor B. Evans. London, Sidgwick and Jackson, 1972.

Lambelin, R. L'Égypte et L'Angleterre vers l'indépendance de Mohammed Aly au Roi Fouad. Paris, P. Grasset, 1922.

Landau, J. Parliament and Parties in Egypt. New York, Praeger, 1954.

Lloyd, Georges Ambrose. Egypt Since Cromer. (2 Vols.) repr. New York, AMS, 1970.

Maakad, Adib. General Principles of the Egyptian Mixed Courts. London, Laureate Press, 1981.

Makarius, Raoul. La jeunesse intellectuelle d'Égypte au lendemain de la deuxième guerre mondiale. Paris, Mouton, 1960.

Marshall, John Edwin. The Egyptian Enigma 1890-1928. London, John Murray, 1928.

McBride, Barrie St. Clair. Farouk of Egypt: A Biography. London, Hale, 1967.

Mellini, Peter. Sir Eldon Gorst: The Overshadowed Proconsul. Stanford, Hoover Institution, 1977.

Mizrahi, Maurice. L'Égypte et ses juifs, le temps rêvolu. Lusanne, L'Auteur, 1977.

Moussa, Faraq. Les nêgociations Anglo-Égyptiennes de 1950-51 sur Suez et le Soudan. Geneva, Librairie E. D. Roe, 1955.

Quraishi, Zaheer Masood. Liberal Nationalism in Egypt: Rise and Fall of the Wafd. Allahabad, Kitab Mahal, 1967.

Reid, Donald. The Odyssey of Farah Antun: A Syrian Christian's Quest for Secularism. Minneapolis, Bibliotheqa Islamica, 1975.

Richmond, J. C. B. Egypt 1798-1952: Her Advance Towards a Modern Identity. London, Metheun, 1977.

Rifaat Bey, Mohammed. The Awakening of Modern Egypt. Lahore, Premier Books, 1976.

Russell, Sir Thomas. Egyptian Service 1902-46. London, Murray, 1949.

Safran, Nadav. Egypt in Search of Political Community. Cambridge (Mass.), Harvard University Press, 1961.

Al Sayyid-Marsot, Afaf Lutfi. Egypt's Liberal Experiment 1922-36. Berkeley, University of California Press, 1977.

Seth, Ronald. Russell Pasha. London, William Kimber, 1966.

Shafiq, Ahmad. L'Égypte moderne et les influences êtrangêres. Cairo, Imprimerie Misr, 1931.

Sharabi, Hisham. Arab Intellectuals and the West: The Formative Years 1875-1914. Baltimore, Johns Hopkins University Press, 1970.

Simiat, Bernard. Suez: 50 siècles d'histoire. Paris, Arthaud, 1954.

Storrs, Sir Ronald. The Memoirs of Sir Ronald Storrs. repr. N. Y., Arno Press, 1978.

Wavell, Archibald Percival, 1st Viscount. Allenby, Soldier and Statesman. London, George Harrap, 1946.

Weigall, A. E. A History of Events in Egypt from 1798 to 1914. Edinburgh, W. Blackwood, 1915.

Wright, Lenoir. U. S. Policy Towards Egypt 1830-1914. New York, Exposition Press, 1969.

Arabic Titles

^{c}Abd al-Hādī, Amīn. Aṣ-Ṣaḥīfa aṭ-Ṭāhira. Cairo, 1923.

^{c}Abd Allāh, Nabīh Bayyūmī. Taṭawwur Fikra al-Qawmīya al-^{c}Arabīya fī Miṣr. Cairo, Al-Hai'a al-Miṣrīya al-^{c}Āmma, 1975.

^{c}Abd al-Qādir, Muḥammad Zakī. Aqdam ^{c}Alā't-Ṭarīq. Cairo, Dār Rūz al-Yūsuf, 1967.

________. Minḥat ad-Dustūr. Cairo, Dār Rūz al-Yūsuf, 1955.

^{c}Abdū, Ibrāhīm and ^{c}Alī ^{c}Abd al-^{c}Aẓīm. Tidhkār Muḥammad Ṭal^{c}at Ḥarb. Cairo, Maktaba al-Ādāb, 1945.

Abū Rās, Ash-Shāfi^{c}ī. At-Tanẓīmāt as-Sīyāsīya ash-Sha^{c}bīya. Cairo, ^{c}Ālam al-Kutub, 1974.

^{c}Afīfī, Ḥāfiẓ. ^{c}Ala' Hāmish as-Siyāsa. Cairo, Dār al-Kātib al-^{c}Arabīya, 1938.

Amīn, Aḥmad. Ḥayātī. Cairo, Dār al-Ma^{c}ārif, 1958.

Amīn, Muṣṭafā. Al-Kitāb al-Mamnū^{c}: Asrār Thawra 1919. (2 Vols.) Cairo, Dār al-Ma^{c}ārif, 1974-75.

Anīs, Muḥammad Aḥmad. Safaḥāt Majhūla min at-Tārīkh al-Miṣrī. Cairo, Rūz al-Yūsuf, 1973.

________. Dirāsāt fī wathā'iq Thawra 1919. Cairo, Maktaba al-Anjlū al-Miṣrīya, 1963.

Al-^{c}Aqqad, ^{c}Abbās Maḥmūd. Sa^{c}d Zaghlūl, Sīra wa Taḥīya. Cairo, Dār al-Ma^{c}ārif, 1936.

Bahā' ad-Dīn, Aḥmad. Ayyām Laha Tārīkh. Cairo, Rūz al-Yūsuf, 1967.

Barakāt, ^{c}Alī. Taṭawwur al-Milkīya az-Zirā^{c}īya fī Miṣr wa atharuha ^{c}Ala'l-Ḥaraka as-Sīyāsīya, 1813-1914. Cairo, Dār ath-Thaqāfa, 1977.

Al-Bishrī, Ṭarīq. Sa^{c}d Zaghlūl Yufāwiḍu al-Isti^{c}mār 1920-24. Cairo, Al-Hai'a al-Miṣrīya al-^{c}Āmma, 1977.

Buṭrus-Ghalī, Mirrit. Siyāsa al-Ghad. Cairo, Maṭba^{c}a ar-Risālāt, 1938.

Ad-Dasūqī, ^{c}Āṣim. Miṣr al-Mu'āṣira fī Dirāsāt al-Mu'arrikhīn al-Miṣriyīn. Cairo, Ma^{c}had al-Buḥūth wa'd-Dirāsāt al-^{c}Arabīya, 1977.

________. Miṣr fi'l-Ḥarb al-^{c}Ālamīya ath-Thānīya 1939-45. Cairo, Ma^{c}had al-Buḥūth wa'd-Dirāsāt al-^{c}Arabīya, 1976.

Faḥmī, ^{c}Abd al-^{c}Azīz. Hādhihi Ḥayātī. Cairo, Kitāb al-Hilāl, 1963.

Faḥmī, Qalinī. Mudhakkirāt. Cairo, Dār al-Kātib, 1934.

Farīd, Muḥammad. Mudhakkirāt. (Edited by Ra'ūf Ḥamīd.) (2 Vols.) Cairo, ^{c}Ālam al-Kutub, 1975-77.

Ḥāfiẓ, ^{c}Abbās. Muṣṭafā an-Naḥḥas wa'z-Za^{c}āma wa'z-Za^{c}īm, Cairo. Cairo, Maṭba^{c}a Miṣr, 1936.

Hamrush, Aḥmad. Qiṣṣa Thawra 1919. (4 Vols.) Beirut, Al-Mu'assasa al-^{c}Arabīya li'd-Dirāsāt wa'n-Nashr, 1974-78.

Haykal, Muḥammad Ḥusayn. Mudhakkirāt fi's-Sīyāsa al-Miṣrīya. Cairo, Maktaba an-Nahḍa al-Miṣriya, 1951-53.

________. Tarājim Miṣrīya wa Gharbīya. Cairo, Maṭba^{c}a Sīyāsīya, 1929.

^{c}Imāra, Muḥammad. Al-Jāmi^{c}a al-Islāmīya wa'l-Fikra al-Qawmīya ^{c}Inda Muṣṭafā Kāmil. Beirut, Al-Mu'assasa al-^{c}Arabīya li'd-Dirāsāt wa'n-Nashr, 1976.

^{c}Īsā, Ṣalāḥ. Ḥikāyāt min Miṣr. (?Cairo), Al-Waṭan al-^{c}Arabī, 1972.

Al-Jazīrī, Muḥammad Ibrāhīm. Āthār az-Za^{c}īm Sa^{c}d Zaghlūl ^{c}Ahd Wizāra ash-Sha^{c}b. Cairo, 1927.

Khākī, Aḥmad. Qāsim Amīn, Tārīkh Ḥayātihi al-Fikrī. Cairo, Maktaba al-Anjlū al-Miṣrīya, 1973.

Lāshīn, ^{c}Abd al-Khāliq. Sa^{c}d Zaghlūl, Dawruhu fi's-Sīyāsa al-Miṣrīya Ḥatta Sana 1914. Cairo, Dār al-Ma^{c}ārif, 1970.

Luṭfī as-Sayyid, Aḥmad. Qiṣṣa Ḥayātī. Cairo, 1962.

Muḥammad, Muḥsin. At-Tārīkh as-Sirrī li-Miṣr. Cairo, Dār al-Ma^{c}ārif, 1979.

Muḥammad, Ra'ūf ^{c}Abbās. Al-Ḥaraka al-^{c}Ummālīya al-Miṣrīya fī Ḍaw' al-Wathā^{c}iq al-Barīṭānīya 1924-53. Cairo, ^{c}Ālam al-Kutub, 1975.

Mujāhid, Mubārak Zakī. Al-A^{c}lām ash-Sharqīya. (4 Vols.) Cairo, Maktaba Mujāhid, 1949-63.

Mu'nis, Ḥusayn. Dirāsāt fī Thawra 1919. Cairo, Dār al-Ma^{c}ārif, 1976.

Muṣṭafā, Aḥmad ^{c}Abd ar-Raḥmān. Taṭawwur al-Fikr as-Sīyāsī fī Miṣr al-Ḥadītha. Cairo, Ma^{c}had al-Buḥūth wa'd Dirāsāt al-^{c}Arabīya, 1973.

An-Naḥḥās, Yūsuf. Dhikrayāt Sa^{c}d ^{c}Abd al-^{c}Azīz Māhir wa Rifāqahu fī Thawra Sana 1919. Cairo, Maṭba^{c}a Miṣr, 1952.

________. Ṣafaḥāt min Tārīkh Miṣr as-Sīyāsī al-Ḥadīth Mufāwaḍāt ^{c}Adlī-Curzun. Cairo, Maṭba^{c}a Miṣr, 1951.

An-Najjār, Ḥusayn Fawẓī. Aḥmad Luṭfī as-Sayyid, Ustādh al-Jīl. Cairo, Al-Hai'a al-Miṣrīya al-^{c}Āmma, 1975.

_______. Luṭfī as-Sayyid wa'sh-Shakhṣīya al-Miṣrīya. Cairo, Maktaba al-Qāhira al-Ḥadītha, 1963.

Naṣr, Muḥammad. Dinshaway wa's-Ṣaḥāfa. Cairo, Maktaba al-Anjlū al-Miṣrīya, 1958.

Qal^{c}ajī, Qadrī. Sa^{c}d Zaghlūl. Beirut, Dār al-^{c}Ilm li'l-Malāyīn, 1946.

Qurrā^{c}a, Sanīya. Namir as-Sīyāsa al-Miṣrīya. Cairo, Maṭba^{c}a Kawstā Tsūmās, 1952.

Ar-Rāfi^{c}ī, ^{c}Abd ar-Raḥmān. Az-Za^{c}īm ^{c}Urābī. Cairo, Dār al-Hilāl, 1952.

_______. Muḥammad Farīd. Cairo, Dār al-Hilāl, 1948.

_______. Thawra Sana 1919. Cairo, Maṭba^{c}a an-Nahḍa, 1946.

_______. Muṣṭafā Kāmil, Ba^{c}īth al-Ḥaraka al-Waṭanīya. Cairo, Maṭba^{c}a an-Nahḍa, 1938.

Ramaḍān, ^{c}Abd al-^{c}Azīm. Aṣ-Ṣirā^{c} bain al-Wafd wa'l-^{c}Arsh 1936-39. Beirut, Al-Mu'assasa li'd-Dirāsāt wa'n-Nashr, 1979.

_______. Ṣirā^{c} aṭ-Ṭabaqāt fī Miṣr 1837-1952. Beirut, Al-Mu'assasa al-^{c}Arabīya li'd-Dirāsāt wa'n-Nashr, 1978.

_______. Al-Jaysh al-Miṣrīya fi's-Sīyāsa 1882-1936. Cairo, Al-Hai'a al-Miṣrīya al-^{c}Āmma, 1977.

Ar-Ra'īs, Muḥammad Ḍiyā' ad-Dīn. Ad-Dustūr wa'l-Istiqlāl wa'th-Thawra al-Waṭanīya 1935. Cairo, Mu'assasa Dār ash-Sha^{c}b, 1975.

Riḍā, M. Rashīd. Tarīkh al-Ustādh al-Imām ash-Shaykh Muḥammad ^{c}Abdu. Cairo, Maṭba^{c}a Miṣr, 1931.

Riḍwān, Fatḥī. Muṣṭafā Kāmil. Cairo, Dār al-Ma^{c}ārif, 1974.

_______. Ṭal^{c}at Ḥarb: Baḥth fi'l-^{c}Aẓama. Cairo, Dār al-Kātib al-^{c}Arabī, 1970.

Ar-Rifā^{c}ī, ^{c}Abd al-^{c}Azīz. Thawra Miṣr Sana 1919. Cairo, Dār al-Kātib al-^{c}Arabī, 1967.

_______. Uṣūl an-Niḍāl ath-Thawra al-Qawmī. Cairo, Dār al-Qawmīya aṭ-Ṭabā^{c}ī wa'n-Nashr, 1964.

_______. Qaḍīya al-Jalā' ^{c}an Miṣr. Cairo, Dār al-Qalam, 1961.

Rizq, Yunān Labīb. As-Sūdān fi'l-Mufāwaḍāt al-Miṣrīya al-Bariṭānīya 1930-36. Cairo, Ma^{c}had al-Buḥuth wa'd-Dirāsāt al-^{c}Arabīya, 1974.

_______. Al-Ḥayāt al-Ḥizbīya fī Miṣr fī ^{c}Ahd al-Iḥtilāl al-Briṭānī 1882-1914. Cairo, Ma^{c}had al-Buḥūth wa'd-Dirāsāt al-^{c}Arabīya, 1970.

Ṣabīḥ, Muḥammad. Baṭal lā Nansā: ^{c}Abd al-^{c}Azīz Maṣrī wa ^{c}Aṣruhu. Beirut, Manshūrāt al-Maktaba al-^{c}Aṣrīya, 1971.

Sa^{c}d, Aḥmad Ṣādiq. Ṣafaḥāt min al-Yasār al-Miṣrī fī A^{c}qab al-Ḥarb al-^{c}Ālamīya ath-Thānīya 1945-46. Cairo, Maktaba Madbūlī, 1976.

As-Sa^{c}īd, Rif^{c}at. Tārīkh al-Munaẓẓamāt al-Yasārīya al-Miṣrīya 1940-50. Cairo, Dār ath-Thaqāfa al-Jadīda, 1976.

_______. Tārīkh al-Ḥaraka al-Ishtirākīya fī Miṣr 1900-25. Cairo, Dār al-Fārābī, 1972.

_______. Al-Yasār al-Miṣrī 1925-40, Tārīkh al-Ḥaraka al-Ishtirākīya fī Miṣr. Beirut, Dār aṭ-Ṭalī^{c}a li'ṭ-Ṭibā^{c}a, 1972.

Shafīq, Aḥmad. Ḥawlīyāt Miṣr as-Siyāsīya. (7 Vols.) Cairo, Maṭba^{c}a Miṣr, 1926-31.

Sharāf, ^{c}Abd al-^{c}Azīz. Muḥammad Ḥusayn Haykal fī Dhikrāhi. Cairo, Dār al-Ma^{c}ārif, 1978.

Shibaykā, Makki. Bariṭānīya wa Thawra 1919. Cairo, Jāmi^{c} ad-Duwal al-^{c}Arabīya, 1976.

_______. Tārīkh Shu^{c}ūb Wādī an-Nīl: Miṣr wa's-Sūdān fi'l-Qarn at-Tāsi^{c} ^{c}Ashara al-Mīlādī. Beirut, Dār ath-Thaqāfa, n.d.

Ash-Shiliq, Aḥmad Zakārīya. Ḥizb al-Umma wa dawruhu fi's-Siyāsa al-Miṣrīya. Cairo, Dār al-Ma^{c}ārif, 1979.

Shinūda, Imīl Fahmī Ḥannā. Sa^{c}d Zaghlūl: Nāẓir al-Ma^{c}ārif. Cairo, Dār al-Fikr al-^{c}Arabī, 1977.

Shinnāwī, ^{c}Abd al-^{c}Azīz Muḥammad. Qanāt as-Suwīs wa't-Tayyārāt as-Siyāsīya Allatī Aḥāṭatbī Inshā^{c}ihā. Cairo, Jāmi^{c}a ad-Duwal al-^{c}Arabīya, 1971.

Aṭ-Ṭabī^{c}ī, Muḥammad. Miṣr Māqabl ath-Thawra. Cairo, Dār al-Ma^{c}ārif, 1978.

Waḥīda, Ṣubḥī. Fī Uṣūl al-Mas'ala al-Miṣrīya. repr. Cairo, Maktaba Madbūlī, 1974.

Zaghlūl, Sa^{c}d. Majmu^{c}āt al-Khuṭāb wa-Aḥādīth. Cairo, Maktab al-^{c}Arab, 1924.

Zaidān, Jurjī. Kitāb Tārīkh Miṣr al-Ḥadīth. Cairo, Dār al-Hilāl, 1911.

Zayīd, Mahmūd. Min Aḥmad ^{c}Arābī ila Jamāl ^{c}Abd an-Nāṣir: Al-Ḥaraka al-Waṭanīya al-Miṣrīya al-Ḥadītha. Beirut, Dār al-Muttaḥida li'n-Nashr, 1973.

Egypt from the Revolution to the Death of Gamal Abdal Nasser

Non-Arabic Titles

Abdel-Malik, Anouar. La pensée politique arabe contemporaine. Paris, Editions du Seuil, 1970.

________. Idéologie et renaissance nationale. Paris, Editions Anthropos, 1969.

________. Egypt: Military Society. New York, Vintage Books, 1968.

Abdul Fath, Ahmad. L'Affaire Nasser. Paris, Plon, 1962.

Agaruishev, Anatoly. Gamal Abdel Nasser: Leben und Kampf eines Staatsmannes. (Translated by G. Leiste.) Frankfurt, Verlag Marxistische Blätter, 1977.

Baddour, Abdel Fattah and Ibrahim el Sayed. Sudanese-Egyptian Relations: A Chronological and Analytical Study. The Hague, Nijhoff, 1960.

Badeau, John S. The American Approach to the Arab World. New York, Harper and Row, 1968.

________. The Emergence of Modern Egypt. New York, Foreign Policy Association, 1953.

Al Barawy, Rashed. The Military Coup in Egypt: An Analytical Study. Cairo, Renaissance Bookstore, 1952.

Barker, A. J. The Seven Day War. London, Faber and Faber, 1964.

Bar Siman-Tov, Ya^{c}akov. The Israeli-Egyptian War of Attrition, 1969-70. New York, Columbia University Press, 1980.

Beaufre, André. The Suez Expedition. (Translated by R. Barry.) New York, Praeger, 1969.

Be'eri, Aliezer. Army Officers in Arab Politics and Society. London, Pall Mall Press, 1970.

Belling, Wilfred. The Middle East: Quest for an American Policy. New York, SUNY Press, 1973.

Berque, Jacques. L'Égypte, impérialisme et révolution. Paris, Gallimard, 1967. Published in English as: Egypt, Imperialism and Revolution. (Translated by J. Stewart.) London, Faber and Faber, 1972.

Bill, James A. and Carl Leiden. The Middle East: Politics and Power. Boston, Allyn and Bacon, 1974.

Binder, Leonard. In a Moment of Enthusiasm: Political Power and the Second Stratum in Egypt. Chicago, University of Chicago Press, 1978.

_______. The Ideological Revolution in the Middle East. London, John Wiley and Sons, 1964.

Bloomfield, L. M. Egypt, Israel and the Gulf of Aqaba in International Law. Toronto, Carswell, 1957.

Bowie, Robert Richardson. Suez 1956. London, Oxford University Press, 1974.

Boroyssou, Rachel and Ralph Casti. Les États-Unis et l'Égypte devant la crise du Proche-Orient. Paris, Documentation Français, 1972.

Büren, Rainer. Nassers Ägypten als arabische Verfassungsmodell. Opladen, Leske Verlag, 1972.

_______. Die Arabische Sozialistische Union: Einheits Partie und Verfassungenssystem der Vereinigten Arabischen Republik unter Berücksichtigung der Verfassungsgeschichte. Opladen, Leske Verlag, 1970.

Calvocoressi, Peter. Suez 10 Years After. New York, Pantheon Books, 1967.

Childers, Erskine. The Road to Suez. London, MacGibbon and Kee, 1962.

Collins, Robert O. Egypt and the Sudan. Englewood Cliffs, Prentice-Hall, 1967.

Cooper, Chester L. The Lion's Last Roar: Suez 1956. New York, Harper and Row, 1978.

Copeland, Miles. The Game of Nations. New York, Simon and Schuster, 1969.

Cremeans, Charles. The Arabs and the World: Nasser's Arab Nationalist Policy. London, Praeger, 1963.

Daumal, Jack and Marie Leroy. Gamal Abd-el Nasser. Paris, Seghers, 1967.

Dekmejian, Hrair R. Patterns of Political Leadership: Egypt, Israel and Lebanon. New York, SUNY Press, 1975.

_______. Egypt under Nasser: A Study in Political Dynamics. Albany, SUNY Press, 1975.

Douek, Raymond Ibrahim. La voie égyptienne vers la socialisme. Cairo, Dār al-Ma^{c}ārif, 1966.

Dubois, Shirley. Gamal Abdel Nasser, Son of the Nile. New York, The Third Press, 1972.

Eayrs, James George. The Commonwealth and Suez: A Documentary Survey. London, Oxford University Press, 1964.

Eden, Sir Anthony. Memories: Full Circle. London, Cassell and Company, 1960.

Estier, Claude. L'Égypte en révolution. Paris, René Julliard, 1965.

Evron, Yair. The Middle East: Nations, Super-Powers and Wars. London, Elek Books, 1973.

Finer, Herman. Dulles over Suez. Chicago, Quadrangle Books, 1964.

Fisher, Sidney. The Military in Middle Eastern Society and Politics. Columbus, Ohio State University Press, 1963.

Flower, Raymond. Napoleon to Nasser. London, Stacey, 1969.

Frescobaldi, Dino. Nasser. Milan, Longanesi, 1970.

Garrett, Sean. The Suez Canal. London, Harrap, 1974.

Georges-Picot, Jacques. The Real Suez Crisis. (Translated by W. G. Rogers.) New York, Harcourt, Brace, Jovanovich, 1978.

Gibbons, Scott. The Conspirators: The Rise of Nasser's Egypt. London, Howard Baker, 1967.

Golan, Aviezar. Operation Susannah. (Translated by P. Kidron.) New York, Harper and Row, 1978.

Gulick, Luther Halsey and Jason Pollock. Government Reorganization in the UAR. Cairo, 1962.

Haddad, George. Revolutions and Military Rule in the Middle East. New York, Robert Speller, 1965-73 (3 vols., of which the second treats Egypt).

Haim, Sylvia. Arab Nationalism: An Anthology. repr. Berkeley, University of California Press, 1974.

Hammond, Paul Y. and S. Alexander. Political Dynamics in the Middle East. New York, American Elsevier Publishing, 1962.

Hanna, Sami and George Gardiner. Arab Socialism. Leiden, Brill, 1969.

Harris, Christina Phelps. Nationalism and Revolution in Egypt. Stanford, Hoover Institution, 1964.

Heykal, Mohammed Hassanein. The Cairo Documents: The Inside Story of Nasser and His Relationship with World Leaders. New York, Doubleday, 1973.

Hofstadter, Dan. Egypt and Nasser. New York, Facts on File, 1973.

Holden, David. Farewell to Arabia. New York, Walker and Company, 1967.

Hurewitz, J. C. Middle East Politics: The Military Dimension. London, Praeger, 1969.

________. Soviet-American Rivalry in the Middle East. New York, Praeger, 1969.

Hussein, Mahmoud. Lutte de classes et libêration nationale. Paris, Maspero, 1973. Published in English as: Class Conflict in Egypt 1945-70. (Translated by M. Chirman et al.) New York, Monthly Review Press, 1973.

Ismael, Tareq Y. The Arab Left. Syracuse, Syracuse University Press, 1976.

________. Governments and Politics of the Contemporary Middle East. Homewood (Ill.), Dorsey Press, 1970.

Jackson, Robert. Suez 1956: Operation Musketeer. London, Allan, 1980.

Joeston, Joachim. Nasser: The Rise to Power. London, Odhams Press, 1960.

Johnson, John J. The Role of the Military in Underdeveloped Countries. Princeton, Princeton University Press, 1962.

Junayd, Abdal Munim. La Rêpublique Arabe Unie: Égypte dans l'unitê arabe et l'unitê africaine. Cairo, Dar al-Kātib al-ᶜArabī, 1968.

Kamil, Mahmud. Tomorrow's Egypt: The Renaissance of a Nation and Its Glory. Cairo, Eastern Press, 1953.

Karpat, Kemal. Political and Social Thought in the Contemporary Middle East. New York, Praeger, 1968.

Kedourie, Elie. Arab Political Memoirs and Other Studies. London, Cass, 1974.

Kerr, Malcolm. The Arab Cold War: Gamal Abdal Nasir and His Rivals, 1953-70. London, Oxford University Press, 1975.

________. Egypt under Nasser. New York, Foreign Policy Association, 1963.

Khadduri, Majid. Arab Contemporaries: The Role of Personalities in Politics. London, Johns Hopkins Press, 1973.

________. Political Trends in the Arab World: The Role of Ideas and Ideals in Politics. London, Johns Hopkins Press, 1970.

Khouri, Fred. The Arab-Israeli Dilemma. Syracuse, Syracuse University Press, 1968.

Kirk, George. Contemporary Arab Politics, a Concise History. London, Metheun, 1961.

Kurland, Gerald. The Suez Crisis 1956. Charlottesville (N.Y.), Samhar Press, 1973.

Lacoutre, Jean. Nasser, a Biography. (Translated by D. Hofstadter.) New York, Alfred A. Knopf, 1970.

_______. The Demi-Gods: Charismatic Leadership in the Third World. New York, Alfred A. Knopf, 1970.

_______. L'Égypte en mouvement. Paris, Éditions du Seuil, 1962. Published in English as: Egypt in Transition. London, Methuen, 1958.

Laqueur, Walter. Struggle for the Middle East, the Soviet Union and the Middle East. Baltimore, Penguin, 1972.

_______. The Middle East in Transition: Studies in Contemporary History. Freeport (New York), Books for Libraries, 1971.

_______. The Road to War. Harmondsworth, Penguin, 1968.

_______. Communism and Nationalism in the Middle East. New York, Praeger, 1961.

Lenczowski, George. Middle Eastern Political Elites. Washington, American Enterprise Institute, 1970.

Lewis, Bernard. The Middle East and the West. New York, Harper, 1964.

Little, Tom. Modern Egypt. New York, Ernest Benn, 1967.

Lloyd, Baron Selwyn. Suez 1956: A Personal Account. London, Jonathan Cape, 1978.

Love, Kenneth. Suez: The Twice-Fought War. New York, McGraw-Hill, 1969.

MacDonald, Robert. The League of Arab States: A Study in the Dynamics of Regional Organization. Princeton, Princeton University Press, 1965.

Mahfouz, Afaf el-Koshêri. Socialisme et pouvoir en Égypte. Paris, Librairie Gênérale de Droit et Jurisprudence, 1972.

Mahgoub, Mohamed. Democracy on Trial: Reflections on Arab and African Politics. London, Deutsch, 1974.

Maltese, Paola. Storia del canale di Suez 1833-1956. Milan, Edizioni il Formichiere, 1978.

Mansfield, Peter. Nasser's Egypt. London, Penguin, 1969.

Marlowe, John. Anglo-Egyptian Relations 1800-1953. Hamden (Conn.), Archon Books, 1965.

Masriya, Y. (pseud.). Zionism in Islamic Lands, the Case of Egypt. London, Institute of Contemporary History, 1977.

_______. Les Juifs en Égypte: Aperçu sur 3000 ans d'histoire. Geneva, Les Éditions de l'Avenir, 1971.

_______. The Arab Role in Africa. Baltimore, Penguin, 1962.

Mayfield, James. Rural Politics in Nasser's Egypt. Austin, University of Texas Press, 1971.

McLauren, Ronald D. and Mohammed Mughisuddin. Foreign Policy Making in the Middle East, Domestic Influences on Policy in Egypt, Iraq, Israel and Syria. New York, Praeger, 1977.

Meyer-Ranke, Peter. Der rote Pharaoh. Hamburg, Christian Wegner Verlag, 1964.

Mezerick, Avraham G. The Suez Canal, 1956 Crisis, 1967 War, 1968-69 Fighting, UN Observers, Action in the United Nations, Positions of Combatants, Big Four and Others, Straits of Aqaba--Causus Belli. New York, International Review Services, 1969.

Moore, Austin L. Farewell Farouk. Chicago, The Scholar's Press, 1954.

Murphy, Robert. Diplomat among Warriors. repr. Westport (Conn.), Greenwood Press, 1967.

Nasser, Gamal Abdel. The Philosophy of the Revolution. New York, Economica Books, 1959.

Nasser, Munir Khalil. Press, Politics and Power: Egypt's Heikal and Al Ahram. Ames, Iowa State University Press, 1979.

Negib, Mohammed (Naguib). Memorie (1919-73). (Translated by C. S. Cerqua.) Firenze, La Nuova Italia, 1976.

_______. Egypt's Destiny: A Personal Statement. Garden City, Doubleday, 1955.

Nutting, Anthony. Nasser. London, Constable, 1972.

_______. No End of a Lesson, the Story of Suez. London, Constable, 1967.

O'Ballance, Edgar. The Electronic War in the Middle East 1968-70. London, Faber and Faber, 1974.

_______. The War in Yemen. London, Faber and Faber, 1971.

O'Rourke, Vernon A. The Juristic Status of Egypt and the Sudan. Westport, Greenwood Press, 1973.

Perlmutter, Amos. Egypt: The Praetorian State. New Brunswick, New Jersey, Transaction Books, 1974.

Pinneau, Christian. 1956 Suez. Paris, Laffont, 1976.

Politi, E. I. L'Égypte de 1914 à Suez. Paris, Presses de la Cité, 1965.

Qayyum, Shah Abdul. Egypt Reborn: A Study of Egypt's Freedom Movement 1945-52. New Delhi, Chand, 1973.

Rejwan, Nissim. Nasserist Ideology: Its Exponents and Critics. New York, Wiley, 1974.

Riad, Hassan. L'Égypte Nasserienne. Paris, Éditions de Minuit, 1969.

Rikye, Indar Jit. The Sinai Blunder, Withdrawal of the UNEF Leading to the Six Day War of June 1967. London, Cass, 1980.

Robertson, Terrence. Crisis: The Inside Story of the Suez Conspiracy. London, Hutchinson, 1965.

Rodinson, Maxime. Marxisme et monde musulman. Paris, Éditions du Seuil, 1972. Published in English as: Marxism and the Muslim World. (Translated by M. Pollis.) London, Zed Press, 1979.

________. Israel and the Arabs. Harmondsworth, Penguin, 1968.

Rondet, Pierre. The Changing Patterns of the Middle East. London, Chatto and Windus, 1961.

Saber, Ali. Nasser en procès: Face à la nation arabe. Paris, Nouvelles Éditions Latine, 1968.

Sachar, Howard. Europe Leaves the Middle East. New York, Alfred A. Knopf, 1972.

Sadat, Anwar al-. Revolt on the Nile. New York, John Day, 1957.

Safran, Nadav. From War to War, the Arab-Israeli Confrontation, 1948-67. New York, Pegasus, 1969.

St. John, Robert. The Boss: The Story of Gamal Abdel Nasser. New York, McGraw-Hill, 1960.

Salama, Abdel Moghny Said. Arab Socialism. New York, Barnes and Noble, 1972.

Seale, Patrick. The Struggle for Syria: A Study in Post-War Arab Politics 1945-58. London, Cambridge University Press, 1965.

Sharabi, Hisham. Nationalism and Revolution in the Arab World. London, D. Van Nostrand, 1966.

________. Government and Politics in the Middle East in the Twentieth Century. London, D. Van Nostrand, 1962.

Stephens, Robert. Nasser: A Political Biography. London, Penguin, 1971.

Stevens, George G., ed. The United States and the Middle East. Englewood Cliffs, Prentice-Hall, 1963.

Stewart, Desmond. Young Egypt. London, Allan Wingate, 1958.

Sykes, John. Down into Egypt: A Revolution Observed. London, Hutchinson, 1969.

Terra Vierra, Blanca. Gamal Abd al-Nasser: Anti-biographia. Madrid, Editions Pueyo, 1962.

Thomas, Hugh. The Suez Affair. London, Weidenfeld and Nicholson, 1967.

Trevelyan, Humphrey. The Middle East in Revolution. London, Macmillan, 1970.

Udovitch, A. L., ed. The Middle East: Oil, Conflict and Hope. Lexington (Mass.), D. C. Heath, 1976.

Ulam, Adam. The Unfinished Revolution. New York, Vintage Books, 1968.

Vatikiotis, P. J. Nasser and His Generation. London, Croom Helm, 1978.

________. Conflict in the Middle East. London, George Allen and Unwin, 1971.

________. The Modern History of Egypt. London, Weidenfeld and Nicholson, 1969; (reprinted as The History of Egypt. London, Weidenfeld and Nicholson, 1980).

________. Egypt Since the Revolution. New York, Praeger, 1968.

________. The Egyptian Army in Politics: Pattern for New Nations? repr. Westport (Conn.), Greenwood Press, 1975.

Vaucher, George. Gamal Abdel Nasser et son équipe. (2 Vols.) Paris, René Julliard, 1959-60.

Vernier, Bernard. Armée et politique au Moyen Orient. Paris, Payot, 1966.

Wald, Peter. Der Vereinigte Arabische Republik. Hannover, Verlag für Litteratur und Zeitgeschehen, 1969.

Warburg, James. Crosscurrents in the Middle East. London, Gollancz, 1969.

Waterfield, Gordon. Egypt. London, Thames and Hudson, 1967.

Wheelock, Keith. Nasser's New Egypt. repr. Westport (Conn.), Greenwood Press, 1975.

Whetten, Lawrence L. The Canal War: Four Power Conflict in the Middle East. London, MIT Press, 1974.

Wynn, Wilton. Nasser of Egypt. The Search for Dignity. Cambridge (Mass.), Arlington Books, 1959.

Zayid, Mahmud. Egypt's Struggle for Independence. Beirut, Khayats, 1965.

Ziadeh, Farhat J. Lawyers, the Rule of Law and Liberalism in Modern Egypt. Stanford, Hoover Institution, 1968.

Arabic Titles

ᶜAbd al-Ḥamīd, Muḥammad Kamāl. Maᶜrika Sinaᶜ wa Qanāt as-Suwīs. Cairo, Dār al-Qawmīya aṭ-Ṭibāᶜī wa'n-Nashr, 1964.

ᶜAbd al-Mawlā, Muḥammad. Al-Inhiyār al-Kabīr Asbāb Qiyām wa Suqūṭ Waḥda Miṣr wa Sūrīya. Beirut, Dār al-Masīra, 1977.

Abū Khāṭir, J. Liqāᶜa maᶜa Jamāl ᶜAbd an-Nāṣir fī Ṣamīm al-Aḥdāth. Beirut, Dār an-Nahār li'n-Nashr, 1971.

ᶜAnbār, Muḥammad ᶜAbd ar-Raḥmān. Sanawāt al-ᶜĀr! Awwal Dirāsa

Mawḍūᶜīya Kāmila li-ᶜAṣr al-Hazā'im. Cairo, Maṭbaᶜa ᶜĀbidīn, 1975.

Anīs, Muḥammad Aḥmad. Thawra Thalātha wa ᶜIshrīn Yūlyū. repr. Cairo, Dār an-Nahḍa, 1977.

_______. Ḥarīq al-Qāhira. Beirut, Al-Mu'assasa al-ᶜArabīya, 1972.

ᶜAshūr, Saᶜīd ᶜAbd al-Fattāḥ. Thawra Shaᶜb. Cairo, Dār an-Nahḍa, 1961.

ᶜAwda, Buṭrus. ᶜAbd an-Nāṣir wa'l-Istiᶜmār al-ᶜĀlamī. Beirut, Al-Mu'assasa an-Nāṣir li-Thaqafa, 1975.

_______. Jamāl ᶜAbd an-Nāṣir: Dawruhu fi'n-Niḍāl al-ᶜArabī. Cairo, Maṭbaᶜa al-Fannīya al-Ḥadīth, 1971.

ᶜAwda, Muḥammad. Al-Bāshā wa'th-Thawra. Cairo, Rūz al-Yūsuf, 1976.

_______. Al-Waᶜy al-Mafjūd. Cairo, Dār al-Qāhira al-Hadītha, 1975.

Badawī, Muḥammad Ṭāha and M. H. Muṣṭafā. Thawra Yūliyū Judhūrahā at-Tārīkhīya wa'l Falsafātuhā as-Sīyāsīya. Alexandria, Al-Maktab al-Miṣrī, 1966.

Baghdādī, ᶜAbd al-Laṭīf. Mudhakkirāt. Cairo, Al-Maktab al-Miṣrī al-Hadīth, 1977.

Basīsū, Mu'īn. Difāᶜa ᶜan al-Baṭal. Beirut, Dār al-ᶜAwda, 1975.

Bilāl, ᶜAbd Allāh. Ta'ammulāt fi'n-Nāṣirīya, Thawra Insanīya Khālida. Cairo, Maktaba al-Anjlū al-Miṣrīya, 1971.

Al-Bishrī, Ṭāriq. Ad-Dīmūqrāṭīya wa'n-Nāṣirīya. Cairo, Dār ath-Thaqāfa al-Jadīda, 1975.

Burj, Muḥammad ᶜAbd ar-Raḥmān. Qanāt as-Suwīs: Ahammīyatuhā as-Sīyāsīya wa'l-Istrātījīya. Cairo, Dār al-Kātib al-ᶜArabī, 1968.

Buṭrus-Ghalī, Buṭrus. ᶜAẓama al-Diblumāsīya al-ᶜArabīya. Cairo, Dār al-Kitāb al-Jadīd, 1969.

Dauḥ, Ḥasan. Ṣafahāt min Jihād ash-Shabāb al-Muslim. Cairo, Dār al-Iᶜtiṣām, 1979.

Fahmī, Fatḥī. Yawmīya ath-Thawra. Cairo, Maṣlaḥa Istiᶜlāmāt, n.d.

Fahmī, Muṣṭafā Abū Zayd. An-Niẓām ad-Dustūrī li'l-Jumhūrīya al-ᶜArabīya al-Muttaḥida. Alexandria, Dār al-Maᶜārif, 1966.

Faraj, Muḥammad. Jamāl ᶜAbd an-Nāṣir wa'l-Mujtamaᶜ al-Miṣrī. Cairo, Dār al-Fikr al-ᶜArabī, 1971.

Al-Ḥadīdī, Ṣalāḥ ad-Dīn. Shāhid cAlā Ḥarb 1967. Cairo, Dār ash-Shurūq, 1974.

Ḥāfiẓ, cUlwī. Muhimmāti as-Sirrīya bayna cAbd an-Nāṣir wa Amrīkā. Cairo, Al-Maktab al-Miṣrī al-Ḥadīth, 1976.

Al-Ḥakīm, Muṣṭafā Muḥammad. cAbd an-Nāṣir Qaḍāyā ... wa Mawāqif. Beirut, Jarīda Ṣawt al cUrūbā, 1971.

Al-Ḥakīm, Tawfīq. Wathā'iq fī Ṭarīq cAwda al-Wacy. Beirut, Dār ash-Shurūq, 1975.

_______. cAwda al-Wacy. Beirut, Dār ash-Shurūq, 1974.

Ḥasan, Ibrāhīm Shihāta. Miṣr wa Sūdān. Alexandria, Al-Hai'a al-Miṣrīya al-cĀmma, 1971.

Ḥasanayn, Jamāl Majdī. Thawra Yūliyū wa Lucba at-Tawāzum aṭ-Ṭabaqī. Cairo, Dār ath-Thaqāfa al-Jadīda, 1978.

Haykal, Muḥammad Ḥasanayn. Qiṣṣa as-Suwīs Ākhir al-Macārik fī cAṣr al-cAmāliqa. Beirut, Maktaba Unkāl Sām, 1977.

_______. cAbd an-Nāṣir wa'l-cĀlam. Beirut, Dār al-Hilāl, 1972.

_______. Naḥnu wa Amarīkā. Cairo, Dār al-cAṣr al-Ḥadīth, 1967.

Huwaidī, Amīn. Ḥurūb cAbd an-Nāṣir. Beirut, Dār aṭ-Ṭalī'a, 1977.

Imām, cAbd Allāh. Ḥikāyāt can cAbd an-Nāṣir. Cairo, Dār ash-Shacb, 1971.

Iskandar, Amīr. Ṣirā' al-Yamīn wa'l-Yasar fi'th-Thaqāfa al-Miṣrīya. Beirut, Dār Ibn Khaldūn, 1978.

Al-Jarf, Tucayma cAbd al-Ḥamīd. Thawra Thalātha wa cIshrīn Yūliyū. Maktaba al-Qāhira al-Ḥadītha, 1964.

Jumca, Rābiḥ Luṭfī. Saḥq al-cUdwān. Cairo, Dār al-Qawmīya aṭ-Ṭabācī wa'n-Nashr, 1962.

Kāmil, Maḥmūd. Ad-Dawla al-cArabīya al-Kubrā. Cairo, Maktaba al-Dirāsāt at-Tārīkhīya, n.d.

Khākī, Aḥmad. Falsafa al-Qawmīya. Cairo, Maktaba al-Ijtimacīya, 1962.

Al-Khawlī, Luṭfī. Dirāsāt fi'l-Wāqica al-Miṣrī al-Mucāṣir. Beirut, Dār aṭ-Ṭalī'a, 1977.

Lotski, Vladimir. A Modern History of the Arab States (in Arabic). Moscow, Progress Books, 1971.

Mallūḥī, ^{c}Adnān. Al-Kitāb al-Abyaḍ fi'r-Radd ^{c}Alā Tawfīq al-Ḥakīm: ^{c}Abd an-Nāṣir wa'th-Thawra bain al-Ḥaqīqa wa'l-Usṭūra. Beirut, Dār an-Nahḍa al-Ḥadītha, 1975.

Al-Marāghī, Aḥmad Murtaḍā. Gharā'ib min ^{c}Ahd Fārūq wa Bidāya ath-Thawra al-Miṣrīya. Beirut, Dār an-Nahār, 1976.

Mar^{c}ī, Sayyid. Awrāq Sīyāsīya. Cairo, Al-Maktab al-Miṣrī al-Ḥadīth, 1978.

Muḥammad, Muḥsin. ^{c}Indamā Yamūtu al-Malik. Cairo, Dār at-Ta^{c}āwun, 1980.

Murād, Maḥmūd. Man Kāna Yaḥkumu Miṣr? Cairo, Maktab Madbūlī, 1975.

Al-Mursī, Fu'ād. Al-^{c}Alāqāt al-Miṣrīya as-Sūvīyatīya 1943-56. Cairo, Dār ath-Thaqāfa al-Jadīda, 1977.

An-Najjār, Ḥusayn Fawzī. Thawrātunā wa'l-Mīthāq. Cairo, Al-Qawmīya aṭ-Ṭabā^{c}ī wa'n-Nashr, 1961.

Nānū, Jān. Mawt Mushīr. Beirut, Dār al-I^{c}lām al-^{c}Arabī, 1968.

Ra^{c}fat, Waḥīd. Fuṣūl min Thawra 23 Yūliyū. Cairo, Dār ash-Shurūq, 1978.

Rāfi^{c}ī, ^{c}Abd ar-Raḥmān. Muqaddimāt Thawra 23 Yūliyū Sana 1952. Cairo, Maktaba an-Nahḍa al-Miṣrīya, 1964.

Ramaḍān, ^{c}Abd al-^{c}Aẓīm. ^{c}Abd an-Nāṣir wa Azma Mārs 1954. Cairo, Rūz al-Yūsuf, 1976.

Riḍwān, Fatḥī. Asrār Ḥukūma Yūliyū. Cairo, Maktaba Madbūlī, 1976.

Riyāḍ, Ẓāhir. Miṣr wa Ifrīqīya. Cairo, Maktaba al-Anjlū al-Miṣrīya, 1976.

Sayf ad-Dawlā, ^{c}Iṣmat. Al-Aḥzāb wa Mushkila ad-Dīmuqrāṭīya fī Miṣr. Beirut, Dār al-Masīra, 1977.

________. Hal Kāna ^{c}Abd an-Nāṣir Dīktātūran? Beirut, Dār al-Masīra, 1977.

Ash-Shahārī, Muḥammad ^{c}Alī. ^{c}Abd an-Nāṣir wa Thawra al-Yaman. Cairo, Maktaba Madbūlī, 1976.

Shākir, T. Th. Qaḍāyā at-Taḥarrur al-Waṭanī wa'th-Thawra al-Ishtirākīya fī Miṣr. Beirut, Dār al-Fārābī, 1973.

Shalabī, Karam. ^{c}Ishrūna Yawman Hazza Miṣr: Dirāsa wa Wathā'iq fī Azma Mārs. Cairo, Dār Asāma li't-Ṭibā^{c}ī wa'n-Nashr, 1976.

Sharqāwī, Jamāl. Ḥarīq al-Qāhira: Qarār Ittihām Jadīd. Cairo, Dār ath-Thaqāfa al-Jadīda, 1976.

Sibā^{c}ī, Yūsuf. Ayyām ^{c}Abd an-Nāṣir: Khawāṭir wa Mashā^{c}ir. Cairo, Maktaba al-Khanjlī, 1971.

At-Tilmisānī, ^{c}Umar. Qāla an-Nās wa lam Aqūl fī Ḥukm ^{c}Abd an-Nāṣir. Cairo, Dār al-Anṣār, 1980.

^{c}Ūda, Muḥammad. Mīlād Thawra. Cairo, Dār al-Jumhūrīya li's-Ṣiḥāfa, 1971.

^{c}Umar, Maḥmūd Fatḥī. Thalātha wa ^{c}Ishrūn Yūliyū. Cairo, Dār al-Qawmīya aṭ-Ṭabā^{c}ī wa'n-Nashr, 1963.

________ and Maḥmūd Ḥāfiẓ. Naẓarāt Ḥawla Falsafa ath-Thawra. Cairo, Dār al-Qawmīya aṭ-Ṭabā^{c}ī wa'n-Nashr, 1961.

Yaḥyā, Jalāl. ^{c}Uṣūl Thawra Yūliyū 1952. Cairo, Dār al-Qawmīya li'ṭ-Ṭabā^{c}ī wa'n-Nashr, 1964.

Zakarīya, Fu'ād. ^{c}Abd an-Nāṣir wa'l-Yasār al-Miṣrī. Cairo, Rūz al-Yūsuf, 1977.

Egypt Since 1970

Non-Arabic Titles

Allen, Richard. *Imperialism and Nationalism in the Fertile Crescent: Sources and Prospects of the Arab-Israeli Conflict.* New York, Oxford University Press, 1974.

Aulos, M. C. *L'Égypte d'aujourd'hui: Permanence et changements.* Paris, Éditions du Centre Nationale de la Recherche, 1977.

Ayouty, Yassin El. *Egypt, Peace and the Inter-Arab Crisis.* Buffalo, SUNY Press, 1979.

Ayubi, Nazih. *Bureaucracy and Politics in Contemporary Egypt.* London, Ithaca Press, 1980.

Baker, Raymond. *Egypt's Uncertain Revolution under Nasser and Sadat.* Cambridge (Mass.), Harvard University Press, 1978.

Burrell, Robert M. and Abbas R. Kelidar. *Egypt: The Dilemmas of a Nation, 1970-77.* Beverly Hills, Sage Publications, 1977.

Dawisha, A. *Egypt in the Arab World: The Elements of a Foreign Policy.* London, Macmillan, 1976.

Dawisha, K. *Soviet Foreign Policy Towards Egypt.* London, Macmillan, 1979.

Dayan, Moshe. *Breakthrough: A Personal Account of the Egypt-Israeli Peace Negotiations.* London, Weidenfeld and Nicholson, 1981.

Dessouki, Ali E. Hillal. *Democracy in Egypt: Problems and Prospects.* Cairo, AUC Press, 1978.

Eidelberg, Paul. Sadat's Strategy. Quebec, Dawn Publishing, 1979.

Frescobaldi, Dina. La Sfida di Sadat. Milano, Rizzoli Editore, 1977.

Fullick, Roy and Geoffrey Powell. Suez: The Double War. London, Hamish Hamilton, 1979.

Glassman, Jon D. Arms for the Arabs: The Soviet Union and War in the Middle East. Baltimore, 1976.

Golan, Matti. The Secret Conversations of Henry Kissinger: Step by Step Diplomacy in the Middle East. New York, Quadrangle, 1976.

Hansen, Bent. Egypt. New York, Columbia University Press, 1975.

Heykal, Mohammed Hassanein. The Sphinx and the Commissar: The Rise and Fall of Soviet Influence in the Middle East. New York, Harper and Row, 1978.

________. The Road to Ramadan. New York, Quadrangle Books, 1975.

Hirst, David and Irene Beeson. Sadat. Faber and Faber, 1981.

Hureau, Jean. Égypte aujourd'hui. Paris, Éditions S. A., 1977.

Israel, Raphael. The Public Diary of President Sadat. (3 Vols.) Leiden, Brill, 1978-79.

Kimche, Jon. There Could Have Been Peace. New York, Dial, 1973.

Lengyel, Emil. Modern Egypt. New York, F. Watts, 1979.

Mansfield, Peter. The Middle East: A Political and Economic Survey. London, Oxford University Press, London, 1973.

McLaurin, Ronald D. and Mohammed Mughisuddin Abdel Wagner. Foreign Policy Making in the Middle East: Domestic Influences on Policy in Egypt, Iraq, Israel and Syria. New York, Praeger, 1977.

Narayan, V. K. Anwar al-Sadat, Man with a Mission. New Delhi, Vikas, 1977.

O'Ballance, Edgar. No Victors, No Vanquished: The Yom Kippur War. San Rafael, Presidio Press, 1978.

Roman, Jochanan Hans. Interpretation und Völkerrechtliche Bedeutung des Sinai Abkommens zwischen Israel und Ägypten vom 4 September 1975. Berlin, Duncker and Humbolt, 1978.

Rubenstein, Alvin. Red Star on the Nile: The Soviet-Egyptian Influence Relation Since the June War. Princeton, Princeton University Press, 1977.

Sadat, Anwar al-. In Search of Identity. New York, Harper and Row, 1978.

Sheehan, Edward R. F. The Arabs, Israelis and Kissinger: A Secret History of American Diplomacy in the Middle East. New York, Reader's Digest Press, 1976.

Shoukri, Ghali. Egypt, Portrait of a President. London, Zed Press, 1981.

_______. Égypte: La contre-révolution. (Translated by M. Morgane.) Paris, Éditions du Sycamore, 1979.

Socialist Union-Egyptian Caucus. Egypt--The January Events. Doncaster, Socialist Union International, 1977.

Stephens, Robert. The Egyptian-Soviet Quarrel in 1972: Russia, the Arabs and Africa. London, Collins, 1973.

Waterbury, John. Hydropolitics of the Nile Valley. New York, Syracuse University Press, 1979.

_______. Egypt: Burdens of the Past, Options for the Future. Bloomington, Indiana University Press, 1978.

Arabic Titles

ᶜAbd al-Majd, Ṣabrī. Al-Masīra aṭ-Ṭawīla maᶜa as-Sādāt ᶜAlā Ṭarīq an-Niḍāl. Cairo, Dār ash-Shaᶜb, 1976.

ᶜAbd al-Munᶜīm, Muḥammad Fayṣal. Hā'ulā'i ar-Rijāl al-ᶜIẓam wa Maᶜrakat al-Mustaḥīla Ḥarb Uktubār 1973. Cairo, Markaz an-Nīl li'l-Iᶜlām, 1979.

ᶜAbd ar-Raḥmān, ᶜAwāṭif. Miṣr wa Filasṭīn. Kuwait, Majlis al-Waṭanī li'th-Thaqāfa wa'l-Funūn wa'l-Ādāb, 1980.

ᶜAbd ar-Rāziq, Ḥusayn. Miṣr fī 18 wa 19 Yanāyir, Dirāsa Siyāsīya wa Wathā'iqīya. Beirut, Dār Ibn Khaldūn, 1979.

ᶜAbd at-Tawwāb, Ismāᶜīl. As-Sādāt bilā Ritūsh. Cairo, Dār ash-Shaᶜb, 1976.

ᶜAbdū, Ibrāhīm. Tārīkh bilā Wathā'iq. Cairo, Mu'assasa Sijill al-ᶜArab, 1975.

_______. Rasā'il min Nifāqistān. Cairo, Mu'assasa Sijill al-ᶜArab, 1974.

Aḥmad, ᶜAbd al-ᶜAṭī Muḥammad. Ar-Ra'īs Anwār as-Sādāt wa Qaḍāyā Nazᶜ as-Silāḥ. Cairo, Mu'assasa al-Ahrām, 1978.

Ayyūbī, Haytham. Ittifāq Faṣl al-Quwāt ath-Thānī fī Sīnā' 1975. Beirut, Al-Mu'assasa al-ᶜArabīya li'd-Dirāsāt wa'n-Nashr, 1975.

Badawī, Mūsā. As-Sādāt, Rajul al-Ḥarb, Rajul as-Salām. Cairo, Dār al-Maᶜārif, 1978.

Basīsū, Mu'īn. Al-Būlduzār. Beirut, Al-Mu'assasa al-ᶜArabīya li'd-Dirāsāt wa'n-Nashr, 1975.

Darwīsh, ^{c}Abd al-Karīm and Laylā Taklā. Ḥarb as-Sā^{c}a as-Sitt. Cairo, Maktaba al-Anjlū al-Miṣrīya, 1974.

Fahmī, Muḥammad ^{c}Alī. Al-Qūwa ar-Rābi^{c}a: Tārīkh ad-Difā^{c} al-Jawwī. Cairo, Al-Hai'a al-Miṣrīya al-^{c}Āmma, 1976.

Faraḥāt, Albīr. Miṣr fī Ẓill as-Sādāt 1970-77. Beirut, Dār al-Fārābī, 1978.

Fu'ād, Ḥamdī. Al-Ḥarb ad-Diblūmāsīya baina Miṣr wa Isrā'īl. Beirut, Dār al-Qaḍāyā, 1976.

Al-Ghiṭanī, Jamāl. Al-Miṣrīyūn wa'l-Ḥarb. Cairo, Rūz al-Yūsuf, 1974.

Ghālī, Ibrāhīm Amīn. Sīnā' al-Miṣrīya ^{c}Abr at-Tārīkh. Cairo, Al-Hai'a al-Miṣrīya al-^{c}Āmma, 1976.

Al-Ḥamāmṣī, Jalāl ad-Dīn. Ḥiwār Warā' al-Aswār. Cairo, Maktab al-Miṣrī al-Ḥadīth, 1976.

Hilāl, ^{c}Alī ad-Dīn. As-Sīyāsa wa'l Ḥukm fī Miṣr. Cairo, Maktaba Nahḍa ash-Sharq, 1975.

Ḥilmī, Maḥmūd. Dustūr Jumhūrīya Miṣr al-^{c}Arabīya wa'l Dasātīr al-^{c}Arabīya al-Mu^{c}āṣira. Cairo, Dār an-Nashr ath-Thaqāfa, 1974.

Ibrāhīm, Shihatā ^{c}Īsā. ^{c}Uzamā al-Waṭanīya fī Miṣr fi'l-^{c}Aṣr al-Ḥadīth. Cairo, Dār al-Hilāl, 1977.

^{c}Īsā, Ḥabīb. Suqūṭ al-Akhīr li'l-Iqlīmīyīn fi'l-Waṭān al-^{c}Arabī. Beirut, Dār al-Masīra, 1978.

Ittifāq Kāmb Dayfīd wa Akhtāruhu: ^{c}Arḍ Wathā'iqī. Beirut, Mu'assasa ad-Dirāsāt al-Filasṭīnīya, 1978.

Jād al-Mawlā, ^{c}Abd aṣ-Ṣamad. Qaḍāyā al-Jabha al-Waṭanīya at-Taqaddumīya fī Miṣr. Beirut, Dār al-Quds, 1977.

Kishk, Muḥammad Jalāl. Kalām li-Miṣr. Beirut, Dār al-Waṭan al-^{c}Arabī, 1975.

Labīb, ^{c}Alī Muḥammad. Al-Qūwa ath-Thālitha: Tārīkh al-Qūwāt al-Jawwīya al-Miṣrīya. Cairo, Al-Hai'a al-Miṣrīya al-^{c}Āmma, 1977.

Luṭfī, Ḥamdī. Al-^{c}Askarīya al-Miṣrīya fawq Sīnā'. Cairo, Dār al-Hilāl, 1976.

Maḥbūb, ^{c}Alī Muḥammad. Miṣr ba^{c}d al-^{c}Ubūr. Cairo, Dār ash-Sha^{c}b, 1975.

Mutawallī, ᶜAbd al-Hamīd. ᶜAlā Hāmish ad-Dustūr al-Miṣri al-Jadīd. Cairo, 1975.

Nawwār, ᶜAbd al-ᶜAzīz, Ṣalāḥ al-ᶜAqqād and Ibrāhīm al-Baḥrāwī. Muᶜtamar Kāmb Dāfīd, Ruᶜya ᶜIlmīya. Cairo, Jāmiᶜa ᶜAyn Shams, 1978.

Ar-Rifāᶜī, ᶜAbd al-ᶜAzīz and Ḥusayn ᶜAbd al-Wāḥid ash-Shā'ir. Al-Waᶜy al-ᶜArabī wa Waḥda Miṣr wa Lībiyā. Cairo, Maktaba al-Waᶜy al-ᶜArabī, 1974.

Ṣabrī, Mūsā. Wathāᶜiq 15 Māyū. Cairo, Maktab al-Miṣrī al-Ḥadīth, 1977.

Shādhilī, Saᶜd ad-Dīn. Ḥarb Uktubār (Mudhakkirāt). Beirut, Al-Mu'assasa al-Waṭan al-ᶜArabī, 1980.

Shalābī, Aḥmad. Miṣr fī Ḥarbayn. Maktaba an-Nahḍa al-Miṣrīya, 1975.

Shalābī, Karām. As-Sādāt wa Thawra Yūliyū: Dirāsa fī Fikr Anwār as-Sādāt. Cairo, Dār al-Mawqif al-ᶜArabī, 1977.

Ash-Shaykh, Ra'fat Ghunaimī. Miṣr wa's-Sūdān fi'l-ᶜAlāqāt ad-Duwalīya. Cairo, ᶜAlām al-Kutub, 1979.

Shukrī, Ghalī. Iᶜtirāfāt az-Zaman al-Khā'ib. Beirut, Al-Mu'assasa al-al-ᶜArabīya li'd-Dirāsāt wa'n-Nashr, 1980.

________. An-Nahḍa wa's-Suqūṭ fi'l Fikr al-Miṣrī al-Ḥadīth. Beirut, Dār aṭ-Ṭalīᶜa, 1978.

Siᶜda, Ibrāhīm. Ar-Rūs Qadimūn. Alexandria, Maktab al-Miṣrī al-Ḥadīth, 1976.

Aṭ-Ṭawīla, ᶜAbd as-Sattār. Al-ᶜAqīd al-Qadhdhāfī ... wa Miṣr! Cairo, Maktaba al-Madbūlī, 1977.

________. Rafḍ ar-Rafḍ: Hiwār maᶜa Jabha ar-Rafḍ al-ᶜArabīya. Cairo, Wakāla Tilstār, 1976.

Yamānī, Sālim. Sīnā': Al-Arḍ, al-Ḥarb wa'sh-Shaᶜb. Cairo, Al-Hai'a al-Miṣrīya al-ᶜĀmma, 1975.

Zikū, ᶜAlī Uthmān. Abṭāl at-Tayyāran fī Ḥaraka Ramadān. Cairo, Al-Hai'a al-Miṣrīya al-ᶜAmma, 1974.

Agriculture and Agrarian Reform

Non-Arabic Titles

Abdel Saud, Hassan. General Aspects of Land Reform in Egypt. Cairo, Anglo-Egyptian Bookstore, 1956.

Brown, Clement Henson. Egyptian Cotton. London, Leonard Hill, 1953.

Burrell, Robert Mitchell, S. Hoyle, K. S. McLachlan and C. Parker. The Developing Agriculture of the Middle East, Approaches and Prospects. London, Graham and Trotman, 1976.

Castle, Mary Ann. Social Reproduction and the Egyptian Agrarian Transformation. Ann Arbor, University of Michigan Press, 1966.

Heyworth-Dunne, G. E. Egypt: The Co-operative Movement. Cairo, Renaissance Bookshop, 1952.

Marei, Sayyid. Agrarian Reform in Egypt. Cairo, Institut Français, 1957.

Poliak, Abraham. Feudalism in Egypt, Syria, Palestine and the Lebanon. Philadelphia, Porcupine Press, 1977.

Radwan, Samir. Agrarian Reform and Rural Poverty in Egypt 1952-75. Geneva, ILO, 1977.

Rivlin, Helen Anne. The Agricultural Policy of Muhammad Ali in Egypt. Cambridge (Mass.), Harvard University Press, 1961.

Saab, Gabriel. The Egyptian Agrarian Reform 1952-62. London, Oxford University Press, 1967.

El Sharki, Mohamed Youssef. La monoculture du coton en Égypte et le dévelopment économique. Genève, Librairie Droz, 1964.

Treydte, Klaus Porter. Genossenschaften in der VAR (Ägypten) Entwicklung, Stand und Struktur des Ägyptischen Genossenschaftswessen. Hannover, Verlag für Literatur und Zeitgeschehen, 1971.

Warriner, Doreen. Agrarian Reform and Community Development in the UAR. Cairo, Dar at-Taawan, 1961.

________. Land Reform and Economic Development. Cairo, National Bank of Egypt, 1955.

Arabic Titles

^{c}Abd al-Fattāḥ, Fatḥī. Al-Qarya al-Miṣrīya: Dirāsa fi'l Milkīya wa ^{c}Alāqāt al-Intāj. Cairo, Dār ath-Thaqāfa, 1973 ff.

Abū'l-^{c}Izz, Sāmī and Muḥammad Abū-Ghār. At-Tamwīl az-Zirā^{c}ī wa't-Ta^{c}āwunī wa Taṭawwuruhu fi'l-Jumhūrīya al-^{c}Arabīya al-Muttaḥida. Cairo, Maktaba ash-Shabāb, 1970.

Aḥmad, Ḥasan Zakī. Al-Quṭn, Taswīquhu wa Tamwīluhu. Cairo, Dār ash-Sha^{c}b, n.d.

^{c}Āmir, Ibrāhīm. Al-Arḍ wa'l-Fallāḥ: Al-Masa'la az-Zirā^{c}īya fī Miṣr. Cairo, Maṭba^{c}a Dār al-Miṣrīya, 1958.

Buṭrus Ghālī, Mirit. Al-Iṣlāḥ az-Zirā^{c}ī: Al-Milkīya, al-Ijār, al-^{c}Amal. Cairo, Dār al-Fuṣūl, 1945.

Gharzūzī, Ivā. Thawra al-Iṣlāḥ bi'l-Arqam. Cairo, Maktaba an-Nahḍa al-Miṣrīya, 1959.

Mar^{c}ī, Muḥammad ^{c}Abd al-Majīd. Al-Iṣlāḥ az-Zirā^{c}ī wa'l-Mīthaq. Cairo, Dār al-Qalam, 1964.

Naḥḥās, Yūsuf. Al-Quṭn fī Khamsīna ^{c}Amān. Cairo, 1954.

_______. Juhūd an-Naqaba az-Zirā^{c}īya al-Miṣrīya al-^{c}Āmma fī Thalīthīna ^{c}Amān. Cairo, Maṭba^{c}a Miṣr, 1952.

_______. Al-Fallāḥ, Ḥālatuhu al-Iqtiṣādīya wa'l-Ijtimā^{c}īya. Cairo, 1926.

Naẓīr, Wilyām. Az-Zirā^{c}a fī Miṣr al-Islāmīya min ^{c}Ahd al-Khulafā' ar-Rāshidūn ila ^{c}Ahd ath-Thawra. Cairo, 1969.

Rashad, Ibrāhīm. Kitāb at-Ta^{c}āwun az-Zirā^{c}ī. Cairo, 1935.

Ṣāliḥ, Ṣāliḥ Muḥammad. Al-Iqṭā^c wa'r-Ra'smalīya az-Zirā^{c}īya fī Miṣr min ^{c}Ahd Muḥammad ^{c}Alī ila ^{c}Abd an-Nāṣir. Beirut, Dār Ibn Khaldūn, 1979.

Art and Architecture

Non-Arabic Titles

Abu Loghod, Janet. *Cairo: 1001 Years of the City Victorious.* Princeton, Princeton University Press, 1971.

Asai, Nobuo. *Cairo.* (Translated by P. Bush.) Tokyo, Kodansha International, 1979.

Balog, Paul. *The Coinage of the Mamluk Sultans of Egypt and Syria.* New York, American Numismatic Society, 1964.

Brandenburg, Dietrich. *Islamische Baukunst in Ägyptens.* Berlin, Verlag Bruno Hessling, 1966.

Colloque Internationale sur l'histoire du Caire, 27 Mars-5 Avril 1969. Cairo, Ministry of Culture, 1974.

Creswell, Sir K. A. C. *The Muslim Architecture of Egypt.* Oxford, Oxford University Press, 1952-60, two vols.

Devonshire, Lady Henrietta. *Moslem Builders of Cairo.* Cairo, R. Schindler, 1943.

Fakhri, Ahmad. *The Oases of Egypt.* Cairo, AUC Press, 1973.

Freeman-Grenville, G. S. P. *The Beauty of Cairo: An Historical Guide to the Chief Islamic and Coptic Monuments.* London, East-West Publications, 1981.

Garçin, Jean-Claude. *Un centre musulman de l'Haute Égypte médiévale: Qūṣ.* Cairo, Institut Français, 1976.

Haldane, Duncan. Mamluk Painting. Warminster, Aris and Phillips, 1978.

Hautecoeur, L., and Gaston Wiet. Les Mosquées du Caire. 2 Vols., Paris, Leroux, 1932.

Hourani, A. M., ed. The Islamic City. Oxford, Oxford University Press, 1970.

Lane-Poole, Stanley. Art of the Saracens in Egypt. repr. Beirut, Librairie Byblos, n.d.

Parker, Richard. A Practical Guide to the Islamic Monuments of Cairo. Cairo, AUC Press, 1973.

Raimond, Jean. Le désert oriental égyptien du Nile à la Mer Rouge. Paris, (for the) Institut Français, 1923.

Russell, Lady Dorothea. Medieval Cairo and the Monasteries of the Wadī Natrūn. London, Weidenfeld and Nicholson, 1962.

Wiet, Gaston. Cairo, City of Art and Commerce. (Translated by S. Feiler). Norman, University of Oklahoma Press, 1964.

Arabic Titles

Al-Bāshā, Ḥasan, ed. Al-Qāhira, Tārīkhuhā, Funūnuhā, Āthāruhā. Cairo, Al-Mu'assasa al-Ahrām, 1970.

________. Fann at-Taṣwīr fī Miṣr al-Islāmīya. Cairo, Dār an-Nahḍa al-ᶜArabīya, 1966.

Fikhrī, Aḥmad. Masājid al-Qāhira wa Madārisuhā al-ᶜAṣr al-Fāṭimī. Cairo, Dār al-Maᶜārif, 1965.

Shāfiᶜī Farīd. Al-ᶜImārā al-ᶜArabīya fī Miṣr al-Islāmīya. Cairo, Al-Hai'a al-Miṣrīya al ᶜĀmma, 1960.

Zakī, ᶜAbd ar-Raḥmān. Bunāt al-Qāhira fī Alf ᶜĀm. Cairo, Dār al-Kātib, 1960.

________. Qalᶜa Ṣalāḥ ad-Dīn al-Ayyūbī wa mā Ḥawlaha min al-Āthār. Cairo, Al-Hai'a al-Miṣrīya al-ᶜĀmma, 1971.

Coptic Studies and Coptic Art

Non-Arabic Titles

Abu Salih al-Armani. The Churches and Monasteries of Egypt and Some Neighbouring Countries. (Translated by B. T. A. Evetts with notes by A. J. Butler.) repr. Oxford, Clarendon, 1969.

Akademie der bilderen Künste. Freïchristliche und Koptische Künst. Vienna, Brüder Rosenbaum, 1964.

Alt, Ernst. Ägyptens Kopt--Eine einsame Minderheit zum verhältnis von

Christen und Moslems in Ägypten in Vergangenheit und Gegenswart. Saarbrucken, Verlag Breitenbach, 1980.

Athanasius, Bishop. The Copts Through the Ages. Cairo, Ministry of Information, 1973.

Badawy, Alexander. Coptic Art and Archaeology: The Art of the Christian Egyptians from the Late Antique to the Middle Ages. Cambridge (Mass.), MIT Press, 1978.

du Bourget, Pierre M. Coptic Art. (Translated by C. Hay-Shaw.) London, Metheun, 1971.

Butcher, Edith Louisa. The Story of the Church in Egypt. repr. New York, AMS Press, 1972.

Butler, A. J. The Ancient Coptic Churches of Egypt. repr. Oxford, Clarendon Press, 1970.

Chaleur, Sylvestre. Histoire des Coptes d'Égypte. Paris, La Colombe, 1970.

Cosmas Indicopleustes. The Christian Topography of Cosmas, an Egyptian Monk. Cambridge, Cambridge University Press, 1909.

Cramer, M. Das Christliche-Kopten Ägypten einst und heuter. Weisbaden, Harrassowitz, 1959.

Al Damanhuri, Shaykh Ahmad b. Abdal Munim. On the Churches of Cairo. (Translated and edited by M. Perlman.) Berkeley, University of California Press, 1975.

Effenberger, Arne. Koptische Kunst: Ägypten in spätantiker byzantinischer und frühislamischer Zeit. Vienna, Tusch, 1977.

Galey, John. Sinai and the Monastery of St. Catherin. London, Chatto and Windus, 1980.

Gayet, Albert. L'Art copte. Paris, Leroux, 1902.

Hardy, Edward Rochie. Christianity and Nationalism in the Patriarchate of Alexandria. New York, 1952.

Hourani, A. D. Minorities in the Arab World. London, 1947.

Kamil, Murad. Coptic Egypt. Cairo, Le Scribe Égyptien, 1968.

Leeder, S. H. Modern Sons of the Pharaohs. repr. N.Y., Arno Press, 1973.

Leroy, Jules. Les manuscrits Coptes et Coptes-Arabes illustrés, Beirut, Institut Français, 1974.

Masriya, Y. (pseud.). A Christian Minority: The Copts in Egypt. Geneva, Centre d'Information et Documentation sur le Moyen-Orient, 1976.

Meinardus, Otto Freidrich. Christian Egypt: Ancient and Modern. Cairo, AUC Press, 1977.

_______. Christian Egypt, Faith and Life. Cairo, AUC Press, 1970.

_______. Monks and Monasteries of the Egyptian Deserts. Cairo, AUC Press, 1961.

Nauerth, Claudia. Koptische Textilkunst in Spätantiken Ägypten. Trier, Spee, 1978.

Plumley, J. Martin. The Scrolls of Bishop Timotheos: Two Documents from Medieval Nubia. London, Egyptian Exploration Society, 1975.

Roncaglia, Martiniano. Histoire de l'église copte. (2 Vols.) Beirut, Dār al-Kalima, 1966-69.

Rondot, Pierre. Les Chrétiens d'Orient. Paris, Peyronnet et Cie, 1955.

Wessel, Klaus. Coptic Art. (Translated by J. Carrol and S. Hallon.) London, Thames and Hudson, 1965.

_______. Christentum am Nil. Rechlingenhausen, A. Borgers, 1964.

Wüstenfeld, Ferdinand. Macrizi's Geschichte der Copten. New York, Olms, 1979.

Arabic Titles

Ḥabīb, Ra'ūf. Tārīkh ar-Rahbana wa'd-Diyāra fī Miṣr wa Āthāruhuma al-Insānī ᶜAlā'l-ᶜĀlam. Cairo, Maktaba al-Maḥabba, n.d.

Studies on the Economy of Egypt

Non-Arabic Titles

Abdel-Fadil, Mahmoud. The Political Economy of Nasserism: A Study in Employment and Income Distribution Policies in Urban Egypt 1952-72. Cambridge, Cambridge University Press, 1980.

Ahmad, Yusuf J. Absorptive Capacity of the Egyptian Economy: An Examination of the Problems and Prospects. Paris, OECD Development Centre, 1976.

Al Barrawi, Rashid. Economic Development in the United Arab Republic. Cairo, Anglo-Egyptian Bookshop, 1972.

Barbour, Kenneth Michael. The Growth, Location and Structure of Industry in Egypt. New York, Praeger, 1972.

Cahen, Claude. Makhzūmiyyāt: Études sur l'histoire économique et financière de l'Égypte médiévale. Leiden, Brill, 1977.

Carmon, Y. The Significance of Egyptian Development: The Egyptian Viewpoint. Jerusalem, Study Group for Middle Eastern Affairs, 1975.

Carr, David William. Foreign Investment and Development in Egypt. N.Y., Praeger, 1979.

Cook, M. A. Studies in the Economic History of the Middle East. London, Oxford University Press, 1970.

Crouchley, A. E. The Economic Development of Modern Egypt. London, Longmans, Green, 1938.

________. The Investment of Foreign Capital in Egyptian Companies and Public Debt. Cairo, Government Press (Bulaq), 1936.

Egypt: Economic Survey Specially Prepared by African Business. London, IC Magazines, 1981.

Farid, Saleh. Top Management in Egypt: Its Structure, Quality and Problems. Santa Monica, Rand Corporation, 1970.

Girgis, Maurice. Industrialisation and Trade Patterns in Egypt. Tübingen, Mohr, 1977.

Gran, Peter. Islamic Roots of Capitalism in Egypt: 1760-1840. Austin, University of Texas Press, 1979.

Hansen, Bent. An Economic Model for Ottoman Egypt, or the Economics of Collective Tax Responsibility. Berkeley, Institute for International Studies, 1973.

________. Economic Development in Egypt. Santa Monica, Rand Corporation, 1969.

________ with Girgis Marzouk. Development and Economic Policy in the UAR. Amsterdam, North Holland Publications, 1965.

Harbison, Frederick and Ibrahim Abdelkader. Human Resources for Egyptian Enterprise. New York, McGraw-Hill, 1958.

Ikhram, Khalid. Egypt: Economic Management in a Period of Transition. London, Johns Hopkins University Press, 1980.

Issa, Hassam M. Capitalisme et sociétés anonymes en Égypte: Essai sur le rapport entre structure sociale et droit. Paris, Librairie Générale de Droit et Jurisprudence, 1970.

Issawi, Charles. Egypt in Revolution, an Economic Analysis. London, Oxford University Press, 1963.

________. Egypt at Mid-Century: An Economic Survey. London, Oxford University Press, 1954.

Johnson, A. C. and L. C. West. Byzantine Egypt, Economic Studies. Princeton, Princeton University Press, 1949.

Al Kammash, Magdi. Economic Development and Planning in Egypt. New York, Praeger, 1968.

Kanovsky, Eliyahu. The Egyptian Economy in the Mid-1960s: The Micro-Sectors. Tel Aviv, Shiloah Centre, 1978.

________. The Economic Impact of the Six-Day War. London, Praeger, 1970.

Kardouche, George K. The UAR in Development: A Study in Expansionary Finance. New York, Praeger, 1966.

Kedourie, Elie, ed. The Middle Eastern Economy: Studies in Economics and Economic History. London, Cass, 1976.

El Khatib, Muhammad Fatallah. The Environment of Management in the UAR. Cairo, 1970.

Kornrumpf, Hans-Jürgen. Vereinigte Arabische Republik: Wirtschaftstrukturwandlung und Entwicklungshilfe. Opladen, C. W. Leske, 1967.

Landes, David. Bankers and Pashas: International Finance and Economic Imperialism in Egypt. repr. New York, Harper and Row, 1969.

Mabro, Robert. The Egyptian Economy 1952-72. Oxford, Clarendon, 1974.

________ and Samir Radwan. The Industrialisation of Egypt 1939-73. Oxford, Clarendon, 1976.

Mansour, Fawzi. Development of the Egyptian Financial System up to 1967: A Study of the Relation Between Finance and Economic Development. Cairo, University of Ayn Shams Press, 1970.

Mead, Donald C. Growth and Structural Change in the Egyptian Economy. Homewood (Ill.), Richard D. Irwin, 1967.

Moore, Clement. Images of Development: Egyptian Engineers in Search of Industry. Cambridge, MIT, 1980.

Musrey, Alfred. The Arab Common Market: A Study in Inter-Arab Trade Relations. London, Frederick A. Praeger, 1969.

Naggar, Said el-. Industrialisation and Income with Special Reference to Egypt. Cairo, Fuad I University Press (Cairo University), 1952.

Nagi, M. H. Labor Force and Employment in Egypt. New York, Praeger, 1971.

Nassef, Abdel Fattah. The Egyptian Labour Force: Its Dimensions and Changing Structure, 1907-60. Philadelphia, 1970.

Neumann, Theodor. Das moderne Ägypten: mit besonderer Rücksicht auf Handel und Volkwirtschaft. Leipzig, Duncker and Humbolt, 1893.

Nossier, Abdel Hamied. Die sozio-politischen Bedingungen der wirtschaftlichen Entwicklung dargestellt am Beispiel Ägyptens 1952-75. Bochum, Studienverlag Brockmeyer, 1979.

O'Brien, Patrick Karl. The Revolution in Egypt's Economic System: From Private Enterprise to Socialism 1952-65. London, Oxford University Press, 1967.

Owen, Edward Roger John. Cotton and the Egyptian Economy, 1820-1914. Oxford, Clarendon, 1969.

Al-Qaissouni, Abdal Moneim. International Economic Development with Special Reference to Egypt and the Arab World. Cairo, National Bank of Egypt, 1974.

Rabi, Husayn Muhammad. The Financial System of Egypt AH 564-741/AD 1169-1341. London, Oxford University Press, 1972.

Radwan, Samir. *Capital Formation in Egyptian Industry and Agriculture, 1882-1967.* London, Ithaca Press, 1974.

Rimawi, Qasim. *The Challenge of Industrialisation in Egypt.* Beirut, United Publishers, 1974.

Tomiche, Ferdinand. *Syndicalisme et certains aspects du travail en République Arabe Unie.* Paris, Maisonneuve et Larose, 1974.

Wallace, Sherman Le Roy. *Taxation in Egypt from Augustus to Diocletian.* New York, Greenwood Press, 1969.

Walz, Terrence. *The Trade Between Egypt and Bilad as-Sudan, 1700-1820.* Boston, 1975.

Arabic Titles

^{c}Abd al-Fāḍil, Maḥmūd. Dirāsāt fi't-Takhṭiṭ ma^{c}a Dirāsa Khāṣṣa li-Tajriba Jamāl ^{c}Abd an-Nāṣir. Beirut, Dār al-Quds, n.d.

^{c}Abd al-Fattāḥ, Muḥammad Shafīd. Āthār as-Sūq al-Urubbīya Mushtaraka ^{c}Ala Iqtiṣādīya Jumhurīya Miṣr al-^{c}Arabīya. Alexandria, Al-Hai'a al-Miṣrīya al-^{c}Āmma, 1974.

Al-Barrāwī, Rashīd. Al-Falsafa al-Iqtiṣādīya li'th-Thawra. Cairo, Maktaba an-Naḥḍa al-Miṣrīya, 1955.

________. Ḥālat Miṣr al-Iqtiṣādīya fī ^{c}Ahd al-Fāṭimīyīn. Cairo, Maktaba an-Naḥḍa al-Miṣrīya, 1948.

Al-Baydānī, ^{c}Abd ar-Raḥmān. Nakhba ash-Shi^{c}ārāt ^{c}Ala' l-Umma al-^{c}Arabīya. Cairo, 1975.

Ad-Dīb, Muḥammad Maḥmūd. Taṣnī^{c} Miṣr 1952-72. Cairo, Maktaba al-Anjlū al-Miṣrīya, 1980.

Al-Ghazzālī, ^{c}Abd al-Mun^{c}im. Tārīkh al-Ḥaraka an-Naqābīya al-Miṣrīya, 1899-1952. Cairo, Dār ath-Thaqāfa al-Jadīda, 1968.

Ḥawwās, ^{c}Iṣām ad-Dīn. Istrātījīya Binā' al-Insān al-Miṣrī. Cairo, Al-Hai'a al-Miṣrīya al-^{c}Āmma, 1980.

Jarītlī, ^{c}Alī. Khamsa wa ^{c}Ishrūn ^{c}Āman. Cairo, Al-Hai'a al-Miṣrīya al-^{c}Āmma, 1977.

________. As-Sukkān wa'l-Mawārid al-Iqtiṣādīya fī Miṣr. Cairo, Maṭba^{c}a Miṣr, 1962.

Al-Kurdī, Maḥmūd. At-Takhalluf wa Mushkilāt al-Mujtama^{c} al-Miṣrī. Cairo, Dār al-Ma^{c}ārif, 1979.

Mursī, Fu'ād. Hādhā al-Infitāḥ al-Iqtiṣādī. Cairo, Dār ath-Thaqāfa al-Jadīda, 1976.

Mutawallī, Maḥmūd. Al-Uṣūl at-Tārīkhīya li'r-Ra'smālīya al-Miṣrīya wa Taṭawwuruhā. Cairo, Al-Hai'a al-Miṣrīya al-^{c}Āmma, 1974.

Najīb, ^{c}Alī Aḥmad. Ra'y fi'th-Thawra al-Waṭanīya: Miṣr. Cairo, Dār al-^{c}Arabī li'n-Nashr wa't-Tawsī^c, 1980.

al-Qaylubī, Aḥmad Fu'ād. ^{c}Ubūr ar-Rūtīn al-Mālī. Cairo, Al-Hai'a al-Miṣrīya al-^{c}Āmma, 1976.

Rabī^c, Ḥasanayn Muḥammad. An-Nuẓum al-Mālīya fī Miṣr Zaman al-Ayyūbīyīn. Maṭba^{c}a Jāmi^{c}a al-Qāhira, 1964.

Riḍwān, Fatḥī. Ṭal'at Ḥarb, Baḥth fi'l-^{c}Aẓama. Cairo, Dār al-Kātib al-^{c}Arabī, 1970.

Rushdī, Muḥammad. At-Taṭawwur al-Iqtiṣādī fī Miṣr. Cairo, Al-Hai'a al-Miṣrīya al-^{c}Āmma, 1972.

Sa^{c}d, Aḥmad Ṣādiq. Fī Ḍaw' an-Namaṭ al-Āsīyawī li'l-Intāj: Tārīkh Miṣr al-Ijtimā^{c}ī al-Iqtiṣādī. Beirut, Dār Ibn Khaldūn, 1979.

Shuhayyib, ^{c}Abd al-Qādir. Muḥākama al-Infitāḥ al-Iqtiṣādi fī Miṣr. Beirut, Dār Ibn Khaldūn, 1979.

Al-Yūzbakī, Tawfīq Sulṭān. Tārīkh Tijāra Miṣr al-Baḥrīya fi'l-^{c}Aṣr al-Mamālīk. Mosul, Jāmi^{c}a al-Mawṣil, 1975.

Literature, Music, Theatre and Contemporary Art

Non-Arabic Titles

Abdel-Wahhab, Farouk. *Modern Egyptian Drama: An Anthology.* Minneapolis, Bibliotheqa Islamica, 1974.

Beyerl, Jan. *The Style of the Modern Arabic Short Story.* Prague, Charles University, 1971.

Fakkar, Rushdi. *Aux origines des relations culturelles contemporaines entre la France et le monde Arabe, l'influence française sur la formation de la presse littèraire en Égypte, au XIXe siècle.* Paris, Guenther, 1972.

Fanjul, Serafín. *El Mawwal egipcio: expresíon literaria popular.* Madrid, Instituto Hispano-Arabe de Cultura, 1976.

Ghanem, Fathi. *The Man Who Lost His Shadow.* (Translated by D. Stewart.) London, Chapman, 1966.

Al Hakim, Tawfiq. *Un substitut de compagne en Égypt: Journal d'un substitut de procureur egyptien.* (Translated by G. Wiet and Z. Hasan.) Paris, Plon, 1974.

________. *Fate of a Cockroach.* (Translated by D. Johnson-Davies.) London, Heineman, 1973.

________. Bird of the East. (Translated by R. Bayly-Winder.) Beirut, Khayats, 1966.

________. The Maze of Justice. (Translated by A. Eban.) London, Havrill Press, 1947.

Hickman, Hans. Orientalische Musik. Leiden, Brill, 1970.

________ and Charles Grégoire, Duke of Mecklenburg. Catalogue d'enregistrements de musique folklorique égyptienne. Strasbourg et Baden-Baden, Heitz, 1958.

Husayn, Taha. An Egyptian Childhood. (Vol. I of Husayn's 3-volume autobiography, translated by E. H. Paxton.) London, Heineman, 1981.

________. The Future of Culture in Egypt. repr. New York, Octagon, 1975.

Ibrahim Hilmy, H. R. H. Prince. The Literature of Egypt and the Sudan from Earliest Times to the Year 1885 Inclusive. London, Trübner, 1886-87.

Ibrahim, Sunallah. The Smell of It and Other Stories. (Translated by Denys Johnson-Davies.) London, Heineman, 1971.

Idris, Yusuf. The Cheapest Nights. London, Peter Owen, 1978.

Ismail, Abdel Monem. Drama and Society in Contemporary Egypt. Cairo, Dār al-Kātib al-ᶜArabī, 1967.

Johnson-Davies, Denys, ed. and trans. Egyptian Short Stories. London, Heineman, 1978.

Keeley, Edmund. Cavafy's Alexandria: Study of a Myth in Progress. London, Hogarth Press, 1977.

Khan, M. An Introduction to the Egyptian Cinema. London, Informatics, 1969.

Khouri, Mounah Abdullah. Poetry and the Making of Modern Egypt. Leiden, Brill, 1971.

Kilpatrick, Hilary. The Modern Egyptian Novel, a Study in Social Criticism. Ithaca, Cornell University Press, 1974.

Long, Richard. Tawfiq al-Hakim, Playwright of Egypt. London, Ithaca Press, 1979.

Mahfouz, Naguib. Children of Gebelawi. (Translated by P. Stewart.) London, Heineman, 1981.

________. Miramar. (Trans. by F. Mousa Mahmud, ed. and rev. by M. El Kommos and J. Rodenbeck.) London, Heineman, 1978.

________. Midaq Alley. London, Heineman, 1975.

________. God's World. Minneapolis, Bibliotheqa Islamica, 1973.

Mahmoud, Fatma Moussa. Women in the Arabic Novel in Egypt. Cairo, Instituto Italiano, 1976.

Masharrafa, M. M. Cultural Survey of Modern Egypt. London, 1948.

Mazyad, A. M. H. Ahmad Amin 1886-1954, Advocate of Social and Literary Reform in Egypt. Leiden, Brill, 1963.

Mitchnick, Helen. Egyptian and Sudanese Folk Tales. Oxford, Oxford University Press, 1978.

Philip, Thomas. Jurji Zaidan: His Life and Thought. Beirut, Franz Steiner Verlag, 1979.

Pinchin, Jane Lagoudis. Alexandria Still: Forster, Durrell and Cavafy. Princeton, Princeton University Press, 1977.

Renaissance du monde Arabe: Colloque international de Louvin sous la direction de Mm. Anouar Abdel-Malik, Abdel-Aziz Belal et Hasan Hanafi. Belgium, Éditions Duclet, 1972.

Sakkut, Hamdi. The Egyptian Novel and Its Main Trends from 1913-52. Cairo, AUC Press, 1971.

Semah, David. Four Egyptian Literary Critics. Leiden, Brill, 1971.

Sharqawi, A. R. Egyptian Earth. London, Heineman, 1962.

Thorval, Yves. Regards sur la cinêma êgyptienne. Beirut, Dār al-Mashruq, 1975.

Wahba, Magdi. Cultural Policy in Egypt. Paris, Unesco, 1972.

Wendell, Charles. The Evolution of the Egyptian National Image from Its Origins to Ahmad Lutfi al-Sayyid. Berkeley, University of California Press, 1972.

Arabic Titles

Abāẓā, Fikrī. Aḍ-Ḍaḥik al-Bākī. Cairo, 1933.

ᶜAbd al-Qādir, Fārūq. Izdihār wa Suqūṭ al-Masraḥ al-Miṣrī. Cairo, Dār al-Fikr al-Muᶜāṣir, 1979.

ᶜĀmir, Munīr. Al-Masraḥ al-Miṣrī baᶜd al-Ḥarb al-ᶜĀlamīya ath-Thānīya bain al-Fann wa'n-Naqd as-Sīyāsī wa'l-Ijtimāᶜī 1945-70. (2 Vols.) Alexandria, Al-Hai'a al-Miṣrīya al-ᶜĀmma, 1978-79.

ᶜĀṭiya, Aḥmad Muḥammad. Tawfīq al-Ḥakīm: Dirāsa fī Fikr al-Ḥakīm as-Sīyāsī. Cairo, Dār al-Mawqif al-ᶜArabī, 1979.

ᶜAṭīya, Naᶜīm. Al-ᶜAyn al-ᶜĀshiqa. Cairo, Al-Hai'a al-Miṣrīya al-ᶜĀmma, 1976.

ᶜAwaḍ, Ramsīs. At-Tārīkh as-Sirrī li'l-Masraḥ qabl Thawra 1919. Cairo, Al-Hai'a al-Miṣrīya al-ᶜĀmma, 1976.

Badārī, Thābit Muḥammad. Al-Ittijā al-Wāqi^{c}ī fi'sh-Shi^{c}r al-^{c}Arabi al-Ḥadīth fī Misr. Cairo, Maktaba an-Nahḍa al-Miṣrīya, 1980.

Badawī, Aḥmad. Al-Ḥayāt al-^{c}Aqlīya fī ^{c}Aṣr al-Ḥurūb aṣ-Ṣalībīya bi-Miṣr wa'sh-Shām. Cairo, Dār an-Nahḍa al-Miṣrīya, 1972.

Buṭrus, Fikrī. A^{c}lām al-Mūsīqā wa'l Ghinā' al-^{c}Arabī 1867-1967. Cairo, Al-Hai'a al-Miṣrīya al-^{c}Āmma, 1976.

Ad-Dasūqī, Muḥammad. Ayyām ma^{c}a Ṭāhā Ḥusayn. Beirut, Al-Mu'assasa al-^{c}Arabīya li'd-Dirāsāt wa'n-Nashr, 1978.

Diyāb, Muḥammad. Qaḍāyā Fikrīya wa Thāqafīya. Cairo, Al-Hai'a al-Miṣrīya al-^{c}Āmma, 1975.

Fannān Ash-Sha^{c}bi. Sayyid Darwīsh. Alexandria, Jam^{c}īya Aṣdiqā', n.d.

Fu'ād, Ni^{c}mat. Shakhṣīya Miṣr. Cairo, Al-Hai'a al-Miṣrīya al-^{c}Āmma, 1978.

________. Umm Kulthūm wa ^{c}Aṣr min al-Fann. Cairo, Al-Hai'a al-Miṣrīya al-^{c}Āmma, 1976.

Ḥamīdā, ^{c}Abd al-Qādir. Layālī Masraḥīya. Cairo, Kitāb al-Idhā^{c}a wa't-Tilifizyūn, 1972.

Ḥaqqī, Yaḥyā. Fajr al-Qiṣṣa al-Miṣrīya. Cairo, Al-Hai'a al-Miṣrīya al-^{c}Āmma, 1975.

Haykal, Aḥmad. Al-Adab al-Qiṣaṣī wa'l Masraḥī fī Miṣr min A^{c}qāb Thawra 1919 ilā Qīyām al-Ḥarb al-Kubrā ath-Thānīya. Cairo, Dār al-Ma^{c}ārif, 1970.

Ḥusayn, Ṭāhā. Mustaqbal ath-Thaqāfa fī Miṣr. Cairo, Dār al-Fikr al-^{c}Arabī, 1944.

Ibrāhīm, ^{c}Abd al-Ḥamīd. Al-Qiṣṣa al-Miṣrīya wa Sūra al-Mujtama^c al-Ḥadīth. Cairo, Dār al-Ma^{c}ārif, 1973.

Ibyārī, Fatḥī, ed. Nabaḍāt al-Qulūb wa Udabā' al-Aqālīm. Cairo, Dār ash-Sha^{c}b, 1975.

Jubrīl, Muḥammad. Miṣr fī Qiṣaṣ Kuttābihā al-Mu^{c}āṣirīn. Cairo, Al-Hai'a al-Miṣrīya al-^{c}Āmma, 1972.

Kamāl ad-Dīn, Muḥammad. Ruwwād al-Masraḥ al-Miṣrī. Cairo, Al-Hai'a al-Miṣrīya al-^{c}Āmma, 1972.

Al-Khāṭib, Muḥammad ^{c}Adnān. Umm Kulthūm Mu^{c}jiza al-Ghinā^c al-^{c}Arabī. Damascus, 1975.

Manḍūr, Muḥammad. Fi'l-Masraḥ al-Miṣrī al-Mu^{c}āṣir. Dār an-Nahḍa al-Miṣrīya, 1971.

Marzūq, Ḥilmī ^{c}Alī. Taṭawwur an-Naqd wa't-Tafkīr al-Adabī al-Ḥadīth fī Miṣr fi'r-Rub^{c} al-Awwal min al-Qarn al-^{c}Ishrīn. Cairo, Al-Hai'a al-Miṣrīya al-^{c}Āmma, n.d.

Muḥassab, Ḥasan. Al-Baṭal fi'l-Qiṣṣa al-Miṣrīya. Cairo, Dār al-Ma^{c}ārif, 1977.

_______. Qaḍīya al-Fallāḥ fi'l-Qiṣṣa al-Miṣrīya. Cairo, Al-Hai'a al-Miṣrīya al-^{c}Āmma, 1971.

Muṣṭafā, Maḥmūd. Al-Adab al-^{c}Arabī fī Miṣr min al-Fatḥ al-Islāmī ila Nihāya al-^{c}Aṣr al-Ayyūbī. Cairo, Wizāra ath-Thaqāfa, 1967.

Rā^{c}ī, ^{c}Alī. Dirāsāt fi'r-Riwāya al-Miṣrīya. Cairo, Wizāra ath-Thaqāfa, 1964.

Sakkūt, Ḥamdī and Marsden Jones. A^{c}lām al-Adāb al-Mu^{c}āṣir fī Miṣr. Cairo, AUC Press, Vol. I, Ṭāhā Ḥusayn, 1975, Vol. II, Ibrāhīm ^{c}Abd al-Qādir al-Māzinī, 1979.

Sakkūt, Ḥamdī. Masraḥīyāt Miṣrīya min Faṣl Wāḥid. Cairo, AUC Press, 1973.

Salām, Muḥammad Zaghlūl. Al-Adab fi'l-^{c}Aṣr al-Mamlūkī, ad-Dawlā al-Ūlā 648-783 hijrī. Cairo, Dār al-Ma^{c}ārif, 1971.

Sharaf, ^{c}Abd al-^{c}Azīz. Ṭāhā Ḥusayn wa Zawāl al-Mujtama^{c} at-Taqlīdī. Cairo, Al-Hai'a al-Miṣrīya al-^{c}Āmma, 1977.

Ash-Sharūnī, Yūsuf. Al-Laylāt ath-Thānīya ba^{c}d al-Alf: Mukhtārāt min al-Qiṣṣa an-Nisā'īya fī Miṣr. Cairo, Al-Hai'a al-Miṣrīya al-^{c}Āmma, 1975.

Ash-Shāyib, Aḥmad. Dirāsa Adab al-Lugha al-^{c}Arabīya bi-Miṣr fi'n-Niṣf al-Awwal min al-Qarn al-^{c}Ishrīn. Cairo, Al-Hai'a al-Miṣrīya al-^{c}Āmma, n.d.

^{c}Umar, Muṣṭafā ^{c}Alī. Al-Ittijāhāt al-Fikrīya fi'l-Adab al-Masraḥī. Cairo, Dār al-Ma^{c}ārif, 1980.

Al-Waraqī, As-Sa^{c}īd. Ittijāhāt al-Qiṣṣa al-Qaṣīra fi'l-Adab al-^{c}Arabī al-Mu^{c}āṣir fī Miṣr. Alexandria, Al-Hai'a al-Miṣrīya al-^{c}Āmma, 1979.

Yūnus, ^{c}Abd al-Ḥamīd. Difā^{c} ^{c}an al-Fūlklūr. Cairo, Al-Hai'a al-Miṣrīya al-^{c}Āmma, 1973.

Zaidān, Jurjī. Mudhakkirāt. (Edited by S. al-Munajjid.) Beirut, Dār al-Kitāb al-Jadīd, 1968.

The Egyptian Press and Press Relations

Non-Arabic Titles

Agha, Olfat. The Role of Mass Communications in Interstate Conflict: The Arab-Israeli War of 1973. Cairo, AUC Press, 1978.

Bustani, Salah ad Din. The Press During the French Expedition to Egypt 1798-1801. Cairo, Anglo-Egyptian Bookstore, 1954.

Elsheikh, Ibrahim. Mass Media and Ideological Change in Egypt, 1950-73. Amsterdam, University of Amsterdam, 1977.

Gendzier, Irene L. The Practical Vision of Ya^cqub Ṣanu^c. Cambridge (Mass.), Harvard University Press, 1966.

Morsy, Hasan Ragab. Die ägyptische Presse: Structur und Entwicklung der ägyptischen Presse der Gegenwart. Hannover, Verlag für Literatur und Zeitgeschen, 1963.

Nasser, Munir Khalil. Press, Politics and Power: Egypt's Heikal and Al Ahram. Ames, State University of Iowa Press, 1974.

Wassef, Amin Sami. L'information et la presse officielle en Égypte jusqu'à la fin de l'occupation française. Cairo, Institut français, 1975.

Arabic Titles

[c]Abd ar-Raḥmān, [c]Awāṭif. Aṣ-Ṣiḥāfa aṣ-Ṣihyūnīya fī Miṣr 1897-1954 Dirāsa Taḥlīlīya. Cairo, Dār ath-Thaqāfa al-Jadīda, 1980.

Abu'l-Layl, Maḥmūd Najīb. Aṣ-Ṣiḥāfa wa'th-Thaqāfa fī Miṣr Khilāla [c]Ām 1970. Cairo, Al-Mu'assasa Sijill al-[c]Arab, 1972.

Abū Zayd, Fārūq. Azma al-Fikr al-Qawmī fi's-Ṣiḥāfa al-Miṣrīya. Cairo, Dar al-Fikr wa'l-Fann, 1976.

Ḥamza, [c]Abd al-Laṭīf. Qiṣṣa aṣ-Ṣiḥāfa al-[c]Arabīya fī Miṣr. Baghdad, 1967.

Khalīfa, Ijlāl. Aṣ-Ṣiḥāfa. Cairo, Dār aṭ-Ṭibā[c]ī al-Ḥadītha, 1976.

Mar[c]ī, Muṣṭafā. Aṣ-Ṣiḥāfa bain as-Sulṭa wa's-Sulṭān. Cairo, [c]Ālam al-Kutub, 1980.

Qabaḍāyā, Ṣalāḥ. Ṣuḥufī Ḍidd al-Ḥukūma. Cairo, Kitāb al-Ḥayā, 1980.

Qabbānī, [c]Abd al-[c]Alīm. Nash'a aṣ-Ṣiḥāfa al-[c]Arabīya fi'l-Iskandarīya 1872-83. Cairo, Al-Hai'a al-Miṣrīya al-[c]Āmma, 1973.

As-Sa[c]īd, Rif[c]at. Aṣ-Ṣiḥāfa al-Yasārīya fī Miṣr 1925-48. Beirut, Dār aṭ-Ṭalī[c]a, 1974.

Shūshah, Muḥammad. Asrār ᶜAlī Amīn wa Muṣṭafā Amīn. Cairo, Mu'assasa Akhbār al-Yawm, 1977.

Islam and Islamic Movements in Twentieth Century Egypt

Non-Arabic Titles

Abduh, Mohammed. The Theology of Unity. (Translated by K. Craig and I. Musa'ad.) New York, Hillary House, 1966.

Adams, Charles. Islam and Modernism in Egypt. repr. New York, Russell and Russell, 1968.

al-Bannā, Ḥaṣan. Five Tracts Selected from Majmū'a al-Imām ash-Shahīd Ḥaṣan al-Banna. (Translated and annotated by C. Wendell.) Berkeley, University of California Press, 1978.

Berger, Morroe. Islam in Egypt Today: Social and Political Aspects of Popular Religion. Cambridge, Cambridge University Press, 1970.

Gibb, H. A. R. Islamic Society and the West. London, Oxford University Press, Vol. I, 1950, Vol. II, 1957.

________. Modern Trends in Islam. Chicago, University of Chicago Press, 1947.

Gilsenan, Michael. Saint and Sufi in Modern Egypt. Oxford, Clarendon, 1973.

________. Studies on the Civilisation of Islam. London, Oxford University Press, 1962.

Heyworth-Dunne, J. Religious and Political Trends in Modern Egypt. Washington, (the Author), 1950.

Hussaini, Ishak M. The Moslem Brethren. Beirut, Khayats, 1956.

Jansen, Geoffrey. Militant Islam. London, Pan Books, 1978.

Kerr, Malcolm. Islamic Reform: The Legal and Political Ideas of Muhammed ᶜAbduh and Rāshid Riḍā. Berkeley, University of California Press, 1966.

Mitchell, Richard P. The Society of the Muslim Brethren. London, Oxford University Press, 1969.

Proctor, J. Harris, ed. Islam and International Relations. New York, Praeger, 1965.

Qutb, Sayyid. Social Justice in Islam. New York, Octagon Books, 1968.

Rosenthal, Erwin I. J. Islam and the Modern National State. Cambridge, Cambridge University Press, 1965.

Smith, Wilfred Cantwell. Islam in Modern History. New York, New American Library, 1957.

Arabic Titles

^{c}Abd al-Ḥalīm, Maḥmūd. Al-Ikhwān al-Muslimūn: Aḥdāth Ṣagha at-Tārīkh. Alexandria, Dār ad-Da^{c}wa, 1979.

Aḥmad, Muḥammad Ḥasan. Al-Ikhwān al-Muslimūn fi'l-Mīzān. Cairo, n.p., n.d.

^{c}Alī, Sa^{c}īd Ismā^{c}īl. Al-Azhar ^{c}Alā' Masraḥ as-Sīyāsa al-Miṣrīya. Cairo, Dār ath-Thaqāfa, 1974.

Amīn, ^{c}Uthmān. Ra'īs al-Fikr al-Miṣrī: Al-Imām Muḥammad ^{c}Abdu. Cairo, Al-Maktaba al-Anjlū al-Miṣrīya, 1965.

Al-Bannā, Ḥasan. Naẓarāt fī Iṣlāḥ an-Nafs wa'l-Mujtama^{c}. repr. Cairo, Maktaba al-I^{c}tiṣām, 1980.

________. 19 Risāla min Ḥasan al-Bannā. repr. Cairo, Dār al-Anṣār, 1979.

Faramāwī, Kamāl. Yawmīyāt Sajīn fī Sijn al-Ḥarbī. Cairo, Dār ath-Thaqāfa, 1976.

Jawhar, Sāmī. Al-Mawtā Yatakallumūn. Cairo, Al-Maktaba al-Miṣrī al-Ḥadīth, 1977.

________. Aṣ-Ṣāmitūn Yatakallumūn: ^{c}Abd an-Nāṣir ... wa Madhbaḥa al-Ikhwān. Cairo, Maktab al-Miṣrī al-Ḥadīth, 1976.

Al-Jundī, Anwār. Ḥasan al-Bannā: Ad-Dā'īya al-Imām wa'l-Mujaddid ash-Shahīd, 1342-68h./1906-49m. Beirut, Dār al-Qalam, 1978.

Khafājī, ^{c}Abd al-Ḥalīm. ^{c}Indamā Ghāba ash-Shams. Kuwait, Maktaba al-Fallāḥ, 1979.

Khālid, Khālid Muḥammad. Min Hunā ... Nabdā'. Cairo, Dār an-Nīl li't-Ṭibā^{c}ī, 1950.

Qal^{c}ajī, Qadrī. Muḥammad ^{c}Abdu, Baṭal ath-Thawra al-Fikrīya fi'l-Islām. Beirut, Dār al-^{c}Ilm li'l Malāyīn, 1946.

Social, Anthropological and Sociological Studies on Egypt

Non-Arabic Titles

Abdel Fadil, Mahmud. Development, Income Distribution and Social Change in Rural Egypt 1952-70. Cambridge, Cambridge University Press, 1975.

Abd ar-Raziq, Ahmad. La femme au temps des mamlouks en Égypte. Cairo, Institut Français, 1973.

Aldridge, James. Cairo. Boston, Little, Brown, 1969.

Ali, Sami. Le haschisch en Égypte: essai d'anthropologie psychoanalytique. Paris, Payot, 1971.

Amin, G. A. Food Supply and Economic Development with Special Reference to Egypt. London, Cass, 1966.

Amin, H. M. Technical Co-operation and Comparative Models of Development: Lessons Drawn from the UNDP Experience in Egypt and Burma. Brighton, Institute of Development Studies, 1977.

Ammar, Abbas. The People of Sharqiya. Cairo, Sociêté Royale de Geógraphie d'Égypte, 1944.

Ammar, Hamad. Growing up in an Egyptian Village. repr. New York, Octagon Press, 1966.

Ayrout, Henry Habib. The Egyptian Peasant. repr. Boston, Beacon Books, 1966.

________. Moeurs et coutumes des Fellahs. Paris, Payot, 1938.

Baer, Gabriel. Studies in the Social History of Modern Egypt. Chicago, University of Chicago Press, 1970.

________. Egyptian Guilds in Modern Times. Jerusalem, Israel Oriental Society, 1964.

________. A History of Landownership in Modern Egypt 1800-1952. Oxford, Oxford University Press, 1962.

Berger, Morroe. Military Elites and Social Change: Egypt Since Napoleon. Princeton, Princeton University Press, 1970.

________. Bureaucracy and Society in Modern Egypt. repr. New York, Russell and Russell, 1969.

________. The Arab World Today. New York, Doubleday, 1964.

Berque, Jacques. Histoire social d'un village égyptien au xxième siècle. Paris, Mouton, 1957.

Besançon, Jacques. L'homme et le Nil. Paris, Gallimard, 1957.

Blackman, Winifred. The Fellahin of Upper Egypt, Their Religions, Social and Industrial Life, with Special Reference to Survivals from Ancient Times. repr. London, Cass, 1968.

Boktor, Amir. The Development and Expansion of Education in the UAR. Cairo, AUC Press, 1963.

Burckhardt, J. L. Arabic Proverbs or the Manners and Customs of Modern Egyptians Illustrated from Their Proverbial Sayings Current at Cairo. repr. London, Curzon Press, 1972.

Callender, Charles and Fadwa El Guindi. Life Crisis Rituals Among the Kenuz. Cleveland, Case Western University Press, 1971.

Carré, Olivier. Enseignment islamique et idéal socialiste; Analyse conceptuelle des manuels d'instruction musulmane. Beirut, Dār al-Mashreq, 1974.

Cleland, W. W. The Population Problem of Egypt. Lancaster (Pa.), Science Press Co., 1936.

Critchfield, Richard. Shahhat: An Egyptian. Syracuse, Syracuse University Press, 1978.

Djavidan, Hanum. Harem Life. London, Douglas, 1931.

Edwards, Amelia Blandford. A Thousand Miles up the Nile. London, Oxford University Press, 1877.

Elgood, Percival George. The Transit of Egypt. repr. New York, Russell and Russell, 1969.

Fakhouri, Hani. Kafr el Elow: An Egyptian Village in Transition. New York, Holt, Rinehart and Winston, 1972.

Fakkar, Rouchdi. Aspects de la vie quotidienne en Égypte à l'époque de Mehmet-Ali, premier moitié du 19e siècle. Paris, Maison neuve et Larose, 1975.

Fathy, Hassan. Architecture for the Poor, an Experiment in Rural Egypt. Chicago, University of Chicago Press, 1973.

_______. Construire avec le peuple, histoire d'un village d'Égypte: Gourna. Paris, Éditions Jérôme Martineau, 1970.

Feddan, Robin. Egypt, Land of the Valley. London, John Murray, 1977.

Fernea, Elizabeth Warnock. A View of the Nile. Garden City, Doubleday, 1970.

Fernea, R. A., ed. Nubian Ceremonial Life. Cairo, AUC Press, 1978.

_______. The Nubians in Egypt: A Peaceful People. Austin, University of Texas Press, 1977.

Fischer, Sydney N., ed. Social Forces in the Middle East. Ithaca, Cornell University Press, 1955.

Gadalla, Saad M. Is There Hope? Fertility and Family Planning in an Egyptian Community. Cairo, AUC Press, 1978.

_______. Land Reform in Relation to Social Development in Egypt. Columbia, University of Missouri Press, 1962.

Gougaud, Henri and Colette Gouvin. Egypt Observed. (Translated by S. Hardman.) London, Kaye and Ward, 1979.

Hall, Sondra. Nubians: A Study in Ethnic Identity. Khartoum, University of Khartoum Press, 1971.

Halpern, Manfred. The Politics of Social Change in the Middle East and North Africa. Princeton, Princeton University Press, 1963.

Hamady, S. *Temperament and Character of the Arabs.* New York, Twayne, 1960.

Hill, Enid. *Mahkama! Studies in the Egyptian Legal System: Courts and Crime, Law and Society.* London, Ithaca Press, 1979.

Harbish, Muhammad Khayri. *Education in Egypt in the 20th Century.* (Translated by A. el Hinnawi.) Cairo, General Organisation for Government Printing, 1960.

Harik, Ilya. *The Political Mobilization of Peasants: A Study of an Egyptian Community.* Bloomington, Indiana University Press, 1974.

Heyworth-Dunne, J. *A History of Education in Mcdern Egypt.* repr. London, Cass, 1968.

Hyde, Georgie D. *Education in Modern Egypt: Ideals and Realities.* London, Routledge, Kegan Paul, 1978.

Ibrahim, Saad Eddin and Nicolas Hopkins. *Arab Society: A Reader.* Cairo, AUC Press, 1977.

Kay, Shirley. *The Egyptians: How They Live and Work.* New York, Praeger, 1975.

Keating, Rex. *Nubian Rescue.* London, Robert Hale, 1975.

Kennedy, John. *Struggle for Change in a Nubian Community.* Palo Alto, Mayfield, 1978.

Laban, Abdel Moneim. *Einige Aspeckte der Akkulturation und des socialen Wandels in Ägypten von 1900 bis 1952.* Frankfurt am Main, Haag Herchen, 1977.

Lane, William Henry. *An Account of the Manners and Customs of the Modern Egyptians.* repr. N.Y., Dover, 1973.

Lerner, Daniel. *The Passing of Traditional Society.* New York, Macmillan, 1964.

Mahmoud, Zaki Naguib. *The Land and People of Egypt.* Philadelphia, Lippincott, 1972.

Mayfield, James. *Local Institutions and Egyptian Rural Development.* Ithaca, Cornell University Press, 1974.

McPherson, Joseph W. *The Moulids of Egypt.* Cairo, N.M. Press, 1941.

El Messiri, Sawsan. *Ibn Balad: A Concept of the Egyptian.* Leiden, Brill, 1978.

More, Jasper. *The Land of Egypt.* London, Botsford, 1980.

Murray, G. W. *Sons of Ishmael, a Study in the Egyptian Bedouin.* London, Routledge, 1935.

Nelson, C., ed. *Women, Health and Development.* Cairo, AUC Press, 1977.

_______. The Desert and the Sown. Berkeley, University of California Press, 1973.

Van Nieuwenhiujze, C. A. The Sociology of the Middle East. Leiden, Brill, 1971.

_______. Social Stratification in the Middle East: An Interpretation. Leiden, Brill, 1965.

Omran, Abdel R., ed. Egypt's Population Problems and Prospects. Chapel Hill, University of North Carolina Press, 1973.

Patai, Raphael. The Arab Mind. New York, Charles Scribner's Sons, 1973.

Promenska, Elizabeth. Investigations on the Population of Muslim Alexandria. Warsaw, Éditions Scientifiques de Pologne, 1972.

St. John, Bayle. Village Life in Egypt. repr. New York, Arno Press, 1973.

St. John, J. A. Egypt and Mohammed Ali, or Travels in the Valley of the Nile. London, Longmans, Rees, Orme, Brown, Green and Longman, 1834.

Staffa, Susan Jan. Conquest and Fusion: The Social Evolution of Cairo 642-1850. Leiden, Brill, 1977.

Sulaiman, Adly. Social Development in the New Rural Communities of Egypt. Cairo, Dar at-Tawin, n.d.

Tachau, Fran, ed. Political Elites and Development in the Middle East. New York, Wiley, 1975.

Tadrus, Hilmi. Rural Resettlement on Egypt's Reclaimed Land. Cairo, AUC Press, 1978.

Thompson, J. H. and R. D. Reischauer, eds. Modernisation of the Arab World. London, D. Van Nostrand, 1966.

Waterbury, John. The Balance of People, Land and Water in Modern Egypt. Hanover, American Universities Field Staff, 1971.

Wikan, Unni. Life Among the Poor in Cairo. London, Tavistock Publications, 1980.

Arabic Titles

ᶜAbd al-Baqī, Zaydān. Al-Mar'a bain ad-Dīn wa'l-Mujtamaᶜ. Cairo, Maktaba an-Naḥḍa al-Miṣrīya, 1977.

_______. ᶜIlm al-Ijtimāᶜ ar-Rīfī wa'l-Qurā al-Miṣrīya. Cairo, Maktaba al-Anjlū al-Miṣrīya, 1974.

_______. ᶜIlm al-Ijtimāᶜ al-Ḥaḍarī wa'l-Mudun al-Miṣrīya. Cairo, Maktaba al-Qāhira al-Ḥadītha, 1974.

Aḥmad, ᶜAlī Fu'ād. Ar-Rīf Yaᶜmal. Cairo, Tārīkh al-Muqaddima, 1958.

^{c}Amāra, Muḥammad. ^{c}Indamā Aṣbaḥa Miṣr ^{c}Arabīya: Dirāsa ^{c}an al-Mujtama^{c} al-Miṣrī fi'l ^{c}Aṣr al-Fāṭimī. Beirut, Al-Mu'assasa al-^{c}Arabīya li'd-Dirāsāt wa'n-Nashr, 1974.

Amīn, Qāsim. Taḥrīr al-Mar^{c}a. repr. Cairo, Dār al-Ma^{c}ārif, 1970.

^{c}Awda, Maḥmūd. Al-Fallāḥīn wa'd-Dawla. Cairo, Dār ath-Thaqāfa, 1970.

Al-Baqlī, Muḥammad Qandīl. Waḥda al-^{c}Ādāt baina Miṣr wa'sh-Shām, Cairo. Cairo, Maktaba al-Anjlū al-Miṣrīya, 1963.

Barrāwī, Rāshid and ^{c}Alī Dilāwar. Mushkilātunā al-Ijtimā^{c}īya: al-Faqr, al-Fallāḥ at-Ta^{c}mīm al-^{c}Ummāl. Cairo, Maktaba an-Nahḍa al-Miṣrīya, n.d.

Ad-Dasūqī, ^{c}Āṣim. Kibār Mallāk al-Arāḍī az-Zirā^{c}īya wa Dawruhum fi'l-Mujtamā^{c} al-Miṣrī (1914-52). Cairo, Dār ath-Thaqāfa al-Jadīda, 1975.

Ghaith, Muḥammad ^{c}Aṭīf. Dirāsa fi'l-Mujtamā^{c} al-Qarawī al-Miṣrī. (?Cairo), Dār al-Ma^{c}ārifa al-Jāmi^{c}īya, 1977.

Ḥabīb, Sa^{c}d ^{c}Abd as-Salām. Mujtama^{c}unā al-Jadīd. Cairo, Dār al-Qawmīya aṭ-Ṭibā^{c}ī wa'n-Nashr, 1963.

Ḥamdān, Jamāl. Shakhṣīya Miṣr. Cairo, Maṭba^{c}a an-Nahḍa al-Miṣrīya, 1970.

Ḥannā, Nabīl Ṣubḥī. Jamā^{c}āt al-Ghajar. Cairo, Dār al-Ma^{c}ārif, 1980.

Ḥāzim, Ḥusām. Al-Jawza wa's-Sarīr wa'l-Mishnaqa. Cairo, Dār al-^{c}Ilm li'ṭ-Ṭibā^{c}ī, 1974.

Ḥusayn, ^{c}Abd Allāh. Al-Fallāḥ wa'l-^{c}Āmil fī Miṣr al-Qadīma. Cairo, Dār al-Qawmīya aṭ-Ṭibā^{c}ī wa'n-Nashr, 1963.

Ibrāhīm, Najīb Iskandar. Qiyamunā al-Ijtimā^{c}īya. Cairo, Maktaba an-Nahḍa al-Miṣriya, 1962.

^{c}Īsā, Muḥammad Ṭal^{c}at. Dirāsāt fī Ijtimā^{c} ar-Rīfī. Cairo, Maktaba al-Qāhira al-Jadīda, 1960.

Khazbak, Muḥammad. Mushkila as-Sukkān fī Miṣr. Cairo, Dār al-Qawmīya aṭ-Ṭabā^{c}ī wa'n-Nashr, 1966.

Al-Kundī, Maḥmūd. An-Numūw al-Ḥaḍarī: Dirāsa li-Ẓāhira al-Istiqṭāb al-Ḥaḍarī fi'l-Miṣr. Cairo, Dār al-Ma^{c}ārif, 1977.

Milayka, Luwīs. Anmāṭ al-Ittiṣāl wa't-Ta'thīr. n.p., Markaz at-Tarbīya al-Isāsīya, 1960.

Al-Miṣrī, Fāṭima. Az-Zār, Dirāsa Nafsīya Taḥlīlīya Anthrūbūlūjīya. Cairo, Al-Hai'a al-Miṣrīya al-^{c}Āmma, 1975.

Muḥammad, Aḥmad Ṭāhā. Al-Mar'a al-Miṣrīya bain al-Māḍī wa'l-Ḥāḍir. Cairo, Dār at-Ta'līf, 1979.

Muṣṭafā, Fārūq Aḥmad. Al-Mawālid: Dirāsa li'l-^{c}Ādāt wa't-Taqālīd ash-Sha^{c}bīya fī Miṣr. Alexandria, Al-Hai'a al-Miṣrīya al-^{c}Āmma, 1980.

As-Sa^{c}dawī, Nawāl. Al-Mar'a wa'ṣ-Ṣirā^{c} an-Nafsī. Beirut, Al-Mu'assasa al-^{c}Arabīya li'd-Dirāsāt wa'n-Nashr, 1972.

Sha^{c}lān, Ibrāhīm Aḥmad. Ash-Sha^{c}b al-Miṣrī fī Amthālihi al-^{c}Āmmīya. Cairo, Al-Hai'a al-Miṣrīya al-^{c}Āmma, 1972.

Shumays, ^{c}Abd al-Mu'nīm. Al-Jinn wa'l-^{c}Afārīt fi'l-Adab ash-Sha^{c}bī al-Miṣrī. Cairo, Al-Hai'a al-Miṣrīya al-^{c}Āmma, 1976.

Ṣubḥ, Aḥmad Ismā^{c}īl. ^{c}Ubūr al-Miḥna. Cairo, Al-Hai'a al-Miṣrīya al-^{c}Āmma, 1975.

^{c}Uwais, Sayyid. Rasā'il ilā al-Imām ash-Shāfi^{c}ī: Ẓāhira Irsāl ar-Rasā'il ilā Ḍarīḥ al-Imām ash-Shāfi^{c}ī. Cairo, Dār ash-Shāya^{c}, 1978.

________. Ḥadīth ^{c}an al-Mar'a al-Miṣrīya al-Mu^{c}āṣira. Cairo, Maṭba^{c}a Aṭlas, 1977.

________. Ḥadīth ^{c}an ath-Thaqāfa ba^{c}ḍ al-Haqā^{c}iq ath-Thaqāfīya al-Miṣrīya al-Mu^{c}āṣira. Cairo, Dār aṭ-Ṭibā^{c}ī al-Ḥadītha, 1970.

Bibliographical Works on Egypt

Non-Arabic Titles

Ahmed, Munir D. Suez Kanal Bibliographie: Eine Auswahl der europäischsprachigen Schriftums seit 1945. Hamburg, Deutsches Orient-Institut, 1974.

Anawati, M. M. and Charles Kuents. Bibliographie des ouvrages arabes imprimês en Égypte en 1942, 1943 et 1944. Cairo, Institut Français, 1949.

Atiya, George N. The Contemporary Middle East: A Selective and Annotated Bibliography. Boston, G. K. Hall, 1975.

Birnbaum, Eleazar, et al. The Islamic Middle East: A Short Annotated Bibliography for High School Teachers and Librarians. Toronto, University of Toronto, 1975.

Blake, G. H. and W. D. Swearington. The Suez Canal: A Comparative Bibliography. Durham, Durham Centre for Middle East and Islamic Studies, 1975.

Al-Chalabi, Samir ᶜAbd ar-Rahim. A Bibliography of Translation and Dictionaries with Special Reference to the Arab World. Baghdad, Al-Mustansiriya University, 1979.

Conover, Helen. Egypt and the Anglo-Egyptian Sudan: A Selective Guide to Background Reading. Washington, Library of Congress, 1952.

Coult, Lyman H. An Annotated Research Bibliography of Studies in Arabic, English and French of the Fellah of the Egyptian Nile. Florida, University of Miami Press, 1958.

Creswell, K. A. C. A Bibliography of the Architecture, Arts and Crafts of Islam. Cairo, AUC Press, 1961-73.

Ettinghausen, Richard. A Selected and Annotated Bibliography of Books and Articles in Western Languages Dealing with the Near and Middle East. repr. New York, AMS, 1974.

Fatemi, Ali Mohammed, S. Abbas Amirie and Panas Kakoropoulus. Political Economy of the Middle East: A Computerised Guide to the Literature. Akron (Ohio), University of Akron, 1970.

Geddes, C. L. An Analytical Guide to the Bibliographies on Modern Egypt and the Sudan. Denver, American Institute of Islamic Studies, 1972.

Guémard, Gabriel. Bibliographie critique de la Commission des Sciences et Arts et de l'Histoire de l'Institut de l'Égypte. Cairo, Institut Français, 1936.

Hansen, Gerda, Ingeborg Otto and Rolf-Digter Preisberg. Wirtschaft, Gesellschaft und Politik Ägyptens: Eine bibliographische Einführung. Hamburg, Deutsches Orient-Institut, 1977.

Harmon, Robert Bartlett. A Selected and Annotated Guide to the Government of Egypt. Monticello (Ill.), American Council of Planning Librarians, 1978.

Hayworth-Dunne, G. E. Select Bibliography on Modern Egypt. Cairo, Anglo-Egyptian Bookshop, 1952.

Hill, Richard L. A Bibliography of the Anglo-Egyptian Sudan from Earliest Times to 1937. Oxford, Oxford University Press, 1939.

Hopwood, Derek and Diana Grimswood-Jones. The Middle East and Islam. Zug, Interdokumentation, 1972; revised by D. Grimwood-Jones, 1979.

Littlefield, David W. The Islamic Near East and North Africa: An Annotated Guide to Books in English for Non-Specialists. Littleton (Colo.), Libraries Unlimited, 1977.

Lorin, Henri. Bibliographie géographique de l'Égypte. (2 Vols.) Cairo, Société Royale de Géographie d'Égypte, 1928-29.

Lyttle, Elizabeth. The Aswan High Dam. Monticello (Ill.), American Council of Planning Librarians, 1977.

Maunier, René. Bibliographie économique, juridique et social de l'Égypte moderne (1798-1916), with 1925 Supplement. repr. New York, Burt Franklin, 1971.

Mayer, Hans Eberhard. Bibliographie zur Geschichte der Kreuzzüge. Hannover, Hahnsche Buchhandlung, 1960.

Pratt, Ida and Richard Gottheil. Modern Egypt, a List of References to Material in the New York Library. repr. New York, Kraus, 1969.

Qazzal, Ayad. Women in the Middle East and North Africa: An Annotated Bibliography. Austin, Center for Middle East Studies, 1977.

Sauvaget, Jean. Introduction to the History of the Muslim East, a Bibliographical Guide. (Second edition, recast by Claude Cahen.) Berkeley, University of California Press, 1965.

Schwarz, Klaus. Der Vordere Orient in den Hochschulschriften Deutschlands, Österreichs und der Schweiz, Bibliographie von Dissertation und Habilitationsschriften 1885-1978. Freiburg im Breisgau, Klaus Schwarz, 1980.

Sherbourne, C. Davis. Bibliography of Scientific and Technical Literature Relating to Egypt, 1800-1900. Cairo, Government Printing Press, 1915.

Simon, Reeva S. The Modern Middle East: A Guide to Research Tools in the Social Sciences. Boulder, Westview Press, 1978.

Toren, Amnon. A Bibliography of Books on Nasser's Egypt, 1952-70. Tel Aviv, Shiloah Centre, 1972.

University of St. Joseph. Arab Culture and Society in Change: A Bibliography of Books and Articles in English, French, German and Italian. Beirut, Dār al-Mashruq, 1973.

Vidergar, John J. Urbanization and Social Welfare Programs in Egypt: A Bibliography. Monticello (Ill.), American Council of Planning Librarians, 1977.

Yarden, Ronit. The U.S. and the Middle East 1967-77, a Selective Bibliography of Publications and Articles. Tel Aviv, Shiloah Centre, 1978.

Arabic Titles

ᶜAlī, Nabīl Ṣādiq. Biblīyujrāfīya al-ᶜUlūm al-Iqtiṣādīya wa'l-Mālīya bi-Jumhūrīya Miṣr al-ᶜArabīya. Cairo, Al-Hai'a al-Miṣrīya al-ᶜĀmma, 1978.

Arab League. Biblīyujrāfīya al-Maṭbūᶜāt al-ᶜArabīya aṣ-Ṣādira fī Majallāt at-Tammīya aṣ-Ṣināᶜīya ad-Dawla al-ᶜArabīya. Cairo, Arab League, 1971.

Badrān, Ḥusayn, et al. Ath-Thabat al-Biblīyujrāfī li'l-Aᶜmāl al-Mutarjama 1956-67. Cairo, Al-Hai'a al-Miṣrīya al-ᶜĀmma, 1972.

Dār al-Kutub al-Miṣrīya. Fihrist al-Kutub al-ᶜArabīya. Cairo, 1927- .

Lawzā, Sārah Fāḥim. Al-Biblīyujrāfīya ash-Shāriḥa li'd-Dirāsāt as-Sukkānīya li-Jumhūrīya Miṣr al-ᶜArabīya Ḥattā 1976. Cairo, Dār as-Sukkān wa'l-Usra, 1976.

Manṣūr, Aḥmad Muḥammad, et al. Dalīl al-Maṭbūᶜāt al-Miṣrīya 1940-56. Cairo, AUC Press, 1975.

An-Nassāj, Sayyid Ḥāmid. Dalīl al-Qiṣṣa al-Miṣrīya al-Qaṣīra Ṣuḥūf wa Majmūᶜāt, 1910-61. Cairo, Al-Hai'a al-Miṣrīya al-ᶜĀmma, 1972.

Wizāra ath-Thaqāfa wa'l-Iᶜlām. Dalīl al-Kitāb al-Miṣrī. Cairo, Al-Hai'a al-Miṣrīya al-ᶜĀmma, 1972- .

Reference Works and General Guides

Non-Arabic Titles

Abdulrazik, Fawzi. Arabic Historical Writing, 1973 (Cambridge, Harvard University Press, 1974); 1974 (Cambridge, Harvard University Press, 1976); 1975-76 (London, Mansell, 1979).

Abstracta Islamica: Bibliographie analytique et sélective d'études islamiques. Paris, 1927- .

Adams, Charles. The Middle East: A Handbook. London, Anthony Blond, 1971.

Additions and Accessions, Centre for Middle Eastern and Islamic Studies. University of Durham, 1970- .

Aktueller Informationdienst, Moderner Orient, 1981- (Fortnightly).

The Arab Historian, a Bulletin of Historical Research. (Arabic and English texts.) Baghdad, 1975- .

Auchterlonie, Peter and Yasin Safadi, eds. Union Catalogue of Arabic Newspapers and Serials in British Libraries. London, Mansell, 1977.

Baedeker's Egypt 1929. repr. Newton Abbot, David Charles, 1974.

Bibliography of Periodical Literature, Middle East Journal, 1974- (Quarterly).

The Cambridge History of Islam. Cambridge, Cambridge University Press, 1970.

Deny, Jean. Sommaire des archives turques du Caire. Cairo, Government Printing Office, 1930.

The Encyclopaedia of Islam. New Edition. London and Leiden, 1960- .

Le Guide Bleu. Paris, Hachette (several editions).

Harris, George L. Egypt. (Country Survey Series.) New Haven, Human Relations Area Files Press, 1957.

Index Islamicus, London, 1958- (Annual).

Journal of the Middle East. Ayn Shams. (Cairo) 1974- (bi-annual).

Library of Congress, Accessions List, Middle East. (Monthly.) (American Libraries Book Procurement Center, Cairo.)

Little, Donald. An Introduction to Mamluk Historiography: An Analysis of Arabic Annalistic and Biographical Sources for the Reign of Al-Malik an-Nāṣir Muḥammad b. Qalā'ūn. Weisbaden, Franz Steiner Verlag, 1970.

Mansoor, Meanhem. Political and Diplomatic History of the Arab World: A Chronological Study. Washington, D.C., NCR Microcards, 1972.

MESA (Middle East Studies Association) Bulletin, New York, 1967- (tri-annual).

Middle East Abstracts and Index. Pittsburgh, 1978- (quarterly).

Periodicals in Review, in the Journal of Palestinian Studies, 1971- (Quarterly).

Précis de l'histoire de l'Égypte. Cairo, Institut Français, 1932-35.

Rivlin, Helen. The Dār al-Wathā'iq in ᶜĀbdīn Palace As a Source for the Study of Modernisation in Egypt in the 19th Century. Leiden, Brill, 1970.

Schäfer, Barbara. Beitrage zur mamlukischen Historiographie nach der Tode al-Malik an-Nasirs. Freiburg im Breisgau, Klaus Schwarz Verlag, 1971.

El Shayyal, Gamal el-Din. A History of Egyptian Historiography in the Nineteenth Century. Alexandria, Alexandria University Press, 1962.

Showker, Kay. Fodor's Egypt. London, Hodder and Stouton, 1979.

Simaika Basha, Marcus with Yassa ᶜAbd al-Masih Effendi. Catalogue of Coptic and Arabic Manuscripts in the Coptic Museum, the Patriarchate, the Principal Churches of Cairo and Alexandria, and the Monasteries of Egypt. (3 Vols.) Arabic and English Texts. Cairo, Government Printing Press, n.d. ?

Smith, Harvey, et al. Area Handbook for the United Arab Republic. Washington, U.S. Government Printing Office, 1970.

Sweet, Louise, ed. The Central Middle East, a Handbook of Anthropology and Published Records on the Nile Valley, the Arab Levant, South Mesopotamia, the Arabian Peninsula and Israel. New Haven, Human Relations Area Files Press, 1971.

Wilber, Donald M. United Arab Republic, Its People, Its Society, Its Culture. New Haven, Human Relations Area Files Press, 1969.

U.A.R. Yearbook (Statistics and General Information). Cairo, Ministry of Information.

Arabic Titles

Amīn, Aḥmad. Qāmūs al-ᶜĀdāt wa't-Taqālīd wa't-Taᶜābīr al-Miṣrīya. Dār al-Kutub, 1953.

Bustānī, Fu'ād Afrām. Dā'irat al-Ma^{c}ārif: Qāmūs ^{c}Āmm li Kull Fann wa Maṭlab. Beirut, 1956- .

Dār al-Kutub. An-Nashra al-Miṣriya li'l-Maṭbū^{c}āt. (Annual, with cumulative editions for 1955-60, 1961-62, 1961-65, 1965-67.)

Hawwārī, ^{c}Iṣmat. Mawsū^{c}a at-Tashrī^{c}a al-^{c}Ummālīya. Cairo, Al-Maṭba^{c}a al-Fannīya al-Ḥadītha, 1970.

Jām^{c}a ad-Dawal al-^{c}Arabī (Arab League). Dalīl Dūr an-Nashr fi'l-Waṭan al-^{c}Arabī. Cairo, 1974.

_______. Dalīl Dūr al-Wathā'iq, Marākiz at-Tawthīq fi'l-Waṭan al-^{c}Arabī. Cairo, 1973.

_______. An-Nashra al-^{c}Arabīya li'l-Maṭbū^{c}āt. (Annual series, 1970- .)

Markaz Buḥūth ash-Sharq al-Awsaṭ. Dalīl Rasā'il al Mājistīr wa'd-Duktūrā al-Muta^{c}alliqa bi'sh-Sharq al-Awsaṭ Allatī Ujīza bi'l-Jāmi^{c}āt al-Miṣrīya. Cairo, 1977.

Sarkīs, Yūsuf. Mu^{c}jam al-Matbū^{c}āt al-^{c}Arabīya wa'l-Mu^{c}arraba. Cairo, Matba^{c}a Sarkīs Misr, 1928-30; repr. 1968.

Non-Arabic Journals Dealing with Egypt, Islam and the Middle East

Arab Report and Record. London, 1966- .

Asian Affairs. London, 1914- .

Bulletin de l'Institut Français. Cairo, 1918- .

Bustan. Vienna, 1960- .

Cahiers de l'Orient contemporaine. Paris, 1944- .

L'Egypte contemporaine, Cairo, 1910- .

The Egyptian Gazette. Cairo (newspaper).

International Journal of Middle East Studies. London, 1970- .

MEED (Middle East Economic Digest). London, 1957- .

Middle East Forum. Beirut, 1954- .

Middle East International. London, 1971- .

Middle East Journal. Washington, 1947- .

Middle Eastern Studies. London, 1964- .

The Muslim World. London, 1911- .

Near East Report. Washington, 1957- .

New Outlook. Middle East Monthly. Tel Aviv, 1957- .

Oriento Moderno. Rome, 1921- .

Progrès Égyptienne. Cairo (newspaper).

Egyptian Newspapers and Periodicals

Egypt has some 400 newspapers and journals published annually; the following are a selection of current major newspapers and journals dealing with historical and cultural topics.

Al-Ahrām (newspaper)

Al-Ahrām al-Iqtiṣādī (journal)

Al-Akhbār (newspaper)

Akhbār al-Yawm (newspaper)

Akhir Sā^{c}a (periodical)

Dirāsāt al-Ishtiraqiya (periodical)

Al-Jumhūrīya (newspaper)

Majalla ash-Sharq al-Awsaṭ (periodical)

Majalla at-Tārīkhīya al-Miṣrīya (periodical)

Majalla ath-Thaqāfa (periodical)

Al-Muṣawwar (periodical)

Oktubār (periodical)

Rūz al-Yūsuf (periodical)

Aṭ-Ṭalī^{c}a